P. Norris

3.95

p 98   AD 70 war of
        Jesus' rejection

SCRIPTURE UNION

THE
DAILY
COMMENTARY

**St. Matthew
to
Acts**

SCRIPTURE UNION
5 WIGMORE STREET
LONDON, W1H 0AD

© 1973 Scripture Union
First published 1974

ISBN 0 85421 389 9

Printed and bound in Malta by
St Paul's Press Ltd

Contents

Co-ordinating Editor: Arthur E. Cundall, B.A., B.D.

Maps: Jenny Grayston

Photographs: Rev. A. Cundall, Rev. J. R. Hill, P. W. Marsh.

Maps and Illustrations

Chronology of the New Testament Period

5 BC	Birth of Christ
AD 29	Commencement of Christ's Public Ministry
AD 33	Death and Resurrection of Christ
AD 35	Conversion of Paul
AD 46	Commencement of Paul's First Missionary Journey
AD 48	The Council of Jerusalem (Acts 15)
	Commencement of Paul's Second Missionary Journey
AD 50/51	Paul at Corinth
AD 53	Commencement of Paul's Third Missionary Journey
AD 54–57	Paul at Ephesus
AD 58	Gospel of St. Mark
AD 59	Paul returned to Jerusalem
AD 59–61	Paul in prison at Caesarea
AD 61	Gospel of St. Luke
AD 62–64	Paul in prison at Rome
AD 65	The Acts of the Apostles
AD 66	Paul's second imprisonment and death at Rome
AD 66–70	The Jewish-Roman War
AD 70	The Fall of Jerusalem
AD 71	Gospel of St. Matthew
AD 90	Gospel of St. John
AD 99	Death of John

Most dates are approximate, especially those of the Gospels.

PALESTINE
in the Time
of Christ

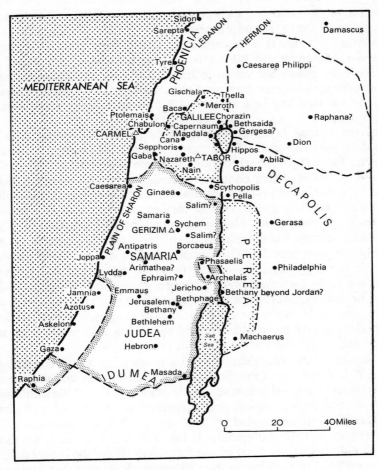

Sidon
Sarepta
Damascus

PHOENICIA
LEBANON
HERMON

Tyre
Caesarea Philippi

MEDITERRANEAN SEA

Gischala
Thella
Baca
Meroth
Ptolemais
GALILEE Chorazin
Raphana?
Chabulon
Capernaum
Bethsaida
CARMEL △
Magdala
Gergesa?
Cana
Dion
Sepphoris
Hippos
Gaba
Nazareth △ TABOR
Abila
Nain
Gadara
DECAPOLIS

Caesarea
Ginaea
Scythopolis
Pella
Salim?
Samaria
Gerasa
Sychem
GERIZIM △
Salim?
Antipatris
Borcaeus
Joppa
SAMARIA
Phasaelis
P
Lydda
Arimathea?
E
Ephraim?
Archelais
R
Jamnia
Emmaus
Jericho
Bethany beyond Jordan?
E
Bethphage
A
Azotus
Jerusalem
Bethany
Askelon
Bethlehem
JUDEA
Salt
Machaerus
Gaza
Hebron
Sea
Raphia
D U M E A Masada

PLAIN OF SHARON

0   20   40 Miles

— — — — — Tetrarchy of Philip

············ Tetrarchy of Herod Antipas

▒▒▒▒▒▒ Under Pontius Pilate

General Introduction

The overwhelming response to the Scripture Union Bible Study Books, when originally issued during the period 1967–71, has led to the demand for their preservation in a more compact and durable form.

It will be recalled that the original intention of this series was to encourage the daily study of the Bible at greater depth than was possible with the Bible Study Notes. This allowed fuller discussion of introductory, textual and background material, whilst still aiming at devotional warmth, sound exegesis and relevance to daily life. It is heartening to know that this aim has, in considerable measure, been achieved. Moreover, the Bible Study Books have been widely used as the basis for group discussion in homes, colleges and churches, and some volumes have even been used as prescribed texts in Bible colleges. It is hoped that the new format will find an equally encouraging reception.

It remains true, however, that the principal aim of this series is to stimulate personal daily Bible study. Each main section contains material for a three-month period. The one exception to this is the section on Mark which contains readings for a two-month period. Where it is suggested that two sections should be read together in order to fit a two or three-month period, they are marked with an asterisk. There is, of course, no obligation to adopt this suggestion. This particular volume, therefore, provides material for a period of approximately fourteen months. The complete series of four volumes will provide for daily readings over a five-year cycle, and will form a complete Bible Commentary. It is appreciated that few students will have the time available for a full consideration of all the questions set for further study. But since these are placed at approximately weekly intervals it would be stimulating and refreshing if time could be set aside once a week for the study of one or more questions.

It is assumed that the reader will be using one of the standard editions of the R.S.V. (or one of the 'Study Bibles' based on it), and will therefore have the marginal references and footnotes of that Bible available; many of these references will not be repeated in these books, and users are therefore recommended to look up the R.S.V. references as a regular part of their daily study. If the R.S.V. is not available, then other modern versions such as the Jerusalem Bible, the New English Bible and The Living Bible, or the well-proven R.V. are recommended.

The authors of the individual sections have been allowed the necessary liberty of approach within the general scope of the series. This provides for a certain variation which we trust will prove stimulating rather than disconcerting. All authors are united within the circle of evangelical, conservative scholarship and are widely respected within this field.

Opportunity has been taken to correct errors which escaped attention in the earlier edition and also to make limited revisions where necessary. The inclusion of further introductory articles, maps, diagrams and charts will, we trust, add to the value of this volume as an aid to the study of God's Word.

List of Standard Abbreviations

AV (KJV)	Authorised Version (King James), 1611.
c. (circa)	about
cf., cp.	compare
e.g.	for example
f.	verse following .
ff.	verses following
Gk.	Greek
Heb.	Hebrew
i.e.	that is
J.B.	Jerusalem Bible, 1966
LXX	Septuagint (Greek Version of the O.T.)
NEB	New English Bible, 1961 and 1970.
NT	New Testament
OT	Old Testament
p.	page
pp.	pages
RSV	Revised Standard Version 1946 and 1952.
RV	Revised Version (American Standard Version) 1885.
s.v.	(*sub voce*) 'under that word'
v.	verse
vs.	verses
viz.	namely

St. Matthew

INTRODUCTION

The Earliest External Evidence

The Gospel according to Matthew, like the three other Gospels, is anonymous. The names attached to the Gospels have been so attached since the first half of the second century at latest, but none of them appears in the body of the work.

Our earliest evidence for the association of Matthew with Gospel-making is a fragment from a lost work of Papias, bishop of Hierapolis in Phrygia (cf. Col. 4.13) about A.D. 130. Papias, who lovingly collected and recorded what remained of oral tradition handed down by those who had seen and heard the Lord in person, wrote in five volumes an *Exegesis of the Dominical Oracles* which is not known to be extant. His work was quoted by various Christian writers of the following generations and centuries. Among these Eusebius, in the third book of his *Ecclesiastical History*, ascribes to Papias the statement that 'Matthew compiled the oracles (*logia*) in the Hebrew speech, and everyone interpreted them as best he could'. Statements by writers later than Papias which name Matthew as the author of the First Gospel appear to be based on what Papias said. But Papias did not say that Matthew wrote the First Gospel, which is a Greek work, but that he compiled the *logia* in the Hebrew speech. It is likely that, when Papias spoke of Matthew as compiling the *logia*, he used the word in the sense which it had in the title of his work. When he composed his *Exegesis of the Dominical Oracles*, the 'oracles' (*logia*) with which he was concerned were the sayings of our Lord, which Papias was so anxious to collect (at one or two removes) from those who had heard them. If the laws of Moses and the utterances of the prophets were recognized as divine oracles (cf. Acts 7.38; Rom. 3.2), the sayings of Jesus, the anointed Lord to whom Moses and the prophets bore witness, were all the more worthy of such recognition.

A Primitive Sayings Collection

Now there is one important element in the *Gospel of Matthew* which has been discerned as just the sort of composition of which Papias speaks—a digest of the sayings of Jesus, conceived after the fashion of those prophetical books of the O.T. which present the prophet's oracles in a minimum of narrative framework, introduced with an account of the prophet's call but not including any account of his death. Such a 'book of the prophet Jesus' appears to have circulated at an early date in the Church, more particularly among

10

Hellenists and Gentile Christians, before any of our present Gospels existed. It underlies the *Gospel of Luke* as well as the *Gospel of Matthew*, being the source of what are conventionally labelled the 'Q' sections in these two Gospels, and has been envisaged as having its contents arranged under four main headings:

1. Jesus and John the Baptist
2. Jesus and His disciples
3. Jesus and His opponents
4. Jesus and the future

Matthew and the Gospel

Who then was the 'Matthew' who is said to have compiled 'the oracles'? Papias was certainly understood by Eusebius (and probably by Irenaeus a century and a half earlier) to have meant Matthew the apostle, and this was a sound interpretation of his words. What Papias was interested in was apostolic testimony, and he gladly recorded anything that came his way on this subject.

Our tentative conclusion is that it was Matthew the apostle who composed the earlier work, 'the book of the prophet Jesus', and, that his name was later attached to our present Gospel, in which that earlier work was incorporated. Happily, our understanding of the Gospel and the interpretation of its contents are independent of such uncertainties as these.

Sources of the Gospel

In addition to 'the book of the prophet Jesus', the Evangelist has drawn upon a parallel compilation of sayings of Jesus, circulating not in the area of the Gentile mission but in the stricter Jewish–Christian communities of Judea. The narrative framework in which the teaching is set reproduces the substance of Mark's record, often telescoped and abbreviated, but sometimes amplified by the inclusion of non-Markan incidents (especially featuring Peter), and rearranged in part (Matt. 7.28—13.58, parallel to Mark 1.21—6.13) to conform with the distinctive design of the *Gospel of Matthew*. This narrative extends from the preaching of John the Baptist (3.1 ff.) to the passion and resurrection of Jesus (chs. 26–28); as in the other Gospels so in *Matthew* the passion and resurrection account is the goal to which everything that precedes leads on. The nativity account in chs. 1 and 2 is peculiar to Matthew and quite independent of Luke's, with which nevertheless it agrees in theology (Jesus' virginal conception by the power of the Holy Spirit), geography (He was born in Bethlehem of Judah although He was later brought up

11

in Nazareth) and chronology (His birth took place in the reign of Herod).

It is all too easy, when considering the sources of information on which one of the Evangelists might have drawn in the composition of his work, to overlook his personal contribution. Matthew was a man of no mean literary ability, and over and above that he possessed in an outstanding degree the spiritual gift appropriate for his particular ministry. 'We must not think of the evangelists as literary hacks producing gospels by stringing other people's work together; they were genuine composers, with gifts as authentic as those of the poet or the musician or the artist, and a good deal more important' (T. W. Manson, *Ethics and the Gospel*, 1960, p. 46).

Leading Themes of the Gospel

> Matthew gives us five discourses;
> In threes and sevens he groups his sources.
> He writes to show what O.T. meant,
> With an ecclesiastic bent.

These four lines do not constitute elevated poetry, but their memorization has proved useful to many examinees who have welcomed the opportunity to expand the basic facts which they summarize when invited to describe the main features of the *Gospel of Matthew*. The 'five discourses' in which the teaching of Jesus is arranged according to affinity of subject-matter (5.1—7.27; 10.5–42; 13.1–52; 18.1–35; 24.1—25.46), dominate the structure of the Gospel. Matthew's tendency to group his material in threes and sevens—from whatsoever sources it may have been derived—is illustrated by the seven parables of the kingdom in ch. 13 and the three in ch. 25. His writing 'to show what O.T. meant' has special reference to the 'formula quotations' from the O.T., appearing throughout his work from 1.22 f. to 27.9 f. As for his 'ecclesiastic bent', not only is he the only one of the Evangelists who so much as mentions the word 'church' (cf. 16.18; 18.17) but he shows an interest in the life, growth and witness of the Christian fellowship.

Character and Purpose of the Gospel

In the first three chapters of the Gospel Jesus is introduced as King of the Jews, heir to David's throne, acclaimed as such by Gentiles and anointed by God. The charge inscribed over His head on the cross, 'This is Jesus the King of the Jews' (27.37), is thus shown in advance to be no false claim but a well-attested fact. Yet in the body of the Gospel the role in which Jesus is chiefly presented is that of Teacher. It is His teaching that constitutes the most

12

prominent feature of this Gospel. Indeed, the Gospel has been envisaged as the 'manual of discipline' of a distinct Christian school (cf. K. Stendahl, *The School of St. Matthew*, 1968), and one can well understand how useful it would have been as a handbook for catechists. It quickly became the most popular of the Gospels: once the four records began to circulate as a collection, the *Gospel of Matthew* invariably occupied the first place, whatever might be the order of the other three. Its position at the head of the N.T. books in their canonical order has a fitness of its own because of the way in which its opening section dovetails into the O.T. narrative.

Its original setting appears to have been a Greek-speaking Jewish–Christian community: we may think of some Hellenistic milieu in Syria which preserved the ideals of those Hellenists who first, in the dispersion that followed Stephen's martyrdom, brought the Christian message to Gentiles. The Gentile mission, entrusted to the eleven apostles, is the note on which this Gospel concludes. It is anticipated earlier in the inclusion of Gentile women in the genealogy of ch. 1, in the epiphany narrative of ch. 2, and in the healings of the centurion's servant (8.5–13) and the Canaanite girl (15.21–28).

The Evangelist himself has his portrait painted in the 'scribe . . . trained for the kingdom of heaven' whom Jesus compares to 'a householder who brings out of his treasure what is new and what is old' (13.52). He was a man of generous mind and comprehensive outlook, including in his record and weaving into a unity material cherished by Christian groups of varying viewpoint: the stricter Jewish Christians and the more liberal Gentile Christians, with the many intermediate gradations, might all find something congenial here.

Date

The date of the completed *Gospel of Matthew* is probably to be fixed quite soon after the destruction of the Temple and city of Jerusalem (A.D. 70). Echoes of the catastrophe and its aftermath can be discerned here and there; moreover, the new situation thus created was an opportunity for Christian consolidation and advance, and to this the *Gospel of Matthew* made its powerful contribution.

Outline

Prologue: Nativity Narrative (1.1—2.23)
      i. Genealogy of Jesus (1.1–17)
     ii. Birth and Infancy (1.18—2.23)
I A   The Beginning of the Ministry (3.1—4.25)

13

St. Matthew 1.1-17   The Line of Succession

The opening phrase binds the gospel narrative which follows securely to the O.T.; as Gen. 5.1 introduces 'the book of the generations of Adam', the Evangelist does the same for the second Adam. He is, however, not concerned to present Him as the second Adam (contrast Luke 3.38) so much as the son of Abraham (and so fulfiller of the divine promises regarding Abraham's offspring; cf. Gen. 22.18) and, more particularly, as the heir to David's throne. The line from David to Joseph probably marks the legal succession rather than biological descent (in some instances 'father' may be used in a formal sense); in Luke 3.23–31 the line from David to Joseph coincides with Matthew's in Shealtiel and Zerubbabel, but otherwise deviates from it completely.

The genealogy from Abraham to Zerubbabel can be constructed from O.T. records; the sources for the links between Zerubbabel and Joseph have not survived. But it was no exceptional thing in those days for a family to preserve its genealogical registers for many generations. The schematic arrangement of the genealogy in three groups of fourteen (17) depends on the omission of certain names—e.g. three between Joram and Uzziah (8; cf. 1 Chron. 3.11 f.) and one (Jehoiakim) between Josiah and Jechoniah (11; cf. 1 Chron. 3.15 f.). The four women mentioned in the genealogy— Tamar the Canaanite (3), Rahab of Jericho (5; her marriage to Salmon is not elsewhere recorded), Ruth the Moabite (5) and Bathsheba, widow of Uriah the Hittite (6)—are all Gentiles: it is thus indicated that the blessing brought by the Son of David is not restricted to one race only (cf. 4.15; 8.5–13; 15.22–28; 28.19).

Notes: The variant reading in v. 16 which a footnote in earlier editions of the RSV reproduced on the authority of 'other ancient authorities' is actually found in one manuscript of the Old Syriac Gospels, and nowhere else; the footnote is omitted in editions from 1962 onwards. V.17: It may be no more than a coincidence that 14 is the numerical value of the three letters making up the name 'David' in Hebrew.

St. Matthew 1.18-25   The Nativity

Matthew's account of the birth of Jesus is completely independent of Luke's; where Luke tells the story from Mary's viewpoint, Matthew tells it from Joseph's, but both evangelists agree in affirming that it was by the power of the Holy Spirit that Jesus was conceived. The law as it affected a betrothed woman in Mary's condition is laid down in Deut. 22.20 f., 23 f.; Joseph's decision not to expose her to the serious consequences of public repudiation marks him out as a man of decent feeling. Here it is he who receives an angelic annunciation and is told to call the child Jesus. The name (the Greek form of Joshua or Jeshua) means 'Yahweh is salvation'; hence its appropriateness, 'for He will save His people from their sins' (21).

Verses 22 f. present the first of several O.T. quotations in this Gospel which are preceded by an introductory formula which, with minor variations in wording, indicates that an event took place to fulfil a certain oracle. This quotation, from Isa. 7.14, comes from Isaiah's address to King Ahaz—when Judah was threatened with invasion from Syria and Israel. Isaiah in the name of God bade Ahaz keep calm, and invited him to name any sign that he might choose to confirm that the threat would vanish; Ahaz, who had already invited the intervention of the Assyrian king, pretended to be too pious to put God to the test by asking for a sign. Isaiah, discerning the truth behind the king's affected piety and foreseeing

15

the disastrous consequences of his overtures to Assyria, gave him the sign of a royal child soon to be born who would not be able to distinguish right from wrong before the two kings Ahaz feared were laid low, but who would grow up to a devastated heritage because of Ahaz's fatal policy. The language of Isaiah's oracle is that of an archaic annunciation form (attested in a text from Ugarit *c.* 1400 B.C. and perhaps echoed in Mic. 5.3). Matthew recognizes its definitive realization in the birth of Jesus, the virgin's son (according to the Greek version of the O.T. which is quoted here) and Emmanuel, 'God with us', in the fullest sense (cf. 28.20).

St. Matthew 2.1-12 The Adoration of the Magi

If Jesus was the fulfilment of the hope of Israel, He was also the answer to Gentile aspirations. The 'wise men from the East' were Gentiles, whose journey the early Church saw foretold in Isa. 60.3: 'nations shall come to your light, and kings to the brightness of your rising'. Hence the festival of their visit on January 6, which is more ancient than Christmas, is called the Epiphany (manifestation) of Christ to the Gentiles; hence, too, their traditional description as 'kings of Orient'—'three kings' probably because of the three gifts they presented (11). But in fact they were magi—a term originally denoting a Median priestly caste but in this context referring to students of the stars. The orbits and conjunctions of planets could be calculated in advance by this time, and one explanation of the star whose rising they saw identifies it with the conjunction of the planets Jupiter (the star of the world ruler) and Saturn (the star of Palestine) in the constellation Pisces (the sign of the last days) in the summer and autumn of 7 B.C. Whether this be so or not, their quest brought them (naturally) to Herod's palace, where it caused great alarm. Herod's reign (37-4 B.C.) was approaching its end, and with each succeeding year he grew more morbidly suspicious. A new king of the Jews was a threat to his throne and dynasty, and must be eliminated immediately. Ascertaining from the chief priests and scribes (interpreters of the sacred law) that, according to Mic. 5.2, Bethlehem (David's birthplace) was to be the birthplace of the Messiah (great David's greater Son), he sent the strangers there to pay homage to the infant King. The reappearance of the star convinced them that they were on the right road; how it led them to the precise house can only be surmised—did they see its reflection in the well of the courtyard?

It is easy, with Origen and others, to read special significance into their respective gifts, 'gold and frankincense and myrrh' (11), fitting donations to One who was both 'King and God and Sacrifice'—but the Evangelist leaves us to carry out such exercises ourselves. He contents himself with the statement that the magi, in response to a divine warning, 'departed to their own country by another way' (12), thus denying Herod the information which would have enabled him also to pay homage to the new King, as he said (8)—or to take what alternative action he thought appropriate.

Note: The mention of 'two years' in v. 16, 'according to the time which he (Herod) had ascertained from the wise men', suggests that they arrived in Bethlehem a considerable time after the birth of Jesus; we may infer that their first sight of the star coincided with His birth, and that their journey was not a short one.

Study: Consider Isa. **60** *in detail and decide how far this event is a 'fulfilment' of its visions.*

St. Matthew 2.13-23   Descent into Egypt

The massacre of the innocents, though unrecorded elsewhere (apart from a possible allusion in a contemporary Jewish apocalypse, which compares Herod's conduct to Pharaoh's plot against the Hebrew infants), is completely consistent with Herod's character in his closing years. The holy family's flight into Egypt was remembered in some Jewish circles; rabbinical tradition preserves a distorted reminiscence of Jesus' sojourn there. Herod died in March, 4 B.C.; his kingdom was divided between three of his sons, of whom Archelaus became ethnarch of Judea. Archelaus inherited his father's vices without his qualities of statesmanship (and his misrule led to his deposition in A.D. 6); Joseph was well advised, on returning from Egypt, to settle in Galilee, where another of Herod's sons, Herod Antipas (cf. **14.**1 ff.), ruled as tetrarch.

This passage is marked by three O.T. quotations with introductory formula (cf. **1.**22 f.). The first (15), from Hos. **11.**1, refers to God's calling Israel, His firstborn son (cf. Exod. **4.**22), out of Egypt at the time of the Exodus. Its application here to Jesus reflects the Evangelist's intention of portraying Him as recapitulating in His personal experience the experience of His people, and being afflicted in all their affliction (cf. Isa. **63.**9). The second (17 f.), from Jer. **31.**15, pictures the matriarch Rachel sitting by the frontier town of Ramah (near which was her tomb, according to 1 Sam. **10.**2), weeping for her children as they were driven off into captivity. Now Rachel, here perhaps symbolizing bereaved motherhood of all ages, weeps disconsolately again as more of her children fall

17

victims to a new tyranny (Matthew may have in mind the alternative location of her tomb near Bethlehem; cf. Gen. 35.19). The third quotation (23) presents a problem: no such text occurs in any edition of the O.T. known to us. The least improbable explanation sees an allusion here to Isa. 11.1, where the Hebrew word translated 'branch' (in reference to the coming ruler of David's line) has the same root consonants as 'Nazarene'. All these oracles are said to have been spoken by the Lord *through* various prophets; they are but His spokesmen (which is the essential meaning of 'prophets').
Questions: (i) How can we explain the fact that God let the Bethlehem babies die? (ii) How does this passage help us to understand the nature of prophecy?

Questions for further study and discussion on St. Matthew chs. 1 and 2

1. Consider the significance of the various ways in which Matthew insists that the birth of Jesus was the fulfilment of divine promise and human hope.
2. What special emphases does Matthew's nativity narrative bring out as compared with Luke's?

St. Matthew 3.1-12   The Ministry of John

Wherever John the Baptist is mentioned in the N.T. he appears as making preparation for the ministry of Jesus. His distinctive theme was the urgent need of repentance, because of the near advent of the Coming One. 'The kingdom of heaven' is a phrase peculiar to this Gospel in the N.T.; elsewhere, and occasionally even in this Gospel, the synonymous expression 'the kingdom of God' is used. It refers more particularly to the universal and everlasting kingdom which, according to Dan. 2.44; 7.14,18,22,27, the God of heaven was about to establish on the ruins of successive pagan empires. On John's lips the expression implies the day of judgement (cf. Dan. 7.9 ff.); the judgement is the fiery baptism to be administered by the Coming One (11 f.); hence the call to repent in time.

It may be that baptism was already established as one of the elements in the initiation of a convert from paganism into the commonwealth of Israel; if so, John warns his hearers that if they are to join the end-time people of God ready to greet the Coming One on His arrival they must first take the outside place, as no better than pagans, and enter the elect community by the baptism of repentance. Descent from Abraham was of no avail (9); here John anticipates

18

Paul (Rom. **9.**7). Those then who confessed their sins were baptized in Jordan.

John shows himself to stand in the prophetic succession (which had been in abeyance for generations) not only by his Elijah-like dress (4; cf. 2 Kings **1.**8) and the convicting power of his preaching but also by the vigour with which he denounces the contemporary religious establishment (7). Worldly Sadducees and observant Pharisees are alike compared to serpents hastening away from the path of advancing flames.

Notes: V. 1: 'In those days': a vague term; thirty years and more have elapsed since the end of ch. **2.** 'the wilderness of Judea': the territory west of the lower Jordan and the Dead Sea; here the community of Qumran and other ascetics had their headquarters at this time. V.3: 'The voice of one crying . . .': this quotation from Isa. **40.**3 originally referred to the glad announcement of liberation for exiles in Babylon. The Qumran community used it as a prophecy of their settlement in the wilderness of Judea. In the N.T. the whole of Isa. **40–66** is treated as a prophecy of the gospel age. V.11: 'He will baptize you with the Holy Spirit': Matthew presents the following ministry of Jesus as in some degree fulfilling this prophecy. V.12: 'His winnowing fork is in His hand': separation is an essential part of judgement (cf. **13.**30, 41 f.).

Question: How can the need for repentance be made relevant to our contemporary society, which is rapidly rejecting authority and therefore any sense of responsibility to it?

St. Matthew 3.13-17 The Baptism of Jesus

John's deprecating answer to Jesus' request for baptism at his hands (14) was natural enough: this was a baptism of repentance and here was One who had no sins to confess: better that John should be baptized by Him. This is merely John's assessment of Jesus' personal character: thus far he had no inkling that Jesus was the Coming One for whom he was preparing the way. But Jesus' reply to John's remonstrance makes clear His purpose in seeking baptism: 'Let it be so for the present; we do well to conform in this way with all that God requires' (15, NEB). These words in a general way express Jesus' constant resolve to do His Father's will. Further, they indicate His recognition that John's ministry was a work of God and His desire to be publicly identified with it. He could not hold aloof from the righteous remnant of Israel which was taking shape in response to that ministry. But more: they declare in a special way His dedication to accomplish the purpose of God in His own

19

ministry, now on the point of inauguration. If His ministry was to be launched by an act of self-identification with sinners, that would mark its course and pre-eminently its climax.

John submitted, and baptized Him. Then came the divine response to His unreserved self-dedication—the opened heavens, the descent of the Spirit and the Father's voice. Here, in the baptism of Jesus, is a moment of divine revelation. The descent of the Spirit points to Him as the One who is to baptize with the Holy Spirit: the Spirit must be received before being imparted to others. Of the Messiah of David's line the prophet had said, 'the Spirit of the LORD shall rest upon Him' (Isa. **11.**2); in introducing His chosen Servant God had said, 'I have put My Spirit upon Him' (Isa. **42.**1). Nor does this exhaust the reference of this narrative to God's introduction of His Servant: if the proclamation 'This is My Son' marks Jesus out as the Messiah addressed in the oracle of Psa. **2.**7, 'Thou art My Son', the following words, 'My Beloved, on whom My favour rests' (17, NEB), equally mark Him out as the obedient Servant of the Lord. The King is anointed, but the circumstances of His anointing show that His royal power and empire must be won by following the Servant's path of teaching and healing, humility and self-sacrifice (cf. **8.**17; **12.**18–21; **20.**28).
Question: If we are to reign with Him, what does this suggest concerning our Christian lives?

Questions for further study and discussion on St. Matthew ch. 3

1. Is there anything in Jesus' ministry which could be regarded as the fulfilment of John's words in v. 12?
2. Consider how Jesus' words to John in v. 15 might serve as an example for us.

St. Matthew 4.1-11   Temptation in the Wilderness

The temptation must be understood in the light of the baptism: the repeated 'If You are the Son of God' (3, 6) harks back to 'This is My beloved Son' (3.17). 'God has called You His Son,' it is implied; 'make Him show that He means what He says; put Him to the test.' The Spirit that descended on Jesus at His baptism leads Him into the wilderness to be tempted; this is part of His appointed probation. Here, too, Messiah recapitulates the history of the messianic people. God's purpose in leading Israel 'these forty years in the wilderness' was 'that He might humble you, testing you to know what was in your heart, whether you would keep His commandments, or not' (Deut. **8.**2). That Jesus recognized this correspon-

20

dence is indicated by His rebuffing the temptation three times from the context of *Deuteronomy* which includes these words. 'You are the Son of God,' says the tempter; 'very well, You have unlimited power at Your disposal; use it for Your own advantage. Turn these flat stones into the cakes of bread that they so much resemble, and satisfy Your hunger.' The reply, 'Scripture says' (4, NEB), quotes Deut. **8**.3 to express Jesus' resolve to act in response to His Father's direction and not from motives of self-interest.

'You are the Son of God,' comes the tempter's voice again; 'do something spectacular and compel Him to intervene miraculously on Your behalf. Throw Yourself down from the Temple roof into the Kidron ravine; no harm will come to You, for *Scripture says* that His angels by His command will see to it that You don't even stub Your toe against a rock—if You can quote Scripture, so can I' (and Psa. **91**.11 f. is pressed into service). Jesus' reply this time (quoting Deut. **6**.16) is a refusal to do the very thing that Israel repeatedly did in that earlier 'day of temptation in the wilderness' when, says God, they 'tested Me, and put Me to the proof, though they had seen My work' (Psa. **95**.9; cf. Exod. **17**.1–7; Num. **14**.22 f.).

The third temptation invites Jesus to attain the world dominion which was Messiah's traditional heritage (cf. Psa. **72**.8) on the devil's terms and by his well-tested methods. Many a would-be world conqueror before and since has sold himself to the devil thus to achieve his ends. The worship and service of the true God alone, prescribed in the words of Deut. **6**.13 with which Jesus repels this temptation, meant for Him obedience to the heavenly voice which marked out the path of the Servant as His messianic way. World-empire more secure and permanent than any other conqueror has won has come to Him in consequence, but it has come to Him by way of suffering and death (cf. **28**.18). The ministry of angels (11) anticipates His present lordship over 'angels, authorities and powers' (1 Pet. **3**.22).

Questions: (i) What does the third temptation tell us about the position of Satan in the world today? (ii) What parallels have these temptations in our experience?

St. Matthew 4.12-25   The Galilean Ministry Begins

'Capernaum by the sea' (13) was a suitable base for Jesus' Galilean ministry because He had only to get on board a ship to cross the Lake and be out of reach of Herod Antipas, tetrarch of Galilee, who had imprisoned John. In the Evangelist's eyes it was suitable also because this is the area where, according to the oracle of Isa.

21

9.1 f., light (associated with the promised Prince of the house of David) is to break forth on those who had endured the darkness of defeat and depopulation. The Gentiles of Transjordan (15) are to share in the messianic blessing (cf. **8.**28 ff.; **15.**29 ff.).

Jesus' message is summed up (17) in the same words as John's preaching (**3.**2), but 'the kingdom of heaven' on His lips had not the same connotation as it had on John's (cf. **11.**2 ff.). Jesus' call to repentance was a call to men to re-assess all personal and social values in the light of the approach of the divine kingdom in His ministry; the nature of this re-assessment appears, for example, in the beatitudes of **5.**3–12.

Right at the beginning of the Galilean ministry He summoned His first four disciples to leave their nets and come along with Him: they were to become 'fishers of men' (19), bringing them into the new order which Jesus announced. The claims of the kingdom of heaven were paramount and imperious; neither family ties nor business interests might stand in their way (22).

Jesus' ministry at this early stage was one of public teaching and healing; the synagogues of Galilee were open to Him for His proclamation that the ancient prophecies were now being fulfilled. The 'gospel of the kingdom' (23) was the good news that God, as He had promised, was visiting His people. The various kinds of physical and mental affliction enumerated in v. 24 were intrusions into God's good creation: the power of the kingdom of heaven was manifested in the relief which Jesus gave to their victims (cf. **12.**28). The news of His ministry naturally travelled far and wide, and crowds flocked to Him from all parts of Palestine and the adjoining lands.

Note: V. 24: The word rendered 'epileptics' literally means 'moonstruck', but it denotes not lunacy (cf. AV 'lunatick') but epilepsy (as also in **17.**15).

Question: Does Christ's choice of despised and isolated Galilee for His ministry suggest a principle in Christian work?

Questions for further study and discussion on St. Matthew ch. 4

1. Consider the tempter's quotation of Psa. **91.**11 f. as an example of the misuse of Scripture in personal guidance.
2. In what circumstances today would it be proper to leave one's work so abruptly as these four fishermen did?

St. Matthew 5.1-12 The Beatitudes

Matthew's first collection of discourse-material, presenting the rule of life in the kingdom of heaven (**5.**1–7.27), is called the Sermon on the Mount (from **5.1** and **8.1**), perhaps in comparison and contrast with Mount Sinai, from which the Mosaic law was promulgated (Exod. **19.1** ff.). It is addressed to the disciples (**5.1** f.) in the hearing of larger crowds (**7.28**).

The opening section (**5.3–10**) pronounces blessings on eight categories of people. The 'poor in spirit' (3) are those who, conscious of their own inadequacy, rely on God's grace; lacking material wealth, they are inwardly rich. The expression occurs also in the Qumran texts (and cf. Isa. **66.2**). The mourners (4) refuse to close their eyes to human sorrow; they sympathize with the tragedy of life. The 'meek' (5) are the opposite of the self-assertive; their reward has been announced already in Psa. **37.11**. Those who 'hunger and thirst for righteousness' (6) are consumed with the desire to see God's will done—in themselves and among mankind at large. The 'merciful' (7), the 'pure in heart' (8) and the 'peacemakers' (9) reflect the character of the God of mercy, purity and peace. In a world where the accepted standards of value are the reverse of these, such people are not likely to have an easy time. In fact, they are almost bound to be 'persecuted for righteousness' sake' (10). But, says Jesus, here is no ground for complaint, but rather for exultation: people such as He describes are the truly happy and fortunate people; on them their friends should press warm and sincere congratulations. The future is with them, not with the hard-boiled 'pushers' who put their own interests first and get on in the world. The rewards are not arbitrary; they are the natural fruit of the qualities that are commended. While eight qualities are mentioned, they tend to be found together; they were manifested in harmonious perfection in our Lord's character. And lest His disciples should miss the practical point of the beatitudes, He repeats the last one in the second person. They will be persecuted and vilified because they are His disciples (11); let them rejoice in this, for it is a sign that they are in the true succession of the prophets (12).

It is only the familiarity of the beatitudes that blinds us to their revolutionary character; they turn the accepted priorities upside down. In their way they were an even more radical challenge to the establishment of the day than were the fiery denunciations of John (**3.7**).

Note: The 'mountain' (1; cf. **8.1**) is probably the gentle slope rising above Capernaum: beneath the ridge parallel to the lake-shore between Tell Hum and et-Tabgha there is a natural amphitheatre. The ridge also satisfies the description of the 'level place' in Luke **6.17**, for one looks down on it (as Luke may have done) when approaching from the west. But above all, 'the mountain' is for Matthew the place of revelation (cf. **17**.1, 9; **28**.16).

*Question: How do we deal with persecution (cf. Jas. **1**.2)?*

St. Matthew 5.13-26   'Not to abolish but to fulfil'

The followers of Jesus must be like salt, preserving their environment from corruption (13); they must be 'the light of the world', dispelling the surrounding darkness (14). Salt that has lost its essential quality of 'saltness' is useless for any other purpose, and what is the good of an invisible light? 'If the New Testament is to decide what is meant by a true Christian, then to be a true Christian in all secrecy, comfortably and enjoyably, is as impossible as firing a cannon in all secrecy' (S. Kierkegaard). 'Our Lord,' remarked George Tyrrell, 'had only one thing to say about making proselytes, and it was not complimentary (cf. Matt. **23**.15); He did say "Let your light so shine before men".' The teaching of v. 16 is echoed in the N.T. epistles—e.g. in Phil. **2**.15 f.; 1 Pet. **3**.1 f., 13 ff.

The Sermon on the Mount does not abrogate the ethical demands of the O.T. law; it completes and sharpens them. The assertion that 'all' that the world needs is the putting into practice of the Sermon on the Mount is naïvely idealistic in a society which finds the Ten Commandments beyond its capacity. According to Paul (who shows himself well acquainted with the ethical teaching of Jesus), it is in those who 'walk by the Spirit' that 'the law of Christ' is fulfilled (Gal. **5**.16; **6**.2). But while the standard is higher, no disciple of Jesus can be content with anything lower. The Pharisees' standard was lofty enough, but it was not unattainable (cf. Matt. **19**.20; Phil. **3**.6). But who can perfectly keep the sixth commandment as interpreted here (21 ff.)? Not only the murderous act but the angry thought, the contemptuous word or the denial of a man's integrity expose one to judgement in the heavenly court (22).

Two corollaries to this interpretation are appended: one insisting that God cannot be acceptably worshipped by those who are not in charity with their neighbours (23 f.) and another reminding the listeners that, since they are all on the way to the heavenly court to give an account of their lives, they should come to terms by means of repentance while there is time (25 f.).

Notes: V. 22: 'everyone who is angry with his brother': the later addition 'without a cause' (AV) is an eloquent commentary on the tendency of Christians to soften their Lord's 'hard sayings'. V. 22: 'whoever insults his brother': literally, 'calls his brother "Raca" '—

24

probably an Aramaic word meaning 'vain' or 'empty fellow'.
V. 22: 'You fool!': Greek *mōre*, which may here be the transcription
of Hebrew *mōreh* ('rebel'), the fateful word used by Moses in Num.
20.10 which excluded him from the Promised Land. The 'hell
(Gehenna) of fire' is an expression for the place of retribution in the
world to come, drawn from the Valley of the son of Hinnom south
of Jerusalem (Jer. 19.2), which served the city as its refuse dump and
incinerator in the post-exilic age.

St. Matthew 5.27-37   Divorce and Swearing Prohibited

Our Lord goes on to interpret further requirements of the Mosaic
law. The seventh commandment, prohibiting adultery, is shown to
forbid also the unchaste thought or glance—a ban enforceable by no
earthly code or court (27 f.). Better lose the eye—or hand—that
tempts to sin than lose the life by yielding to sin (29 f.; cf. 18.8 f.).

To this admonition is appended (31 f.) Jesus' interpretation of the
law affecting divorced persons in Deut. 24.1-4. The meaning of
'some indecency' in Deut. 24.1 was debated in the rabbinical schools:
some (e.g. the school of Shammai) restricted it to evidence of pre-
marital unchastity; others (e.g. the school of Hillel) allowed it to
embrace a wide variety of features which might displease a husband.
For reasons detailed later in 19.3 ff., Jesus rules that marriage is
binding for life; the exceptive clause (32) refers to the situation in
which the parties are so closely related that their marital union
would be technically 'fornication' in Jewish law (cf. 1 Cor. 5.1;
the RSV rendering 'unchastity' is far too vague to convey the precision of the original wording). A divorced wife had no means of
redress or appeal against her husband's arbitrary decision, and as
her existence in independence of a man to support her was practically impossible in that society, she was more or less bound to
remarry and thus involve herself and her new husband in a relation
which was illicit by the standard here set up.

Next Jesus reinterprets the law regarding oaths, based on the
third commandment and elaborated in Lev. 19.12; Num. 30.2;
Deut. 23.21-23, and lays down a new procedure for His followers
(33-37). They must not swear oaths at all: they should be known as
men of their word, so that their simple 'Yes' or 'No' will be believed.
To debate whether Christians, in view of this ruling, should or should
not take the oath in courts of law is to indulge in casuistry foreign
to its spirit. Some Christians indeed, notably the Society of Friends,
apply Jesus' words literally in such a situation; but their public
reputation is such that most people would accept the bare word of a

25

Friend before the most vehement oaths of many others. The point is that all the followers of Jesus should have this kind of reputation.

The various oaths mentioned in vs. 34–36 were substitutes for oaths sworn by God, perhaps in the vain supposition that their breach did not incur such solemn perjury as the breach of an oath taken in God's name. The folly of such 'limited liability' swearing is exposed.

'Anything more than this comes from evil' (37): perhaps 'from the evil one' (the devil), but more probably from sinful human nature (cf. Jas. 5.12, which echoes this injunction of Jesus).

St. Matthew 5.38-48   'But I say . . .'

A third time Jesus goes beyond what 'was said to the men of old' with His 'I say to you'—the authority implicit in this emphatic 'I' must not be overlooked. The prophets of old said 'Thus says the LORD'; the rabbis were never happier than when they could quote a legal ruling in the name of some illustrious teacher of the past, but Jesus appeals to no authority higher than His own when He brings out the inward sense of the divine law.

The law of retaliation, 'An eye for an eye . . .' (Exod. 21.24 f.; Lev. 24.19 f.), originally marked an advance in civilized behaviour when it replaced the unlimited blood-feud; henceforth the rule was 'one eye (and one only) for an eye; one life (and one only) for a life'. But Jesus' teaching marks a further advance: His followers should not retaliate at all. On the contrary, they should take the initiative in repaying evil with good: the man who volunteered to carry a soldier's pack for a second mile after being compelled to carry it for one mile showed himself a free person and not an involuntary automaton. The spirit in which these directions are obeyed is the important thing: one could even turn the other cheek in a provocative manner (38–42).

'You shall love your neighbour as yourself' (Lev. 19.18) sums up the law of Israel; its application depends on our answer to the question 'Who is my neighbour?' The added words '. . . and hate your enemy' (43) are not quoted from the O.T.; their spirit can be recognized, for example, in the Qumran literature, where love for fellow members of the community and 'everlasting hatred for all the men of the pit' are alike enjoined. There is nothing extraordinary about loving (i.e. doing good to) one's friends: unregenerate human nature does that as a matter of course. The followers of Jesus must be marked by kindness towards their enemies; in this they will show themselves true sons of God, who dispenses the blessings of creation impartially.

'You, therefore, must be perfect . . .' (48): this recalls 'You shall be holy; for I the LORD your God am holy' (Lev. **19**.2, etc.), but the special reference here is to perfection in mercy (cf. Luke **6**.36). This is no law to be enforced, but a pattern to be emulated.

Note: It has been suggested that a blow on the right cheek (39) would imply that the striker was left-handed (contrast Luke **6**.29, where neither right nor left is specified). But if we wish to insist on such precision, we might consider the possibility that a back-handed blow is envisaged, which would be more painful and perhaps even more insulting.

Questions: (i) Can I trust God enough to leave my vindication with Him? (ii) Which of the commands in vs. 21–48 is most difficult for me?

Questions for further study and discussion on St. Matthew ch. 5

1. Discuss some familiar techniques for evading the uncomfortable directness of the Sermon on the Mount.
2. Compare the words about the permanence of the law in v. 18 with Paul's teaching about Christ as 'the end of the law' (Rom. **10**.4).

St. Matthew 6.1-8   Public and Private Piety

The 'piety' (literally 'righteousness') of v. 1 covers the principal forms of religious practice—almsgiving (2–4), prayer (5–15) and fasting (16–18), which were largely left to the discretion of the individual. In fact, the word is sometimes used with specific reference to almsgiving (cf. Psa. **112**.9, quoted in 2 Cor. **9**.9, and the close association of 'practising righteousness' with 'showing mercy to the oppressed' in Daniel's advice to Nebuchadnezzar, Dan. **4**.27).

The point of Jesus' teaching is that those who do such things to gain a public reputation for piety get precisely that—and no more. Practised with this motive, they are not truly religious acts. Let them rather be done so that God alone knows about them, and He will bestow an appropriate reward—the opportunity for the further practice of such piety (cf. 2 Cor. **9**.10 f.). The AV addition 'openly' at the end of vs. 4,6,18 perverts the meaning of the promise: publicity is as inappropriate in the bestowal of the reward as in the pious action.

The primacy of almsgiving among the forms of piety mentioned in these paragraphs is quite in line with O.T. teaching: 'he who is kind to the poor lends to the LORD, and He will repay him for his deed' (Prov. **19.**17)—a text on which Dean Swift preached one of the shortest sermons on record: 'If you like the security, down with the dust.'

As for prayer, there is a place for public and 'synagogue' prayer, but there is something specially distasteful about praying ostensibly to God but actually in order to be heard or seen by others and so to gain the reputation of being a man of prayer. We recall the newspaper report of 'the most eloquent prayer ever delivered to a Boston audience'. The Christian to whom prayer is 'vital breath' and 'native air' will pray when no one is around, and his (or her) public prayer will take character from habitual secret prayer. The heaping up of 'empty phrases' (7) may refer to the Gentile practice of including all the deity's designations so as to make sure of not omitting the appropriate one; it has its counterpart in the grandiloquent phraseology which some Christians today imagine God prefers to the simple word 'Father'. We do not acquaint God with our needs when we pray (8); we remind *ourselves* of them, and adopt that dependent attitude of heart which can receive His mercy in a spirit of grateful trust.

Note: 'Hypocrites' (2; cf. vs. 5,16; **7.**5; **15.**7; **22.**18; **23.**13–15) means literally 'play-actors'; people who go through the motions of almsgiving and prayer 'that they may be seen by men', without any inward sense of charity or devotion, are simply acting a part which does not express their attitude of heart.

Question: Is any part of my religion play-acting?

St. Matthew 6.9-18   Prayer, Forgiveness and Fasting

The Lord's Prayer, given to the disciples as a pattern to follow, summarizes as in a nutshell Jesus' teaching about the kingdom of God. It 'can be repeated in less than half a minute, contains petitions which range from the common bread-and-butter needs of our breakfast tables to the ultimate achievement of the age-long purposes of God; puts God's glory first, our needs second, does not rule out material matters as too trifling to pray about, yet insists on the supremacy of the spiritual, and emphasizes the basic condition of the disciples' enjoyment of the Father's forgiveness' (C. F. Hogg and J. B. Watson). The clauses 'Hallowed be Thy name, Thy kingdom come, Thy will be done' are probably three forms of what is basically the same petition; to each the words 'on earth as it is in heaven' are applicable. Whether we render 'our daily bread' or 'our bread for the morrow' (margin), the petition of v. 11 is content

28

with 'rations' for one day at a time. In Aramaic 'debts' and 'debtors' (12) are idiomatic terms for 'sins' and 'sinners'; the reminder that only the forgiving can ask for forgiveness is reinforced in vs. 14,15 (cf. **18.23–35**). 'Lead us not into temptation' (13) may mean 'grant that we may not fail in the test'—the supreme crisis which puts one's faith and loyalty to the crucial test (cf. **26.41**). The 'evil' from which we should pray to be delivered is probably the 'evil one' whose aim is to destroy faith in the people of God. The doxology which follows the prayer in AV does not belong to the original text but preserves very early church practice: a few decades after the publication of this Gospel it is appended to the prayer in the *Didache* ('Teaching of the Twelve Apostles').

This document, the *Didache*, has a significant gloss on the next paragraph, on fasting (16–18), which shows how easy it was then, as now, to miss the point of our Lord's teaching: 'let not your fasts be with the hypocrites, for they fast on Mondays and Thursdays (cf. Luke **18.12**), but do you fast on Wednesdays and Fridays.' Fasting, like almsgiving and prayer, should be a private and voluntary undertaking between the worshipper and God, not a means of acquiring credit with men.

When we read our Lord's criticisms of the scribes of His day, we should consider whether we are not prone to treat His words with the same wooden legalism as they manifested in their application of the O.T. law. Is it not possible for Christians today to fulfil their religious exercises as if they were so many rules to be kept, and to regard the fulfilment of them as constituting a stronger title to God's approval than is available for others who are deplorably lax in these matters? In what way are such Christians better than the 'play-actors' who incur our Lord's censure?

St. Matthew 6.19-34   The Carefree Mind

This section of the Sermon inculcates a freedom from anxiety, rising from implicit confidence in a heavenly Father's love and care. Verses 19–21 constitute a perfect poem in Aramaic, showing unforced rhythm and even rhyme. The uncertainty of treasure laid up on earth is illustrated by the parable of Luke **12.15–21**. 'Character is the only garment you can weave in this world and wear in the next.' An unsound eye, in the sense of v. 23, is an envious eye, which is apt to accompany concentration on earthly treasure; a sound eye (22) betokens a generous spirit, such as God Himself shows (cf. **5.45,48**). 'Mammon' (24) is an Aramaic word, etymologically denoting anything in which men put their trust, but in practice

29

standing for material gain, which can so easily take the central place in life that is due to God alone. We may recall the apostolic equation of covetousness with idolatry (Col. 3.5). In spite of the plain warning that God and mammon cannot be served together, a surprisingly large number of Christians try their best to prove that it can be done—and succeed in demonstrating the truth of our Lord's words. The Father who feeds the birds and bedecks the grass can be trusted to provide His children with enough to eat and wear (25–34). We cannot be sure whether 'span of life' or 'stature' is the better translation in v. 27; in favour of the former is the consideration that worry has little effect on one's stature, but is more likely to shorten life than to prolong it. The Gentiles (32) were supposed by Jews to have little or no spiritual appreciation: our Lord warns His hearers that they are liable to live on the same level as the Gentiles. Verse 33 shows the true priorities. An African ruler a few years ago modified this precept in a public inscription to 'Seek ye first the *political* kingdom . . .'; he soon discovered his mistake. Many Christians make their own more private modifications of the precept; they, too, are destined to discover their mistake. To seek God's kingdom and righteousness first is to take the Sermon on the Mount seriously.

Questions for further study and discussion on St. Matthew ch. 6

1. How does the injunction about praying in private (5,6) square with Daniel's praying at his open window (Dan. 6.10)?
2. What is the meaning of fasting for a Christian?
3. Is the trust in God for food recommended in vs. 25–33 feasible in famine-stricken areas, when adequate provision for the needs of one would mean so much less for others?
4. Does the difficulty of reconciling v. 34 with the duty of providing for one's dependants suggest that some of these precepts were intended for an interim and exceptional period?

St. Matthew 7.1-12 The Golden Rule and its Corollaries

The Golden Rule (12) is the quintessence of the greater part of these twelve verses. Our Lord was not the first teacher in Israel to sum up 'the law and the prophets' in such terms as these, although the earlier formulations of the Golden Rule are negative rather than positive. For example, a generation earlier, Rabbi Hillel said to a proselyte who asked for a brief summary of the law: 'What is hateful to yourself, do not to another; that is the whole law, everything else is commentary.'

The exhortation against judgement (1,2) forbids not a judicious discernment but a censorious spirit which delights in finding fault with others. The picture of a man with a log in his own eye volunteering to remove a splinter from his brother's eye (3–5) is a delightful sample of our Lord's humour. A proper use of discernment is enjoined in v. 6, which incidentally is an example of chiasmus; the swine will trample the pearls underfoot and the dogs (pariah dogs, of course) will bite the hand that feeds them, even if it be with consecrated meat. This injunction does not refer specifically to the withholding of sacraments from the unworthy or unbelieving; still less is it (as some contemporary exegetes have suggested) a judaizing warning against offering the blessings of the gospel to Gentiles. It means, more generally, that spiritual mysteries are not to be pressed on those who are unready or unwilling to appreciate them.

The encouragement to prayer in vs. 7–11 reaffirms the teaching of 6.5–15, and does so by means of the 'how much more' argument which Jesus loved to use. If even a reluctant and sleepy head of the house will rise at midnight to give his neighbour three loaves for the sake of peace (Luke 11.5–8, immediately preceding the Lukan parallel to our present paragraph); if even an unjust judge will give an importunate widow her rights to avoid being pestered to death (Luke 18.1–8); if even earthly fathers, sinful men though they are, give their children food when they ask for it and do not put them off with useless or dangerous substitutes, *how much more* will God, the heavenly Father, give His children good things, not harmful things, when they ask Him? Therefore 'ask . . . , seek . . . , knock'.

St. Matthew 7.13-29   A Matter of Life and Death

There is a note of urgency, even sternness, about these verses which is overlooked by those who make facile remarks about the Sermon on the Mount as an ethical ideal. By insisting on the two gates, the two ways, the two destinies (13,14), the two kinds of tree and fruit (15–20) and the two foundations (24–27), Jesus presents His way as the path of life, and the refusal to follow it as the straight road to disaster. The *either–or* of His words is inescapable. In the day when all things are shaken, stability and salvation, for individuals and communities alike, can be secured only by accepting the way laid down in His teaching and exemplified in His life. Those who teach otherwise, however fair their approach and plausible their reasoning, are 'false prophets', wolves in sheep's clothing (15). The repeated 'you will know them by their fruits' (16,20) is a principle of universal

31

application—'by their fruits', commented William James, 'not by their roots.'

To claim the status of disciples, to call Jesus 'Lord' by way of lip-service only, to preach, exorcize and even do mighty works in His name will not avail unless there is genuine inward obedience to the Father's will as He made it known. Only those who are thus obedient will gain entrance to His kingdom (21-23). The obstacle to such obedience is not outrageous wickedness but some of the most familiar human tendencies. 'It will simplify the discussion if we admit the truth at the outset: that the teaching of Jesus is difficult and unacceptable because it runs counter to those elements in human nature which the twentieth century has in common with the first—such things as laziness, greed, the love of pleasure, the instinct to hit back and the like. The teaching as a whole shows that Jesus was well aware of this and recognized that here and nowhere else lay the obstacle that had to be surmounted' (T. W. Manson). The fulfilment of the righteous requirements of the Sermon, as of the older Law, is possible only to those who 'walk not according to the flesh but according to the Spirit' (Rom. 8.4)—the Spirit of Christ Himself.

The crowds might well be 'astonished at His teaching' and recognize the authority of His words (28,29), but that is not the same thing as accepting His teaching or submitting to His authority. There is rarely an inconvenient throng around the narrow gate.

Questions: (i) Could you rewrite v. 22 using modern terms and modern situations? (ii) What does v. 23 teach about the essence of Christianity and about the final reckoning?

Questions for further study and discussion on St. Matthew chs. 5-7

Consider the following statements in the light of the Sermon on the Mount:

1. 'The moral standard set up by Jesus is a standard of example rather than precept' (T. W. Manson).
2. 'Christianity has not been tried and found wanting; it has been found difficult and not tried' (G. K. Chesterton).
3. 'It would be a great point gained if people would only consider that it was a Sermon, and was *preached*, not an *act* which was passed' (James Denney).

St. Matthew 8.1-13

Blessing for Gentiles as well as Jews

Having given prominence to the Sermon on the Mount as the programme of our Lord's ministry, Matthew now relates detailed incidents from the earlier Galilean phase of His ministry (8.1—9.34). The healing of the leper illustrates His compassion and disregard for the isolation imposed on one whom the law pronounced 'unclean' (Lev. 13.46), for He 'touched him' (3); at the same time it shows that He had no desire to overrule the recognized procedure, for the cured man was directed to offer the prescribed sacrifice and so obtain a priestly declaration that he was now 'clean' (4; cf. Lev. 14.2-32). Conflict with the religious establishment came soon enough, but it was not of Jesus' seeking.

The leper was cured by the healing touch of Jesus' hand: by contrast, the centurion's servant, like the Canaanite girl in 15.28, was healed at a distance (5–13). This may serve as a parable of the fact that Jesus' active ministry on earth, with rare exceptions, was confined to Jews. With them He lived in close physical contact. The blessing which in due course He bestowed in unstinted measure on Gentiles was communicated not by personal contact of this kind but from the heavenly throne of glory through the agency of His disciples (cf. 28.18 ff.). Jesus did not withhold His sympathy from Gentiles; He was ready to 'come and heal' the centurion's paralysed servant (7), and He saw in the centurion's faith, which made His doing so unnecessary, a foreshadowing of the day when 'many' would come from the Gentile lands and share the blessings which the patriarchs of Israel would enjoy in the new age. The ingathering of the Gentiles was an 'eschatological' sign—a sign of the age of fulfilment of what the prophets had foretold (cf. Psa. 102.15; Isa. 60.3). Jesus' ministry marked the inauguration of this new age, but not until the Son of Man was raised from the dead would its full power and outreach be manifested (contrast the commissions of 10.5 and 28.19). The centurion, recognizing that Jesus had unseen powers at His command which could obey Him at a distance (8 f.), exhibited a quality of faith such as Jesus had met in no one else; hence His delighted response (10). The hard saying about 'the sons of the kingdom', i.e. those who were the natural heirs of Abraham, Isaac and Jacob (12), is absent from the parallel in Luke 7.2–10, but the same lesson is taught in the Nazareth sermon of Luke 4.23–27. The 'outer darkness' (12) continues the picture of v. 11; those who expect to head the list of guests find themselves, because of their lack of faith, excluded from the brightly-lit banqueting hall, grinding their teeth in vexation in the darkness outside.

St. Matthew 8.14-22

Healing the Sick and Screening Volunteers

The healing of Peter's mother-in-law from her fever—again by the touch of His hand—is mentioned as a sample of the many cures effected by our Lord that day in Capernaum (14–16). (The mention of Peter's mother-in-law provides an 'undesigned coincidence' with 1 Cor. 9.5, where Paul confirms that he was a married man.) The 'word' with which He relieved those who were victims of demonic powers (16) was the word of command which expressed His authority as Lord of all creation. The quotation of Isa. 53.4 in this healing context (17) emphasizes the Servant's removing the infirmities and diseases of men rather than (as in its O.T. context) His enduring them vicariously; the verbs used can bear either sense. He bore His people's sins; there is no suggestion that He shared their sicknesses, especially as demon-possession is included among these. Yet we cannot miss the note of sympathy which accompanies the power of His word and action: this is no dispassionate visitant from another realm who cannot be touched with a fellow-feeling for the ills of humanity, but One who is man among men, bone of their bone and flesh of their flesh.

In vs. 18–22 samples are provided of the tests which Jesus applied to discourage would-be disciples whose commitment was less than total. His reply to the scribe who volunteered to follow Him wherever He went raises a question about the meaning of the title 'Son of man'. If it is here little more than another way of expressing the first personal pronoun, then He says that whereas wild animals have their resting-places He Himself can never be sure of a bed for the night or a roof over His head and His companions must similarly be prepared to have no fixed abode. But there were homes where Jesus was most welcome. The suggestion that it is a proverb contrasting the plight of man with the creatures which by instinct construct suitable homes for themselves has little to commend it. Perhaps the point is that 'everybody is at home in Israel's land except the true Israel. The birds of the air—the Roman overlords, the foxes—the Edomite interlopers (cf. Luke 13.32), have made their position secure. The true Israel is disinherited by them: and if you cast your lot with Me and Mine you join the ranks of the dispossessed, and you must be prepared to serve God under those conditions' (T. W. Manson). The other volunteer promised total commitment when his last family obligation was discharged. Jesus' reply assures him that he need not fear that his father will be left unburied when he dies; the business of the kingdom of God is urgent and brooks no reservation or delay.

Question: What excuses do men make today for not following Christ?

St. Matthew 8.23-34   Tempests Without and Within

Matthew describes this storm on the lake by a very strong word, literally meaning 'earthquake' (24), and it is a pity that translators have not given it its proper force, for Matthew intends its proper force to be understood. The stilling of the tempest, recorded by the three Synoptists, not only portrays Jesus as Lord of wind and wave, but does so in such a way as to recall the ancient Near Eastern motif of the Creator's victory over the unruly sea, portraying the forces of chaos. Matthew's choice of the word 'earthquake' deliberately emphasizes this aspect of the matter: the upsurging of the deep (the 'abyss' of Luke 8.31) symbolizes all the demonic powers which rise to overthrow the kingdom of God but which are overthrown by that kingdom. The lesson which this incident teaches in the realm of nature is taught again by the following incident on the human level. It is the spirit of man that is the principal target of demonic hostility, as is shown in the description of the two possessed Gadarenes. The multiple schizophrenia and complete loss of personal identity from which they suffer have their counterparts in contemporary society, where one's capacity for responsible decision can so easily be killed by the trend-setting legion. 'If it is true that we are the contemporaries of Christ, as the gospel of the resurrection teaches us, then we can see how He moves through our consumer society and asks the anonymous member of the mass, "What is your name?" A ring at the doorbell; and an indistinct murmur of voices from within: "We are many, we are many . . ." ' (Olov Hartman). The juxtaposition of the 'consumer society' with demon-possession is seen in the reaction of the Gentile population, more concerned about the loss of their pigs than about the healing of souls. A strange story in modern ears, no doubt; but it is our modern predicament that it uncovers.

Note: There is considerable variation between Gadarenes, Gerasenes and Gergesenes in the manuscript tradition of this passage and its parallels in *Mark* and *Luke*. Gadara was 7 miles south-east from the lake, separated from the area indicated here by the Yarmuk gorge. The best-known Gerasa was modern Jerash in Transjordan, nearly 40 miles south-east of the lake. The readings Gerasenes and Gergesenes apparently preserve the ancient name of the modern village of Kersa or Kursi, on the east shore of the lake, at the only point on that coast where the steep hills come down to the shore. The incident should probably be located there.

St. Matthew 9.1-8   The Authority of the Son of Man

Matthew's account of Jesus' healing of the paralytic of Capernaum (here called 'His own city', i.e. the city which He now made His headquarters; cf. Mark 2.1) is greatly compressed in comparison with those of the two other Synoptists (nothing is said here of the man's being let down through the roof); but the essential lessons are retained. This is not only a miracle story but a 'pronouncement story', one which is told for the sake of the dictum to which it leads up—in this case: 'the Son of man has authority on earth to forgive sins' (6). It is as easy to *say* 'Your sins are forgiven' as to say 'Rise and walk'; but the spectators could immediately see the effectiveness of the latter command, whereas the validity of the former utterance belonged to the inward and spiritual realm. The scribes were justified in thinking that Jesus was exercising a prerogative of God; but some of God's prerogatives can be delegated if He pleases. So in Dan. 7.13 f. His prerogatives of dominion and judgement are delegated to 'one like a son of man' (cf. John 5.22,27), and it is as this Son of Man that Jesus now speaks. Yet, as the sovereign interpreter of the will of God, He claims for the Son of Man the authority not to *judge* sins but to *forgive* sins (cf. John 3.17; 12.47b). He to whom God has delegated the judgement of the world can exercise that authority by pronouncing acquittal as well as by sentence of condemnation, and such is the good pleasure of the Son of Man. Not only so, but Matthew envisages this authority as shared in some sense with others, unless we are to treat the plural 'men' at the end of v. 8 as purely a generalizing plural. Here we have Biblical precedent for the familiar assurance that God 'hath given power, and commandment, to his Ministers, to declare and pronounce to his people, being penitent, the Absolution and Remission of their sins'; it is theirs to proclaim the forgiveness which the Son of Man has procured.

St. Matthew 9.9-17   Controversy Grows

The story of the call of the tax collector raises some interesting questions. Why, for example, is it only in the Gospel traditionally associated with Matthew that this tax collector (referred to as Levi by Mark and Luke) is called Matthew? And why is it in the apostolic list of this Gospel only that Matthew (mentioned by his bare name in the parallel lists of Mark and Luke) is distinguished as 'Matthew the tax collector' (Matt. **10.3**)? It is only from this Evangelist that we learn that the Twelve included a former tax collector. That he should have become a colleague of the fishermen is noteworthy enough—'if ever cursing was justifiable, it was when such as Peter the fisherman cursed Matthew the publican' (W. M. Christie)—but that he should have been a member of the same group as Simon the Zealot is a near-miracle. For while it was not for the Romans, but for the administration of Herod the tetrarch, that Matthew collected taxes in his toll-booth on the Capernaum quayside, tax-farmers as a class were regarded as unpatriotic characters, no better than robbers, and tax evasion carried no moral stigma with it.

The appended incident (10–13) is a pronouncement story, told for the sake of the concluding utterance, in which Jesus defends His association with such disreputable persons by appealing to a great prophetic declaration (Hos. **6.6**; cf. Matt. **12.7**) and to the well-known fact that it is sick people, not healthy people, who need the doctor's care. 'I came not to call the righteous, but sinners' (13b) is one of the greatest single-sentence summaries of the gospel.

The fasting incident is another pronouncement story. Regular fasting (apart from the observance of the few fast-days of the Jewish year) was a voluntary act of religious devotion (cf. **6.16–18**), undertaken by many religious groups in Israel but not by the disciples of Jesus. Jesus' defence of their behaviour in this regard (15a) may have implications for His own understanding of His person and role. The additional words (15b) point to the later period, when His disciples did fast, and explain this change of practice. But during His ministry their deviation from the fasting procedure of other religious groups underlined the difference made by the proclamation of the kingdom and the incompatibility of this new order with that which preceded it—an incompatibility illustrated by the two short parables of vs. 16,17.

St. Matthew 9.18-26 Jairus' Daughter

Like the narrative of the paralytic, the account of the raising of Jairus' daughter is greatly compressed in this Gospel as compared with the parallels in *Mark* (5.22–43) and *Luke* (8.41–56). It is from these parallels that we know that 'ruler' (18) means 'ruler of the synagogue', as also that his name was Jairus. The rulers of the synagogue (except where the title was honorary) exercised general supervision over the building itself and over the services which were

37

conducted in it; they were commonly elders of the congregation and, since the synagogue served as the community centre, would be persons of considerable local importance. No doubt only the most desperate need would have driven such a man to implore the help of Jesus, who was no longer in good odour with the synagogue.

The woman with the persistent haemorrhage who touched Him on the way had not merely to endure the physical distress of her condition; according to the law (Lev. **15**.25) she was in a permanent state of ceremonial defilement, with all the social and religious disadvantages which this involved. The fringe of Jesus' cloak which she touched (20) was one of the tassels prescribed by the law of Num. **15**.38; Deut. **22**.12.

The flute-players of v. 23 were professional mourners, hired for the sad occasion. It has sometimes been argued that our Lord's assurance, 'the girl is not dead but sleeping' (24), means that those who thought she was dead were mistaken: but cf. John **11**.11 (that the Greek word for 'sleep' there is different from that used here is immaterial). It is implied that He raised her from death as easily as He might have roused her from sleep. Both the incidents in this section illustrate Jesus' ready response to faith—the ruler's and the woman's.

Meditation: 'Maturity and youth . . . much faith or little faith, touching or being touched, Jesus was the answer to men's needs' (Ellison).

St. Matthew 9.27-38   The Galilean Harvest Field

The duplication of the blind men (cf. Mark **8**.22–26) probably emphasizes the note of witness (cf. Deut. **19**.15), as with the two demoniacs of **8**.28 and the two blind men of Jericho in **20**.30–34 (an incident closely similar to this). This incident also illustrates the power of faith (28 f.). The 'stern charge' of v. 30 is like that laid upon the leper (**8**.4a), but much more vigorously expressed (although the verb used here of the charge to the blind men is used in Mark **1**.43 of the charge to the leper). The expression conveys a sense of indignation, and may combine anger at the forces which afflicted men with eager desire to prevent the misunderstanding of His real mission which could too easily arise from the blazing abroad of His acts of healing.

The exorcizing of the dumb demon and the imparting of the power of speech to its victim (32–34) occasions the mocking charge that one who exercised such mastery over the demons must be in league with their prince—a charge repeated in similar circumstances in

38

12.24, where it is refuted in detail. No silence can be imposed this time, because the cure was seen by crowds of bystanders. The two actions together represent a fulfilment of Isa. **35.5** f.:

'Then the eyes of the blind shall be opened . . .
and the tongue of the dumb sing for joy.'

When the crowds mentioned in the generalizing summary of vs. 35 f. are compared to 'sheep without a shepherd', we should remember the precedent of 1 Kings **22.**17 and conclude that what is meant is not a congregation without a pastor but an army without a captain—'a maccabean host with no Judas Maccabaeus, a leaderless mob, a danger to themselves and everyone else' (T. W. Manson). Jesus knew very well how readily they could be led to disaster if they found the wrong kind of leader. The political unrest in Palestine in this period was due in large measure to the desperate economic plight of the population and the high level of unemployment. The majority of them refused the leadership of Jesus because He would not be the kind of leader they wanted—one who would promise them political independence and economic rehabilitation—and in due course were led to disaster by others who made these promises without being able to fulfil them. But at the moment these leaderless multitudes presented, in Jesus' eyes, a ripe harvest-field waiting to be reaped for the kingdom of God, if only sufficient harvesters were available for the task (37 f.).

Questions for further study and discussion on St. Matthew chs. 8 and 9

1. Discuss the various manifestations of faith in the narratives of these two chapters.
2. 'The calling of a tax collector was a "sign" of the gospel—that God does not demand righteousness according to the Law, but gives the kingdom to those who have no righteousness of their own' (J. C. Fenton). What further 'signs' of this kind can be found in this Gospel?
3. Compare the two passages in this Gospel (**9.**13; **12.**7) where Jesus quotes Hos. **6.**6 ('I desire mercy, and not sacrifice') and consider the relevance of the quotation in both places. What is the point of 'sacrifice'?

St. Matthew 10.1-15   Mission of the Twelve

Into the ripe harvest-field, then, the Twelve are sent two by two, and the Evangelist takes the opportunity to list their names (2–4; cf. Mark **3.**16–19; Luke **6.**14–16; Acts **1.**13). There are variations between the lists given by the several Evangelists, but if the Twelve are divided

39

into three groups of four, each group of four invariably begins with the same name: Simon Peter, Philip, James the son of Alphaeus. Thaddaeus (cf. Mark 3.18) must be equated with 'Judas the son of James' of Luke 6.16; Acts 1.13 (cf. 'Judas not Iscariot' of John 14.22). 'Cananaean' (not 'Canaanite', as in AV) here and in Mark 3.18 represents the Aramaic word which corresponds to 'Zealot' (Gk. *zēlōtēs*, Luke 6.15; Acts 1.13), denoting a member (or former member) of the militant party of resistance.

The commission to the Twelve constitutes Matthew's second body of discourse material. They were to function as an extension of their Master's ministry, speaking and acting in His name. With the message of v. 7 cf. 4.17. The time was limited, and they must concentrate on 'the Jew first'. That Jesus was willing to help Gentiles we have seen already (8.5 ff.) and His friendly contacts with Samaritans are chronicled in other Gospels; but the time for their unrestricted access to His grace was not yet (cf. John 12.24,32). That the present restriction betokens no exclusive outlook on the part of the Evangelist himself is plain from the post-Easter commission of 28.19 f., spoken when the earlier restrictions have been removed. The reference to 'the lost sheep of the house of Israel' (cf. 9.36) implies that Jesus offered Himself to them as their true Shepherd (cf. John 10.1–16, echoing Ezek. 34.23 f., where the son of David fulfils this role).

The Twelve were to take no provisions for their journey but to depend on charity. The dictum that 'the labourer deserves his food' (10) has echoes elsewhere in the N.T. (cf. 1 Cor. 9.14; 1 Tim. 5.18). The expectation that in any town or village one 'who is worthy' will be found recalls what Josephus says about the travelling Essenes —that they could always rely on the hospitality of resident Essenes. Jesus knew that sympathizers with the message of the kingdom might be found in many places; some at least of these would have been influenced by the preaching of John the Baptist (cf. 3.5 f.).

The 'peace' of v. 13 is that of the greeting 'Peace be with you'. So terrible a judgement will be experienced by the place which refuses the gospel they bring that its dust must be shaken off as they depart lest that judgement extend to it and so to them (cf. Acts 13.51; 18.6).

Consider: The Twelve had first to witness to their own people. It is a serious delusion to think that the 'flop' at home will be a shining success in the mission field.

40

While the charge of vs. 5–15 relates to the immediate mission of the Twelve, that of vs. 16 ff. looks forward to a later period, to their ministry in the period between A.D. 30 and 70. This section is parallel in part to 24.9–14; it is valuable for the degree of light it sheds on the Palestinian disciples' largely unchronicled mission to the Jews during these years (cf. Gal. 2.7–9). Their defence was to lie not in force but in wisdom and innocence (cf. Rom. 16.19); the animals mentioned in v. 16 served as standard symbols for the qualities indicated. The 'councils' of v. 17 are 'sanhedrins' (Gk. *synedria*)—mainly the local sanhedrins rather than the supreme Sanhedrin at Jerusalem (although it was by the latter that James the Lord's brother was sentenced to death in A.D. 62)—and the flogging inflicted in synagogues would be the 'forty stripes save one' (cf. 2. Cor. 11.24; Deut. 25.3). The 'governors and kings' of v. 18 might be Roman governors and Jewish kings (like Herod Agrippa, whose action against James the son of Zebedee and Peter is recorded in Acts 12.1–4). The general sense of vs. 18b–20 is illustrated by the earlier Christian martyrologies, where Christians on trial for their faith exhibit a ready eloquence in reply and defence which astonishes their accusers (cf. also Acts 4.13; 1 Pet. 3.15 f.). The warning about domestic division (21) is repeated in vs. 35 f. (cf. also Mark 13.12). With v. 22 we should compare Tacitus' description of Christians as 'a class of men loathed for their vices' and especially for their 'hatred of the human race' (*Annals* 15.44).

With v. 23a compare the action of Paul and Barnabas in Acts 14.5 f., 19 f. The interpretation of v. 23b has been a debated issue for long and the debate continues (one interpretation supplied the main foundation of Albert Schweitzer's solution to the *Quest of the Historical Jesus*) but in the context the coming of the Son of Man can scarcely be dissociated from the fall of Jerusalem in A.D. 70 (see notes on 16.27 f.; 24.3 ff.). That this is Matthew's intention is more likely than the view which dissociates it from vs. 16–22 and attaches it to vs. 5–15, as though the Twelve on their immediate mission were Jesus' forerunners, preparing for His coming to the 'towns of Israel' which they visited in advance of Him (cf. Luke 10.1, where the seventy are sent 'into every town and place where He Himself was about to come').

St. Matthew 10.24-42   Words of Encouragement

Some further sayings of Jesus for the encouragement of His disciples are appended. The persecutions in store for them are no greater than what He Himself must endure (cf. John 13.16; 15.20; 16.2; also Luke 6.40). There may be two plays on words in v. 25 if Jesus spoke in Aramaic: 'it is enough for the disciple' would be *shewi le-shewilya* (if 'disciple' be understood in the sense of 'apprentice'), and the name Beelzebul itself may mean 'master of the house' (Jesus is referring back to the taunt of 9.34). But if the servants share their Master's sufferings, they will also share His vindication: He Himself will be their advocate with God, as He will be the prosecutor of the faithless (cf. Mark 8.38; Luke 12.8 f.). They are to be His heralds, proclaiming the 'secrets of the kingdom' (cf. 13.11) without fear or favour (26 f.); if only they fear God, they need fear no one else (28). With the comparison of men and sparrows in v. 31 cf. 6.26.

The warning that His mission would divide families (34 ff.; cf. v. 21) echoes Mic. 7.5 f.; such domestic dissension was to be one of the woes of the end-time. The lack of sympathy which Jesus found in His own family circle may have taught Him by experience how 'a man's foes' could be 'those of his own household' (36; cf. Mark 3.21; John 7.5). That the claims of the kingdom of heaven take precedence over all family ties (37) is repeatedly emphasized in the Gospels (cf. 8.22; 12.46–50; 19.29). To take up one's cross (38) was in the circumstances of those days no easy metaphor for the endurance of this or that vexatious burden: it meant that Jesus' followers must be prepared to be crucified, as He was (cf. 16.24). The repeated 'is not worthy of Me' may reflect the same Aramaic phrase as the parallel 'cannot be My disciple' in Luke 14.26 f. But life lost in His service would be life gained; life gained at the expense of loyalty to Him would be life lost (39; cf. 16.25–27).

The final paragraph in this section (40–42) was as applicable to the immediate mission of the Twelve as to all time following: the treatment meted out to His followers is accepted by their Lord as meted out to Himself (cf. 25.40,45; Mark 9.41; Luke 10.16; John 13.20). With v. 41 cf. 1 Kings 17.8 ff.; 2 Kings 4.8 ff. The reference to 'little ones' in v. 42 anticipates the teaching of 18.5–14.

Thought: There is nothing in this section which does not apply to us. See how it was worked out in Acts. Are we prepared to take this teaching seriously today?

Questions for further study and discussion on St. Matthew ch. 10

1. How would you answer those preachers who maintain that the directions of vs. 5–15 should be followed as closely as possible by evangelists and missionaries today? How would you interpret these verses in terms of your own neighbourhood?

2. Consider actual examples of the way in which the claims of the kingdom of heaven may still cut across family loyalties.

St. Matthew 11.1-15   Jesus and John the Baptist

We have not been told thus far of the imprisonment of John the Baptist: it is related as a 'flash-back' in **14.3** ff. John had announced that the Coming One would carry out a ministry of judgement, but the reports of Jesus' activity which reached him in the cell at Machaerus had little to do with judgement. Was Jesus, he wondered, the Coming One after all? Had he himself perhaps been mistaken in so identifying Him? When he sent his messengers for reassurance on these questions, Jesus performed before their eyes many of the signs which, according to the prophets, would mark the new age (cf. Isa. **35**.5 f.; **61**.1); when they told John what they had seen, his faith would be confirmed, and he would not feel that Jesus had let him down (for this is what 'take offence' amounts to in v. 6.)

Jesus' witness to John sets John on a pinnacle by himself. Those who remembered John's appearance and demeanour must have laughed as they heard the inappropriate metaphors of vs. 7 and 8. Jesus confirmed the general belief that John was a prophet—'and more than a prophet', He added (9), for John, the last prophet of the old order, was the herald of the imminent kingdom (cf. **3**.2), the messenger of Mal. **3**.1 who would prepare the way of the Lord (cf. Isa. **40**.3 quoted in Matt. **3**.3) and the returning Elijah foretold in Mal. **4**.5 f., whose advent would precede 'the great and terrible day of the LORD'. At the end of the old age of 'the prophets and the law' John stood and announced the dawn of the new age, without himself entering that new age; therefore, unsurpassed as he was in personal stature, he was surpassed in privilege by the least in the new age (11). The reference in v. 12 may be to the Zealots and other militant nationalists, who endeavoured to hasten the new age by force of arms. They, too, were liable to 'take offence' at Jesus when He refused to exploit His popularity by putting their policy into practice; and indeed, in this day as in that, all who find that He will not accommodate Himself to their preconceived pattern do well to pay heed to the beatitude of v. 6.

St. Matthew 11.16-24
The Doom of the Lakeside Towns

Those who found fault with John the Baptist for his ascetic way of life were equally ready to criticize Jesus for a way of life which was very different from John's. (Whatever inner significance the title 'Son of Man' may bear elsewhere, in v. 19 it cannot be understood otherwise than as a circumlocution for the personal pronoun 'I'.) There was no pleasing such people: they were like children playing out-of-doors, at odds with one another because one half wanted to play weddings while the other half wanted to play funerals. (If v. 17 is turned back into Aramaic, it has the form of a jingling rhyme.) But the wisdom of God was vindicated equally in John's asceticism and in Jesus' eating with 'tax collectors and sinners' (19).

For all the popular excitement which the Galilean ministry had aroused, it found little genuine or lasting response from those lake-side towns where Jesus had been most active. Chorazin is commonly identified with modern Kerazeh and Capernaum with Tell-Hum, while Bethsaida may be et-Tabgha or Mas'adiya, according as it is to be located on the west shore of the lake or east of the point where the Jordan enters it (the latter is the more probable). Gentile cities in O.T. times had experienced prophetic denunciation (like Tyre and Sidon; cf. Ezek. 26.1—28.23) and divine judgement (like Sodom; cf. Gen. 18.20—19.28), without a hundredth part of the knowledge of God which these lakeside towns had been given during recent months: the judgement of the latter on the great day would be correspondingly greater than that of those more ancient communities; and indeed in their case the eschatological doom was anticipated when the Romans crushed the revolt in Galilee in the spring of A.D. 67. The opening words in the denunciation of Capernaum echo those addressed to the king of Babylon in Isa. 14.12–15. The greater the privilege, the greater the responsibility.

St. Matthew 11.25-30   The Yoke of Wisdom

While Jesus deplored the unbelief of the majority of His hearers, He reserved warm words of commendation for the minority that did respond to Him, and—'babes' in intellect though they might be alongside the alumni of the rabbinical schools—were enabled nevertheless to appreciate the revelation of the Father which He imparted. This reversal of worldly standards was no innovation in the dealings of God with man: Jesus acknowledged it to be His Father's will. Verse 27 (cf. Luke 10.22) has been described as an 'aerolite from the Johannine heaven' because its style and content are so similar to what we find in the Fourth Gospel; yet it belongs to the earliest literary stratum of our Gospel material. Our Lord speaks here as the Son and Revealer of the Father (cf. John 1.18) and as One whose person and commission are known in fullness to the Father only. In the 'comfortable words' which follow He speaks in the role of the Divine Wisdom (cf. note on 23.34). A striking parallel in Jewish wisdom literature is provided by Sirach 51.23–30, where the author issues an invitation to draw near and lodge in his school in order to learn wisdom. 'Put your neck under the yoke', he says, for under that yoke, he adds, 'I . . . found for myself much rest.' He was a learner and teacher of wisdom; Jesus is Wisdom incarnate (cf. 1 Cor. 1.24–30).

'Take My yoke upon you' (29) means 'Enrol yourselves as My disciples'; with His 'easy' yoke we may contrast the burdensome yoke to which Peter refers in Acts 15.10. On the lips of another the claim to be 'gentle and lowly in heart' would not have the ring of truth. If it is said that the claim is unlikely to have been made by Jesus in person we may reflect (*i*) that generations of readers or hearers of the Gospel have been conscious of no incongruity here, (*ii*) that it agrees with objective testimony (cf. 2 Cor. 10.1) and (*iii*) that, as has been said, it is uttered in the character of Divine Wisdom.

Thought: The yoke is a sign both of Christ's lordship and partnership.

St. Matthew 12.1-14   Sabbath Controversies

Our Lord's final break with the synagogue establishment arose from the sovereign freedom with which He reinterpreted the sabbath law in His teaching and action alike. The wording of the Fourth Commandment, 'in it (the seventh day) you shall not do any work' (Exod. 20.10; Deut. 5.14), called for a more precise definition of 'work'; the rabbinical schools distinguished 39 classes of activity which were forbidden on the sabbath. The disciples' actions fell within these prohibitions, for plucking the ears of grain was a form of reaping, and rubbing them in their hands to extract the kernels (cf. Luke 6.1) was a form of threshing. Our Lord's reply to the Pharisees' criticism, with His appeal to the precedent of David (1 Sam. 21.1 ff.) and quotation of Hos. 6.6 (cf. Matt. 9.13), amounts to this: the law of God in general, and the sabbath law in particular, were intended to be a blessing to men, not a burden, and a fulfilment in the letter is no true fulfilment if it infringes the spirit and purpose of the law. Human need takes precedence over the best-intentioned religious casuistry, and the Son of Man's authority includes the right to interpret and fulfil the sabbath law in accordance with the divine provision.

The second sabbath controversy (9–14) had its setting in 'their synagogue'—an indication, perhaps, that He was no longer welcome there. If an act of healing were necessary to preserve life, the rabbini-

45

cal schools permitted it on the sabbath; if there was no such urgency, the proper course was to wait until the sabbath was past. But Jesus maintained that the sabbath was the most appropriate day to relieve men and women from sickness and other afflictions, because such acts honoured the purpose for which the day was instituted. It is assumed that the Pharisees would relieve an animal in distress on the sabbath (11); the Qumran community was so much more strict that in its sabbath regulations precisely such a humane action is forbidden.

Note: 'the priests in the temple profane the sabbath' (5), i.e. by continuing their work on that day, in fact by offering more sacrifices on it than on ordinary days.

St. Matthew 12.15-21   Behold My Servant

That the breaking-point between Jesus and the synagogue was the conflict over sabbath observance is attested by the Synoptic narrative and the Fourth Gospel alike (cf. John 5.9 ff.). Withdrawing from the synagogue, Jesus was followed by many who needed His help even more than they needed the synagogue ministrations, 'and He healed them all' (15). This pattern of withdrawal from the synagogue and detaching disciples from it is repeatedly re-enacted in the apostolic age (cf. Acts 13.46 ff.; 17.4 ff.; 18.6 f., and especially 19.8 f.). Again the secrecy motif appears (cf. 8.4; 9.30); on this occasion the Evangelist adduces O.T. authority for it. It is noteworthy that the citation of Isa. 42.1–4 comes at this point. The religious leaders of Judaism have repudiated Jesus, but the crucial question is: what is God's estimate of Him? This question is answered in the terms of what we know today as the first of the four Isaianic Servant Songs. Its opening words were echoed by the heavenly voice at the baptism (3.17). Jesus is presented by God as His Servant, and the words cited here convey divine approval of the kind of ministry He has been accomplishing, including the avoidance of publicity which characterizes it. The wording of this Greek citation in vs. 18–21 is closer to the Hebrew text of Isa. 42.1–4 than the common 'Septuagint' version is; it is probably an independent translation of the Hebrew used, or perhaps actually composed, by the Evangelist.

While the four Servant Songs in Isa. 42—53 were not distinguished as such before the end of the 19th century, it was inevitable that the two passages beginning 'Behold my servant' (42.1–4 and 52.13—53.12) should be related one to the other as referring to one and the same person. A citation from the second of these two passages (the fourth Servant Song, as we call it) has already appeared in 8.17

(see also notes on 20.28; 26.28). The final clause of the present citation (21) points on to the post-resurrection Gentile mission (cf. 28. 19 f.)

St. Matthew 12.22-37   The Beelzebul Controversy

The authorities had decided that Jesus' attitude towards the Law (especially the sabbath commandment) excluded all possibility of His acting by the commission of God. Yet He undoubtedly performed works of mercy and power, like the exorcizing of the demon from the blind and dumb man of v. 22 (cf. Luke 11.14). The common people might find in this further evidence of His divine authority—'Son of David' (23) means 'Messiah' (cf. John 7.31,42)—but the Pharisees felt compelled to seek the source of His power elsewhere. Their charge that He expelled demons by the power of their prince, Beelzebul (anticipated in 9.34), was refuted by Jesus as self-contradictory (25 f.). Beelzebul was an ancient Canaanite deity ('lord of the high place' or 'master of the house'; cf. 10.25); long since demoted to this inferior status. 'Your sons' (27) means 'your pupils' (cf. the 'sons of the prophets' in 2 Kings 2.3; 6.1, etc.). The Pharisees and their pupils exorcized demons; why should not they derive this power from the same source as Jesus? The truth was far otherwise: it was by the power and 'Spirit of God' (28; Luke 11.20 has 'finger of God') that Jesus expelled demons, and this meant two things. It meant (a) that the kingdom of God had come upon them unawares, for such actions were tokens of its power at work in their midst, invading the kingdom of evil and releasing its prisoners (29; cf. Isa. 49.24 f.; 61.1); it meant (b) that they were ascribing the work of the Spirit of God to the prince of darkness, and this deliberate shutting their eyes against the light was the one irremediable and therefore unpardonable sin. It was not that they were misled to a false conclusion; people in that condition can be shown their mistake and helped to appreciate the truth. It was rather that, with clear evidence of the Spirit of God at work before their eyes, their presuppositions made them refuse to accept it. Other sins might be forgiven; even the opponents of the Son of Man could be brought to a better frame of mind; but if people have made up their minds not to accept the witness of the Spirit, what further witness will convince them?

Verses 33-37 comprise a number of sayings, some of them proverbial, which drive home the point of vs. 25-32.

Consider: The best proof that a man has not sinned against the Holy Spirit is the fear that he has.

47

The 'sign' which the scribes and Pharisees sought must have been something different from the works of healing and exorcism which Jesus performed. These could be explained away as wrought by demonic power; they wanted some sign that would compel recognition that Jesus was sent by God—perhaps such a sign as He refused to give when He was tempted in the wilderness (4.5–7). Such a sign, were it possible, would leave no room for faith. The 'sign of Jonah', which alone they would be given (39), is interpreted here in terms of our Lord's resurrection (40). The Ninevites who repented when Jonah came to them from 'the belly of Sheol' (Jon. 2.2) would be in a position to condemn the unbelief of Jesus' contemporaries at the last judgement (41), as also would the queen of Sheba (42). The 'something greater' than Jonah or Solomon (41, 42) is the kingdom of God, present in Jesus' ministry (cf. 'something greater than the temple' in v. 6).

The parable of vs. 43–45 implies that the communities which had benefited temporarily from the ministry of Jesus would be in a worse state afterwards than they were before because they did not respond to it in wholehearted repentance and faith. 'This evil generation' (45) recalls the language used in the O.T. of the wilderness generation (Deut. 1.35, etc.); its additional characterization as an 'adulterous' generation in v. 39 implies its unfaithfulness to God.

The incident of vs. 46–50 emphasizes not only that earthly relationships must give way to the demands of the kingdom of heaven (cf. 10.37) but also that Jesus' true family comprises all who, like Him, do the will of God, and that means in the first instance those who had abandoned the synagogue order and all that went with it in order to form His new community (cf. v. 15). The 'brothers' of Jesus are named in 13.55.

Study: Consider the relationship of Jesus to His mother.

Questions for further study and discussion on St. Matthew chs. 11 and 12

1. What features of John the Baptist's character and ministry might have justified the description of him as unsurpassed 'among those born of women'?
2. What practical guidance for our own conduct can we derive from Jesus' teaching about the sabbath day?
3. Consider in detail the relevance of the portrayal of the Servant quoted in Matt. 12.18–21 to the facts of our Lord's ministry.

St. Matthew 13.1-9 Parable of the Sower

Chapter 13 brings together seven 'parables of the kingdom', two of which (the sower and the mustard seed) are paralleled in *Mark* and *Luke* and one (the leaven) in *Luke*, while four (the weeds, the hidden treasure, the pearl and the dragnet) are peculiar to *Matthew*.

By his statement that Jesus 'went out of the house' (1) before He spoke in parables, Matthew indicates that the context of the parables —at least of these parables—is the situation following on Jesus' rejection by the synagogue (cf. 12.15). The 'crowds' (2) are distinct both from the religious authorities and the disciples; they are still relatively uncommitted.

The first parable (3–9) is one of the 'parables of growth', describing an experience familiar to all Galileans. From v. 18 it is commonly called 'the parable of the sower'; its main point, however, has to do with the four kinds of soil on which the seed was sown. If the modern reader in the west feels that the waste of so much seed is due to the carelessness of the sower in not avoiding unpromising patches of ground, it must be remembered that in traditional Palestinian procedure sowing precedes ploughing. The sower therefore deliberately scatters his seed on the track beaten by the feet of passers-by and on the thorny ground because path and thorns alike are to be ploughed up; as for the rocky ground, this was concealed by a thin covering of soil and would be detected only when the ploughshare struck it. So the message of the kingdom had been broadcast indiscriminately, to receptive and unreceptive hearers alike; the fact that some hearers were unreceptive did not mean that the proclamation was in vain, for the fruit that it produced in the lives of the receptive hearers made it abundantly worth while. The threefold figures of v. 8 may indicate the yield in different parts of the good soil: the harvest was plentiful over its whole area, though even more plentiful in some parts than in others. A 'hundredfold' crop would certainly be exceptional, but not at all miraculous. Matthew may have thought of the dimensions of the Church of his day by contrast with the small beginnings of Jesus' ministry, as a result of gospel preaching (cf. Col. 1.6, 'bearing fruit and growing').

St. Matthew 13.10-17 An O.T. Situation Reproduced

In these verses repeated reference is made (13,14f.) to Isa. 6.9 f., in which Isaiah at his inaugural vision receives his commission as a prophet to his people but is warned that they will pay no attention to him: in fact, all his speaking to them will but serve to make them the more insensitive and unresponsive to his message and the more incapable of enjoying the divine relief which repentance and obedience would have brought. This situation was being reproduced in Jesus' ministry, since the majority of His hearers refused His message. The Aramaic term for 'parable' can also mean 'riddle' and Jesus' words may have meant that whereas 'the secrets (or mysteries) of the kingdom of heaven' were readily accessible to faith such as the disciples had, they remained 'riddles' to the unbelieving multitudes. It is a truth of common experience that things which are easily understood by those who approach them in the proper attitude are unintelligible to others. But Matthew, narrating the parables against the background of Jesus' rejection, makes the telling of them the consequence of the multitude's unbelief: *'because* seeing they do not see . . .' (13). The general echo of Isa. **6.9** f. in v. 13 is followed by the formal quotation of the passage in vs. 14 f., in a form resembling that of the Greek (Septuagint) version of the O.T. The allusion to the O.T. passage in v. 13 is paralleled in the same context in Mark **4.11** f. and Luke **8.**10; it is quoted in different contexts in John **12.**40 and Acts **28.**26 f. as an O.T. 'testimony' in advance to Israel's failure to accept the gospel. The whole saying of Jesus in vs. 11 ff. is amplified by the inclusion of two utterances from other contexts: v. 12 is appended later to the parable of the talents (**25.29**), and vs. 16 f. have a parallel in Luke **10.**23 f., following on the return of the seventy from their mission. But the two additional utterances help to fix the sense of the accompanying words here.

> *How blessed are our ears*
> *That hear this joyful sound,*
> *Which kings and prophets waited for,*
> *And sought, but never found!*
>
> *How blessed are our eyes*
> *That see this heavenly light!*
> *Prophets and kings desirèd long,*
> *But died without the sight.*
>
> *The Lord makes bare His arm*
> *Through all the earth abroad;*
> *Let all the nations now behold*
> *Their Saviour and their God.*

St. Matthew 13.18-30

Interpretation of the Four Soils;
Parable of the Weeds

The interpretation of the parable of the sower (18–23) is given to the disciples, not to the crowds: it makes the 'mystery' plain. The parable is explained in terms of what happens when the 'word (message) of the kingdom' is proclaimed, whether by Jesus during His ministry or by His disciples later. Some have their minds diverted from it before they have time to consider it; some are attracted by it until they discover that it may involve them in persecution and other forms of trouble, and then they are 'put off' or feel themselves 'let down' (the same word as in 11.6); others allow secular interests to stifle the power of the message in their lives. But those who accept it intelligently and hold to it firmly in spite of hardships or counter-attractions produce abundantly the 'fruit' of the kingdom; that is, God's will is fulfilled in their lives.

The next parable, Matthew's second 'parable of growth' (24–30), tells of 'weeds' sown by 'an enemy' in a man's wheat-field; the 'weeds' (AV and RV 'tares'; NEB 'darnel') were so like the wheat until each began to ripen that they could not be uprooted at an earlier stage without endangering the good crop. But when the harvest came, there was no difficulty in distinguishing the two. In the rabbinical schools darnel (*Lolium temulentum*) was regarded as degenerate wheat and its Hebrew name was fancifully related to a similar-sounding word meaning 'fornication'; there could therefore be a connexion in our Lord's mind between its appearance in this parable and His reference to an 'adulterous generation' in 12.39; 16.4. However that may be, the harvesters bundled up the weeds and burned them before reaping the wheat. Evidently a situation is envisaged in which, for the time being, true 'sons of the kingdom' and 'mere professors' cannot be told apart.

Consider the statement: 'Pressing spiritual meaning on all details of a parable is highly dangerous.' How do we determine the limits of interpretation in any given parable?

St. Matthew 13.31-43

Mustard Seed and Leaven;
Interpretation of the Weeds

The parable of the mustard seed (31 f.), Matthew's third 'parable of growth', is a reminder that a great enterprise may have very small beginnings; there may be a contrast between the modest following that Jesus secured during His ministry and the wide extent of the

Church when this Gospel was published. The 'birds of the air' are probably the Gentiles, as in Dan. 4.12,21, where the language is similar. Any reader who is concerned about the botanical exactitude of the phrase 'the greatest of shrubs' (32) may reflect that the literal rendering is 'greater than the herbs' (RV).

The parable of the leaven (33) also points to the far-reaching results that may come from small beginnings; in addition, the fact that the woman 'hid' the leaven in the meal may suggest the unobtrusive growth of the kingdom, as in Mark's parable of the seed growing secretly (Mark 4.26–29). So Jesus was launching the kingdom of heaven on earth by His ministry: 'now let it work!'

> *When he first the work begun,*
> *Small and feeble was his day;*
> *Now the word doth swiftly run,*
> *Now it wins its widening way;*
> *More and more it spreads and grows,*
> *Ever mighty to prevail,*
> *Sin's strongholds it now o'erthrows,*
> *Shakes the trembling gates of hell.*

According to vs. 34 f. parabolic language was (henceforth) Jesus' regular—indeed invariable—mode of addressing the 'crowds', as distinct from His disciples (see comment on v. 2); and in this the Evangelist sees the fulfilment of Psa. 78.2, where 'parables' is equivalent to 'dark sayings' or 'riddles' (see comment on v. 13); the emphasis of vs. 10–15 is thus underlined.

The interpretation of the parable of the weeds (36–43) is (like that of the parable of the sower) given privately to the disciples. If the life-setting of the telling of the parable is the ministry of Jesus, that of its interpretation may be the Christian mission of the Evangelist's day. 'The field is the world' (38), which in Dan. 7.14 is made subject to the Son of Man: it is His 'kingdom' (41) in a wider sense than the kingdom of the Father (43), which is the kingdom of heaven consummated at 'the close of the age' (39) with the final execution of judgement by the Son of Man (41). The dualism between 'the sons of the kingdom' and 'the sons of the evil one' (38) is radical so long as it lasts, but it is brought to an end when at last the Son of Man establishes His universal sovereignty, to which the latter must submit as completely as the former. With v. 43 compare Dan. 12.3.

*St. Matthew 13.44-52
The Treasure, the Pearl and the Dragnet

The parables of the hidden treasure (44) and the costly pearl (45 f.) are companion-pieces, each stressing the paramount value of the kingdom of heaven. The fact that the first man hit upon the treasure by chance, while the merchant was engaged in the search for 'fine pearls', is probably irrelevant to the main lesson. It is better that a man should let everything else go than that he should miss this, for to enter the kingdom of heaven is to possess eternal life. The disciples, who had left everything to follow Jesus (cf. 19.27), had learned the lesson of these parables; here and now they were initiated into 'the secrets of the kingdom of heaven' (11) and in the new world they would inherit eternal life (cf. 19.28 f.). What seemed to outsiders to be folly was in fact the highest wisdom.

The parable of the dragnet (47–50) is a companion-piece to the parable of the weeds (24–30); in both the separation of the good from the bad is interpreted of the judgement at 'the close (consummation) of the age' (39,49). In much rabbinical thought of that time the present age would give place to the age to come: the transition from the one to the other would be marked by resurrection and judgement. In some phases of thought the period of Messiah's reign would intervene before the dawn of the new age. Christian thought modified this scheme in view of the belief that Jesus was the Messiah; His reign began with His triumph over death and exaltation by God and would continue until His advent, which would accordingly mark the 'close of the age' (cf. 28.18–20). But even in His earthly ministry, and still more from His passion onwards (cf. 26.64), the powers of the new age were already at work (cf. 11.5; 14.2; 15.30 f.).

Whether in fact the disciples understood 'all this' as fully as they supposed (51) may be doubted. But the Evangelist, whose own self-portrait has been recognized in v. 52, sets forth the ideal for all who would be scholars and teachers in the school of Christ; to them, unlike the unbelievers, the parables would convey the instruction they required concerning the kingdom of heaven. The source of the instruction was 'old' (it went back to the visions and oracles of prophets in earlier days) but the mode of its impartation was 'new' (it was interpreted in the light of the coming of the kingdom and fulfilment of the prophecies in the ministry of Jesus). Matthew has much to say in criticism of the Pharisaic 'scribes' (exponents of the law), but he holds up the picture of the true scribe for the emulation of his readers.

*St. Matthew 13.53-58   Without Honour at Nazareth

The formula at the beginning of v. 53, marking the end of a body of discourse, is similar to those in **7.28** and **11.1** (cf. **19.1**; **26.1**). By 'His own country' or 'His home town' (54) Nazareth is meant (cf. **2.23**; Luke **4.16**). His fellow townsmen, instead of feeling pride in the fame of a local boy, 'took offence' at Him (57; cf. **11.6**; **13.21**) because they did not see why a member of a well-known but undistinguished family of the place should gain such a reputation for 'wisdom' and 'mighty works' (54); why should He be better than any of themselves? Since 'the carpenter' is not named (55), he may no longer have been alive. The proverb of v. 57 appears in the same context in Mark **6.4** and Luke **4.24**; in John **4.44** it seems to refer rather to Judea. Verse 58 implies that in spite of their unbelief He did one or two mighty works there; cf. Mark **6.5**: 'He laid His hands upon a few sick people and healed them.' But Matthew probably wishes to show that with His inhospitable reception in Nazareth the record of Galilean rejection is complete.

Self-examination: The Galileans' prejudice prevented their looking squarely at all the facts. What are the implications of this for me with regard to personal relationships, local church life, ecumenical movement, etc.?

Questions for further study and discussion on St. Matthew ch. 13

1. There has been no space to discuss different interpretations of the parables from those suggested in the foregoing notes, but consider:

   (*a*) the view that the mustard-seed portrays the kingdom as ceasing to be the lowly institution which it was to have been in the divine plan and becoming 'a great corporation, a visible and comfortable sphere of operations for wicked spirits', represented by the 'birds of the air' (G. H. Lang, *Pictures and Parables*, p. 122);

   (*b*) the view that the parable of the leaven describes the growth of evil within the kingdom (in the light, e.g. of 1 Cor. **5.6**; Gal. **5.9**);

   (*c*) the view that the merchant of vs. 45 f. is our Lord, and that the 'pearl of great value' is the Church, or the individual soul.

2. How far can we distinguish those elements in ch. 13 which relate to the actual ministry of Jesus and those which relate to the developing life and service of the Church?

3. In the application of Isa. **6.9** f., compare 'because' of Matt. **13.13** with 'so that' of Mark **4.12** and Luke **8.10**.

'Herod the tetrarch' was Herod Antipas, the youngest and politically ablest son of Herod the Great and the full brother of Archelaus (cf. 2.22); after his father's death in 4 B.C. he became ruler of Galilee and Peraea and retained this position until he was deposed by the Roman Emperor in A.D. 39. Herodias was not only the wife of his half-brother Philip (a private Roman citizen, not 'Philip the tetrarch' of Luke 3.1) but also the daughter of his half-brother Aristobulus. Marriage with a brother's wife was forbidden by Lev. 18.16 (apart from the 'levirate marriage' of Deut. 25.5 ff.); it was the more heinous when (as in this case) the brother was still alive. John's denunciation of this illicit match was quite in the O.T. prophetic tradition, and his influence with the people was such that Herodias could not feel her position secure while he was alive. Herodias' daughter (6) was probably not Salome, who by this time was the wife of Philip the tetrarch, but a younger daughter, otherwise unrecorded—'girl' in v. 11 is a diminutive ('little girl'). The 'prison' where John was held (cf. 11.2) was the fortress of Machaerus, east of the Dead Sea, as we learn from Josephus, whose narrative of John's imprisonment and death supplements the Gospel account (*Antiquities* 18. 116–119).

The events of vs. 3–12 took place some months before those of their context; they are recorded here to explain Herod's reference to John's death in v. 2. The account of Jesus' activity, and no doubt of His disciples' Galilean mission (10.1 ff.), made him feel that this was John the Baptist all over again; the 'powers' of which he spoke were the supernatural powers by which Jesus' mighty works were performed (cf. 12.28).

St. Matthew 14.13-21   Five Thousand Fed

The words 'when Jesus heard this' (13) refer not to the death of John, which was not fresh news, but to Herod's unwelcome interest in Jesus Himself, recorded in v. 2. When the evidence of all the Gospels is put together, it appears that the disciples, during their Galilean mission, had at times spoken or acted with more enthusiasm than discretion. It was best therefore to withdraw to a 'lonely place' east of the Lake, out of Herod's jurisdiction. But even there Jesus was followed by crowds, whose urgent desire was that He would put Himself at their head, overthrow their oppressors, and inaugurate a new era of liberty and abundance. To this desire He would not accede, but in His compassion (cf. 9.36) He healed the sick among them and then performed one of the greatest of His mighty works.

'Can God spread a table in the wilderness?' asked the unbelieving Israelites in Moses' day (Psa. **78**.19). They had their answer then; a similar answer is given now. (Another O.T. parallel is the incident of 2 Kings **4**.42–44, in Elisha's day.) Over the produce of the land and the produce of the sea Jesus pronounces the blessing; the traditional Jewish grace before meat takes the form, 'Blessed art Thou, O Lord our God, King of the universe, who bringest forth bread from the earth'. The lifting of one's eyes heavenward in prayer seems to have been a general practice (its omission is noted as exceptional in Luke **18**.13).

The feeding of the 5,000 is narrated by Matthew, as by the other Synoptists, with an economy of language which leaves the reader with the impression that there is much more here than meets the eye. The inner significance is brought out in the dialogue of John **6**.26–58. But even in Matthew's account it is possible to read between the lines and see Jesus revealed as the second Moses, the prophet of the end-time (cf. Deut. **18**.15–19), feeding His people in the wilderness, and as the true Messiah, giving them (in symbol at least) the food which sustains the life of the age to come. There is first-century evidence for the Jewish expectation that the gift of manna would be renewed when the Messiah was revealed.

The 'twelve baskets' (20) correspond, probably intentionally, to the sum-total of the tribes of Israel (as also do the twelve apostles). Matthew alone of the Evangelists adds the phrase 'besides women and children' (21; cf. **15**.38). An army of 5,000 men would not have been contemptible, had Jesus been minded to use the multitude thus.

Question: How far should the Christian help directly to feed men?

St. Matthew 14.22-36   Walking on the Sea

After the feeding, Jesus *compelled* the disciples to embark and make for the other side of the Lake; the Greek word shows unambiguously that compulsion was required. The probable reason was that they were becoming infected with the militant enthusiasm of the crowds. His withdrawal for solitary prayer after He had persuaded the crowds to disperse may suggest that for Him this had been a new 'temptation in the wilderness' (cf. John **6**.15).

Verses 22–33 record a second storm on the Lake, not unlike the earlier one of **8**.23–27. The main differences between the two are (*a*) that the former voyage was from west to east, the present one from east to west, and (*b*) that on the former occasion Jesus was with the disciples in the boat throughout, whereas on this occasion He came walking for their relief over the water during the 'fourth watch'

56

(i.e. the three hours immediately preceding dawn). Matthew amplifies his record at this point with an incident in which Peter figures (28–32)—the first of three or four such passages peculiar to this Gospel (cf. **16.**17–19; **17.**24–27; **18.**21 f.). Perhaps the church in which this Gospel took shape had a special interest in Peter (the church of Antioch claimed him as one of its apostolic founders; cf. Gal. **2.**11!). Peter's sinking through lack of faith, and his restoration by Jesus, is paralleled by the story of his denial (cf. **26.**33–35, 69–75); together with the whole context of the storm-tossed boat and ensuing calm when Jesus entered it the incident lent itself admirably to practical exhortation. The disciples' worship and confession (33) go beyond the earlier language of amazement (**8.**27); yet perhaps in their relief they hardly knew what they were doing or saying. No such importance is attached to this as to Peter's confession in **16.**16 (cf. also **27.**54).

Gennesaret (34, modern Ginossar) is the fertile plain north-west of the Lake. With the generalized language of v. 35 cf. **4.**24; with v. 36 cf. the incident of **9.**20 f.

Thought: Peter walked on the water as long as Jesus filled his thoughts.

St. Matthew 15.1-20 Traditional Barriers Removed

The breach with the scribal establishment in Galilee is followed by a breach with representatives of the same establishment in Jerusalem itself, who came (at the invitation, perhaps, of their Galilean colleagues) to assess this disturbing movement and its suspect Leader. 'The tradition of the elders' (2) was the cumulative corpus of oral law by which the written law of the O.T. was interpreted, supplemented and applied to the changing circumstances of Jewish life. While its intention was to safeguard the written law, its effect could be to nullify some of its fundamental principles. Jesus interpreted the written law differently—by appealing to the purpose for which this or that commandment was originally given (cf. **12.**1 ff.; **19.**3 ff.). The Jerusalem deputation's criticism that Jesus' disciples ignored the ritual hand-washing before eating (cf. Luke **11.**38) attracts the counter-criticism that the tradition of the elders, by ruling that the law concerning vows (Deut. **23.**21–23) took precedence over reverence to parents, neutralized the fifth commandment (Exod. **20.**12; Deut. **5.**16; cf. also Exod. **21.**17; Lev. **20.**9). Property vowed to God, it was ruled, must not be used for other purposes, and if, after making such a vow, a man had nothing left for helping his parents in need, that was too bad. (The spirit of Jesus' criticism

57

was generally accepted among the rabbis by the end of the first century A.D., when the judgement prevailed that, if a vow adversely affected relations between parents and children, it might be annulled.) Such frustration of the divine intention is said (8 f.) to fulfil Isaiah's denunciation of his contemporaries who paid lip-service to God but failed to render Him heart-obedience (Isa. 29.13). This contradiction between lip and heart calls forth the designation 'hypocrites' (7; cf. 6.2 ff.). Pharisees themselves recognized the presence of a hypocritical element in their fellowship, and the Gospels do not suggest that the designation applied to Pharisees as a whole (cf. 23.13 ff.). Verse 13 is reminiscent of the parable of the weeds (13.24–30); with v. 14 cf. Luke 6.39 (also Matt. 23.16, 24).

But the teaching of vs. 10–20 goes farther than a criticism of the oral law; it amounts to an abrogation of the written law, so far as concerns its food-regulations. According to Lev. 11, various kinds of forbidden meat were 'unclean' and 'abominable'; Jesus rules that defilement is conveyed not by food but by moral evil in thought, word and deed (including infringements of the sixth, seventh, eighth and ninth commandments). The defilement that matters is ethical, not ritual. But this teaching set at naught not only the Pharisaic ideals of purification but (in principle, at least) the whole basis of separation between Jew and Gentile.

St. Matthew 15.21-28   A Canaanite Woman's Faith

The Evangelist relates this incident against the background of the implied lowering of Jewish–Gentile barriers in vs. 10–20. He knows that the Gentile mission proper could not start until after Jesus' death and resurrection (28.19 f.; cf. 10.5 f.) but he records the healing of this woman's daughter as an exceptional occurrence in the period before His death, like that of the centurion's servant (8.5–13). It has already been suggested that there is symbolical significance in the fact that these two healings were effected at a distance. The woman, called 'a Greek, a Syrophoenician' in Mark 7.26, is here called a Canaanite: the Tyrians, Sidonians and other Phoenicians were Canaanites who retained their independence for centuries after the other Canaanites lost theirs. Matthew's readers might recall another Gentile woman in that area whose child was healed by the power of Israel's God in Elijah's day (1 Kings 17.17–24; cf. Luke 4.25 f.). It is Matthew alone who records the woman's appeal to Jesus as 'Son of David' (22; cf. 9.27, but the plea is of doubtful appropriateness on Gentile lips), the disciples' advice to 'send her away' (23) and His reply (to them, evidently) that He 'was sent only

58

to the lost sheep of the house of Israel' (24; cf. **10.6**), which suggests that they meant 'Do what she wants and let her go'. Jesus was indeed minded to do what she wanted, but with nobler motives than to get rid of a mother's noisy importunity. His further interchange with her was calculated to bring quite an exceptional expression of shrewd and determined faith. By Jewish standards Gentiles were 'dogs', unclean creatures; it may be of importance that in Greek (the language in which presumably this conversation was carried on) the word used in vs. 26 f. is a diminutive which denotes not the pariah dogs out of doors but the puppies indoors, the children's pets. The phrase 'their master's table' (27) may imply the woman's readiness to take a place of inferiority to Jews (Mark **7.28** speaks of 'the children's crumbs'). For the instantaneousness of the cure (28) cf. **8.13**.

Meditation: Faith does not query the truth of Christ's statements: it argues from them.

St. Matthew 15.29-39 Four Thousand Fed

This passage presents a close parallel to **14.13–22**; in both passages great crowds come to Jesus and have their sick folk healed, and then are miraculously fed. The healings described in vs. 30 f. may recall the prophecy of the new age in Isa. **35.5** f. (cf. **11.5**). The glorifying of 'the God of Israel' (31) suggests that these people were Gentiles.

As for the two feedings, the intention of the two Evangelists (Mark and Matthew) who record both was probably discerned by Hilary and Augustine when they interpreted the former as Christ's communication of Himself to the Jews, and the latter as His self-communication to the Gentiles. If blessing to the Gentiles is indeed symbolized by the feeding of the 4,000, this narrative comes very aptly here, after the teaching of vs. 10–20 and the incident of vs. 21–28. The various numbers appearing in the narrative (which constitute its main difference from the feeding of the 5,000) have been allegorized in this sense, including the 'three days' of v. 32, as though they reminded the reader that Christ's unrestricted self-communication to the Gentiles could not take place until He was raised from the dead (cf. **28.19**). It has even been pointed out that two distinct Greek words for 'basket' are used in **14.20** and **15.37**, and that the word used in the former passage had a specially Jewish association, whereas that in **15.37** is a quite general word for 'fish-creel'. Another verbal variation appears when 'blessed' in **14.19** is compared with 'having given thanks' in **15.36**; the former denotes the ascription of blessing to God, while the latter is *eucharisteō*,

59

but this should not be taken to imply a eucharistic significance, for it is to this day the commonest Greek verb meaning 'to thank'.

The whereabouts of 'Magadan' (39) is as uncertain as that of the parallel Dalmanutha in Mark **8**.10; the AV 'Magdala' represents a later attempt to replace an unknown place-name by a familiar one. Some point west of the Lake is probably indicated.

Questions for further study and discussion on St. Matthew chs. 14 and 15

1. It has been suggested that in this Gospel Jesus' 'withdrawals' are usually followed by some new revelation in word or action. Can this be supported from these (and other) chapters?
2. Consider the view that the bringing of gospel blessings to the Gentiles is anticipated in the three main divisions of ch. **15**.

St. Matthew 16.1-12   Pharisees and Sadducees

The request for a 'sign' has already been made in **12**.38; a 'sign from heaven' might have taken the form of a public and conclusive announcement by God. But even such an announcement could have been explained away by those unwilling to accept it. Jesus' answer was that, as they could foretell tomorrow's weather by today's sky, they ought to be able to see the outcome of contemporary trends— e.g. the disaster to which the increasing mood of rebellion against Rome would inevitably bring the people unless they saw where their true peace lay and changed their temper accordingly. With v. 4 cf. **12**.39.

Matthew conjoins Pharisees and Sadducees more frequently than the other N.T. writers (cf. **3**.7); thus in v. 1 he adds 'Sadducees' to Mark's 'Pharisees' (Mark **8**.11) and in v. 6 has 'the leaven of the . . . Sadducees' in place of 'the leaven of Herod' (or 'of the Hero-dians') of Mark **8**.15. The paragraph vs. 5–12 is thus tied more closely to vs. 1–4. The Pharisees and Sadducees of Jesus' day had little enough in common: the Sadducees rejected the oral tradition of the scribes and insisted on the literal rigour of the written law, and dismissed as a 'fond thing vainly invented' the Pharisees' belief in hierarchies of angels and demons together with their doctrine of bodily resurrection (cf. **22**.23 ff.; Acts **23**.8). But both parties opposed Jesus, though for different reasons. The Pharisees' opposi-tion to Him was essentially theological; while the Sadducees also objected to Him on theological grounds (as they objected to the Pharisees too), their main objection to Him was political. It was to their party that most of the chief-priestly establishment belonged, and they feared that His activity might upset their *modus vivendi* with Rome and precipitate the downfall of the Jewish commonwealth. 'The teaching of the Pharisees and Sadducees' (12) was no unified body of doctrine, but the scepticism of their demand for a sign (1), and the hostility which it barely concealed.

Jesus' reply to the disciples in vs. 8–11 confirms the impression given by the Evangelist that there is more significance than meets the eye in the feeding narratives (14.15–21; 15.32–38); this deeper significance (relating to their Master's person) had thus far escaped them. But new light was about to dawn.

Meditation: Christians are not meant to despair at their apparent lack of equipment for life's journeys; they travel with One who will provide.

St. Matthew 16.13-20   Peter's Confession

Caesarea Philippi (modern Banyas) was the capital of Philip's tetrarchy, situated at one of the principal sources of the Jordan; Jesus and the disciples were coming to the end of their visit to the territory bordering Galilee on the north and east. The question of v. 13 is perennially interesting: by the account people give of Jesus they may not add to our knowledge of Him but they throw much light on themselves. For His identification with John the Baptist cf. 14.2; for Elijah cf. 11.14; 17.10 ff. As for Jeremiah (in this Gospel only), we may recall his language about the Temple (Jer. 7.4, 11 ff.; 26.2 ff.; cf. Matt. 21.12 f.; 24.2; 27.40a) and his counsel of submission to the Gentile power (Jer. 38.17 f.; cf. Matt. 5.41; 22.21). But the personal question of v. 15 was the crucial one. The disciples may have thought of Him as the Messiah earlier (cf. John 1.41), but Jesus had shown Himself so unlike the Messiah of common expectation that they might well have changed their minds. Peter's declaration that He was, nevertheless, the Messiah, implied that the Messiah-concept was being modified in his thinking into conformity with what Jesus actually was and did and taught. At this stage 'the Son of the living God' may have meant little more than that Jesus was the Anointed One to whom, in Psa. 2.7, God says 'You are My Son'.

Jesus was filled with joy: that Peter, in spite of all appearances to the contrary, should have reached this conviction was a proof of divine illumination (17). Now He could make a beginning and found the new Israel (18). The resemblance between 'Peter' and 'rock' in Greek (*Petros* and *petra*) was even closer in the Aramaic in which these words were probably spoken (*Kepha . . . kepha*); cf. French 'tu es *Pierre* et . . . sur cette *pierre* je bâtirai mon église' (Segond).

It is not Peter in his own right, but Peter the confessor, that is the rock. The Church to be built on this rock is the company of those who share Peter's confession. 'The powers of death' = (literally) 'the gates of Hades'; the realm of the dead is pictured as a prison-house whose gates will never close on the new community so that it is irretrievably extinguished. The 'keys' (19) are given to the chief steward as his symbol of authority (cf. Isa. 22.22). The binding and loosing (forbidding and permitting in rabbinic idiom) may point here to the declaration of forgiveness in the gospel (with the corollary of judgement for the impenitent) and the exercise of Church discipline (with the assurance of ratification in the heavenly court); cf. 18.18. Later we see Peter opening the 'door of faith' to Jews in Jerusalem (Acts 2.14 ff., 38 ff.) and to Gentiles in Caesarea (Acts 10.34 ff.). For the preservation of secrecy (20) cf. 8.4; 9.30; 12.16.

St. Matthew 16.21-28   First Prediction of the Passion

Peter's confession marks a watershed in Jesus' ministry: 'from that time' He began to speak to the disciples about His impending passion. They had begun to fill the traditional concept of Messiah with new meaning, but they were not prepared for the radical reinterpretation which Jesus now began to impart to them. A suffering Messiah was a contradiction in terms—so much so that Peter expostulated with his Master for speaking like this (22), and the disciple who had just been greeted as the recipient of a divine revelation was now reproved as an adversary ('Satan') and a hindrance (23). In Peter's well-meant remonstrance Jesus recognized a repetition of the wilderness temptation—the temptation to achieve His messianic destiny by some other path than that of the Father's will (cf. 4.8–10). Peter's reaction was natural: he thought of Jerusalem as the place of Messiah's enthronement, not of His humiliation. In the event, the humiliation and the enthronement were bound up together, but this was beyond the disciples' comprehension at present. The warning of what lay ahead at Jerusalem had to be repeated at frequent intervals (cf. 17.22 f.; 20.18 f.).

If suffering and death was to be their Master's lot, the disciples would have to reassess their own position. They might well be involved in His fate. To 'take up one's cross' (24) was no mere figure of speech for some minor inconvenience: a man who took up his cross was on his way to be crucified, and had 'denied' himself in the sense of bidding a last farewell to all personal interests, hopes and ambitions (cf. 10.38 f.). But the assessment should be made not by worldly standards but in the light of the day of final review and reward. In the light of that day, the man who lost his life by following Jesus would gain life eternal; the man who saved his life by turning back would incur total loss, even if he gained the whole world in the meanwhile. The Son of Man's coming in judgement (27) is the occasion foreseen in Dan. 7.13 f. But v. 28 need not mean that *this* coming would take place in the lifetime of some standing by: there might be earlier occasions for the manifestation of the Son of Man's authority (cf. 24.30; 26.64); and the language of this verse is Matthew's interpretation of 'the kingdom of God coming with power' of Mark 9.1, which would be the sequel to the Son of Man's passion (we may think of Pentecost; c.f. Acts 1.8a).

Note: If we consider the literal sense of the word translated 'hindrance' in v. 23, we may see the 'stone' image being carried on from v. 18: the disciple who has been hailed as a foundation stone is now described as a stumbling stone.

St. Matthew 17.1-8   The Transfiguration

The transfiguration is not the fulfilment of the promise of 16.28 (one does not say of something due to happen within the week that it will take place within the lifetime of some hearers), but it anticipates that fulfilment in the form of a vision. The Son of Man was manifested in glory before the three disciples' eyes. They might not have been able to say whether they themselves were in the body or out of the body (cf. 2 Cor. 12.2 f.) but they were enabled to see in advance their Master's 'body of glory' (cf. Phil. 3.21). There are some striking resemblances between this narrative and those of the resurrection appearances. Jesus had told them of His impending death and resurrection; this experience was calculated to confirm the significance of His words and show them something of the new age which these events would inaugurate. Moses and Elijah represent the law and the prophets, the old order now being superseded by the new (cf. 11.13). The passing of both of them from earthly life had been attended with mystery (Deut. 34.5 f.; 2 Kings 2.11 f.), and something of that mystery still attaches to them as they reappear to bear final witness to Him to whom law and prophecy alike pointed forward. Now He has come, and they say, in effect, 'This is He!' before receding into the background. They have said their say, but now, says God, 'This is My beloved Son, . . . *listen to Him*' (5). To the announcement of the heavenly Voice at the baptism (3.17) there is now added the exhortation referring to the promised prophet like Moses (Deut. 18.15). All that God has to say is embodied in Him. The 'bright cloud' (5) from which the Voice spoke bespeaks

63

the presence of the divine glory, the *shekinah*. At the end of Jesus' ministry, as previously on its threshold, His Father's approbation is expressed: with this assurance He will set out for Jerusalem.

For Peter and his companions, this was the moment of truth. If only they could hold it, and prevent the vision from dissolving! But the whole point of the vision meant that they could not stay on the holy mount, good as it was to be there. They must descend to the plain and take the Jerusalem road: not until the Son of Man had accomplished His 'Exodus' there (Luke 9.31) could the Kingdom come with power and glory.

Note: The RSV 'it is well that we are here' (4) rightly avoids the self-regarding tone of the AV 'it is good for us to be here'; Peter's meaning may be: 'It is good for You and Moses and Elijah that we are here, because we can erect booths for the three of you'.

St. Matthew 17.9-20 (21)   Little Faith

As on other occasions, secrecy is imposed: not until the resurrection of the Son of Man would the three disciples understand the vision well enough to speak about it intelligently to others (9). The question about Elijah (10) was prompted by that prophet's appearance in the vision. The fulfilment in John the Baptist of the prophecy that Elijah would be sent to discharge a special ministry before the coming of the great day (Mal. 4.5 f.) has been mentioned already in 11.14. Here it is expounded in greater detail: what the first Elijah's enemies attempted in vain to do to him (1 Kings 19.2) the second Elijah's enemies had succeeded in doing to him (14.3 ff.). In John's death Jesus saw His own foreshadowed (12).

From the exalted experience of anticipated glory the company now returned to the suffering and frustration of everyday life. The 'faithless and perverse generation' (17) must be understood here as a reference to the disciples, who for all the length of their companionship with Jesus showed themselves still unable to exercise the authority He had given them (10.1). The phrase is drawn from Deut. 32.5, where the wilderness generation is thus described (cf. 12.45; 16.4). As with several other healing incidents in *Matthew*, this account of seven verses is greatly compressed as compared with the Markan account of sixteen (Mark 9.14–29). 'Jesus rebuked him' (18): i.e. the demon that possessed the epileptic boy. The purpose of the story is to emphasize the all-importance of faith; the 'little faith' of the disciples has been reproved before (cf. 6.30; 8.26; 14.31). The point about the 'grain of mustard seed' (20) is illuminated by the parable of 13.31 f. 'This mountain' (20) in the present context would be the mount of transfiguration (traditionally Mount Tabor, though some have thought of Mount Hermon); when the saying recurs in 21.21 the reference is to the Mount of Olives. Verse 21 (AV; cf. RSV note) is not an original part of this Gospel: it was added from a later form of the text of Mark 9.29.

Thought: Faith: it is not the size of the mustard seed but its ability to grow that matters.

St. Matthew 17.22-27   The Temple-Tax

This further prediction of the passion (22 f.) was calculated to remind the disciples of the gravity of their situation: the first prediction (16.21) might well have begun to fade from their memories, especially the memories of the three who had witnessed the transfiguration (despite their Master's words in v. 12).

The incident of vs. 24–27, recorded in this Gospel only, would have been valued by Jewish Christians in the period between A.D. 30 and 70, when they considered whether or not they should pay the annual tax of half a shekel, contributed by every male Jew between the ages of 20 and 50 for the maintenance of the Jerusalem Temple. Their Master's action served them as a precedent: they were no longer under a divinely imposed obligation to pay it—with the coming of the kingdom 'something greater than the temple is here' (12.6) and they were 'sons of the kingdom' (13.38)—but out of consideration for their fellow Jews, who would be scandalized if they withheld payment, they should continue to do so as a voluntary courtesy.

The fish, which is incidental to the main point of the story, is presumably the *musht* or 'comb' fish of the Lake of Galilee, which is prone to have glittering objects in its gullet; the coin in its mouth was actually a stater or Tyrian tetradrachm, equivalent in value to a Jewish shekel and therefore sufficient to pay the temple-tax for two.

Question: How do you relate vs. 24–27; 22.15–21; Rom. 13.7?

Questions for further study and discussion on St. Matthew chs. 16 and 17

1. Consider some of the answers that might be given today to the question 'Who do men say that the Son of Man is?' (16.13).
2. How would you answer the question of Matt. 16.15, from your own experience and in your own language?
3. Are there features of contemporary life which could be explained as due to contemporary disciples' 'little faith' (17.20)?
4. In what present-day situations would the principle 'not to give offence to them' (17.27) be valid?

The 'discourse' contained in this chapter consists of a number of Jesus' sayings to the disciples dealing with various aspects of fellowship in the kingdom of heaven. The disciples appear to have been repeatedly concerned about the achievement of greatness in the kingdom. Here Jesus' answer to their question, showing that true greatness in the kingdom consists in true humility, is illustrated by the example of a child, too young to have lost the unassuming trustfulness of infancy. Far from being greatest in the kingdom, they cannot even enter it unless they change their outlook completely and abandon all thought of self-seeking (1–4). To 'turn' (3) or 'be converted' (AV) is not to be understood in the restricted sense which the latter term has acquired in popular evangelical parlance.

Our Lord's practical identification of a child's well-being with His own (5; cf. 25.40,45), coupled with His warning of the sure damnation incurred by teaching a child to sin (6), leads on to a further warning against all sources of temptation to sin (7–9; cf. 5.29 f.). The 'hell of fire' (9) is Gehenna, as in 5.22,29 f. The dignity of children is emphasized by the statement that their guardian angels (or angelic counterparts; cf. Acts 12.15) have direct access to the presence of God (cf. Luke 1.19; Rev. 8.2); their helplessness calls forth a special degree of divine interest and protection (10). 'Little ones,' said one of the rabbis, 'receive the presence of the Shekinah' (cf. 19.14). The lesson is further inculcated by the parable of the hundredth sheep (12 f.), appearing here in a different context from that of Luke 15.3–7. As for v. 14, it has been well described as 'a text to display in the nursery of every Christian home' (Sir Robert Anderson, *The Entail of the Covenant*, p. 18).

Question: What ways are there, today, of making little ones stumble?

These verses present us with a short 'manual of discipline' regulating the conduct of Jesus' followers one to another. In v. 15 the words 'against you' are probably a later addition (cf. NEB): it is the duty of a disciple who sees his brother commit a fault to try to put the matter right privately or, failing that, in the company of one or two others. (The reference to 'two or three witnesses' in v. 16 is a quotation from Deut. 19.15.) To ignore the fault would be unfair both to the offender and to the community as a whole (cf. Lev. 19.17 for an O.T. precedent and Gal. 6.1; Jas. 5.19 f. and 1 John 5.16 for N.T.

applications of the principle). But publicity must be avoided if at all possible. Only if the offender remains obdurate must the community at large be informed. The 'church' in v. 17 is (unlike that of **16.**18) a local company of disciples. The situation envisaged is one that would arise after Jesus' death and resurrection. Refusal to accept the verdict of the Church amounted to self-exclusion from its fellowship. If we reflect on Jesus' attitude to Gentiles and tax collectors, we may conclude that the Church would consider it had a duty to win this self-constituted outsider back into its communion. But the verdict of the Church, reached in accordance with Jesus' teaching, was assured of heavenly validation (18); the authority conferred on Peter in **16.**19 is here extended to the whole body of disciples.

The mention of 'two or three witnesses' (16) is followed by an assurance given to 'two or three' united in prayer in Jesus' name: their concerted petition will be granted by God, for Jesus Himself is among them (19 f.). The reference is to His unseen presence after Easter rather than to His visible presence during His ministry, when He could be only in one place at one time. We may compare the dictum of an early second-century rabbi: 'When two sit and the words of the Law are between them, the Shekinah rests between them.' It would be incredible, if it were not confirmed by experience, that any single group should try to monopolize the Lord's assurance of v. 20, which was intended for all His disciples.

Peter's question about the limits of forgiveness (21) suggests (what is perfectly true) that to forgive the same person seven times would be a mark of exceptional patience (cf. Luke **17.**3 f.). Jesus' reply, counselling unlimited forgiveness (22), perhaps expresses a deliberate antithesis to the 'seventy-sevenfold' (or seventy times sevenfold) vengeance of Lamech's song (Gen. **4.**24). The disciples must emulate their heavenly Father's all-embracing forgiveness (cf. **5.**43–48; **6.**12).

Question: What is the N.T. motivation for our forgiving?

*St. Matthew 18.23-35   The Unforgiving Servant

The number of parables which have their scene set in a royal court reminds us that Herod Antipas had his palace at Sepphoris, some four or five miles distant from Nazareth, until in A.D. 22 he built himself a new capital at Tiberias, by the lakeside. The happenings at his court would be the common talk among Galilean countryfolk and fishermen. The present parable enforces Jesus' words to Peter about the brotherly duty of unlimited forgiveness; it might also be regarded as an expansion of **6.**14 f.

The first servant, whose debt ran into millions, must be envisaged as the king's grand vizier: no other 'servant' could have incurred so colossal a debt. Nor would the confiscation of all his property come anywhere near defraying the sum. His promise to make repayment in full (26) was a mere form of words: he could never have done it. This his master knew full well, but in his compassion he cancelled the whole amount. The forgiven servant showed immediately how little he shared his master's merciful nature by enforcing the law against his fellow servant who owed him a trifling sum (28-30). On hearing of this, the king revoked his cancellation of the enormous debt, and treated him as he had treated his fellow servant. Lest it should be said, 'But this is just a detail in the story; God would not do that', Jesus emphasizes that this is precisely what God will do to any unforgiving servant of His. If we find it difficult to accommodate v. 35 within our theological system, we should modify our system to make room for it rather than try to make v. 35 mean something different from what it says.

'So ends the fellowship section of the Gospel, and one of the greatest chapters in the New Testament' (J. A. Findlay).

Questions: Am I my brother's keeper? What does an affirmative answer imply?

Questions for further study and discussion on St. Matthew ch. 18

1. Is it right to conclude from vs. 1-4 that while adult disciples may need to 'turn', children have no such need, because they have the proper attitude already?
2. When are disciples gathered together 'in the name' of Jesus, in the sense of v. 20?
3. Should we infer from v. 35 that an unforgiving believer will have his pardon cancelled by God, or that by his conduct he shows that he never was a true believer? Or is the attempt to make such a distinction an evasion of the challenge of the parable?

St. Matthew 19.1-12   Ruling on Divorce

Our Lord's ruling on the divorce debate, which has already been recorded in 5.31 f., is repeated here in reply to the Pharisees' question. Now it is made clear that His ruling is based on an appeal to first principles: the divine purpose in marriage is implicit in the creation ordinances. Two passages are quoted, the last clause of Gen. 1.27 and the narrator's comment in Gen. 2.24, following on the account of the formation of Eve—and note that this comment is treated as something 'said' by God, since it is part of Holy Writ. From these passages the inference is drawn that marriage is an institution of God, designed to be permanent, and not to be annulled by man. To the natural question why in that case divorce is permitted in the law of Moses (Deut. 24.1), the answer is given that this was a concession to 'hardness of heart' but a departure from the Creator's ordinance, which Jesus reaffirms. The words 'except for unchastity' (9) have the same technical force as the similar exceptive clause in 5.32.

In the social context of that time and place, Jesus' ruling had the further effect of redressing an inequitable balance in favour of women. The disciples' reaction (10), expressing a thoroughly male point of view, suggests that they felt His ruling bore hardly on men, by depriving them of the right of divorce (a right which Jewish women did not share).

Those 'who have made themselves eunuchs for the sake of the kingdom of heaven' (12) are those who have remained unmarried in order to devote themselves with undivided mind to the service of God, especially in view of the impending crisis (cf. 1 Cor. 7.26–35). The unmarried members of the Essene orders provided a contemporary example, which in due course was to be abundantly paralleled among Christians.

Question: How would you present and defend the N.T. teaching on marriage and divorce in the contemporary 'permissive' society?

St. Matthew 19.13-22
Children and the Rich Young Man

Whatever the historical relation may have been between the two incidents recorded in these verses—the blessing of the children (13–15) and the conversation with the rich young man (16–22)—their juxtaposition in the Synoptic narrative in the setting of 'Judea beyond the Jordan' (1), i.e. Peraea, is deliberate. They illustrate respectively the simple, childlike confidence which is an indispensable qualification for the kingdom of heaven (cf. 18.1–4) and the attachment to material interests which keeps one out. Those who brought the children may have felt that the touch of the Prophet of Nazareth would in itself impart a blessing to them: Jesus' response probably points to children's unsophisticated readiness to ask and receive, as an example of the attitude His disciples should have towards their heavenly Father (cf. 7.7–11).

In vs. 16,17 there is a significant change in the relation of the term 'good' from that in Mark 10.17 f. and Luke 18.18 f. 'Eternal life' is practically synonymous with 'the kingdom of heaven'; to enter one is to enter the other (cf. Mark **9**.43,45 with 47). For the keeping of the commandments as the way to life cf. Lev. **18.5**; Deut. **30**.15–20. Those enumerated in vs. 18,19 form the second table of the decalogue, man's duty to his neighbour, summed up in the second of the two great commandments (Lev. **19**.18; cf. Matt. **22**.39). The young questioner, like Paul, could honestly claim to be blameless in respect of legal righteousness (cf. Phil. **3**.6); yet he was conscious of the need for something more. It is one thing to observe a series of specific precepts which are mainly negative; it is another to fulfil perfectly the all-embracing injunction to love one's neighbour as oneself. For the sense of 'perfect' (21) cf. **5.48**. Even the selling of his goods and giving the proceeds to the poor would not exhaust the meaning of the law of love (cf. 1 Cor. **13**.3), but it would be a first step towards fulfilling it and would show that the man was in earnest. Jesus knew just where his readiness needed to be tested, and he proved unequal to the test. (For 'treasure in heaven' cf. **6**.20.) The young man's sorrow was genuine enough; Jesus' probing words revealed to him the limitations of his eagerness to be utterly devoted to the doing of God's will. If the incident makes us also feel a bit uncomfortable, good; that is what it is intended to do.

St. Matthew 19.23-30
The Camel and the Needle's Eye

Our Lord's assurance that 'it will be hard for a rich man to enter the kingdom of heaven' (23) is rarely taken seriously, despite the solemnity with which it is introduced. Even at the time He found it necessary to drive it home by means of a vivid metaphor (paralleled in rabbinical teaching), and we must not make it a little easier for the rich man by supposing that the 'needle's eye' is a small gate within the large city gate or that He meant 'cable' and not 'camel'. The disciples' surprised question (25) may have been prompted by their remembrance that in much of the O.T. riches are a reward for piety and a token of divine blessing (cf. Deut. **28**.1–14; Psa. **128**, by contrast with those later texts in which 'poor' and 'righteous' are almost synonymous). Entry into the kingdom is difficult for all, but especially for those attached to material encumbrances: only with divine aid can it be achieved (26). But the apostles had given up all such things to follow Jesus: for them not only entry into the kingdom but high responsibility in the kingdom was reserved. The reference to 'twelve thrones' in v. 28, which must not be dissociated from the lesson of **18**.1–4 and **20**.25–28, implies the establishment of the believing community or 'Israel of God' (cf. Gal. **6**.16) in the 'new

70

world' or 'regeneration' (to be inaugurated by Jesus' death and resurrection)—the 'Church' of **16**.18—m which the apostles would exercise the authority promised in **16**.19; **18**.18. For this use of 'the twelve tribes' cf. Jas. **1**.1; see also Luke **22**.28–30. The number of the apostles (cf. **10**.1 f.) is significant in this regard. For the Son of Man's 'glorious throne' cf. **25**.31.

Moreover, all (not only the apostles) who gave up possessions and earthly ties for Jesus' sake would 'inherit eternal life' and be abundantly recompensed—though the recompense was not one which by worldly reckoning would make the sacrifice worthwhile. The assessment in the light of the coming Day is implied here, as it is expressed in **16**.25–27: then it will be seen that the first (by secular standards) are last (by the standards of the kingdom) and vice versa (cf. **20**.16).

St. Matthew 20.1-16 Last come, first served!

This parable may be placed here because it illustrates another aspect of the principle that the 'first will be last, and the last first' (**19**.30; cf. **20**.16). Its details reflect the high unemployment resulting from the desperate economic state of Palestine in N.T. times. At harvest or (as here) vintage time there was always a large pool of potential casual labour. The work began immediately after sunrise; the third, sixth, ninth and eleventh hours (3–6) were about 9 a.m., 12 noon, 3 and 5 p.m.; the wages were paid (8) when work ceased at sunset (about 6 p.m.). The fact that a denarius (a silver Roman coin roughly equivalent to 5 p. or a dime) was the daily wage for a casual labourer illuminates other references to money in the Gospels. We can readily understand the heightened hopes and consequent disappointment of those who had toiled for twelve hours, enduring 'the burden of the day and the scorching heat'—language bound to excite the sympathy of all who have had experience of unshaded noonday in a Palestinian summer. If the story had been told for its own sake, its moral might be that the men who, through no fault of their own, had been idle for the greater part of the day, required a living wage to support themselves and their families as much as the others did: 'to each according to his need' (cf. John Ruskin, *Unto This Last*). But it is introduced as a parable of 'the kingdom of heaven'; what is the point of comparison? Since it is not explicitly stated, we cannot be sure. The complaint of vs. 11 f. might remind us of the scribes and Pharisees, who disapproved of Jesus' proclamation of pardon and acceptance to doubtful characters whose record of righteous achievement bore no comparison with theirs. But perhaps the lesson was intended more particularly for the disciples, lest they should claim special merit for having 'left everything' to follow Jesus (19.27) and object to sharing the rewards of the kingdom with others whose commitment appeared to be neither so continuous nor so unreserved. In any case, the chief emphasis of the parable is laid on the householder's generosity. Those hired at daybreak had agreed to accept a denarius as their wage; those hired later agreed to be paid at his discretion (4). 'It is fortunate for most of us that God does not deal with us on the basis of strict justice and sound economics. . . . God's love cannot be portioned out in quantities nicely adjusted to the merits of individuals. There is such a thing as the twelfth part of a denar. It was called a *pondion*. But there is no such thing as a twelfth part of the love of God' (T. W. Manson).

Thought: What is my real motive for service?

St. Matthew 20.17-28   On the Jerusalem Road

Our Lord's third prophecy of His passion is more detailed than the preceding ones (16.21; 17.22 f.); His being handed over to the Gentiles (i.e. the Romans) for execution is explicitly mentioned for the first time, although it may already have been implied in the reference to the cross (10.38; 16.24). They are now on the way to Jerusalem, and the twelve must have the imminence of the crisis impressed upon them. But the fact that here (as in Mark 10.35 ff.) the incident of James and John's request follows immediately suggests that, in the Evangelists' opinion, the disciples' minds were not yet sufficiently attuned to their Master's to appreciate the solemnity of His warning.

The part played in the incident by Salome (cf. 27.56 with Mark 15.40) is peculiar to Matthew's account. Mothers are sometimes more ambitious for their sons than the sons themselves. The lesson of greatness in the kingdom (cf. 18.1–4) was hard to learn. Had James and John in due course been crucified on either side of Jesus instead of the two robbers, their request would have been in a fair way to being realized; but such distinction as this was far from their thoughts. The 'cup' of v. 22 was their Master's passion (cf. 26.39); they professed themselves ready to share it, and in a sense they did, as Jesus assured them they would, but long after He Himself endured it (cf. Acts 12.2 and possibly Rev. 1.9). As Jesus Himself was subject to His Father's good pleasure, so His followers must be content to accept those places in the Kingdom which the Father assigns them. The indignation of the ten was due, not to the impropriety of James and John's request in itself, but to the feeling that they had stolen

72

a march on them: the honour was one which each would have coveted for himself. So once again they had to be taught the secret of true greatness: their pattern must not be the Gentile rulers who command service but the Son of Man who gives lowly service. And the place of honour is not a reward or compensation for the service: the service *is* the honour. Is there any greater honour than to be allowed to serve God—and our fellow men? So the Son of Man rendered the lowliest and simultaneously the noblest service of all by becoming 'a ransom for many'. It is as His people's Saviour that He receives highest honour, and the shameful cross to which He was fastened has become the object of His people's chief glorying (Gal. 6.14). The language in which this service is described is reminiscent of the oracle of the Servant who gave His life as a 'reparation offering' and thus 'bore the sin of many' (Isa. 53.10,12).

> *'Bearing shame and scoffing rude,*
> *In my place condemned He stood;*
> *Sealed my pardon with His blood:*
> *Hallelujah! what a Saviour!'*
> Philip Bliss

St. Matthew 20.29-34   Blind Men of Jericho

The last lap of the journey to Jerusalem was the road from Jericho, leading up the Wadi Qelt. On either side of the lower reaches of the wadi lay N.T. Jericho, a new foundation built by Herod the Great as his winter residence, in imitation of contemporary Roman town-planning and architecture. Its site (Tulul Abu el-Alayiq) was about a mile south of O.T. Jericho (Tell es-Sultan). The incident of vs. 29–34 is Matthew's counterpart to the narrative of the healing of blind Bartimaeus in Mark 10.46–52; however, it features two blind men where Mark (cf. Luke 18.35–43) has only one. (For a similar Matthaean duplication cf. the two Gadarene demoniacs of 8.28 ff. alongside the one of Mark 5.1 ff. and Luke 8.26 ff. But such duplication is not restricted to *Matthew*; compare the 'two men' of Luke 24.4 with the 'young man' of Mark 16.5 and the 'angel' of Matt. 28.2.) A further point to consider here is the close resemblance between the present incident and the earlier one of 9.27–31; here, however, there is no stern warning not to broadcast the act of healing, for it was performed in full view of the 'great crowd' of Galilean pilgrims going up to Jerusalem for the Passover. As on the earlier occasion (cf. also 15.22), Jesus does not refuse to be called 'Son of David', though He is not recorded as laying claim to the title Himself. One Old Syriac manuscript makes the blind men say:

73

'Lord, let our eyes be opened and let us see Thee' (33). The incident illustrates the perseverance of the blind men in face of discouragement, the compassion of Jesus, and the power of God which inhered in His word and touch. On receiving their sight, they not unnaturally joined the others who were following Him up to Jerusalem.

Questions for further study and discussion on St. Matthew chs. 19 and 20

1. Can the ruling on marriage and divorce in **19**.3–9 be applied without modification today (a) to 'Christian civilization' in general; (b) to committed church members?
2. What bearing has the incident of **19**.13–15 on the doctrine and practice of infant baptism?
3. What relation can you find between the parable of the labourers in the vineyard and the gospel of salvation by grace?
4. Compare **19**.28 with **20**.26 f. Does the principle of lowly service as the true greatness apply to the age to come ('the new world') as much as to this age?

St. Matthew 21.1-11 The Entry into Jerusalem

The steep ascent from Jericho to Jerusalem has almost been completed; Jesus and the pilgrim crowd have reached the Mount of Olives, which lies to the east of the city. Bethphage ('the place of young figs') was a village near Bethany, on the eastern side of the Mount, barely 2 miles from Jerusalem. There Jesus had made advance arrangements for His entry into the city. Matthew's mention of two animals (2,7), over against the other Evangelists' one (Mark **11**.2 ff.; Luke **19**.30 ff., John **12**.14), is 'duplication' of a different kind from that in the preceding paragraph; here he emphasizes the express fulfilment of the prophecy of Zech. **9**.9, in which 'an ass' and 'a colt, the foal of an ass' appear in synonymous parallelism (5). The other Gospels make it plain that it was on the unbroken colt that Jesus rode into Jerusalem. The introductory formula of v. 4 in this instance implies Jesus' deliberate plan to give effect to the oracle —probably to see what the response of the Jerusalemites would be to His peaceful approach. It was not encouraging.

It was the pilgrims thronging around Jesus who uttered jubilant shouts—perhaps with more enthusiasm than understanding (9). 'Hosanna' ('save now', 'give victory now') is the festal cry of Psa. **118**.25; 'Hosanna to the Son of David' is as much as to say 'God save the (messianic) King'. The words of welcome ('blessed is he who comes in the name of the Lord') come from the same context

74

(Psa. 118.26). The phrase 'in the highest' is a substitute for the name of God: 'Save now, (Thou who dwellest) in the highest (place).' But when the people of Jerusalem ask the cause of all the commotion, the crowds claim nothing more for Jesus than that He is the prophet of Nazareth. Prophet or King, would the city have Him on His own terms? Would it recognize Him as the Shepherd of Israel, ready to 'devote' Himself for His people's salvation, or would it prefer others who would involve it in ruin?

St. Matthew 21.12-22 Activity in Jerusalem

The expulsion of the traders from the Temple (i.e. from the 'court of the Gentiles') is best understood as a prophetic action like those of O.T. times in which a message is vividly driven home. Jesus' attitude to the Temple of His day is similar to Jeremiah's attitude to Solomon's Temple (cf. 16.14). His words of rebuke are partly drawn from Jer. 7.11 ('Has this house, which is called by My name, become a den of robbers in your eyes?') and partly from Isa. 56.7 ('My house shall be called a house of prayer for all peoples'). The bazaars may have been installed there temporarily but, useful as they probably were to many visitors, they were occupying ground which ought to have been used for the worship of God. The protest was directed against the Temple authorities, and they fully recognized this (cf. v. 23).

Whereas the rule had been laid down in the days of David that 'the blind and the lame shall not come into the house' (2 Sam. 5.8), it is reversed when 'great David's greater Son' appears (that the rule was not enforced for the outer court is evident from Acts 3.2). This use of the Temple area for healing, and the children's taking up of the Galilean pilgrims' shout of greeting, scandalized the authorities, who invited Jesus' co-operation in moderating what they regarded as disorder; but He invoked Psa. 8.1 f. in the children's defence. The implication of v. 17 is probably that He spent each night during this Jerusalem visit in Bethany (cf. 26.6).

The withering of the fig tree (18 ff.), which is here telescoped into a short time (by comparison with Mark 11.12–14, 20 ff.), is a further prophetic action, in which the tree (cf. Luke 13.6–9) may well represent Jerusalem, so unresponsive to Jesus' overtures (cf. also v. 43). The fact that at this time of year it bore only leaves, without any *taqsh* (the precursor of coming figs), showed it to be fruitless. To the disciples the incident is made the basis of a lesson on the power of faith (cf. 17.20). In the present setting 'this mountain' (21) must be Olivet; the fact that Olivet was to be the centre of a major

convulsion on the day of the Lord, according to Zech. **14.**4, stamps
the setting as authentic and suggests the interpretation: 'If only you
have sufficient faith, the new age will be inaugurated sooner than
you think.'

Questions: What does the cleansing of the Temple signify (a) *for
the individual* (1 *Cor.* **6.**19)? (b) *for the church* (1 *Cor.* **3.**16)?

St. Matthew 21.23-32   'By what authority?'

While Jesus spent the nights in Bethany, He spent the days teaching
in the Temple area. The 'chief priests and the elders' would be
members of the Sanhedrin, the supreme court of Israel (cf. **26.**3,47;
27.1,3,12,20); in particular, the ultimate responsibility for maintaining order within the sacred precincts lay with the captain of the
Temple, who was a member of one of the chief-priestly families
and ranked next to the high priest. Hence the question of v. 23,
which related not only to His teaching and healing (15) but perhaps
especially to His expulsion of the traders (12). But what answer
would have satisfied them? If spiritual authority—the kind of
authority by which the prophets spoke and acted—is not recognized
as self-authenticating, no amount of argument, not even a sign from
heaven (cf. **12.**38; **16.**1), will validate it. The questioners perhaps
suspected that He did these things because He claimed to be the
Messiah, but at this stage He does not voice such a claim. Instead,
He asks them what they thought of the authority of John the
Baptist—was it derived from God or self-assumed? The true answer,
of course, was 'From God'—and even more evidently this was the
true answer regarding the authority of Him whose forerunner John
was. But they would not commit themselves to this course of reasoning and so their question remained unanswered.

The next episode, in which Jesus asks the opening question, also
involves an appeal to John. (The variant, but inferior, reading in
v. 31, where the answer given is 'The last', may point to a society
in which politeness is more important than obedience.) John's 'way
of righteousness' (32) required 'fruit that befits repentance' (**3.**8),
and this was produced by those who at first said 'I will not' (the
tax collectors and harlots) rather than the religious leaders who
undertook to do God's will but did not carry out their undertaking.
Is there a counterpart to this situation in our own religious life?

St. Matthew 21.33-46   Parable of the Vineyard

As in Isaiah's parable, so here 'the vineyard of the LORD of hosts is
the house of Israel, and the men of Judah are His pleasant planting'

(Isa. **5.**7). The rulers of the people could not miss the point; they and their predecessors were the tenants (45). The 'servants' (34–36) are the prophets (cf. **23.**37), and the significance of the owner's sending his son (37) as a last resort cannot be overlooked. Of all the Gospel parables, this one (exceptionally) comes nearest to being an allegory, in which there is a series of correspondences between the successive details of the narrative—the 'parables' (plural) of v. 45—and the reality to which it points. The killing of the son after he is cast out of the vineyard (39; contrast the order in Mark **12.**8) reflects Jesus' being put to death outside Jerusalem. By the 'other tenants' (41), i.e. the 'nation producing the fruits' of the vineyard (43), the Church, the new Israel, is intended; its leaders (cf. **19.**28) will replace the present rulers in Israel from whom the kingdom is to be taken away. The reference to 'fruits' makes the same point as the fig-tree incident of v. 19. The 'miserable death' of the tenants (41) may anticipate the disaster of A.D. 70.

The quotation in v. 42 (Psa. **118.**22 f.) is from the same festal psalm which provided the acclamation of v. 9; it is treated as a messianic 'testimony' repeatedly in the N.T. (cf. Acts **4.**11; 1 Pet. **2.**7), together with the other 'stone' passages (Isa. **8.**15; Dan. **2.**34 f.) alluded to in the doubtful v. 44 (RSV footnote). What is said of the multitude's assessment of Jesus in v. 46 echoes their assessment of John according to v. 26. In both places the multitudes are probably the pilgrim crowds rather than the residents in Jerusalem; at Passover the visitors might outnumber the residents by three to one.

St. Matthew 22.1-14   Parable of the Marriage Feast

This parable is superficially similar to the parable of the 'great banquet' in Luke **14.**16–24, but its meaning is closer to that of the vineyard in Matt. **21.**33–43. The proclamation of the kingdom of heaven is compared to a royal command, sent out to people already invited in advance to a marriage feast at the palace, to come and take their places, since the feast was now about to begin. (Since no emphasis is laid on the king's son in v. 2, he need not be allegorized as the Messiah.) The command, being unheeded, was repeated, but was received with deliberately offensive indifference—or worse, as when the servants who summoned the guests were beaten up or killed (cf. **21.**35 f.). The punishment of the murderers (cf. **21.**41a) and burning of their city (recorded parenthetically in v. 7) point to the siege and destruction of Jerusalem in A.D. 70; the first invited guests thus represent the religious establishment in Jerusalem. As in the parable of the vineyard the owner, after putting the first tenants to death, let out the vineyard to more trustworthy tenants, so the king here conscripts guests who had not been previously invited to come and fill the wedding hall and enjoy the feast. (The punitive action of v. 7 was not necessarily completed before the second lot of guests were gathered: otherwise the good things provided would have become cold and stale.) The second guests correspond to the 'nation' of 21.43—the new society of Jewish and Gentile disciples—to which the kingdom was to be transferred.

So far so good, but the appended incident (11-14) presents a problem. It probably prefigures the final judgement, when every man will be repaid 'for what he has done' (16.27); the 'wedding garment' is best understood as the way of life that shows the genuineness of the initial repentance (cf. 3.8; Rev. 19.8). For the man's expulsion from the banqueting hall into the darkness outside cf. 8.12; 25.30. The problem lies in the difficulty of fitting some elements in the incident into the whole narrative, for which reason it has been thought that two originally separate parables have been telescoped here. The moral of v. 14 is not to be understood in the sense of 'effectual calling' (cf. Rom. 8.28-30); it simply means that not all to whom the invitation is extended enjoy the banquet (the blessings of the kingdom). When a limited number of vacancies must be filled, several candidates may be short-listed and called for interview, but not all of these are appointed.

St. Matthew 22.15-22   Tribute to Caesar

In 17.24–27 responsibility regarding one form of tax was discussed: the tax which figures in the present debate constituted the hottest political question of the day in Judea. It did not arise in Galilee, which was governed by a Jewish prince (Herod Antipas); but when Judea became a Roman province in A.D. 6 it became directly tributary to the Emperor. Some Jews maintained that the payment of taxes to a pagan ruler constituted high treason to God, the true King of Israel, and revolted against Rome under Judas the Galilean (cf. Acts 5.37). The revolt was crushed, but its spirit survived among the Zealots (cf. 10.4). The Zealots' viewpoint enjoyed much popular support, whatever was thought of their violent methods (cf. 11.12). The Pharisees and the Herodians were strange bedfellows, but if the Herodians (who do not appear elsewhere in this Gospel) maintained the claims of the Herod dynasty to rule all Palestine, they would have had at least theoretical objections to the payment of tribute to Caesar. It was hoped that the question would impale our Lord on the horns of a dilemma: if He said it was right to pay the tribute,

He would forfeit general popularity; if He said it was wrong, He could be reported to the Roman administration for sedition (cf. Luke 23.2). For Him, however, 'the things that are God's', the interests of His kingdom, were primary; they would not be adversely affected if a pagan monarch received back the denarius (cf. 20.2) which was self-evidently his. There were some Jews so scrupulous that they would not touch such a coin, because the imperial image infringed the Second Commandment. Jesus' words may suggest that such coinage was fit only for Gentiles to handle: Caesar's money was best designed for paying Caesar's tribute. Let them make God's kingdom and righteous requirements their principal concern (cf. 6.33). Thus Jesus not only avoided the dilemma but turned it to emphasize the central theme of His own teaching.

Note: By 'hypocrites' (18) we are (as in 6.2 ff.) to understand 'play-actors', whose words and actions do not express their personal thoughts. The reference is probably to the complimentary gambit of v. 16, which masked a desire to set a trap for Jesus.

Question: What, in the modern world, is Caesar's?

St. Matthew 22.23-33   How are the Dead Raised?

The Sadducees, the aristocratic party to which most of the chief-priestly families belonged, regarded themselves as conservatives in theology and rejected the Pharisaic 'tradition of the elders' (cf. 15.2), sticking to the literal application of the written law. They repudiated the doctrine of bodily resurrection as a post-exilic innovation (cf. Acts 23.8). They understood resurrection (as indeed some of its proponents envisaged it) in terms of a restoration to the conditions of bodily life on earth; hence their improbable story (25-27) with the following question (28) was intended to expose the absurdity of such a belief. The command of Moses summarized in v. 24 is the law of levirate marriage (cf. Deut. 25.5-10; Ruth 3.1 ff.). No doubt the conundrum was one with which they were accustomed to embarrass their Pharisaic rivals. But Jesus assured them that their question revealed ignorance both of the nature of resurrection (as an act of divine power) and of their own Scriptures. Resurrection did not mean the resumption of former conditions of biological life and reproduction, but a new order of existence (cf. 1 Cor. 15.35 ff.), sexless as the angels (30). It is inaccurate to say, as has sometimes been said, that the Sadducees' canon was restricted to the Pentateuch (this was true rather of the Samaritans); but they would certainly venerate it as supremely authoritative, and Jesus appealed to it rather than to (say) Isa. 26.19 or Dan. 12.2 (the latter of which they may well not have acknowledged as canonical). Instead of quoting this or that proof-text, He grounded the doctrine of resurrection securely in the being and character of God. The God who could call Himself the God of men long since dead (Exod. 3.6) showed by doing so that in relation to Him they were not dead: 'He is not God of the dead, but of the living' (32). 'What does not die to God does not die to itself' (Augustine).

St. Matthew 22.34-46   Debating with Pharisees

The Pharisees could not but applaud Jesus' answer to the Sadducees; now they tested His judgement on the kind of question which they debated among themselves. Some of them distinguished 'heavy' (more important) from 'light' (less important) commandments (cf. 23.23), but that did not mean that they could treat the latter less seriously, for God's relative assessment of His commandments might be different from theirs. Was there one commandment which could be regarded as the greatest and, if so, how was it to be recognized? Jesus in reply quoted the injunction of unreserved love to God (Deut. 6.5) which included the doing of all His commandments (cf. 1 John 5.3a), and coupled with it (by the rabbinical exegetical method of 'equal categories') the injunction of unreserved love to one's neighbour (Lev. 19.18b), which begins, like the former, with 'you shall love'. Of this twofold injunction the words might well have been spoken which Hillel used of the golden rule (see note on 7.12). All that God requires in the whole volume of written revelation is comprehended in these two injunctions. (It is noteworthy that in Luke 10.27 these two are quoted by a 'lawyer' as a summary of the divine law, in response to our Lord's question.)

Our Lord's turn now comes to put a counter-question to the Pharisees. He and they believed that Psa. 110 was composed by David and referred to the Messiah. According to them, the Messiah was to be the son of David (cf. 1.1). But in Psa. 110.1 David refers to the Messiah as 'my Lord', and does so by inspiration. How can the Messiah be both David's Son and David's Lord? Those early Christians who heard or read this incident would feel that this question, which the Pharisees found unanswerable, presented no problem to them: they knew that Jesus, Son of David (cf. Rom. 1.3), had been highly exalted by God and made both Lord and Messiah (Acts 2.36), thus receiving 'the name which is above every name' (Phil. 2.9-11). Throughout the N.T., Psa. 110.1 is the principal O.T. 'testimony' for the acknowledgement of Jesus as Lord and for

His session at God's right hand (cf. Acts **2**.34 f.; Rom. **8**.34; 1 Cor. **15**.25; Eph. **1**.20; Col. **3**.1; Heb. **1**.13; 1 Pet. **3**.22; Rev. **3**.21).

Questions: Is it possible to fulfil vs. 37–39? *How can we test our obedience?*

St. Matthew 23.1-12 An Example to be Avoided

Not all Pharisees were willing to engage with Jesus in friendly debate. This chapter brings together a number of criticisms of tendencies to which people of Pharisaic attitude (today as in the first century) are specially prone. Where stress is laid on strict law-keeping as an expression of heart-devotion to God, it is possible for some to emulate the outward law-keeping and so gain a reputation for a heart-devotion which is not there (cf. **6**.1 ff.). The Pharisees themselves were well aware of this, and while seven categories of Pharisee are enumerated in the rabbinical writings, only one of these—he who is a Pharisee for love of God—receives unqualified commendation. Jesus warns His hearers, and especially His disciples, against the temptations to which Pharisees were exposed—setting up a standard of legal righteousness impossible of attainment for ordinary working men ('the people of the land', as they called them) and receiving deferential treatment because of their reputation for piety. The 'phylacteries' of v. 5 are parchments containing four passages from the O.T. (Exod. **13**.1–10; Exod. **13**.11–16; Deut. **6**.4–9; Deut. **11**.13–21) in parallel columns, placed in leather containers and worn on the forehead and left arm in literal fulfilment of Deut. **6**.8 (before A.D. 70, as the Qumran discoveries indicate, the ten commandments were also included). The 'fringes' were the tassels prescribed in Num. **15**.38 f.; Deut. **22**.12 (cf. Matt. **9**.20; **14**.36). Extra-large phylacteries and tassels (like an extra-large Bible carried under the arm) might be regarded by unthinking people as signs of exceptional piety. Jesus bids His followers avoid such ostentation, and dispense with the use of honorific titles. In this regard, as in some others (cf. **5**.34 ff.), His instructions have been taken with serious literalness by the Friends. This part of the discourse ends with a repetition of His characteristic insistence on service and humility as the hall-marks of His disciples (11 f.).

Note. At a rather later date 'Moses' seat' (2) was the actual chair in the synagogue in which a rabbi sat as he taught (cf. Luke **4**.20), but probably not so early as this. Here the expression probably means that they expound the law which Moses received on Sinai.

Thought: Somebody must have the place of honour: it is wanting, not having, the front seat that is wrong.

JERUSALEM
at the Time of Christ

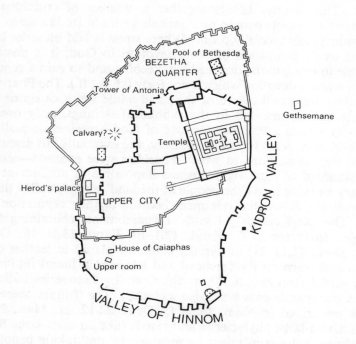

Pool of Bethesda

BEZETHA
QUARTER

Tower of Antonia

Gethsemane

Calvary?

Temple

KIDRON VALLEY

Herod's palace

UPPER CITY

House of Caiaphas

Upper room

VALLEY OF HINNOM

Akeldama

═══════ Present wall of old city

─────── Probable location of walls

0   500 Yards

St. Matthew 23.13-28   Lament for the Scribes

The seven 'woes' of vs. 13–32 can be read as laments rather than denunciations: 'Alas for you!' rather than 'Woe to you!' It is not implied that 'scribes and Pharisees' are inevitably 'hypocrites'; the reference is to hypocritical or 'play-acting' scribes and Pharisees, whose 'piety' was a matter of outward show. Such conduct is possible only in a context of sincere Pharisaism, such as is exemplified in the N.T. by Nicodemus, Gamaliel and Saul of Tarsus. The charge in v. 13 refers to those who opposed Jesus' preaching of the kingdom themselves and discouraged others from paying heed to it. Verse 15 bears witness to the active proselytization in the Dispersion at this time (cf. G. Tyrrell's remark quoted in note on 5.16). Verses 16–22 amplify 5.33–37 and expose the inconsistency of distinguishing between binding oaths and invalid oaths. The Pharisees were particularly scrupulous about tithing; in addition to tithing the main fruits of the earth (grain, wine and olive oil) specified in Deut. 14.22 f., they interpreted Lev. 27.30 to cover garden herbs (23). But those who paid more attention to such minutiae than to 'justice and mercy and faith' (cf. Mic. 6.8) were aptly described as straining out midges from their drink while swallowing camels without noticing them (cf. 7.3–5). The two 'woes' of vs. 25 f. and 27 f. return to the theme of outward respectability camouflaging inward sin. Tombs were whitewashed to draw attention to them, so that people who would incur ceremonial defilement by accidental contact with them—e.g. the high priest (Lev. 21.11) or a Nazirite (Num. 6.6)—could easily avoid them.

Question: Rephrase these 'laments' to express contemporary attitudes and actions. Do any of these apply to me?

St. Matthew 23.29-39   Lament for Jerusalem

For the argument of vs. 29–32 we may compare Stephen's charge in Acts 7.51 f. The language of v. 33 is similar to the Baptist's in 3.7; 'hell' is 'Gehenna' (as in v. 15; cf. 5.22, 29 f.). The question could be answered in one phrase, 'By repentance'; but it is implied that no sign of repentance was forthcoming. In vs. 34–36 Jesus speaks in the role of Divine Wisdom; the words might well be put within quotation-marks, as in Luke 11.49–51. In the traditional order of Hebrew Scripture (which ends with 1 and 2 *Chronicles*) Abel (Gen. 4.8) is the first martyr and Zechariah (2 Chron. 24.20–22) the last. In the course of transmission the son of Jehoiada has apparently been confused with the son of Berechiah (Zech. 1.1). For the emphasis on 'this generation' cf. 12.39, 41 f.,.45. The horrors of the war of A.D. 66–70 were greater than the sins of one generation could have incurred as a penalty. In Luke 13.34 f. the lament over Jerusalem (which in both Gospels implies previous unrecorded visits) follows the remark: 'it cannot be that a prophet should perish away from Jerusalem'. The words 'you will not see Me again' (39) apply to the Temple, which Jesus now leaves for the last time, rather than to the city in general. Verse 38 may recall the gradual departure of God's glory from the earlier Temple before its destruction by the Babylonians (Ezek. 8.4; 9.3; 10.4, 18 f.; 11.23); the day foretold in v. 39 would then be linked with the return of the glory to the restored house (Ezek. 43.1–5) and identified with the coming of the Son of Man (Matt. 24.27, 30 f.).

Questions: How much of this chapter could you apply to the Church today? Can you suggest evils in the Church which Christ would have to condemn?

Questions for further study and discussion on St. Matthew chs. 21–23

1. What can be gathered from these chapters about our Lord's attitude to the Temple?
2. Can we discover emphases in Jesus' Jerusalem ministry which distinguish it from His Galilean ministry?
3. What practical lessons can we learn from Jesus' replies to His questioners in ch. 22?
4. Does the severe language of ch. 23 justify us in expressing ourselves similarly about people whose religious beliefs or practices we consider to be wrong?

St. Matthew 24.1-14   Convulsions Preceding the End

The fifth and last discourse in this Gospel, dealing with the consummation of the kingdom (chs. 24,25), begins with the Olivet prophecy (paralleled in Mark 13 and Luke 21.5 ff.), which is concerned largely with events associated with the destruction of the Temple (2). Whatever the disciples' ideas of the future were in A.D. 30, it was possible by the time this Gospel was written to distinguish 'this' (3)—i.e. the destruction of the Temple, which had taken place—from Jesus' coming (*parousia*) and 'the close of the age' (cf. 13.39, 49), which still lay in the future. In the following verses we expect an answer to both parts of the disciples' question, but we cannot divide the prophecy neatly so as to make part refer exclusively to the nearer event and part to that which was more remote.

The Temple restored by Herod from 19 B.C. onwards was internationally renowned for its architectural splendour. The lower courses of masonry on the western wall survive to bear witness to its vanished glories. No wonder that the disciples drew their Master's attention to the buildings (1). It was His prediction of the overthrow (2) that prompted their question as they looked across to the city and Temple from the slopes of Olivet (3). His reply in the first instance warns them not to be misled by false Messiahs (4 f.), many of whom attracted large numbers of enthusiastic devotees in the period between A.D. 44 and 70, and encourages them not to be dismayed by wars and natural calamities (6 f.; cf. Rev. 6.2–8). These will be but harbingers of the birth-pangs of the new age (8). Then He prepares them for persecution and apostasy (cf. Dan. 11.33 ff.) amid increasing wickedness (9–12) but holds out the promise of final deliverance for those who maintain their loyalty to the end (13). Verses 9–14 largely repeat 10.16–23; the assurance that the world-wide proclamation of the good news of the kingdom must precede the end (14) is parallel to the enigmatic 10.23b; but what was there restricted to 'the towns of Israel' is here 'a testimony to all nations' (cf. 28.19), which indeed became a historical reality in the decades before A.D. 70.

> Plague, earthquake and famine, and tumult and war
> The wonderful coming of Jesus declare.

St. Matthew 24.15-28
Desolating Sacrilege and Great Tribulation

The 'desolating sacrilege' of Dan. 8.13; 9.27; 11.31; 12.11 was an idolatrous installation in the Temple of God. The event predicted here can scarcely be equated with the victorious Romans' sacrificing to their standards opposite the east gate of the Temple in A.D. 70 while the building was still ablaze; it precedes the outbreak of war. The attempt to set up an imperial image in the Temple in A.D. 40 would have been a fulfilment had it not been called off. The language suggests some distinct act of colossal blasphemy which would usher in unprecedented distress for the people of God; we may compare what is said of Antichrist in 2 Thess. 2.4. 'Let the reader understand' (15) is as much a challenge to discernment today as it was then (Rev. 13.18); it implies that there is more in the reference than lies on the surface. Instant flight will be necessary, and it will bear hardly on expectant and nursing mothers (19); winter would make speedy escape more difficult and a sabbath would limit the distance that could be covered (20; cf. Exod. 16.29b). The historical departure of the church from Jerusalem before the siege of the city appears to have been more leisurely than what is envisaged here. The 'great tribulation' was already foretold in Dan. 12.1, together with deliverance for the elect; the means of deliverance is here stated to be the shortening of its allotted duration (cf. Dan. 12.6 ff.). As for vs. 23–26, the 'deceivers' whose rise is foretold in v. 5 multiplied as the doom of Jerusalem became more imminent, promising victory when there was none. When the Son of Man comes (cf. Dan. 7.13), His advent will be as sudden and unmistakable as the lightning-flash (27). Verse 28 means that where a situation is ripe for judgement (as then in Jerusalem), there the judgement will fall. The mention of 'eagles' instead of the expected 'vultures' may be an allusion to the Roman legionary standards.

Question: What is our underlying attitude to the Second Coming?

St. Matthew 24.29-35   The Sign of the Son of Man

Such cosmic phenomena as are described in v. 29 appear in the O.T. as metaphors for disasters like the overthrow of cities; cf. Isa. 24.1 ff., which depicts in this way the downfall of a hostile city (Isa. 24.10–12; 27.10). The tribulation of siege and warfare will be followed by the fall of Jerusalem, and 'all these things' will be completed within the lifetime of 'this generation' (34). Here is the answer to the disciples' first question, 'when will this be?' (3). There is no need to make difficulties about 'this generation', as though it meant 'this race' (the Jews) or the generation of the end-time; the phrase is identical with that in 23.36 and the two passages point forward to the same sequence of events. Unlike the advent of the Son of Man (27), the fall of Jerusalem will be heralded by signs which cannot be mistaken by those who have eyes to see: just as the appearance of leaves on the fig-tree is a token of the approach of summer, so the events of vs. 5–14, and especially the 'desolating sacrilege' (15) and attendant signs (24), betoken the imminent destruction of the city and Temple (in v. 33 we might render with AV 'it is near' rather than 'he is near'). The coming of the Son of Man, the subject of the disciples' second question (3), follows the fall of Jerusalem. Matthew alone speaks of 'the *sign* of the Son of Man' (30), which harks back to 'sign' in v. 3. Since the Son of Man comes without preceding signs (27,37–44), His 'sign' in v. 30 may be Himself—the sign which is the Son of Man. Like Jonah, the Son of Man is His own 'sign' (cf. 12.39). The expression was early interpreted as the sign of the cross in the sky, but this is improbable in the present context. His coming 'on the clouds' with power and glory (cf. 16.27; 26.64) is based on Dan. 7.13; the trumpet-call for

86

the ingathering of the elect (31) on Isa. **27.**13, and the wailing of 'all the tribes of the earth' on Zech. **12.**10 ff. As in Rev. **1.**7, the original reference to the wailing of the families of Israel is given a world-wide extension. The words of Jesus have the same binding and permanent validity (35) as the words of the law (**5.**18).

St. Matthew 24.36-51 — Call to Vigilance

While the fall of the Temple and city will take place before the passing of 'this generation' (34), no time indication can be given for the Son of Man's advent. While the Son's subordination to the Father is seen in His not knowing 'of that day and hour', His supremacy over all created beings is expressed by His being mentioned after 'the angels of heaven' (36). As no warning signs preceded the flood of Noah's day, so none will precede the coming of the Son of Man (37–39): it will overtake people as they pursue their everyday activities and separate one from the other in judgement (40 f.; cf. **25.**32 f.). No opportunity now for flight!

The necessity of vigilant readiness, in view of the Son of Man's unpredictable coming (42,44), is illustrated by two parables—the thief by night (43) and the returning master (45–51). The parable of the thief by night recurs throughout the N.T. (cf. 1 Thess. **5.**2; 2 Pet. **3.**10; Rev. **3.**3; **16.**15); his nefarious plan succeeds only when the house is not adequately guarded. When the chief steward whose master leaves him in charge during his absence has no idea when his master will return, that ought to keep him on his toes: only a very foolish steward would abuse his authority and neglect his duty in such a situation. If, even so, he does misconduct himself, his master's return will mean for him not commendation and reward (47) but flogging and dismissal (51). The reference to 'the hypocrites' in v. 51 suggests that the defaulter played the part of a faithful steward only when his master was around; the parallel in Luke **12.**46 has 'the unfaithful'.

Questions: (i) How can we be ready for the Second Coming? (ii) Why did Christ not make it clear that we should have to wait so long?

St. Matthew 25.1-13 — Late for the Wedding Breakfast

To the Olivet prophecy with its short appended parables Matthew adds three longer parables re-enforcing the lessons of vigilance, faithfulness and kindness.

In the first parable the ten maidens appear to be the bride's attendants (cf. Psa. **45.**14) who are to go out to meet the bridegroom when, with his friends, he arrives at her house, and then escort the couple with a torchlight procession to the bridegroom's home for the marriage feast. If, however, we read 'the bridegroom and the bride' at the end of v. 1 (cf. RSV footnote), then the maidens are girls of the neighbourhood who plan 'to light up the approach to the bridegroom's house as a welcome, in return for which they would hope to have some share in the rather promiscuous hospitality of an oriental festivity' (F. C. Burkitt). It is best not to allegorize the parable and determine whom the maidens stand for and what the oil represents. For example, if we allegorize the two sets of maidens, we have to reckon with the fact that they all fell asleep. And if we allegorize the oil, we have to reckon with the fact that the foolish maidens had oil to begin with as well as the wise, and that when it gave out they succeeded in buying some more, even though it was past midnight. What matters is that, by the time they bought a fresh supply, they were too late for the procession and when they reached the bridegroom's home the doorkeeper would not let them in. So they had to go back tired and disappointed, because they were not ready when the bridegroom arrived. The story is a parable, not an allegory; the lesson for the hearers is: Don't be like those foolish girls; keep awake and be prepared. To the words 'you know neither the day nor the hour' (13) the 'received text' (followed by AV) adds 'when the Son of man comes'; this is no doubt sound exegesis, although it forms no part of the original text. But there are partial comings of the Son of Man before the final *parousia* (cf. **16**.28; **26**.64); and the text as it stands bids the reader be ready for any hour of testing that may come upon him unannounced. Be ready to resist the temptation (whatever it may be), to meet the crisis, to grasp the opportunity. Yesterday's oil will not keep our lamps alight today; past experience will not suffice for present or future need.

St. Matthew 25.14-30   Parable of the Talents

The parable of the talents elaborates the theme of the parable of the returning master (**24**.45-51). It bears a general resemblance to the parable of the pounds in Luke **19**.11-27 but there are material differences in detail. A talent was not a coin but a weight, roughly equivalent to half a hundredweight or 25 kilograms of silver or gold, tied up in bags (cf. NEB). It is from this parable that the word has acquired its extended meaning of spiritual endowment or faculty. There are not so many five-talent or two-talent people going about; the work of the kingdom of God is done mainly by those who have one talent—and use it. The phrase 'to each according to his ability'

88

(15) expresses an important principle: no one is responsible for talents which he has not been given. Why did the third servant not trade with his talent? He probably reckoned that trading carries a risk with it—you may gain more, but if you invest unfortunately, you may lose. The safest course therefore was to keep his talent intact by burying it. When safe deposits were not so readily available, this was a common way of guarding valuables against loss (cf. 13.44). But nothing venture, nothing win. The kingdom of heaven involves placing everything at hazard (cf. 10.39; 16.24–27). The portrayal of the day of judgement in terms of a master investigating his servants' accounts (cf. 18.23) is familiar in rabbinical literature. 'The reward of a duty performed is a duty to perform', said a first-century rabbi. So here the reward of the two faithful servants consists in opportunities for further service more responsible in character. 'The joy of your master' (21,23) is probably the banquet of the resurrection age (cf. 8.11). The unprofitable servant excuses his lack of enterprise as best he can, blaming it on his master's harsh exploitation of his employees' labour. But his excuses are not accepted; he is ejected from the merry-making of his master's 'welcome home' feast and left outside in the dark with his frustration and remorse. Verses 28 and 29 convey a subsidiary moral, already taught in another context in 13.12, which is of abiding application and does not refer to the time of the end. The penalty of neglected opportunity is the loss of further opportunity.

Thought: A servant is known by his master's absence.

St. Matthew 25.31-46   The Sheep and the Goats

The setting of this judgement scene was familiar to the hearers and probably to the readers: the coming of the Son of Man with attendant angels (cf. 16.27) and His sitting on His glorious throne (cf. 19.28), the gathering of all nations for judgement (cf. Joel 3.2,11–14) and the allocation of bliss or doom were themes of contemporary apocalyptic literature, derived ultimately from O.T. revelation. It is in the criterion on which the verdict is based that the distinctive feature of the parable consists. The parabolic element, strictly speaking, is confined to the words: 'as a shepherd separates the sheep from the goats, and He will place the sheep at His right hand, but the goats at the left' (32 f.). A mixed flock of sheep and goats is not uncommon in Palestine: superficially they may look alike, apart from their tails, but from time to time they must be separated.

They may be gathered as nations but they are judged as individuals. And this, says Jesus, will be the principle of judgement: how have they treated Me in the person of 'the least of these My brethren'? He is fittingly called 'the King' (34,40) because of His enthronement. The expression *these My brethren* suggests that they are present: the followers of the Son of Man, 'the saints of the Most High', are associated with Him in the judgement (cf. Dan. 7.22; 1 Cor. 6.2 f.). His kingdom is their inheritance (21.43), but here it is revealed that it has also been prepared 'from the foundation of the world' for those who have treated them kindly (34 ff.) and in so doing are deemed to have shown this kindness to the King Himself (cf. 10.40–42; 18.5). No wonder these Gentiles are amazed (37); readers of this passage have been amazed in generation after generation, and have found difficulty in fitting the teaching here given into their theological scheme. But which must be altered— the teaching of Jesus, or our theological scheme? For the same essential insistence on the care of those in need cf. Gal. 6.10; Heb. 13.2 f., 16; Jas. 2.15 f.; 1 John 3.17. Those on the left hand are as surprised by their condemnation (44) as the others are by their acceptance; but the awards are completely impartial. As elsewhere in Scripture (cf. 16.27; Rom. 2.6–11) divine judgement is rendered to men according to their works, be they good or bad. The 'eternal fire' (41) is probably Gehenna (cf. 5.22, 29 f.; 18.8 f.). As 'eternal life' (46) is the life of the age to come (cf. 19.16), so 'eternal punishment' consists in exclusion from that life; for those so sentenced there is no portion in the age to come.

Question: What are the equivalents in the western world of the acts described in vs. 35, 36?

Questions for further study and discussion on St. Matthew chs. 24 and 25

1. Can you think of events in this century which can be treated as significant epochs in the outworking of God's increasing purpose, as the fall of Jerusalem was in the first century?
2. How far can the parables of the ten maidens and of the talents be used as 'gospel texts' in the current evangelical sense?
3. Do modern agencies such as V.S.O., Christian Aid, War on Want and 'Shelter' qualify for the commendation of Matt. 25.40?
4. How would you respond to the suggestion that the parable of the sheep and the goats teaches salvation by works?

St. Matthew 26.1-13   Anointing at Bethany

Jesus' teaching ministry is over: His passion is about to begin. The Sanhedrin (or at least its 'steering committee') resolved, at a meeting convened in the high priest's palace, to arrange for His arrest and execution, but felt that His popularity, especially with the visiting pilgrims, was such that their plan could not be carried out until after the seven days' festival of Unleavened Bread (which was inaugurated by the Passover meal). An opportunity was unexpectedly given them to carry it out much sooner.

We cannot be sure why the incident at Bethany (6–13) should have stimulated Judas to offer to put Jesus into the chief priests' power (14–16). He seems to have voiced the disciples' indignation at the 'waste' of ointment which would have cost a labourer's wages for a year (cf. Mark **14.**5; John **12.**4–6). Perhaps, in addition, he took the woman's anointing of Jesus to be a form of coronation (cf. 1 Sam. **10.**1; **16.**13; 2 Kings **9.**1–13) and was dismayed that Jesus should lend Himself to this display of popular messianic enthusiasm. Whatever the woman's motive was, Jesus accepted her devotion as 'a beautiful thing' done in anticipation of His burial: if she saw the cross looming ahead, she would know that it was not always practicable to perform the last rites for those crucified as criminals. The prediction of v. 13 has been fulfilled by the very inclusion of her act in the Gospel narrative; there may be the further thought that when the worldwide proclamation of the gospel was consummated (cf. **24.**14), her good deed would be recorded to her credit on the great day.

Notes: 'Simon the leper' v. 6—meaning possibly 'the *former* leper'—may have been the father of the well-known family at Bethany, if we put this Matthaean narrative (and its parallel in Mark **14.**3–9) alongside John **12.**1–8 (Mary and Martha appear only in *Luke* and *John*, and Lazarus only in *John*). V. 11: 'You always have the poor with you' does not state a binding economic rule; it simply means that the poor would still be available as recipients of their charity when He was no longer there.

St. Matthew 26.14-25   The Last Supper

Whatever provided the stimulus, Judas immediately made his way from Bethany to seek an audience of the chief priests and undertook to enable them to lay their hands on Jesus. Matthew is the only evangelist who names the price of the betrayal as 'thirty pieces of silver'; the last clause of v. 15 is almost a quotation of the last clause of Zech. **11.**12, where thirty shekels (12 oz. or 342 grams) of silver are the derisory wages paid to the prophet for tending the flock of Israel (cf. **27.**9 f.). This was the price fixed in Israel's earliest law-code as compensation paid to the owner for a slave gored to death by someone else's ox (Exod. **21.32**), and God assures the prophet that the implied insult is directed primarily at Him.

Jesus knew that there was a traitor in the camp; hence His care to make the arrangements for eating the Passover meal with the disciples as secret as possible. The venue had evidently been fixed in advance with the master of the house (18). There were more ways than one of calculating the date of the Passover and other feasts, and it is possible (though this does not affect the study of Matthew's narrative in itself) that Jesus and His circle followed a different reckoning from that which regulated the temple calendar (cf. John **18.28; 19.14**). In that case they must have dispensed with the paschal lamb, which could be slaughtered only in the Temple on the official date (and no mention is made of Jesus and His disciples' eating the lamb); but every Passover meal eaten away from Jerusalem lacked the lamb in any case.

During the meal, at which all reclined (the proper Passover posture), as is indicated by the Greek word rendered 'sat at table' (20), Jesus reveals the presence of a traitor. None but Judas knows who is meant; each of the others wonders if he himself has inadvertently said or done something to his Master's disadvantage. The words of v. 23 echo Psa. **41.9** (actually quoted in John **13.18**), but as all were dipping their hands in the same dish the traitor's identity was not thereby divulged. There may be an implication that, as the Son of Man's way of suffering had been 'written of Him' (24)— a reference perhaps to Isa. **52.13—53.12** and similar O.T. scriptures —so the traitor was a subject of prophecy (cf. Acts **1.20**). At any rate, he is the most unenviable of men. When Judas repeats his fellow disciples' question, the responsibility for the answer is thrown back on himself (25): he had still time to renounce his plan. Here and in v. 49 'Master' is actually 'Rabbi'; in this Gospel Judas is the only one to address Jesus by this title.

Thought: Is it merely coincidence that money was involved in the downfall of both Judas and Ananias (Acts **5.1–6**)?

St. Matthew 26.26-35 The New Memorial

The new memorial is instituted within the context of the memorial of the ancient redemption from Egypt. Unleavened bread was broken and eaten after a blessing in the course of the Passover meal: Jesus, at the head of the table, takes the initiative in doing this, but adds words which give the act a new significance (26). No longer is this 'the bread of affliction which our fathers ate when they left Egypt', as the Passover liturgy declares (cf. Deut. **16.3**), so that the partici-

pants year by year might share the experience of the Exodus generation. 'Take, eat,' says Jesus; 'this is My body.' If the lamb was in
fact missing from the table, His words might mean 'I Myself am
your Passover sacrifice' (cf. 1 Cor. 5.7b); indeed, some such meaning
is suggested whether the lamb was there or not. As the Passover
sacrifice preserved Israel from the angel of death and effected their
deliverance from Egyptian bondage, so Jesus devotes Himself to
death for the preservation and deliverance of His people. The cup
(27) appears to have been the 'cup of blessing' (cf. 1 Cor. 10.16),
drunk when grace after meat had been said at the end of the Passover
meal. The drinking of wine was of the essence of this meal, and the
wine was usually red, thus providing a visible point of comparison
between the contents of the cup and the new significance which
Jesus gave it in the words of institution (28). The 'blood of the
covenant' is probably deliberately reminiscent of Exod. 24.8, where
the old covenant at Sinai was ratified by sacrificial blood; the
covenant now ratified is the new covenant foretold in Jer. 31.31–34,
even if the adjective 'new' (as in the best authorities) does not
explicitly appear here, and it is ratified by no animal sacrifices but
by the life-blood of Jesus, 'poured out for many' (cf. 20.28, an echo,
probably, of Isa. 53.12). Matthew's added phrase, 'for the forgiveness
of sins' (cf. Jer. 31.34), makes explicit what the parallel records
imply. Verse 29 suggests that Jesus Himself did not take the cup:
He looks forward to a renewal of table-fellowship with them on the
other side of death, in the new age.

The 'hymn' (30) was perhaps the second part of the 'Great
Hallel' (Pss. 114/115–118) with which the Passover concluded; the
Mount of Olives was included by religious law within the city limits.
Jesus, speaking as the Shepherd of Israel, foretells the imminent
fulfilment of Zech. 13.7, but promises to return from death, gather
His scattered sheep again and lead them forth to Galilee (cf. 28.7).
The disciples, led by Peter, stoutly assure Him that they will not
'fall away' or feel disillusioned on His account; they will die with
Him if need be. He knows them better than they know themselves;
nevertheless, His promise remains.

St. Matthew 26.36-46   Consecration for Sacrifice

Gethsemane lay on the west slope of Olivet. Peter, James and John,
who had witnessed His glory on the mount of transfiguration, now
witness His agony, as He nerves Himself for the impending ordeal
and dedicates Himself definitively for the accomplishment of His
Father's will. For 'cup' (39) in the sense of 'lot' cf. 20.22 f. While

the spiritual conflict was something which He must endure alone, He craved sympathetic companionship, but this even His closest friends among the Twelve were unable to supply. If they felt themselves to be in the presence of a mystery so awe-ful that they were quite unequal to its demands, the reader of the narrative can share something of their feeling. 'Watch' (38,40 f.) means 'keep awake' both in the literal sense and in the sense of vigilance against the assault which was about to be made on their souls by the forces of evil. Their resolution to stand firm and share His ordeal (35) was good; their capacity to abide by it when the test came was questionable (41). 'Pray that you may not enter into temptation' (that you may not fail in the test) is reminiscent of the Lord's Prayer (6.13) as is also 'Thy will be done' (42; cf. 6.10). Jesus rose from His vigil prepared in spirit for the test that He had to face; it would be a test for them too, and how they acquitted themselves under it is recorded tersely in v. 56b.

'Are you still sleeping and taking your rest?' (45) is rightly punctuated as a question; treated as a command, it fits the context (especially v. 46) with difficulty.

The kingdom of God as proclaimed by Jesus could not have been more completely embodied than in Him who said 'not as I will, but as Thou wilt' (39)—and acted accordingly.

St. Matthew 26.47-56   Arrest in the Garden

The 'crowd' which came under Judas' guidance to arrest Jesus consisted of temple police, whose commander was the captain of the Temple (see note on 21.23); their services were at the disposal of the Sanhedrin. The word rendered 'kissed' in v. 49 is more intensive than that in v. 48, suggesting the show of affection or enthusiasm which Judas puts into the act. As in v. 25, Judas addresses Jesus as 'Rabbi'; Jesus in turn calls him 'Comrade' (the same expression as is used in 20.13; 22.12) and adds words which, because of their elliptical construction, are of uncertain force to us (contrast RSV text and footnote) but which, from their appearance on a first-century glass goblet (probably from Syria), may be intended to remind Judas of their recent table-fellowship. Some show of resistance was put up by the disciples (as in *Mark*, the identity of the sword-wielder is not divulged); then their nerve failed and they took to their heels. Jesus' rebuke in vs. 52–54 is for the most part peculiar to *Matthew*. He submits to His captors in the conviction that thus it is written and that the prophetic scriptures pointing to this hour must be fulfilled (cf. v. 24). Yet He points out the incongruity of their having come to take Him by surprise at night, as though He were a bandit-leader, a Zealot terrorist, when day by day throughout the preceding week He had been teaching publicly in the Temple court. 'I sat' (55) refers to the customary posture for instruction (cf. Luke 4.20).

Note: The 'twelve legions of angels' (53) may be understood, in the light of the Qumran texts, as hosts of militant angels under the command of the Prince of light, such as co-operate with the human 'sons of light' in the eschatological warfare against the 'sons of darkness'. But Jesus renounces recourse to angelic force as much as· that to human or material force.

Thought: Consider Peter's mistake in drawing his sword—misplaced zeal leads Christians to do the wrong things in the wrong place, and to do them badly.

St. Matthew 26.57-75   High-priestly Inquisition

Members of the Sanhedrin awaited Jesus at the high priest's residence. Joseph Caiaphas, son-in-law of Annas (who had held the high-priesthood A.D. 6–15), was appointed high priest by the Roman governor Valerius Gratus in A.D. 18 and remained in office for what was in those days the unusually long term of 18 years. On Jesus' arrival, Caiaphas and his colleagues were not so much concerned to try Him formally as to find evidence against Him of which the Roman governor would take cognizance. Since the sanctity of the Temple was protected by Roman authority, a threat to its safety would have been an offence against Roman provincial law, but the attempt to convict Jesus of having uttered such a threat was unsuccessful, and Jesus refused to say whether or not He had spoken such words as the witnesses alleged. An attempt to fasten quite a different charge on Him was (from the high priest's viewpoint) more successful. Challenged to say whether or not He claimed to be the Messiah (acclaimed by God as His Son in Psa. 2.7), He replied in effect that the expression was the high priest's, and that He did not necessarily make the claim in the sense which the high priest intended: what He did claim was that 'from now on'— 'henceforth' rather than 'hereafter'—the Son of Man would be seen enthroned at the right hand of the Almighty and coming with the clouds of heaven (64). In thus combining Dan. 7.13 f. (cf. 16.27 f.; 24.30) and Psa. 110.1 (cf. 22.43 f.) He was understood (rightly) to be speaking of Himself. The reference is not so much here to His advent at the end-time as to the triumph and exaltation which would follow on His present humiliation and condemnation: vindicated by God, He would visit His people in judgement or blessing, according to their attitude of heart, and they would see the kingdom of God established in power. His judges could scarcely believe their ears: this voluntary affirmation was tantamount to a claim to be the peer of the Most High, and thus constituted a capital offence in Jewish law (blasphemy) as well as providing evidence which could be presented to the Roman governor as a clear basis for the death-sentence. The tearing of the clothes (65) was a prescribed expression of horror at hearing blasphemy. The actions of vs. 67 f. are probably those of the police who guarded Jesus (but cf. Acts 23.2).

Peter's denial, which is inserted effectively between Jesus' appearance before the high priest and His accusation before Pilate, fulfils the prediction of v. 34. His following at a distance and mingling with the crowd by night in the palace courtyard is much to his credit; if his courage failed in the moment of sudden testing, it was a further proof of his Master's saying: 'the spirit indeed is willing, but the flesh is weak' (41). His repentance (75), unlike Judas' (27.3), was the making of him. 'Godly grief produces a repentance that leads to salvation and brings no regret, but worldly grief produces death' (2 Cor. 7.10).

St. Matthew 27.1-14   Enter Pilate, Exit Judas

While the Sanhedrin under Roman occupation could not execute sentence of death, its leaders did not go to Pilate to have their own sentence ratified but rather to have Jesus convicted and condemned by him on a charge of sedition. In whatever sense He claimed to be the Messiah, such a claim could readily be represented to Pilate as political in character, involving rebellion against the Roman Emperor. In Jewish eyes the Messiah, the Lord's anointed, was by definition the King of Israel. From Pilate's question (11) it is plain that Jesus was charged before him with setting Himself up as 'King of the Jews' (the Roman equivalent of 'King of Israel'), and it was on this ground that He was executed (37). He admitted the charge when Pilate put it to Him, although 'You have said so' (as in 26.64) implies that the form of words is His questioner's, not His own, and that He does not necessarily accept them in the sense intended by the questioner. But to the charges pressed against Him by His accusers He has nothing to say (12,14; cf. 26.63a); it looks as if He is resolved to make the issue of His kingship the decisive one. Pilate governed Judea from A.D. 26 to 36; an inscription from his term of office discovered at Caesarea in 1961 shows that his technical title was 'prefect' rather than 'procurator'. He quickly acquired a reputation for ruthlessness and obstinacy.

The Judas episode (3–10), like that concerning Peter (26.69–75), provides a dramatic interlude. Judas had served the chief priests' purpose and they had no further interest in him. But they had the responsibility of disposing of the thirty shekels which he left in the Temple before taking his life. To understand the following narrative, we must realize that in Zech. 11.13 there is a variant reading, *'oṣar*, 'treasury' (cf. RSV) for *yoṣer*, 'potter' (cf. AV). It is almost as if the chief priests said: 'Which reading of this prophecy shall we fulfil? Shall we give the money to the *treasury* or to the *potter*? We cannot put it in the temple *treasury* because it is blood money; let us give it to the *potter* in exchange for his field.' So they bought the potter's field with it as a burial-place for foreigners, and because it was bought with blood money it was called 'Blood Acre' (8, NEB; in Aramaic *Akeldama*, according to Acts 1.19), traditionally located on the ridge south of the Valley of Hinnom. The quotation of Zech. 11.13b is ascribed to Jeremiah (9,10) probably because in an early Christian collection of O.T. 'testimonies' it was attached to one or more passages from Jeremiah (18.2 f. with 32.6–15, perhaps, or 19.1–13).

Thought: There must have been a point in Judas' life when treachery, greed, dishonesty were first tolerated. Small surrenders to the enemy have far-reaching effects.

St. Matthew 27.15-31   Not this Man, but Barabbas

The Barabbas incident, mentioned in all four Gospels (cf. Acts 3.14), is associated with a custom not elsewhere attested (15). In vs. 16,17 some textual authorities read 'Jesus Barabbas' instead of simply 'Barabbas'; this fuller reading may be right, and is specially effective in v. 17. It is strange indeed that the man released had been rightly convicted of the very charge of sedition on which Jesus was wrongly condemned. The episode of v. 19 is recorded by Matthew only. If Pilate's tribunal was set up within the Antonia fortress, north-west of the temple area (which would thus for the time being have constituted the 'praetorium' or 'governor's headquarters' of v. 27), then his wife's message may have been sent from more comfortable quarters in Herod's palace on the western wall. Such a message would be taken seriously; every knowledgeable Roman was aware that Julius Caesar would not have been assassinated on the Ides of March, 44 B.C., if he had paid heed to his wife's dreams and stayed at home instead of going to the senate. 'Let Him be crucified' (22,23) may imply 'Let Him have the cross which was designed for Barabbas'; in any case, crucifixion was the regular penalty for sedition except where the accused was a Roman citizen. Scourging (26) was a normal preliminary to crucifixion; it was a murderous torture in itself, and strong men sometimes died under it.

The incident of Pilate's hand-washing (cf. Deut. 21.6–9), with the people's response (24 f.), is peculiar to *Matthew*. The people's response (25) is seen by Matthew as fulfilled in the siege and destruction of Jerusalem (cf. Luke 19.41–44; 23.28–30). The Jewish commentator who wrote of the 'oceans of human blood, and a ceaseless stream of misery and desolation' occasioned by these words, was right in so far as they have been grossly misapplied as though fastening messianic blood-guilt on the whole people of Israel in successive generations. That Christian readers have too often misinterpreted the words in this sense is sadly and shamefully true. Nor is there any ground for supposing that the call for Jesus' crucifixion came from those who had shouted 'Hosanna' on Palm Sunday: the city mob must be distinguished from Galilean pilgrims.

The soldiers' barrack-room horse-play, caricaturing their prisoner's kingly claim (27–31), is commonly and perhaps rightly believed to have been enacted on the 'pavement' beneath the Convent of the Sisters of Zion, where the Antonia fortress then stood. The 'scarlet robe' (28) was a military cloak; the thorns (29) may have been those of a species of date-palm whose thorns or spikes are sometimes twelve inches long, arranged in the form of a 'radiate crown' as affected by 'divine rulers' in the Hellenistic world.

Thought: Moral fibre: the Christian faith can give a man vision and courage to do the right thing, when the right thing is costly to the point of appearing disastrous.

St. Matthew 27.32-44 Christ Crucified

The 'cross' carried by the condemned man, or (as here) by someone commandeered by the military to carry it for him, may have been the cross-beam, to be fixed to the upright post at the place of execution. 'Golgotha' (33) represents Aramaic *gulgolta*, 'skull'; there is no certain explanation of the giving of this name to the place, which lay just outside the north wall of the city. The 'gall' of v. 34 recalls Psa. 69.21; a reference has been seen here to the soporific drink which charitable women of Jerusalem provided for men about to be crucified, but this involves a sudden change of subject, which otherwise from v. 27 to v. 37 is 'the soldiers'; perhaps the soldiers offered Him some of their own sour wine. Verse 35 fulfilled Psa.

22.18, but the incident is not manufactured out of the O.T. text; what was on the condemned man's person became his executioners' perquisites, and dicing was the natural way to determine the allocation. In the wording of the charge inscribed over His head Matthew, like the other Evangelists, sees a proclamation of the truth: Jesus is the Messiah of Israel, the kingliest King of all, 'reigning from the tree'.

The 'two robbers' or bandits crucified along with Him (38,44) were probably nationalist insurgents, perhaps Barabbas' lieutenants, originally intended to flank their leader on either side. The crosses were planted by the roadside, so that people passing in or out of the city gate could see and talk to the crucified men at close quarters. The derisory words addressed to Jesus by various passers-by (40,42,43) echo one or another of His claims, real or alleged. With vs. 39,43 cf. Psa. **22.**7 f.

The taunt 'He saved others; He cannot save Himself' (42), might serve as a motto for the whole scene—especially if 'cannot' be replaced by 'will not'.

Thought: Consider v. 44 in the light of Luke 23.39–43.

St. Matthew 27.45-54   'This was the Son of God'

Attempts (attested as early as the middle of the first century) to explain the midday darkness of v. 45 as due to a solar eclipse are put out of court by the fact that the Passover was celebrated at full moon. The cry of dereliction from Psa. 22.1 is quoted in Aramaic (although a few texts replace *sabachthani* by the original Hebrew form). It is not for us to rush in with an answer to our Lord's question, since He left it unanswered Himself; but His use of this psalm established its recognition in the Church as a principal O.T. 'testimony' of His passion and triumph (for the triumph cf. Heb. **2.**12). If *Eli* ('my God') was pronounced like *Eliya* (a pronunciation for which some Qumran manuscripts provide evidence), the by-standers' misunderstanding His utterance as a call for Elijah would be intelligible. It was popularly believed that Elijah, who had never died, could make himself available to help people in desperate trouble. The vinegar (sour wine) may have been intended to alleviate His thirst or to enable Him to speak more distinctly. The statement that He 'yielded up (dismissed) His spirit' (50) suggests that He remained in control of events to the end.

The rending of the Temple curtain (probably the curtain separating the inner shrine, the holy of holies, where the invisible presence of the God of Israel was enthroned, from the outer compartment)

signifies that the hitherto hidden God is fully revealed in the death
of Christ: its rending 'from top to bottom' (51) indicates that this
full revelation is God's own act. The statement of vs. 51b–53 (made
only by Matthew) is mysterious, and not only because of the time-lag
between the first stirring of the O.T. 'saints' and their 'coming out
of the tombs after His resurrection' (they could not come out earlier
because, as 1 Cor. 15.20 affirms, Christ is 'the first fruits of those
who have fallen asleep'). There is a suggestion that the death of
Christ caused a radical disturbance in the realm of the dead; His
victorious supremacy is attested over the grave, for 'to this end
Christ died and lived again, that He might be Lord both of the dead
and of the living' (Rom. 14.9).

The centurion's testimony (54) is impressive: Jesus' death confirms His claim to be the Son of God.

> Now discern the Deity.
> Now His heavenly birth declare!
> Faith cries out, 'Tis He, 'Tis He,
> My God, that suffers there!

St. Matthew 27.55-66
Vain the Stone, the Watch, the Seal

Of the three women mentioned in v. 56, only the mother of the sons
of Zebedee has appeared earlier in this Gospel (20.20); for Mary of
Magdala (west of the lake of Galilee, between Capernaum and
Tiberias) cf. Luke 8.2, and for 'Mary the mother of James and
Joseph' (called 'the other Mary' in v. 61 and 28.1) cf. John 19.25,
where she is said to have been the wife of Clopas (possibly a variant
of Alphaeus), and Mark 15.40, where her son James is called 'James
the younger' (perhaps to distinguish him from James the Lord's
brother who figured so prominently in the Jerusalem church until
his death in A.D. 62).

Once Pilate was satisfied that Jesus was really dead (cf. Mark
15.45), he had no objection to allowing Joseph of Arimathea to
take away His body for burial. He had no further interest in Jesus,
and was not impressed by the Jewish leaders' anxiety to forestall
further trouble. He knew his soldiers, and experience had taught
him that if they certified that a man was dead, there was no question
of his walking again. But the high priest and his companions could
not get the words about rising 'after three days' out of their minds—
had Judas told them, or did they have some idea that this was the
point of the saying about rebuilding the Temple in three days (26.61)?
If they wanted to secure the tomb, said Pilate, by all means let them

do so; they could use their own temple police, for Roman soldiers could not be spared for such a frivolous exercise. 'A guard of soldiers' (65) represents Latin *custodia*, 'watch', used as a loanword in Matthew's Greek. Matthew is the only Evangelist to mention the guarding of the tomb and its sequel (28.4,11–15). The 'Preparation' (62) was Friday of Passover week; the tomb, by Matthew's account, was left unguarded over Friday night.

Thought: Joseph acted when, humanly speaking, it was too late. But he was stepping towards the resurrection. The antidote to despair is to do the duty which lies nearest.

Questions for further study and discussion on St. Matthew chs. 26 and 27

1. Examine those sections of Matthew's passion narrative which are unparalleled in the other Gospels. Do they throw any light on a special viewpoint from which this part of Matthew's record was composed?
2. Consider those features of the crucifixion and events leading up to it, as related by Matthew, which bring out the fact that our Lord remained in control of the situation throughout.
3. Where in these two chapters do we have some indication of the saving purpose of the death of Christ?
4. How are the characters of (*a*) Judas, (*b*) Peter, (*c*) Caiaphas and (*d*) Pilate brought out in these two chapters?

St. Matthew 28.1-15 The Empty Tomb

The morning star was rising on the day after the sabbath when the two Marys visited the tomb. The verb 'was' in v. 2 should probably be rendered 'had been' (pluperfect): in that case the earthquake was past and the guards had disappeared by the time the women arrived: only the angel of the Lord remained. His words and the empty tomb, accessible now that the stone was rolled back, bore witness to the fact that the body of Jesus was no longer there. It is worth bearing in mind that no N.T. writer tries to describe Jesus' resurrection or His leaving the tomb. The women are invited to inspect the ledge on which His body had been laid on Friday night and directed to report His resurrection to the disciples. 'He is going before you to Galilee' (7) repeats Jesus' own promise before His arrest (26.32). The promise is repeated again by the risen Lord Himself when He meets the women leaving the tomb, but whereas the angel had said 'tell His disciples' (7), the Lord says 'tell My brethren' (10; cf. John 20.17). Perhaps the word 'brethren' is intended to embrace not only the disciples but the members of our Lord's own family. They did not believe in Him during His ministry, but were numbered among His followers in the days immediately following the ascension (Acts 1.14); to one of them, James, He appeared personally in resurrection (1 Cor. 15.7).

The incident of vs. 11–15 is proof enough that the guards were not Roman soldiers; no intervention by the chief priests would have kept Roman soldiers out of trouble for such dereliction of duty. The tale they were instructed to tell was feeble enough, but the chief priests 'knew what they could get away with' (A. Lunn). If they had thought that some more probable story would hold water, they would not have been reduced to spreading this one. It was still circulating, however, when this Gospel was written, and it may have been responsible for an imperial decree published in Palestine some years earlier, forbidding interference with tombs on pain of death.

'The early Christians did not believe in the resurrection of Christ because they could not find His dead body. They believed because they did find a living Christ' (C. T. Craig).

St. Matthew 28.16-20
The Exalted Lord Sends out His Ambassadors

There is no account of the ascension in Matthew's Gospel. The 'mountain to which Jesus had directed' the disciples (16) is traditionally identified with the mount of transfiguration (17.1) and is so commemorated on the summit of Tabor. In any case, here as in 17.1 the mountain is a place of revelation (cf. also 5.1). The statement that 'some doubted' is ambiguous in Greek, in that it might refer to others than the eleven, but not certainly so. But Jesus reveals Himself to them as the exalted Lord, vested by God with universal authority, and in the exercise of that authority He commissions them to be His ambassadors among 'all nations' (cf. 24.14). No longer is their mission restricted to 'the lost sheep of the house of Israel', as it was during the Galilean ministry (10.5 f.); all limitations have now been dropped. Their mission is to be mainly one of instruction—making disciples of all the nations and teaching the disciples thus made to keep all the commandments which they themselves had received from their Lord. For the later prosecution of this teaching ministry this Gospel provided an excellent manual. The baptism into 'the strong name of the Trinity' was specially appropriate for Gentile converts who 'turned to God from idols'; Jewish converts and others who already worshipped the living and true God were called to believe in Jesus as the Messiah and were therefore baptized specifically in (into) His name (Acts 2.38; 8.16, etc.). In the discharge of their commission the disciples are given the assurance of their Lord's continuing presence with them 'to the close of the age' (20).

William Carey, addressing the Northamptonshire Association Ministers' Fraternal in 1791, proposed Matt. 28.19, 20 as the subject for discussion, and in particular: 'Whether the command given to the Apostles to teach all nations was not obligatory on all succeeding ministers to the end of all the world, seeing that the accompanying promise was of equal extent.'

Questions for further study and discussion on St. Matthew ch. 28

1. Compare Matthew's narrative of resurrection appearances with those of Luke, John and Paul (1 Cor. 15.5–7).
2. Consider the commission of the eleven disciples to teach all nations in the light of Paul's account in Gal. 1.16; 2.1–10, which indicates that the Jerusalem leaders were entrusted with the evangelization of Jews, leaving Paul and Barnabas to evangelize Gentiles.
3. Are we justified in taking the commission to the eleven disciples as binding on all Christians?
4. How was Matthew's Gospel adapted to serve as a handbook for such a teaching ministry as is envisaged in 28.19 f.?

St Mark

INTRODUCTION

By almost universal consent this is the oldest written account of the life of Jesus which we possess, composed some thirty years after His death in or for the Church at Rome by John Mark, the 'interpreter' of Peter.

The book presents Jesus as the Son of God who gave His life as a ransom for many, in terms obviously geared to the Roman, Gentile mind.

This, the shortest of the Gospels, is a vigorously written evangelistic tract, portraying Jesus as the early Christians saw Him. And like every tract its contents call for a response to the facts it presents. While it is true that almost everything Mark records has been scrutinized by sceptical critics who are prepared to deny the historicity of the major proportion of Mark's story, there are excellent historical grounds for accepting the reliability of his record.

St. Mark 1.1-3 The Preface

Mark begins his book by telling us what he is going to do in it. V. 1 gives the title and theme: it is the **good news** of **Jesus,** the good news which He proclaimed and whose essential content is Himself. Since, however, the theme of the good news is a particular person, the book looks like a biography, although the interest is concentrated on those parts of the life of Jesus which constitute the good news. Moreover, the good news is a piece of history, although Mark does not stop to prove its historicity.

The theme, then, is Jesus Christ, the Son of God. Each part of the name is significant. Jesus was a name common among the Jews; for its meaning see Matt. 1.21. Christ is the Greek equivalent of 'Messiah', i.e. 'anointed'; the deliverer of His people. 'Son of God' gives us the deepest secret of the person of Jesus. The rest of the Gospel should be read as a justification by Mark for these titles being given to Jesus.

'The beginning' probably refers to the whole story of Jesus as the origin of the Christian good news, and the ensuing quotation is used to put the beginning of the ministry in its proper Scriptural context. The words quoted are a compound from three places in the Old Testament—Exod. 23.20; Mal. 3.1 and Isa. 40.3 (hence the correction of the text in later manuscripts recorded in RSV mg). The first part is taken from a passage in which God promises to send His angel to guide His people to the promised land. In the Old Testament itself the Exodus from Egypt was seen as the pattern for God's future acts of redemption. The second part of the quotation (Mal. **3.1**) itself echoes the language of Exodus as it speaks of the coming of the Lord in judgement preceded by His messenger. The combination of this verse with Mal. **4.5** suggested that this messenger would be a second Elijah (cf. **9.13**). Finally, Isa. **40.3** summons captive Israel to prepare a way for the Lord in the desert along which He would lead them to redemption. Thus the coming of Jesus is placed in a setting of redemption and judgement.

St. Mark 1.4-11   John and Jesus

Although John was popularly known as 'the baptizer', his work is described here as preaching (cf. 1 Cor. **1.17**). He announced that God offered forgiveness of sins to those who would display their repentance in the act of baptism. He insisted on the connection of baptism with repentance, i.e. 'a coming to one's senses resulting in a change of conduct'.

In appearance John resembled Elijah (2 Kings **1.8**), like Elijah he heralded the coming of a mightier One (Mal. **3.1**; **4.5**).

V. 8 is not too easy to understand. When used with the word 'water' the meaning of 'baptize' is 'dip' or 'wash' for a religious purpose. But one can hardly speak of dipping people in the Spirit; 'baptize' must be taken in a metaphorical sense to signify cleansing in which the Spirit purifies the 'inner man' just as water cleanses outwardly.

But to what was John looking forward? In Matt. **3.11** and Luke **3.16** John speaks of a coming baptism with the Holy Spirit and with fire. This may be understood as the cleansing effect of the Spirit in those who repent, being like fire in its effects (cf. Acts **1.5**).

Mark does not tell us why Jesus submitted to John's baptism (Matt. **3.14** f.). He is more interested in the spiritual event for which the baptism provided the form. But we see in His baptism His willingness to share in the lot of sinful Israel and to bear its sin.

The Spirit descended upon Jesus, and a voice spoke to Him from the opened heavens. For the coming of the Spirit we are reminded of such passages as Isa. **11.2**; **42.1**; **61.1** which speak of the Spirit being given to certain people as their anointing for kingly and prophetic service. The significance of the heavenly voice is less clear. Probably we have a combination of two texts, Psa. **2.7**, in which God addresses the anointed king as His Son, and Isa. **42.1**, in which God addresses His Servant in whom He delights and upon whom He has put His

Spirit. Thus the heavenly voice addresses Jesus as the Son of God who must perform the ministry of the Servant of God, and this declaration is confirmed by the anointing of the Spirit. God's seal is set upon the vocation of Jesus and He goes forth in the power of the Spirit.

*St. Mark 1.12-13   The Temptation of Jesus

Mark gives only the briefest account of the event that immediately followed the baptism of Jesus (contrast Matt. 4.1–11; Luke 4.1–13). After Jesus had received God's commission and power for His work, He was sent by the Spirit farther into the wilderness, away from human contacts, and there He faced Satan in single combat. Satan appears in the New Testament as the one who tempts men to turn aside from the will of God, accuses them before God when they fall, and seeks their destruction. He is the prince of this world, and it was to defeat him and set his prisoners free that Jesus entered upon His ministry.

The position of the story suggests that the temptation was a preparation or probation for the ensuing ministry. Jesus encountered the prince of evil personally before attacking his minions. Support for this view has often been sought in the 'forty days' which are regarded as being parallel to the forty years of Israel's journeyings in the wilderness (Deut. 8.2,16) or to the forty days of Elijah's journey to Mount Horeb (1 Kings 19.8); but neither of these Old Testament periods was one of temptation by the evil one, and it is probably best to conclude that forty days is simply a round number meaning a 'long-ish' time with no typological significance.

The 'wild beasts' suggest the loneliness and evil associations of the area, far removed from civilization (Isa.13.20 f.; 34.9 ff.; Psa. 22.11–21). There may perhaps also be the thought that the wild beasts are subject to Jesus (Job 5.22 f.; Psa. 91.13; Isa. 11.6–9). On the other side, the angels are the allies of Jesus (Psa. 91.11 f.) who aid Him in His contest (cf. 1 Kings 19.5,7); 'ministered' need not be confined to providing food, especially since Mark does not mention that Jesus fasted, but has a more general sense.

So the story ends, but not the temptation. See 8.11; 10.2 and 12.15 for the recurrence of temptation in a less obvious fashion, for here it comes through men rather than in a wilderness from an agent who may be more easily recognizable.

We are not told explicitly that Jesus overcame the tempter, but the fact is obvious from the way in which the story continues (see the comment on 3.27).

*St. Mark 1.14-15 The Gospel of the Kingdom

Jesus had already been active before John was arrested (John 3.22–24), but this event marked the commencement of His own work proper in the area around Galilee. Galilee was a comparatively small area, some 50 miles long and 25 wide.

His work is fully summed up as 'preaching the Gospel of God'. Although the Gospel of Mark concentrates chiefly on what Jesus did, he was fully aware that Jesus brought a message of good news about God by word and deed.

We have here a précis of that message. It was that the time of waiting and expectation (cf. Dan. 7.22) had ended and the kingdom of God had drawn near. Here, 'kingdom' really means kingship or rule. To the Jews this phrase denoted that God is the eternal King in heaven who expects men to obey His royal law. They cherished the hope that one day God would act visibly and powerfully to set up His kingly rule in a rebellious world. This act would be one of redemption for those who obeyed God as king (the Jews themselves!) and of judgement upon those who oppressed them (e.g. the Romans!). The announcement of its coming was therefore truly a piece of good news (Isa. 52.7).

Jesus' announcement contained two revolutionary points. First He stated that the kingdom was 'at hand'; the Greek verb may mean that it had actually arrived or (more probably) that it was very near. Jesus saw His ministry as the inauguration of a new era of salvation in whose coming Calvary and Pentecost were decisive stages. This new era would lead inevitably to the consummation of God's kingship in an open and glorious manner in the future. There would be two stages, the inauguration of the era of salvation in Jesus' earthly ministry and the Church, and the consummation of God's rule with the final judgement upon all who refused God's salvation offered through Jesus.

The second revolutionary point was that Jesus summoned the *Jews* to repent in view of this great announcement .They as much as the Gentiles were not fit for God's rule. In this He was like John; but whereas John could only look forward to the coming of the mightier One, now the mightier One Himself called them to believe the good news and prove for themselves that salvation really had come.

St. Mark 1.16-20 Response to the Gospel

It is no accident that the summary of the gospel message is followed by the story of the call of the first disciples of Jesus. It is thereby made crystal clear that to repent and believe in the gospel is nothing other than to follow Jesus. It is through Jesus that the gospel comes to men, and the witness of the whole New Testament is that the gospel cannot be separated from Him. If He is the preacher of the gospel, He is equally the content of the gospel, and one cannot believe in the gospel in any other way than by making a personal commitment of oneself to Him.

It is Jesus Himself who calls men to be disciples. Plainly this does not rule out previous contact with or knowledge of Him. We know from John 1 that some of these men had already met Him. If we are told nothing about this here and almost gain the impression that Jesus' call came 'out of the blue', it is because the story has been so abbreviated and sharpened as to bring out the one essential lesson that Jesus calls men to respond to the gospel by following Him. The fishermen are thus brought into the story without any detailed introduction, and we learn nothing of the circumstances which enabled them to down tools and follow Jesus on the spur of the moment; vs. 29 ff. (cf. 5.18 f.) show that a radical break with home and its associations was not involved.

The call of Jesus was to follow, i.e., accompany Him, and to share His task. He was the first fisher of men. The metaphor was obviously suggested by the daily occupation of the new disciples, and those scholars who argue that Jesus could not have used the metaphor in a good sense because elsewhere it is used in a bad sense (Jer. 16.16; Ezek. 47.10) prove nothing beyond the wrong-headedness of their scholarship.

To follow Jesus as a disciple did not always require literal walking in His footsteps through Palestine, but it did demand that a man should own Jesus as his Master and work out his whole life afresh in the light of that relationship (8.34 f.). There is nothing intrinsically wrong in fishing as an occupation—Jesus Himself joined in fishing on occasion (Luke 5.1–11)—but following Jesus may mean saying 'No' even to what is normally legitimate when He has a task for us to do. The big question is: does He call all His disciples to be fishers of men, or was this simply a special call to the apostles?

St. Mark 1.21-28 The Authority of Jesus

The scene which follows the calling of the fishermen is very different in character, but is equally important in showing us at the outset the nature of Jesus' mission. If the preceding story told how men responded to the authoritative call of Jesus, this incident shows how His authority extended even to the world of evil spirits.

Jesus had gone into the synagogue and received an invitation to preach such as might be given by the leaders to any man whom they considered competent to address the people (Acts 13.15). All the emphasis lies on the fact that Jesus taught (i.e. preached) with a note of authority which was not characteristic of the other religious teachers of the day; what has survived of the teaching of the scribes or rabbis shows that they loved to quote their predecessors. The congregation's amazement at this prophetic type of utterance turned to astonishment and alarm as a man with an unclean spirit loudly interrupted the proceedings by challenging Jesus to His face (cf. 1 Kings 17.18 for the words). Jesus rebuked the spirit and called it to come out of the man.

To modern people demon possession is one of the most difficult things in the Gospels. Several times Jesus was confronted by men suffering from what we would be inclined to diagnose as some kind of mental or psychosomatic illness, and He cured them by a word. But demon possession differs from mental illness in that the possessed showed uncanny insight into the true identity of Jesus as the holy One (Psa. 16.10; John 6.69) or Son (3.11; 5.7) of God.

Now stories of similar phenomena are found in pagan sources, and the temptation of the critic is to dismiss the Gospel stories as having been modelled on these pagan patterns. But is this so? Reports of demon possession in the Biblical sense sometimes occur today, and some modern thinkers are coming to realize the existence of a world of evil that transcends the world of men and exercises a baleful influence upon it. We may also ask with regard to the Biblical stories whether there may not have been a concurrent activity of unclean spirits in the mentally ill to give them their strange insight into the identity of Jesus just as we speak of the concurrent activity of the Holy Spirit in the minds of the inspired writers of Scripture

St. Mark 1.29-34 Jesus the Healer

The day on which Jesus came into Peter's home and cured his mother-in-law of a fever would be indelibly impressed upon his memory. The healing action of Jesus arose from His compassion and His determination to carry the rule of God into effect over physical evil, just as He had already demonstrated its authority over the demonic powers. His power was further demonstrated that same evening.

What is the place of Jesus' healing power in the gospel message today? An older form of Christian apologetic used to argue: because Jesus worked miracles, He must have been divine. Today, others, more sceptical about the very possibility of miracles, prefer to work in the opposite direction: if Jesus was divine, then He could have worked miracles. In other words, if they believe on other grounds that Jesus was divine, they will be prepared to consider the possibility that He wrought miracles.

The following points are relevant. 1. The popular modern supposition that 'miracles do not happen' is only a supposition and is scientifically unprovable. The scientist's assumption that nature behaves uniformly is a necessary one if he is to pursue his scientific research, but it is only an assumption, and it cannot be used to rule out the occasional, apparently arbitrary irruption of the supernatural into the world. 2. Granted, however, that miracles are not impossible events, the factor that weighs most with many scholars is Hume's celebrated argument that it is in general much more likely that the witnesses were lying or mistaken (a very common occurrence!) than that a miracle occurred. Can we trust the witnesses on whose evidence the stories of Jesus' power rest? On this point all that we can do here is to note that so critical a scholar as G. Bornkamm, who would admit the presence of much legend in the miracle stories, says plainly that it is hard to doubt that physical power to heal emanated from Jesus. 3. It was possible for men to see the miracles of Jesus and yet not to believe that He was divine or commit their lives to Him. In a sense they were not compelling signs (John 12.37). 4. Jesus performed His miracles not as wonders to impress people with His supernatural power but as signs of the gracious presence and kingly power of God. It was their spiritual significance that mattered ultimately, *but they could never have had any significance whatsoever if they had not taken place.*

St. Mark 1.35-45   Prayer and Healing

The story of this day in the life of Jesus concludes with the account of Jesus rising early in the morning to pray quietly before the day's work. This was no doubt His normal practice. For His prayer life, study 6.46; 14.32–39; 15.34; Luke 3.21; 5.16; 6.12; 9.18,28 f.; 11.1; 23.46; Matt. 19.13; John 11.41 f.; 12.27 f.; 17. The force of His example was profound: His disciples asked to be taught to pray as He did (Luke 11.1–4), and He gladly responded to their request: see Mark 9.29; 11.17, 24 f.; 12.40; 13.18.

Probably Jesus prayed especially on this occasion because He was seeking guidance for the future. It was not an easy decision to leave a place of successful ministry and excellent prospects (37), but Jesus had to go to the surrounding towns ('villages' is a better translation):

it was, He said, for this task of *preaching* to all Israel that He had come out, i.e. been sent by God.

So Jesus embarked on a wider ministry, although He returned more than once to Capernaum. One final incident is related, typical of this period of work. Leprosy is a word loosely used to cover a number of skin diseases ranging from true leprosy (Hanson's bacillus) to ringworm. Jesus' motive in healing was again compassion (41); the NEB, following a different Greek text, has 'in warm indignation', which would refer to Jesus' anger at the work of evil in the world.

An important element in the story is that Jesus sternly commanded the man to keep quiet about his cure, except for registering himself with the priest who acted as the health official in a community where the physical and religious effects of unclean diseases were closely linked (Lev. 14.1–32). Frequently Jesus sought to keep His miracles as secret as possible and silenced the demons who revealed His identity, but His wishes were hard to put into effect (45). Why Jesus sought to work in secret has become the major problem of interpretation in this Gospel. It is most reasonable to believe that Jesus Himself was anxious not to make a public display which would precipitate a popular uprising. The people were looking for a Messiah who would fit in with their own preconceived ideas and would readily rally to Jesus if He gave them any excuse to do so. He made a 'secret revelation' of Himself so that those with eyes to see might recognize Him as God's messenger, and to those who accepted Him He revealed Himself more fully and openly. The way in which even they often misunderstood Him showed how right He was to adopt this manner of working.

Questions for further study and discussion on St. Mark chapter 1

1. Is there a relationship between the baptism of Jesus and the baptism of the Christian? Discuss the similarities and the differences.
2. In what ways is the Holy Spirit the Spirit of judgement?
3. How would you preach the gospel today using 1.14 f. as a text?
4. Are the miracles a help or a hindrance in preaching the gospel today?
5. What place did the miracles occupy in the ministry of Jesus, e.g. in relation to His preaching? Does your answer to this question throw any light on the place of a healing ministry in the Church today?

111

Photo: Synagogue at Capernaum

Photo: Sculpture depicting the Ark of the Covenant in which the scrolls in the synagogue were kept

St. Mark 2.1-12 The Forgiveness of Sins

From a very early date the ministry of Jesus, whose general character
we have now seen, aroused controversy and opposition; the next
section of the Gospel (2.1—3.6) brings together a series of incidents
which illustrate this conflict.

The present story, therefore, is told not simply to demonstrate
the healing power of Jesus (contrast the earlier stories), but rather
to demonstrate the deeper issues. It begins by carrying further the
lesson on the need for faith which was implicit in 1.40 ff. Palestinian
houses had a flat roof, used for additional living space, which was
reached by an outside stair. Faith was seen in persistence and determination to reach Jesus by this unusual route.

But with v. 5 the story takes a surprising turn. Instead of healing
the man in response to his faith, Jesus declared to him the forgiveness of his sins. Did this imply that the man was a notorious sinner
(cf. John 5.14)? Or was this particular disease a consequence of
sin? We cannot tell. Jesus explicitly denied that disaster and disease
are necessarily caused by sin (Luke 13.1-5; John 9.2 f.). But sin and
disease are both effects of evil, and Jesus took this opportunity to
show God's opposition to evil in the whole man.

The scribes responded to the declaration perfectly correctly.
Only the offended person can forgive the offender, so that only God
can forgive sin. A prophet could speak in His name (2 Sam. 12.13),
but could Jesus be a prophet in an age when prophecy had died out?
Surely He was behaving blasphemously by violating the power and
authority of God? Jesus, therefore, sought to give visible proof of
His authority and ability to grant the invisible (and therefore un-
verifiable) act of forgiveness by performing the act of healing that
was equally God's prerogative and impossible for an ordinary man.
This would show that He did possess authority, but not simply that
of a prophet. He claimed the authority of the Son of man. The
Aramaic phrase which Jesus here used could apparently be understood as a substitute for 'I' (like 'this poor man' in Psa. 34.6) or as a
title for a divine being (cf. Dan. 7.13). Jesus chose this ambiguous
form of expression so as to leave an air of mystery around His
identity.

St. Mark 2.13-22 The Universality of the Gospel

The call of Levi resembles that of the four fishermen, but its lesson
is not so much to show how men should respond to the call of Jesus
as to indicate the kind of men Jesus called. Levi, otherwise known
as Matthew (3.18; Matt. 9.9), was a tax-collector, engaged in

collecting customs dues for Herod Antipas on goods passing in and out of Galilee, and the kind of company that he kept consisted of tax-collectors and 'sinners'. The tax-collectors were, in general, in the pay of the Romans and fleeced their fellow Jews; they mixed freely with Gentiles, so that they were ritually unclean, and their morals were not above question (Luke **19**.8). The 'sinners' were either persons of open immorality or perhaps simply that section of the populace who made no effort to live up to the rigid standards of the Pharisees. For Jesus to consort with such people was to bring Him into direct conflict with the Pharisees who were the most influential religious party in the country. The theme of the story is therefore Jesus' defence of His gospel of divine grace and of His mission in bringing it to those who needed it most. To ask whether v. 17 implies that there are some righteous is to miss the point; the implication is surely that Jesus would welcome the Pharisees if they realized their need.

Although the Old Testament prescribed fasting for all Jews only on the annual Day of Atonement (Lev. **16**.29), the Pharisees prescribed fasting on Mondays and Thursdays (Luke **18**.12). Unlike John, Jesus had not taught His disciples to fast frequently. He defended them with three parables. 1. 'Can you expect wedding-guests to fast in the bridegroom's presence?' (Phillips). Wedding imagery is often used for the era of salvation (Hos. **2**.19; Ezek. **16**.7 ff.; Isa. **54**.4 f.; **62**.4 ff.). The Jews did not think of the Messiah as the heavenly bridegroom, but Jesus evidently so regarded Himself, and v.20 is surely an allusion to His coming death (cf. Isa. **53**.8; John **16**.20). 2. The ministry of Jesus was the time not only of joy but also of newness. To try to bind the new movement to the old religion of Judaism would be like attaching a new, unshrunk spare collar to an old shirt; disaster at the first wash! 3. It is equally foolish to contain new, fermenting wine in old wineskins; as the wine expands, both it and the skins will be lost. The joy of the new message is not to be checked by Jewish legalism.

St. Mark 2.23—3.6 Keeping the Sabbath

The fourth and fifth stories of conflict are concerned with observance of the Sabbath. The Old Testament law forbade ploughing and reaping on the Sabbath (Exod. **34**.21). The Pharisees' detailed interpretation of this law had been transgressed, and they demanded an explanation from Jesus. He referred them to David's action at Nob; a clear transgression of Mosaic legislation (Exod. **25**.23–30; Lev. **24**.5–9). It is often said that David was breaking the law of God

in a case of necessity, and that Jesus was justifying the same procedure on the part of His disciples. Rather, He was showing that
David's action is one that was not condemned by Scripture: similarly, His disciples were not breaking any Scriptural law but only the
Pharisaic, pedantic interpretation of it. Two new positive principles
are established. First, the Sabbath exists for man's benefit, and
man-made rules which make it a burden to observe are wrong.
Second, if the Sabbath is made for man, how much more has man's
lord and representative, the Son of man, authority over its use.
Note the deeper implication of this statement: in the Old Testament
the Sabbath is the *Lord*'s day, so that by claiming lordship over it
Jesus is implicitly claiming equality with God.

In the story in 1 Sam. **21**.1–6 the priest's name is Ahimelech; no
fully satisfactory explanation as to why the better-known Abiathar
is mentioned here exists. The value of the story is not affected.

In Jewish law a man was warned rather than punished as a 'first
offender' since, it was argued, he might be acting unwittingly; if he
transgressed a second time, he was obviously wilfully ignoring the
warning and was then liable to punishment. This may be the background to this second story about sabbath breaking. Healing was
permitted on the Sabbath only if life was in danger. Opinions
differ about v.4: did Jesus simply mean by 'do harm' and 'kill', 'not
to heal', or was He not thinking of the malicious plotting of the
Pharisees? The latter were rapidly hardening their hearts against
the grace of the Kingdom (cf. **6.**52; **8.**17). The Herodians were
supporters of Herod Antipas, and an alliance between them and the
Pharisees was utterly inconceivable; evil can unite men as well as
good (6)!

St. Mark 3.7-19   The Choice of the Twelve

Although Jesus may have found it judicious to 'withdraw' because
of the Pharisees' opposition to His work, He was certainly losing
none of His popular appeal. Crowds were coming from areas outside
Galilee—from the south (Judea, Jerusalem and Idumea), the east
(Transjordan) and the north (Tyre and Sidon). The impact of His
healing miracles was so intense that He had to retreat to a boat in
order to fulfil His task of preaching.

With this increased spread in His influence the time had come
for Jesus to appoint twelve men as His special helpers. They were
first of all to be with Him in order to learn from Him, and only then
were they to go out and extend His work. These twelve were the
nucleus of the later and wider group of apostles. Their number is

significant; we cannot help comparing the fact that there were twelve tribes of Israel (Matt. **19.**28), and also that Moses appointed twelve spies to go into Canaan—and gave one of them a new name (Num. **13.**8,16). We are justified in seeing here the beginning of a new Israel. It is also significant that Jesus Himself was not one of the twelve.

The list as Mark records it indicates how some of the twelve received new names. Simon became Peter (Greek for 'rock'; the Aramaic equivalent is Cephas), an allusion to the character of life and function which Jesus envisaged for him. James is the same name as Old Testament Jacob. The name 'Boanerges' continues to tease scholars. It is often taken in a derogatory sense (cf. **9.**38; Luke **9.**54,55), but it seems unlikely that Jesus would have given such an uncomplimentary designation to His disciples: was their witness to Jesus to be as loud as thunder? Andrew and Philip have Greek names, showing how far Greek culture had been assimilated in Palestine. Bartholomew is probably Nathanael (John **1.**45 ff.). 'Thomas' is from Aramaic *Teoma* (a twin), identical in meaning with the Greek 'Didymus'. James, the son of Alphaeus, is probably 'James the younger' (**15.**40), possibly the brother of Levi/Matthew. For Thaddaeus, Luke has 'Judas the son of James' (cf. John **14.**22). 'Cananaean' has nothing to do with Canaan, but means a Zealot or extreme Jewish nationalist. 'Iscariot' may mean 'man of Kerioth' or be connected with Latin *sicarius*, an assassin.

It is common to note what a mixed catch the Great Fisher had taken and how He brought them together in harmony. Christian unity begins at this individual level.

St. Mark 3.20-35   Opposition to Jesus

The spread of Jesus' fame was constantly accompanied by misunderstanding and opposition. Two new groups now appear who swelled the opposition of the local religious leaders.

The local religious leaders had presumably invited an official deputation to come from Jerusalem and give a verdict. While even to His friends Jesus' conduct seemed strange, to His enemies it appeared that He was under the power of the devil. 'Beelzebub' was the name of an ancient Canaanite deity ('Baal the prince'), probably understood as meaning 'lord of the high place' or 'lord of the dwelling' (cf. Matt. **10.**25); here it denotes Satan. Jesus felt obliged to defend Himself, and used a series of parables or similitudes. He argued that if the demons were Satan's minions, then His exorcisms would be due to Satan acting against his own allies, and this would obviously speedily lead to his downfall. Consequently, to say that Jesus was in league with Satan was to be illogical. In fact the opposite was the case: the plundering of Satan's house by Jesus implies that He is in opposition to Satan and has bound him. The argument resembles that in Isa. **49.**24 f. (cf. perhaps Isa. **53.**12): just as a hunter might overpower a wild beast and then release his prey, so God delivers His people.

But when did Jesus bind Satan? Elsewhere the defeat of the evil powers is associated with the cross (Col. **2.**15; John **12.**31). Was Jesus thinking of the temptation and conflict in the wilderness? Or was He simply using the comparison to show that the exorcisms proved that He must be opposed to Satan? In any case, the saying brings out how Jesus knew Himself to be the Stronger One.

Then in vs. 28–30 Jesus takes the offensive. To suggest that Jesus' works, done in the power of the Spirit, were really the work of Satan came perilously near to committing a sin that cannot be forgiven. This sin is the attitude that regards good as evil and evil as good; such a person has so sunk in moral insensibility that he cannot repent and be forgiven. It follows that the person who worries lest he has committed this sin is unlikely to have committed it.

The final lesson of the section was occasioned by the presence of Jesus' family. Spiritual relationships, says Jesus, matter every bit as much as physical ones. Those who obey God and hence know Him as their Father find themselves to be brothers (Matt. **23.**8 f.).

*St. Mark 4.1-9   The Parable of the Sower

One of the most characteristic features of the teaching of Jesus was His use of parables; they were collected together by His hearers, and this chapter gives such a collection of stories which were no doubt told frequently in many places. The present occasion was a return to the lakeside where once again Jesus had to find an improvised pulpit (cf. **3.**9).

In the Old Testament we find a considerable number of sayings which might be described as parables—pithy proverbs (1 Sam. **24.**13), riddles (Psa. **49.**4), proverbial examples of disaster (Deut. **28.**37), oracles (Num. **23.**7), and fables, tales and allegories (Ezek. **17.**2–10). Almost any kind of non-literal statement could be called a parable. Parables are, therefore, unusual ways of speaking that convey a sharp and pointed lesson. The parables of Jesus include proverbs (Luke **4.**23), metaphors and similes (Mark **2.**21 f.; **3.**23), typical events (e.g. the Sower) and stories of particular incidents (e.g. the Good Samaritan). Sometimes there is only one main point, sometimes a more extended lesson.

Here is such a story, demanding the reader's full attention as much as that of the original hearer (3,9); make sure you get to the bottom of this, says Jesus, for it is not simply a lesson in agriculture! The story itself is perfectly clear with its description of the farmer sowing his seed broadcast over different parts of the field. But what does it mean? For the moment forget that there is an 'explanation' later in the chapter. The crowds did not hear that explanation: what would they have made of the parable? Was Jesus comforting His disciples who saw little result from the mission and promising that a glorious harvest was coming? Or was He telling the people to listen to the message with care, so that they might be like good ground? Or was He reflecting on the very mixed success of His work and concluding that, just as in agriculture, this was only to be expected? Or what? 'He who has ears to hear, let him hear.'

*St. Mark 4.10-20   The Meaning of the Parables

At this point in the chapter there is an interlude which relates how on a later occasion Jesus gave His disciples a private explanation both of the parables in general and of the parable of the sower in particular. V. 10 shows that the disciples of Jesus were a wider group than the Twelve.

The words of Jesus in vs. 11 and 12 are not easy. The word 'secret' almost means the opposite of what it usually means in English! It refers to the plan of God, long kept secret, but now *revealed* to the men of His choice. God's plan to act in kingly power for the salvation of men has now been made known to the disciples, and they should understand what is taking place in the ministry of Jesus. But to those outside this circle everything that takes place in the ministry of Jesus happens in 'parables' or riddles; they cannot understand what is going on. The result is that the prophecy of Isa. 6.9 f. is fulfilled; they see and hear what is happening, but they do not perceive its inner significance, and consequently they do not repent and receive God's forgiveness. There are two difficult points here. First, it appears from this statement that the parables—and indeed the whole ministry of Jesus—are meant to conceal the 'secret' rather than to reveal it. But it is a Biblical principle that 'from him who has not, even what he has will be taken away'; when men close their minds to the truth, God takes away from them the chance of responding to it. The parables were meant to provoke people to probe after their deeper meaning; but if they refused to make the

118

effort, and thought that there was nothing in them, the form of the parables would effectively conceal the truth from them. Second, it looks as though Jesus is here dividing men into two rigid groups; there are those to whom God has revealed the truth and those from whom He has concealed it. This, however, is not so. Throughout the ministry of Jesus it was open to any man to pass from the group of 'outsiders' and become a disciple. The revelation in the teaching of Jesus was for all, and it was only the people who persistently closed their minds to His teaching who found their opportunity of understanding it being taken from them.

The explanation of the parable of the sower shows that the parable is an appeal to men to be careful how they hear the teaching of Jesus. The seed is good, but the ground may vary in quality.

St. Mark 4.21-34   Further Teaching in Parables

With v. 21 we return to the public teaching of Jesus. A brief series of parabolic sayings is followed by a further two parables and a conclusion to the whole section in which Mark reiterates how Jesus used the parables to speak to the crowds.

In the opening sayings (21-25) the second part is easier to understand; it confirms our view of the parable of the sower by urging the people to take heed how they listen to the words of Jesus, for the way in which they listen will determine what they get out of them. Lack of attention will lead to loss, but keen attention will be rewarded by an even fuller measure of understanding.

But what of the preceding verses? Jesus says that lights are not meant to be hidden but to be placed where they will give illumination. If, therefore, a light is hidden, this can only be for a temporary period and in the end it will shine forth. Now in Matt. 5.15; 10.26 f. where the same metaphor is used, the point is that the disciples must not conceal the message entrusted to them, for one day it will be openly revealed to the world. Here, however, the point is rather that at present the parables (and the whole mission of Jesus) are not easy to understand, but one day the meaning will be clearly revealed. Jesus worked secretly, as it were, in His earthly ministry, but the meaning of His ministry was to be revealed in due course as God gloriously vindicated Him and brought in His kingly rule in power.

This fits in with the two parables that follow. Once man has sown seed, the way in which it grows and inevitably comes to fruition without human intervention is God's secret. The ministry of Jesus was the time of sowing; that seed would certainly grow and lead to a glorious harvest. Similarly, the parable of the mustard seed contrasts the tiny beginnings of the kingship of God—the preaching of an unknown prophet in a corner of Palestine—with the greatness of the end result; perhaps the birds are meant to symbolize the Gentiles, but they may simply be meant to indicate the great size of the tree. Let not men, therefore, be misled by the smallness and quietness of the beginnings, but let them make sure that they penetrate the mystery of the rule of God and themselves enter in.

Questions for further study and discussion on Mark 2.1–4.34

1. Consider Levi as an evangelist.
2. What difference does the 'law of Christ' (1 Cor. 9.21) make to our interpretation of the Fourth Commandment?
3. What does Jesus mean by 'doing the will of God' (3.35)?
4. What further aspects of God's secret purpose (4.11) are revealed by Paul? See Eph. 3.1–6; Col. 1.26 f.; 2.2 f.; Rom. 11.25–27; 1 Tim. 3.9,16; 1 Cor. 15.51 f.
5. In what ways is the parabolic teaching method of Jesus relevant to the Church's work today?

St. Mark 4.35-41   The Master of the Storm

After the day of teaching by the lakeside, Jesus resolved to cross over to the south-east corner. Probably He wished for rest and quiet, and therefore sought an area where fewer Jews resided. The story continues in the next chapter as if everything took place on the same day; this would certainly overcrowd the remaining hours of the day, and it is likely that the journey took place overnight or that there is an unmentioned interval somewhere in the story.

The journey was interrupted by one of those sudden squalls which are characteristic of the lake, hemmed in as it is by steep mountains and narrow valleys down which the wind is funnelled upon it. Was this squall so severe that experienced sailors were worried? Or was it rather the land-lubbers in the boat who panicked? V. 38 may suggest that the sailors expected Jesus to do something to save them (Matt. 8.25) rather than that they were simply complaining that, while they were working for dear life to bale out the boat and bring it under control, one passenger, like Jonah before Him, was unconcerned and asleep. Yet when Jesus did act to rebuke the wind and the sea in masterful tones, they were stunned with surprise. They rightly asked, 'Who then is this?' Their question is to be answered from the Old Testament where it is God who controls the elements (Psa. **89**.8 f.; **93**.3 f.; **106**.8 f.; **107**.23–30; Isa. **51**.9 f.). It was His power that was revealed in Jesus. But whether the disciples fully realized this is uncertain.

Some readers try to preserve the meaning of the miracle (the power of God revealed in Jesus) without accepting its historicity. It should be plainly said that if the miracle did not happen then the power of God was not revealed in this event; if the miracle did not happen, and yet the early Church believed that the power of God was revealed in this incident, then their belief was mistaken and is worth nothing. You cannot have your cake and eat it.

St. Mark 5.1-20   The Gerasene Demoniac

It is no doubt bad enough to be a Dr Jekyll and Mr Hyde type of person, alternating between two different states of personality. It is much worse to be the victim of a whole series of simultaneous conflicting impulses and demonic powers, as was the case with this man who knew himself to be inhabited by a whole legion of demons. He suffered from what today would be called a particularly severe manic-depressive psychosis which rendered him incapable of living a normal life in human society; we get a grim glimpse of the only cure that the ancient world knew for such poor sufferers—restraint and confinement. Once again, however, the illness was not purely physical, for the man possessed the uncanny knowledge of the demon-possessed as to who Jesus was.

Three points of difficulty arise in the story. First, where did it happen? The manuscripts give different possibilities. Gerasa was some thirty miles south-east of the lake; its 'country' must have stretched to the lake side. Gadara (Matt. 8.28) was six miles from the lake. Gergesa (RSV mg.) is modern Khersa on the lake side, and the cure took place near here.

Second, the aftermath of the cure. Many people have found it difficult to credit the story of the demons passing from the man into the swine. So far as the moral difficulty of the destruction of the swine is concerned, it is sufficient to say that one man is of much greater value than many swine. Attempts to give a rational explanation of what happened are all conjectural. The vital point is the effects of the cure on the local people. They showed themselves to be much more interested in their swine than in the cure. When every allowance is made for their loss of livelihood, can their attitude be justified? Note that the old argument that, as Jews, they shouldn't have been keeping swine, is dubious; the people concerned were possibly Gentiles.

121

Third, why was the man not told to keep silent about his cure? Was it because it was Gentile territory? Or because Jesus Himself did not intend to work in that area Himself?

Thought: Do you have any vested interests that would be disturbed if Jesus was working powerfully in and around your life?

St. Mark 5.21-34 The Woman with a Haemorrhage

Some indication of the pressure under which Jesus worked is given by this story of two people appealing for His help simultaneously. Jairus was a man responsible for the management of the synagogue. (The actual work was done by the 'hazzan' or beadle mentioned in Luke 4.20.) His appeal to Jesus shows that by no means all the religious leaders of Galilee were opposed to Jesus. Knowing the power of Jesus he had the faith to seek healing for his sick daughter. According to Matt. 9.18 Jairus said that she had already died, but this difference is due to the fact that Matthew abbreviates the story and does not mention the servants who brought this news to Jairus (Mark 5.35).

As if to strengthen the faith of Jairus while the party made its way to his house, there took place the healing of a woman who had had a haemorrhage for twelve years. The reference to the doctors is not meant to cast a slight upon an honoured profession, but to show how intractable the disease was. The woman was shy of appearing in public and especially before a religious teacher because her disease rendered her unclean. She hoped to take advantage of the crowd to touch the garment of Jesus and slip away unobserved. The uncharitable may say that she was superstitious. Perhaps in some measure she was, but Jesus is greater than superstition, and in response to her real faith she received healing. The way in which her cure is described indicates a certain supernatural quality about the person of Jesus. It is wrong to think that the power passed involuntarily from Him, just as a battery might be accidentally short-circuited by contact with a piece of metal. The spiritual power of Jesus is not to be narrowly confined within human categories of interpretation and consequently misunderstood. Jesus Himself made sure that there could be no remaining ground for superstition in the woman's mind, and brought her into the open so that she might recover her self-respect and know healing for her soul as well as for her body. He showed His love and care for her as an individual, and spoke a healing word which transformed what might have been a mechanical act into a personal relationship.

There is a lesson here for all who help people. Care—*even spiritual care*—is incomplete if it is unaccompanied by love.

St. Mark 5.35-43   The Daughter of Jairus

The arrival of the sick woman and her cure may have been providentially intended to sustain the faith of Jairus. He may not have seen it in this way. After all, she was taking the attention of Jesus away from him, and with every moment that passed his little girl could be getting worse. His fears were confirmed by the arrival of the message that she had died. This was surely the end. To cure illness was one thing; to raise the dead was quite another. It is surely more likely that Jesus 'overheard' (RSV mg.) rather than 'ignored' the fatal message, and promptly acted to relieve the anxiety of the sorrowing father.

At the house the elaborate ritual of Jewish mourning had already commenced; in an eastern climate the whole business of burying the dead was accomplished with the utmost speed (Acts 5.5-7). Jesus upbraided the mourners because, He said, the child was not dead but asleep. That is enough for the rationalists! Obviously the girl had never died at all and was only in a coma; only later was the story heightened by saying that she had died. But notice that Jesus had not yet seen the child, and He was not in the habit of making medical diagnoses. On the other hand, He cannot simply be describing death as sleep. He means that she is in a state from which she can be awakened, death and yet not final, irrevocable death. Here, then, is promise of His power.

The miracle is simply described. The words of command are no magic formula, but the actual Aramaic phrase that Jesus used. His thoughtful care is seen in the command that she be given some food. The injunction that nobody should know what happened is strange. Surely a cure like this could not be kept secret? But Jesus was concerned with the actual act of healing which He conducted in privacy. The people outside the room could speculate about what had happened, but they could never be certain. Only in the presence of faith did Jesus show His power. Even the pagan Plato once wrote: 'To find the maker and father of this universe is a hard task; and when you have found him, it is impossible to speak of him before all people.'

*St. Mark 6.1-6   Unbelief at Nazareth

Mark's picture of the ministry of Jesus contains sharp contrasts between success and failure, acceptance and opposition, understanding and misunderstanding; it is a reminder to the Church not to expect a path of uninterrupted, smooth progress. Of all places, Nazareth, where Jesus was brought up, might have been expected to give a warm welcome to its son, just as a modern country town might celebrate the return of some distinguished man who has won a reputation in the wider world. But when Jesus went into the synagogue on the Sabbath and accepted an invitation to teach, the mood of the audience was sceptical; they were surprised, but not impressed. There was nothing that Jesus could do beyond healing a few sick. That he could do no mighty work there means that to have worked miracles in the absence of faith or potential faith would have been contrary to His purpose. All that He could tell the people was the proverbial comment that great men are not appreciated at home. It is a proverb which has many exceptions, but it applies especially to prophets whose words are unwelcome. Note how Jesus tacitly assumes the rank of a prophet (Luke 13.33).

The brothers and sisters of Jesus (cf. 3.31–35) were almost certainly the children of Mary and Joseph born after Jesus. Two other theories about them arose in the early Church. One view, associated with Jerome, is that they were cousins of Jesus, but this is an unsupported and unlikely supposition. The other view is that they were Joseph's children by a previous marriage. This is, to say the least, improbable in view of Luke 2.7 and Matt. 1.25 which imply that Mary had other children.

The fact that Joseph is not mentioned here or elsewhere very probably means that he was now dead, and it has been conjectured that the reason why Jesus did not begin His work until the age of thirty was that He had to be the breadwinner while His brothers were still young. There may, however, be a deeper significance in this verse (3). To describe a person's parentage without naming his father was tantamount to hinting at illegitimacy. If so, the language of the people contained a calculated insult—and the knowledge that there was something unusual about the birth of Jesus.

*St. Mark 6.7-13   The Mission of the Twelve

Despite the lack of response at Nazareth, the work of Jesus had now reached such proportions that the Twelve could be sent out on their own to do the same work as their Master, preaching, exorcizing and healing. The use of oil to anoint the sick was not simply because of its curative properties (Luke 10.34) but was meant also as a sign, possibly to demonstrate that the disciples were not acting by their own strength.

The Twelve were sent out in pairs. This was common practice both in Judaism and in the early Church. In addition to the vital function of providing for companionship and mutual help in dangerous country, it enabled the missionaries to proclaim a message which was confirmed by two witnesses and did not depend on a single testimony (John **8.**17 f.; cf. Deut. **17.**6; **19.**15).

The instructions for the journey sound strange to us. The disciples were to travel as lightly as possible. They were permitted to wear sandals and use a staff; but even these two concessions are forbidden in the account in Matt. **10.**10; Jesus was giving principles, not invariable rules. We are probably to think of a brief tour within a limited area, so that it was possible to live without any elaborate equipment. The disciples were to avoid anything that might smack of luxury and ease, and perhaps they were to take care not to look like other wandering preachers who made a good thing out of a gullible public.

In their evangelism the disciples were to make one home their base rather than make a series of social calls. The acted parable of shaking the dust off their feet as they departed was an action which pious Jews performed on leaving Gentile territory; here it was meant to warn the Jews that they were behaving like Gentiles in rejecting the message of God (Acts **13.**51). Here also the principles involved must be distinguished from the Jewish customs in which they found expression.

Questions for further study and discussion on Mark 4.35–6.13.

1. Are there situations in which we think that Jesus is asleep (4.38)? What are they intended to teach us?
2. If Jesus wished the raising of Jairus' daughter to be kept a secret, why did He openly raise a dead man at Nain (Luke **7.** 11–17) and at Bethany (John **11.**42,45 f.)?
3. Is our unbelief the only reason why we do not see Jesus working in great power in our midst (6.5 f.)?
4. Why did the early Church especially remember the instructions for evangelists given in 6.8–11 rather than details of how to preach the message? How are the principles to be applied today?
5. In what circumstances is a modern evangelist justified in leaving an unsuccessful area of work (6.11; cf. Acts **13.**46)?

St. Mark 6.14-29   The Martyrdom of John the Baptist

Among those who were talking about Jesus at this time was Herod, 'King Herod' as he styled himself, although he was not entitled to this rank (cf. Luke 9.7). Of the various popular explanations of who Jesus was which were current, Herod's bad conscience inclined him to accept the one which identified him with John the Baptist risen from the dead. John had done no mighty works in his lifetime (John 10.41), but if he were risen from the dead, he could be expected to have supernatural powers.

In explanation of Herod's allusion to his beheading John we are now given a 'flash-back'. The event had taken place only a short time before (cf. Matt. 14.12–21). Josephus tells us that John was imprisoned at Machaerus, a grim fortress near the Dead Sea with magnificently spacious and beautiful apartments. John had criticized Herod regarding his second marriage. Herod, who was the son of Herod the Great and Malthace, had first married a daughter of King Aretas of Arabia. Then he fell for his own half-niece Herodias, the granddaughter of Herod the Great and Mariamne; she had been married to Herod's half-brother Philip (who was probably the son of Herod the Great and *another* Mariamne!). Herod the Great had been the archetypal Bluebeard, and his family were not much better as far as morality was concerned. John attacked Herod on the grounds of Jewish law (Lev. 18. 16; 20.21). Herod had some respect for John, but Herodias had no such scruples and when she obtained a suitable opportunity put a scheme into action. Her own daughter, Salome, performed a dance at the birthday party which was sufficiently provocative to lead the king to make his rash offer. Those critics who allege that such a dance—it would have been on the level of a strip-tease act in a night-club—would have been impossible for a *princess* are forgetting the moral (or rather, immoral) quality of Herod's family. In his half-drunk state the tetrarch was perfectly willing to part with a kingdom which he did not even possess (cf. Esth. 5.3,6), but the girl, primed by her mother, asked for less: 'Please may I have the head of John the Baptizer on a plate, and please can I have it now.' The voice of John was silenced, but his condemnation of the king still stood, sealed by his blood. From now on a deep shadow hangs over the ministry of Jesus (cf. 9.12 f.).

St. Mark 6.30-44   The Feeding of the Five Thousand
The Bible leaves us in no doubt that God created the good things of this world for the enjoyment of men; if it emphasizes the duty of work, it also speaks of the privilege and delight of rest. But there are occasions when even well-earned rest must be postponed for further service. This was one such occasion. Jesus, filled with compassion for the crowd who thronged about Him, *taught* them (contrast

126

8.2). They resembled an army gone forth to war without a commander (Num. **27.**16,17; 1 Kings **22.**17; Ezek. **34.**5), and Jesus took His place as their leader.

When it was late the question of food arose. (The problem of accommodation for the night [Luke **9.**12] was of secondary importance. People then improvised much more readily than our modern generation which requires its caravans, tents and sleeping bags). The disciples' suggestion was the sensible one. Jesus' rejoinder must have sounded quite mad; it aroused a sarcastic reply, for we may be sure that the disciples did not have so much money with them (the denarius was a labourer's daily wage). Then Jesus acted. The people were seated in groups of 50 and 100 (or does it mean a hundred rows of fifty each?). Jesus said the usual grace before a meal; note that He blessed *God* and not the *food*—there is no justification here for blessing the bread and wine in the Lord's Supper. Then He divided up the scanty food available so that all were satisfied and the twelve disciples were each able to gather up a basket of fragments.

What is the significance of the story? In John **6** the miracle is a picture of Jesus' ability to give the bread of life freely and abundantly to all who believe in Him. Is this the point in Mark? Is there a repetition of the miracle of the manna in the wilderness or an anticipation of the heavenly marriage supper of the Lamb? The early Church interpreted the feeding in the light of the Lord's Supper, and some commentators have gone so far as to speak of the Galilean Lord's Supper, but we may wonder whether this was the intention of Jesus. The Lord's Supper was for disciples only and was closely linked with the death of Jesus; neither of these elements is present here. Perhaps there is a clue to be found in Jesus' comments in 8.14–21.

St. Mark 6. 45-56   The Lord of the Sea

There is good reason to think that Jesus sent the disciples away while He dismissed the crowds because the latter were in the mood to adopt Him as their leader for an uprising there and then (John **6.**15). Jesus may have feared that His disciples, who still understood His purposes so imperfectly, might be led astray by the crowd. Perhaps He Himself also felt the pull of temptation, for He retreated into the hills to pray, and the fact that His prayer is mentioned so seldom (though we know it was His regular custom) suggests that this day was one of crisis.

Meanwhile the disciples were making little headway at sea against the wind. By the Roman method of reckoning four night watches (see 13.35 for their names; the Jews reckoned only three divisions in the night, Matt. 24.43; Luke 12.38) it was between 3 and 6 a.m. when they saw Jesus walking on the sea. To calm their terror Jesus came near and spoke words of reassurance. Their significance is to be explained from the Old Testament. 'Take heart; have no fear' is God's word to His people in their distress (Isa. 41.10,13 f.; 43.1; 44.2). 'It is I', literally 'I am', may simply be self-identification, but there may just possibly be an echo of the Old Testament form of revelation of God, 'I am (He)' (Exod. 3.14; Isa. 41.4; 43.10; 52.6). Finally, mastery of the sea is a divine attribute, and this incident ranks with the earlier one in 4.35–39 in showing that the power of God is revealed in Jesus (Job 9.8; Psa. 77.19; Isa. 43.16—note the occurrence of Isa. 43 in each of these three sets of references). Were they beginning to realize the truth? Mark says that they were 'utterly astounded', but Matthew states that they worshipped Him, saying, 'Truly You are the Son of God' (Matt. 14.33). Does Mark mean that they were 'taken by surprise' at this revelation of the divine power of Jesus because they had failed to understand the significance of the feeding of the multitude?

Although the boat had set out from the north-east corner of the lake for the nearby village of Bethsaida Julius at the head of the lake, the disciples finally landed farther round to the west at Gennesaret (the region around Capernaum), and once again the crowds began to throng around the disciples. The 'fringe' was a border of blue tassels worn on the outer cloak (Num. 15.37 ff.; Deut. 22.12), and it was this that the woman with the haemorrhage touched (Matt. 9.20); Jews who liked to be thought especially pious made them unnecessarily long (Matt. 23.5).

St. Mark 7.1-13   Counterfeit Religion

With this chapter we return to the theme of conflict between the Pharisees and Jesus, and the two types of religion for which they stood are clearly drawn and contrasted. Two related themes run through the chapter; the question of religious purity and defilement, and the authority of religious rules and traditions.

Writing for Gentile readers Mark explains the ceremonial ablutions of the Jews. Although these rules may have had a useful hygienic result, the Pharisees were not concerned with dirt but defilement, which they regarded as something that could be spread by touch. Jesus did not follow the party line, and He was called to account for the conduct of His disciples.

128

He dealt first with the origin and authority of the custom (6–13) and only later with the true nature of defilement—sin (14–23). He began enigmatically by quoting Isa. **29**.13 and applying it to His questioners. They were hypocrites (the Hebrew word means 'godless') because although they made an outward fuss about worshipping God they did not give Him true heart worship; scrupulosity in the things that He had not commanded was accompanied by subtle evasions of what He did command. Such worship could only be in vain.

Indeed, they were not above breaking God's law in the interests of their own human rules. For example, the Old Testament law quite clearly laid down the obligation to honour one's parents (Exod. **20**.12; **21**.17; cf. Deut. **5**.16). Such honour would include practical care for their needs (this is what 'honour' means in 1 Tim. **5**.3,17). Through their 'tradition' it was possible for a man to declare his possessions to be 'corban' (a Hebrew word meaning 'dedicated' or 'an offering') and give them to the Temple, so absolving himself from the Fifth Commandment. Jesus strongly condemned this attitude which encouraged religious donations at the cost of religious duty to parents. This was to set human tradition above divine command.

The matter may have been even more disgraceful. The practice of corban is surrounded by much obscurity, but one view is that a man might make such a vow without taking proper thought for the future and then wish to retract it; this the Pharisees would not let him do. According to another view, the whole thing was a legal fiction, and the money dedicated to the Temple was actually kept by the man, and he continued to enjoy the use of it.

What were the 'many other such things' which the Pharisees practised? Their restrictive Sabbath legislation was certainly one. More important, does the Church today fall into the same trap? 1 Tim. **5**.8 should not be forgotten by those consumed with zeal to dedicate their possessions to God.

St. Mark 7.14-23   The Origin of Sin

Having dealt with the question of religious authority, Jesus returned to the issue originally raised: religious cleanliness. From castigating the Pharisees for their personal rejection of God's law He turned to give a general principle which applied to everybody ('the people', 14). The principle was expressed in a brief and somewhat cryptic parabolic saying which required the careful attention of the audience (14b). The disciples asked for an explanation privately (cf. **4**.33 f.), only to be told that they should have grasped the meaning for themselves. As v. 19 makes clear, Jesus was thinking of foods entering the body and being evacuated. They do not enter a man's heart and therefore cannot make him religiously unclean. It is a man's *heart*—the word refers to the whole inner personality of man and not simply to his emotions—which is the source of the evil thoughts listed by Jesus, and it is the appearance of these which defiles him.

Thus Jesus makes certain basic lessons clear. 1. God is concerned with the moral behaviour of mankind. This truth was plain to read in the Old Testament, but Pharisaic pettifogging had effectually obscured it. It is conduct that matters, and not all the religious ritual in the world, sacrifices, ablutions, fasting and penance, can alter the colour of a man's heart in God's sight (Psa. **51**; Isa. **58**; Amos **5**.21-24). 2. By this declaration Jesus rendered obsolete all distinctions between clean and unclean foods, vessels and people. A whole section of Old Testament legislation, which had served a purpose in its time, was thus 'fulfilled' and finished by Jesus. Yet the early Church was slow to realize the implications of Jesus' words. There were to be anxious debates whether Jewish Christians might eat with uncircumcised Gentiles, and what the Christian attitude was to be to foods sacrificed to idols. Paul surely knew this saying of Jesus (Rom. **14**.14) and applied it to the problem, but it took a long time for its truth to be recognized. 3. Jesus here speaks in the plainest terms about human sin and its source in the human heart. He did not use the word very often (**2**.5,9 f.; **2**.17; **3**.28; **8**.38 and **14**.41 are the only uses in Mark), but the idea was a prominent one in His teaching. In what other ways does He speak of it (see **3**.4 f.; **4**.24 f.; **6**.6,11,52)?

St. Mark 7.24-30   The Gospel and the Gentiles

One of the things which may strike the modern Christian as strange in the ministry of Jesus is the way in which He confined His work to the Jews and to Jewish territory. There are few exceptions to the rule which He expressed in the words 'I was sent only to the lost sheep of the house of Israel' (Matt. **15**.24—note the context! cf. Matt. **10**.5 f.). Yet the preceding discussion, in which Jesus firmly declared the invalidity of rules regarding religious cleansing, has as its logical corollary the declaration of the invalidity of Jewish particularism. There must, therefore, be some other explanation of Jesus' conduct than simple rejection of the Gentiles. The present story clearly bears on this problem; as with some earlier stories

130

(e.g. 2.1–12), its significance lies not so much in the miraculous power to which it testifies, as in the conversation which is recorded.

The mother who sought the help of Jesus for her daughter is described as a Greek from Syrian Phoenicia; it was so called to distinguish it from Libyan Phoenicia, i.e. Carthage in N. Africa. Jesus met her with what sounds like a harsh refusal: the children (Jews) must be fed, their bread must not be thrown to the dogs (Gentiles). Now 'dogs' was a well-known term of opprobrium for Gentiles, but it is going against all that we know of Jesus to imagine that He could have voiced this insult. What, then, did He mean? Did He say the words with such an expression on His face and tone in His voice that they sounded gently ironic? Note how He talked of 'little dogs' (the Greek word is a diminutive) which were allowed in the house (E. V. Rieu translates as 'house-dogs'), and He qualified His statement by saying 'first'. Was He trying to lead the woman to *faith*? If so, her response was immediate: recognizing the prior rights of the Jews she claimed the crumbs and her child was cured in an instant (Matt. 15.28).

The problem of Jew and Gentile is not wholly solved by this incident. It is clear that Jesus responded to those Gentiles who sought.Him with His customary compassion, but in the economy of God His calling was to the Jews first. It was to the Church that He committed the task of the Gentile mission. Today the Church has learned the lesson of 'to the Jew *and to the Greek*' so well that it has almost managed to forget the Jews.

Questions for further study and discussion on Mark 6.14–7.30.

1. How would you justify Jesus' estimate of John the Baptist (Matt. 11.11)?
2. 'You cannot preach to a man with an empty stomach.' What is the scope of the Christian's responsibility for the physical needs of the unconverted?
3. Can the gospel be preached without any reference to human sin?
4. What evidence is there other than Mark 7.24–30 for Jesus showing compassion to the Gentiles?
5. How is the principle 'to the Jew first' to be applied in evangelism today?

St. Mark 7.31-37   The Healing of a Deaf Mute

The route followed by Jesus here is a peculiar one. He went from the area of Tyre to the Sea of Galilee (south-east of Tyre) via Sidon (farther north of Tyre on the coast) and through the region of

Decapolis (which lay east and south-east of Galilee). Certainly this was one of the most indirect routes that Jesus could possibly have taken back to Galilee! Some manuscripts have instead 'from the region of Tyre *and* Sidon' (see AV–KJV); this would simplify the geography and leave us with a journey round the north of the Sea of Galilee to Decapolis. The purpose of the journey was evidently unknown to Mark, and we can only guess why Jesus stayed in these parts. But 3.8 speaks of His fame spreading to this area, and He may well have ministered here; there were Jews throughout these areas, so that it is not necessarily implied that He went to the Gentiles.

Whether the deaf and dumb man was a Gentile is uncertain. He lived in a predominantly Gentile area, but Jesus' use of Aramaic to speak to him and the quotation from Isaiah in v. 37 may be pointers that he was a Jew. He is described as having an impediment in his speech (32,35), but it was apparently so bad that he was virtually dumb (cf. 37). The various gestures of Jesus were meant to indicate to the man by sign language what He intended to do. 'His tongue was released' (35) is a paraphrase of the Greek which literally says 'The bond of his tongue was loosed'. Did Jesus regard the man as enslaved by evil or Satan (cf. Luke 13.16)? Once again Jesus commanded silence about the miracle, but the wonder was so great that it could not be kept secret.

What is the point of the story? It lies in the comment of the spectators. Their exclamation embodies the words of Isa. 35.5 f., a passage that prophesies the coming of the era of salvation. The miracle was a sign that that age was dawning. If so, the question becomes all the more pressing: who is this whose presence brings the signs of the age of the Messiah? Matt. 11.2–6 is a good commentary on this incident.

For meditation: The witnesses of this miracle could not be constrained to obey Jesus' command to keep quiet about it, but our temptation is to disobey His command to us to blaze the news abroad.

St. Mark 8.1-10   The Feeding of the Four Thousand

It will not surprise those who are familiar with the vagaries of Biblical criticism to find that the majority of critical scholars today believe that the stories of feeding a multitude recorded by Mark are variant versions of one and the same basic story. The reasons for this hypothesis are of differing strength. Apart from the refusal of some scholars to believe that Jesus could ever have said the same thing twice or performed two closely similar acts, the principal difficulty is the dullness of the disciples in not realizing that Jesus could feed the crowds again after what had happened on the previous occasion. This is far from being an insuperable difficulty, for all along Mark has been showing us how very dull and uncomprehending the disciples could be.

The story is very similar to the previous one; the telling of each would influence the form of other, and the often quoted illustration of how a policeman will use almost identical language in describing two quite different street accidents is a relevant one. Note, however, the differences. On this occasion the compassion of Jesus is linked to His *feeding* of the crowd. They had been with Him three days, a phrase which (as in the resurrection story) need not mean literally 72 hours but one whole day and parts of the immediately preceding and following days. As a result they exhausted their supplies of food. The numbers of people and loaves differ, as do the number and type of baskets of crumbs. Here large hampers were used.

The identity of the crowd remains a mystery. The indications are that the miracle took place in Decapolis, and if so, the crowd may have been composed of Gentiles. In this case, the purpose of the story is to show how Jesus fed the Gentiles after He had fed the Jews (cf. 7.27!). This would explain why Mark has used his precious space to report two very similar occurrences, but it must be admitted that the Gentile nature of the crowd remains uncertain.

In v.10 'Dalmanutha' is a name not otherwise known, and the various manuscripts give different guesses at what the name of the place was. Magdala on the west side of the lake remains the most likely possibility.

St. Mark 8.11-26   Problems of Belief

In the first of the three incidents in this section the Pharisees asked Jesus for some kind of divine authentication of His message. Not even the feeding of hungry crowds was enough to convince them (cf. John 6.30). This suggests that although the Pharisees were asking Jesus for proof of His divine power they had made up their minds in advance. A belief which depends simply upon the compulsion of mighty deeds is not true belief, and involves no real change of heart (cf. Luke 16.30 f.).

Nevertheless, Jesus had performed mighty works and would continue to do so. His words (12) must be taken to mean that although He would not perform conjuring tricks to overawe the unbelieving, He would continue to perform His works of compassion and salvation through which those who were prepared to believe might perceive the gracious rule of God at work in Himself and find their faith confirmed.

Then Jesus set off with His disciples for Bethsaida. He was trying to instruct them to beware of the evil influence of the Pharisees and of Herod (why is *he* mentioned here? Is there a clue in Luke 13.31f. ?), but their minds were taken up by what they thought was a much more pressing problem: there was no food on the boat! For the third time they failed to realize that with Jesus on board their wants were fully taken care of, and they had fallen into that hardness of heart which ought not to have been found in disciples (4.10–12). Jesus strongly reproached them: had they forgotten His power to provide enough *and to spare* for their needs?

Finally, there is the brief story of the healing of the blind man. The healing of the blind, like that of the deaf and dumb, is a sign of the era of salvation (Isa. 35.5). The story is unique for its two-stage cure, and commentators have wondered if there is something symbolic about it. The story comes just before the incident at Caesarea Philippi in which Jesus gave His disciples a *deeper* insight into His person. Is, then, the two-stage cure a picture of two stages in their understanding of Jesus? This is rather speculative, and it is safer simply to see in the stories of the opening of the ears of the deaf and the eyes of the blind a commentary on the opening of the ears and eyes of the disciples (8.18!).

St. Mark 8.27—9.1   The Way of the Son of Man

This incident is undoubtedly the central point in the Gospel. Jesus and His disciples were again in the north, in the vicinity of the 'new town' of Caesarea Philippi some 25 miles from the lake. Here He asked them to sum up their impressions so far. The crowds do not seem to have thought of Him as the Messiah, but Peter, speaking for the disciples, made this confession. Four important points now follow.

First, Jesus accepted the title as true, but He did not wish it to be generally known. An open claim to Messiahship would cause trouble with the authorities and lead to wrong ideas in the minds of the people.

Second, Jesus revealed a new fact about Himself. Referring to Himself as the Son of man (a title which included and transcended that of Messiah), He spoke of a path foretold in Scripture and divinely appointed for Himself. As the messianic Son of man He must undergo the fate of the righteous sufferer in the Psalms and especially of the Servant of Yahweh in Isaiah (Psa. 22; 69; 118;

Isa. **50**.4 ff.; **52**.13—**53**.12; Zech. **13**.7). But the shock was too great for the disciples. The one who so readily recognized the Christ, swiftly assumed the role of Satan.

A still bigger shock awaited the disciples, for the third thing that Jesus said was that they must go the same way of suffering and rejection (and resurrection) as Himself. The reference to the multitude (34) is strange; the circle is silently enlarged and all are addressed who would follow Him. A disciple must be ready even for martyrdom like Jesus. He must be prepared to give up his hopes of 'life' in this world with all that it has to offer in terms of success, wealth, enjoyment and so on, for none of these things can stand comparison with the value of eternal life. A man's soul or life is of inestimable value and if he loses it it cannot be redeemed from death (Psa. **49**.5–9,15). How does a man lose his life? By refusal to follow Jesus, for at the parousia or coming of the Son of man He will be ashamed of all who refused to follow Him on earth. In other words, a man's ultimate destiny depends on whether he accepts discipleship now.

Fourth, a word of reassurance (**9**.1). Admittedly it is very enigmatic. At first sight it implies that the coming referred to in **8**.38 will come in the lifetime of some of Jesus' hearers (cf. **13**.30). But this is unlikely, for Jesus expected a longer interval than this before the coming. Moreover, the reference is to the coming of the '*kingdom of God*' (**1**.15). It is therefore more satisfactory to see an allusion to the resurrection and exaltation of Jesus and the coming of the Spirit. At the same time, however, the saying seems to bear some relationship to the story of the transfiguration which immediately follows it; an event which in itself prophesies the revelation of God's kingly power in Jesus.

St. Mark 9.2-13   The Transfiguration of Jesus

The 'high mountain' on which Jesus was transfigured before the inner group of His three disciples is usually thought to be Hermon (9000 ft.). This was close to the Caesarea Philippi area; the scene of Peter's recent confession.

How should we interpret the incident? Peter was at a loss, and his suggestions are disregarded. The final emphasis on 'Jesus only' (8) points away from venerating Moses and Elijah and confirms Jesus as the central character. Most probably the incident was to be a confirmation of Peter's confession by showing a glimpse of the glory which was to follow the sufferings of Jesus—His transformed person, glistening garments, the heavenly voice and the cloud,

135

symbolic of God's presence (Exod. 24.16)—all exalt Him. The scene is therefore an anticipation of the exaltation and the second coming of Jesus, these two events being 'run together' as happens in Biblical prophecy with its foreshortened pictures of the future, and thus confirms that God's rule is at work powerfully in Jesus. At the same time the transfiguration shows that Jesus had not lost His heavenly glory on earth, though normally it was hidden from sight. The picture thus presented is of Jesus as the Son of God and the Son of man.

But what are Moses and Elijah doing here? They may perhaps be regarded as representatives of the law and the prophets which bear witness to Jesus, but Elijah certainly and Moses possibly were expected to appear before the end of the age, and there may be a reference to this role here.

On the way down from the mountain Jesus again issued a command to keep silent about what had happened until after the resurrection. This puzzled the disciples. They realized that Jesus must mean a special resurrection of the Son of man before the general resurrection, and this was a strange idea. For the moment the problem remained unsolved, and a second difficulty was raised: The Jews expected the return of Elijah to prepare for the coming of God or of the Messiah (Mal. 4.5 f.). Now, if the Messiah had come in Jesus, as Peter had confessed, what had happened to Elijah? Jesus' answer contained three points. 1. Although Elijah was to come first to prepare the people, this did not remove the Scriptural necessity for the Son of man to suffer. 2. In fact 'Elijah' had already come, for Jesus saw his role fulfilled in the work of John. 3. Just as this 'Elijah' had suffered, so the Son of man would suffer. It is not certain what Scripture is referred to in v.13; possibly 1 Kings 19.2,10.

St. Mark 9.14-29   The Power of Faith

We are back again in the world of human need where there are no more visions to sustain men, and they must live by faith rather than by sight. The Jesus who was revealed as the Son of God on the mountain top is now to be seen as the Son of God with power to heal and save.

The story apparently takes place in Galilee, for the scribes are said to have been disputing with the disciples. We never learn what they were arguing about: clearly it cannot have been very important! When Jesus reappeared, the people were greatly amazed. This has sometimes been taken to mean that heavenly glory still clung to Him (cf. Exod. 34.35), but it is more likely that they were simply surprised

136

by His sudden return, especially at a moment when His presence was urgently needed. A man had brought his son, suffering from a demoniac attack associated with epilepsy, to the disciples, and they had been unable to cure him despite the commission in 6.7. Jesus reproached the people for their lack of faith in words modelled on Deut. 32.5, and spoke directly to the father who sought His help with the words, 'If you can help, save us'. Jesus at once seized on his word: 'You say, "If you *can*"? All things can be done by the one who believes.' The answer evoked the noble response of the man in which he confessed his weak faith and sought the help that Jesus is ready to give those who find it hard to believe. Thereupon the boy was healed.

Preachers often handle this story in terms of the mountain top and valley experiences of life. Surely, however, the *primary* point in the story is faith in Jesus. Jesus reproached the whole company present for their lack of faith. He instantly responded to the appeal of a man who sought His help. When the disciples asked why they had failed, He replied that prayer, which is the spoken expression of faith and the active appeal for faith to God, was the one essential. (The addition 'and fasting' in some manuscripts is probably not original.)

This is the lesson of this story. Mountains and valleys, the visible presence and absence of the Lord—these should be of no account. Faith is what matters. And where faith is weak, Jesus will draw near and help those who call upon Him.

St. Mark 9.30-37   Suffering and Humility

The end of Jesus' work in Galilee was drawing near; He made His way southwards to Capernaum (9.33) and then towards Judea (10.1). From this point onwards He devoted more of His time to instructing the disciples and teaching them about what lay ahead. Only they could be entrusted with the revelation that He now brought, but even they failed to understand it. For the third time He reminded them of the coming passion of the Son of man, repeating the pattern of words used in 8.31. We shall meet the same pattern again in 10.33 f.

The sceptics have disputed the authenticity of these prophecies of the death and resurrection of Jesus. 'Can there be any doubt', asked R. Bultmann, 'that they are all *vaticinia ex eventu*?' i.e. history disguised in the form of prediction and created by the early Church.

Behind these objections is often an unwillingness to admit the possibility of knowledge of the future by Jesus. Yet, even at the human level surely Jesus must have seen that some such fate awaited

Him if He pursued His present path. At the same time, we have seen sufficient already in this Gospel to realize that purely human categories are quite insufficient to explain this Person and that we cannot set arbitrary limits to what He may or may not have said. Furthermore, the mystification of the disciples was by no means odd. It was against all Jewish expectation that the Messiah should suffer, and the disciples could not bring themselves to share the insight of Jesus. British people will remember how very few were capable of believing the prophecies of Sir Winston Churchill about the menace of Hitler in the 1930s. Men are slow to believe what they do not want to believe.

Vs. 33 ff. show this clearly. The disciples were more interested in status than in suffering. They needed a strong lesson, and Jesus gave it to them. The ambitious person, He said, must be prepared to take the meanest place. (The lesson evidently needed repetition! See Matt. 23.11 f.; Luke 22.26; John 13.13–16.) Children were regarded as insignificant in the ancient world. To be prepared to care for the insignificant is a mark of estimate you place on yourself. More than that, it is to receive Jesus, who Himself thus takes the insignificant place (10.45), and yet—*here is the amazing paradox*—to receive Him is to receive God. Here is hidden the secret of who Jesus really is (see Matt. 10.40; Luke 10.16; John 12.44 f.; 13.20).

Questions for further study and discussion on Mark 7.31–9.37

1. In what ways is the dullness of the disciples seen in Mark? Does it have any parallels in our lives? What is the cure for it?
2. How do we set about convincing modern Pharisees of the truth of Jesus' claims? Does it make any difference in our approach to them if they do not believe in 'heaven' (8.11)?
3. What evidence can you find in Mark 1—8 to substantiate the confession made by Peter in 8.29? Was Peter's confession an adequate one?
4. What is the significance of the transfiguration for our understanding of the person of Jesus?
5. What should be the modern equivalent of curing the demon-possessed?

St. Mark 9.38-50   Hard Sayings

The little story in vs. 38–41 is meant for those of us who think that we alone are 'sound' and follow Jesus truly, and who do nothing to help the work of other Christians whose understanding of the Faith may be different from our own. Here was a man doing effective work in the name of Jesus—unlike the exorcists in Acts 19.13–16.

Was he not a disciple at all or simply not one of the Twelve who had been commissioned by Jesus to do this work? Surely the latter was the case. But Jesus gladly receives those who follow Him even when the organized Church despises them. Those who are not against us in Christ's service are on our side. At the same time a person who is not for Jesus is against Him (Matt 12.30); there can be no neutrality.

Then Jesus makes His promise of reward for all who care for the disciples by throwing in their lot with them, especially in time of persecution. It should be clear that Jesus is not here speaking of rewards for non-Christians, but is challenging men to personal commitment to Himself and His followers.

The following sayings cover such a variety of topics that it is probable that they were spoken on several different occasions and then gathered together as a result of the presence of certain key-words in them (e.g. 'sin' and 'salt'). V.42 stands in strong contrast to v. 37. Whether it refers to disciples young in years or in faith is neither clear nor important. Then Jesus speaks of the danger of a man letting himself be led into sin by hand, foot or eye. The imagery used to describe the sinner's fate is drawn from Gehenna, a per-petually burning rubbish dump outside Jerusalem, and from the slow eating of dead bodies by worms (Isa. 66.24). Since this is imagery associated with *bodies*, it would be wrong to press it to refer to literal fire for *souls* after death, but Jesus does say that the fate of the sinner will be every bit as bad as Gehenna.

Vs. 49, 50 must be taken on their own. V. 49 is an allusion to the purifying effect of tribulation and suffering. A second saying about salt comes in v. 50a. Matt. 5.13 suggests that it refers to the witness of the disciples which must not be allowed to become insipid. V. 50b says in effect: have the salt of the gospel in your own lives, and then you will live at peace with one another instead of bickering for precedence (34). Here is that same combination of grace and gumption which we find in the Sermon on the Mount.

St. Mark 10.1-16   Family Life

At the beginning of chapter 10 we come to a change in the location of Jesus' work. From Galilee He moved to Judea and Perea, the region east of the Jordan (cf. John 10.40; 11.54). At this point Mark concentrates on the teaching of Jesus rather than on His deeds. The opening themes are marriage, children and possessions.

In asking Jesus about divorce the Pharisees may have been putting a catch-question to Him: would He in His answer offend King Herod, as John had done, or would He contravene the law of Moses? Or perhaps they wished to know whether He agreed with the more strict or lax schools in Pharisaism. As was so often, Jesus directed them to the authority of the Old Testament law, and then proceeded to elucidate it. The law in Deut. 24.1ff. did not represent God's ideal for mankind, but was enacted to prevent worse situations arising. Recognizing the existence of human sin and frailty, it took measures to keep it in check. But alongside this frank recognition of the possibility of divorce Jesus placed two radical statements. First, marriage is intended to be a partnership for life in which the couple become 'one flesh' (RSV mg.), i.e. 'one person' or 'one kindred'. Therefore, a stern warning, reminiscent of 9.42, is issued to all who tempt others to matrimonial infidelity (9). Second, Jesus stated that if a man divorces his wife to marry another, he is committing adultery against the first wife. This was a new and radical saying, for Jewish law did not regard the misdemeanours of *men*, but only those of women, as adultery. Jesus here puts woman on an equality with man. The second part of the saying (12) which says the same thing about the wife probably has Gentile society in mind, since divorce by a woman was almost unheard of in Judaism.

A story about Jesus' attitude to children follows appropriately. It tells how He received and blessed them, just as any Jewish rabbi might do. But His words go further than mere blessing. The Kingdom of God is only for those who come trustingly and humbly to Jesus like children. Later the story was used in the Church in connection with the baptism of infants, but of course there is no reference to baptism as such in it. It simply asserts that Jesus welcomed children, and just as surely did He welcome any adult who came with the right attitude of mind and heart.

St. Mark 10.17-22 — Jesus and a Rich Man

The rich man addressed Jesus in an unusual manner by calling Him 'Good Teacher'—a term never used for a rabbi. It could be regarded as flattery giving a man a higher status than is his due, for true goodness is the prerogative of God. Jesus' question was designed to test whether the man really knew what he was saying. Is there here a veiled claim to divinity?

This, however, was incidental to the main theme. The questioner was concerned about the future destiny of the individual as he sought after the experience variously called 'inheriting eternal life', 'entering the Kingdom of God' or 'being saved'. All these expressions refer to entering the bliss of the age to come instead of being condemned to punishment. The orthodox Jewish answer was simple: salvation was for circumcised Jews who kept the commandments. Jesus' reply to the rich man was at first entirely orthodox. He cited the so-called second table of the ten commandments not because the first table is unimportant, but because obedience to the second table is more easily tested by a man's outward conduct. The rich man claimed, like Paul (Phil. 3.6), that he had obeyed them perfectly. There was here evidence of religious devotion, of an apparently sincere desire to serve God truly, and Jesus' heart went out to His questioner. But a two-sided commandment still remained! On the one hand, Jesus bade the rich man to realize his assets and give the proceeds to the poor. Here he failed. Why? He loved himself and his money more than he loved the poor. He was breaking the first commandment of all, for he had made an idol of himself and consequently could neither worship God truly nor love his neighbour fully.

On the other hand, Jesus, who is significantly described at the beginning of the story as 'setting out on His journey' *to Jerusalem and crucifixion*, called him to follow Him. This is the condition for inheriting eternal life, discipleship. Here too he failed. He was not ready for total commitment to God. This was his fundamental error.

Does Jesus call all rich men to give up their riches if they would be saved? No: it is not the possession of riches but the desire for them that keeps a man from salvation. But is this a complete interpretation of Jesus' words? Is there in fact any New Testament evidence that Christians may enjoy their riches themselves instead of sharing them fully and freely with the needy?

St. Mark 10.23-31   Riches and Rewards

We now have Jesus' comments on the story of the rich man. That story demonstrated clearly that it is hard for a *rich man* to enter the Kingdom. The statement amazed the disciples because it was accepted Jewish thinking that a man's earthly prosperity was some index of his spiritual state, even although this fundamental proposition was inevitably crossed by others which took notice of the variety of human experience. To this Jesus replied with the more fundamental statement that it is *hard* for *anybody* to enter the Kingdom of God. Indeed, He said (reverting to the case in hand) it is as *impossible* for a rich man to enter the Kingdom as for a camel to go through the eye of a needle. (It should not need to be said that Jesus meant literal camels and literal needles, just as in the similar Jewish proverb about an elephant and a needle.) Who then can be saved? The answer is: *nobody*. From a human point of view salvation is impossible. All this fits in with what we have already learned, that

141

men are afflicted with blindness and hardness of heart and cannot of themselves respond to the message of Jesus. But where men cannot act, God can and does. He can bring men to a change of heart, open their eyes to understand the truth, and grant them to believe. This may sound like the doctrines of total inability and irresistible grace, but it would be wrong to harden what Jesus says here into rigid theology. Mark says nothing to restrict the scope of God's grace or make it irresistible.

What is the significance of vs. 28 ff.? Is Peter saying, 'We are all right; we have given up our possessions to follow You'? This sounds very self-righteous in the context, but Peter was very human! Anyhow, Jesus responds with a promise that those who have taken this step will receive their reward. Here in this life they will share in the fellowship of the disciples with all its blessings in human relationships (cf. 3.35), and in the next world they will enjoy eternal life. There are two caveats. Jesus was too much of a realist not to mention the fact that persecution will come from outside the fellowship to those who join themselves to it. At the same time He issues a warning against setting one's heart on reward: there will be reversals as well as rewards in the Kingdom.

For meditation: does the promise of v. 30 come alive in your experience? Are you making it a reality for other disciples?

St. Mark 10.32-45   The Way of Service

Reward and position are still the themes in this section. Now they are set in the context of our fourth reminder that Jesus is on His way to His passion. The awestruck disciples' fears are confirmed by this further detailed prophecy of His impending suffering.

In sharp contrast James and John, still thinking only of the traditional glory of the messianic kingdom, sought for themselves the places of supreme rank. The bitter 'cup' and the 'baptism' of the cross which Jesus set before them were both metaphors utilizing Old Testament language referring to suffering and distress; the former especially was associated with bearing retribution and wrath (Psa. 75.8; Isa. 51.17,22; cf. Mark 14.36; Rev. 14.10; 16.19), the latter has as its background the idea of being engulfed in calamity (Psa. 69.1–3; cf. Luke 12.50). To the disciples these metaphors may have conveyed the thought of a messianic battle, and they professed themselves willing to fight in it. Jesus promised that they would. As for the rewards for which they asked, these were not His to bestow, but are 'prepared'—by God.

The rest of the disciples, though more backward in seeking

honour, were no less covetous of it, and Jesus had to take them all to task. Wanting to be like Gentile rulers, they understood leadership in terms of commanding slaves and exacting service from them. That is not the way in the Kingdom of God. The person who wants to be first must take the lowest place and serve his fellows. This is not a recipe for success; it is a command to find happiness in service *instead of* being served, in loving others *instead of* commanding them. It finds its inspiration in the example of Jesus Himself. At this point, as in 1 Pet. 2.18–25, the thought moves from the example of Jesus to the saving results of what He did. His service was to give His life as an offering instead of the many. The background to this saving will be found in Psa. 49.7–9 and Isa. 53.10–12. It plainly teaches substitution: the 'many' not only benefit from what is done on their behalf (representation), but gain what they could never have achieved for themselves through One who loved them and gave Himself for them. It equally plainly teaches a universally available atonement, for 'many' is a Hebrew way of saying 'all', and all who will may take advantage of what is offered to them. No saying from the lips of Jesus in Mark is more precious.

St. Mark 10.46—11.11   From Jericho to Jerusalem

Bartimaeus is the great example in the Gospels of a man who was conscious of his need of Jesus and let nothing stand in the way of having his need met. He recognized in Jesus the Son of David (the title is very probably messianic; see Isa. 11.1–5; Jer. 23.5 f.; Ezek. 34.23 f.; Mark 12.35), and believed that He could help him as He had helped others. When Jesus summoned him and asked what he wanted done for him, there was no hesitancy (contrast John 5.6 f.). Thereafter Bartimaeus joined the company that was following Jesus. The story is an excellent parable of the meaning of discipleship.

Jesus had reached Jericho after crossing over the Jordan from the region to the east (10.1). He now continued farther to the south-west up the steep road to Jerusalem which He approached via the two villages on its east side. Here He made His plans for a symbolic entry. It is not certain whether the instructions about the colt reflect a previous arrangement or supernatural knowledge. But it seems strange to describe the incident in such detail if it were simply a prearranged plan.

The significance of the entry is to be gathered from the cries of Jesus' companions. 'Hosanna' is an Aramaic word meaning 'Save now' which was used as a greeting for pilgrims; it was probably shouted without people being aware of its meaning, just as people

143

today may say 'Hallelujah' without realizing that they are saying 'Sing praise to Jehovah'. Then Psa. 118.26a is quoted: this was originally a blessing pronounced upon pilgrims, but here it may possess a deeper sense. This would be confirmed by v. 10, which speaks of the coming of the messianic kingdom.

What, then, did it all mean? Did Jesus take the bold step of entering Jerusalem as the Messiah, yet in such a way that the people might realize that His ideas of Messiahship differed completely from those popularly held? Did some of the people realize the significance of the colt as a pointer to Zech. 9.9? Did their cries mean more than they realized at the time? John 12.16 suggests that something like this was the case. There was a mixture of understanding and perplexity among both the crowd and the disciples. For the moment there was nothing on which the authorities could lay the finger.

For meditation: How would you reply to Jesus' questions in 10.36 and 51?

St. Mark 11.12-19　　　　　The Cleansing of the Temple

During festival periods the city of Jerusalem was so crowded that many people had to stay outside in the vicinity, and Jesus followed this practice (Luke 21.37).

The fig tree bears its fruit in April to June, but earlier in the season (late March to early April) it bears a crop of small knobs which are edible and are a sign that the tree will later bear fruit. Either Jesus found no knobs on the tree and deduced that it would not bear fruit later, or else He deliberately acted in a strange way by looking for fruit out of season in order to arouse the attention of His disciples. We may safely dismiss the view that He was simply looking for food. Nor is the significance of the incident simply the power of prayer. It was an acted parable, and its point was that Israel, which had failed to produce the fruit that it should have done, would endure the curse of God (Jer. 8.13; Hos. 9.10, 16 f.; Mic. 7.1–6; Luke 13.6–9).

This interpretation is confirmed by the close link with the story of how Jesus entered the Temple. In the Court of the Gentiles the various requisites for sacrifice were sold, and money could be exchanged for the special coinage in which the Temple dues had to be paid; it would be naïve to imagine that these dealings were free from corruption and graft. Jesus' action had a three-fold significance. 1. The Temple was not meant to be desecrated into a place of commerce and profiteering (Jer. 7.11). 2. Jesus' quotation from Isa. 56.7 shows that He was attempting to make room for the Gentiles

144

in the place allotted to them. It was an act which stressed the universalism which ought to have been part of the Jewish religion. 3. The cleansing of the Temple was an act of the Messiah (Mal. 3.1 ff.; cf. Ezek. 40–48; Hos. 9.15; Zech. 14.21). For those with eyes to see, this was a claim to Messiahship. In itself it was not a condemnation of the Jewish religion, but only of its abuses. The lesson, however, was not heeded, and the prophecy in chapter 13 followed inevitably. The Temple authorities began to talk of doing away with Jesus.

Questions for further study and discussion on Mark 9.38–11.19

1. What has Mark 9.39 to say to evangelicals in the present Church situation? What other New Testament teaching is relevant to this problem?
2. What is the bearing of the New Testament teaching on the remarriage of divorced persons?
3. Does the saying of Jesus in Mark 10.14 throw any light on the problem of whether young children can undergo an experience of evangelical conversion?
4. Should the disciples of Jesus be motivated in their service by the hope of reward?
5. Do we do anything that keeps modern 'Gentiles' out of the Church of Jesus (11.17)?

St. Mark 11.20-33
Teaching on Prayer; the Authority of Jesus

The morning after Jesus had cursed the fig tree it was found to have withered away. Peter was surprised by the fulfilment of the word of Jesus and remarked on the incident. Jesus replied with some remarks on the broader theme of faith and prayer. After proclaiming a general principle (22), He gave an example to show what He meant. 'This mountain' would be the Mount of Olives or the Hill of Zion, and the sea would be the Dead Sea which can be seen from there on a clear day. The saying is one of Jesus' vivid, hyperbolic statements (like Matt. 23.24) which are not meant to be taken literally. It is to be taken metaphorically like Zech. 4.7 and simply confirms the practical principle in v. 24 (cf. Matt. 17.20; Luke 17.6). This principle is one of vital importance in prayer (John 14.13 f.; 15.7; 16.23; 1 John 5.15), but there is a condition which must also be fulfilled, expressed in v. 25 (cf. Matt. 6.14 f.). Note how Paul makes the same point (1 Cor. 13.2). V. 26 is omitted in the best manuscripts; similar words occur in Matt. 6.15 to which v. 26 may owe its origin.

There now follows a series of incidents in which the conflict between Jesus and the religious authorities flared up for the last time and led to their decision to do away with Him. In the first of these incidents what seems like an official delegation came to question the credentials of Jesus. What was His authority, whether as a rabbi or as a prophet, to teach and act as He did, especially in the Temple? Jesus' reply, with a counter-question, neatly placed them in a dilemma and implicitly claimed the same direct authority from God as John had possessed ('heaven' is a Jewish periphrasis for the name of God, cf. **8.**11). Note how Jesus here places Himself alongside John; there is never any hint that the two men saw each other as rivals.

St. Mark 12.1-12   The Parable of the Vineyard

When Jesus began to speak to the leaders of the people about a vineyard, it is probable that they would be reminded of a parable told by Isaiah in which 'the vineyard of the Lord of hosts' was the house of Israel (Isa. **5.**1–7), and the application of Jesus' words would not be lost on them (12).

The 'mechanics' of the story seem to be that in certain cases an estate which belonged to a foreigner or proselyte who died intestate could pass to anybody, and the tenants here were determined that they would be the ones to benefit. But although the general build-up of the story can be explained naturally in this sort of way, a number of features suggest irresistibly that the story is an allegorical one, cleverly designed to give a picture of Israel and the way in which it had treated the messengers of God. There are small differences in the way in which this is done in Matthew and Luke. It is, however, a moot point whether the hearers would have realized that 'son' had an allegorical significance. Certainly Jesus meant Himself by this term and was hinting at His divine Sonship, but the people at large, who did not commonly think of the Messiah as the Son of God, may not have grasped the point. However, Jesus' main purpose was not to reveal who He was but rather to show the consequences of repeated rejection of God's messengers—and of His last Messenger. Salvation would be taken away from Israel and given to others (cf. Matt. **21.**43). The closing quotation from Psa. **118.**22 f. stresses how the rejected Son is God's Messenger and will be exalted by Him.

Meditation: Consider love and hate in the light of v. 12 (how it influenced the history of Israel—and ourselves). Perfect love casts out fear; so ultimately does perfect hate.

146

We have already met the extraordinary combination of the Pharisees and Herodians in opposition to Jesus (3.6). Now they reappear with a question regarding the duty of Jews to the Roman government. The word translated as 'taxes' is 'census'. This was a poll-tax levied on all the people and paid directly into Rome's treasury. It was a particularly hated tax, since it was one of the most obvious evidences of Jewish subjection to a foreign power, and there had been riots at its introduction (Acts 5.37). The question posed was a trap: was Jesus prepared to lose the sympathy of the people who paid the tax so unwillingly or to face a charge of subverting the people and even of inciting them to rebellion? Was the Messiah going to declare Himself? Jesus' answer, which skilfully evaded the dilemma, depended upon the fact that His questioners themselves used Roman coinage in daily life. This was why He asked *them* to produce the coin.

The coin bore the Emperor's head on one side and an image of the goddess of Peace on the other, with an inscription which read in translation: 'Tiberius Caesar Augustus, son of the divine Augustus, Chief Priest'—all of which was repulsive to Jewish (and later to Christian) sentiment. Jesus elicited the fact that His questioners recognized that the coin belonged to Caesar: it bore his image and inscription. Therefore, He argued, they were bound to pay him for the use of his money and, presumably, for all other benefits of his rule. One commentator stresses that the word 'render' really means not simply 'give' but 'give back'; the money was Caesar's and must be repaid to him.

The point was made, and Jesus could have stopped there. But He added, 'And give back to God the things that are God's'. This could be taken literally of paying to God the temple tax which was due to Him (Matt. 17.24–27), but there is surely a deeper meaning. Men are 'God's coinage', bearing His image, and what belongs to God must be paid back to Him.

Thus the two duties are put side by side. The position of Caesar *vis-à-vis* God is not clarified. That is not the purpose of this story, and other passages of Scripture must be consulted when the problem of the Christian and the State is discussed. What is stressed here is that the disciple of Jesus has a duty to the community of which he is a member, and, inasmuch as he cannot live without receiving the benefits of the community, so he must make his contribution to it, even if he disapproves of it.

St. Mark 12.18-27 Life after Death

After the discomfiture of the Pharisees and Herodians it was the turn of the Sadducees to question Jesus. They were the materialists of their day, alike in their denial of the resurrection, angels and spirits (Acts 23.8), and in their worship of wealth and worldly position. In later years they were overshadowed by the Pharisees, whose greater religious zeal made them the leaders of Judaism at a time when the people had no national future; but in the time of Jesus the Sadducees occupied a powerful place in the Sanhedrin, and it was from their ranks that the high priests came.

Their question arose from a palpably absurd story based on the Old Testament principle of levirate marriage (Gen. 38.8; Deut. 25.5 f.; the name has nothing to do with 'Levite' but comes from Latin *levir*, a brother-in-law). Such complicated problems are found in Jewish discussions of the time. The purpose of this story was to ridicule the doctrine of the resurrection by a *reductio ad absurdum*; the modern parallel is when people ask what happens at the resurrection to a man who has been eaten by cannibals. In His reply Jesus enunciated two principles (24).

First, the Sadducean question ignored the power of God to create a new order of life in the heavenly world in which the earthly relationship of marriage would be transcended. The saying of Jesus has appeared hard to many, but the suggestion of C. F. D. Moule is helpful, that 'the exclusive loyalty of husband and wife in this life may prove to be a way forward into a wider and more inclusive fellowship in that other life'.

The other part of Jesus' reply was framed especially to answer the Sadducees, for they based their denial of the resurrection on its alleged absence from the books of Moses, which alone were authoritative for them. But there God, speaking to Moses, affirmed 'I—the God of Abraham' (Exod. 3.6). There is no verb present in the Hebrew text, as is normal in such a statement. Jesus implies that a present tense 'am' must be supplied (as in the Septuagint). If God thus spoke of Himself to Moses, then He was implying that these men were still alive because He was still their God. He who was their God in their lifetime would not abandon them in death; they still live to Him. Thus the hope of immortality and resurrection depends upon the character of God.

St. Mark 12.28-37 The Great Commandments

There was at least one man who asked Jesus a sincere question during this time of testing and who would not fall under the condemnation in vs. 38–40. He was a scribe or rabbi, a professional teacher of the law, and he asked Jesus a question which was a frequent subject of debate in scribal circles. Could all the commandments in the law—there were reckoned to be 613 of them—be summed up in one, or could the more important ones be picked out? A famous rabbi, Hillel, had said: 'What you hate for yourself do not do to your neighbour: this is the whole law: the rest is commentary; go and learn.' Jesus agreed with that sentiment (Matt. 7.12), but here He gives a different, and more penetrating answer. He quoted what was called the 'Shema' (Hebrew for 'Hear!'), the passage from Deut. 6.4 f. which Jews recited daily, and to it He added a second commandment drawn from Lev. 19.18. Note especially how the call to obedience here is grounded in the nature of God, grace preceding the commandment. In making this reply Jesus was saying nothing very new, for there is evidence that this combination of commandments had already been arrived at by pious Jews. What Jesus was saying agreed with the insight into the spiritual and moral nature of true religion already found in the Old Testament (1 Sam. 15.22; Hos. 6.6).

But Jesus went a step further. He placed the scribe not *in* but only *near* the Kingdom. Was this because the Kingdom was still distant? Or was it not rather because the scribe lacked some qualification? Is not the answer that the scribe had still to learn to follow Jesus (10.21) and so be in the presence of the 'Kingdom Incarnate'?

The second incident here tells how Jesus took up the common teaching of the scribes that the Messiah was to be an earthly descendant of David (2 Sam. 7.12 f.; John 7.41 f.) and suggested that this could not be the *whole* truth. If David, in Psa. 110, spoke of the Messiah as 'my lord', how could the Messiah be simply his son? Some have thought that here Jesus was repudiating the Davidic descent of the Messiah; rather He was showing that 'Son of David' is an inadequate title for one who is David's lord and trying to make the people think more carefully about Messiahship and what it involved. An ancient J. B. Phillips might well have written a book for the scribes entitled 'Your Messiah is too small'!

St. Mark 12.38-44   False and True Piety

A third paragraph dealing with the scribes now follows. It contains a warning against their brand of religion. The scribes, especially those of them who belonged to the Pharisaic party (others were Sadducees), were the 'keen' religious people of their day. They knew the Scriptures well and were ready to teach from them. Their distinctive dress of a teacher's long robe bore silent testimony to their zeal. They not only prayed, but prayed at length. Yet the virtues of their religion easily became vices. Instead of directing men's attention to God and serving Him humbly, they claimed credit for themselves. They enjoyed wearing their robes and receiving the compliments of men. They sat in their special seats facing the rest of the congregation in the synagogues, and like many a modern choir or kirk session (or its denominational equivalents) they glowed in the public esteem which they received. With it all, they were not free from corruption. Such religion is no religion.

The list of criticisms could easily be extended; see Matt. 23; Luke 11.37–52. While we should not forget the better members of this class, including the one who came to Jesus by night and heard of a new birth, we should not ignore the lesson that zealous faith may easily be corrupted into a pride which delights in its own piety and flaunts itself before the world. It is a good question: when does Christian witness become exhibitionism?

The following story is obviously meant to provide a contrast, whether or not it actually happened immediately after these scathing remarks. Free will offerings made by the people at the Temple were put into thirteen collection boxes shaped like trumpets. Rich people put in their money ostentatiously and loudly; it cost them little to do so. The poor widow put in a gift that meant self-sacrifice, for she gave her whole livelihood, and had to do without other things that the money might have bought. This indication of her faith and devotion earned the praise of Jesus.

We had better ask; should our Christian faith lead us to give spontaneously our 'whole living' to the service of God, and, if so, what does this mean in practice for us in our different individual situations?

St. Mark 13.1-8   The Beginning of the End

This is the most difficult chapter in Mark for the interpreter, telling as it does of strange, future events and portents. A comment on the grandeur of the newly built Temple, prompted Jesus' prophecy that this great structure would be razed to the ground. The deeper implication of the prophecy is that the Temple and all it stood for had had its day, but how much did the disciples understand then? When Jesus was alone they asked two questions. First, when would the Temple be destroyed? Second, what would be the indication when 'these things are all to be accomplished'? This second question

150

seems to refer to the coming of the end of the present age (cf. Matt. **24.**3), and suggests that the disciples were associating the destruction of the Temple with the end of the age.

Many scholars doubt whether the discourse that now follows was actually spoken by Jesus on this one occasion, and it is possible that sayings spoken at different times have been gathered together (as in the chapter of parables or in the great discourse in Matthew) to give a fuller conspectus of His teaching on this theme. The first part of His reply (5–8) was a warning not to be led astray by events which suggested that the end had already come or that it was never going to come.

On the one hand, false teachers would lead the people astray. The phrase 'in My name' suggests that they would either appear as representatives of Jesus or even pretend to be Him. They would say, 'I am He!', which could mean 'I am the Messiah' or 'I am God'; Simon Magus made claims like these (Acts **8.**9 f.). They would persuade men that the end had come, and turn their minds away from Jesus.

On the other hand, the outbreak of wars and natural disasters could tempt the faithful to believe that God had forgotten them and that the end would never come. Such events, however, were part of the 'programme', and must be seen as the travail which precedes the joy of birth.

We have seen the destruction of the Temple, but close on two millennia have passed since then and the end has not yet come. The fall of Jerusalem in A.D. 70 is theologically part of the end, and yet the end still tarries. Throughout this chapter the events of A.D. 70 and A.D.? are closely woven together by a prophetic foreshortening which links essentially similar and related events to each other. The reason for this may become clearer further on in the chapter. For the moment, the warning in v. 7 is as relevant for us as it was for Jesus' first hearers.

Questions for further study and discussion on Mark 11.20–13.8

1. What is the significance for us of Jesus' teaching on prayer in Mark **11.**22–25?
2. Does the Bible give any guidance to a Christian who feels that the taxes which he pays to the State are being used for purposes (e.g. development of nuclear weapons) of which he cannot approve?
3. How would you answer somebody who says that love for God is fully summed up in love for your neighbour? Is there only one 'great commandment' or are there two (**12.**29–31)?

151

4. What difference does a belief in the second coming of Jesus make to the Christian life? Why is it not enough simply to have the fact of His living presence with us now?

5. What kind of things may lead us astray (13.5) as we look forward to the second coming of Jesus?

St. Mark 13.9-23   The Need for Perseverance

If the lesson of the first part of Jesus' discourse was 'Do not be led astray', that of the second part (9–13) is 'Stand fast'. The disciples are not only to take care not to be misled by the signs of the times; they must also hold out resolutely to the end, no matter how difficult circumstances become. Persecution will take place both through official channels (religious and civil courts) and through personal enmity as families are divided among themselves. In this situation three facts must be remembered. First, the disciples are to be *witnesses*. When they are tempted to despair and to give up their witness, they must remember that the end will not come until the gospel has been brought to all the nations. Second, they are promised the *help of the Spirit* in making their witness in the courts. Third, they are to persevere in their faith right *until death or the end* if they would attain salvation.

The next section prophesies definite events (14–23). The phrase 'desolating sacrilege' is the Greek rendering of the Hebrew 'the abomination that desolates', i.e. 'the fearfully abominable thing' found in Dan. 9.27; 11.31; 12.11. This prophecy was regarded as fulfilled in the desecration of the Temple by Antiochus of Syria in 168 B.C.; the phrase is applied to this event in 1 Maccabees 1.54. Now a further fulfilment is prophesied. This fulfilment was the destruction of Jerusalem and its Temple in A.D. 70 (cf. Luke 21.20). The coming of this event was to be the signal for flight from the ensuing scenes of battle and carnage in Judea. Yet even these terrible events would not mean the immediate coming of the end, and men would still need to beware of being led astray by false Messiahs (such as Simon ben Koseba who appeared in A.D. 132).

The whole of this section fits excellently the events in and around A.D. 70 when the sufferings of Jews were indescribably cruel. It is doubtful whether we are to expect a further fulfilment of the prophecy (evil follows a pattern, just as God's deeds conform to one) or simply to see these events as part of the sufferings associated with an end which has still not come. On either view of the passage, the warnings and advice given here are still relevant to Christians, and come alive especially at those times and in those areas where evil follows the pattern described here.

St. Mark 13.24-37   The Coming of the Son of Man

Whatever be our interpretation of the previous section, this paragraph (24–27) unmistakably brings us to the end of the age. Language almost fails Jesus as He indicates the cosmic significance of the coming of the Son of man in the traditional language of prophecy (Isa. **13**.10; **34**.4). The very heavens are affected by His appearance and hide their glory before Him. Then comes the climax, the appearance of the Son of man, as prophesied in Dan. **7**.13. The clouds, power and glory all indicate that He is invested with the attributes of God. His coming has a double purpose. On the one hand, the One who comes is the Son of man who suffered humiliation and death on the earth and was raised and exalted by God. He now comes as God's viceregent and is fully vindicated before men (cf. **14**.62). On the other hand, He comes to bring about the final fulfilment of the Old Testament promise that God's people will be gathered together from all the earth so that they may be in His presence and enjoy His salvation (Deut. **30**.4; Zech. **2**.6).

And this is all that is revealed. Jesus says nothing about the future age or the millennium, and there is no mention at all of the fate of those who do not belong to the elect. There is no encouragement to speculate about the fate of unbelievers. Instead, Jesus turns to exhortation. Having answered the two questions raised in v. 4, He now makes three further points. 1. *The time is near.* When the disciples see these signs coming to pass, they are to draw the glad conclusion: the end is at hand—as surely as the sprouting fig tree heralds summer. 2. *The time is unknown.* But just how near is the end? Now 'this generation' (30) probably means the contemporaries of Jesus, but 'these things' (29) surely mean the *signs* of the end rather than the end itself. Jesus Himself said that He did not know when that final day would come; He did know that His own coming and the events He prophesied here were all part of God's final intervention in the history of the world. 3. *Therefore, be ready.* Servants cannot afford to be slack when the master is away.

Once again the question arises: Where is the promise of His coming? It was asked by the contemporaries of Peter (2 Pet. **3**.4), and is now even more pressing. May it perhaps be that the time is dependent on the response of His disciples to His words in v. 10? So the Church must watch and pray, and Immanuel will come.

St. Mark 14.1-11   The Plot against Jesus' Life

With the long discourse about the future, the ministry of Jesus to the people and to His disciples had come to an end, and events moved swiftly to their conclusion. The point at issue with the chief priests and scribes was not whether to kill Jesus, but how and when. Their problem was answered by the offer of Judas to enable them to take Jesus quietly, so avoiding the tumult they feared (2).

The chronology of these days is highly complicated, and some brief clarification must be given. The two feasts of the Passover and Unleavened Bread were closely linked together. The former was celebrated on Nisan 15 with a solemn supper at the beginning of the day, i.e. in the evening, for the Jews regarded the new day as beginning at sunset rather than at midnight. The preparations for this feast, including the slaughter of the lambs, took place earlier in the afternoon of the same day by our reckoning; but this was in fact the end of Nisan 14 by Jewish reckoning. The feast of Unleavened Bread ran from Nisan 15 to 21 inclusive, both of these days being reckoned as special festival sabbaths (Lev. 23.4-8). According to Mark Jesus held His Passover supper at the normal time on Nisan 15 and died later on that same Jewish day (which was of course the following day, Friday, by our reckoning).

While the Jewish plot was being hatched, there took place an act that stands in complete contrast to it. A woman whom we know to have been called Mary (John 12.1-8) anointed Jesus with a lavish quantity of very precious ointment or perfume (worth 300 times a labourer's daily wage). It represented an act of devotion to Him personally. Almsgiving was a worthy act (5), but this act was even more worthy (by Jewish standards, quite apart from the uniqueness of this particular situation) since it was really an anointing for His burial (8). We do not know if Mary realized the full significance of her action, but it seems that at least one person had begun to understand something of the mystery of a Messiah who must die.

The act is worth remembering (9). In a world where some would have us believe that the first of the two great commandments is adequately fulfilled simply by obedience to the second, we need this reminder that personal devotion to Jesus Himself is of primary importance. Loving our neighbour is only part of what it means to love God.

St. Mark 14.12-21   The Passover Meal

During the afternoon of Nisan 14 Jesus made His preparations for what He knew would be His last Passover meal. The feast required a suitable room in Jerusalem, and the food (the lamb, bread and bitter sauce) and wine. The story of how the room was obtained suggests a prior arrangement made in the interests of holding the meal in privacy and peace rather than an act of supernatural foreknowledge. A man carrying a water jar would be a sufficiently unusual sight to be a means of recognition. The room is often identified with that in Acts 1.13 (possibly in the house of Acts 12.12).

The meal was duly held in a context of tension and suspicion. Over the table hung the shadow of betrayal, a betrayal all the more awful because it meant breaking up the fellowship of the sacred meal (Psa. 41.9; John 13.18). The disciples were all sufficiently aware of their weakness to ask anxiously which of them Jesus had in mind as He uttered His fateful prophecy. But He refused to name the offender, merely indicating that it was one of those present who was dipping his bread in the same dish of bitter sauce as Himself. (The identification in Matt. 26.25 was probably made in quiet reply to Judas himself, or else he might have been lynched on the spot: Peter had a sword!)

The New Testament does not speculate on why Judas behaved as he did. Jesus said that the way appointed for the Son of man to tread was that laid down by God in Scripture for Him (cf. comment on 8.31), but this necessity in no way diminished the awful responsibility of the man who freely chose to betray Him. That man's fate would be so dreadful that he had better never have been born. Here the factors of divine sovereignty and human responsibility are brought together in a way which denies the reality of neither but simply states the mystery of their juxtaposition. More important than speculation into that mystery (which we shall never be able to understand this side of eternity) is to observe how Jesus freely chose to follow the path laid down for Him.

Thought: The highest exercise of free will is submission to God's will.

St. Mark 14.22-31 The Lord's Supper

The account of the Passover meal is confined to those essential details which showed how the Church was to continue to perform the rite in memory of its Lord. The normal course of the meal would be as follows: 1. An inaugural blessing and prayer were followed by a dish of herbs and sauce and the first of four cups of wine. 2. The account of the institution of the Passover was related, Psa. 113 was sung, and a second cup of wine was drunk. 3. After a grace the main meal of roast Passover lamb with unleavened bread and bitter herbs was eaten, and after a further prayer the third cup of wine was drunk. 4. Psa. 114–118 were sung, and the fourth cup of wine was drunk.

The narrative here does not even mention the Passover lamb and the symbolism of the Exodus associated with it (for the *Christian* symbolism see 1 Cor. 5.7), but concentrates its attention on how Jesus attached a new significance to the bread eaten with the main course and to the third cup of wine and made a solemn vow in connection with the latter. In the saying over the bread the word 'is' (which would in any case be omitted in Aramaic idiom; cf. 12.26) must mean 'represents', since Jesus Himself was actually performing the act. The word 'body' is variously interpreted to mean the flesh of Jesus or His whole self. The symbolism suggests that Jesus was thinking of Himself as being offered in sacrifice like the Passover lamb on behalf of the disciples (1 Cor. 11.24). The wine symbolizes the death of Jesus. Three thoughts are bound up with it. First, it is covenant blood (cf. Ex. 24.8), the new covenant, prophesied by Jeremiah (Jer. 31.31–34). Second, it is therefore sacrificial blood, for the covenant is inaugurated by a sacrifice in which God and man are reconciled. Third, it is the blood of the suffering Servant of God who lays down His life 'for 'many', i.e. for all men (Isa. 53.12; Mark 10.45). The sacrifice is vicarious and substitutionary, and the disciples receive its blessings symbolically by receiving the bread and wine. Finally, in His vow (25) Jesus looked forward to the full coming of the Kingdom of God, which was possible only through His death, and to the messianic banquet of which the Supper is a foretaste: 'You proclaim the Lord's death *until He comes.*'

After singing the appointed Psalms the little company went outside Jerusalem, and through the gloom of impending betrayal and desertion shines the hope of Jesus in His resurrection and the coming of the Kingdom.

St. Mark 14.32-42   The Cup of Agony

Gethsemane was an olive plantation at the foot of the Mount of Olives. Jesus came here with the intention of praying and took three of His disciples aside with Him to be His close companions in this hour of anguish. His words, 'My heart is ready to break with grief' (NEB), show that He was conscious of the approach of the hour of suffering and death and that He would willingly have avoided it. He therefore prayed that the hour might pass from Him, i.e. might never come to Him. He addressed His Father with the familiar, tender term 'Abba', which is the confident word of a child to a father who understands his needs. He confessed the omnipotence of the One who answers prayer, and made His request. The word 'cup' (10.38; Isa. **51.** 22) indicates that He saw what lay ahead not simply as suffering (would He have shrunk from that?) but as the cup of God's wrath which He must drain on behalf of sinners. Then He freely put Himself in God's hands. Was His prayer answered? Heb. **5.**7 says that it was. How?

Jesus had instructed His companions to stay by Him and remain awake. Did He want them to wrestle in prayer on His behalf or simply to have an object lesson in facing temptation? His words to them show that they were not equipped to face temptation either then or afterwards. It is not enough to have a strong desire to overcome it; the flesh and its conflicting impulses must be brought under control. It is surely significant that the personal rebuke, 'Simon . . .' (37) is recorded in 'Peter's Gospel'.

The scene was repeated twice, as if to show the continuing strength of the temptation which Jesus faced. Then came the end. The disciples had slept and rested long enough (the meaning of v. 41a is very obscure). Now the betrayer had come, and in the strength won by prayer Jesus went forth confidently to meet him: 'Up, let us go forward!' (NEB).

For meditation: If Jesus knew the reality of temptation and had to resist it with all His might, how much more do we need to beware of it and to seek His victory.

St. Mark 14.43-52 The Act of Betrayal

The enormity of Judas' act is emphasized in the description. He was 'one of the twelve', he addressed Jesus as 'Master', he gave Him the kiss of affectionate greeting. The Gospels make no attempt to whitewash his character but are unanimous that he was a traitor. His motives can only be guessed; most probably he was disappointed that Jesus had not attempted a *coup d'état* by force because he had never been truly converted to an understanding of the divine way of redemption.

He was accompanied by a rabble horde from 'the chief priests and the scribes and the elders', i.e. 'the government', to whom he had given information as to where and when they might quietly arrest Jesus. The band had instructions to arrest Jesus alone, and they made no attempt to prevent the flight of His followers, even though one of them (the Greek implies 'somebody whose name I could tell you') made an attempt at armed resistance (cf. John 18.10). Jesus' one recorded comment stresses the incongruity of treating like a brigand One who had done nothing to cause trouble but had taught quietly in the Temple. The Scripture which Jesus had in mind was probably Isa. 53, especially vs. 3 and 12.

The only reason for the inclusion of vs. 51 f., which contribute nothing to the main story, must be that they refer to the person who told the story; the young man was therefore Mark or somebody well known to him. 'Naked' may mean that he was wearing only a light undergarment, but quite probably it should be taken literally. In his hurry he had merely thrown a cloth around his shoulders. It has been suggested (assuming the last supper to have been held in Mark's mother's house) that the young man slipped out of the house when he should have been in bed, followed Jesus and the disciples to Gethsemane, and so, incidentally, overheard the prayer of our Lord's agony while the disciples slept, and thus subsequently became an eye-witness to the betrayal and arrest.

Questions for further study and discussion on Mark 13.9–14.52

1. What weapons other than persecution does the non-Christian world of today use to tempt Christians to give up their faith? In what ways does the Holy Spirit (13.11) help us to bear witness and endure in our situation?
2. Can you think of any reasons why the crowds who supported Jesus during His ministry in Jerusalem (11.18; 12.12,37; 14.2) failed to help Him at the end?
3. How can we follow the example of the woman who anointed Jesus (14.3–9)?
4. How can we celebrate the Lord's Supper so as to lose none of the meaning which Jesus intended us to find in it?
5. What does it mean for us to enter into the 'fellowship of His sufferings' (Phil. 3.10; cf. Col. 1.24)? Does the story of Geth-semane shed any light on this aspect of the Christian life?

St. Mark 14.53-65   The Jewish Trial

From the scene of arrest Jesus was hurried away to be tried by a variety of 'courts'. The brief mention of Peter at the beginning of the scene reminds us that he was present throughout it and prepares us for vs. 66–72. The scene here took place at night before the members of the Sanhedrin (seventy-one members, comprising

158

representatives from the priestly families, the scribes and the laity). Since a further consultation was held in the morning, it is fairly certain that here an unofficial, even an illegal, meeting was held, 'packed' with the high priest's friends.

The purpose was simple. It had already been resolved to put Jesus to death; the only problem was to find some justification for condemning Him on a capital charge. Jewish law required that concurrent testimony be given by at least two witnesses, and the charges against Jesus broke down because of conflicting evidence. Even the 'Temple' charges were too garbled to stand. That Jesus had spoken about it is clear (13.2; 15.29; John 2.19 ff.), and His words about erecting a new temple could be construed as a claim to Messiahship (2 Sam. 7.13; Zech. 6.12 f.). Perhaps this was what gave the high priest his cue to question Jesus Himself. Finally, when the high priest asked Him whether He claimed to be the Messiah, the Son of God, Jesus replied with an unequivocal 'Yes'; for the first time He made a plain, public avowal of His status. Then He proceeded to elucidate His statement by declaring, in words based on Psa. 110.1 and Dan. 7.13, that His human judges would see the Son of man exalted and coming with the clouds of heaven. This prophecy does not fix the second coming as taking place in the lifetime of Jesus' hearers; its point is that the exalted Son of man will one day act in judgement against the judges of Jesus.

The answer was enough to throw the high priest into a feigned paroxysm of horror at the blasphemy of Jesus claiming a seat at God's right hand, and the council forthwith condemned Him to death. But the sentence would need to be confirmed by a formal meeting, and it could be carried out only by the Roman governor since the Jews did not possess the right to inflict the death penalty (John 18.31). Meanwhile, some of the rougher characters began to goad Jesus to perform acts of 'second-sight', thus fulfilling Isa. 50.6.

For meditation: Bearing shame and scoffing rude,
In my place condemned He stood.

St. Mark 14.66-72　　　　　　　　　Peter denies Jesus

The record of the disciples in this Gospel is a sorry one. They had persistently misunderstood the teaching of Jesus, they had all forsaken Him and fled, one of them had turned traitor, and now the leader of the group openly denied Jesus.

The place where Jesus was tried was evidently a building with a central open courtyard from which the various rooms opened off.

Here Peter sat with the guards and servants beside a fire, and in its dim light a servant girl recognized him as somebody who had been seen in the company of the Nazarene—the title is here used contemptuously. In this dangerous situation, when a wrong word from Peter might have led to his being placed alongside Jesus in the court room, he chose the easy way out (which we would no doubt have chosen too) and denied that he knew anything about Jesus. Then he moved away to avoid further questioning. But he soon discovered that one lie leads to the necessity to tell others. The merciless interrogation went on as the maid, not easily to be put off, voiced her suspicions to the bystanders, and they turned on the unfortunate Peter. Somebody noticed his 'north country' accent which indicated plainly his association with Galilee where Jesus had won most of His support, and advanced this as a piece of evidence against him. Peter, caught out, began to protest vehemently that he did not know Jesus, and even called God to bear witness against him if he were not speaking the truth. Then the cock crew, and Peter remembered— and repented.

Peter, through Mark, humbly reveals himself at his weakest and worst. Not only for the early Church but for those of subsequent centuries it has provided a vital lesson for Christians under persecution. It does not condone Peter's denial, but it shows that even for such sin there is the possibility of repentance and forgiveness. 'If we are faithless, He remains faithful' (2 Tim. 2.13).

St. Mark 15.1-15   The Roman Trial

Business began very early in the day in the ancient world, and it would have been no more than about 6 a.m. when the Sanhedrin met officially to confirm its previous night's informal proceedings. The prisoner had then to be handed over to the Roman government for confirmation and execution of the sentence. Pontius Pilate, the prefect of Judea, was in Jerusalem for his customary visit during the Passover festival, and Jesus was brought before him. The charge against Him had now to be reframed and presented in a way that would make out Jesus to be a political danger to the Roman government. It was, therefore, as a pretender to the throne that Jesus appeared before Pilate.

C. H. Dodd has illuminated the non-committal answer of Jesus to Pilate by quoting from Scott's *Old Mortality*. Lauderdale, trying the Covenanter Ephraim Macbriar as a rebel asks: 'Were you at the battle of Bothwell Bridge?' 'I was.' 'Were you armed?' 'I was not— I went in my calling as a preacher of God's word, to encourage them that drew the sword in His cause.' 'In other words, to aid and abet the rebels?' *Thou hast said it.* So Jesus' answer was a disclaimer, although of course, in a deeper sense than Pilate could understand, the answer was 'Yes' (John **18**.33–38).

The chief priests then made further accusations, to which Jesus offered no reply, and Pilate probably realized that they were trumped-up charges. His plan to release Jesus misfired because the chief priests incited the crowd to seek the release of Barabbas, a revolutionary.

The flagrant disregard for justice shown by Pilate can easily be paralleled from the behaviour of other Roman governors: one has only to think of the picture of Verres in Sicily painted by Cicero. But many have felt that Pilate shows here a weak vacillating character quite out of harmony with the description of 'inflexible, merciless and obstinate' given to him by a contemporary. It is, however, by no means unlikely that Pilate should have baited the Jews over their desire to have him execute an innocent man and then adopted the course which seemed likely to cause least disturbance; in any case human life was cheap. It was a perfectly ordinary act of injustice, only this time it was the Son of God who suffered in person, as He does indirectly when the innocent are wronged (Matt. **25**.41–46).

St. Mark 15.16-32   The Crucifixion of Jesus

The crucifixion itself was preceded by mockery from the Roman soldiers who dressed up Jesus in a soldier's red cloak and a crown of thorns in imitation of the Emperor's purple robe and diadem and then proceeded to bully Him. He had claimed to be a king; let Him receive royal homage! The incident is precisely what would be expected from rough men of the time. The palace where the incident took place was either the fortress of Antonia built adjacent to the temple or the palace of Herod on the west of the city, probably the former. Equally uncertain is the site of the crucifixion; the vicinity of the Church of the Holy Sepulchre on the north of Jerusalem has the best claims. The fact that the sites of Jesus' death and burial are so uncertain shows how little importance was attached to these so-called holy places by the first Christians; they knew that what really mattered was that He was alive from the dead.

The cross was normally carried to the scene of execution by the condemned man himself (John **19**.17), but Jesus could not sustain its weight, and a passer-by was requisitioned to help. His sons are named because they were known to Mark's readers and could vouch

for the story; perhaps the Rufus in Rom. **16.**13 was one of them.
The wine was offered as a soporific. The condemned man's
clothes were customarily given to the executioners. The use of a
'titulus' to indicate the charge against the criminal was also customary. To the by-standers the crucifixion was the culminating proof of
Jesus' self-deception, but for Christian readers their words are
strongly ironical: in the weakness of the cross the power of God is
hidden (2 Cor. **13.4**).

So the story is told with stark simplicity. No obvious attempt is
made to interpret it as an atonement for sin. Yet the interpretation
of the story is written into it for those who know their Old Testament.
A study of Isa. **50.**6 f.; **53.**3,5; Prov. **31.**6; Psa. **69.**21; **22.**18; Lam.
2.15 and Psa. **22.**7 f. will show how heavily the narrative is impreg-
nated with allusions to the Old Testament descriptions of the
righteous sufferer and the suffering Servant. His death was according
to God's plan and purpose (Acts **2.**23). The fact that He was so to
suffer for us and for our salvation has already been made clear in
10.45 and **14.**24.

For meditation: Psalms 22 and 69.

St. Mark 15.33-39 The Death of Jesus

Jesus was crucified at the third hour, i.e. 9 a.m. At noon the land
became dark (possibly—it has been suggested—as the result of a
sirocco wind laden with thick dust from the desert obscuring the
sun) by divine decree. Its coming was perhaps symbolical of the
separation which Jesus felt from His Father and which He expressed
in the words of His cry from Psa. **22.1**. The words are given both in
Aramaic and in translation. The plain and obvious sense of the
words is as a cry of dereliction in which Jesus expressed His sense of
separation from God. They imply, on the one hand, that He expected God to deliver Him, and, on the other hand, that He felt
Himself cut off from God by being identified with the sin of the
world (2 Cor. **5.21**; 1 Pet. **2.24**).

The bystanders misunderstood the cry. There was a tradition that
Elijah would come to the help of pious Jews in distress, and some
deduced that Jesus was praying to Elijah. One man offered Him a
sponge dipped in the cheap wine that soldiers drank, to allay His
thirst (cf. Psa. **69.21**); if the action is not the same as that recorded
in Luke **23.36**, it may have been meant as a rough kindness. But the
end had now come, and Jesus breathed His last.

In direct connection with His death Mark records the splitting of
the Temple curtain. The event may have a twofold significance; was

it a sign that the prophecy quoted in v. 29 would be fulfilled, as well as a clear indication that the way into the presence of God was now opened for men (cf. Heb. 9.8–14; 10.19 f.)?

A second incident in connection with the death of Jesus was the saying of the Roman centurion in charge of the execution squad. His words can be translated as 'This man was *a* son of God' or 'This man was *the* Son of God'. The centurion *may* have meant only the former limited sense of the words, but Mark reckoned that, if so, he spoke more wisely than he knew, and regarded this as the supreme confession of Jesus in his Gospel. This is the message of the cross: it reveals Jesus as the Son of God who was obedient to God even to the point of death.

St. Mark 15.40-47   The Burial of Jesus

At first sight the brief note giving the names of the various women who were present does not add anything to the telling of the story and simply duplicates the list of names in 16.1. Its vital significance, however, is to show that the women who were the first witnesses of the resurrection, themselves saw Jesus die and consequently were not likely to be deceived as to the fact that He had really died. We are also reminded of the care which they gave to Jesus and His comrades in Galilee and on the way to Jerusalem (Luke 8.1–3). Three women are mentioned, Mary from Magdala on the west shore of Galilee, Mary the mother of James the younger (probably the same as James the son of Alphaeus, 3.18) and of Joses (Matt. 27.56 has 'Joseph'), and Salome, the wife of Zebedee (Matt. 27.56).

Normally the bodies of crucified criminals were left hanging and eventually cast into a common grave, but the friends of Jesus saw to it that He was saved from this indignity. Just before the Day of Preparation (Thursday sunset to Friday sunset) ended and ushered in the Sabbath, Joseph took measures which ensured that the Sabbath was not defiled by the crucifixion. Crucifixion was usually a painful, drawn-out process during which the victim might hover between life and death for two days or more. Pilate was therefore surprised by the speedy passing of Jesus, but when the fact of death had been confirmed, he readily allowed Joseph to give the body a decent burial according to the normal Jewish custom which Mark clearly describes for the benefit of Gentile readers who might well be unfamiliar with it.

Joseph of Arimathaea appears in this story as a true follower of Jesus who was 'looking for the kingdom of God' (43). Now this is a phrase which could be used of any Jew, since all Jews hoped for the intervention of God in their history to overcome the Romans. The fact that the phrase is used here especially of Joseph must indicate that he had a more spiritual view of the kingdom and accepted the teaching of Jesus about it. There is no reason whatever to suppose that he, any more than Nicodemus, approved of the Sanhedrin's decision to execute Jesus (John 7.50 f.), and we may be fairly sure that neither of them was wakened from his bed to take part in that illegal council meeting by night.

St. Mark 16.1-8   The Resurrection of Jesus

Although Jesus had spoken about His resurrection to His disciples, they had not understood what He meant, and nobody expected what actually happened. The disciples were plunged into grief (cf. 2.20), and the women prepared to carry our the last rites as soon as possible; it may seem strange that they waited so long in view of the haste with which decomposition proceeds in warm countries, but John 19.39 f. may suggest that the body was embalmed. What was to be a final display of devotion ended in a flight of fear. Note the points of emphasis: *amazement* at the removal of a massive stone, heightened by an angel's presence and message, culminating in '*trembling*' and '*astonishment*'—'they were *afraid*' and '*fled*'. A sense of terror overwhelms a message of triumph.

If you were writing a Gospel for the first time, where would you end the story? With the death of Jesus, with the announcement of the resurrection, with the resurrection appearances of Jesus, with the ascension, with the story of His continuing spiritual presence with the Church, or where? Here at the end of v. 8 is where the Gospel of Mark apparently concludes, and the problem is whether this is where Mark intended to conclude it or whether he wrote (or intended to write) more (as the writer of the supplement in vs. 9–20 evidently believed). Is this a fitting conclusion?

Whatever be the answer to these questions, this is where the Gospel ends according to the best manuscripts and it is appropriate to see what this abrupt ending has to teach us. The fear and amazement which the first witnesses felt is in sharp contrast to what we almost regard as an expected and necessary occurrence. They were *terrified*. Here was revealed the power of God.

Second, the story puts before us the fact of the empty tomb; the women saw that there was no body there. This is of infinite importance. *If the tomb was not empty, then Jesus had not risen.* Of course the empty tomb by itself is not the sole or sufficient proof of the resurrection, but without it there could not be a resurrection.

Third, the story promises the appearance of Jesus to His disciples without actually recording an appearance which might seem to fix His risen presence to one particular spot in history. Still today He continues to reveal Himself to His disciples in their hearts, and they know that He is alive. Can you confess 'He lives—within *my* heart'?

St. Mark 16.9-20   The Appearances of Jesus

Our best ancient authorities for the text of the Gospel of Mark end at 16.8, and there can be no doubt that what follows (written as it is in a different style) does not come from the pen of John Mark. But very early the Gospel was felt to be incomplete, and more than one attempt was made to provide it with a fitting conclusion. The most popular of these attempts appears as vs. 9–20 in our older English versions.

We are here given a brief résumé of the appearances of Jesus after His resurrection. Vs. 9–11 summarize the appearance to Mary of Magdala (Luke 24.1–11; John 20.11–18), and vs. 12f. obviously refer to the story of the walk to Emmaus (Luke 24.13–35); the note that Jesus appeared 'in another form' explains why the disciples did not recognize Him, and the statement that the others did not believe is probably based on Luke 24.41. The final paragraphs (14–20) join together the contents of Matt.28.16–20 and Luke 24.36–53, but add some fresh information. Here alone we have the fuller note on the significance of baptism as the proper outward expression of Christian belief. Note that condemnation is for those who do not *believe*; while baptism is the proper expression of faith, lack of it does not lead to condemnation. The unspoken corollary is that baptism without faith has no saving power. Here too there is the promise of the miraculous powers which the early Church experienced as it preached the gospel.

Noteworthy in this section is the emphasis on the unbelief of the disciples. It required the most rigorous evidence to convince them of the resurrection. Faith must rest on firm foundations, and the foundations for faith in the resurrection have been carefully tested and shown to be built on solid rock. A second point is that the disciples were slow to realize the implications of going to 'the whole creation' (15) and at first confined their attention to the Jews.

So the story ends. But v. 20 makes it clear that the story is still in progress. The same Lord is still at work to confirm the message. Is this Gospel a 'good news' for us personally and for the world in which we live? If we do not pause to ask and answer this question we have missed the whole point of what we have read.

Questions for further study and discussion on Mark 14.53–16.20

1. What was the difference between the betrayal by Peter and the betrayal by Judas? Why was Peter forgiven and not Judas?
2. In what ways do the Gospels show that Jesus suffered as an innocent victim?
3. How were the Scriptures fulfilled in the incidents surrounding the death of Jesus (see references in note on 15.16–32)?
4. Have opponents of the resurrection any grounds for arguing that Jesus never really died?
5. If Mark's Gospel had perished, what would we have lost from our knowledge of Jesus that cannot be found in the other Gospels? What is distinctive in Mark's portrait of Jesus?

St. Luke

The Author. All the evidence supports the view that the third Gospel was written by the physician Luke, friend and fellow-traveller of Paul. Style, outlook and language identify him as the writer of the Acts of the Apostles. External evidence, from archaeological and epigraphical studies, marks the same writer as one familiar with the world of the first century, and as the careful historian which he claims to be(1.1–4).

Granted that Luke wrote both books, a plain reading of the text supports the statement that he was familiar with medical literature, and was with Paul during part of his travels (note the pronoun 'we' in Acts **16.**10–17; **20.**5–15; **21.**1–18; **27.**1–**28.**16). If so, Luke's close connection with Philippi is clear, a fact which in no way denies a familiarity with Antioch.

Luke was probably the only Gentile contributor to the New Testament, a fine historian in his own right, an admirable reporter (read The Walk To Emmaus, The Riot in Ephesus, The Wreck of the Grain Ship) and an ardent Paulinist, who appreciated the great apostle's global outlook, and, in the light of it, was attracted by the universality of Christ, His appeal to high and low, His interest in Gentiles, and the attraction of His gospel for women.

The Patron. Luke begins both of his books in the manner of a Greek historian, and with a dedication. For this reason alone Theophilus must be regarded as a real person. He may have been an official of standing, whose support Luke needed to win, for a project he had was to establish the fact that Christianity was not seditious. He also sought to win him to Christ, and the apparent growth in familiarity between the two dedications, suggests that Luke may have indeed won his friend. There is no means of knowing who Theophilus was.

The Authorities. While Paul was in Roman custody at Caesarea in the late fifties, Luke had time to find eye-witnesses. He penetrated the circle of John the Baptist, and may have interviewed the aged Mary. Hence the precious opening chapters with their unique hymns; hence the flash of light on the Lord's childhood.

He may have had access to Mark's material, which, if the recent fragment from Qumran proves of early date, could have been circulating by the mid-century. Luke was with Paul when Mark was present (Col. **4.**10,14; Philem. 24). He met James, such unknown disciples as the Emmaus couple, and many others of the 'Third Force' in Palestine, whose testimony went back to the Baptist's wilderness revival.

The Book. Hence a book in Greek of some polish with tracts of new

167

information, clusters of stories like that of The Prodigal and The Samaritan, the opening chapters, the Emmaus walk. There are new emphases already mentioned, on prayer, on the ministry of womankind, on gentleness. He spares Peter the record of his 'cursing' (22.54–62), and his petulant word on physicians, passed to Mark (8.43, see Mark 5.26)... It is a great book, the second of the narratives to see publication—probably very early in the sixties, and a by-product of Paul's imprisonment. It had a Gentile public in mind, and was a major contribution to Paul's ministry.

St. Luke 1.1–25

Verses 1—4 are a remarkable piece of Greek written in the manner of the best Greek historians. Luke was conscious that he was engaged upon a task of vast historical importance. He dedicated to it all he had—a polished style, diligence, and a careful, ordered mind. God does His work with human qualities, human skills and human worth committed to His creative hands.

Verses 5—7 tell of beauty and tragedy. "In the days of Herod the king", in his last days, in fact, when a cruel and cynically evil life was hastening to its dissolution in madness and blood, there were good and godly folk in Israel. So it had always been (1 Kings **19**.18). The Remnant is always alive, and it is an honour, in any Herod's day, to belong to the Few.

Verses 8—13 record a wondrous experience (see Exod. **30**.7,8). All members of Aaron's tribe were priests and took a turn to make the daily sacrifice, and call a blessing upon the assembled multitude. It was a rare privilege, the high moment of his career, and, when Zechariah's great day came he went, no doubt, with consciousness of the awesome occasion and a heart prepared. God met him in the place of duty and the hour of worship. He brought the burden of his childlessness to the altar and found his burden lifted there.

Verses 14—17 throw light on the fulfilment of prophecy. The closing words of Hebrew scripture (Mal. **4**.5,6) had promised the return of the fiery Elijah. The Lord Himself pointed out (Matt. **11**.14) that this oracle was fulfilled in the fiery John (John **5**.35). It is an interesting study to list the similarities between the two careers, eight centuries apart, and to note the likenesses of character between the two men.

Verses 18—23 reveal more of the good man. Voiceless and over-whelmed, Zechariah nevertheless continued to the end of his tour of duty. He gave the people the formal blessing and needed no words to convey a message which overawed them. A personality committed to God and owned by His Spirit can itself touch and sanctify other lives. *Note:* In His new revelation, God does not break with the past: He uses a *priest*, in the *temple*, in fulfilment of *prophecy*. The Old is the cradle of the New.

St. Luke 1.26–45

Verses 26—38 tell the story of the Virgin Birth. Read Matt. **1**.18—25, and it must immediately be obvious that the New Testament asserts that the birth of the Lord was miraculous. There is no "controversy" as some are ready to assert. The narrative must be accepted as true or rejected as false. And if the Christian faith began thus in deception or in subterfuge it is difficult to see how Christianity can defend its validity, or the New Testament retain its authority. Read Luke's account with care, lingering over verse 35, and it will be seen that he agrees entirely with Matthew. John, by implication, says the same (John 1.14). Let it also be remembered that it stands proven, especially from his second book, that Luke was a careful and painstaking historian. While Paul was imprisoned in Caesarea (Acts 24,25) he had two years to pursue his researches and to question witnesses. In this account there stands obviously what the apostles believed and what Mary stated.

Verses 39—45 present a vivid picture cf Mary. She too was one of the Remnant, and was chosen for her faithfulness—not doubting for a moment the promise of God (45). The "blessed" virgin has sometimes been denied her proper due of reverence and regard by those rightly anxious to avoid the attribution of divine honours to a human person. She had to face the malice and slander of men (John 8.41). When God entrusts one of His servants with a task it is seldom easy. It is always glorious.

The significance of the Virgin Birth is deep. God thus demonstrated a connection with mankind and a discontinuity with it; or, in other words, that the Messiah was one with the men He came to save but unique in His heavenly origin. And strong support of that unique entrance into the human state is given by the fact that the human life which follows was like no other life. It is "a touchstone of faith in the mystery of God incarnate" (V. C. Grounds). Can effective faith survive its rejection?

Notes: V. 26: Nazareth was the original home of Mary, not the adopted home, as one might assume from Matt. 2.23. V. 28: "O favoured one", said Gabriel. The Latin version translates "O full of grace", and on this appellation has been based the teaching of her mediatorship. However, these words imply the *reception* of "grace" or favour, and not the ability to bestow it.

St. Luke 1.46–56

Mary was stirred to song, and the pattern of the hymn was poetry and imagery from the Old Testament. Study carefully Hannah's hymn of praise in 1 Sam. 2. Follow also the theme of "God's poor" into Isaiah. The *Magnificat*, as this song is called from its first word in the Latin version, is an answer to those who allege a division between Christ and the common man, and a reproach for those who, from time to time through the ages, have sought to sequester the faith, as both

Sadducee and Pharisee did with Judaism, and make it the sole preserve of the privileged in wealth or knowledge.

Mary spoke as one of the common folk of Palestine (51,52). It was a land of shocking poverty, overcrowded, pressing hard upon its poor resources of food and water, as ravaged with hunger and want as India is today. And yet it was among the masses of the land that the deep currents of faithful religion ran. From Elijah to Amos God had spoken through the simple people of the countryside. He was not without witness in high places, and Isaiah is an illustration; but His word found readier resting place where no affluence had bred sloth and materialism, and where the sharp pressure of need had kept men humble and dependent. It is a subduing study to trace through Isaiah to Amos, to the gospels and James' epistle, the condemnation of wealth. Consider this theme. The Bible has its men of substance, from Barzillai to Joseph of Arimathea. What is the decisive factor, and the aspect of wealth, which Christ despised, and God condemns, and which man should fear? Why do the rich go empty away (53)? Empty of what good things? Which parables point this vital question?

Consider Mary in conclusion. Her true status should be recognized. While denying her worship, Christians do well to honour Mary as the noblest woman of all time. Verse 48 envisages Mary's own expectation that all history would regard her as favoured above all her kind. Gabriel and Elizabeth had voiced like opinions. Her devotion, humility, and utter self-surrender are the marks of her worth. Observe God's care for her, and His provision of help in the hour of undoubted trial.

Mary's authority, it should be remembered, lies behind this account. Analyse the chapter, and note its careful construction of speech and fact, poetry and prose. Luke's researches are nowhere better illustrated. They vindicate his claim to write "in order" (1.3).

St. Luke 1.57—80
John means "God's gift" or "God is gracious", and marks the humble thanks of a devoted couple for the privilege of bringing life into the world. A simple faith deepens joy and makes all living significant. Man loses the finer facets of his mind when he thinks of his life as aimless, as meaningless beyond his narrow span of years, and his actions as without responsibility to God.

After the Virgin's hymn comes that of the priest, rich in his pondering over the great prophecies of his race, and solemn with the cadences and poetry of the Old Testament. Take a reference Bible, and follow word by word back into the Hebrew Scriptures the

171

thoughts and phraseology of Zechariah's song of worship and of praise. Rich dependence on Scripture is the mark of a good hymn, and the analysis of this priestly poem might conclude with some consideration of what hymns in our own collections best conform to the lofty standards set in the chapter.

Zechariah had high ambitions for his son, but they were interwoven with his zeal for God. With the old oracle of Malachi (4.5) in view, the good priest understood that his son was the forerunner of the Messiah. He probably understood as little as his son did after him the true nature of the Messiah's ministry. Consider soberly this thought. A full, clear understanding of what God is doing or outworking in life and duty is not necessary for the faithful prosecution of the task laid upon His servants. He always does "exceeding abundantly above all we can ask or think"; His ways ("plans", Moffatt translates it) are always infinitely above ours (Isa. 55.9). How inevitable it is that finite and time-bound man should be baffled by the thoughts and purposes of infinite wisdom, and how necessary that humility, which follows step by step, and does immediately what lies ready to do, should be the quality most needed.

John, the chapter concludes, was "in the deserts" until his tremendous ministry began. The Qumran community by the Dead Sea was one only of many such groups which were at home in the wilderness (e.g., Isa. 40.3; Heb. 11.9), and John undoubtedly owed much to the "Protestants of the Wilderness". Whether he knew Qumran, and drew his knowledge of Isaiah from the actual scroll which reposes in the Hebrew Shrine of the Scrolls, and has been seen in a number of centres in the West, is an interesting speculation.

St. Luke 2.1—20

Verses 1—7. A tattered piece of papyrus found in Egypt contains the sort of notice which Joseph, the carpenter, must have read in Nazareth. It commands all people living away from their place of origin to report back to their home town authorities for the census. Before the torn document breaks off it speaks of provisioning arrangements for overcrowded conditions. The Egyptian document dates from a century later than the enrolment conducted by the Roman diplomat Quirinius (Cyrenius). This event probably took place in the autumn of 5 B.C., for those who, as late as A.D. 525, established the chronology of Christianity, made a slight error in calculating the date. (Those who seek further information will find it in an appendix to *The Century of the New Testament*, by the writer of these Notes.) But ponder awhile the human situation. Joseph, at this time of stress of

172

waiting, had to take his wife to Bethlehem. He did not realize that, in fulfilling the normal and irksome obligations of daily life, he was also fulfilling a plan of God. The first obligation of godly living is to do properly that which we are obliged to do "Live worthily as citizens of the Gospel of Christ," says Paul (Phil. **1**.27).

Verses 8—15. It was fitting that the proclamation of the Messiah's coming should first be made to the simple folk of the land. The story of the New Testament moved through the cities of the world. Some twenty-three cities appear in it. The Old Testament moves through wilderness and countryside. Four cities only have prominence: Babylon, symbol of evil; Nineveh, the capital of the hideous Assyrians; Samaria, city of Ahab and Jehu, flayed by Amos; and Jerusalem, which, in the Lord's phrase, "slew the prophets". Amos came from a peasant's task; Elijah lived on Carmel; John preached in the wilderness. The shepherds were the old stock of Israel, uncorrupted by wealth, unspoiled by city living. God bypassed established religion and announced Christ's coming to the peasants. *Notes:* Vs. 1—5: Sir Wm. Ramsay's *Was Christ Born in Bethlehem?* shows how Luke's trustworthiness as a historian can be vindicated here. V. 7: possibly the best 'guest room' was occupied by Bethlehem's most distinguished contemporary, Hillel, the great Pharisee, with Simeon his son—they were of David's line. V. 8: not a winter scene— Dec. 25 was chosen in the 4th century to overlay a pagan festival. V. 9: the "glory of the Lord"—compare Exod. **24**.16, Num. **14**.10.

St. Luke 2.21–35

Verses 21—24. The theme of the previous paragraph resumes. Joseph was a simple man whose whole life and religion consisted of doing what he ought to do—honestly, faithfully, and uncomplainingly. God needs more men like him. The Law prescribed certain obligations, and in its mercy brought the requirements of sacrifice within the reach of God's poor (Ex. **13**.12; Num. **8**.17; Lev. **12**.8). Jerusalem was on the way home, a fact for which the good man, no doubt, thanked God. He travelled north over the hills to Jerusalem, saw the fine view of the city and its temple from the high ridge of the Mount of Olives, went in through the gate which was to be called Saint Stephen's gate, after Christ's first martyr, and brought the Child to the temple. The consecration of the firstborn was a provision of the Law designed to cut at the root many foul practices of child sacrifice in the cults of paganism. It was a moving moment when the Lord came thus to His temple. He was to come again "like a refiner's fire".

173

Verses 25—35. One sensitive soul penetrated God's secret. Faith was not dead in the land, for all the cynical commercialization of religion by the Sadducees, for all the cluttering of simple things by man-made regulation by the Pharisees. The Remnant of the Old Testament is a theme for study. God has always had His few. We have already met Mary and Joseph, and the parents of John the Baptist. The religion of pomp and ceremony turned on Christ, and sought to carry on Herod's work of destruction. The faithful, undistinguished, and unrecognized of men received Him. Simeon was one of the honoured few. He was familiar with the Scriptures. Note his quotation of Isaiah (42. 6 and 7), which puts him in the tradition of John the Baptist. It is also a fact that the people of Qumran, the wilderness sect who hid the Dead Sea Scrolls, were devotees of Isaiah. The insight of Simeon flowed from his knowledge of the Word. Such insight always will.

Note: V. 25: the image is that of a servant bidden wait through the darkness and announce the day—*cf.* Isa. **60.**1,2; Mal. **4.**2. V.35: the challenge of Christ causes men to reveal their true attitudes. Think of the trial scene and how it revealed the secret selves of every actor in it.

Prayer: Give us, O Lord, understanding of Thy Word, that through its wisdom we, too, may be wise.

St. Luke 2.36—52

Verses 36—40. Another of God's Remnant enters the story, this time an aged woman, but with insight akin to Simeon's. There is no end to usefulness. John wrote his gospel in his nineties. Anna was 84. Or, if the phrase means that she had been a widow for that total of years, she could have been well over a century old. She gave her life to prayer, and the old can always serve in this way. But let it be borne in mind that most people, for good or ill, are much the same in age and declining years as they have been through life. If Anna's extreme old age was prayerful, it is a fair inference that she had always been prayerful. Thanks to the triumph of medicine it is given to more and more to know long retirement and old age. God's plan for the evening should be the concern of the afternoon. Spend some time studying the old folk of the Bible.

Verses 41—52. This is a revealing picture of the pious Nazareth family, journeying to Jerusalem and remaining for the full length of the festival. Perhaps there was strong reason for this visit. A Jewish boy was accounted of responsible age at twelve years. He became "a son of the Law", and assumed a dress more proper to maturity. Joseph and Mary were forced to abandon the Galilee caravan which ensured their safety, and hasten back only to find a Child Whom they must have felt they hardly knew. A new dignity had come upon Him, and there was now a part of Him which they were unable to penetrate. Mary "kept all these sayings in her heart", and we can almost hear her telling Luke the story. But is not Christ always thus? Could any earthly character have engaged the wonder, the love, and the questing of man as He has done? Does any earthly character grow ever more awesome, as He did among those that knew Him, without ever revealing flaw, fault, or weakness? The character of Christ is the strongest proof of the Deity of Christ. Consider this.

Notes: V. 48: in civil law and everyday language Joseph was the father. Specious arguments against the miraculous birth are founded upon this verse. Luke saw no contradiction between the words and what had already been written, nor is there any. V. 49: the R.V. rendering, "in My Father's house", is correct.

Questions for Further Study and Discussion on St. Luke chapters 1, 2.
1. In what ways did John fulfil the prophecy of Malachi 4.5,6?
2. How do John and Paul support the doctrine of the Virgin Birth (*e.g.*, John 1, 3, 10; Rom. 5; 1 Cor. 15)?
3. How do these chapters illustrate the character of those "in whom He is well pleased"?
4. How does John in his gospel and first epistle develop the image of light and darkness (1.79, etc.)?
5. To whom does God reveal Himself? What are the barriers to such revelation?
6. How do the opening chapters of Luke link together the two Testaments? Consider scenes, character, expression.

St. Luke 3.1–9

Verses 1—3. Here is Luke, the careful and exact historian, speaking. It has been demonstrated, first by the scholarship of Sir William Ramsay, that he was precisely that. He lists the rulers who held sway, from the old Emperor Tiberius to Caiaphas, priest of Jewry. The princes and prelates did not know that they formed merely the background for the events which really mattered. Of deep and lasting significance was the great religious revival led by John. It was no less. His preaching-place was the wide river-valley of the lower Jordan near Jericho. It is likely enough that John had spent years of preparation in the company of the sects of the wilderness. A few miles from the place of baptism was the community of Qumran, the people of the Dead Sea Scrolls. It is possible today, in the Hebrew University of

Jerusalem, to see their roll of Isaiah, one of the many documents which they hid in the caves when the Romans were pacifying the Jordan valley in the Great Rebellion of A.D. 66—70. It is possible that John himself saw it, for it was in use in his day.

Verses 4—9. Isaiah was more than once upon John's lips. He knew that his preaching was a fulfilment of prophecy. Using the splendid poetry of the prophet, he pictured himself as the herald of a king. There was a note of fierceness in the preaching of John which bears the mark of the Old Testament rather than of the New. Snatching a figure of speech from the scrub fire of the Jordan wilderness, from whose running flame the hidden vipers of the undergrowth darted to safety, John castigated the Pharisees and Sadducees (Matt. 3.7), thrashed Jewish nationalism and pride, and demanded repentance. Israel's largest forest-land, the Jordan jungle, provided him with the image of the axe. Repentance, its reality and demonstration, was his theme, and gentler and more loving though the persuasion of the Christian evangelist may be, repentance is still the prerequisite for all blessing, for acceptance, for salvation. *Demonstrate this from Christ's teaching.*

Notes: Vs. 1,2: compare Matt. 3.1, and note how carefully Luke links his gospel to world history. Annas had been deposed by the Romans, but was recognized by the people. V. 3: Baptism had been confined to proselytes, but it was familiar as a symbol of purification (Ezek. 36.25*ff.*, Zech. 13.1). Vs. 7,8: no substitute for repentance!

St. Luke 3.10—20

Verses 10—14. The call to repentance which was the point and appeal of John's preaching was no abstract doctrine. Boldly and simply John showed that religion had a form and shape in the conduct of every man, and in each day's living. Each mode of life has its peculiar temptations. Some are more prone to, and more exposed to, the temptations of the flesh; others to the faults of the spirit. Each personality, each trade or profession, has its own pitfalls. A genuine desire to have done with sin—and repentance is nothing else than this —finds its first expression in the immediate environment, in the first and nearest confrontation with the enemy of good. It is for society to adapt itself to the requirements of the Gospel, not for the Gospel to adapt itself to society. That is what those who journeyed to the west bank of the Jordan to hear John found.

Verses 15—20. The response of those who heard the desert preacher was as it has always been. There were those who saw the hand of God, and heard the accents of the Holy Spirit. They questioned, indeed, whether the great event of God's ultimate revelation might not have come. For them John had a clear and unequivocal word. Christ was another, and Christ was coming, and Christ would, by His very presence, reveal the worthless and the worthy, and separate the evil from the good. But others reacted as men still do. Fearlessly John had rebuked sin in high places. Herod had with him, in illicit union, the ambitious, scheming woman who had been married to Philip (a brother to be distinguished from Philip the tetrarch, who lived quietly in Rome). When Herod was in Rome, Herodias trapped him, and fled with him. She was to ruin his life. Her story is worth reading for its warning. It would have been better had Herod listened and repented.

Note: V. 11: the injunction to charity had its place in the fiery prophet's preaching. There is a world of difference between due severity in the preaching of the Gospel, and that bitterness which only engenders hardness of heart. Not all who renounce the world do so with sound motives, and where these are twisted the condemnation of sin becomes an exercise in hostility.

St. Luke 3.21–38

Verses 21, 22. The words mean no more than that Jesus waited until the mass movement of John's revival was past. He sought no spectacular publicity. John's thought moved in the orbit of the great Isaiah, and God, as He ever does, met him on the level of his thought: "Oh, that Thou wouldst rend the heavens and come down," the prophet had cried (**64.**1), and so it came to pass.

Verses 23—38. The genealogy makes dull reading for us. To the Jews it would have been of the utmost importance. Detailed records were kept at Jerusalem. Hillel, who lived at this time, had no difficulty in demonstrating his Davidic descent. There are Polynesians, alive today, who, without written records, can recite their descent to remote centuries. The difficulty of Matthew's variant genealogy is felt only by the modern world, inadequately informed about Jewish practice. It is obvious that Matthew and Luke, with access to the same information, and writing in the same generation, would not knowingly contradict each other. It is clear that they must have followed different plans. Matthew gives Joseph's line, while making it clear that Jesus was not Joseph's son, because Joseph was Jesus' legal father, a point important for more than one reason in Jewish law. It was also necessary to establish the fact that Mary had married within the tribe. Legislation mentioned in the closing chapters of Numbers shows the necessity for this to be clear. Luke almost certainly gives the genealogy of Mary. Joseph, not Mary, is given as the immediate descendant of Eli because Joseph authenticated Mary's inheritance by the Numbers legislation (27.1—11, 36.1—13). It is probable that more exact information would establish some ritual of adoption in such cases. Note that Matthew takes the line back to David; Jesus was *King*. Luke takes it to Adam; Jesus was the *Son of Man*, the world's Saviour, not the Jews' alone. Luke, the friend of Paul, has the world in view. He has just spoken of the baptism, necessary only as the sign of the identification of the Sinless One with sinful man. *We* have our part and place here.

Note: For a full discussion of the issues raised by the genealogy, see Gresham Machen's *The Virgin Birth*, pp. 203*ff*.

St. Luke 4.1–13

Behind the palms, cypress, and jacaranda of the town of Jericho, a mile back from the arid mound which covers the remains of a dozen ancient fortresses on the old, historic site, stands a harsh, bare mountain on the edge of the Judaean wilderness. This is the traditional place of Christ's temptation.

How was He to conduct His ministry? As the wonder-worker, able to feed a hungry multitude and turn the stones to bread? The host will follow those who feed them, as He Himself once said (John 6.26). Was He to seek the path of worldly influence and power in wider spheres than the little land? And as He wrestled with this thought perhaps He saw what He had often seen from the high uplifted edge of hills where Nazareth stood. The vast level floor of Esdraelon lies beneath. It was a highway of all nations. Egyptian, Assyrian, Babylonian, Greek and Roman had marched that way. Alive and vivid in His memory was the vision of the "kingdoms of the world", seen again "in a moment of time". Palestine was small, obscure, trampled by the vast empires.

And then Jerusalem. Should He stand aloft on the temple top, and shatter all the scorn and incredulity of men by demonstrating His faith in Scripture, and His own Messiahship? The storm raged through Him, for He was "tempted in all ways as we are", and it is only those who do not yield who know the ultimate impact of the testing.

Matthew changes the order of the trials. And how true it is that temptation is repetitive, varied, resourceful. A mind is behind temptation, organizing the attack, in open confrontation or in ambush, varying the assault, probing for the weak places, returning, switching the attacking thrust now here, now there. . . . And for long weeks it continued as He threw back the fierce invasion, and answered with Scripture each twisted argument. We are safe when we can so reply.

Notes: Heb. **4.**15 suggests that this was not the only temptation. The temptation in the wilderness was an assault on Jesus as Messiah rather than as Man. Vs. 5—8: the repudiation of the Jewish idea of the Messiah is involved here. V. 10: Psalm **91.**11,12 was regarded as addressed to the Messiah.

St. Luke 4.14–22

He Who came from Nazareth, and belied the reputation of the town (John **1.**46), came back again. Luke begins his story of Christ's ministry at this point, but much had already happened to bring fame and reverence to His name. The times are uncertain, but events recorded up to Mark **6,** Matthew **13,** and John **4** had probably already taken place. Verse 23 shows that Luke was aware of this.

Isaiah was an appropriate book. Since John's ministry Isaiah had been active in the minds of men. The passage read was Isa. **61.**1,2, with a phrase from Isa. **58.**6, though, perhaps, in the roll from which the Lord read, those words were included in the later passage. The Lord thus took up the theme of John, with one significant variation. John had spoken, and rightly spoken, of judgment. The Lord stressed the fact that the Day of God's grace postponed the final hour of retribution.

His method was dramatic. The passage should be read in Isaiah where, in all versions, it will be plain that the Lord broke off His reading in the midst of a verse. He can only have meant that "the day of vengeance of our God" was not yet. He could have chosen no more effective demonstration to impress upon all that a new age of God's grace was opening, and that no liberating crusade against the enemies of Israel was at hand.

Mercifully the day of acceptance continues. The poor are still found in an affluent society, though, like those of Laodicea, "rich and increased with goods", they are not always aware of what God deems poverty (Rev. **3.**17); the broken-hearted are multitudinous—lives soured by rejection, chilled by disappointment, disillusioned by love, because true love was misconceived; the captives, bound by evil habits, day and night under the mastery of alcohol, nicotine, drugs, or the masterful lusts of the flesh; the blind, who see no pervasive Presence in the loveliness of the world, no wider life beyond the grave, nothing save that which can be felt, looked at, heard or tasted; the bruised in spirit are a multitude who still need liberty from obsessive fears, gnawing hate, imprisoning bitterness . . . *Christ's offer stands.*

179

Notes: The incident here is very probably that described in Mark **6.1—6** and Matt. **13.53—58.** V. 17: "there was given to Him"—Gk., "further handed to Him"—*i.e.*, after the reading of the Law. V. 18: a free version, based on the Septuagint.

St. Luke 4.23–30

Luke is often a master of succinct irony. Look at his quiet description of the crowd at Ephesus (Acts **19.32**). The same hand wrote verse 22. Charmed in their despite, the folk of Nazareth wondered at the gracious words of Christ. Then in an upsurge of bitter jealousy they realized that He was one of them, "Joseph's son", who worked with plane and saw along the street. The utter irrelevance of the thought is the centre of its tragedy.

So it comes about that those nearest to the proffered blessing fail often to lay hold of it. Others—the Phoenician widow, the Syrian soldier—receive it. And it is here evident why Luke, the associate of Paul, who shared the great apostle's vision of a global Gospel, chose to set this incident in the forefront of his story. Here was the Jewish response to the evangel, which was repeated with monotonous regularity throughout the ministry of Paul, revealing its tragic shape thus early in the ministry of Christ. The mention of Zarephath and Naaman suggested the appeal to the Gentiles.

This prospect was revolting to the nationalistic Jew. The Lord had refused an idle demonstration of His power in Nazareth. That is what they demanded, and the explanation of His words in verse 23 lies here. Matthew (**13.58**) remarks that their unbelief prevented His doing such deeds among them. And now His reference to the faith of Gentiles supplied the spark. In a flame of hate they thrust Him to the cliff-top with murder in their hearts. Nazareth lies in a hollow in a ridge of hills. The Mount of Precipitation, a likely enough site, presents a precipitous face to the Esdraelon plain. A score of biblical sites ring the vast landscape. The Nazarenes added another. Compare Acts **13.46,50; 22.21,22.**

The Lord departed, as He departed from Gadara. It is possible to reject salvation in the very presence of Christ. And with fatal finality. He never came back to Nazareth. Carefully compare the story in the other two gospels.

Notes: There is no contradiction between vs. 22 and 28. When the crowd began to talk, the evil words of the jealous (23) gained control. The morality of a crowd tends to be that of its lowest components. V. 29: "throw Him down headlong"—a form of stoning, the punishment for blasphemy.

St. Luke 4.31–44

Verses 31—37. The ruins of Capernaum lie at the head of the lake whose level waters gleam through the screen of trees. There is a large remnant of an ancient synagogue. Hadrian tore down all the synagogues of Galilee when he finally crushed the second Jewish rebellion in A.D. 132 and 133, but foundations are not easily destroyed. There is little else—a few broken columns and shattered walls, some worn fragments of olive presses. The lizards run over the warm stone (Matt. **11**.23).

The "devil-possession" mentioned in the story must not be too lightly dismissed. There are phenomena of evil not adequately explained by psychology. The horrors of Voodooism, with the sudden seizure of bystanders by some alien influence, which obliterates personality, changes the voice, and imposes modes of behaviour quite remote from normal, is one manifestation of something unseen not easily explained in familiar scientific terms. Other exotic cults, ancient and modern, display similar inexplicable phenomena. But suppose the "devil-possessed" of the New Testament narratives were actually suffering from forms of recognizable mental illness—how else could the Lord have cured them save on the level of their knowledge and their faith? He healed one blind man on the basis of his belief that the spittle of a saint was curative (John **9**.6). It is part of His grace that He meets us where our faith can operate. Otherwise, indeed, "how helpless and hopeless we sinners had been."

Verses 38—44. This passage has inspired many hymns. The hot sun had dropped behind the hills of Galilee. The lake was silver in the twilight, and the snow of Hermon to the north-east pink in the last light. He came from Peter's house where His cool touch had healed a good woman of her sickness, and though it was late found time to put His hands "on each one of them" (40). He did not heal in groups, but met each one in the place of need. Where love and grace meet faith and hope, at that point is salvation. We gather together for worship, but we meet Christ alone for the soul's healing.

Notes: V. 34: "us"—note the plural personality implied. Compare other similar occasions. Vs. 38,39: as an efficient doctor, Luke distinguishes, as the textbooks did, a great from a small fever. Vs. 40,41: the Sabbath ended with sunset. V. 43: the "kingdom"—the "kingly rule".

St. Luke 5.1–11

Forms of mystic interpretation which make Scripture strange and remote have done their worst with this human story. The deep water

181

(4) is represented as the Gentile world; Peter's reluctance to put out as a foreshadowing of the story in Acts where he was led in his despite to bring the message to the Gentiles, a hesitation only overcome by the Lord's specific command . . .

Such strained exegesis harms preaching and withdraws the Gospel from ordinary men and women, who desperately need it. The Bible is meant to be understood, and any form of interpretation which destroys simplicity may be commonly dismissed forthwith as human perversity.

The story, in fact, is exquisitely simple. The low shore of the lake runs south towards Tiberias in a wavering line, once crowded with the busy fishermen of Capernaum. It was here that the first disciples were called, vigorous and able men, active in Galilee's chief industry, and converts, it seems, of John's great religious awakening, which had deeply marked the common people of the land. Christ taught in the place of business, amid all the coming and going along the line of little bays. So the Church's message, rightly emphasized, touches all life. Christ, Who had preached in Capernaum's synagogue, went also to Capernaum's fishermen at their place of labour.

Peter obeyed, though he saw no meaning in the command, and in the great haul of fish he saw, as he had never seen before, not even at the time of healing in his home, the glory of the Lord. His first reaction was like that of Isaiah (Isa. 6.5), an overwhelming consciousness of unworthiness, inadequacy, and sin. Ever ready in such emergencies to rush to speech (Mark 9.5,6; John 21.3), Peter begged Christ to leave him. It is the heart's desire (Psa. 37.4) which God regards, not the stumbling fashion of our words. Look on to verse 32. Let us bow the head with Peter: *Lord, touch our lives with healing. Be with us, a challenging and cleansing Presence, where we work. Let us hear Thy voice in business. Let our unworthiness wither in Thy fellowship.*

Note: Observe several marks of Luke's authorship: he calls Gennesaret a "lake"—his less-travelled fellow-evangelists call it a "sea"; he uses a technical medical term ("full of leprosy"); he gives prominence to the call of Peter, the apostle in whom the Gentile world was particularly interested.

Questions for Further Study and Discussion on St. Luke chapters 3—5.11.

1. How does Luke's gospel reflect the world outlook of Paul?
2. What conclusions are to be drawn from ch. 4 about (*i*) the existence of Satan, (*ii*) his power, and (*iii*) the limits to that power? In what ways does this incident help us when we are tempted?

3. In the Satanic quotation of Psalm **91.**11,12. what was omitted, and why?
4. Why do those who might be willing to honour the Man Jesus find a stumbling-block in Christ the Saviour (John **6.**51—66)?
5. "To consort with the crowd is harmful", said Seneca. How do these chapters relate to that statement?
6. Who else reacted as Peter did in the presence of God? See Judges **13.**22; Exod. **20.**19; 1 Sam. **6.**20; 2 Sam. **6.**9; 1 Kings **17.**18; Job **42.**5,6; Isa. **6.**5.

St. Luke 5.12–26

Verses 12—16. In this story the Lord both disregards and conforms to the regulations of the Law. He touches the leper, an act which was forbidden, but He bids the cleansed man show himself to the priests (Lev. **14**). He conformed when love permitted. When love demanded something deeper than formality, He brushed formality aside.

The reason for the Lord's request in verse 14 is found in Mark **1.45.** The Lord sought to avoid a mass movement and an epidemic of emotional enthusiasm. He sought to lay His foundations firmly in the rank and file of the land and in understanding, dedicated lives. Is not this still the better way?

Verses 17—26. The gathering of the religious leaders was part of the process mentioned by Mark, the spurious or hostile interest which He had sought to avoid. Enthusiasm which lacks tact and obedience can harm the work of Christ.

The experts had come to criticize; the prejudiced, in most situations, can find food for their prejudice. The advice of the practical Peter, and an armful of rope from his boat, may lie behind the drastic methods of the four friends who brought the sick man to Christ. Unorthodox methods are not always wrong, but should not be sought for their own sake. Let us use the door if it is there. Applicable, is it not, to evangelism?

The whole story shows that the Lord recognized the link between a troubled soul and a broken body. Most of our ills can in some way be shown to arise from disturbance in the spirit, and there is no deeper disturbance than sin, a nagging conscience, and corrupted thought.

Read Matt. **9.**2—8 and Mark **2.**1—12. Note the minor differences in words and detail, remembering always that more words were said than those reported, and that what was said was in Aramaic. Even the basic Greek is itself a translation.

Note: Vs. 17—26: Luke's theme, unfolded in ordered sequence, is the self-revelation of Christ. The Messiah Who has demonstrated

His lordship over sickness, demons and Nature, now shows His authority in forgiving sin.

St. Luke 5.27–39

Verses 27—29. God looks more deeply than man. Capernaum saw only the cynic who despised his people enough to sell his services to the Roman or Herodian tax corporations. There were wide opportunities for bribery, exaction and all manner of corrupt and cruel practice in the ancient systems of tax-collection, and the class who lent themselves to a mode of livelihood so despised and debased were outcasts from their community and the subject of savage jibes and bitter sayings. Christ only, among those who passed the tax-booth, saw something more, the pathetic figure of a man in need of love, who longed for help to break free from a life he hated, a soul in desperation. And Christ was seeking entry into the submerged class of Matthew's kind. They were many in Capernaum, for the town was the customs-post for traffic up the lake.

Verses 30—35. There was little privacy in ancient society. Matthew's dinner party was no doubt observed by the critics, and their carping question evoked the Lord's ironical remark. Ironical it is, and must be so read. He by no means implied that there are righteous folk who need no repentance, much less that the critics themselves were such people.

Verses 36—39. Hence the Lord's method, which may be further illustrated by later encounters with the same strong opponents. He passed to the offensive. Read chapter **20**, and observe the same method. It is not good to be always on the defensive. Pass to the attack, but only with skill, confidence, and understanding of the foe. The Lord's method was drastic. He thrust straight at their foundations. Their whole order, tattered and outmoded, was to pass away. Christianity was to be no makeshift patch on an ancient garment, no new ferment in the old containers. Luke, who had caught from Paul the vision of a global Gospel, appreciated this, though the parable is also recorded by Matthew and Mark.

Note the attempt to divide John and Jesus on a minor issue of practice (33)—a favourite device of the enemy. V. 35: "taken away"—the first indication that Jesus expected a violent end.

St. Luke 6.1–11

The two incidents in this passage illustrate Christ's clash with the legalists in their jealously guarded province of Sabbath regulation.

Christ's point in both cases is that in the Old Testament the Sabbath was a beneficent institution. The scribes and Pharisees had turned it into a burden to be borne, and not infrequently a system of cruelty.

Verses 1—5. According to the humane provisions of the Law, as Moses laid it down (Deut. 23.25), it was lawful thus to eat another's corn. But the Pharisees, infinitely elaborating and embroidering the simple laws of Sabbath-keeping, had listed such manual stripping of an ear of wheat and removal of the husks, as both reaping and threshing. Such absurdities were manifold. A chair, which could be moved on a firm floor, could not be moved on soft earth on the Sabbath, lest the furrow left prove to be ploughing and sowing should a chance seed fall in it.

Verses 6—11. An ox or ass which fell into a pit on the Sabbath had to be fed and bedded for later rescue. If it was injured it could be drawn up and killed. The Pharisees, in their system of escape clauses, which made it possible for the initiated to avoid their own burdensome regulations, had decreed that one could lift the beast on the declared intention to destroy, and then, finding it uninjured, let it go free. The Lord's point was that the critics of His men, and of His own compassionate healing, could twist their laws for a beast, but not for a man. They had laid it down that medical help could be given on the Sabbath only in a case of life or death.

Pharisaism still lives where a movement once beneficent degenerates into a set of rules, postures, and attitudes; wherever self-seeking, pride, love of place, reward or advantage find a place in religion; wherever man-made rules, exclusivism, and absurdity clash with the splendid sanity of Christ; wherever men are preoccupied with doctrine and tolerate sin, deny God's good gifts to the needy, forget love or refuse mercy . . .

Notes: Vs: 1—5: Luke takes his theme one stage further—the Son of Man is Lord also of the Sabbath. V. 6: Dr Luke notes that it was the *right* hand. V. 7: "watched"—the word implies close and continuous scrutiny.

St. Luke 6.12–19

Worn by the conflict with the Pharisees the Lord withdrew for a time of close communion with His Father from Whom He always drew strength and sustenance. Such times of peace and withdrawal are necessary nourishment and healing. Abraham went to "the place where he stood before the Lord", Habakkuk to his "watchtower". A walk alone can be a time of rich fellowship with God, and Nature an aid to such communion.

He sought not only the refreshment of withdrawal from the place of bitterness and conflict and the disturbing presence of evil. He was seeking the mind of His Father for the great task of choosing His men (John 15.16). Perhaps He faced the dread problem of Judas. It sometimes seems as if God can act on two planes, that which His omniscience knows will be, and that which might have been but for the rebel will of man. Judas, perhaps an able man, had his great opportunity.

Read the lists in Acts 1.13, Matt. 10.2—4, and Mark 3.16—19. The Nathanael of John 1.45 is Bartholomew, a surname meaning "the son of Ptolemy". Matthew is Levi, and Judas, the son of James, is Thaddeus. Peter is always mentioned first and Judas from Kerioth (Iscariot) last. These men were not the "band of ragamuffins" of Frederick of Prussia's phrase. They were all busy men as far as we can envisage their daily life, not without property, successful in their way of life, and with much to give up (Mark 10.28—31).

They were called apostles, "special messengers" or "envoys". The word means "one sent". The word implies a goal and a purpose and a task to perform. "I have chosen you, and so placed you, that you should go and produce fruit . . ." runs John 15.16, literally rendered. And look again at the renewal of the commission in Acts 1.8.

These were the men who were to change the course of all history. It is instructive to study them individually. Many are mentioned more than once. To keep a notebook and list all incidences and utterances of each apostle under his own name is to be impressed with the distinct and recognizable character which takes shape. God takes us as we are and variously expresses Himself through the differing facets of our personality. Our unreserved committal is what He requires of us.

St. Luke 6.20–29

This is not the Sermon on the Mount reported at length by Matthew. Luke is clear in verse 17 that "He came down and stood in the plain". Some of the same sentiments find expression, but what preacher uses a sermon only once, and surely this address was worth repetition? Hence, too, some slight variety of utterance. The poor and the hungry, for example, find fuller definition in Matthew, but no Eastern listener, in the context of the speech, would misunderstand the briefer words. They are "the poor in spirit" and "the hungry for righteousness." The Lord was not promising a social and a material millennium, true though it is that His message came to the scorned and rejected of society, those neglected by the remote and aristocratic custodians of a corrupt religion.

186

The Dead Sea Scrolls have thrown some light on the meaning of the former expression. The "poor in spirit" are the tender-hearted. In one of the scrolls they appear as the opposite of the hard-hearted. There is no blessing in God for those who lack pity and mercy, and are not moved by the spectacle of human sorrow, the pathetic helplessness of little children, the sight of suffering and pain, and the pathos of man's plight. The imagery of the Bible sometimes loses its cutting edge outside its context of time and place. Palestine was a stricken land, with deep need in its little towns and villages, and the power of the alien heavy in the life of men.

It was also a hot land. It is still a hot land, with water so precious that international strife between Arab and Israeli has frequently loomed over its distribution. Real thirst, when the sun dries the very fibres of the body, parches mouth and tongue, and fills the whole person with a longing for relief, is a commoner experience in Palestine than in more rain-blessed lands. But is it thus that we long for the will of God in our lives, is it with such insistence, passion and desire that we seek for righteousness?

Christ had little comfort for those who thought they had all life could give; or for the worldly popular. "What have I done wrong," said Socrates once, "that this bad man should speak well of me?"
Notes: A "saying" of Jesus, found in 1897, runs, "I found all men drunken and none found I athirst among them." (See John 7.37: Matt. 5.6.) V. 22: "hate . . . separate . . . reproach . . . cast out your name" —the four stages whereby a Jew was excommunicated from the synagogue. V. 24: the word for "have received" is that used to receipt a bill in the Greek of the period—"They are quit, their reward paid in full."

St. Luke 6.30–38

Verses 30—35. In the interpretation of such passages certain principles are to be consistently observed. First, realize that the East speaks in poetry, with image and illustration woven into the text in pictures rather than concepts. The West is logical, seeking abstract expression. Matthew's parallel passage bids the Christian give the coat also to one who demands a cloak, to turn the other cheek to the smiter, to go the second mile. The fact that two of these expressions have been usefully absorbed into Western speech shows how truly they describe Christ-like gentleness and disarming meekness. And, of course, the true meaning is here. The Christian is not to be stripped bare by a cynical and greedy world, is not expected to double his contribution to Income Tax, while the Lord Himself is illustration of

187

what He meant by "turning the other cheek" (John 18.22,23). The whole drift and purport of this teaching is selfless generosity, utter self-control under persecution, absolute compassion, and Christ-like love. It is completely daunting. Secondly, remember that Scripture must be balanced by Scripture. The Christian who strips himself of necessary resources in spectacular or emotional giving may be falling short in other bounden obligations, in providing, for example, for his own family, a theme on which Paul has a stern word to say (1 Tim. 5.8. Read also chapter 6 for a statement of Paul).

Verses 36—38. Similarly with judgment. The Lord judged the Pharisees (Matt. 23), and a function of judgment is committed to the Church and to its leaders (1 Cor. 5.2—5). But remember that the Lord was in a position to judge in a manner denied to men. He could pronounce that there were those who had sinned beyond possibility of repentance (Mark 3.23—29). No man dare assume such certainty. What the Lord condemns in verse 37 is the censorious attitude which forgets personal shortcomings just as grave as those condemned, a ludicrous self-righteousness which adopts a pose of condemnation without knowledge of the circumstances of another's temptation or sin, and which sheds all love in criticism. It is the theme of love which He is continuing and developing. Let us pray: *Help us, holy Lord, to remember how far we ourselves fall short, and to be tender to the beaten, the desperate, and the defeated in life's battle.*

St. Luke 6.39—49
Three parables close the sermon.

Verses 39—42. The blind were primarily the corrupt priesthood and religious plutocracy. "Beam" is to be understood as a piece of Oriental hyperbole. The "mote" was a scrap of chaff blown from the threshing floor and a common autumn nuisance.

Verses 43—45. The point of the illustration is that a change in nature is required if a tree is to change its fruit. The parable looks on to John 3.

Verses 46—49. The picture probably includes two ways of life. The dry river valleys of the Middle East, the "wadis" of Arabia, were the highways of trade, but subject to occasional disastrous floods. Going with the crowd, seeking the moment's advantage, intent on gain, one man risks danger and builds on the sandy floor. The other, more concerned for security, builds on the "crag". (48, literally). His position is lonely, less convenient for trade, buffeted by the winds, but safe. So in life. The wrong foundations, chosen for the same reasons, are self-confidence, material wealth, social position. Hence, in the flood of life's testing, moral, and often mental, collapse. The true foundation is defined in 1 Cor. 3.11. Read also Eph. 6.11—13.

This entire section emphasizes the principle that conduct depends on character. And it is what a man believes that makes him what he is. Recent controversy has emphasized this: the so-called "new theology" was inevitably followed by the "new morality"—although it is straining language to employ the terms "theology" or "morality" to such nebulous concepts.

Note: V. 48: Gk.—"like a man building a house, who dug and kept on deepening . . ." emphasizes the tedious persistence involved.

St. Luke 7.1–10

The centurion was a Roman seconded for special duty in a sphere of Herod Antipas' administration. It is a notable fact that the Roman officers who find mention in the New Testament are, all five of them, men of standing and visible integrity. Palestine was a turbulent province. Rome was seeking to hold it with a garrison of 3,000 men, which, as the ultimate disaster of the Great Rebellion was to prove, was totally inadequate. Hence Rome's cultivation of the Herodian house, and the collaborating priesthood and aristocracy. Hence, too, the obvious fact that officers picked for duty in Palestine were men of character and strength. It is not strange to find an officer of this type attracted to Judaism, whose lofty view of God, and stern standards of moral conduct, appealed to many pagans who found the religions of the Greek and Roman world unsatisfying.

It is also clear that the centurion was a man of insight who could see past the obtuse religious leaders, proud, bound by their own legalism, and suspicious of Christ. He saw the worth and wonder of the Lord, and came to seek Him with courtesy, reverence, and faith. It was inevitable that he should conceive God in the forms and terminology of his own soldier's profession. So it happens with every believer. An astronomer will think of God as a great mathematician, a poet will see His glory woven into simple things, and the common bush aflame with Him. The infinite Creator is infinitely varied, and each believer has his own contribution of understanding to make. But supremely, God would have us see Him in the face of Christ. Here is His grace, His love, His ultimate revelation (John 1.18).

When Luke wrote his gospel, much of the career of Paul was already over. Peter's dramatic meeting with Cornelius, the centurion of Caesarea, was more than twenty years behind. The door was open to the Gentiles, but there were those in the Church, the heirs of the carping Pharisees, who still resisted the gift of the Gospel to the world.

189

Luke was pleased to tell the story of a Gentile's faith, for it revealed in Christ's own experience and purpose that which Paul had woven into his world-wide ministry. In Christ was neither Jew nor Gentile, just as in Him there is neither black nor white . . .

Notes: V. 3: "elders of the Jews"—the leaders of the local synagogue who ministered its affairs under the "ruler" (8.41). V. 9: note how this is expanded in Matt. 8.11—13.

St. Luke 7.11–18

A good map is always an interesting aid to the study of Scripture. The position of Nain is worth noting. It lies ten miles as the crow flies south-east from Nazareth, across the eastern extension of the lovely Esdraelon plain. A few miles south-west lies Shunem where Elisha similarly brought an only son back to life (2 Kings 4). At the same distance in the other direction lies Endor, scene of the doomed Saul's grim encounter with the dead. The village is called Nain today and there are rock-cut tombs nearby which may have been the goal of the sad procession which the Lord met coming from the gate.

It was a grievous sight. A woman utterly desolate, her husband gone, her only son dead. The widow of Nain need not have been over forty years, perhaps even less, and a long wilderness of left-over life stretched ahead of her, to live in the loneliness and anxiety which the ancient world regarded as the widow's lot. It is a vivid little scene as the Lord stopped the cortege of noisy mourners and touched the dead. Those who seek to "demythologize" Scripture and eliminate tales of miracle fail to explain the artless marks of truth on such narratives, how, in a community which could draw no advantage from mendacity, invention, or deception, the stories found origin at all, or why a competent historian, as Luke undoubtedly was, came to include them in his narrative after due investigation (1.3), and no doubt the interview of eye-witnesses. The New Testament is to be accepted or rejected. It cannot be rejected, and any semblance of Christianity retained. Honesty before God must at least face those alternatives.

In verse 13 Christ is called "the Lord" for the first time. The setting is significant. Luke was writing thirty years after the incident, and uses the term which had become current in the Church. It should be our habitual usage.

St. Luke 7.19–30

Verses 19—22. Tormented and in prison, John fell into doubt. Doubt not infrequently arises from a discrepancy between our view of what God should do, and what He actually does. John had expected a conquering Messiah, Who would cleanse the land of evil, and give the people their ancient liberty. He would burn wickedness and oppression away. Even after the daunting recognition of the Messiah in the person of his own relative (John 1.31—33), the old preoccupation persisted. Surely He would soon "reveal Himself", and "give back the kingdom to Israel" (Acts 1.6).

John did with doubt what should always be done with doubt, he brought it frankly to Christ. Observe the frequency with which David acts in this way in the Psalms. The Lord gave no special revelation. He sought to reveal Himself in His works, and still called for faith. He was reminding John of the other foreshadowings of Himself in the great prophet whom he loved (Isa. 35.5,6; 61.1). On this John was bidden rest.

Verses 23—30. When the envoys were gone the Lord pronounced His great eulogy of John. He was no river reed, or tussock of the Jordan plain, bent under the wind's blast like any weak and pliant thing, nor some princely visitant delicately clad, whom the crowds gather to applaud at the palace gates. John was the greatest of the prophets, because he closed the whole prophetic line, and saw the fulfilment of all messianic prophecy with his own eyes. And yet he was to die before God's final revelation in the atoning death and the empty tomb. In that he lacked what the least of Christians had. He was without the last insights into God's great plan.

How should a Christian deal with doubt? He should ask first what he is doubting, and find whether it is something which he was never called to believe. He should also realize that doubt is temptation, and that temptation is not sin. Sin is cherishing doubt, and falling to temptation. He should take his doubt to Christ, and be prepared then to wait for an answer, alert for God's demonstration.

Notes: V. 20: "He that should come"—"the Coming One". At this moment John saw in Jesus neither the wielder of fan and axe (Luke 3.9,17), nor the fulfilment of Isa. 53.

St. Luke 7.31–40

Verses 31—35. The record of the gospels is darkened by the lengthening shadow of the attitude of the religious leaders. They rejected John because the great movement of the Spirit which God brought to pass through him took no thought of the existing framework of established religion. The Baptist, indeed, had only fierce scorn for them (Matt. 3.7,12). Jesus mingled with the society He came to in-

191

fluence, meeting the sinner where the sinner was to be found, but like John paying no reverence to the leaders of religion. With like savagery they turned on Him and reviled Him for His association with the outcasts of society. Whimsically, He referred to a children's game with its accompanying ditty. It is not clear what it was, but wedding and funeral seem to have been similarly rejected. Time tells, the Lord concluded, for foolishness and wisdom find expression in action and history, and men ultimately see plainly who is wise and who is foolish. Christ and John stand vindicated.

Verses 36—40. The Lord was no rigid proletarian. He was without class-consciousness as every follower of the Lord should be. He had dined with the tax-gatherers at Capernaum. He now dines with a Pharisee, who treated his guest rudely, with an eye, no doubt, to the comment of his critical fellows. People from the street could freely penetrate the public rooms of large houses, and so it came about that the woman came in and ministered to Christ.

The incident is not that recorded in Matt. 26.7—13, Mark 14.3—9, and John 12.1—8. Simon the cleansed leper is not Simon the Pharisee. Similarity of names is always possible. If the records were largely destroyed, historians of a distant future might find it difficult to believe that Admiral Cunningham, General Cunningham and Air Vice-Marshal Conyngham commanded simultaneously in the eastern Mediterranean in the 'forties of this century. In Luke, the incident apparently takes place in Galilee, and the woman is not known. In the others it is Mary of Bethany. Incidents can be repeated, as words also can, without the narrative being suspect, or the narrator careless or mendacious.

Questions for Further Study and Discussion on St. Luke chapters 5.12—7.40.
1. How are Christians today in danger of Pharisaic restrictions on spiritual freedom? What self-imposed limits did Paul observe? Is there *any* place for fasting in the Christian life?
2. What do we learn about evangelism from Matthew's example?
3. What place has the hope of reward in Christian living?—see Rom. 8.17; 2 Tim. 4.7,8; James 1.12. What interpretations fit the image of the flood of ch. 6, v. 48?
4. Why are riches regarded as spiritually perilous? Consider this in both an O.T. and a Christian setting.

St. Luke 7.41–50

The simple human story of the woman in the Pharisee's house provoked the parable of the two debtors. Simon saw the point and rightly, if a trifle disdainfully, answered that gratitude in human affairs is commonly proportionate to benefit received. Simon, too, claimed forgiveness for his sins. The whole Jewish ritual to which he subscribed had atonement and reconciliation for its end. But forgiveness for Simon was part of a legal transaction between man and God. His sins were of the subtler sort, sins of the mind and spirit rather than the flesh—pride, disdain, discourtesy, self-esteem, and contempt for lesser folk. He was like the Pharisee who went up to the temple to pray (Luke 18.9—14). He would, as a matter of course, admit a condition of sin, and claim that, by the processes of the Law, he was forgiven. He had never known the bite and viciousness of gross sin, sin which soils all life and ruins happiness.

The broken woman, on the other hand, had found something in the Lord which convicted her and brought her to His feet for cleansing. That one could so refashion and redeem, could so care and pity, filled her with a love which overflowed in passionate thanksgiving. Christ had brought God to her in such guise that she saw the mercy of the Most High, and His willingness to save. She believed that God must be like Christ, and therefore accepted the Christian Gospel, although Calvary, its last and complete manifestation, was yet without its cross. And so it was her faith which saved her as the last verse says.

It remains a fact difficult to explain that carnal sin fills the repentant with deep horror, and its forgiveness evokes the corresponding depth of love, while the hateful blemishes of the outwardly respectable, equally guilty in God's eyes, remain the theme of casual confession and small exercise of heart and mind. *Lord and Master, make us sensitive to sin, and aware what it cost Thee to redeem us.*
Note: V. 47: this does not teach justification by works; she is not forgiven *because of* her love; her love is the evidence of the forgiveness she has received. Love is weak where consciousness of sin is weak.

St. Luke 8.1–8

Galilee today is not the most crowded part of Israel. In the first century it was much more densely populated, almost as full of busy little towns and villages as the Decapolis on the other side of the lake. To cover Galilee with a preaching mission was an arduous task.

The work of the women is mentioned only in Luke. Women are prominent in his gospel. In his busy collection of material of interest, while Paul lay imprisoned at Caesarea, Luke must have made contact with a group of devoted women, perhaps Mary's circle, who provided him with much information. There is also a glimpse into the Lord's means of sustenance. Joanna, wife of Chuza, is mentioned only once more in the New Testament (24.10), Susanna does not appear again. Mary of Magdala is prominent in the narratives of the resurrection. She is not the "sinful woman" of the last chapter. The strange phrase about the seven devils means that there was a battle for Mary's soul, whatever else it means. And is it not a matter of personal experience that God's grace again and again restores, that God does not let the sinner go, but returns as often to reclaim as evil returns to its attack?

It is a fact which women should note with humble gratitude that, although there are numerous references in the gospels to the ministrations and the reverence of women, there is no single example of a woman hostile to Christ. Traitors, cynical schemers, self-seeking cowards, brutes and hypocrites among men can find their counterparts in Judas, Caiaphas, Pilate, the soldiers who wove a crown of vicious thorns, and the Pharisees, but women who reject Christ and scorn His name can find no types or predecessors in the pages of the gospels. Even Pilate's wife revered Him.

Perhaps women have suffered more cruelly from sin, perhaps the care of innocence in little children has made them more tender. Let us thank God for the ministry of women in family, society, and church. *Notes:* V. 3: Joanna's presence indicates the early links Jesus' followers had with Herod's court—**9.9, 23.8**, and Acts **13.1**.

St. Luke 8.9–15

The parable of the sower sums up the Lord's experience in Galilee. The use of parabolic teaching now becomes more frequent, not in order to conceal the truth, for verse 10 does not mean this, but to separate those willing to learn and follow truly from the merely curious, or the seekers for personal advantage and reward.

The parables are all earthly little stories, full of the life and daily activity of Palestine. They come vividly to life in the land of their birth with its outcrops of stone.

Some of the seed is trodden to death by passing feet. All unconsciously a material society makes much preaching vain. Secure and affluent, content in the familiar pattern of society, multitudes see no relevance in Christ because they have all they need. The preacher seeks in vain to stir concern for the things of the spirit or the life hereafter.

Some of the seed falls where the moist earth is thin and warm on a bed of rock. In such soil the seed quickly germinates, only to wither at the breath of drought. There are those who feel the stirrings of nobler desire but weakly allow old forms of life to reassert themselves, and allow the tender new growth of sweeter and more lofty aspirations to wither and fail in the arid world's hostile air.

Some of the seed falls among thorns. There are those like Pilate who cannot escape from the evil crop which they have allowed to grow. The thicket of cultivated sin, old compromise, and base partnership is too dense to allow room for better growth.

Some of the seed sprouts, proves fertile, and fulfils its divine purpose. It is variously fruitful, some more productive, some less. . . . And so it has ever been. But remember that all analogies fall short. The place of sowing, good or bad, is passive. The human field determines its own destiny. Man is free to choose. Hearing is an urgent business. Let each man attend to it. Verse 8 says as much.

Notes: V. 10: the quote from Isa. **6.9** occurs six times in the N.T.— Matt. **13.**14,15, Mk. **4.**12, John **12.**40, Acts **28.**26,27, Rom. **11.**8, and here. *Cf.* also the references to the Word of God as "seed".

St. Luke 8.16—25

Verses 16—18. The ancient lamp was small and feeble enough. It gave little illumination from its tiny wick of flax or tow. To set it forth to best advantage was common sense. So with the Christian's feeble testimony. The requirements of a lamp are that it should burn and burn steadily and consistently. It is a thought worth taking to heart.

Verses 19—21. The Lord's brothers and sisters are mentioned several times in the New Testament (Matt. **12.**46, **13.**55,56; Mark **3.**32, **6.**3; John **2.**12), and He Himself is called the "first-born". There can be no doubt that they were the children of Mary. The story that they were the children of Joseph by an earlier marriage, or even cousins of the Lord, was an invention of Jerome and other later writers who were adopting the absurd hostility to marriage and sex which is no part of Christianity but a feature of the obscurantism of the Middle Ages.

Before imagining harshness in the Lord's attitude, consider both the brevity and the purpose of the story. There are fifty-six words in the Greek text. The visitors were not necessarily rejected nor dismissed unkindly. The Lord delayed the commencement of His ministry until Mary's other children were sufficiently independent to sustain her, or to be no burden on her resources. He does, however, use the occasion to speak of the brotherhood and close relationship of all believers, and it is a fact of experience that those who are one in Christ can be more intimately linked than blood relations who do not

195

share their faith. It is also a sad situation, later to pass away, that at one stage the Lord and His family were not at one (John 7.1—5).

Verses 22—25. It was late in the day (Mark 4.35) when the band of disciples pushed out into the lake. The hills on the far side rise blue and steep not many miles away, but far behind them is the desert spawning-ground of winds. Hence sudden storms. It was an awesome experience to see the turmoil of air and water fall still at His word. Let it be true of the soul's tempest.

Notes: Vs. 16—18: an important complement to v. 10. The Lord turns from the imperious multitude to enlighten the Twelve. V. 24 note the development of Luke's theme—Christ is Lord of the elements.

St. Luke 8.26–39

Gadara lay across the lake somewhere on the eastern shore where the hills rise steeply near the Yarmuk Gorge. By this time it must have been almost dark, an eerie time to meet a violent maniac emerging with a yell from the tombs. In the cool presence of Christ the distraught creature became harmless, and begged the Lord to depart. He was Legion, he cried, torn and rent by a possessing host of evil things, tramping, tramping through his hot brain like a marching regiment of Rome.

Perhaps he had once hidden, a terrified child, or ran screaming from some blood-stained village street, when soldiers of the garrison systematically cut down parents and playmates in reprisal for the murder of some Roman soldier. And there were graves of the Tenth Legion in Gadara. Sir George Adam Smith, the geographer of Palestine, found the headstones on the site. Cast out from society, and haunting the tombs, the broken-minded man saw the hated name and went mad with passion, breaking bonds asunder and tearing his body with stones.

The Lord had to prove to the stricken creature that he was healed. It cost two thousand swine. How valuable is peace of mind? How precious is a soul redeemed? ... The folk of Gadara, preoccupied with swine, bade Him urgently to depart. They were in the presence of Christ and preferred swine. They had God's salvation within reach, and chose swine.

Christ forces Himself on no man. He went, but left behind the first apostle to the Gentiles, the healed lunatic. It was the Decapolis. A million Gentiles lived in its ten towns. The first missionary, in his borrowed fisher's cloak, set out to evangelize.

Notes: V. 31: "abyss"—the abode of wicked spirits (Rom. 10.7; Jude

6; Rev. **20**.3). V. 39: there was no need for secrecy here to avoid a false Messianic rising; this area was predominantly Greek, not Jewish, which helps to account for the presence of the swine.

St. Luke 8.40–56

The little ship came back across the lake, perhaps to Tiberias, which lies half-way down the western shore. Here Jairus sought His help, and the Lord began to make His way through the thronging streets, and the crowds who were glad to see Him return. There is a strong, vivid verb in verse 42. The multitude "were suffocating Him", it says.

It was a desperate situation. The little girl was dying, and the desperation of Jairus can be imagined, as the party made its slow progress along the packed street.

And then came fatal interruption. The woman with the humiliating and long-standing blemish in her body surreptitiously touched His garment. God met her, as God will, on the level of her faith, and she was healed.

Then came the message which Jairus dreaded. It was too late. The child was dead. The cruel delay which had ended thus fatally must have been hard to bear. What was the woman's burden compared with the life of a loved child? Jairus faced the uttermost of temptation.

But as with the Bethany family, the Lord's delay was purposeful (John 11.4,6). He wished to give Jairus not less, but more, than he asked, not a little one restored, but one brought back from the dead, and a deep lesson which would colour all life and faith. God is never too late, and Jairus learned that in the room of death.

It is still true, or our faith is vain. He does not cancel today the law of death, but what is death as God sees it? He still appears to time-bound man to linger and tarry, but it is in order to strengthen the fibres of our faith, to give understanding which we might otherwise lack, to purge and ennoble our prayers. And yet He does not forbid the prayer: *Lord, make haste to save us.*

Notes: V. 42: "one only daughter"—Luke notes this detail; *cf.* 7.12, **9**.38. V. 43: a literal interpretation of Leviticus **15** would make her an outcast always, and Pharisaic severity would no doubt strengthen the prohibitions against her. Mark **5**.26 adds a satiric comment on physicians, which Dr Luke omits; inspiration does not obliterate personality (similarly Luke omits the rebuke of Matt. 8.26). V. 44: "ceased", "stanched", a medical term.

St. Luke 9.1–9

Verses 1—6. The mission of the Twelve was to train them for their life-long task of evangelism without Him visibly by their side.

197

Bultmann has suggested that this passage was imported into the record to justify the later efforts of the Church. Needless to say there is not a shred of evidence to support this. It is an example of the methods of criticism tolerated in New Testament studies which would be dismissed as ridiculous in any other branch of literary or historical criticism.

The directions laid down are still applicable in principle, though not in detail. The abandonment of all provision for the journey was practicable in the small area which they were called to traverse, and formed an object lesson in haste and complete dependence. The message was simple: the Kingdom of God, by which is meant God's rule and government in life, the acknowledgement of Him as Lord. Good deeds and the alleviation of suffering were to accompany the proclamation. The Church should keep a balance between the two. The message is richer now that Calvary and the New Testament are woven into it.

Verses 7—9. The Lord's own progress through Galilee, and now the consolidating mission of His closer followers, occasioned in the north of the land something like the stir which the preaching of John in the lower Jordan valley had created in Judea. Herod was disturbed. The student of the New Testament should study the background history, and learn to distinguish the five members of the remarkable royal family who appear in its pages. Herod Antipas was a man who might have found salvation. Mark tells us that he had been moved by John's testimony (6.20). Herodias ruined his life. Unable to break free from a vicious entanglement, and claim liberty and forgiveness, he had descended to the crime which now filled his guilty mind with fear. It is impossible, as the stricken Macbeth remarked, "with the deed to trammel up the consequences." Man cannot sin in a vacuum.

Notes: V. 5: "shake off the dust"—the action of a rabbi after travelling in Gentile territory. V. 7: lit., "utterly perplexed". Luke had sources of information at Herod's court (8.3).

St. Luke 9.10—17

Bethsaida Julias is a mile north-east of the lake across the Jordan, a quiet countryside, where the Lord sought rest for His weary men (Mark 6.31). The eager multitude followed, and the Lord ministered to them. The weary Christian worker should note His example. To toil is part of dedication.

There is no bypassing the miracle. It is told by all four evangelists, and it is instructive to compare the accounts (Matt. 14.13—21; Mark 6.30—44; John 6.1—13). There is no difficulty provided Christ was the One He claimed to be, and if He was less than that the whole fabric of Christian doctrine disintegrates. Creative hands increased that which was surrendered, and made it useful to a multitude (John 1.1—3).

A divine principle of action is apparent in the incident. God seems to demand some point of entry into the world, some bridgehead in the spirit of man. To bring blessing to mankind He seems to require some surrendered trifle, some shred of experience, a widow's mite, a handful of bread and fish, a sorrow, a pain, a joy. Given utterly to God the small gift becomes miraculous in His hands. David's and Isaiah's agony break the barriers of time, merge with the pain of Calvary, and become Psalm 22 or Isaiah 53. Habakkuk's perplexity becomes a book of poetry and prophecy built round a text which echoes on to Paul and Luther (Hab. 2.4; Rom. 1.17). The key is verse 16. That which God blesses, infinitely multiplies.

The blessing was no doubt the beautiful Jewish form of grace: "Blessed art Thou, O Lord our God, King of the universe, Who bringest forth bread from the earth." Affluent societies, rich and increased with goods, should remember that multitudes still lack the necessities of life, and should hold their plenty with humble, grateful and generous hands. And note, in the midst of such creativity, the Lord's care for the fragments left in His possession. The Jew on a journey carried a 'cophinos' or rush-woven basket so that he might avoid buying his bread from Gentiles. The disciples were thus equipped, and each of the Twelve gathered provision for the morrow. There was no waste, and a society prodigal of material goods, as no society has ever been before, should note the fact. No blessing lies on it.

Let our small gifts be not wasted, Lord, but multiplied at Thy touch.

Questions for Further Study and Discussion on St. Luke chapters 7.41—9.17.

1. What are the factors which lead to the under-estimation of sin?
2. What are the lessons of the Parable of the Sower for those engaged in evangelism?
3. On what wrong attitude towards Christ is the worship of Mary founded?
4. How does ch. 8, vs. 41—56 help us to accept adversity with patience?
5. Should the rules for the preaching and conduct of the Twelve apply today?

St. Luke 9.18–26

Verses 18—22. If Matthew and Mark are compared, it will be seen that there is a large gap in Luke's narrative at this point. This passage corresponds with Matt. **16.**13—28 and Mark **8.**27—**9.**1. The events of almost two chapters in the two other gospels are omitted. It is quite absurd to suppose that Luke's abridgement of the story was not intentional. It is surprising that Luke did not include the story of the northern journey, the only excursion outside Israelitish territory, which is so prominent in Mark. One who shared the vision of Paul might have made much of the visit to Gentile territory, the story of the Syrophenician woman, and the implications of a Gentile share in the regard of Christ. Perhaps Luke had nothing new to add, and chose at this point to make one of the drastic abbreviations which are to be seen in Acts. It is a mark of his style of writing that he liked room to expand when the subject seemed of major importance and that he provided space by heavy pruning elsewhere. There was the simple consideration of the practicable length of a roll of papyrus. In both of his books Luke uses a roll of maximum length. We would surely prefer him to include the story of the Prodigal Son, and associated parables, than tell again what the other evangelists have told. And we would agree that space kept for the walk to Emmaus was well used. Writers on the New Testament become too complicated in their theorizing on these points. Luke could explain it all by unrolling one length of papyrus, rolling it again, and allowing us to try its weight, one stick in each hand, rolling and unrolling as each column is read.

Verses 23—26. The longer narratives in the other gospels make it clear that these events were a climax to weeks of fellowship and instruction in the Decapolis, where the Lord sought to prepare His men for what was to happen in Jerusalem. They have recognized Him as the Christ, but the implications of that confession were not to be what they had envisaged. The Cross comes into the life of the one who kneels before the Cross to seek forgiveness. The Cross stands for sacrifice, for love to the uttermost, for surrender, and sometimes for the scorn of men.

Notes: V. 18: Luke refers to Jesus praying in six places where the other gospels make no comment (**3.**21, **5.**16, **6.**12, **9.**18,29, **11.**1). All occasions are the preface to momentous words or actions. V. 20: "Christ"—Greek *christos*—Heb. *messiah*, "anointed", the title given to the chosen Servant of God foretold in the Old Testament. V. 22: "rejected"—Gk. implies examination and rejection. The three classes stated formed the Sanhedrin.

St. Luke 9.27–36

The statement in the opening verse must be closely linked with the story which follows. The Transfiguration was the prelude to the return to Jerusalem, the Passion Week, Christ's death and resurrection. So, in the truest sense, came "the Kingdom of God"—not the consummation of all things, but the completion of God's self-revelation in Christ.

Dire testing and temptation lay ahead, and as a climax to weeks of spiritual preparation in the villages round Caesarea Philippi, the Lord chose to strengthen three of His men for the trial which lay before them, and the tense weeks in which their leadership was to count for much. Hence the night journey up Mount Hermon, the beautiful 9,000 foot mountain which lies fourteen miles north of Caesarea Philippi.

The temptation which threatened would inevitably be to doubt whether the victim of Roman and priest could be the Coming One. Hence the strange scene on the mountain which showed Christ first as the consummation of Old Testament history. Moses was the great law-giver, Elijah the first of the prophets. Both were associated in prophecy with the Messiah. (Deut. **18.**15—19; Mal. **3.**1; **4.**5,6.) Minds alert for Old Testament reference, soaked from childhood in its imagery and thought, would be conscious of other parallels: the cloud indicating the divine presence (Ex. **40.**34, 35), the cloud of Sinai, the cloud of Carmel. They would remember that both Moses and Elijah had strange endings on the east of Jordan where they now were, and that Horeb was in the experience of both. Moses led the exodus. And the conversation, runs the Greek text literally, was concerning "the exodus which He was to accomplish at Jerusalem". Secondly the vision of John was confirmed, and Christ was shown to be the Beloved Son.

God sometimes fortifies the soul of those who are to face trial and testing for His sake with some special experience of grace, some deeper revelation of Himself. It behoves us to remember in the darkness that which God taught us in the light. God's method is often the rehearsal of familiar truth. Compare **7.**22. Read something of Moses and Elijah again and try to imagine the impact on the minds of the three watchers.

Notes: V. 27: three interpretations of this are suggested—the resurrection; the transfiguration; or the fall of Jerusalem in A.D. 70 which swept away the remnants of the old dispensation. V. 28: Matthew and Mark say six days: Luke's eight days is on the Roman inclusive reckoning. V. 31: the same word, "exodus", occurs in 2 Peter **1.**15. V. 35: quoting Psa. **2.**7 and Deut. **18.**15.

St. Luke 9.37–45

The chill world of difficulty and defeat was waiting at the mountain's foot. Mark tells the story a little more fully, and it appears that the nine men who had not shared the journey up Hermon were the centre of a curious crowd which included some of the religious leaders of Caesarea Philippi. The district was strongly Gentile in character, but also had a large Jewish population who watched with critical or interested eyes the doings of Christ.

The epileptic boy, like the blind man at the gate (John 9.2), was a theological problem to the disciples, a case for exhibition, not a spectacle of dire need and an object for sacrificial love. Hence their helplessness. It is not difficult to gather a crowd, and those who have a flair for doing so too commonly meet the crowd at its own level, set themselves in the centre of the stage, and dissipate real usefulness.

Mark tells the story at greater length, for Peter, Mark's informant, must have been deeply impressed by the spectacle of need and failure. Luke's briefer account still catches the dull tone of the stricken father's hopelessness. There is little in earthly pain to match the agony of a parent over the affliction of a beloved child. Let those called thus to suffer hold fast to the thought that in such experience they touch the edge of the love of God. The thought of God's suffering is an awesome one. The hymn is surely wrong which says: "No trouble, nor sorrow, nor care, Lord, hast Thou." It is enough for us to remember that God was "in Christ reconciling the world to Himself".

The man sought Christ in his distress, and found the Church. In one he should, no doubt, have found the other, but too often, in the common scene, the Church stands in the way. Like too many, the man saw that the Church was helpless to aid him in his dire need, and imagined that Christ too was unable to help him . . . *Help us, Lord and Master, not to hide Thee from our fellows, and blunt the aspirations of those who seek or need Thee by our dulness, impotence and self-esteem.*

Notes: V. 41: "Perverse"—see also Acts 20.30, Phil. 2.15. V. 42: again Luke thinks of the family—*cf.* 7.15. Vs. 43,44: "said"—repeatedly: see Mark 9.31.

St. Luke 9.46–53

The chapter might properly have ended at verse 50, because at this point Luke inserts a long tract of material not found in the other evangelists. In his usual fashion he has abbreviated on either side to make room for it. From 9.51 to 19.44 there is an account of the Lord's words and doings as He moved forward first in Galilee, then down the

Jordan valley, and up from Jericho, on His last journey to Jerusalem. Luke has concentrated much material here, and it is not necessary always to assume a strict chronological sequence.

Verses 46—48. Conscious that a climax was near, and still not grasping the spiritual nature of "the Kingdom", the Twelve were becoming sensitive over matters of prestige and precedence. The choice of three for the mystic experience on Hermon may have accentuated certain tensions in the group. The Lord's quiet patience and continued confidence in them is a daunting spectacle. It is thus that He bears with others, equally obtuse and insensitive to His outworking purpose.

Verses 49 and 50. If these verses follow in time sequence, which may not be the case, they reveal how little John had heeded the talk on childlike simplicity. Verses 54 to 56 are an even sharper demonstration. In life and in death the Lord illustrates how all evil in God's hands can be made an occasion of good. Such was the supreme lesson of Calvary, and again and again some fault, failing, or sin produces immortal words or acts. John's narrow sectarianism, which seeks smugly to elicit the Lord's commendation, produces the statement of verse 50, the rebuke of all intolerance. The contrary remark reported two chapters later (11.23) is not a repudiation or an afterthought, but a principle which applies to another situation. The two attitudes stand in tension, not in contradiction, and steady the Christian between two extremes. His fellowship must be wide, but not at the expense of fundamental truth and conviction, a fact which some, over-eager for a spurious unity, forget.

Verses 51—53. The Samaritan boorishness may have been disappointment. The stern mood of verses 51 to 53, so apparent in Mark's story, was upon Him, and may have chilled their desire to retain Him. Jerusalem and the Cross were in full view. We must watch with reverence.

Notes: V. 46: the reasoning may have been their reaction to Jesus' prediction of v. 44; they wonder who will succeed to the leadership. V. 48: the service of love is tested by its operation towards the most insignificant. V. 51: *cf.* Mark 16.19, where the Gk. verb is used whose noun form occurs here. V. 53: for Samaritan hostility, see Ezra 4.1–5; Neh. 2.19,20.

St. Luke 9.54–62

Verses 54—56. As on the earlier occasion a demonstration of intolerance produces a precious saying. Sixty years later, the same John wrote the fourth gospel and the letter which accompanied it, a

203

document which is full of the plea for love which marked, according to tradition, the old man's last days. "Little children, love one another," he pleaded in Ephesus. "Why, master, do you always say this?" they asked. "Because," the aged apostle replied, "if you do that, it suffices." Experience had tamed the "Son of Thunder".

Verses 57 and 58. On sudden impulse or a burst of emotion, a scribe (Matt. 8.19) promised to follow Christ. He had not counted the cost, and we are not told the result when he came to count it. The Lord offers joy, not comfort. He makes no promises of material reward. He calls to strife, and has to offer, He might have told them, "nothing but blood and tears and sweat". He wants no one to follow Him under any illusions, with any false hopes, any selfish or ill-considered motive.

Verses 59 and 60. The man surely would not have been there had his father been lying dead at home. The demands of an Eastern funeral would have preoccupied him. He must mean: "Let me wait, like Abraham at Haran, until my father dies, and I can follow without offending him." The Lord must have priority if duties conflict. It is easy to decide when good and evil are the alternatives. The pain and difficulty of decision lie where good conflicts with good.

Verses 61 and 62. Another who came to Christ (5.29) did precisely this. Levi gave a farewell banquet to his friends, but in order to introduce them to Christ. This man had a divided mind. Like Lot's wife, he "looked back". In such is no stability. The good ploughman fixes his eye steadily on a distant goal, takes firm grip on the plough, throws the whole energy of his body into the act, and does not stop, pause, or waver until the long furrow is clean and straight to the end. Such are those whom the Lord would have follow Him. *Help us, O Lord of the field and the harvest, to drive our furrow straight today.*
Notes: V. 56: "another"—*i.e.*, not Samaritan. V. 62: "the light ploughs of the East, easily overturned, require constant attention" (Farrar).

St. Luke 10.1–9

The mission of the Twelve was to Galilee, the mission of the Seventy extended to Judaea. The two projects of evangelism must not be confused, but may profitably be compared. As the Twelve represented the missionary function of Israel's twelve tribes, so the Seventy perhaps suggested the seventy members of the Sanhedrin, the land's prime religious assembly whose purpose was ideally to prepare the land for the coming of the Messiah. Jerusalem Jewry had neglected Trans-Jordan, and it was through this strip of territory, with its admixture of Gentiles, that the Seventy were to go, if they were to "go before His face".

The detailed directions given were proper to the urgency of a brief pioneering mission, and are not universally applicable in Christian work. Time was short, and the Lord forbade detailed preparation. He told them not to waste time in social activities, for salutation in this context is not the passing courtesy of friend meeting friend but the endless formalities of Eastern hospitality (see 2 Kings 4.29). Since the area to be traversed held many non-Jews, it was also directed that no exhibition of Jewish sensitivity over dietary prohibitions should be allowed to create awkwardness or spoil the visitor's testimony. Note Paul's application of this sensible rule in the case of Corinth (1 Cor. 10.27) where conscience could make a problem of food.

The principles which lie behind the instructions given to these first evangelists do contain points of universal application. The Christian preacher must be gentle in a harsh and hostile world (3), must go earnestly about his business, must be contented, and courteous and careless of material comfort, must be simple in his message, and the envoy of his Lord. Paul must have read and heeded words like these, for his whole conduct as a missionary shows his effort to apply the Lord's directions. He sought no personal advantage, but was not ashamed to accept Christian hospitality (1 Cor. 9.7—18; 1 Tim. 5.18; Acts 18.1—3; Phil. 4.10—19). But let the Church at large not presume upon the self-sacrifice of those who serve it. The Church has also its obligations, not listed here.

Notes: V. 1: it has also been pointed out that the Jews thought of the Gentiles as seventy nations. V. 2: *cf.* Matt. 9.37; John 4.35.

St. Luke 10.10—21

The lakeside towns had been uniquely blessed. In Capernaum the Lord had lived, and to many communities He was a familiar presence. To have lived in the light of the truth and to have neglected it is a dire responsibility. As though in illustration of the words of doom, the northern and north-eastern coasts of Galilee lie bare today. The level blue of the lovely lake laps empty shores. Capernaum is a ruin among its trees. Other sites are gone, or represented in a garbled name. Kerazeh, for example, may be Chorazin, but none can be sure. On the far side extends the eastern shore, its busy little ports all gone, and the Decapolis behind a wide scatter of ruined towns. Only Amman, the ancient Philadelphia, carries some semblance of the teeming life of the first century.

When the faith and principles round which a nation builds its strength and usefulness decay, inevitably disaster follows. Above all, the English-speaking nations should heed the warning. Uniquely privileged, enlightened beyond others, blessed with long centuries of faithful Christian witness, they abandon the old faith and prate of new moralities at their direst peril . . .

The Seventy returned in jubilation. The Lord's remark about the fall of Satan was designed to check the insidious growth of pride. It is a phrase in the style of Jewish apocalyptic poetry. "Yes, I watched Satan fall from heaven like a flash of lightning," runs Moffatt's paraphrase. Satan fell by pride, and minds taught in such imagery would see immediately the point of the warning. Success in their preaching mission could so easily lead to arrogance. In similar apocalyptic vein, and not likely to be taken literally by Eastern minds, is the remark about serpents and scorpions. They are symbols of cunning and vicious enemies. Then in sharp simplicity the Lord bids His men take humble thought of their privilege and not their power. And He speaks to all.

Notes: V. 12: "that day"—Sodom's final judgment was still to come. V. 15: "Hades"—the abode of departed spirits. Note question form as in R.S.V. V. 19: *cf.* Gen. 3.15, Isa. 11.8, Rev. 9.5. V. 21: the contrast in the prayer is not between the educated and the uneducated, but between those who vaunt their understanding and those of simple faith.

St. Luke 10.22–29

Verse 22, which is found again in Matthew (11.27), is alone and apart from all other evidence proof that the three synoptic gospels do not present a different picture of Christ from John. John undoubtedly takes up the theme more fully. It required re-emphasis at the end of the century when he was called to write. But here in Luke, where it is an integral part of the text, these words are testimony to the Son's oneness with the Father.

Such claims are not traceable to any accretion of myth or legend. They enter into the very substance of all He said. Consider, for instance, what is involved in His quiet use of the plural "We", when He speaks of Himself and God: "We will come unto him and make Our abode with him" (John 14.23). Consider what is implied in the necessity which He seems to feel to explain: "My Father is greater than I". Whenever He mentions God it is in tones of unique and superhuman intimacy. If we seek to prune such words away, to remould His speech, and find the human Christ which some have imagined might be found, a holier John Baptist, a more homely Elijah, Who speaks and thinks and acts like a saint of earth, nothing at all is left. This impossibility to reduce Him to human proportions without obliterating Him is an unanswerable argument for deity. Reject this simple conclusion and the alternatives are these. Either —and its impossibility has been demonstrated—four ordinary men created this astonishing character, and by four little books of simple Greek changed the history of the world, or else it was an unbalanced man who spoke like this, a deluded being for whom mankind's best have lived and died, and from whose teaching the sweetest things of life have ever flowed. Yet, for nearly two thousand years, up and down a sceptical world swift to bring down in derision the airs of high conceit, these claims have been preached. Men have turned away, have blasphemed and rejected. None has called Him mad. And the world shall one day bow the knee before the Son of God. *Notes:* V. 22: typical references in John's gospel—**1.**18; **14.**6; **3.**35; **6.**44 – 46; follow these themes through with a concordance. V. 25: the lawyer's aim was two-fold—to trap the Master *and* to justify himself. The second aim is often hidden in a seemingly objective enquiry about Christianity. "Inherit eternal life"—another Johannine concept. **18.**18*ff*. shows it to be synonymous with entering the kingdom. V. 26: "how readest thou?"—implies a reproach.

St. Luke 10.30–37

The parables in Luke's gospel are not parables in the strictest sense of the word. They are stories which could be true, pieces of life. This story bears all the marks of truth. From Jerusalem, 2,600 feet above the sea, to Jericho is the great rift valley. Even today the long sweeps of sealed highway curve and bend through howling wilderness. It was a place for bandit and highwayman, with boulders on the barren hillsides to hide the waiting thief, and deep desert to contain and to conceal his flight.

It was human enough for the priest and Levite to pass furtively by. The inert figure in the roadside dust might have been a decoy. The high priest at Jerusalem might have counselled caution and non-involvement. How many good people in some sombre modern slum would care to repeat the scene of the Samaritan's act of mercy with danger lurking in every corner of the sinister environment? To pass by, to shirk responsibility, to avoid a compromising entanglement in a situation of unknown difficulty, is a natural enough instinct.

The Samaritan was a compassionate man. He was also an uncommonly brave man. He belonged to a race despised by the Jews.

Assyria overran and depopulated the northern kingdom of Israel, and by their cruel policy of population-transfer denuded the land of its inhabitants. To keep the province from complete social and economic collapse, the Assyrian king repopulated Samaria with aliens (2 Kings 17.24—41). Instead of regarding the newcomers as objects of Jewish evangelism, the people of Judah, which survived in independence till Nebuchadnezzar took Jerusalem a century later, turned away in contempt, and the racial division between Samaritan and Jew began its bitter course.

In answering the lawyer, the Lord struck racial prejudice a stinging side-long blow. He also defined a "neighbour"—one who helps when and where he is needed, and who helps wherever he has opportunity to help, irrespective of rank, race or religion. And neighbourhood is co-extensive with humanity.

Notes: V. 31: "by chance"—the usual Greek word is avoided in the N.T.; for the duty of mercy see Deut. 22.4, Isa. 58.7. V. 34: "oil and wine"—Isa. 1.6, Mark 6.13, James 5.14. V. 35: "penny"—*denarion*, a labourer's normal daily wage. V. 37: the lawyer cannot bring himself to utter the loathed word "Samaritan".

St. Luke 10.38–42

John 10.22 suggests that the Lord visited Jerusalem briefly during the last months of His life, apart from the historic journey up from Jericho to the final encounter with the hierarchy, the Passion and the Cross. This was no doubt the occasion of the visit to Bethany and the incident here vividly described.

It is possible that the visit took Martha by surprise, and like a good hostess she set busily to work to entertain her guest worthily. Nor was there anything reprehensible in this. John, writing over half a century later, took occasion to remind the Church that Jesus loved Martha (John 11.5). The rebuke to Martha, kindly and affectionate enough, must not be taken as a licence for casual entertainment of an honoured guest, or diminished care and generosity in Christian hospitality.

But Martha was at fault in losing control of the situation and herself. She was "distracted", came and "stood over them" (40), and rebuked her Master: "Don't you care that my sister has left me to serve by myself? Tell her then to lend me a hand." The Greek text, which no doubt renders the Aramaic conversation well, is racily vivid. "There is need only of one thing," He replies, "and Mary has chosen the good part which shall not be taken away from her." The reference may be to the dish of honour such as that placed before Benjamin in Joseph's banquet (Gen. 43.34). Briefly the Lord's meaning was: we can be deprived of food and comfort without real harm. That which we cannot safely lack is communion with our Lord. To be robbed of this is to starve indeed. The lesson for us? Unhurried calm in the press of duty, and priority for prayer. It is worth considering how the Martha and Mary incident relates to the parable of the Good Samaritan—two very different reactions nevertheless show love for the same Lord. Note the further implication—unruffled attention to what the Master has to say leads to truest service.

St. Luke 11.1–13

Verses 1—4. The Lord was never more simple than when He taught men to pray. There are those who turn prayer into an exercise in resignation, a form of quietism, a ritual of meditation, or a process of psychological therapy. If Christ is to be heard on the theme, prayer is simply speaking to "our Father in Heaven", and He would never have called God "Father" had He not intended those who heard Him to take the word for what it means. God is infinitely wise, infinitely loving, and may be approached as an earthly father may be approached by his anxious child. A father yearns for some interchange of love from his children, he treasures their complete confidence, he listens with sympathy to their smallest requests; although in his wider wisdom he does not always grant them, he is never deaf to their appeals, unmoved by their fears, or untouched by their anxieties, even though he may know that the appeals are unwise, the fears without foundation, and the anxieties groundless. If an earthly father fails to respond thus, to that extent he lacks wisdom or lacks love. God, our Father in Heaven, is all-wise, all-loving. If, therefore, we cannot approach Him as a child comes to his parent, prayer is not what Christ taught it to be, and if He was wrong, it is futile to seek another basis. The prayer which He gave was not intended to be a hasty gabble of words. It is a series of headings, by which a time of prayer, long or short, may be guided. It calls for pauses, in which the phrase of worship or supplication is related to all life, its varied needs, its personal problems. "Thy will be done" are words not to be uttered without committal, "our daily bread" involves more than mere food, "temptation" and "evil" have their private echoes in our own special circumstances.

Verses 5—10. By this everyday story, the Lord did not mean that God, like the weary neighbour, could be brought by importunity to a different frame of mind. What Christ meant was that in earthly relationships people are not put off by delay or a first refusal, if their desire is deep enough, or their confidence firm enough in another's ability to give. Should we be less earnest with God, while at the same time examining our prayer, and seeking His purpose in delay?

Verses 11—13. The words reinforce the previous contention that the Fatherhood of God is no mockery. All good which comes in the normal, simple relationships of life from a loving parent, comes also from God, only magnified, timely, wisely. If man can be, in love, the author of good, how much more so will the all-loving God give—Himself. For is not the Holy Spirit God?

Notes: V. 2: "hallowed"—treated as holy; "name" includes character. V. 3: "daily" here means "for the coming day"—it is a morning prayer. Most of the prayer can be paralleled from rabbinical sources; it is not new words but a new spirit which is all-important. V. 8: "importunity"—"shamelessness" (N.E.B.). V. 10: *cf.* Matt. 7.7—11, Mark **11**.24, John **16**.23. V. 13: "who are evil"—sinful by disposition. Vs. 11,12: the round desert stones of Palestine resembled loaves.

St. Luke 11.14–23

It is part of the viciousness of human nature to shut the eyes to good. Some perversity of mind corrupts the whole outlook of the determinedly rebellious. An ingenuity of wickedness suggests some means of rejecting good. It is part of human free will. Conviction is forced on no one. Nothing is so compellingly proved, that the obstinately sceptical has no alternative to faith. They saw the healing touch of Christ on distracted minds, were unable to deny the visible and factual evidence, but sought a base and evil explanation of it all.

What then is faith? It is not blind credulity. There is evidence on which the questing mind can build a structure of confidence. There is enough to satisfy the reason which seeks enlightenment, not enough to beat into submission the mind which is eager for a way out and fertile in objections. Alternatives stand before the seeker. He must, in point of fact, take one or another path of faith. For let the one who rejects God and His Christ realize that he is not done with faith. If he pleads insufficient proof to warrant acceptance, he must equally admit that the contrary choice also lacks final proof. The last act is the committal of the life to the likelier alternative, and the choice of likelihood is often, indeed invariably, determined by the desire that this way or that be true. The moral choice, therefore, at last determines the balance of the intellectual choice. Perhaps this gives a glimpse of.why faith saves. But, again, let the one who rejects Christ not delude himself into imagining that he avoids faith. He has committed his life to that which he cannot prove. For the one who accepts, the promise of John 7.17 proves true.

Notes: Note here how the accounts in Matt. **12** and Mark **3** supplement each other and Luke's account; especially the strong words of Matt. **12**.31,32. V. 14: the tense is significant—it suggests that the cure was not in this case instantaneous. V. 15: Be-elzebul—in N.T. = Satan. Possibly derived from Baal-zebul—"Lord of the high place", a Canaanite deity. V. 19 "sons" = pupils. V. 23: see note on **9.50**.

St. Luke 11.24–32

Verses 24—28. The brevity of the narrative sometimes blurs the connection of thought, but consideration will sometimes recover it. The drift of the controversy, with determined wickedness obstinately set on rejecting Christ, suggested the possibility of neutrality. What of the man who is cleansed of the evil in his life, but does not fill the vacuum with Christ? Old sin will reassert itself, the defeated invaders of the soul will sweep back in force. The psychologists sometimes condemn the practice of repression, predicting a more damaging outbreak for evil pressed down and forcibly restrained. Christianity advocates no such half measures. Most evil in the human personality is misdirected good. Beneficent impulses, desires, emotions, are bent and distorted by self-seeking and godless abuse into tyrannous and harmful things. Christianity advocates sublimation, the lifting and restoring of the damaged personality, the restoration of its sanctioned functioning. Christ, and all Christ means, takes control, and fills and purifies.

Verses 29—32. Two historic instances illustrate the point made in the previous discussion of faith. The choice is often determined by the moral attitude of the person. Men set on evil asked in vain to be convinced. "The sign of the prophet Jonah" was manifest in Nineveh of all places, the stronghold of the grim Assyrians. Sheba's Queen, likewise, the daughter of an alien civilization, came with open mind, seeking for conviction. She found it.

Note, in the same connection, Christ's astonishing claims. He is "greater than Solomon . . . greater than Jonah". What sort of man was this Who could claim such eminence and yet leave, as He did undoubtedly leave, the impression of meekness, and an authority which daunted and silenced all opposition?

Notes: Vs. 24—26 had a particular application to the Jews, who had known the blessings of the Old Covenant and were now being called upon to accept the Messiah, following John the Baptist. The next half-century provided grim fulfilment of vs. 23 and 26. V. 29: Gk. "were

211

gathering thickly". V. 30: the reference to Jonah is filled out in Matt.
12.40, which also relates to the hint contained in the future tense here.
V. 31: "something greater than Solomon"—the Greek pronoun is
neuter, N.E.B. translates, "what is here is greater than . . .". Jesus
is the Prophet and the King.

Questions for Further Study and Discussion on St. Luke chapters 9.18—11.32.

1. How, according to the New Testament, does the Christian share
   in the cross?—Follow the theme through with a concordance.
2. In what ways should the Christian's relationship to Christ affect
   his treatment of others? See 1 John 4.20,21.
3. Does fully committed Christian service eliminate conflicts of
   duty or loyalty? If so, how?
4. What principles of prayer are taught in 11.1—13?
5. What new aspects of Luke's theme, the self-unveiling of Christ,
   are developed in chs. 9 and 10?

St. Luke 11.33–44

Verses 33—36. This passage looks like a fragment of the Sermon on
the Mount. The Lord's teaching, like all good teaching, was repetitive, and this period of His ministry was one of arduous teaching,
preaching and controversy. The light was most certainly not hidden.
From Galilee down to Jerusalem the light was shining, openly, clearly,
and with no attempt at concealment. So should the Christian shine in
the world's murk, and the smog of a self-poisoned society.

The strange saying about the eye touches another aspect of truth.
There were many blind in Palestine. Bartimaeus was waiting down
at Jericho. The light of heaven's sun was blazing in the Jordan valley,
and sharpening the shadows of all Jericho's palms and balsam trees.
Bartimaeus saw nothing. His eyes were not functioning. If light is to
flood the mind, the eye must receive and interpret the conditions
without. God's grace is the waiting illumination of the sun. The eye is
the faith which receives. Where grace and faith meet, at that point is
salvation.

Verses 37—44. The washing which the Lord omitted was not a
simple act of cleanliness. It was the ceremonial of the Pharisee, a
ritual act, ordained and regulated to the smallest detail by the complicated laws which the Pharisees had invented. The amount of water
was specified, the movements and attitudes by which it was poured

from finger-tip to wrist, and the manner in which hand was rubbed in hand. The regulations governing the cleanliness and uncleanness of table-ware were equally detailed. This was the clutter of nonsense which the Lord treated with contempt.

Pharisaism, as His denunciation shows, had much to say of rule and regulation, little about the positive duties of mercy and love. It is still active in the world. To reduce religion to a set of prohibitions and attitudes, while neglecting the committal of the whole person to Christ, is a common fault of man. To judge another for non-conformity with rules and man-made demands which have no root or sanction in Scripture is a by-product of the same pernicious attitude. And yet the Pharisees began well. Thanks to them, in the stern days of exile, the Law was garrisoned and kept. But human institutions can introvert, become an end in themselves, lose their spirit, and perish.

St. Luke 11.45–54

The Pharisees were laymen, fanatically preoccupied with details of the Law. The lawyers were professionals, the "scribes", associated with the Pharisees in their fantastic legalism. It is difficult to draw a sharp line between the two classes. They are linked in condemnation.

Verse 46 is the core of the charge. The lawyers had made the simple and beneficent Mosaic Law a complicated web of regulation too difficult for ordinary folk to follow. It is always true that any system of interpretation or of teaching which makes religion hard to follow or to comprehend, irrelevant to life, or remote from common experience, is forthwith wrong. But the lawyers had also made it possible for those who knew the way to evade their own burdensome obligations.

Examples may be quoted in multitude from rabbinical literature. The Sabbath day's journey is an illustration. It was limited to about one thousand yards. This was of little use, but one could extend the distance by pushing out the limits of one's legal home. A rope across the end of one's street, no doubt briefly put in place, constituted the whole enclosure of one's "home". The "journey" could begin at that point. Or if greater licence still were needed, a parcel of food, concealed or placed, on Friday, at the end of the prescribed distance, constituted a second "home". One could begin again, and proceed for another Sabbath day's journey.

It is easy to see how a personality thus preoccupied would become utterly corrupt. The spirit of man cannot endure, undamaged, hypocrisies like these. Hence the attitude which the Lord condemned. They honoured the tombs of the prophets who had denounced spiritless legalism (Isa. **1**.11—15), but their forbears had persecuted the same prophets, and they themselves were unable to recognize One greater than all the saints of old. Consider John 3.17—21 as a commentary on all this.

Notes: V. 47: dead saints are always more popular than living ones. V. 49: "wisdom of God"—*cf.* Matt. **23**.34. V. 50: "shed"—"being constantly poured out". V. 51: these incidents span the whole of O.T. history. V. 52: a key was the law-teacher's badge of office, his work being to open the Scriptures to others—see Isa. **22**.22. V. 53: note the forceful language.

St. Luke 12.1–12

It is difficult to say whether Luke has concentrated at this point a number of utterances, or whether this is a condensed summary of one address. Teaching was repetitive and the same illustrative material or metaphor could have been used with more than one point of exhortation.

The disciples are bidden to avoid the dissimulation of the Pharisees. The vice of the Pharisees was the concealment of an unsanctified life behind an exterior of complicated holiness. They acted a part, and that is precisely what hypocrisy means. But "play-acting" can have other interpretations. It can find a place in the Christian who conceals his real convictions, and tries to hide his faith. If conviction is real and faith genuine, such dissimulation is vain (2). Therefore anticipate the inevitable, and boldly speak out about the truth (3).

And why do people hesitate to do this? Fear of man is the inhibiting force (4), which should take second place, natural though it is, to reverence for God (5). Consider Joseph's "fear" of God (Gen. **39**.9), Ezra's (**8**.22), Nehemiah's (**6**.11). God knows and understands (6,7). By the roadside still in Lebanon the vendors of small birds stand, with the tiny feathered creatures hanging pathetically in dozens upon uplifted sticks. They were sold two a penny, said Matthew; five for twopence, says Luke. So worthless were the small birds that an extra carcass was thrown in for the larger sale. But even such trivial death does not elude God's knowledge. Let those who trust such a God value above all God's honour and acknowledgement (8). To deny Him is to forfeit such acceptance (9).

Indeed, denial can be rejection, and this thought must have led in the context of the full discourse to the solemn theme which Matthew and Mark develop more fully, the "sin against the Holy Spirit". It is obvious that this must mean ultimate, deliberate, and final rejection of Christ as Saviour, the self-willed and conscious repression of the movement of God's convicting Spirit in the heart and conscience, wilfully imputing to the workings of Satan that which is manifestly of the grace of God. Denying God can end in such disaster (10).

Notes: V. 5: "hell"—*Gehenna*, Gk.; the valley of the sons of Hinnom, outside Jerusalem, where fires burned continually to consume rubbish (see Josh. **15.**8, **18.**16; 2 Kings **23.**10, Jer. **7.**31). The name was used metaphorically for a place of punishment after death. V. 8: on confessing Jesus, see Matt. **10.**32; Rom. **10.**9; Phil. **2.**11; 1 Tim. **6.**13; Rev. **3.**5.

St. Luke 12.13–24

The stern rebuke to the man who brought his problem of injustice to Christ must be looked at within its context. There is no reason why such difficulties should not be brought reverently to Christ, along with all our problems of conduct, suffering, and perplexity. It seems, however, apparent, from the drift of a highly condensed narrative, that the man interrupted a serious discourse on dependence upon God with an untimely intrusion. Deaf to the immortal words which he might have heard to his eternal profit, the fellow blundered tactlessly forward with his financial problem. All he could think about in the presence of Christ was money. Hence the rebuke.

And hence the parable about the fool who could not see past material things. In other respects there is nothing to indicate that he was a bad man. He was a successful farmer. Palestine generally is not good agricultural country, save on the coastal plain. The chocolate-brown soil of the valley bottoms is fertile enough, but the boulder-strewn hillsides are hungry and difficult to farm. The Parable of the Sower gives a fair picture of the land. But the man in the story, no doubt both by good fortune and good management, had built up high prosperity. He was rich.

Unlike some rich people, he also saw that riches were meant for use and enjoyment. He knew when to retire. There is nothing to show that anyone grudged him this pleasure. He had paid his labourers. He owed no man anything. His wealth was fairly won. But his fault is apparent. In a land marred by poverty, inequality, and suffering, he had no thought of stewardship. It was "*my* barns," "*my* fruits," "*my* goods". No other was to share. Lazarus might lie at the gate with the sores of malnutrition tormenting his body, but there is no relief from the comfortable and insensitive farmer. He has no mercy.

He has no thought, in fact, but for himself. And life for him is "eat, drink, and be happy". (This is the meaning of the word: *e.g.*, "God rest you merry", which of course means: "God keep you happy".)

215

Happiness was a state confined to self, and limited to eating and drinking. His error was threefold: (*i*) he imagined that he was in full control; (*ii*) he mistook his body for his soul; (*iii*) he confused means and end. Here is the very essence of materialism.

Notes: V. 13: "inheritance"—Deut. 21.15—17. V. 14: "divider"— "arbitrator".

St. Luke 12.25–34

The thought flows on from the parable just told, and some teaching from the Sermon on the Mount is introduced. Life is more than food and mere physical necessities. All such matters must be kept by the Christian in due proportion. This is no call to a hermit's life and the spectacular abandonment of all possessions and modes of normal living, as the authorities of later centuries perversely regarded it. "God knows that we have need of all these things" is the closing thought.

Two points must always be borne in mind when reading the Bible. The first is that it is an Eastern book, and speaks in poetry as readily as in prose. For the same reason, it must also be expected that paradoxical and striking statements will be made.

Secondly, text must be balanced with text, and Scripture with Scripture. Verse 33 seems a drastic statement until it is measured against fact. The disciple John had a home, for thither he took Mary when bidden by the Lord on the cross to treat her as his mother. The family at Bethany had a house and a competence wherewith they entertained Christ. What then did Christ mean? Look at the whole context of His remark. He began with comment on the rich fool who thought that the end of all life and activity was an abundance of food and drink. He passed from this to the preoccupation with the necessities of daily living, which excludes and quenches higher and more vital concerns.

With the rich farmer the acquisition of material goods was a life-long and absorbing passion. There are poorer and more enlightened men who also think too much about such things. Cast care and anxiety aside, Christ urges them. After all, does worry effect much? A "three-cubit man" and a "four-cubit man" were common terms for short and tall, and one of the twain cannot make himself into the other by anxiety. Who will deny that worry is a problem? None the less we should seek to quench it by faith; it is unreasonable for the Christian (22—24), useless (25), and irreligious (28).

Notes: V. 29: "anxious mind"—the Gk. expresses the tossing of a ship—literally, "raised between heaven and earth". V. 34: "heart"—

a comprehensive term; thoughts, affections, actions. For the idea of being "rich toward God", see Matt. **6.**19—21; 1 Tim. **6.**17—19; Jas. **2.**5.

St. Luke 12.35–48

The doctrine of the Lord's Return haunts Scripture. Note how frequent reference to it is in both the teaching of Christ and that of His apostles. It was once called the "blessed hope", but has not today as prominent a place in the teaching of the Church as once it had. At the human level, the reasons for this are two. The Second Advent has so frequently been central in the teaching of sectaries extravagant in their interpretation, given to date-fixing and crudity, that those jealous for the integrity of Scripture, anxious for the good name of the Church and the effectiveness of evangelism among intelligent people, have grown suspicious of the doctrine. The second reason is the comfort of an affluent society. The Church tends to be "at ease in Zion". The sting of trouble and anxiety, chaotic times which reveal the instability of the social order and the fragility of civilization, turn the minds of men towards the intervention from above which alone could end all strife and bring the warring world to peace.

The doctrine of the Second Advent is nevertheless an integral part of the New Testament. No time is specified. The manner of the advent is not clear. The fact remains.

Nor is this ever stated merely as a theme for speculation. Rather, as here, it is a matter which prompts zeal, and calls for urgency and dedication. Like servants alert for the return home of their master, so the followers of Christ must be ready for their Lord's Coming. The best preparation for the consummation of all things, for the secret hour which shall end the long tumult of history, is to be busy with the task at hand. "He'll find me picking cotton when He comes" runs the old Negro song. Compare 1 Cor. **4.**1*f.*; Jas **4.**17; 2 Pet. **2.**21.

Notes: It is important to consider why the teaching about Christ's Return occurs at this point in the gospel, and how it arises out of the preceding verses. V. 37: "gird himself"—see John **13.**3*f.* Vs. 41*f.*: note how Christ frequently answers one question by posing another. Much here is applicable to leaders in the Church. V. 45: *cf.* 2 Pet. **3.**8*f.* Vs. 47, 48: an incidental remark indicates variety in punishment. "Knew not" means partial enlightenment, not total ignorance.

Questions for Further Study and Discussion on St. Luke, chapters 11.33—12.48.

1.   Why is it equally impossible for man to serve two masters and to serve no master?

2. In what ways is it possible to sin today in expecting "signs" from God?
3. What is the significance of such statements as that found in **11.31** and others like it? Consider it in the light of the Lord's deity.
4. Why do healthy religious movements decay? Consider the Pharisees and the rabbinical schools of law.
5. What form does the "leaven of the Pharisees" take nowadays?
6. What is the Old Testament significance of the title "Son of Man"?
7. What place does the Second Advent hold in the doctrine of the New Testament? How and when should it be preached?

St. Luke 12.49–59

Verses 49—53. The words again must be taken in their context. It is a fact that Christ brought peace, peace between man and God, "peace that passes understanding", peace between man and man, for those who applied His teaching and lived in the blessed light of it. It is also a fact that socially Christ sets man at variance with man. A binding and a demanding loyalty challenges some old allegiance. A new-born love clashes with old affection, and divides one person from another. Fire (49) both burns and purifies. "He who is near Me is near the fire" runs a saying of Christ, reported by Origen. Fire can never be disregarded. It cannot be approached without due calculation. Neither can Christ.

Verses 54—59. There is a clear division here. These words are addressed to the crowds. They were alert enough for the signs of the weather. The wind out of the west rolled in such water-laden clouds from the Mediterranean as Elijah's servant saw (1 Kings **18.44,45**). Out of the Arabian Desert the south and west wind brought the scorching heat. Worldly wise in such matters of simple observation and common prudence, they shut their eyes to "the signs of the times". Hence the designation used: 'hypocrites''. There was pretence, the blindness of obstinacy and pride. Like a man doggedly determined to push a bad or a hopeless case to the last arbitrament of the law-courts (57,58), instead of seeking a just and reasonable accommodation out of court, the people were blundering on towards the disaster which lay ahead.

The signs of the coming Great Rebellion of A.D. 66 to 70 multiply in the New Testament. This warning is one of them. Wilfully blind, the Jewish people refused to heed the voice of prudence, and beat their nation to pieces against the iron wall of Rome. Among the few who survived in liberty were Christians who heeded such words as these.

Notes: V. 50: "constrained"—see the other use of this word in the N.T.—2 Cor. **5.**14; on the picture of baptism, see Mark **10.**38, and the language of Psalms **18.**16, **42.**7, **124.**4,5. V. 58: "the officer"—lit., "the exactor". V. 59: the coin was the Jewish *lepton*, the smallest coin in circulation.

St. Luke 13.1–9

Verses 1—5. Mention of Pilate's Galilean massacre, and the disaster of the Siloam Tower, flows from the words on judgment which closed the last chapter. It was no doubt suggested that the victims of the two catastrophes were under some special judgment of God. Not so, Christ replies. Man is exposed to the vicissitudes and chances of life, and God does not always intervene to protect the innocent from disaster. A little reflection will show why. Continual guarding of the good would make it *profitable* to be godly, on the lowest level of that word. If man is richly to believe it must be in spite of all, without special patronage or ready reward.

The mention of the atrocity at the altar is a glimpse of Pilate's rough-handed government. From the New Testament, from Josephus, and from Philo, a group of similar incidents may be collected. The same arrogant character, with its streak of cowardice, may be discerned throughout them all. It was a similar incident in Samaria which led finally to the procurator's recall in A.D. 36, and his disappearance from the pages of history.

Verses 6—9. Hos. **9.**10 and Joel **1.**7 are probably the key to the imagery. In verses 3 and 5 the Lord had used the chilling word "perish". How could a "chosen people" perish, was the spoken or unspoken response. The little parable is the answer. Fig trees were planted in spare corners of vineyards and it was natural to expect signs of fruit after three years. The truth which the Lord sought to emphasize was that national privilege carried national responsibility. To those taught to think in the imagery of the Old Testament, it was plain that Israel was the fig tree. Israel, the similitude suggested, would stand only while she fulfilled the historic purpose for which she came into being. This is true of all living. Every privilege carries a responsibility. A duty attaches to every endowment which man enjoys. Historically the respite might represent the early ministry of the Church in Palestine.

Notes: V. 1: possibly men who caused a riot when Pilate used money from the temple treasury to build a 25-mile aqueduct into Jerusalem; the incident may have caused the enmity between Pilate and Herod (**23.**12). Did the questioners expect Jesus, as a Galilean, to take sides for personal reasons? V. 7: literally, "for three years I have kept coming".

St. Luke 13.10–17

This story bears all the marks of direct reporting. It is the last instance in this gospel of an appearance in the synagogue. The places of regular assemblage were closing to the Lord's teaching, as the opposition of the Pharisees grew. The woman, the text runs, had a "spirit of infirmity". Luke could speak only in the language of his day, if he hoped to be understood by the people of his day. Dr Rendle Short points out that the woman's affliction was arthritic, with severe rigidity and deformation of the spine. The sense of firm and painful resistance to all efforts to straighten the back gave rise to the figure of speech: "a spirit of infirmity".

The leader of the synagogue emerges vividly from the brief account. He was chairman, in common Jewish practice, of a local board of ten men, who were in charge of the synagogue of the neighbourhood. He does not dare to confront his visitor directly. He rebukes Him indirectly (14) with an exhortation to the congregation on Sabbath-keeping. It was pharisaical "play-acting" of the first order, and earned the Lord's prompt retort. Sham and posing was a sin which stirred His righteous indignation. Compare Matt. 23.

The detailed Talmudic provisions for the care of stock on the Sabbath laid it down that water could be drawn for ox or ass on the seventh day, but that it must not be brought to the animal's mouth. Men who reduced religion to such meticulous absurdity could look with indifference both on human affliction and human deliverance. Hence the confounding of His adversaries, and the joy of those who found the religion of their leaders an anxiety and a burden.

Notes: V. 11: in spite of her infirmity, she attended the house of God —does this rebuke us? V. 12: the language of faith—it anticipates the fact. V. 16: a "daughter of Abraham"—physically *and* spiritually ("she praised God"). "Whom Satan bound"—not a concession to superstition: the spiritual "first causes" of infirmity are often under-rated.

St. Luke 13.18–30

Verses 18 and 19. This appears to be the only instance of parabolic teaching connected with the synagogue ministry . . . The grain of mustard seed was the smallest kind of seed sown by the farmers of the land, and grew to be the largest of their seed crops. It was a picture of history. All the story of the gospels took place in an area no bigger than Wales, the State of Vermont, or the northern peninsula of New Zealand. Twelve men, one of whom defected, were chosen from obscure towns of Galilee to stage an assault on the world. Those who have found liberty, release, joy, and fulfilment in Christ are "a multitude no man can number" (Rev. 7.9).

Verses 20 and 21. Those who regard leaven as a symbol of corruption in Scripture (see 12.1, 1 Cor. 5.6—8, Gal. 5.9) are in difficulties with this little parable. There is no doubt that it follows on the last, and carries a similar significance. There is no need to suppose that the same word or image must always be interpreted in one way. The picture here is surely the hidden working of a principle of life which permeates an inert mass. So works the Gospel in society and in the personality. To be sure, the New Testament does not teach that the world will be completely Christianized by the preaching of the Gospel, but parables are not to be pressed beyond their primary meaning.

Verses 22—30. The burden of these words is urgency. The Lord was moving down the Jordan valley and its associated territories. He never came that way again. The Cross is in clear view. Opportunity came and went, and some who saw the multitudes pass on their indifferent way, and the few who came to a live faith, were constrained to ask whether but few would be saved. The question was rejected as irrelevant. There is one urgent need—to take advantage of the hour's opportunity, and to meet the challenge of the moment. The Jewish nation were failing at this point, and others were laying hold of their privilege.

Notes: Vs. 18—20: the catacombs contain 4,000,000 Christian graves from the first three centuries; statistical analysis suggests that there were generations in which one third of the Roman population professed Christianity. V. 21: three measures—about $4\frac{1}{2}$ pecks. V. 24: "strive"—"do your utmost" —see 1 Tim. 6.12; "fight" is same word. V. 25: possibly a wedding feast, held at night, with a porter at the door, checking the guests. V. 28: an unexpected allusion to the place of the Gentiles in God's scheme of things. V. 29: *cf.* Isa. 49.12, 45.6.

St. Luke 13.31–14.6

Verses 31—33. The Lord must still have been within the boundaries of Herod's territories, which embraced both Galilee and Peraea (see "hence", 31). A map will help understanding at this point. It is impossible to say whether the Pharisees' warning was sincere concern, or a subterfuge to be rid of the Lord, to drive Him into Judea. Some among the Pharisees did not deserve the reputation which the majority had earned—e.g., Nicodemus and Gamaliel. Jesus evaded Herod, sent him a message of contempt, and when brought face to face with him, had nothing further to add.

Verses 34, 35. Luke anticipates. The sad remark about Jerusalem leads him to record here the lament over the city which was delivered from the summit of the Mount of Olives some weeks later. It must be remembered that a tidy and ordered narrative, with visible historical and geographical sequence, was not necessarily Luke's first object. The prime need was to record. There was a sense of urgency in his mind. He was free while Paul lay in custody at Caesarea to collect and set down the precious information. He died, if sudden silence bears that interpretation, before he could write the sequel to Acts, and much of his material may have been left in the form in which he first recorded and classified it. Hence some puzzles for commentators.

Verses 1—6. The strict Jew ate three times on the Sabbath. This was probably the midday meal. It is not impossible that the presence of the afflicted man was designed to trap Christ into yet another Sabbath violation. He used again the devastating argument of the legislation over the care of animals which did contain the elements of mercy and compassion (compare 13.15 and John 5.17). They gave to the beasts that which they denied to suffering man. The beasts, after all, cost money. Human life was cheap. Where Christianity wavers, it grows cheap again. *Grant, O Lord, that mercy may not die among men. Help us to honour Thee by compassion for our fellows.*

Notes: V. 32: "fox"—noted for slyness and cruelty. "Today and tomorrow"—"a brief time longer". 14.1: lit., "kept on watching Him"; Gk. implies close scrutiny with suspicious motive. The guests would be invited as a religious duty. V. 5: once again Jesus answers their thoughts. Notice "immediately"—they would treat *this* as a case for urgency.

St. Luke 14.7–24

Verses 7—14. There is a touch of irony in this table-talk. The gathering was a crowded one, and the competition for places of importance among the guests was embarrassingly evident. The Lord lays down some simple rules for such occasions, whimsically enough, but with serious rebuke for pride beneath it all. Compare John 5.44.

"How is it," asks C. S. Lewis, in his chapter on The Great Sin, "that

222

people who are quite obviously eaten up by pride can *say* that they believe in God and appear to themselves to be very religious? I am afraid it means that they are worshipping an imaginary God. They theoretically admit themselves to be nothing in the presence of this phantom God, but are really all the time imagining how He approves of them . . . this does not come through our animal nature at all. It comes direct from Hell. It is purely spiritual: consequently it is far more subtle and deadly . . ." The whole chapter (*Christian Behaviour*, pp. 42—47) should be read.

Verses 15—24. (Compare carefully with Matt. 22.1—10.) The first man had business which could not be delayed. He was insincere. No man would buy a farm without inspecting it beforehand. He really wanted to enjoy his farm, and there was nothing wrong in the desire. The man's system of priorities was wrong. Harmless pursuits, hobbies, enthusiasms, pleasure—all these can deprive us of Christ.

The second man likewise was eager to see the brown earth turning as his new team drew the plough. A deep interest in profession or trade, one's studies or one's work, can shorten the vision and dry up the soul.

The third man had the Law behind him. A Mosaic regulation freed a newly married man from military service for a year. With conscious rectitude he "cannot come", like the man who "cannot" be a Christian because the Church is "reactionary", the "tool of the governing class" . . . or perhaps because he has some substitute for faith and worship in some form of public service. "I cannot come" in all cases is "I will not come". Rebel man shirks, but shirks in vain, the responsibility for his withholding.

Notes: V. 12: lit., "Do not always invite your friends". V. 15: the hope of every Pharisee—to earn the reward of sitting at the Banquet of the Righteous. Vs. 16,17: Israel had received the first invitation through the prophets; the customary (in Eastern practice) second invitation had been given by John and Jesus Himself. V. 23: the compulsion is not that of force, but of loving earnestness—see same word in Matt. 14.22 and Mark 6.45. V. 24: "you"—the disciples.

St. Luke 14.25—35

Verses 25 and 26. No verses could more strikingly illustrate the need for Western readers to realize that they are reading the poetic language of the East. Hyperbole, or purposeful exaggeration, is a recognized figure of speech. The words cannot be taken literally, because the One Who bade His followers love their enemies would not call them in fact to hate their own folk. The expression merely establishes absolute priorities, and its use in this context flows from the third

223

excuse of the man in the story of the ungrateful guests. Loyalty to Christ is so demanding that it takes precedence over all other claims however natural and legitimate, upon the life. It overrides all other obligations. See 12.51, 53.

Verses 27—30. Christianity is an arduous, toilsome, and costly business. It is like engaging on a building project, a metaphor taken up by Paul (1 Cor. 3.10—15). It demands dogged perseverance, and continuance to the end.

Verses 31 and 32. Christianity is also a battle, a figure of speech also taken up by Paul (Eph. 6.11—17). The warring monarch count the cost of hostilities. Let no one forget that the Christian life is challenge to the powers of evil, which will undoubtedly be taken up. It is a warfare which never ends, and recruits should count the cost.

Verses 34 and 35. Those who do count the cost, and are ready to pay it, are like salt; they preserve the mass from utter corruption. The rock salt of Palestine is said to have lost its sharpness and usefulness by some form of chemical breakdown in the place of storage. It was henceforth of no use save as a form of gravel. The Christian who has lost his usefulness, his antiseptic function in a corrupt society, his sharp distinctive flavour, is of no use at all. For Christian discipline compare Rom. 8.13, Phil. 3.7*f.*, Col. 3.5.

Lord and Master, help us to count the cost, but enable us to pay it, to build well, battle well, and keep our savour.

Notes: V. 25: *en route* for Jerusalem, Jesus, as a potential Messiah was increasingly thronged—but plainly discouraged a mass movement. Vs. 29,31 refer possibly to the Herods indirectly, their building ambitions, and Herod Antipas' defeat by Hareth of Arabia. V. 33 "renounce"="say goodbye to", 2 Cor. 4.2.

Questions for Further Study and Discussion on St. Luke chapter 12.49—14.

1. How is the theme of "fire on earth" to be reconciled with the angels' message of "peace on earth" (2.14—see John 14.27)?
2. Follow through the Biblical references to Israel as the "fig tree" —what do they teach?
3. What light does 13.1—9 throw on the problems of providence
4. Are there any limits to Christian humility? Must it ever be qualified? In what way?
5. "The purest humility is in him who is never conscious of it"—is this true?

St. Luke 15.1–10

The key word for this chapter is "lost". The sheep was lost, the coin was lost, the son was lost—and all were found. The Lord put a new meaning into the word, brought into relief and clarity its pathos and its tragedy. The proud custodians of "religion" had no pity nor regard for the outcast crowd who saw with wistful eyes the new world, the new prospect, which Christ offered.

Folly, failure to mark the danger which lurked in the world of every day, thoughtless preoccupation with the petty needs led the sheep astray. From the beginning of the Bible to the end, the shepherd's calling and the shepherd's flock have formed an image. Moses was trained in the desert for the leading of the flock of God, the Lord is the Shepherd in the most heart-warming of all psalms. He claims the title in the last book of the Bible to be written. It would make an interesting study to follow the thought, with the aid of a concordance, through all Scripture.

The similitude of the sheep is not flattering for arrogant man. The sheep is a foolish animal, helpless before bold and ruthless predators, needing protection—the crook which restrains as well as the staff which defends. Sheep go blindly in crowds, are prone to stampede, and fatally apt to wander. "All we like sheep are gone astray . . ."

The shepherd's care is the notable part of the little parable; see Matt. 9.36, Rom. 5.6. To the Eastern shepherd sheep are individuals, not a nameless flock. There is significance in the fact. If only one of all mankind had strayed, the whole plan of God's salvation would still have been necessary, or God would have shown Himself that much less than all-loving.

The woman searching for the lost coin reveals another aspect of the same truth. The ten pieces of silver were no doubt the poor woman's dowry, worn about her neck as a precious possession. The nine which remained were no joy to her while her one was lost. The point of the story is again God's care for the individual, for each one of us.

Notes: V. 1: "were drawing near"—*i.e.*, repeatedly. V. 8: the silver *denarius* was the equivalent of a day's wage for a working man. Dark Eastern houses and a rush floor would make the search difficult.

St. Luke 15.11–24

Through the south-eastern districts of Galilee, where the Lord appears, at this time, to have been teaching, ran the road to the Decapolis, the crowded half-Gentile region of the Ten Towns, astride the southward-swinging caravan routes and the highways of trade and activity. The ruins of Gerasa, streets, houses, temples, remarkably well preserved, give a vivid picture of one of the towns of this busy land.

The Prodigal did not necessarily go far. He was able to reach home half-starved, in time of famine. A far country is not necessarily remote geographically. The rebel boy was as alienated and separated in heart and mind even in his father's household. He merely translated a mental attitude into fact, when he laid premature hands on that which he might later have enjoyed in fulness and in peace.

Perhaps some wandering Greek philosopher had proved to him the illogicality of faith, that the idea of God was "meaningless", and that life, after all, is only the experience of the senses—as many teach today. He did not tell him that philosophy is a constantly changing speculation, and can by sleight of words argue its own self out of existence, and destroy with words the very words in which it finds expression.

Famine came. It was periodic in the first century. A papyrus letter from A.D. 100, written by a prodigal just such as this young man to his mother, brings the story of the boy from Galilee very close to us. He was outcast, in rags, rejected. There is no evidence that the mother forgave. But the father in the Lord's story is a picture of God. The boy's motives for returning are low enough, but he had faith enough to rise and go. And when faith moves out, grace more than meets it. The father did not keep him waiting at the door, or receive him gruffly, ironically, sarcastically . . . He ran to meet him. It is the Parable of the Wonderful Father.

Notes: V. 12: "his living"—Deut. **21**.17, one third. V. 13: Gk. "living ruinously". V. 15: "feed swine"—abhorrent to a Jew; sin degrades as well as alienates. V. 19: "hired servants"—lower status than slaves; could be dismissed at will. V. 22: "robe"—sign of honour; "ring"—sign of authority; "shoes"—mark of sonship.

St. Luke 15.25–32

The story is also the Parable of the Unforgiving Brother. Like the Pharisees, who would have been horrified to jostle with Gentiles in the oval forum of Gerasa, the prodigal who had never left home claimed perfect obedience. Obedience? Yes. He had fulfilled meticulously the letter of the Law, and felt he had earned much from his father.

But it was a purely legal relationship, service rendered without love, and with no understanding of his father's heart. The elder brother also needed to kneel and say: "Father, I have sinned against

226

Photos: Forum and Amphitheatre at Jerash

heaven and against thee, and am no more worthy to be called thy son." But he had no sense of sin, no realization of his merciless heart no conviction of his bitter jealousy. "This son of *yours*," he said repudiating all bonds of brotherhood. He is a repelling picture. Note the rebuke in v. 32—"this *your* brother".

Let us give the parable a third name. It is the Parable of the Waiting Father. God sent His Son into the far country to pursue the prodigal. The elder brother might have done just this. The father in the story had no one whom he could send. He simply waited, as God still waits. Those whose children wander may take comfort here. They share the grief of God.

"O Lord, make haste to save us," runs the ordered prayer, and it is a cry natural enough. Indeed, the Prayer Book takes it from the Psalms. And yet it shows the situation from the angle of time-bound man alone, and not as it is seen from Heaven. God waits for the sinner's return. God is ready in grace to meet the sinner's inch with His mile. (See Isa. 55.7; Jer. 3.12; Eph. 2.4*f.*) The parable ends without a word of the future. The Pharisees are left free to make their own ending.

Let Heb. 10.22 in the N.E.B. rendering conclude: "*So let us make our approach in sincerity of heart and full assurance of faith, our guilty hearts sprinkled clean, our bodies washed with pure water. Let us be firm and unswerving in the confession of our hope, for the Giver of the promise may be trusted.*"

Notes: V. 28: "kept intreating him"—the father displays the same love to both sons. V. 30: note the direction in which the elder brother's suspicion at once turns ("harlots").

St. Luke 16.1–13

The story of the unjust steward is an excellent illustration of the basic principle in the interpretation of parables. The parable must not be pushed beyond its specific purpose. In other words, a parable is not an allegory. In an allegory *every* portion has symbolic significance. It is important to understand the difference. In the Oxford English Dictionary "allegory" is given as one of the meanings of "parable". This does not apply to the New Testament. None of its parables is an allegory.

The story is true to life. Among the papyri recovered from the sands of Egypt are many which illustrate such corruption. A hoard of letters found as part of the packing of a mummified crocodile proved to be the office file of a scamp named Menches, who held a petty official's post in an Egyptian town in the second century. It is obvious that he

vas busy with embezzlement, took bribes, and used his position for
base monetary ends.

The unprincipled fellow in the Lord's story was just such a man.
He miscalculated, as such villains sometimes do, and saw retribution
coming. With wicked agility he set to work to use his master's money
to secure advantage after his inevitable dismissal. The "lord", note
carefully, was the master of the man, not Christ.

But the whole point of the story is that worldly rogues will use
money to secure friends. On the basest levels of humanity money is
seen to be useful only for what it can do. And yet there are those who
should know better who seek money for its own sake. Christ despised
money. That fact is evident everywhere. Jolting His hearers to
attention with the strange story, Christ is asking them why they are
not as inventive in a better cause. Earthly wealth is a loan and a trust
which may at short notice be withdrawn. Heavenly possessions do not
diminish nor fail. The Christian is expected to manage well and
honestly the getting of money, to use money sanely, generously, and
usefully, but never to love money, never to trust it, never to use it for
base ends.

Notes: V. 1: unlike ch. 15 this is addressed specifically to disciples.
V. 6: the "measure" (Gk. *baton*) was about 22 litres. V. 7: "measure"
Gk. *koros*)—about 86 gallons. V. 9: "mammon"—an Aramaic word
meaning money; the opposite of "true riches" in v. 11. V. 13: "hate"
—see **14.26.**

St. Luke 16.14–31

Verses 14—18. These verses form a highly condensed account of a
clash with the Pharisees. As a class they loved money. As one commentator remarked: "Money-making generally agrees well with
religious separation among the Jews and Christians alike." Compact
groups of sufficient size and disparity provide a common market and
a mutual aid society which can be financially very effective. The
Pharisees, to be sure, paid their tithes, but mechanical giving can be
without grace, and can mean nothing in real terms of godliness.

The word on divorce (18) no doubt came from the same discourse
on the legalism of the Pharisees. The liberal school of Hillel allowed
divorce on the most trivial grounds. The stricter school of Shammai
was not the target of this implied reproach.

Verses 19—31. The parable of the Rich Man and Lazarus must be
interpreted in the manner already stressed. It is designed to teach that
the place and time of opportunity is here and now, that the measure
of earthly prosperity, social standing, and wealth is no indication of a

229

man's standing before God. The Rabbis regarded riches as a special
mark of God's favour. Obviously the details of the picture are
figurative. Paradise and Hell are not visible each from each, with
facilities for communication but none for transfer. "Abraham's
bosom", "the great gulf fixed", "this flame"—all are apocalyptic
details, and not intended to teach physical realities.

This fact by no means strips the story of its deep significance.
Heaven is not won by charity, but the rich man's callous carelessness
for the sad need in sight was an indication of his hard and alien heart,
a sure measure of his lovelessness; love awoke too late (28).

Misery had not turned the poor man to God, for want is no more a
way to Heaven than plenty, and it was the grace of God rejected or
embraced which reversed circumstance in the other world. Like his
brothers the man had God's Word. Hence the sad prophecy: those
who failed to heed the Word failed also to heed when One indeed
came back from the dead.

Notes: V. 16: *cf.* Gal. 3.24, Matt. 11.12. V. 23: "Hades" (O.T. Sheol)
in Jewish belief an abode of all the dead, but in N.T. the place where
unbelievers await final judgment. Vs.24,25,28: note the evidence for
continuance of personality and place of memory. V. 29: the O.T. is
adequate to point to Christ.

St. Luke 17.1–10

Verses 1—4. These crowded chapters in which Luke presents material
from the last discourses of Christ read sometimes like notes taken by
hearers or disciples. Indeed that is what they may have been. Much of
the teaching of the philosopher Aristotle survives in what appear to
be notes taken by his students, and only roughly edited. Luke, eager
to record and to preserve the precious words of the Lord, packed this
portion of his book with all the sayings he could find, and the connect-
ing thread is not always to be found. It is, however, there, more often
than not. Forget the artificial intrusion of a chapter heading, and let
the story run on. Woe, indeed, to such men as the merciless rich man
who allowed a helpless beggar, one of God's "little ones", to lie in
unrelieved and unpitied misery. Better by far had he been drowned
before the years piled guilt's weight or burden on his soul.

Verses 5 and 6. This section, as the opening words show, is part of a
discourse between the Lord and the Twelve. The language is Eastern.
Rooting up a tree (the sycamine had deep roots) and planting it *in the
sea* is an impossible process. It is intended to underline the vast power
of faith: its reality, rather than its quantity, is what matters.

Verses 7—10. This difficult little parable can only be rightly understood if the principles of interpretation already stressed are rigidly applied. Note first that this is a picture from life. This is what happens, or happened in that world of master and man, and before such assumptions of superiority produced the egalitarian reactions of today. The servant had to be prepared to "labour on, spend and be spent". This is not a picture of God, nor of God's way with men. It merely stresses the fact that one who serves goes on serving past the point of weariness. The servant of God must be prepared to serve as doggedly, to expect no special rewards, to know and realize that his performance is nothing more than he owes. The lesson is humility. Surely we should give to God without grumbling that which man, without complaint, gives man. The rest of the story is not told here. See Rev. 3.20.

Notes: V. 3: note there is a place for the loving rebuke. R.S.V. omits "against thee". V. 4: "seven"—see Matt. 18.21; the Rabbis said that a man was perfect if he forgave three times. V. 6: "sycamine" = mulberry. V. 10: "unworthy servants"—see 19.17, and compare Paul's experience (1 Cor. 9.19, 2 Tim. 4.7,8).

St. Luke 17.11–19

The geography is difficult, and this section perhaps has been displaced, and should have appeared earlier in Luke. In 9.51,52 and 13.22 we are assured that these events take place on the journey from Galilee, by way of the Jordan valley, to Jerusalem. Verse 11 is correct in R.S.V. The Samaritans had been hostile, and denied Him passage through their territory (see 9.51—53). He therefore passed out of Galilee through Bethshan, crossing the river where it winds through the flat valley floor not far south of the lake, and then proceeding down the eastern bank almost to the Dead Sea. He recrossed the Jordan at Jericho, at or near the place of His baptism. A map will help.

Somewhere on the road which threaded the Galilean border the band of lepers met Him and found healing. Of their number one returned and rendered thanks, and he found, not only cleansing for his body, but salvation for his soul.

Gratitude is the heart's memory. "It is a fruit of great cultivation," said Samuel Johnson, "you do not find it among gross people." "It is not only the greatest of virtues," said the Roman orator Cicero, "but the parent of all the others." By this he meant that the cold and the thankless heart can never know humility, can never surrender, and therefore can never know God.

231

There are mean souls who would agree with Henry Ward Beecher, that "next to ingratitude, gratitude is the most painful thing to bear". It warms the heart to receive that unexpected response, the open joy of the one in ten, who is able to render thanks in simplicity and joy. It warms but humbles. There are meaner souls who are unable to entertain, to give, or utter thanks, and yet are ready enough, human fashion, with complaining and reproach. How frequently is the problem of unmerited suffering discussed; how seldom unmerited good. Consider Psalms 50.14, 100.4, Phil. 4.6, Col. 2.7. *Make us mindful of our benefits, O Lord, thankful for Thy touch of cleansing, grateful for abundant life in Thee.*

Notes: V. 15: the Samaritan would go to his priests at Gerizim. V. 18: the wording suggests a mixed crowd of lepers—the community of suffering breaks down barriers. V. 19: his return sealed the connection "which his cure had formed between Jesus and him" (Godet).

St. Luke 17.20–37

This highly compact passage can only be understood if taken with Matthew's fuller account of the Lord's teaching on last things. The Lord answers the Pharisees negatively (20) and positively (21). Verse 20 is a difficult saying, but must mean that no one can predict the coming of the Lord as one *can* predict the movements of the sky. Meticulous observation fixes sunrise and sunset and the phases of the moon. It will not fix and date the Second Advent. Compare John 1.26. But trouble awaits (22), and stressful circumstance, which will make Christians long for God's decisive intervention, but at the same time expose the careless and the thoughtless to false Messiahs (John 1.10—12). Of such were Theudas (Acts 5.36), and Bar-Kochba, the leader of the last ruinous and desperate Jewish revolt in A.D. 132.

The consummation of all things comes upon a world utterly preoccupied with its worldly pursuits (26), without regard for the minority, the Noah, the Lot, who look for other things than the carnal round of each humdrum day. Suddenly God breaks in. The word "suddenly" is worth studying in the Bible. God's judgment is as the lightning, flashing unexpectedly forth, visible, decisive (24).

And it is judgment which seems to be in view in verse 31, with its specific warning. In Matthew's gospel it is striking to observe how, in the parallel account, the nearer and remoter events of history are intermingled. This verse seems to embody a warning about the calamity which was to come upon the land in the awful four years which closed the sixties of the century. The mob had called down judgment on themselves (Matt. 27.25). The Christians of Jerusalem did "remember", and escaped in large numbers to the Decapolis as the Roman army closed the ring round Jerusalem. The eagles of verse 37 may be a symbol of the legions, each with its eagle standard at the head (see note below). Let one clear message emerge: the end of the age will be God's intervention. Christians should watch, work, and hold the material world with light hand.

Notes: V. 21: R.S.V. "in the midst of you" is correct. V. 25: "generation"—some commentators see this as reference to the Jewish nation. V. 33: "preserve"—Gk. "bring to new birth". V. 34: possibly husband and wife ("men"==humans). V. 37: "eagles"—vultures. "Where the spiritually dead people are, there the judgement will be executed" (Geldenhuys).

Questions for Further Study and Discussion on St. Luke, chapters 15—17.
1. What principles of evangelism can be deduced from Luke 15?
2. What light is thrown on the nature of God in Luke 15—17 (John 1.18)?
3. What principles of interpretation are suggested by the parables of Luke 15—17?
4. What do we learn about the sources of failure in Christian service from the passages considered in the last six studies?
5. What did the Lord mean by the words "lost" and "saved"?

St. Luke 18.1–8
Here is another of the forceful stories which Luke discovered and preserved. Yet again it illustrates the need, in the interpretation of parables, to keep the central meaning in view, and to recognize the details which have no doctrinal significance. The story is manifestly from life. Here, perhaps, is the godless and arrogant petty magistrate of some Galilean community denying a widow woman the simple benefits of justice. The widow is chosen as the victim of the scoundrel's callous disregard because the widow was the weakest and the most pitiably helpless unit of that sad society.

She was a dogged woman who worked upon one simple conviction. The magistrate's duty was to dispense justice with impartiality and to all. She was determined to hold him to his task, and so besieged his court day by day. Preoccupied with more profitable cases—those which, on the evidence of the papyri, were rich in the profits of

bribery and corruption—the judge adjourned the widow's case, until
at last her very importunity forced him to act.

God is no unjust judge, but for other reasons He appears to delay,
and to leave His children to suffer the injustices of the world. If a
village woman in some local court can be sufficiently convinced of
ultimate action and final justice to go against all discouragement to
final success, how much more should Christians persevere in faithful
petition! They at least can be assured that the delay which seems so
often to confront their desire is not the delay of selfishness and
corruption, but of wisdom and beneficent purpose (read Rom. 8.28
in Phillips' rendering).

*Review, at this point, the series of illustrative stories which Luke has
recorded. Note their characteristics, their realism, their characters.
Observe how the characters talk to themselves (the prodigal, the steward,
the judge). It is part of the dramatic machinery. And out of the evil of
common life the Lord draws a lesson of good.*

Notes: V. 2: the judge breaks both the great commandments. V. 3:
note R.S.V., "kept coming". V. 5: Gk., lit., "gives me a black eye".
V. 8: "speedily"—not "soon", but "by a decisive intervention".
The reference to faith indicates that this parable is not concerned with
God allowing Himself to be bullied into answering prayer; He is
encouraging us to hold on by faith in times of adversity.

St. Luke 18.9–14

The last degeneracy of prayer is self-congratulation. The Pharisee's
God was too small. Like those of Psalm 50.21, he had made himself a
God in his own image.

The picture is vividly drawn and is again from life. The Pharisee
"takes his stand", the text runs literally. He had his place, doubtless a
place most carefully chosen, where his words could be heard by all,
for this man was guilty of that vast irreverence, not unknown in the
prayer meeting—self-advertisement in the holy place.

He "prayed thus with himself". His prayer was for himself and
about himself. It did not reach the ear of God. He prayed aloud so that
all could hear. This was common practice in the ancient world.
Horace, the Roman poet, pictures just such a hypocrite making a
public petition in the temple of Apollo, and adding to the impeccable
prayers which others can hear the whispered private petition that
Heaven's blessing fall upon his trickery and deceit.

Pride is everywhere evil. In the holy place it approaches blasphemy
The pompous creature was not as other men. With a curled lip of
contempt, he even draws God's attention to the poor publican. The

wondering crowd were expected to look from the richly robed figure gazing up to God to the bent and downcast form of the broken man who sought forgiveness.

He came with the first requisite of forgiveness, "a broken and a contrite heart", which God does not despise (Psalm 51.17), as He certainly despises the arrogance and sham of self-satisfied hypocrites. (See Job 40—42.6; Isa. 2.22.) The publican heard what the Pharisee said about him. He did not utter a word of reproach. He cried with bowed head: "God be merciful to me *the* sinner." Why the Authorized (King James') Version says "*a* sinner" is without explanation. The definite article is plain enough in the Greek. "Yes, Lord," he said, "I am the sinner of whom he speaks. Thy mercy, Lord." If we desire justification it is found thus and in no other way (1 John 1.9).

Notes: V. 12: "twice in the week": Mondays and Thursdays, a practice imposed by tradition, and a work of supererogation; the Law ordained one fast day only (Lev. 16.29); "all that I get"—*cf.* Deut. 14.22,23 with Luke 11.42. V. 13: "be merciful"—Gk., "be propitiated".

St. Luke 18.15–23

Verses 15—17. The worth of humility is the thought which links this section to the last. At this point Luke's account rejoins those of Matthew and Mark. A glance at Mark's account (10.13—16) will show that Luke tones down a little the rebuke of the Twelve. This is a characteristic of his writing. After all, he was not as free to speak as Matthew and John, who were themselves members of the apostles' band, or Mark who wrote under the specific direction of Peter. It is instructive to collect from the gospels the Lord's sayings about children. He stands in some contrast with the Jews generally, whose attitude towards children tended to be disciplinary in the narrower sense, and severe. Christianity is the charter of freedom for both women and children. A papyrus letter dating from about the time of Christ's birth throws vivid light on this. It is an affectionate note from a Greek workman in Egypt to his wife in Alexandria, who was expecting a child during her husband's absence. "If it is a girl, throw it out," he concludes casually. And such was the way of the hard pagan world. The unwanted children died on the city rubbish heap, or were diligently picked up by slavers and other vermin.

Verses 18—23. The theme of self-abasement continues into another story. "Good Master," cries the young man, without consciousness of the true significance of the term. The Lord's reply is not a repudiation of goodness, but an attempt to bring the young man face to face with

235

realities. The answer should have been: "I call You good because You are the Son of the Living God, the Messiah." A pause . . . and the Lord, having failed here to elicit a true answer, challenges the youth with the commandments, only to meet a naïve claim to perfection. He had certainly not understood the commandments as Christ interpreted them in the Sermon on the Mount. The Lord thrust home to this unsurrendered corner of his life. It was the technique of John 4.16. Unable to face such a test of self-abnegation, the young man withdrew. It is a sad picture.

Notes: V. 19: the emphasis is on "Why". See Matt. 16.13—19. Note tne difference in the way Jesus answers here from the case of the lawyer in 10.25—28.

St. Luke 18.24–30

The Lord looked with grief after the retreating figure. He was like so many, pleasant to know, upright in character, generous, no doubt, and a useful member of the community, but unwilling to follow Christ. The dominant power in the young man's life was his wealth. The guarding, cherishing, and maintaining of his fortune must have been the main preoccupation of his life. Had this not been the case, the Lord would not have recommended such drastic surgery.

His attitude must, in fact, have been unusually severe, for it puzzled the Twelve, especially when the strange saying about the camel and the needle was added. Much ingenuity has been expended on the phrase. Some suggest a gate into Jerusalem so small that it was called the "Needle's Eye", the access point in the hours of darkness when the main gates were shut. A camel could pass through only if its load were removed. There is no evidence that such a gate ever existed.

Another explanation is that the words for "cable" and "camel" were alike. The Greek for camel is *kamelos*, with a long 'e' pronounced like "air" or "aye". If the word for cable or ship's hawser was *kamilos*, with a long 'i', confusion would be easy, since vowels in Greek were already undergoing the transformation which has made them all sound like 'i' in modern Greek. This is an attractive explanation: "It is as hard for the wealthy to make a full committal of their life to God as it is to thread a cable through a needle." The only doubt lies in the paucity of evidence for the existence of the word *kamilos*.

The simple explanation is Eastern hyperbole, or picturesque exaggeration. The West always finds such poetic language difficult. Even the Twelve found it disconcerting. The Lord's enigmatic word in verse 27 means: "God sees things differently—sees possibilities lost on us, openings for grace which elude us."

236

Notes: V. 24: "entering the kingdom of God" is synonymous with "inheriting eternal life" (18), and "being saved" (26). V. 28: Gk., "abandoning our homes". V. 30: "age to come"—"in the age which is being realized".

St. Luke 18.31—43

Verses 31—34. They were nearing Jericho. To the left was the blue level of the salt sea. The green river valley, flat-floored and covered with farmland, green patches of the "jungle of Jordan", trees and crops, were at their feet. The oasis of Jericho formed, as it still forms, a splash of verdure in the midst of the plain. Perhaps they could see the beginning of the road which climbs from the deep-set plain, 1,300 feet below the level of the sea, to Jerusalem, perched 2,600 feet above the Mediterranean.

It was the road to the Cross. It is clear from the other gospels that the Lord had spent much time training His men to meet that which was to be. They had understood little of what He had to say (see 9.22, 44; 13.33). This must have been a lonely time for Him, with none to mark and know. and understand, in love and fellow-feeling, the burden which He bore . . . The road dropped to the valley floor, crossed the Jordan near the place where He had been baptized, and bent slightly north towards the green of Jericho.

Verses 35—43. The healing of the blind man (a contrast to the blindness of the disciples, 34?) took place as the party entered Jericho. Mark speaks of Bartimaeus, and Matthew of two blind men who found healing as the Lord left the town. Those anxious to discover "contradictions" in Scripture have made much of this. If the three accounts are read precisely as they are set down, it will be clear enough that three or perhaps four men were healed, one of whom was named Bartimaeus. Incidents took place on both sides of the town. What is more likely than that the news of the first healing, and the words which claimed attention, should spread through the crowd and provoke other requests? Others see a confusion between Old Jericho, the mound which covers the Canaanitish city-fort, where the excavations may be seen today, and New Jericho, Herod's foundation, the modern tree-filled town. There is no careless reporting. It is the brevity of Scripture which causes misunderstanding.

Notes: V. 32: Mark 10.33 emphasizes Jewish responsibility. V. 33: Jesus always speaks of the Crucifixion in the context of Resurrection. Vs. 38,41: compare Isa. 11.1 and 35.4,5. V. 39: "cried"—a different word from that in v. 38, signifying more intense emotion. V. 43: Luke makes a special point of recording doxologies.

St. Luke 19.1–10

Much trade passed through Jericho. It lay on the highway from the fords of Jordan to Judea, an east–west artery of commerce. At such points there was much to gather in customs dues. Jericho, with its balsam groves, was itself a rich place. Jericho was a desirable place of residence, apart from the sultry heat, which may have been less burdensome in those days than now. There are some indications that the temperature of the whole Mediterranean area has risen over the last 2,000 years.

Zacchaeus' eagerness to see the Lord is some indication of his deep longing for something better than the despised calling of a hated tax collector, with its temptations, corruptions, and ostracism. It is an extraordinarily vivid scene, not without its humour, as the small man, forgetful of dignity, outdistances the crowd and climbs just such a roadside tree as those which may be seen in Jericho today, palms and jacarandas. The story may have been first written in Aramaic. There are numerous "ands" and turns of phrase which suggest such an original. It would be interesting to know Luke's informant.

Observe the Lord's warm response to the man whose humble wish was only to see Him. Zacchaeus wanted a glimpse of another world, a world of peace with God and a heart at rest. He did not realize how close such a realm lies to the turmoil of common life. Like one who turns aside from some roaring motorway to picnic in peace behind a hedgerow down some quiet English lane, so those who will can step from the tumult of the world into the peace of God. The delight of the poor man is evident. Christ cannot come truly as a guest into a home without cleansing it. He cannot enter a life without bringing sanctification. It all illustrates **18.24,27**.

Notes: V. 3: the crowd express their hostility by keeping Zacchaeus from seeing Jesus. V. 5: Jesus knows about Zacchaeus' home. V. 8: Zacchaeus repays on the scale of Exod. **22.1** rather than Exod. **22.4,7, 9**; Lev. **6.5**; Num. **5.7**. V. 9: "son of Abraham"—spiritually as well as physically—Rom. **4.16**.

St. Luke 19.11–19

When that clever scoundrel Herod the First died, his will divided the kingdom between his sons. Judea was part of the portion of Archelaus, and this was why Joseph and Mary, returning from Egypt, did not go back to Bethlehem, but went north to Nazareth in the realm of Herod Antipas (Matt. **2.22,23**).

Archelaus, who had a full share of his father's vices, without the first Herod's diplomatic astuteness, began his rule over Judea with the sanguinary suppression of disorders in Jerusalem. A widespread Jewish uprising necessitated the armed intervention of Varus, the governor of Syria. It was at this time of tension that Joseph and Mary returned from Egypt, and the disturbed state of the country was abundant reason for their change of residence.

But it was vital for Archelaus to have his authority confirmed by Augustus in Rome, and necessary, in consequence, for him to hurry to the capital before reports from Palestine, and especially the despatches of Varus, presented the condition of affairs in Judea in too unfavourable a light. A Jewish embassy, and Herod Antipas in person, opposed Archelaus' appointment. Augustus, surprisingly, did confirm his title to Judea, but refused the appellation of "king".

Archelaus, then, was the "nobleman" who went abroad to "receive a kingdom", and it was natural enough for the Lord to use the incident as a parable in Jericho, because this was his starting-point. Archelaus had a large palace in Jericho, and the sight of its white marble and terraces suggested the pointed story.

It is a further striking illustration of the necessity of dissociating the incidental machinery of a parable from the moral or doctrinal significance. There could be no greater contrast between the Lord, leaving behind Him His followers with responsibilities, and the villain of the Herod family, whose tyrannical rule until A.D. 6 altogether failed to justify the confidence which Augustus had placed in him. We shall look further at the exegesis in our comments on the next section.

St. Luke 19.20–27
This parable is not another version of the Parable of the Talents told in Matt. 25.14–30. Jesus must not be supposed to have taught each lesson only once and in the same form and context. The differences between the two stories and their teaching should be carefully listed. For example, the unprofitable servant is not cast out in this case.

The reason for this parable is given in verse 11. There was excitement among the Twelve, and Mark's account of incidents on the journey up to Jerusalem (Mark 10.32–45) reveals the mood of expectation. "The kingdom" was at hand—the kingdom as they disastrously conceived it, with an earthly Messiah dispensing the rewards of victory.

The parable hints first at long delay. The ruler went to "a far country". The servants of the ruler had one task to perform in his absence. It was a test of fidelity and capacity when he gave each a modest sum, and left them to demonstrate in the arena of trade their fitness to serve in a wider field, and their concern for his work . . .

239

Archelaus may, indeed, have done something like this, and, when he returned from Rome in a bitter mood of frustration over Augustus' refusal of the royal title, he may have meted out just such savage punishment as Luke here records. At any rate, the rough and ready method of examination did reveal to him those who gave and those who grudged their service to the new regime.

The second point which the parable teaches is the inevitability of the day of reckoning. Archelaus inevitably returned. The certainty of God's judgment day is yet more sure. The servants of the Lord are called to long and arduous service, to dogged day-by-day prosecution of their task, to inventiveness and to endeavour. Faithfulness in the hard trial of Christian living will determine wider opportunity to serve, and every man, before the judgment seat of Christ, will give an account of the service rendered (1 Cor. 3.12–15; 2 Cor. 5.10). *Prepare our souls, O Lord, for that great day.*

Notes: V. 23: *cf.* a traditional saying of Jesus—"show yourselves approved bankers". V. 26: those who use spiritual opportunities will be given even more; those who fail to do so will lose the ones they had. For the Christian's attitude while waiting for the Lord's return see Eph. 5.16, Col. 4.5, 2 Tim. 4.1,2.

Questions for Further Study and Discussion on St. Luke, chapters 18.1—19.27.

1. How and why do men fall into the error of making God in their own image?
2. What does 18.1—14 teach about the proper approach to God in prayer? How do we know when to persist in prayer and when to recognize that it is mistaken?
3. What has Luke's gospel to say about the peril of riches?
4. Begin with 18.16,17, and follow through the subject of ministration to children in the N.T. Is Protestant practice satisfactory?
5. In what respects did the young man of ch. 18 differ from Zacchaeus in his approach to Christ?
6. What details do chs. 18 and 19 add to the development of Luke's theme?

St. Luke 19.28–40

The long climb up from Jericho reaches its highest point on the Mount of Olives. It approaches the summit by way of a long uplifted ridge on which the village of Bethany still stands. The mountains of Moab are a pale blue rampart above the Dead Sea, which lies out of sight in its great trench. In the other direction, still screened by the Mount of

Olives, lies the Holy City. The modern road skirts the foot of the hill. The ancient road lay right over its summit, no doubt in order to give approaching travellers from that direction the magnificent panorama of Jerusalem which the hilltop offers.

The Lord probably had some arrangement about the ass. He deliberately fulfilled a prophecy of Zechariah (9.9) when He chose the ass for His triumphal entry into Jerusalem. It was on an ass that the ancient monarch rode when he came on a mission of peace. A horse was the beast of war. On that momentous day He was offering Himself to Jerusalem, not as the Messiah of war, which their carnal expectation desired, but as the Prince of Peace. He wanted no illusions.

He wants no illusions today in the minds of those who serve Him. Churchill, in the grim days of 1940, offered nothing but "blood and toil and tears and sweat". Christ offers more than that—the peace which passes understanding, His presence and His championship; but He would not have those who follow Him imagine that they will be favoured with material advantage, protected from all ill, exempt from the world's spite and bitterness.

The cheering multitude saw the coming of One Who would perhaps lead them to victory over the occupying power, would form a rallying point for the proletariat against the priesthood and the collaborating aristocracy. Hence the change of mood a week later. The Lord was offering Himself as He always does on His terms. So many were accepting Him on theirs. And yet, unwittingly in many cases, they uttered truth. Hence His closing words.

Notes: V. 29: Bethphage—an outer suburb; Bethany—2 miles away. V. 35: a royal honour (2 Kings 9.13). V. 37: the raising of Lazarus (John 11.45) had intensified the interest and excitement.

St. Luke 19.41–48

Verses 41—44. From the high swell of the Mount of Olives Jerusalem may be seen entire. Over the valley of the Kedron the ancient walls top the stony ridge on whose slopes Stephen was to die. The packed roofs of the old city fill the view. Hence the Lord's distress. The veil of the years grew thin before Him and He saw what the Roman ballista teams saw from the same spot almost forty years later. In the stark vision of forty years on there were no grey-green olives on the slope, only blackened stumps, there was no going and coming on the road below. The gates were closed. The walls were marred and scarred by the catapult stones ... And not long afterwards the city was a ruined heap of ash and blackened stone covering a multitude of dead. It was a day of visitation indeed. When the Lord spoke there was still a choice

241

between the terror which was seeping through Palestine, the growing power of hate, the rising tide of violence, and the acceptance of Christ, with a rôle in the world which might have changed all history in some unimagined way. But "they would not".

Verses 45—48. From Mark **11**.11 and 15 it appears that Jesus crossed the Kedron, entered the city, and went straight to the temple. It was only a few hundred yards to the left of His place of entry. He observed the situation there. The old abuses had crept back to the holy place since the earlier occasion, described by John (**2**.13—17), when He had driven out the traders and money-changers. He then retired to Bethany for the night, came back to the city the next morning, and cleansed the temple afresh. This seems the best reconstruction of events. The Sadducean priesthood, who authorized this vulgar but lucrative bazaar in the Court of the Gentiles, were hesitant to act because of the popular support for the Lord among the multitude. It required a few days for them to develop a plan of campaign. They waited cunningly for the onset of disillusionment in those who had expected a spectacular demonstration of messiahship; they cornered Pilate, and circumvented the rest. But what of the temple of our lives (2 Cor. **6**.16,17)? Note also Isa. **56**.7, Jer. **7**.11, Zech. **14**.21, Mal. **3**.1,2.

Notes: Compare Christ's lament with **13**.34,35. V. 41: "wept"— aloud; contrast the silent tears over Lazarus (John **11**.35). V. 46: "cave of brigands" (Gk.)—*cf.* Isa. **56**.7, Jer. **7**.11. Birds and animals for sacrifice were sold at exorbitant prices; Greek, Roman and Tyrian coins had to be changed into Jewish money—at a premium, of course.

St. Luke 20.1–18

Verses 1—8. The imposing group from the Sanhedrin "came upon Him". It is the same verb as that which is used in **10**.40 of Martha's sudden and exasperated approach to the Lord. They came on Him suddenly, they came and stood over Him: both of these meanings are in the word. It is used again in **21**.35 for the coming of judgment. The dilemma of the authorities is apparent. What authority had He to empty and to appropriate the temple court for His preaching? At this point they were fumbling for a charge against Him. He countered with a devastating question, and the example is one to note. Controversy is sometimes inevitable, although it should never be sought. If such strife of words is thrust upon the Christian, it is well for him not to stand on the defensive. Be ready, by all means, to give a reason for faith (1 Pet. **3**.15), but counter question with question. The opponent of the Gospel has many questions to answer. He also has a faith for which he must give a reason, for he too has staked his life upon a belief—a belief that Chance ruled creation; that the world and all things visible are a great joke played by no one or everyone; that all the best of all the centuries was built upon a delusion or a fraud, that evil has chosen the better part . . .

Verses 9—18. This parable is closer to being a full allegory than most of the other parables in the New Testament. There was no doubt in the minds of the religious leaders at whom it was directed. The image of the vineyard was deep in Scripture (Deut. 32.32,33; Psalm 80.8—16; Isa. 5.1—7; Jer. 2.21; Ezek. 15.1—6, 19.10—14; Hos. 10.1; Joel 1.7). History was woven bitingly into the story. Those who were entrusted with the guardianship of the vineyard looked upon it as their private preserve, and neither Israel nor Israel's rulers, who were the twin objects of the parable's twofold significance, held a prerogative here. The parable passed from history to prophecy in verses 14 and 15. Verse 17 is from Psalm 118.22, a song said to have been sung at the completion of the walls of Jerusalem in 444 B.C. The Lord showed the true content of the words. The Early Church remembered this—see Acts 4.11; 1 Pet. 2.7,8; Rom. 9.33.

Notes: Mark 11.12,20,27 suggests that this Day of Questions was Tuesday in Holy Week. Each of the main groups puts a question reflecting their dominant concern—the Pharisees (authority, 1—20); the Herodians (political responsibility, 21—26); the Sadducees (speculative theology, 27—38).

St. Luke 20.19—38

Verses 19—26. Since A.D. 6 the land had been under procuratorial rule. A procurator was a minor governor directly responsible to Caesar himself, so Roman rule was immediate and clear. The tribute was, however, its clearest and most irksome symbol. The silver denarius, bearing Caesar's image and superscription, was issued for the purposes of taxation. The legal fiction was that coinage so stamped belonged to the Emperor, who, in receiving tribute but recovered his own. It was a subtle point, but not without its usefulness among the legally-minded Jews, who avoided in this way some of the impact of direct payment of dues to an alien, and also the reproach of accepting a form of "graven image". Taxation, however, and the use of the embossed coinage, was a burning problem, and the trap thus set was a deadly one. It would have been fatal to answer either way. The reply which the Lord gave established an abiding principle. Those versed in the Old Testament could not well ponder the words without realizing that man too bears an image—that of God, in Whose likeness he was made. "Give back to Caesar what Caesar owns, but give back to God that which is His—your persons and all that which you are."

Verses 27—38. The Sadducees were a worldly sect who controlled the priesthood, and formed the core of collaborating Jewry. They accepted only the five books of Moses, and so among the vital doctrines which they had rejected was that of the resurrection. Their question was an attempt to make both teacher and teaching appear ridiculous, a not uncommon method of attack. The Lord replied to the absurd question with dignity. A future life must not be crudely regarded as a material continuation of the present life. It is another mode of existence, altogether different but utterly blessed (1 Cor. **2.**9). It is the perennial fault of man to conclude that there can be no reality outside the competence of his five senses to apprehend. In fact he is the prisoner of those senses, and can only break free by faith. The Sadducees applied the limited faculties of sense and mind to spiritual matters, reached absurd conclusions, and rejected truth. Later Pharisees used the argument of v. 37.

Notes: V. 19: they resist the plain truth of Christ's parable, and so are led—as always—to greater wickedness. V. 21: note the flattery. V. 22: "lawful"—by Moses' law. V. 24: Jewish coins bore agricultural emblems. V. 25: "render"—Gk., "pay what is due".

St. Luke 20.39–21.4

Verses 39—47. The Lord's use of Scripture was one with which His opponents and questioners were quite familiar. The Christian authentication of Christ rests on other grounds—His resurrection, and all that which the New Testament has to say on its significance. The Church has the gospels, also, and the record of His life and death. The prophecies of the Old Testament, with their clear indications of Davidic descent, were much more significant as arguments in a Jewish context (2 Sam. **7.**8—29; Isa. **9.**5—7; Mic. **5.**2; Psalm **110.**1, *etc.*). It is well to remember that a messianic meaning in these places is not precluded by some other or local significance which may have had a place in the Scripture concerned. It is often the case that a passage of Scripture has both primary and secondary meaning. The Lord was also speaking within the context of the Jewish interpretation of the Old Testament, and confounding His critics with their own doctrine and methods of exegesis.

Verses 1—4. After distasteful conflict on the levels of their choice, the Lord appeared to turn with relief to a spectacle of humble

244

devotion. "He looked up and saw . . ." He had been sitting, weary, with downcast eyes, and was refreshed to see the poor widow's sacrifice. She little knew the magnitude of her gift, its vast fruitfulness, the fame it was to win, and the joy it gave to the Lord Himself.

Gifts are relative. Legalistic tithing systems, indiscriminatingly pressed by some churches, take no thought of this. Money, like all else, is held in trust. There are priorities in its use. A man's family must first be properly provided for. Children made unwisely to suffer by a father's financial sacrifices are more difficult to win for Christ; and to win one's own family is the first and most essential duty of a Christian parent. And let it also be observed that a tithe is no sacrifice for others. The New Testament gives no authority for tithing. Christian giving is a far less mechanical obligation.

Notes: Vs. 45–47 may well sum up the condemnation of Matt. **23** (cf. Matt. **22**.41–45; Luke **20**.41–44). Vs. 42,43: note the use of these in Acts **2**.34,35. V.2: the temple authorities prescribed *two* gifts; hence this was a minimum. The "mite" (*lepton*) rated 128 to the denarius.

St. Luke 21.5–19

The group was inside the building. The "goodly stones" were the marble walls; the gifts included a table from Ptolemy of Egypt, a chain from Agrippa, a golden vine from Herod. Tacitus, the Roman historian, who told of the siege of Jerusalem, called the temple a "shrine of immense wealth". It was a shock to the hearers to be told that destruction awaited the mighty and beautiful place. But a "greater" had been rejected; judgment was inevitable (Deut. **18**.19, **32**.35; Lev. **26**.31—33; 1 Kings **9**.6—9; Mic. **3**.12).

The prophetic words of Christ gave a grim preview of terrible years which lay ahead. They telescope the centuries in the frequent fashion of prophecy, but have first in view the two dark generations of judgment which followed the rejection of Christ. The mad challenge to the might of Rome, in the days of the Empire's ruthless strength, was already taking shape in the time of Christ. (See the account of the Great Rebellion in *The Century of the New Testament*, by the writer of these notes.)

The warning of verse 8 is the core of this section. There was to be persecution, but delusion was a greater danger. Those who heed the Lord's words will not readily be led astray by the heresy, exhibitionism, and folly which have so often spoiled and marred the blessed hope of the coming of the Lord.

The special directions given to the persecuted were probably intended to meet their immediate need. There was no New Testament, with its rounded body of doctrine, no record of the experience of the Church. Simple and unlettered men were often called upon to make their defence before the learned and the great, and the promise of the Spirit's aid was intended for them, and for all who at all times were similarly challenged. The words are not meant to excuse those who are equipped and able to prepare from proper attention to defence and proclamation. God can and will guide in preparation as well as in utterance.

Notes: Vs. 10,11: an earthquake ravaged Phrygia in A.D. 61 Vesuvius erupted disastrously in A.D. 63; worldwide famines occurred in the 50s and 60s; there was war in Britain, Parthia, and Palestine; A.D. 69 saw *four* emperors (Nero died in A.D. 68). Vs 12—17 all find fulfilment in the Book of Acts.

St. Luke 21.20—38

Verses 20—24. The local garrison were quite unable to deal with the first passionate outbreak of revolt. The Roman army group which watched over the eastern and north-eastern frontiers was located in Syria, because Rome regarded the Parthians as the gravest menace on this flank. The Jews in consequence had notable initial success in A.D. 66. But inexorably the strength of the Syrian legions was brought to bear on the situation. Under the capable Vespasian, who was to emerge from the complex civil war of A.D. 69 as Emperor of Rome the disciplined armies of the eastern command began to deal with Palestine. The conquest was methodical and complete, with Jerusalem left until the countryside had been combed and subdued. Hence the relevance of the warning. The city could appear deceptively as a place of refuge to the rural population of Judea. But all who were trapped there found death or slavery. A million Jews died; 97,000 went into servitude. Eusebius describes the escape of Christians to Pella.

Verses 25—28 have a main reference to "last times" at the end of the day of grace, the "times of the Gentiles" (Rom. 11.25). The closing words of verse 25, "the sea and the waves roaring", is clear enough indication that the Lord is using "apocalyptic" language, a recognized type of poetic symbolism, the meaning of which was plainer to the Jews than it is to us. The sea has been an image for the restless surge of nations in more than one language. The heavenly bodies are an image for those in authority (*e.g.*, Gen. 37.9). The rise and fall of kings and tyrants has been a commonplace of history, but seldom more strikingly than in the first century and the twentieth.

Verses 29—36 seem to refer back primarily to the Fall of Jerusalem The word "generation" in verse 32 illustrates the dual meaning of this passage of apocalyptic poetry. It can mean those living at a given time, and also "race" or "stock". Both meanings are common through all the range of Greek literature. It is true that there were those living who saw the horror descend on Palestine. It is also true that the Jewish race has outlived all attempts to obliterate it, and it is the Lord's prophecy that it will be living still at the consummation of man's history.

Meanwhile let us heed verse 34, stand alert, and be prepared in heart, for the Day could be today. 2 Peter 3.1—14 is relevant.

St. Luke 22.1–13

Verses 1—6. In this sombre narrative note two points. Judas was "of the number of the twelve". To be numbered with a group can be of small significance. It is sympathy, love and fellowship which bind a man to his fellows. Judas had long been alien in heart. Betrayal opened a way for a successful attack from without. The Church can fall only by betrayal from within, the sabotage of standards, the decay of faith. Judas plays his part in all centuries. And "they were glad" (5), for Jewry, gathered in vast hordes round Jerusalem, was a formidable force (see Mark **14.**2). The one deterrent had been fear. Injustice, false witness, unutterable cruelty wreaked on the innocent and good, treachery—all these vicious and noxious things were taken in their stride by men who feared for comfort and prestige. God was "sifting out the souls of men before His judgment seat", and these men were demonstrating the depth of their perdition.

Verses 7—13. The house thus honoured was probably that of Acts **12.**12, the home of Mark's mother, or perhaps of both his parents. If Mark's father was still alive at this time, his co-operation in the Lord's plan must have been one of the last deeds of his life. The evening cannot be better spent than in such service. The Lord was aware of Judas' plotting, and was seeking to conceal the place of the Last Supper for as long as possible. It was easy enough for the faithful two, Peter and John, to distinguish their host among the many pilgrims in the crowded streets, for it was quite unusual for a man to be seen carrying a pitcher of water. Women carried pitchers, men skins . . . The room shown today as the "cenaculum" in one ancient corner of Jerusalem is medieval, but could occupy the site. It is a blessed home which entertains Christ and keeps open table for His men. Its young people are the likelier to follow Christ, for it was thus that Peter won Mark. (Motto at Oak Hill College, London: *It became known that He was in the house.*)
Notes: V. 1: a colloquial explanation; the Feast of Unleavened

247

Bread lasted from 14 to 21 Nisan, and 15 Nisan was the Day of Passover. V. 4: "captains"—the Levitic Captain of the Temple and his force.

St. Luke 22.14–23

The order of events is described in Matthew. Mark and the first Corinthian letter show some variation but this has no significance. A Syrian manuscript of Luke is different again, and may represent an ancient tradition: "And He took bread and gave thanks over it, and brake and gave unto them, saying, This is My body which I give for you; this do in remembrance of Me. And after they had supped He took the cup and gave thanks over it, and said, Take this and share it among yourselves. This is My blood, the New Testament. For I say unto you that henceforth I will not drink of this fruit, until the Kingdom of God shall come." It is also a fact that several cups of wine were drunk at the Passover feast. If a full and detailed account had survived, the details of all accounts would no doubt be integrated.

It was a time of solemn fulfilment. The symbolism of the Paschal lamb was deeply relevant to the last hours and coming sacrifice of the Lamb of God. The Passover feast was the most colourful of all Jewish ceremonies, a demonstration in dramatic ritual of substitutionary sacrifice, and of God's own saviourhood. It was about to be replaced by a Christian ceremony which speaks as eloquently of God in flesh appearing, and of life sacrificially outpoured.

The hand of the traitor was on the table with Him, and the fact stirred the conscience of the other men who were abashed by the divisions which had appeared among them. John tells how the Lord had washed their feet, and the deep rebuke of that moving action still lay on their hearts and made them sensitive to sin. This, indeed, should be the mood in which we draw near to the table. The bread and the cup are for sinners, and none can approach the feast with perfection of heart. All can come with Christ's righteousness (1 Cor. 1.30), for His perfection is granted by God's grace to those who claim it. It was still not too late for Judas to abandon his unholy treachery and rebellion, to cry for His forgiveness and to be forgiven. *Let our hand, O Lord, when it rests by Thine on the table, be innocent and clean of evil. Forgive and restore, we pray.*

Notes: V. 17: in Talmudic directions, the wine preceded the breaking of the Passover bread, so this would not be the "cup of the New Testament" (1 Cor. 11.25). Luke knew well the established practice of the Early Church, and of Paul himself.

St. Luke 22.24—38

The dissensions among His men, which made the long walk up from Jericho a lonely one, and darkened the Lord's last hours, appear in all four narratives. (Matt. 18.1—5, 20.24—28; Mark 9.33—37, 10.41—45; Luke 9.46—48; John 13.2—20). Dispute may have arisen again as they sat down to the Paschal feast. There were positions of honour (14.7—11), and perhaps there was unseemly competition at the table. John's narrative of the footwashing (John 13) appears at this point. There was some range of age among the men, as verse 26 suggests. Peter was the eldest. He was a married man with his own home (4.38), when he joined Jesus as a disciple, and calls himself an "elder" in the sixth decade of the century (1 Pet. 5.1). John, who lived until the death of Domitian in A.D. 96, was probably the youngest of the band.

Verse 30 is apocalyptic language, and those trained in this poetic mode of communication should not have taken the words literally. Verse 31 was a reference to the dramatic opening of Job. Peter, like the Old Testament character, was to pass through a period of darkness and temptation, from which he was to emerge toughened and trained, and fitted to help his brethren. Note the use of "Simon", the name of frailty. It is in this fashion that we should approach such experience: "God has allowed this to happen. What beneficent purpose has He in view? What do I lack which this trial can give me? How can it be turned to ultimate usefulness, and made fruitful in my life?"

The reference to the sword is again to be taken as apocalyptic speech. Since the Lord later that night repudiated the use of one of the fisher's knives, which were produced in answer to His words, it is obvious that He cannot have intended them to be taken literally. As with the parables, He was seeking to evoke a more spiritual attitude, and turned away with weary words from the sight of their puny weapons. He sought to show that they were called now to courage and to testing. Their soldiering for Christ was about to begin. And they did not know. "Enough," He said, "enough of dull misunderstanding, of trial and weariness!" It was late, later than they thought.

Notes: V. 29: "appoint"—Gk. "make a bequest"; the Lord's last will and testament. V. 38: "swords"—*machairai*, long knives or swords (used for preparing the Passover Lamb?).

St. Luke 22.39—53

Verses 39—46. A remnant of the Garden of Gethsemane still lies across the Kedron on the lower slopes of the Mount of Olives. Two or

Photo: Golden Gate from the Garden of Gethsemane

three trees of immense age stand there, their short but enormous trunks gnarled, twisted, and eroded with the passing of centuries. The hill was bared of all growth and greenery in the two great rebellions, but olives are the most tenacious of all trees. They will spring again from their ancient roots when all visible portions of the tree are burned and shattered. The roots of the trees visible today could have been those which gripped the stony ground when the Lord knelt in prayer, and put for ever into all prayer the words which every true follower of His must observe: "Nevertheless, not My will, but Thine . . ."

That Jesus, knowing what was to be, should yet shrink in horrified humanity from the fearsome reality of shame and agony, is not strange. In Him deity and humanity were perfectly blended. Here we see the Perfect Man, perfectly understanding, and in the grip of suffering unimaginable to duller, imperfect minds (Heb. 5.7—9). The haematidrosis, the rupturing of tiny blood vessels into the sweat-glands, is a known medical phenomenon, and indicates the fearful stress of the mind's agony.

Verses 47—53. Only John reveals that it was Peter who turned to violence. When John wrote, almost forty years later, it was safe to reveal the name. Peter was long since dead. John also, acquainted as he was with the high priest's house, knew the name of the injured servant. It was like Peter to turn to action in a moment of bewilderment or distress. This trait more than once appears in the gospels. And so they led Him away, and Judas' name became a name of treachery and base betrayal. For what will our names be remembered?

Notes: Who heard and reported the prayer? The three intimates (see Matt. and Mark) probably heard much of it; and Mark, if he were the mysterious young man of his own account, may have heard it all (Matt. 26.37,38; Mark 14.51,52). V. 42: see Matt. 20.22; Psalm 75.8. V. 47: the kiss was a customary way for a disciple to greet his rabbi.

St. Luke 22.54–71

Luke consistently spares the apostles, whenever it was possible to do so. Matthew and John were themselves of the number of the Twelve, and Mark wrote under Peter's direction. Luke showed fine feeling in his understandable reserve. Here he omits Peter's outburst of bad language.

Peter perhaps should not have been there, though it was natural enough that he should follow. Besides, John, his closest personal friend, had access to the high priest's house, and tells very naturally

251

the story how Peter came to be there (John **18**.15—18). He should not
have sought comfort at the fire of God's foes. It is well to estimate
carefully the nature and impact of temptation, to know the weak-
nesses and capacities of our own personality, and to avoid localities,
situations, and all company which is likely to try the spirit or the flesh
beyond the point of possible resistance. There is no disgrace in
evading temptation.

Luke is reaching the length of narrative which a maximum-sized
papyrus roll could conveniently contain. He had material such as the
story of the Emmaus walk which could not be abbreviated without
loss. Hence a certain sketchiness and telescoping of narrative in such
sections as this, a device visible enough in the Acts, Luke's second
"treatise".

In verse 69 the Lord is again speaking in the accepted forms of
apocalyptic language. The reference is to the resurrection. The
"glorifying" of the Son of Man began with the crucifixion (John
13.31). The phrase "Son of Man" was a recognized Messianic title
(Dan. **7**.13) and was so taken by those who heard. Hence the direct
question of verse 70. Mark renders the same reply: "I am". This is
indication enough that the formula of verse 70 is one of assent. See
also Acts **2**.33—35; Rom. **8**.34; Heb. **1**.3,4; 1 Pet. **3**.22; Rev. **3**.21,
12.5. It is important to understand how, and in what sense, the
Sanhedrin took Christ's words. Western minds are prone to literalism
and to logical statement. The East spoke in imagery with greater ease.
The important point is that the Jewish leaders clearly understood that
Jesus claimed to be the Messiah.

Notes: Vs. 63—71: Luke tells of five trials of Jesus; comparison of
this first one with Mark **14**.53—64 suggests that the Sanhedrin met
with Annas to draw up their charges against Jesus, and then (as they
were not supposed to meet by night) the morning's business was a
mere formality. Even so, the proceedings were irregular. Witnesses
for the defence should have been summoned first and solemnly
adjured to speak from knowledge; the meeting should not have been
held on a feast day; sentences of condemnation should have been
held over for 24 hours. V. 69 would recall Psalm **110**.1.

St. Luke 23.1–12

Verses 1—5. Pilate, as a procurator, was directly responsible to
Tiberius himself. Arrogant and heavy-handed conduct of his office
had left him vulnerable to threats of complaint to Caesar. Above all,
Caesar wanted peace in Palestine. It was a vital corridor of communication between the valleys of the Nile and the Euphrates. Egypt

and Syria were provinces of immense importance. Palestine linked them. Pilate would undoubtedly have been commanded to cherish the collaborators, especially the Sadducean priesthood, to handle the rank and file with circumspection, and to manage relations with the petty kings of the area with wisdom. Pilate had done none of these things, and his failure was known to the grim old emperor. Pilate could not afford another complaint. It was obviously the best policy for those who sought to be rid of Christ to represent Him as a subversive agitator. Note the development in the nature of the charge —see Mark **14**.57,58,61—64. In spite of this Pilate actually pronounced acquittal (4). At this point he could have played the man, but clamour reached the stratum of cowardice in him and he turned with relief to the thought that the tetrarch of Galilee might take the case off his hands. He could also demonstrate unusual courtesy.

Verses 6—12. Herod was in Jerusalem for the feast—he kept up appearances. He had once listened gladly to John (Mark **6**.20), and had John's murder heavily on his conscience. Some curiosity made him eager to see the prophet from Galilee, perhaps to silence his fear that John might be alive again (Mark **6**.14). Herod had known his day of opportunity. He had openly chosen his vicious course. Christ does not speak to those who have set their will against Him. But Herod was too practised a diplomat to be caught by Pilate's trick. This was the Roman's responsibility. John had been burden enough on his murderer. He was not prepared to take measure against a Galilean with half Galilee in Jerusalem for the feast. It is idle to try to force someone else to make decisions which we ourselves should make.

Notes: In John's account Pilate appears to disconcert the priests by opening the trial in legal fashion—perhaps under the influence of his wife. V. 11: "gorgeous apparel"—a white festal gown to add to the mockery. V. 12: see **13**.1. For this entire passage, see 1 Peter **2**.21—23.

St. Luke 23.13–26

Luke only, of the four evangelists, tells of the visit to Herod, and records it as an acquittal. He had some first-hand source of information (see **8**.3), from which he derived such details as these, and those of Acts **12**.20 and **13**.1.

The struggle between Pilate and the priests is intensely dramatic and is told in Luke's most vivid manner. In Acts he is eager to show that Roman magistrates, as well as experienced local rulers, found nothing subversive in Christianity. His treatment of the trial of Christ clearly anticipates this preoccupation of his later work.

Pilate stresses the dual acquittal, and should have released his prisoner under safe conduct. In verse 16 his streak of cowardice is visible. There was no case for scourging if the prisoner was innocent. Scourging is what is meant here by chastisement, and it was a shocking punishment, ending often in death. Nor need he have given any indication that the release was the customary Passover favour.

Observing the hesitation, the priests, shrewd and ruthless men aware of their advantage, renewed their clamour. The chanted chorus: "Crucify! Crucify!" drove Pilate to a weak reopening of the case. "What evil has He done?" It was a case for peremptory dismissal, and a calling out of the guard, and this could have been done before the mob, abroad now in the streets, took up the cry for Barabbas.

To call for Barabbas, the terrorist, was illogical enough in those who had brought Jesus before the Procurator on a charge of subversion and disturbance of the peace. It was a significant choice. It was still not too late for the nation to choose the way of peace, and escape the holocaust towards which the land was moving. Midnight struck when they chose Barabbas. It was no longer the eleventh hour. It was too late.

Notes: Rome prided herself on her justice; Jewry on her religion. Here both reveal fatal flaws, yielding to the pride and fear of sinful men. V. 13: at Gabbatha, the Pavement. V. 18: Barabbas—"son of a rabbi". V. 26: Simon of Cyrene—see Mark 15.21, and, possibly, Rom. 16.13. He may have come for the Passover—Acts 6.9 shows that the Jews of Cyrene had their own synagogue in Jerusalem.

St. Luke 23.27–38

It has been suggested that the place of the crucifixion could have been the skull-shaped knoll, north of the city, not far from the Damascus Gate, known as Gordon's Calvary. Gashes in the rock-face represent eye-sockets and the shattered features of a skull. The Jordanians built a bus-terminal hard against the knoll where battered vehicles moved in and out, and crowds rushed for seats or hurried away. The traditional site, under the Holy Sepulchre Church, has to be sure some archaeological support, but whatever the exact location, at some such place the most significant event of history was enacted, and that fact must at least be conceded by all. Vast issues were decided at the Place of the Skull. Notice the dignity and the restraint of Luke's narrative; the physical horrors of crucifixion are passed over.

But at Calvary the issues of eternity also found their climax and consummation. The story has only to be read in its simplicity to see the first lesson of the cross. Could man's rebellion against God and good be more shatteringly demonstrated than it was that day? The brutal soldiery, the leaders of religion mocking the spectacle of despair and agony, cruelty which no beast would practise upon beast, were a spectacle which a world inured enough to blood and horror was never to forget. Here is man when sin has done its worst with him.

What was not yet so clear was that here too was God. "God was in Christ reconciling the world to Himself." Some were soon to see this scene with other eyes, for here was the spectacle of God Himself involved in human sin. *Lord, make us understand it.*

Notes: Vs. 27—32: Luke gives a large place to women, and their presence in the story both illustrates his sources and throws light on the Early Church. V. 27: the women may have come to offer drugs (Prov. 31.6). V. 34: the Lord asks forgiveness not so much for the soldiers as for the people at large; 40 years of opportunity for repentance were given. V. 38: the varied versions of the superscription result from its being written in three languages. If Matthew's version is turned into Latin, Luke's into Greek, and John's into Aramaic, lines of nearly equal length result.

St. Luke 23.39–49

Verses 39—45. There is of course no clash between this narrative and that of Mark. Both criminals at first soiled their last hours of life with abuse and blasphemy (Mark 15.32). One observed the Lord's demeanour, heard His words, and in the midst of his unimaginable pain found a Saviour. Forgiveness was immediate and complete. The broken creature, already bleeding and gasping to death, had no chance or opportunity to do anything to remedy or compensate for a life's misdeeds. He could only cry for pardon, and pardon he received. There could be no more striking demonstration that salvation is of grace, "and not of works" (Eph. 2.8).

The rending of the temple veil (45) was a sign of deep significance to the Jews. The writer of the Epistle to the Hebrews makes much of it in his masterly exposition of the Christian significance of the Hebrew ceremonies. He relates the symbolism to Christ in 9.3—8,11,12 and 10.9—22. Access to God became the right of all. The curtain which indicated separation was divided, and no priest nor mediator other than Christ can come between.

Verses 46—49. The story of these awful minutes is told at greater length by the other evangelists. Perhaps Luke found it too painful to be other than brief. He heard the story perhaps from the women who had followed Christ (49).

The awesome solemnity of the moment seems to have subdued the crowd. It is a fact of mass psychology that crowds are subject to sudden changes of mood, and the fact is demonstrable in the story of the Passion Week from Palm Sunday to Calvary. The ribaldry died and "they smote upon their breasts", some, no doubt, in saving sorrow and repentance (18.13). It was finished, and salvation won for all who chose to repent, believe, and follow Christ.

Notes: V. 43: "Paradise"=garden: the abode of the blest spirits awaiting the general resurrection (*cf.* 2 Cor. **12.**4, Rev. **2.**7). V. 44: the darkened sun was a sign to the Gentile, the rent veil to the Jew. The sun was not darkened by an eclipse, which cannot take place at full moon; the event was supernatural.

St. Luke 23.50–56

An indication that Gordon's Calvary is the place of the crucifixion is found hard by. The ridge of rock which ends in the skull-shaped knoll runs back to form a low cliff. In the cliff-face is cut an ancient tomb. It is a squared chamber with a low ledge on the side nearest Calvary. A great groove shows where a wheel-shaped stone once rolled to close the entrance. A walled garden on two levels encloses the place and gives an air of simplicity and sanctity not to be found in the great church, cluttered with the tawdry symbols of devotion, which covers the alleged site now within the city walls.

It is refreshing to meet another of the Lord's "remnant". They are of all ranks of society. Joseph was a Sanhedrist, who now with uncommon courage went to the Roman governor, who was, no doubt, still tense and irascible from the day's frustrations, and begged for the body of Christ. He gave it reverent and honourable burial, and the women were there also, an intent and observant audience. Hence perhaps the fuller account in Luke. He who was more brief than either Matthew or Mark about events on Calvary, gives more detail here, and in so doing provided material for much Christian art.

Luke had other purpose than mere narrative in view. The resurrection was the first prominent feature of the Christian Gospel, as the earliest preaching shows. Scepticism, faced with the empty tomb, would find its readiest argument in the statement that the Lord was not really dead. It is a theory recently revived by a medical man. Luke was also a medical man, and took some care over this matter. Such witnesses could not have been deceived. Joseph and those with him could have no doubt that it was a dead man with whose mortal remains they were dealing. The great stone was rolled in front and the garden emptied, until the tramp of the guards resounded, set to watch the tomb.

Notes: Had Joseph not intervened, the body of Jesus would have been thrown out for the dogs and vultures. We do not know whether he openly opposed the condemnation of Jesus or merely absented himself from the Council. V. 53: see Isa. **53.9.**

Questions for Further Study and Discussion on St. Luke, chapters 22, 23.
1. What details do chs. 22—23 add to the development of Luke's theme?
2. In what significant features does the Communion Service differ from the Passover Feast?
3. What light do chs. 22 and 23 throw on the motives and methods of persecution?
4. What are the chief prophetic scriptures which find fulfilment in chs. 22 and 23?
5. Do the Lord's words in 23.28 reveal a faulty attitude in modern teaching on the Passion of Christ?
6. At what points could Pilate have extricated himself from his vicious course of conduct, and why, at each crisis, did he fail to do so?

St. Luke 24.1–12

Luke chose to record the appearances of Christ associated with Jerusalem. There is no reason at all why he should not have been selective in his recording of events. It would have been held against him with equal cogency had he merely traversed ground covered by the other evangelists. The alleged discrepancies in the narrative are likewise of little consequence. Luke, for example, mentions two men in the tomb. Mark (**16.5**) mentions only one. Mark was writing in great haste, and appears, indeed, to have been unable to finish his account before violence or arrest interrupted him. He naturally mentions the spokesman of the two visitants. Such words in no way deny the fact of two appearances recorded by Luke. Two contains one, as the greater contains the less. For a detailed study see N. Geldenhuys' Commentary on Luke, pp. 626—628.

Luke's informants are again apparent. Joanna (**8.3**) probably gave him such details as those set down in this story, as she no doubt gave him those of **23.8**—12. When Luke was combing Palestine for surviving witnesses of the resurrection, twenty years later, the

apostles were abroad. The women were a more stable group. It is also
to be remembered that Luke was a close friend and travelling com
panion of Paul who was in prison at Caesarea, but accessible to hi
associates. In 1 Corinthians 15.1—7 Paul penned what is probably th
first account of the resurrection, for the epistle antedates Mark. It i
quite impossible to imagine that Luke did not know of the event
which Paul enumerated. He was deliberately selective.

Observe also verse 12. As Mark omitted one angel, so Luke omit
one apostle from his account. He had no doubt heard Peter describ
the event: "I ran to the tomb, stooped and looked in. I saw the grav
clothes . . ." John (20.3—10) naturally tells a fuller story.

Notes: The alternative to sane and honest reporting by the gospe
writers is pious fraud; such a tainted source would have smoothe
out the apparent differences. Note how the behaviour of the disciple
likewise militates against the theory that the story was fabricated
V. 8: contrast 22.61. V. 10: Mark 16.1 adds Salome to the list. V. 11
"idle tale"—a medical word for "delirious babbling".

St. Luke 24.13–24

This exquisitely told story is peculiar to Luke. Two Christian me
(they were not apostles) lived at Emmaus, perhaps the moder
Kalonich, to the north-west of Jerusalem. They were walking home i
animated discussion, with the light of the sloping sun in their eyes,
when a Stranger joined them. Here is a simple translation of the verses
which follow, choosing a reading for the end of verse 17 found in the
Codex Sinaiticus and one other ancient and important manuscript.
"He said to them: 'What words are these that you are tossing back
and forth as you walk along?' They stopped and looked sadly at Him.
And one of them named Cleopas replied: 'Do you live alone in
Jerusalem, seeing you do not know what happened there in these last
days?' He said to them: 'What sort of things?' They said to Him:
'Concerning Jesus of Nazareth, a man Who spoke the words of God, a
man of power in word and deed before God and all the people, and
how the high priests and our rulers handed Him over to be condemned to death, and crucified Him. And we were hoping that it
might have been He Who was going to redeem Israel . . .' "

The word for "redeem" is allied to that of 1.68. The whole reply
rings with the hopelessness of the disciples after the crushing events
of the week's ending. Set this broken spirit over against the triumph
and the jubilation of the days which followed. Only some cataclysmic
event could have so transformed a shattered group of men. One and
all must have been utterly convinced about the central fact of their

faith. How pathetic before such certainty seems the speculation of the philosophic school of post-Christian theologians. "It does not matter," wrote one of them in 1964, "whether the empty tomb created the faith of the disciples, or whether the faith of the disciples created the empty tomb." The experience on the Emmaus road was no illusion. It was no group of deluded enthusiasts who were thus transformed. Of course it matters. If the tomb was not indeed vacated by a risen Christ, there is no Christian faith, and theologians who deny the fact might more appropriately seek less compromising employment.

Note the clear and specific report of events in verses 22 to 24. These were not gullible men. They admit only what their eyes have seen. Their animated discussion when the Stranger joined them was probably about the interpretation of those observed facts.

St. Luke 24.25–35
The story moves naturally and convincingly to its climax. It has been widely rendered in art, especially that of the stained-glass window. And in such representation it is not the arid Judean landscape which finds a place, but the trees of Europe and America, "the oak, and the ash, and the weeping-willow tree." It is altogether appropriate. Christ still walks the road with those who are eager for His company. They are still dull and slow of heart to apprehend all His plans and purposes. He thrusts His presence on none, but is glad to be the Guest of any home which opens doors of welcome to Him. "Thoughtless men," He said. "Fools" is too strong a word. It must have been a lesson indeed to hear the risen Christ unravel the thread of His own foretelling from the Old Testament. Before turning from this vivid gospel, an hour should be found with concordance and reference Bible to retrace some of the path of that late afternoon's instruction.

Realization burst upon them as He broke the bread. Perhaps it was only then that they saw the torn and ravaged hands. Perhaps a familiar gesture revealed Him. Weariness forgotten, they hurried the seven miles back to Jerusalem to find the Eleven. They, too, were agog with strange and thrilling news. The appearance to Peter, mentioned here and in 1 Cor. 15.5, is nowhere detailed in the New Testament. Perhaps Mark would have told it, had he had time to finish his hastily concluded gospel. Perhaps the words of that interview were too painful or private, perhaps too personal, for common knowledge and publicity.

But note the artlessness of the whole narrative. It is told naturally and gracefully. Word and incident bear the marks of truth and the manner of the eyewitness. This is not fiction. Prose fiction, indeed, was hardly born and its rare examples in Mediterranean literature have none of the simple and delightful realism which mark this narrative. Nor could the walkers of the Emmaus road, and the group which they sought in Jerusalem, be easily deceived in such collective fashion. *O Risen Lord, walk with us this day on the road which leads to sunset. Abide with us when falls the eventide.*

Notes: V. 26: they had failed to link the idea of the Suffering Servant with that of the Victorious Messiah. V. 27: see refs. in R.S.V. margin. V. 34: see Mark **16**.7.

St. Luke 24.36–45

There can be no doubt at all that the New Testament teaches that the Lord rose physically from the dead. The witnesses were clear that they were not in communication with a spirit. He ate food in their presence. Verse 39 is part of their testimony.

The witnesses to this first appearance of Christ to the apostles themselves are Luke, John (**20**.19—23) and Paul (1 Cor. **15**.5). In Luke, as we observe, the narrative links with the Emmaus story. In John it is a distinct episode, and adds the important detail that the men were assembled behind closed doors, "for fear of the Jews". John, of course, was there, and his account supports the authenticity of Luke. Only Luke speaks of the fish and the honey-comb, but John speaks of the Lord's eating with them on the beach in a Galilean resurrection story told only by him.

The greatest care has been taken by the evangelists, as has been already noted, to establish the fact that the body in which Jesus appeared was a real body, no phantasm or manifestation of the spirit. It was the body of the cross and the tomb, still bearing the marks of suffering. On the other hand, it belonged to a different order of existence. It appeared and disappeared. Something about it baffled immediate recognition, though identity became evident when He so willed it. It is sixty years since James Orr, in speaking of this phenomenon, hazarded the guess that "physicists are not so sure of the impenetrability of matter as they once were". Physics since then has demonstrated that matter is only apprehended by sight and touch in the form appropriate to those senses. Its overwhelming proportion of empty space, if that term itself makes sense, the fantastic motion of seemingly motionless material, all emphasize the fact that we see only that which we see, and that there is an order of existence beyond comprehension on such levels of evidence. This does not explain the resurrection appearances of the Lord, but does suggest the thought that there are other orders than those of common experience.

Notes: V. 41: "disbelieved for joy"—a realistic observation; compare 22.45. V. 44: "still with you"—points to the difference between His pre-resurrection presence and His post-resurrection appearances. His abode now was elsewhere. "Moses . . . the prophets . . . the psalms"—the three great divisions of the Old Testament.

St. Luke 24.46–53

Luke concludes his gospel with notable brevity, because he was already planning his second "treatise", and intended to enlarge on some of the events of the forty days in that place. Hence his rapid treatment of the period of instruction (44—48), and of the Galilean appearances mentioned elsewhere. 40 days precede verse 50.

They came back to the city "with great joy," says Luke. Let it be again emphasized that Luke had spoken with these men. Literary theories aimed at destroying the tradition of his authorship, and along with it the authenticity of his narrative, fall far short of their object. Luke was a competent historian, and sifted his evidence. Moreover, the life of peril and toil which necessarily followed his holding such convictions was not the life which one would choose apart from the drive and compulsion of a commanding faith.

Paul, too, was in the background. Luke knew him intimately. He must often have heard from Paul himself about the events which transformed the persecutor of the Church into its greatest apostle. Paul, too, applied the powers of his keen analytical mind to the evidence for the empty tomb in the garden, and the simple explanation of that overwhelming fact.

The "great joy" of the group who came back from Bethany was also translated into historic fact. The Church was born of it, and the Church in the first century, indeed in the generation after the ascension of its Founder, is a solid reality. Some tremendous conviction gave power and coherence to a feeble, scattered group. The earthly ministry of Jesus ended in apparent defeat. The powers of evil and dissolution seemed victorious. Look again at verse 21 and catch the atmosphere of broken hopelessness. Doubt was dispelled, despair quenched, fear cast out, defeat turned into a victory manifest in history. How? There can be only one explanation. *"Blessed be the God and Father of our Lord Jesus Christ, Who, according to His great mercy, begat us again unto a living hope, by the resurrection of Jesus Christ from the dead, unto an inheritance incorruptible, undefiled, which fadeth not away."*

261

Questions for Further Study and Discussion on St. Luke, chapter 24.

1. What Scriptures might have been expounded on the way to Emmaus?
2. Why did the Lord appear only to His own?
3. What evidence for the resurrection is to be derived from (*i*) the early chapters of the Acts of the Apostles? (*ii*) the career of Paul? (*iii*) the story of James, the Lord's brother?

St. John

INTRODUCTION
There are many different theories about the origin and meaning of this Gospel, and the following summary will indicate only the standpoint adopted in this book. For other views commentaries or reference books should be consulted.

The Gospel was traditionally believed to have been written by John, the son of Zebedee, who is thought to have lived at Ephesus *I* until about the end of the first century. Because John is nowhere mentioned by name (there is only a reference to the sons of Zebedee in **21**.2), and because the Baptist is simply referred to as 'John', there seems little doubt that the evangelist intends the readers to suppose that 'the beloved disciple' is the apostle John. It would seem likely, then, that John was the real author of the Gospel, even if he did not necessarily pen or dictate every word of it. While some scholars suggest that ch. **21** was added later as a sort of postscript, possibly after he died, others maintain that this chapter too is very substantially the work of John. In either event, even if the date of publication is late, the material in the Gospel, coming from an eyewitness, will have as much historical value as that in the Synoptic Gospels.

The purpose of the Gospel is similar to that of any Gospel. It is to present a selection of the deeds of Jesus in such a way that people will come to put their faith in Him as the Son of God and find eternal life, and that those who have done so will be built up in the faith (**20**.31). It may have been written in the first place for Greek-speaking Jews who lived outside Palestine, but its message has gone home to men of every race in every age.

The relationship of the Gospel to the Synoptic Gospels presents a large number of problems, few of which are dealt with here. Some scholars have held that John knew *Mark* and adapted that Gospel for his own purposes. Others have suggested that he is independent of *Mark* and that any resemblances go back to Peter and John who were eyewitnesses of the same events. Recent study has suggested that all the evangelists were interested in the facts and in their interpretation. While John makes the interpretation more obvious, he is not necessarily less interested in the facts. Archaeological discovery has done a certain amount to confirm that a number of

263

things found only in *John* fit well into the background of the times
It is often difficult to know when John intends things to be taken
symbolically, and imagination must not be allowed to run riot! But
the discovery of a symbolic meaning for something does not automatically mean that it was not also a historical fact.

There are seven 'signs' in the Gospel which present in dramatic
form the challenge of the person and work of Christ. There are
seven 'I am' sayings which are evangelistic appeals. In the Gospel
many people recognize Jesus partially, but only the confession of
Thomas after the resurrection, 'My Lord and my God!' (**20.**28), is
adequate. One of the features of the Gospel is the divine irony.
Men say and do all sorts of things with deeper significance than they
realize. God's own people put God's own Son to death. ('The
Jews', who are mentioned frequently, seem to be the Judeans, the
people who live in the promised land and have a vested interest in
the old order of things.) The supreme paradox is the way in which
the shameful death on the cross reveals the glory of the Father and
the Son.

The Gospel may be divided as follows: The Prelude (**1**); The
Book of Signs (**2–12**); The Book of the Passion (**13–19**); The
Resurrection and Epilogue (**20–21**).

There are many useful commentaries on the Gospel. B. F.
Westcott's is the classical one of modern times. W. Temple has a
vast amount of helpful devotional material. R. V. G. Tasker and
A. M. Hunter have both produced very good short commentaries.
J. C. Fenton's *The Passion according to John* is full of insight into
chs. **18** and **19**. C.K. Barrett's commentary is the finest modern one
on the Greek text, but takes a generally low view of John's historical
reliability. Two books by C. H. Dodd, *The Interpretation of the
Fourth Gospel* and *Historical Tradition and the Fourth Gospel*, give a
great deal of detailed information and help to establish John as an
independent witness to the ministry of Jesus. But no books about
the Gospel can be a substitute for careful study for oneself of one
of the greatest books of all time. For here in a unique way we meet
the Word of Life.

St. John 1.1-5

The Prologue (**1.**1–18) gives us a preview of some of the great themes
of the Gospel and sets the earthly ministry of Jesus in its heavenly
perspective.

When did Jesus become the Son of God? The resurrection was
the great event which confirmed His divine Sonship (Acts **2.**36;

Rom. **1**.4). But a voice had declared it before that at His transfiguration (Mark **9**.7) and even earlier at His baptism (Mark **1**.11). *Matthew* and *Luke* show that He was divine from His birth and His conception (Matt. **1**.20–23; Luke **1**.35; **2**.10 f.). Yet all these events were but stages in the revelation of an eternal truth. 'In the beginning was the Word'—long before He took human flesh in the person of Jesus. *Mark's* 'beginning' (Mark **1**.1) is the beginning of the saving ministry culminating in the death and resurrection of Jesus. *John's* 'beginning' is the beginning of everything. If God *created* 'in the beginning' (Gen. **1**.1), the uncreated Son *was* 'in the beginning'.

'The Word'. This would mean something to Greek readers for whom *logos* meant 'reason'. For Jews 'the Word' was the revelation of God's character, expressed in increasingly personal terms in the O.T. 'The Word was with God', i.e. in personal relationship with Him. 'God' has the definite article, marking this out as a reference to the first person of the Trinity. 'The Word was God'—here there is no article since the Word is not said to be the same person as God but to have the nature of God. The NEB paraphrases well: 'What God was, the Word was'. This is the starting point for the evangelist, but in the Gospel story he shows how people failed to recognize the full deity of Jesus until Thomas' confession of faith (**20**.28), which is in some ways the climax of the Gospel.

After reaffirming the pre-existence of the Word and His relationship to God (2), the evangelist goes on to describe His work in creation (cf. Col. **1**.15–20; Heb. **1**.1–4). Through Him everything came into being—not just material things but life itself. So we meet two of the great themes of the Gospel—life and light. The light shines on (present tense). The darkness made an attempt to master it, but failed decisively (past tense). In that fact lies our salvation. *Note:* In v. 4 follow the RSV rather than the margin.

St. John 1.6-13

Vs. 6–8. The first paragraph has seen the Word and His work in the divine perspective. Philosophers of various cultures and religions might have used similar terms, at least, to some extent. In the second paragraph, we come to earth with a bump! For the great philosophical truths have been brought into focus in human history. The drama has been played out with human actors. 'There was a man sent from God, whose name was John.'

The Gospel begins with John the Baptist as does *Mark* (Mark **1**.1–11). *Matthew* and *Luke* give additional material about the birth of Jesus. But here, at least, is the essential starting point of the apostolic proclamation (the *kerygma*) (Acts **1**.21 f.). John is the forerunner (Mark **1**.2 f.) and the link between the old and the new covenants (Matt. **11**.13; Luke **16**.16). In *John*, especially, he is the witness to the incarnation rather as the apostles were to the resurrection (cf. **1**.15,32,34; **3**.26; **5**.33). He was sent from God with divine authority as a prophet. (Jesus, too, was sent from God— **4**.34; **5**.37 f., etc.—but unlike John He *was* God.) John was sent with the purpose of testimony which had as its purpose faith. He was the lamp (**5**.35) but not the light itself. No higher privilege could be given to any man.

Vs. 9–13. The significance of Jesus Christ is world-wide. He was the genuine light in contrast to the many false lights that seemed to shine, and He came to lighten every man. His sphere of activity had to be the world—made through Him (3) and loved by Him (**3**.16) but refusing to acknowledge Him. So in the Gospel 'the world' often comes to mean human society organized apart from God. The rejection by the world of its Maker is brought into sharper focus in the rejection by God's people of their Messiah. His own home (theologically) is Judea (**4**.44; contrast Mark **6**.4). His own people were the Jews, and again and again in the Gospel the emphasis is on their being Judeans, living in the promised land. But God's purposes are not frustrated. The Gospel goes to the whole world and all who receive Him in faith are given legitimate authority to become members of God's family. Their birth, like that of Jesus, is not natural but supernatural. Only those who have experienced it can understand. But there is a human element. The two verbs, 'received' and 'believed' (12) do not indicate two separate actions but, rather, two aspects of the total response to the Saviour.

Note: V.9: 'coming into the world' is rightly taken by the RSV to refer to Jesus rather than to 'every man'.

St. John 1.14-18

Whatever the Greek philosophers might have said about the cosmic operations of the *logos*, they could never have said that it 'became flesh'. This is the startling assertion of John. The eternal Word became flesh—became man in all his weakness, sharing our nature, living and visible in our midst. It was not God taking over a human being, nor the Word ceasing to be God in order to become man. Somehow, in the most profound mystery of all time, He remained God and yet became man. One who was with God (**1**.1), dwelt among us as in a tent, for His permanent residence was not here (cf. 2 Cor. **5**.1). He was no ordinary man, for He was full of grace

266

(which shows the generosity of the action of God) and truth (which shows the reality of it). These had been demonstrated partially in the O.T., now they are displayed perfectly. Christ fulfils the redemption and the revelation of God. His glory is the outshining of the divine nature. This had been seen in the divine presence in the Tabernacle (Exod. **40**.34), and in the Temple (1 Kings **8**.11). Such men as Moses (Exod. **33**.22) and Isaiah (Isa. **6**.3) had caught glimpses of it. But its fullness was reserved for the future (Isa. **60**.1) and here it is shown in the divine presence incarnate among men. This He brings as the unique Son of God (cf. **3**.18; **5**.16,18).

The evidence of John is re-emphasized in order to show that though Christ 'came' after him as far as His birth and His ministry were concerned, He 'was' before him (**1**.1). The fullness of grace was for all to receive as they received Him (**1**.12). Grace was unlimited. The contrast with Law is more a feature of Paul than of John, but he is concerned to show the superiority of the new to the old even though that too was given by God. No one ever yet saw God, not even Moses (Exod. **33**.20). We live in a privileged position (Matt. **13**.16 f.). Jesus has explained Him by who He was and what He did. One day we shall see Him as He is (1 John **3**.2).

Notes: V. 14: the consonants of the Greek word for 'dwelt' are the same as for the Hebrew *shekinah*—the divine presence among the people. The divine glory was no longer in Tabernacle or Temple (cf. **2**.21) but in Jesus. 'We have beheld' may mean the apostolic Church as a whole, but suggests eyewitnesses. His glory was seen especially in His signs (**2**.11; **11**.4,40). There is no account of the transfiguration in *John*.

A challenge: Do we live like 'children of God' (12)? If we, like the disciples, 'have beheld his glory' (14) do we reflect it? The secret is not in ourselves but in the fullness of His boundless grace (16).

St. John 1.19-34

One of the most important themes of the Gospel is that of the evidence that Jesus is the Son of God. Here is the evidence of John, whose ministry had the essential purpose of giving testimony to Him (cf. **1**.7,8,15). He was the last of the prophets, but while they had spoken in general terms of the Messiah, it was John who was actually to identify Him. He is the first to give evidence that Jesus is the Son of God, in order to induce that faith which is the object of the Gospel (**20**.31).

John's evidence is in the first place negative (19–21). His ministry and unusual appearance and habits had aroused curiosity. What did

267

it all mean? Who was he? He explains in shorter and shorter sentences that he is neither Messiah, nor Elijah reincarnate, nor the prophet promised by Moses and said to be like Moses (Deut. **18.**15). In answer to repeated questioning he claimed the role of forerunner (22 f.) as shown in Isa. **40.** The emphasis was not on his person but on his message. He insists on directing attention away from himself (cf. **3.**30).

The supplementary question inevitably followed. Why then was he baptizing? For a ministry of baptism was generally thought to be the preparation for the messianic age (24 f.). He replies that his baptism is only an outward symbol and his own dignity is nothing compared with the coming One (26 f.).

The Gospel does not mention the baptism of Jesus, and the evangelist may assume that it is well known to his readers (cf. also the omission of the transfiguration and the institution of the Holy Communion). He does, however, record John's allusion to the descent of the Spirit on Jesus to commission Him for His work, and his description of his own baptism as a foreshadowing of the baptism with the Holy Spirit (29–34). The title which he applies to Jesus, 'the Lamb of God', is of considerable importance and may combine ideas of the lamb of the sin offering, the Passover lamb (cf. **19.**36) and the suffering servant of Isa. **53.** He deals not just with individual *sins*, but with the *sin* of the whole world. Such was the price of our rebellion against God! John's solemn declaration (29), probably coming immediately after Christ's temptation (Matt. **4.**1–11), would underscore vividly His renunciation of any short cut to success. Christ's ministry *began* under the shadow of the Cross. The *promise* contained in John's statement must not, however, be eclipsed by this note of foreboding. The Cross, finally, was a place of triumph.

Note: V. 21: in the Synoptic Gospels, John is said to be Elijah, but this was presumably in a typological sense (Matt. **11.**14; **17.**10–13; Luke **1.**17). Jesus fulfilled the role of the prophet like Moses (Acts **3.**22).

St. John 1.35-51

The evidence which John the Baptist gave, that Jesus was the Son of God and the Lamb of God, led to two of his own disciples leaving him and following Jesus. This was a literal following which was also to become a spiritual following in due course (cf. **8.**12; **12.**26; **21.**19,22). But it was not to be simply on second-hand evidence.

Jesus invites them to come and see for themselves, and to stay with Him. (For a spiritual *coming* to Jesus, cf. **3.**21; **6.**35, etc.; for a spiritual *seeing*, cf. **14.**9; for a spiritual *staying* or *abiding*, cf. **15.**4–10.) Notice that John was concerned not to attach disciples to *himself* (unlike the leaders of many modern cults and schisms) but to Jesus. He could even rejoice in their transferred allegiance (**3.**29 f.); a sure indication of his spiritual greatness.

Christ-centred testimony is infectious. Each 'carrier' has a vital part to play. Andrew's first thought is to share his new experience with his brother. Finding him was, as William Temple said, 'perhaps as great a service to the Church as ever any man did.' Simon (perhaps the name has overtones of hearing and obeying) will become Cephas (Peter, the rock man). Little could either of them see what Jesus would make of him!

Andrew had found Simon for Jesus, now Jesus Himself finds Philip, and Philip in turn finds Nathanael—the Israelite without any touch of the guileful Jacob (Gen. **32.**28). To every misconception about His true origin (that His true home is Nazareth or that His real father is Joseph), there is the answer of experience—'Come and see.'

The titles ascribed to Jesus in this passage are probably, as Temple puts it, 'rather an outburst of exalted hope than a rooted conviction of faith.' But 'Rabbi' (38), 'Messiah' (41), 'Him of whom Moses . . . and the prophets wrote' (45), 'Son of God . . . King of Israel' (49) are all inadequate because they are limited by the preconceptions of the time. Jesus prefers the cryptic title 'Son of Man' (51). Only after He rose from the dead did true Christian faith come. Only then could Jesus be seen as Jacob's ladder (Gen. **28.**10–17), as the house of God (cf. **2.**19–22) and the gate of heaven (cf. **10.**7,9; **14.**6).

Notes: V.35: 'The next day'—suggests different days in a momentous week. V. 40: 'one of the two.' The most natural assumption is that the other was John. V.41: 'first'—there are three possible meanings here: *(a)* that Andrew sought out Peter the very first thing on the next morning; *(b)* that having found Peter he then found someone else for Christ, possibly Philip (cf. v.44); *(c)* that while Andrew was the first to find *his* brother, John the evangelist, probably the second of the two questioners, also found *his* brother, James. All three alternatives have something to say to us! V.47: Nathanael is probably the same as Bartholomew (Mark **3.**18). Being under the fig tree implies studying the Law.

It seems likely that the preliminary meetings with the Apostles recorded here were the reason for their immediate response to

269

Jesus' call in Mark **1**.16–20. So today there may be other meetings with Christ before the time of committed discipleship.

St. John 2.1-12

Jesus, having acquired some disciples, is now invited with them to a wedding. Cana is probably the modern Khirbet Qana, eight or nine miles north of Nazareth. And the presence of Jesus' mother there suggests that some friend or relative of His family was being married. The wedding celebrations might last several days and it seems as if Jesus and His disciples did not arrive until near the end. It may be that the presence of a number of extra guests put a strain on the resources and the wine ran out. Jesus' mother (she is never named in the Gospel, cf. **6**.42; **19**.25–27) mentions the need to Him as a simple statement of fact. The seeming rebuff was not one of disrespect—but, nevertheless, a clear indication that He would not be 'pressured into action'. His power was not to be controlled merely by a mother-son relationship.

The six stone jars were used to provide water for the washing of hands and of vessels. Jesus' command to fill them is put into effect completely. Then there occurs what is undoubtedly described as a miracle and no attempt at 'rationalizing' looks convincing. God, who is always turning water into wine, now does so in a 'speeded-up' way (cf. C. S. Lewis, *Miracles*, p. 163 f.). It is not clear whether all the water in the pots was turned into wine or only what was drawn out.

The miracles in John are described as *signs*—that is, they have a deeper significance than just the action itself. Here the old flat water of Judaism is turned into the sparkling new wine of the gospel. This has been kept 'until now'. Christ comes as the heavenly bridegroom (**3**.29; cf. Mark **2**.19–22), who by His presence enriches the social occasions of life and points us forward to the marriage feast of the Kingdom (Matt. **22**.1–14). His glory is revealed at other times in the Gospel (**11**.4,40) and the purpose was to bring those to faith in Him who had eyes to see. The majority were ignorant about what had happened, the servants knew and expressed wonder, but the disciples saw and believed. How often we fail to have the eye of faith!

Notes: V.4: 'O woman, what have you to do with Me?' seems harsher in English than in Greek. Perhaps it is best to render 'Mother', with the NEB. Jesus emphasizes His independence from human influence in carrying out the will of His Father at His hour (cf. **17**.1). We too may pray but never force His hand.

*For meditation: This incident suggests that mundane, domestic problems such as the dislocation of a wedding feast and the embarrassment of the host are not outside the range of interest of the Lord of Glory. Does this encourage you to share **all** your problems with Him?*

St. John 2.13-25

Jesus now goes up to Jerusalem, where John shows that He presents the challenge of His person and work to the Jewish leaders. He has just demonstrated, by His sign at Cana, the superiority of the new religion over the old. Here He makes a symbolic purification of Jewish worship as an indication of the coming of the Messianic age. The Lord of the Temple comes suddenly into His Temple (Mal. 3.1–3). He finds at the very heart of Judaism, in the very place which the Lord had chosen to make His name dwell, commercial exploitation and corruption. This allowed for a kind of 'instant religion' where everything was on hand—convenient for the 'worshipper', no doubt, but governed mainly by the profit motive. True religion withers in such an atmosphere, as many, visiting so-called 'shrines', have discovered. The prophecy of Zech. **14**, which had spoken of the Lord's reign over all the earth and the pilgrimage of all nations to Jerusalem to worship Him, ended with the words 'And there shall no longer be a trader in the house of the Lord of hosts on that day' (Zech. **14**.21). The zeal of Jesus for God's house and honour was such that He was prepared to use strong methods to drive out those who were profiteering from the need of the people to have animals and birds for sacrifice. There are times when Christians too may be called to forceful action.

The Jews demand a sign to authenticate His action and He gives them an answer which they misunderstand (cf. Mark **14**.58). The Temple, as the symbol of God's presence with His people, was theologically redundant, as the Word had become flesh and was tabernacling among men (**1**.14). It was doomed to destruction in due course, paradoxically through their possessive attitude to it (**11**.48; cf. Luke **13**.35, '*your* house'). But the new temple of Christ's body had to go through death to resurrection before it could be a spiritual temple and body of believers (1 Cor. **3**.16; **12**.27). As always there was a mixed response to Him and some very superficial 'belief'. At that stage Jesus was not ready to trust Himself to them as He now so graciously trusts Himself to us.

Note: The chronology of the cleansing of the Temple creates a problem as the Synoptic Gospels place it just before the Passion. The evangelists were not bound to write in a strict chronological

271

order, and it may be that John has put it here as a 'programmatic' incident symbolizing the nature of Christ's mission, or that the others have put it for conciseness in the one visit to Jerusalem which they record. But there are sufficient differences of detail to allow the possibility of two separate cleansings (see, e.g. Westcott).

Questions for further study and discussion on St. John, chs. 1 and 2
1. What attitude ought we to have to One who was both God (**1.1**) and flesh (**1.14**)? Do we hold the two in proper balance?
2. What does it really mean for us to *see* the glory of Christ today (**1.14**) and to receive from His fullness (**1.16**)?
3. 'Come and see' (**1.46**). How far does this express the basis of evangelism?
4. In what ways can we apply the lessons of patience, trust and obedience shown in **2.1–11** to our own Christian work?
5. In what way does Christ wish to come and cleanse our spiritual lives and the spiritual life of His Church (**2.13–22**)? Why is it 'His own people' who so often do not recognize Him (**1.11**)?

St. John 3.1-8

If the Messiah brings a new beginning for the nation and its religion, He also brings one for the individual and his religion. Nicodemus was a member of the Sanhedrin, the Jewish Council. He was probably both theologian and diplomat. He comes by night in anonymity. His questions show an inability to understand the spiritual significance of the gospel. Eventually he is 'faded out' of the scene and Jesus is left talking to a baffled Judaism and to puzzled and uncommitted religious men as a whole.

Nicodemus' approach is cautious. He not only comes by night, so as not to commit himself (cf. Joseph of Arimathaea in **19.38** f.), but his opening gambit is also non-committal. He recognizes in a general way ('*we* know') Jesus as a rabbi, doing signs and sent by God in some sense. When 'Jesus answered him' (3) it was his thoughts rather than his words. He calls directly for a radical response—a completely new start. Without a new birth a man cannot even see the Kingdom of God—cannot begin to understand what it is all about. Nicodemus probably takes Jesus literally, as others do mistakenly (cf. **6.42,52**; **8.33**). But perhaps he does see that it is figurative and protests that a new spiritual start is impossible.

If understanding the Kingdom is impossible without new birth, how much more is the commitment of entering it! Men must be

272

born with water, and the reference in the first instance is perhaps to the baptism of John as an external rite signifying repentance (cf. **1**.26,31–34). From there the extension may be made to Christian baptism, which in its turn must be linked with the internal experience of new life in the Spirit. Two worlds are shown to us in the Gospel—flesh and spirit, the earthly and the heavenly (cf. **8**.23). Even a man's religion may be on the level of 'flesh'—human effort. It is not surprising that spiritual life needs spiritual birth. The Spirit is like the wind—free, powerful, unseen, unpredictable—but its results may be observed. The power of the Spirit goes far beyond the physical realm to every sphere of life. He both illuminates and empowers the believer. There is no area of our lives where this influence cannot be effective. Let us never seek to limit His power.

Notes: V. 3: 'born anew', cf. RSV margin 'from above'. The Greek word can mean either, and both may be in mind. 'Kingdom of God' means His reign rather than His realm. V. 8: both Hebrew *ruah* and Greek *pneuma* mean wind or breath as well as spirit.

Prayer: 'Breathe on me, Breath of God.'

St. John 3.9-15

The new analogy of the wind and the Spirit which Jesus introduces baffles Nicodemus further. 'How can this be?' he asks, not so much, it seems, wanting to know how to take the step of faith himself, as unable to comprehend what it is all about. Jesus expresses surprise that someone appointed as a theological teacher of God's chosen people should be so out of his depth. The idea of birth by water and the Spirit was foreshadowed in the O.T., especially in such a passage as Ezek. **36**.25–28.

Jesus speaks not only from Scripture, but also from experience. On the basis of both He gives His testimony. But Nicodemus and those like him did not receive it. An earthly analogy was meant to clarify the heavenly reality. It would be impossible to speak directly of unseen heavenly things to those who cannot understand what they see. In fact there is only one interpreter of heavenly things, the Son of Man. His origin is heavenly, He has a foot in both camps, He bridges the gap between heaven and earth in His own person (cf. **1**.51; 1 Cor. **15**.47). Man could never ascend to meet God. God had to descend to meet man.

Not only was the incarnation necessary to reveal the life of heaven to men, the atonement was also. The bronze serpent on the standard was a symbol of healing (Num. **21**.4–9). The Son of Man was likewise to be lifted up (in a double sense—cf. Gen. **40**.12 f., 18–22; see also **8**.28; **12**.34; **18**.32). As the One lifted up was not a bronze serpent but the living and dying Son of Man, so the benefits were far greater. Here was no temporary cure but eternal life as the result of faith.

Notes: V. 11: 'We speak of what we know'. This may refer to Jesus' disciples, and John the Baptist possibly, as well as to Jesus Himself. No words of a Christian are worth listening to unless they spring from inner conviction. V. 13: 'who is in heaven'. NEB: 'whose home is in heaven'. Some MSS omit this. Jesus did not cease to be God when He became man.

St. John 3.16-21

Here is an important paragraph which summarizes some of the main themes of the Gospel. It shows the purpose and effect of the mission of the Son and the reason why it did not meet with a full response.

Verse 16 has been described as 'the gospel in a nutshell'. It tells us that the love of God was the motive force behind the incarnation and passion of Christ. It was a love great enough to embrace the whole world—a world which was made through the Son but which did not recognize Him (**1**.10) and even hated Him (**7**.7). It was love shown not just in sentiment but in giving. God's gift was the greatest that could ever be made—His only Son (cf. Gen. **22**.2,16). It was a love which required a response of faith, a commitment, in return. The relationship resulting from this could be described as eternal life, the life of the age to come experienced in the present.

Light inevitably casts shadows. Though the purpose of the Son's mission was salvation (rescue and health), the effect of it was often judgement. (He can even say that in one sense its purpose was judgement—**9**.39.) This was not something arbitrarily imposed but it resulted naturally from a refusal to be exposed and to face realities. It is something which, like the offer of eternal life, is taking place already. It is even now showing up what is genuine and what is shoddy and mean. Light and the process of discrimination are inseparable. How terrible it is that for some the offer of life should almost become the means of death!

Superficially, the act of belief appears a very small factor to determine the difference between salvation and destruction, but in reality this is not so. Belief is indicative of a fundamental change of life. It involves the open acknowledgement of sin, whereas, as

274

Christ observes, a man's corrupted nature impels him to avoid the light of exposure (19 ff.). It also involves a sense of need, an awareness of a personal insufficiency and the appropriation of God's provision. All this includes the acceptance of His estimate and standards. So conversion should mark the beginning of a walk in the light—a concept which John develops in his first epistle.

Note: It is not certain whether vs. 16–21 are a continuation of the words of Jesus (RSV margin, NEB) or a comment by the evangelist (RSV). As punctuation marks were not used in the N.T. manuscripts, it is a matter of individual interpretation according to the context. A similar problem is found concerning vs. 31–36.

St. John 3.22-36

Vs. 22–24. The ebb and flow of the ministry of Christ can be seen in the movement between Jerusalem, Judea and Galilee. Jesus has made His first challenge to Jerusalem and His claims have been misinterpreted. Now He goes into Judea (22) before returning to Galilee (**4.**3). In the Jordan valley He began a ministry of baptism parallel to that of John. This was not performed by Jesus Himself but by His disciples (**4.**2), but it was done with His authority.

Vs. 25,26. The ministry of Jesus was inevitably controversial, and there were occasions where controversy occurred amongst those who should have been His supporters. The Jew involved here (25) is unknown (some MSS read 'Jews' and it has even been suggested that there could have been a scribal slip in copying an abbreviation for 'Jesus'). The issue, so common amongst religious people, was one of pastoral jealousy. It seemed to John's disciples that he had precedence over Jesus, whose growing popularity they probably resented (cf. **12.**19 and the attitude of the Pharisees).

Vs. 27–30. John shows great wisdom in understanding his role as 'best man'. His precedence was one of service and preparation (**1.**30 f.). He never claimed to be the Christ (**1.**20). His privilege was to make arrangements for the uniting of the Messiah with His bride Israel. Far from causing jealousy, the God-given success of Jesus was a source of joy to him: There is no other success that matters in Christian work today.

Vs. 31–36. These verses may be a comment by the evangelist (see previous day's note). John's ministry is essentially on a human and earthly level. Jesus has a heavenly origin and His testimony is about heavenly things (cf. **3.**11 f.). Sent and loved by God, He speaks the truth of God and imparts the Spirit of God. The response which men make to Him is decisive for life or for wrath (God's implacable

275

hostility to sin). God's relevation of Himself in Christ cannot be trifled with. Our duty, as believers, must always be the humble, self-effacing part of witnesses to Christ. But v.34 has its application to us also, we have superhuman reinforcement for a superhuman task!

Notes: V. 23: 'Aenon near Salim'—'Aenon' means 'Fountains' and was chosen because of the water there. 'Salim', meaning 'Peace', may have had symbolic significance. V. 24: John does not record the Baptist's imprisonment and this allusion suggests that he expects his readers to know something of the subsequent story. V. 31: 'from above'. The Gospel uses the picture of 'up there' to show the 'transcendence' (otherness) of God and Christ. It also shows the One in whom is life (**1.4**) to be 'immanent' ('the ground of our being').

A challenge: Does John's magnificent affirmation truly reflect your own attitude?

St. John 4.1-15

Jesus was anxious not to provoke a major clash with the Pharisees until 'His hour had come'. He therefore left Judea to which He had made His challenge (almost 'left it to its fate') and went back to Galilee. Geographical necessity took Him through Samaria, for this was the shortest route home, though Galilean pilgrims often took a long way round to avoid it. But, as so often in the life of Jesus, the action of divine providence could be seen also, for it gave Him the opportunity to present to the sectarian Samaritans the true way to worship God. In His own human weariness and thirst He was able to offer them true satisfaction of all their needs.

The story illustrates, vividly and at some length, the way in which Jesus dealt with individuals (cf. also **9**.1–41; **11**.1–44). It has often been used as a pattern for personal evangelism. (For a fine exposition see Temple, *Readings in St. John's Gospel*, ad loc.). Jesus meets a Samaritan woman on the level of felt and shared human need. He begins by asking her a favour, which caused considerable surprise. There was a barrier of race and of sex which would normally have prevented anything but a superior and scornful attitude by a Jewish rabbi to a Samaritan woman who may have been an outcast in her own community. The manner of our approach to others reveals how much we care for them as people.

The surprising thing did not, however, lie in this encounter but in the fact of His identity and the spiritual offer which He was making. But talk of living water is understood by her on the literal

276

level (cf. **6.**52; see also Jer. **2.**13; Zech. **14.**8; Ezek. **47.**9). How can a tired stranger be greater than Jacob the ancestor of the race (cf. Abraham in **8.**53)?

Jesus had to open up a completely new dimension. The rabbis sometimes used 'water' as a figure of the Law, sometimes of the Spirit. Jesus speaks of the water of eternal life which satisfies people at the deepest spiritual level (**6.**35; **7.**37 f.).

Notes: V. 5: 'Sychar'—probably modern Ashar near Mount Ebal. 'Jacob's well' may still be seen. V. 9: probably read with NEB: 'Jews and Samaritans, it should be noted, do not use vessels in common.'

A testimony:

> I heard the voice of Jesus say,
>   'Behold I freely give
> The living water—thirsty one,
>   Stoop down, and drink, and live.'
> I came to Jesus, and I drank
>   Of that life-giving stream;
> My thirst was quenched, my soul revived,
>   And now I live in Him.

A prayer: 'Sir, give me this water, that I may not thirst ...'

St. John 4.16-26

Before the woman can receive the living water, Jesus tells her to call her husband. The gift of God is personal but not private—it has to be shared. She had probably not come to draw water just for herself—the water of life was to be for others too. The partner in marriage is the first with whom it needs to be shared.

The mention of her husband brings a denial that she has one, and Jesus shows (presumably by supernatural insight) that He knows all about her marital and extra-marital relationships. Her sin had to be acknowledged before she could experience the new life of God. There is no faith without repentance.

The woman's reaction is natural. Someone with such insight is a prophet. He can therefore solve the great denominational dispute. Is Mount Gerizim or Mount Zion the right place to worship? So often will people try to deflect the personal moral challenge of the gospel to a question of general interest.

Jesus shows that Gerizim and Zion are temporary local symbols. When God's hour comes worship will be universal and its location irrelevant. That, however, is not to say that all religions are the same. Samaritan worship in many points was in ignorance, Jewish was with knowledge. God's saving actions had been among Jews, and the Jewish people, as a cradle for the Messiah, were the means of salvation for the world. Yet even Judaism pales before the worship opened up now.

God's nature is spiritual not local. He is the living God and seeks living worship. Men's worship must therefore be not in Jewish letter but in spirit (that aspect of man which answers to God and is made alive by the Holy Spirit), and not in Samaritan falsehood but in truth (in sincerity which depends on the reality of God's revelation in Christ). As she does not understand, the woman pushes off the challenge until later, when the Messiah comes. Back comes the startling reply: 'I am He'. The enjoyment of His presence is still the key to worship.

Note: V. 18: 'five husbands' may refer to the five peoples with their heathen 'baals' ('baal' meant 'husband') who were the ancestors of the Samaritans (2 Kings **17**.24–33). If this were so, it would explain why the woman raised the question of the right place to worship.

St. John 4.27-38

The private personal conversation which Jesus has with the woman has to come to an end with the arrival of the disciples. They are still at the stage of being surprised at His attitude to women, but have become aware that they are in no position to question His actions. The woman left her waterpot and went off to spread the news of her meeting with someone so remarkable that He might even be the Messiah.

If the woman has made a possible discovery after misunderstanding, the disciples continue to misunderstand. They are rightly concerned about Jesus' physical welfare, but cannot appreciate His spiritual metaphor. He was sustained by doing His Father's will (**5**.30; **6**.38) and completing His work (**5**.36; **17**.4; **19**.28–30). Others too were to be sustained (and still are) by His obedience to the uttermost (**6**.51).

In the natural world there may have been four months between the end of sowing and the beginning of harvest. In the spiritual world sowing and reaping may seem almost simultaneous. The work of the gospel is teamwork, and there are always different parts for different people to play in its furtherance (cf. 1 Cor. **3**.6). As far as the presentation of the gospel to the Samaritans was concerned, John the Baptist and his disciples had done their part, Jesus and His disciples were now doing theirs, and in due course Philip and the others were to do theirs (Acts **8**.5–25). Each group and individual is helping in the mission of the Son and of the Spirit. No comparison should be made between the importance of the spiritual work of one group and that of another.

Notes: V. 28: she left her jar probably because she was in a hurry to tell her friends and come back. It was not necessarily because her mind was totally absorbed with what she had heard. V. 35: although this could have been a proverbial saying there is no precise evidence that it was. It might simply be that the scene was set four months before harvest. The fields were 'white' probably with the head-dresses of the Samaritans.

For meditation: One simple, factual testimony led many to 'come and see' (29f.). Does your testimony provoke such a response?

St. John 4.39-45

There is no stopping the testimony to Christ. Despite the unbelief of the Jews (**1**.11), knowing all that they did of God (**4**.22), we see the Samaritans believing in Jesus. This was not yet a full Christian faith. In the first instance it was based upon what the woman had said about a man who had some sort of supernatural knowledge of her life. Nevertheless this was testimony—part of the unfolding of the whole testimony to Christ in the Gospel. The testimony of God (**5**.37), or of Christ Himself (**3**.32), or of His deeds (**5**.36), or of some other person (**1**.7) is one of the bases of faith in the Gospel.

The Samaritans gave Jesus an invitation to stay with them. There is no hint that a stay in Samaria was in Christ's original plan, but He was sufficiently flexible to meet an obvious need (40). Are we adaptable enough to make the most of *our* time and opportunities (Col. **4**.5)? So the Samaritans moved on from acceptance of testimony at second-hand to experience of Jesus at first-hand. It was the word of Jesus which they heard for themselves which brought life (cf. **4**.53; **5**.24). The Jews, from whom was salvation (**4**.22), were preceded by the Samaritans in the confession of the Messiah as Saviour of the world. There is no order of ecclesiastical precedence in spiritual enlightenment. *Prejudice* could have viewed Jesus as a Jewish, nationalistic prophet—*personal experience* proved that He was the Christ.

Samaria is a stop on the road to Galilee (**4**.3) and Jesus continues His journey. Here too He will have more honour than in Jerusalem. In fact, the Galileans welcomed Him because they had seen for themselves at first-hand His signs in Jerusalem (**2**.23). Here is the irony of faith and unbelief—the Samaritans believed without a sign,

279

the Galileans with a sign, and the Judeans (His own people) not at all despite a sign.

Notes: 'because of the woman's testimony' (39); 'because of His word' (41); 'because of your words' (42). The same Greek preposition is used to denote the means through which faith comes (cf. **1.7**; **17.20**). It should be our privilege today to be those 'because of' whom others believe, even if we do not always know it. V. 44: in *John*, if Galilee is where Jesus lives, Judea is theologically His own country (cf. Mark **6.4**). It is to Jerusalem that the challenge is repeatedly made and it is the Jews (seen usually as the Judeans) who as a whole do not believe.

Questions for further study and discussion on St. John, chs. 3.1—4.45
1. What can we learn about personal evangelism by comparing Jesus' dealings with Nicodemus and with the Samaritan woman?
2. What temptations to jealousy do we face in our Christian work (**3.25** f.)? Do we really practise teamwork (**4.36–38**)?
3. In what lies the greatness of John the Baptist? (See also **10.41**.)
4. How do we see light and darkness at work in people's lives today (**3.16–21**)?
5. What are the distinctive marks of Christian worship (**4.16–26**)?

St. John 4.46-54

Jesus returned not only to Galilee but more especially to Cana, the scene of His first sign. The general pattern of His movement is repeated—departure to Galilee (**1.43**; **4.43**), arrival at Cana (**2.1**; **4.46**), going up to Jerusalem for a festival (**2.13**; **5.1**). Here at Cana He performs another sign. This shows His power, even at a distance, to heal and rescue from the gates of death.

The official was probably an officer at the court of Herod Antipas. It is not clear whether he was a Jew or a Gentile. He must have known of Jesus' reputation as a miracle-worker, so he left his sick son at Capernaum and came to ask for Jesus' help in his desperate plight. Jesus' reply seemed off-putting (cf. **2.4**). He addresses not only the official but others like him ('you' in v. 48 is plural), deploring their dependence upon spectacular miracles before they believe. But the man's urgent need shows that there is faith of a kind in the power of Christ to help. It is an appeal from the heart which does not go unheeded. Jesus confidently assures him that his son will live.

The man took the first step to faith by believing Jesus' word and acting on it. Confirmation of his faith was provided by his servants with their news of the boy's recovery. Natural curiosity compelled him to seek the extent of the connection with the word of Jesus. The discovery that the healing was instantaneous and simultaneous with it brought him and his household to a committed faith in Jesus. For it is His word which brings life from the gates of death (5.24). So, in the second sign (54) as in the first (2.11), individual faith and obedience were matched by Christ's response, and led to belief in a limited sphere. Is there a principle of abiding relevance here?

Notes: Many commentators have suggested that this is a different version of the story of the healing of the centurion's servant found in the Synoptic Gospels (Matt. 8.5–13; Luke 7.1–10). There seem, however, to be sufficient differences in detail between the two to make it more likely that this was another, though similar, event.

The vivid phrase 'Your son lives' comes three times (50, 51, 53; cf. 1 Kings 17.23). It is better taken as present (with AV and Phillips) than as future.

Some have seen the descriptions of 'an official' (46), 'the man' (50) and 'the father' (53) as indicating a progressive revelation of his real self and situation as he drew nearer to Christ. In our spiritual dealings with people we should likewise find them becoming increasingly real to us.

St. John 5.1-9

The word which has recently given life in Galilee now gives healing in Jerusalem. There the emphasis had been on the rescue from the jaws of death, here there is the return of lost powers. Once again water plays a prominent part. At Cana water was turned into wine (2.1–11), at Sychar water was unable to satisfy true human thirst (4.13 f.), and now at Jerusalem water cannot make a man's paralysed limbs function again. As 'water' was one of the terms used by the rabbis to describe the Law, there is probably an implied contrast between the impotence of the Law and the life-giving power of the word of Christ.

The Pool of Bethesda was a shrine for sick people who wished to be healed and, presumably having despaired of a cure by other means, came in the superstitious hope that they might be able to benefit from the mysterious powers of the pool. Some MSS include vs. 3b,4 which state that an angel of the Lord went into the pool and troubled the water and the first person in after that was cured. This is no doubt simply a deduction from the authentic text and describes what was believed to happen. Jesus comes to this scene of helplessness and superstition and as always His eye picks out an individual in special need of help. He altogether removes the idea of

Photo: Crusader Church of St. Anne

Photo: Pool of Bethesda

healing from the realm of chance and puts it in the realm of will. The man proves his real desire to be healed by his obedience to Jesus' startling threefold command to rise, take up his bed and walk (cf. Mark **2.**11). But there is one snag, forgotten no doubt by the man in his joy. It is the Sabbath.

*Notes:*V. 1: it is uncertain which festival is referred to but it was not a major one. V. 2: MSS differ as to the name of the pool. It may be Bethzatha, Bethesda or Bethsaida. The pool seems to have been discovered just north of the Temple. 'Five porticoes'—some see this as symbolic of the Law with its five books. V. 5: some have seen symbolism in the thirty-eight years, for this was the time of Israel's wandering in the wilderness (Deut. **2.**14). The primary reason for its mention is to show that he had been ill a long time.

St. John 5.10-18

John traces Jewish reaction to the person and ministry of Christ as it was unfolded in His actions and words. The true Light had come into the world (**1.**9), and men whose habitat was darkness rather than light (**3.**19) were disturbed, eventually they were to attempt to extinguish the Light.

If Jesus has really come to give new life in a way that the old order could not, then He is bound to clash with the guardians of the old order concerning their religious institutions. He has tried to show them the true significance of the Temple (**2.**13–22), now He has to reveal to them the true meaning of the Sabbath. In one sense there was no urgency about this miracle, one extra day could hardly have made much difference, and it may be that its performance on the Sabbath (cf. Matt. **12.**9–15; Luke **13.**10–17; **14.**1–6) was a direct challenge to the Jews. The Sabbath, intended for man's benefit and enjoyment, had been so hedged about with petty restrictions, many enforceable by death, that man was shackled in legalistic bondage. But the question of the Sabbath could not be solved without going back to the more fundamental point—the origin and authority of Jesus Himself.

The healed cripple is the first object of their attack. To carry his bed on the Sabbath was against the Law (Jer. **17.**21). He has the feeling that the man who gave him healing has also authority in other matters, and defends himself by referring to Jesus' command. Naturally enough they wish to know who it is who gives such illegal orders. But Jesus had not been ready to reveal Himself and had slipped away, so that, like countless others, the man was ignorant that Christ was the source of the blessing which had come to him. Jesus does not wish to leave him in ignorance, and after finding

283

him gives him a solemn warning. The spiritual lesson must reinforce the physical healing. There is a far worse fate for persistent sinners than even the pathetic condition of paralysis. What the man made of this we do not know, but he dutifully gave the authorities the information for which they had asked. This attitude to the Sabbath became a main cause of the persistent hostility of the Jews towards Jesus. Yet He takes the matter further—God His Father does not stop working on the Sabbath, nor does He. Such apparent blasphemy turns Jewish hostility into a desire to kill Him.

Notes: V. 14: this does not imply that the man's illness was directly the result of his own sin (cf. **9**.3). It does mean that spiritual warnings are to be taken from physical evils (cf. Luke **13**.1–5). Too easily we fail to see and heed them. V. 17: God's Sabbath rest (Gen. **2**.2) did not mean that the Creator of the world was inactive. He was seeking to give life on the Sabbath; they were seeking to kill. There was no doubt which was God's work (cf. Mark **3**.1–6).

St. John 5.19-29

The real issues have now been revealed. They concern the relationship of Jesus to the Father and His consequent right to exercise the divine prerogatives of giving life and judging. This is a struggle which cannot reach the point of decision until life comes through His death (**12**.23–26) and until judgement comes upon the unbelieving world and its ruler through the sentence passed upon Him (**12**.27–33).

Vs. 19–24. Jesus speaks of His authority in the first instance as far as His incarnate nature is concerned. In this it is derivative, and in a sense imitative. But it comes from the close relationship of love which exists between Father and Son. There is in a way little to marvel about in the healing of a cripple. They could begin to marvel when they saw the Son raising the dead and giving them life, for that was the work of God alone (cf. 2 Kings **5**.7). God the Father who is judge of all the earth (Gen. **18**.25 ; Psa. **94**.2) in fact delegates His judicial office to the Son. With these prerogatives there logically follows a title to divine honour, a denial of which shows failure to honour the Father. To hear the Son's word and to believe the Father gives life on an eternal plane, bypassing the terrors of judgement.

Some men, like the Jews, have rejected outright those tremendous claims. After all, no prophet, not even Moses, had assumed such prerogatives. Most men have given them token acceptance. But if they are true, then Christ's claim on our love and our allegiance must be taken seriously—God Himself is knocking at the door of our lives and claiming them. Note the conditions of acceptance (24) and compare them with **1**.12.

Vs. 25–29. Having stated the general principle, Jesus now shows that these will be given concrete expression in the future and even in the present. Those who believe receive spiritual life now, those who are physically dead will come into the fullness of the resurrection. How easily Christians forget the amazing extent of their salvation!

Notes: V. 19: 'whatever He does'—the Son is associated with all the work of the Father (cf. **1**.3). V. 20: 'greater works'—specifically the raising of Lazarus (ch. **11**); and the resurrection (ch. **20**). V. 25: 'the hour is coming, and now is'—a characteristic phrase of Jesus in the Gospel (cf. **4**.23; **16**.32). It shows the way in which divine and human time-scales overlap in the ministry of Jesus. V. 27: the Son of man, as a human figure with divine origin, was particularly well qualified to act as judge (cf. Dan. **7**.9–14).

St. John 5.30-47

Such a claim to authority cannot be accepted without evidence. There follows therefore a presentation by Jesus of the evidence upon which He bases it. Again He states that it is derived authority, and adds that the unselfish nature of His motives reinforces His claim to the truth (30). A man's own evidence is not sufficient, and the Law did not allow it without corroboration (Deut. **19**.15). But Jesus has another witness of whose testimony He is sure (31 f.).

On the human level there is the evidence of John the Baptist (33–35). His mission is described in similar terms to those used before (**1**.6–8). He was a lamp which was kindled and shone temporarily, but he was not the light itself (**1**.8). His evidence could have led to salvation, but it was not the real evidence that mattered in the case. The real evidence was that the Son was doing the works of His Father (36–38). This was supported by the Father's witness both in Scripture and in experience. This was unavailable to the Jews because they could not see or hear Him directly, and they did not accept His Son who gave perfect expression to Him. So there came about the extraordinary situation that those who possessed, read and professed to trust in the Scriptures were unable to recognize the One to whom the Scriptures were referring (39 f.).

As so often, failure to understand has a moral cause (41–44). The Jews were blinded by prejudice towards Christ. In His attack on them He had shown that they had no personal knowledge of God (37b). Of course, no man could expect to see God physically, but

He *was* revealed in the Scriptures and through Christ, and here the Jews had a massive blind-spot. They were motivated by a preference for human approval over divine approval (cf. **11**.42 f.). The irony is that those who professed to be Moses' disciples (**9**.28) were going to have Moses in the witness box testifying for Jesus and against them (45–47). When a man is blind to the spiritual truth which lies before his eyes, there is little hope for him (cf. Luke **16**.31).

Notes: V. 32: 'another' is the Father rather than John. V. 39: 'you search' almost certainly indicative rather than imperative. V. 45: 'on whom you set your hope'—they had fallen into idolatry by confusing the sign (the Law) with the thing signified (eternal life with God through the Messiah). The temptation to do this has not disappeared. Some modern-day evangelicalism is in danger of elevating the Scriptures above the Christ, but life is not in the Scriptures themselves but in the One to whom they point. The Scriptures are the *signpost* to Christ the Saviour.

Questions for further study and discussion on St. John, chs. 4.46–5.47
1. Why did Jesus heal some people and not others? Why is this still so?
2. In what ways today are people ignorant of Christ as the source of blessings which they enjoy (cf. **5**.13)?
3. In what ways are the questions about the origin and authority of Christ discussed in the Gospel still relevant today?
4. Do we ever honour but not obey the Scriptures (**5**.39 f., 45–47)?
5. What temptations do we have to receive glory from other people rather than from God (**5**.44)?

St. John 6.1-15

We have seen Christ as the provider for human need (**2**.1–11) and the giver of life (**4**.46–54). Now in providing again for human need He demonstrates that He is not only the giver but also the gift of life. He is the bread which alone can sustain men's souls. He reveals this spiritual truth through a miracle in which, as at Cana, He brings into focus in a single dramatic act what God is always doing in multiplying bread and fish.

The Passover setting of this miracle, and the discourse which follows it, are of considerable importance. Under the old covenant the great act of redemption was the Exodus from Egypt. This had associated with it the feeding of the people with manna in the wilderness, which was a sign to the people and a temporary provision for their need. As a continual remembrance of this redemption the annual festival of the Passover was held in which each succeeding generation identified itself with those whom the Lord had brought out of Egypt. So under the new covenant the great act of redemption is the cross and resurrection of Christ. This has the Lord's Supper as its permanent festival of remembrance. But it also has a temporary sign parallel to the feeding with manna, namely, this feeding miracle. Both old and new covenants point forward to the final Messianic banquet. It would be a mistake to think that the chapter is essentially about the Holy Communion. Rather, it seems to be about the central theological facts of the divine redemption to which also the Holy Communion points. When we partake of the Lord's Supper in faith we link ourselves up with all that Christ has done for us.

Notice in this incident the various reactions to Christ. *(i)* Philip calculated human need in terms of cash, and in the unlikely event of their having such an amount it would only blunt the edge of the crowd's hunger (7). Yet he was in the presence of the Son of God, with His unlimited resources! *(ii)* Andrew was more hopeful. He noted the scanty, inadequate provision, but appears to have left the question open, as does Ezekiel in **37**.3. In the presence of God *nothing* is impossible. *(iii)* The crowd, seeing possibly the fulfilment of Moses' prophecy (Deut. **18**.15–19), were about to respond (15). But all they sought was a Messiah of their own devising who would fill their stomachs (26). Note how resolutely Christ dealt with this temptation to short-circuit Calvary (15, cf. Matt. **14**.22f). Temptations can come in attractive guise, and to entertain them even momentarily is to court disaster.

Notes: V. 1: a gap must be presumed after chapter **5**. V. 5: this is the only miracle recorded in all four Gospels. John seems to have an independent account which illuminates, and is illuminated by, the others. V. 10: 'men' means males. Their possible military formation (Mark **6**.39 f.) suggests there might have been an attempt at a Messianic uprising as it was Passover time. Jesus will have none of it (15). V. 12: some see this as a picture of the gathering of the remnant of true believers (cf. **11**.52). V. 15: when His hour came men did come and take Him by force (**18**.12), and made Him King (**19**.1–22).

St. John 6.16-24

Vs. 16–21. After the feeding of the five thousand Jesus again demonstrates that He is Lord over nature by walking on the surface of the Sea of Galilee. Some have suggested that there is a further

287

point of Exodus typology here and that this symbolizes a new crossing of the Red Sea. The evidence for this is rather slim and it is better to take it as showing the power of Christ to help and guide even in the face of adverse natural conditions (cf. Mark **6.**45–51). His presence banishes fear and guarantees arrival at their destination.

Vs.22–24. These verses give a somewhat complicated explanation of how the crowds on the east shore of the lake discovered that Jesus and His disciples had gone over to the west shore and how they followed across as soon as there was transport available for them. They were sufficiently impressed by what He had done to be anxious to search for Him, though their motives were materialistic (26). We need to have a proper assessment of such seekers today.

Notes: V. 16: they were presumably given instruction by Jesus in order to avoid the attentions of the crowd. V. 17: they expected Jesus to join them somehow. V. 19: the lake was about eight miles across, but this may have been a shorter crossing near the northern end. 'On the sea': the Greek phrase could mean simply 'on the seashore'. The story in Mark **6.**45–51 and the general context here make it most unlikely that this is what was intended. (Even less probable are the 'rationalizing' theories concerning the feeding miracle which suppose that when the boy took out his sandwiches many of the others followed suit!) V. 20: 'It is I'. The Greek *ego eimi* may mean this, or simply 'I am', or 'I am He' (**18.**5). In view of the 'I am' sayings in the Gospel and such a claim as is found in **8.**58, it is probable that there are intended to be overtones of divinity in the expression.

St. John 6.25-34

There now follows a long discourse of Jesus with the Jews about the meaning of the sign which He has performed. This is similar to the discourse in **8.**12–59 concerning the light of the world and related themes which precedes the healing of the blind man in ch. **9.** In each of these dialogues there is an 'I am' saying of Jesus and a failure by the Jews to understand His meaning.

A query as to when He had come across the lake is met by a rebuke to those who had found Him, on the grounds that they wanted Him for the wrong reason—merely as a purveyor of bread for the hungry. He had already rejected this as an adequate Messianic programme (Matt. **4.**2–4). Like water (**4.**13 f.), food is a sign of spiritual sustenance. It must be worked for, yet paradoxically it is the gift of God. Work of this kind is therefore not an external striving but faith in the Son.

288

The people then want a further sign, as if the feeding were not enough for them. (No one depending on seeing wonders will ever be satisfied. Paradoxically, however, the greater the objective proof supplied, the less is the demand for the faith which Christ requires.) Their ancestors had been fed with manna in the wilderness. A repetition of this was expected to be one of the marks of the Messianic age. Jesus reminds them that the source of the manna was not Moses but God, and that the manna was not the genuine bread from heaven. This was to be sought, not in anything temporary and corruptible, but in something of heavenly origin which could bring life to the whole world. This sounded so good that they wanted to have it always available to themselves (cf. 4.15). The mystery is still hidden from them.

Notes: V. 26: 'saw signs'—they did see the actions but not their significance. V. 30: they depend on physical sight, but the physical sight which they have already had has not turned into spiritual sight. V. 31: the Christian manna is referred to in Rev. 2.17 and may be alluded to in the Lord's Prayer (Matt. 6.11).

St. John 6.35-46

The Jews have been looking on Jesus as one who claims to give sustenance. Now comes the startling assertion that He is the sustenance itself. His claim to be the bread of life is the first of the seven 'I am' sayings in the Gospel (cf. 8.12; 10.9,11; 11.25; 14.6; 15.1). Each of them is a statement about the person of Christ coupled with a consequent promise of what He offers to the believer. The emphatic 'I am' may carry overtones of deity (cf. Exod. 3.13 f.). This saying is an offer of complete and eternal satisfaction to those who trust in Him (cf. 4.14). O taste and see!

The offer to faith reveals as ever the problem of unbelief. Men could see without believing, for true faith depended not upon physical sight but upon the gift of God. The identity of will between Father and Son is such that those given by the Father will be received by the Son and brought to eternal life in the present, and resurrection at the end. The twofold reference to 'the last day' (39f.) would remind the Jews of the Old Testament concept of the 'day of the Lord' (e.g. Amos 5.18) when God's purposes would be consummated. Christ's claim that this was in His control was a further assertion of His deity.

A claim such as this could hardly fail to be disputed. The most obvious objection to it was that this was a local young man of known parentage. It was a preposterous thing for Him to say! But

Jesus stands His ground concerning His Father's calling people t·
Him. Living experience of the Father inevitably leads to faith in th
Son, though true sight of the Father is reserved for the Son alon·
(cf. **1.**18).

Notes: V. 37: the ground of Christian assurance is not a man'
own actions or feelings but the unfailing purpose of God. Nothin;
less is a safe foundation for life. David Livingstone described thi·
promise as 'the words of a perfect gentleman'. V. 39: some connec·
this with the gathering of the pieces of bread (12 f.). V. 41: 'th·
Jews'—the scene is in Galilee, but, in every other instance in th·
Gospel apart from v. 52, they seem to be Judeans. V. 42: as so ofte·
in the Gospel they think that they know His origin, but they see ·
only from the human side (cf. **7.**27,41; see also Mark **6.**3). Ou·
Lord shows that their misunderstanding was the result of ignorance·
firstly, of any genuine work of God in their hearts (44), and·
secondly, of the Old Testament revelation which, properly under·
stood, would lead to Him (45).

St. John 6.47-59

Jesus repeats some of what He has said before in a slightly differen·
way in order to reinforce His message (47–51). Faith is the way t·
life, to be enjoyed in the present (cf. **3.**15). He alone in His perso·
can give true spiritual sustenance of a permanent kind whic·
enables men to avoid death and brings them into a new spiritua·
realm. But the bread must be given—in death—for the life of th·
world. And the bread is His flesh. It is by His incarnation an·
passion that the world can be sustained.

There is inevitably misunderstanding not only of His person bu·
also of His offer. It is taken as a literal promise of His giving Hi·
flesh for them to eat, which sounds very much like cannibalism. I·
reply Jesus makes no attempt to soften the language which He ha·
used. Rather He strengthens it. He speaks of eating His flesh an·
drinking His blood as being essential for life and for resurrection·
He describes it as the true food and drink. He asserts that it is th·
means of union with Him and mutual indwelling. He claims tha·
those who 'eat' Him will have His life in them as He has the Father'
life in Himself. He reminds them once more of the temporary effect·
of the feeding with the manna, and contrasts the heavenly origi·
and eternal effects of this bread. The language is supposed to b·
strong and startling. The metaphors, eating and drinking, clearl·
point to that act by which one 'comes' and 'believes' in Chris·
(**6.**35), and through which he is made one with Him. His flesh an·

290

blood alone provide our spiritual sustenance. This is clearly demonstrated in the Lord's Supper, but the sacrament is not the source of this experience nor is it the only place where this spiritual truth is realized. The believer knows it as a permanent reality, and enjoys a closeness of identification with Christ, parallel to His relationship with His Father, drawing upon His unlimited resources in a relationship of absolute love, dependence and obedience.

Notes: V. 52: 'How can ...?' This question is not answered directly (cf. 3.5,9). V. 54: 'eats'—the word is a harsh one almost meaning 'munches', V. 59: perhaps the synagogue lesson was the story of the manna.

St. John 6.60-71

Jesus' ministry has already for some time been causing controversy with 'the Jews'. Now dissension comes to the disciples as well. There were clearly a good number of people who followed Jesus in some way or other during His ministry, for He was able to send out seventy on a mission as His representatives (Luke 10.1). Amongst those associated with Him would be some whose commitment was very loose or who had badly mistaken ideas of what sort of ministry the Messiah would have. Possibly we can hardly understand the 'cultural shock' on men with the traditional Jewish background of allegiance to the law, religious observances and good works. Instead, Christ claimed their complete loyalty to *Himself* as the repository of spiritual life. The harshness of His statements shocked them because of their materialism and maybe also because of their implication that life came through death. To their objections Jesus makes a twofold reply. On the one hand, the return of the Son of Man to heaven, after His death and resurrection, will show them the true meaning of what He is talking about. On the other hand, they had left the Spirit out of account. He is not talking about anything merely carnal nor is He offering automatic salvation through mechanical participation in a sacred meal. The Spirit gave life and the word He spoke was the living interpretation of this figure. But because they did not believe it was lost upon them.

We are now faced clearly with the issue of faith and unbelief amongst His disciples. Jesus knew who would be faithful, and true faith was the gift of the Father. Some separated themselves from Him at this stage. But disloyalty and unbelief have gone further. The Twelve are now challenged about their position. Simon confesses Him on their behalf as the Holy One of God, but even then Jesus must describe one of them as 'a devil'.

291

Notice the great place which testimony is given in John's Gospel (68 f., cf. **1**.29–36,41,45; **4**.29). Has this any significance for our generation? Observe, too, that opposition often serves to clarify truth and sharpen our awareness that Christ is what He claims to be, the one Source of true satisfaction.

Notes: V. 60: the NEB paraphrases: 'This is more than we can stomach! Why listen to such words?' There are many truths which we find it no easier to receive. V. 67: this is the first mention of 'the Twelve' as such. Jesus uses the expression in v. 70 to emphasize the fact of their being the chosen inner circle. The evangelist repeats the phrase in v. 71 to show the tragedy of the betrayal (cf. Mark **14**.10, 20,43). In the Greek these words come with vivid dramatic effect at the very end of the sentence. The problems of predestination and moral responsibility and their relationship are found in as acute form in the case of Judas as anywhere in the Bible.

Questions for further study and discussion on St. John ch. 6
1. Have you a doctrine of the Lord's Supper? How does it square with this chapter?
2. Why did St. John not include the story of the institution of the Holy Communion?
3. What was the point of the walking on the water and what is its relevance to us today?
4. In what ways (honestly!) do we find our lives sustained by the Bread of Life?
5. What do we make of the hard sayings of Jesus (**6**.60)? Which ones have we wrestled with and applied recently?

St. John 7.1-13

The clouds of conflict increasingly overshadow the ministry. Jesus still continues with His offer of life for His own people and for the world. His own people have decided upon His death. Jesus pauses for a while in Galilee. When the Feast of Tabernacles comes round Jesus' brothers are most anxious that He should go and reveal Himself in Judea. For this was one of the great festivals at which there would be present pilgrims from all over the world. But His brothers, who had still not come to faith in Him, were arguing with purely human strategy. Galilee, to them, was an unimportant backwater; Judea was where He ought to be if He was to gain acceptance. Let Him be venturesome and dazzle men with an open display of power! Jesus is concerned about the divine strategy. The thing that really matters is whether His hour has come. We are no more entitled to try to push Him into action.

In the end, after a delay in Galilee, Jesus went up to Jerusalem, not publicly, as He did for the final Passover when the issues had to come to a head, but privately. The people had expected that He would come and there was a great deal of excited informal discussion about Him, though largely at a superficial level which failed to wrestle with the challenge of His claims. Clearly, at this juncture there was much uncertainty, influenced by official hostility which muzzled discussion (12 f.). Both opinions expressed were somewhat nebulous. The discourses which follow show Jesus presenting Himself to God's people as life and light for themselves and for the world, and being rejected (1.4 f., 9–13).

Notes: V. 2: the festival was held in September or October and was the most popular in the calendar. It was a thanksgiving for harvest (Exod. **23**.16) and for the provision which God had made for the people when He led them through the wilderness (Lev. **23**.39 –43). To commemorate this the pilgrims erected tents all over Jerusalem and lived in them for eight days. V. 3: 'His brothers'— the natural assumption is that they were sons of Joseph and Mary born after Jesus. V. 8: the apparent difficulty of reconciling this statement with v. 10 seems to have led to a scribal alteration of 'not' to 'not yet'. But it may be that the word 'go up' carries with it the sense of going up to the Father by way of the cross (**3**.13; **6**.62; **20**.17). V. 13: 'fear of the Jews'—cf. **19**.38; **20**.19.

Question: Is it right for any religious body to stamp its authority on a particular issue, doctrinal or practical, so as to stifle or preclude personal conscience?

St. John 7.14-24

The Gospel shows that the festivals were the most significant occasions, and the Temple the most significant place, for Jesus to present His challenge to Judaism (**2**.13–22; **5**.1; **10**.22–39; **12**.12– 36). So about the middle of this feast He went into the Temple and taught. His ability to engage in rabbinic argument was a considerable source of surprise, for He was without formal education in that discipline. What should have impressed them was not the style of His discourses but their content. Intellectually they had to acknowledge His skill, spiritually they were blind to His authority. Jesus' authority should have been accepted as God's authority because His motive was clearly God's glory. They could not accept it unless they were willing to obey God's will. In this controversy Christ appears as the one person completely sure of Himself,

293

His origin and His mission. Notice the practical test which He offers (17 f.)—honest investigation, with the *will* directed to seek God's truth (cf. Philip's 'Come and see', **1**.46).

The question of authority can be pinned down more specifically—those who claimed to accept the authority of the Mosaic Law did not even keep it themselves. They made a great issue of His breaking the Sabbath by His healing of the cripple while they themselves practised circumcision on the Sabbath. Moreover their lawlessness was such that they wished to kill Him. No wonder that He has to impress upon them the need for just, rather than superficial, judgements! It is so much easier to be superficial.

Notes: V. 14: the Lord whom they sought (11) came suddenly into His Temple (Mal. **3**.1). V. 15: the same charge of lack of rabbinic education is made against Peter and John (Acts **4**.13). V. 18: 'seeks his own glory' (cf. **5**.30,41–44). V. 20: 'the people'— they may be different from 'the Jews' and may have been ignorant of plots against Him. V. 23: if a ritual operation may legally be performed on one part of a man's body on the Sabbath, how much more may a man's whole body be healed. There must be some conflict of laws, and it should be clear to all but petty legalists which was the more important. V. 22: Moses gave the law about circumcision (Lev. **12**.3), but the practice originated in Israel with the patriarchs (Gen. **17**.10).

St. John 7.25-36

From the more superficial questions which have been raised, the discussion passes to the question of who Jesus really is. Some know Him only as a wanted man and, when they find Him teaching without being arrested, they wonder if the authorities have decided that He is after all the Messiah. This solution, however, seems to be ruled out by the fact that they know His origin. Jesus retorts that that is precisely what they do not know. His true origin is from His Father and it is for that reason that He comes with the authority of His Father.

The Jewish leaders decide that after all they must try and arrest Him but Jesus is protected by the fact that it is not yet His hour. Many of the people are sufficiently impressed by the number of His miracles to believe that He is the Christ after all, what more could be expected of the Messiah (31)? Their estimate of Christ was shallow, with little understanding of His person and nature. But it was at least a movement towards truth. The authorities accordingly make another attempt to arrest Him. But they cannot stop His ministry. For Jesus is confident not only of His origin but also of His destination and of His time. His destination is one that is out of reach of the unbelieving Jews. They think that the barrier is a geographical one and fail to see that it is a spiritual one.

Notes: V. 26: despite His having visited Jerusalem privately, He teaches, as always, openly (**18**.20). Phillips: 'Surely our rulers haven't decided that this really is Christ!' V. 27: they cannot believe He is the Messiah because they knew where He came from (cf. **6**.42; **7**.41 f.). They did not know about His birth at Bethlehem, which is not mentioned in the Gospel. Others did not believe because they did not know where He came from (**9**.29; **19**.9)! It is amazing what excuses unbelief can find. V. 28: 'You know Me, and you know where I come from?' The question mark brings out the irony. V. 35: 'the Greeks', this need not mean the Gentiles. It could be a term used by the 'Jews' (Palestinian Jews) about the Jews of the Dispersion (cf. **12**.20). It was inconceivable that the Messiah would go where they (the Jews who actually lived in the promised land) could not find Him. Our ecclesiastical pride can be as great.

St. John 7.37-52

It is only on the last day of the feast, the 'climax of the festival' (Phillips), that Jesus is ready to make an astonishing offer to His people and to the world. On this occasion water from Siloam's pool was solemnly offered in the Temple, probably this was an ancient rite invoking God's help in bringing the refreshing 'former rains' to end the long summer drought. Jesus seized this opportunity; any thirsty soul was invited to find deep and lasting refreshment through faith in Him. The blessing which He offered was to be made available through the Holy Spirit, who had not yet been given in a new way to believers.

As usual there was a mixed reaction. For some this offer marked Him as the promised prophet (Deut. **18**.15; John **1**.21; **6**.14). For others it showed Him to be the Christ. Those who knew their Scriptures knew that Christ had to come from Bethlehem. So there was a division among them, with one party relying on Scripture and the other on experience, and neither probably aware that had they known the facts Scripture and experience could have been reconciled! Again a desire to arrest Him fails. The Temple police find that there is something about Him and His teaching which marks Him off as unique. But ignorant men can soon be crushed, without any need of reasoned argument, by an appeal to superior office and knowledge. When Nicodemus does dare to raise his voice in protest in the name of the very Law which they professed to uphold, he too is scornfully dismissed as having baseless provincial sympathies. Galilee of all places!

Notes: V. 37: this was probably the eighth rather than the seventh day. The punctuation of the saying of Jesus is uncertain. It is probably better to follow the RSV margin and NEB in making two parallel invitations and then referring the quotation to Jesus Himself rather than to the believer. The Scripture in question may be Zech. **14.**8, which was part of the lesson appointed for the Feast of Tabernacles. It is no longer Jerusalem but Christ who is the source of blessing. V. 39: the Spirit had been active in the world from the beginning but was not to be given to the believer in the full Christian sense until Pentecost. The phrase is literally 'the Spirit was not'. The third person of the Trinity had to wait for His full personal revelation in the world as did the second person. V. 43: divisions are also described in **9.**16 and **10.**19. V. 50: Nicodemus' visit to Jesus by night had suggested timidity (**3.**1 f.). Now as 'one of them' he plucks up courage to speak up, even if tentatively, for Jesus. V. 52: had they forgotten Jonah? (2 Kings **14.**25).

Thought: Jesus is still a perplexing figure to those who refuse to accept Him at His own estimate as Son of God and Saviour. Why is this?

St. John 7.53—8.11

This story did not originally belong here nor indeed anywhere in St. John's Gospel. This is clear both by the evidence of the MSS and by the style. It was probably inserted by a scribe at this point as an illustration of the principle enunciated in **8.**15. Some MSS put it elsewhere in *John*, others after Luke **21.**38. There is no reason, however, to doubt that it is a genuine story about our Lord's ministry.

There is a close parallel between the story and that of the tribute money (Mark **12.**13–17). Each of them represents an attempt to force Jesus into a position where He makes a pronouncement which will put Him out of favour with either the Romans or the Jews. His accusers, hypocritically pretending to be scandalized by this woman's conduct, were using her, not as a person, but as a political pawn. In this case to advocate stoning would be to usurp the power of the Roman authorities, who alone were allowed to carry out death sentences. To do otherwise would be to contravene the Law of Moses which ordered stoning in such circumstances.

The answer which Jesus gives is a model. He transgresses neither Roman nor Jewish authority. Instead He turns an attempt to trap Him into a penetrating moral challenge to those who were prepared to play politics with human sin and misery. His point is well enough made both with them and with her. Note how conscience works in the presence of the sinless One; these men, convicted of their hypocrisy, soon made their exit. In the end all know themselves to be sinners, and the one who has committed the greatest sin in letter and probably the smallest in spirit leaves with His word of counsel and exhortation.

Notes: V. 3: 'adultery'—only in the case of fornication by a betrothed virgin was stoning laid down as the punishment (Deut. **22.**23 f.). The same punishment was laid down for the man, but the woman seems to have been an easier victim for their scheme. V. 6: it may be that He was writing the sentence as the Roman judge would do and that the words were what He then spoke to them. Any suggestion is pure guesswork. V. 11: Jesus does not condemn her; the witnesses having left, He is in no position to pass judgement according to the Law. By implication He offers her forgiveness but does not excuse her conduct. For she is to go and not to sin again.

Prayer: Lord, make **me** *sensitive to Your presence, aware of my own sinfulness, and help me to 'walk in the light' (1 John 1.7).*

Questions for further study and discussion on St. John chs. 7.1— 8.11

1. What principles do we use in trying to decide between different laws (e.g. the Sabbath law and men's need of healing)?
2. How do we resolve conflicts between Scripture and experience (7.40–52)?
3. In what ways do we set up ourselves, at least in our private thoughts, as more worthy of the gospel than others (7.35)?
4. Was Nicodemus' position to witness stronger or weaker by his being 'one of them' (7.50)?
5. What is our attitude to those guilty of sexual sin? Can we avoid condemning or condoning (8.3–11)?

St. John 8.12-20

The scene continues in the Temple at the Feast of Tabernacles. This festival commemorated, amongst other things, the pillar of fire which had been given as light to the Israelites in the wilderness (Exod. **13**.21 f.), and one of its most impressive ceremonies was the lighting of the golden candelabrum. The light was said to be so brilliant as to illuminate every courtyard in Jerusalem. It was a festival of light. And the Law was also held to be light (Psa. **119**.105; Prov. **6**.23). But neither ceremonial nor even Scripture is the true light. It was God who was the light of His people (Psa. **27**.1), and Jesus therefore comes to direct men's attention away from the symbols to the reality—God's own presence in His person in their midst.

His great claim to be the light of the world is challenged on the ground that it is testimony in His own case. Jesus replies that there is a validity about such evidence in this instance because He had a knowledge of His origin and destination which they did not share. Their idea of judgement was governed by purely human rules. He had in fact the testimony of His Father in support of Him, a fact which they could not understand because they did not know Him.

Notes: V. 12: 'the light of life'—the light which has and gives life (cf. **1**.4 f.). This is given not to those who simply gaze in admiration but to those who follow. It was the destiny of the Servant of the Lord to be a light to the nations (Isa. **49**.6). The theme of light is forgotten until the next chapter. V. 13: the argument concerning evidence is similar in many ways to that in **5**.31–39. V. 15: the question of judgement is one of the most paradoxical themes in the Gospel. It was not Jesus' purpose to judge men (**3**.17; **12**.47), and yet it was (**3**.18; **12**.48; **5**.22; **9**.39). V. 17: '*your* law' perhaps implies that they had treated it as their own preserve. Such spiritual possessiveness is still with us. V. 19: 'Your Father'—they may think He is speaking of Joseph. V. 20: the treasury was just beside where the Sanhedrin met, but even so because of the divine purpose they could not arrest Him.

St. John 8.21-30

The long discourse, which follows to the end of the chapter, is connected with themes which have already been introduced. Here are discussed His origin, His destination, His parentage and His identity. The contrast is made between what He claims to be, and in fact is, and what the Jews in fact are, despite their claims.

Jesus speaks first of going away. His destination is somewhere that they cannot reach (cf. **7**.33–36). Their tragedy is that death will overtake them before their sin is forgiven. The probable allusion to

Plan of Herod's Temple

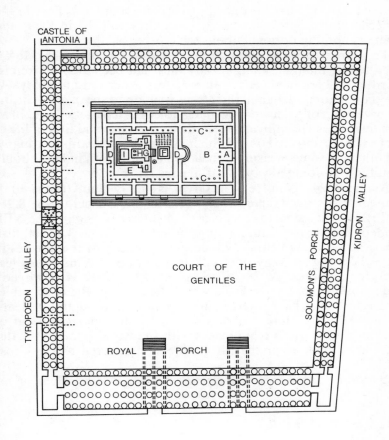

A   Beautiful Gate (Gate of Nicanor)
B   Court of the Women
C   Women's Gallery
D   Court of Israel
E   Court of the Priests
F   Altar of Burnt Offering
G   Porch
H   Holy Place
I   Holy of Holies

299

death is picked up by the Jews, but they suspect that He is planning suicide. Jesus goes on to point the contrast between Himself and them. There are two worlds, one above and one below. His origin, unlike theirs, is from the one above. Their failure to believe in His supernatural origin is the reason why they will die in their sins. There is nothing optional about the Gospel of Christ.

To a direct question about His identity, Jesus replies that He has been telling them all along if only they had been able to exercise spiritual discernment. His authority was a derived authority. As they could not understand this, Jesus went on to speak of the lifting up of the Son of Man which would authenticate His message. In all circumstances He enjoyed His Father's presence and lived a life of perfect conformity to His will. Such claims, though baffling to many, led others in some measure to believe in Him. Faith in Him should result in our doing always what pleases His Father.

Notes: V. 24: 'I am He'. The Greek is simply 'I am' (*ego eimi*). It is used on its own three other times in the Gospel (**4.**26; **8.**28; **13.**19). Here it seems to carry clear overtones of deity and the NEB renders 'I am what I am', giving the echo of Exod. **3.**14 (cf. also Deut. **32.**39; Isa. **43.**10). V. 25: Jesus' reply may be rendered as in the RSV margin, 'Why do I talk to you at all?' This seems less likely in the context. V. 28: 'lifted up' (cf. **3.**14; **12.**32,34). It already had a double sense in the O.T., where the heads of Pharaoh's chief butler and chief baker were 'lifted up' in exaltation and in death (Gen. **40.**20 ff.). Here it obviously marks an important point of transition in Christ's relationship with the world (cf. **3.**14). Later on, Christ made clear that this expression referred to His Cross (**12.**32 ff.).

Question: How does Calvary show Jesus as 'the Light of the world'?

St. John 8.31-47

The debate moves on from the question of authority to that of freedom. The basis for the proper enjoyment of this most treasured human possession is discipleship and truth. But few concepts are so much misunderstood as freedom. National pride revolts against the suggestion that they are in need of liberation. Is not the fact of their ancestry sufficient guarantee of their freedom?

The assertion of their descent from Abraham gives Jesus an opportunity to discuss the real issues of their ancestry and His. Only the Son of God is able to offer them the true liberty of God. Whatever their physical ancestry, their rejection of His offer shows their failure to enter into that liberty and their consequent enslavement by sin. To be Abraham's children in the true sense required moral conformity to Abraham, and this they clearly did not have. They must, spiritually, have another father. Oh, yes, they agree about that. Their father in that sense is, of course, God. No, says Jesus. If that were true they would recognize God's message which He had come to proclaim. Their complete failure to do so marked them off as children of the devil with all his hatred and falsehood. They could find no moral fault in Him, yet they did not believe Him. Their attitude proved quite plainly that they did not belong to God.

Notes: V. 31: 'believed in Him'—as the discourse shows, they must have been nominal believers. True discipleship is shown in continuing obedience to Him and only in this way can true freedom be attained. V. 33: despite periods of foreign domination, such as the Roman occupation at this time, they always thought themselves to be truly free as Abraham's sons. For reliance upon their descent from him, cf. also Matt. **3.**9; Luke **3.**8. It is similar to their reliance upon being Moses' disciples (**9.**28). Pedigree is no substitute for faith. V. 34: 'commits sin'—lives a life of sin (cf. 1 John **3.**4,8). V. 35: the position of servants and sons in a house and their relationship with God are often contrasted in the N.T. (Heb. **3.**2–6; Gal. **4.**1–6). V. 41: the emphatic *'we'* suggests that there may be a charge against Him of physical illegitimacy after He has accused them of spiritual illegitimacy. V. 43: they cannot understand the *words* He speaks because their heart is not open to His *word.*

To ponder: It has been well said that God has no grandsons. What is meant by this? How is it possible for **apparently** *God-fearing men to be so spiritually enslaved as to merit the condemnation of v.44? How can we avoid this?*

St. John 8.48-59

Most of us are familiar with the alleged marginal note against a portion of a written sermon; 'argument weak here—raise voice and thump pulpit'! There is something of this attitude in Christ's adversaries who, unable to combat His teaching, resort to slander and invective. They cannot understand Jesus' claims or accept them in so far as they do understand them. They therefore accuse Jesus of being a demon-possessed Samaritan. Jesus will not allow them to get away with such slanderous suggestions, for the fact is that He is honouring His Father in doing His work, and it is God who will make the truth plain. Obedience to His word is a passport through death.

Such an assertion settles the question of demon-possession as far as the Jews are concerned. Abraham, the great ancestor of the race, had to die. How could a man like this promise immortality? Jesus has to remind them again that what He does and says is not simply His own whim, for His mission is inspired and authenticated by His Father. It would be false for Him to say less than the truth of His relationship with God. Abraham had rejoiced to see His day, for even before Abraham was born He was there in His eternal being. This is sheer blasphemy and an attempt is made to stone Him for it, but again, for the moment, He escapes.

Notes: V. 48: to be a Samaritan was one step worse in their eyes than being a Galilean. The Samaritans' ancestry was mixed (2 Kings **17**.24) and this may be a further charge of illegitimacy (cf. **8**.41). He is accused of having a demon in **7**.20 and **10**.20. It is only here that He refutes the charge. How easy it is to conduct our theological arguments by 'labelling' people and then thinking we have refuted their views! V. 53 'Are You greater . . . .?' The woman of Samaria asked the same question with relation to Jacob, and the answer given was indirect, as it is here. 'Who do You claim to be?'—literally 'make Yourself' (cf. **5**.18; **10**.33; **19**.7,12). He made Himself nothing, what He was He was by the will of the Father. V. 56: Jewish tradition said that Abraham saw the whole history of his descendants and the messianic age. V. 57: 'have You seen Abraham?' is the best reading. It shows how the Jews misquoted His claim, still assuming that Abraham is the greater of the two. V. 58: Abraham not only died but was born. Christ *is* eternally. Here, as the reaction shows, there must be a claim to deity (Exod. **3**.14). V. 59: By hiding Himself, Christ was, in effect, passing judgement on them: they had rejected Him and stood condemned (cf. **3**.18).

For meditation: Note Christ's desire throughout this chapter to glorify the Father, and not Himself. Are we as self-less in our lives and service?

St. John 9.1-12

While the sign of the feeding of the five thousand had preceded the discourse about the bread of life, the sign of the healing of the blind man succeeds the discourse about the light of the world. John does not record many miracles compared with the other Gospels, but when he does, it is usually with full detail and careful explanation, in order to illustrate a divine truth. It was one of the marks of the Messiah that He would open the eyes of the blind (Isa. **35**.5; **61**.1 f.; Luke **4**.18; **7**.21 f.). Here Jesus is shown in

302

Photo: Pool of Siloam

Photo: Looking south down the Kidron Valley towards the Pool of Siloam

action demonstrating the truth of His claim that He is the Messiah and the light of the world.

As Jesus was going along, perhaps from the Temple on the last day of the festival, He noticed a man who was blind from his birth. This pitiful condition is assumed by the disciples to be punishment for sin. As the man was born in this state the possibilities were that he had committed some ante-natal sin (Gen. **25**.22; Psa. **51**.5), or that he had sinned in a previous existence. If neither of those explanations seemed satisfactory, then it must be assumed that parental sin was the reason (Exod. **20**.5). Such speculation failed to take into account the fact that, while there is a connection between human sin and human suffering as a whole, there is not necessarily a direct connection between a man's suffering and his own sin. (This was pointed out in the Book of Job.) Jesus in any event looks not to the past (as we usually do) but to the future and sees it as an opportunity to glorify God (cf. Luke **13**.1–5). He had only limited time to work in His role as the light of the world. He therefore anointed the man's eyes and sent him off to wash. When he returned with his vision restored, so incredulous were those who had known him that they questioned his identity.

Notes: V. 1: 'from his birth'. He had never known the realm of sight for himself. This illustrates men's spiritual condition. V. 3: Jesus does not deny that either party are sinners but asserts that this is not the point at issue. V. 6: this was an ancient remedy but its use on the Sabbath was specifically forbidden by Jewish tradition. V. 7: 'Sent'—the mention of the meaning of the name suggests symbolic significance. The name was due to the water being sent from another pool. Jesus, the source of living water, is also 'sent' (**3**.17; **4**.34; etc.). As the Jews 'refused the waters of Shiloah' (Isa. **8**.6) so they refused Him. The pool was the source of the libations at the festival.

*For meditation: 'We must work the works of Him who sent me, while it is day' (4). The plural 'we' emphasizes both the privilege of the disciples in being associated with the work of the Master and the responsibility we all have to use our time to the best advantage (cf. Eph. **5**.16).*

St. John 9.13-23

The acquaintances of the man were baffled by the whole business so they took him to the Pharisees in order to investigate further the issues raised by the incident. In particular there was the fact that the cure had taken place on the Sabbath. The Pharisees asked the man what had happened and he gave them a straightforward, factual reply. There was a division among them. On one side were those who knew the religious traditions and on the other those who could see the evidence which lay in front of them (cf. **7.**40–43; **10.**19–21). They decide therefore to ask what the man himself thinks. He replies bravely, but inadequately, that he thinks Jesus is a prophet.

The Jews then revert to the position his neighbours had adopted. This was a case of mistaken identity. Sensibly they ask his parents to tell them. They are perfectly prepared to vouch for his being their son and his having been born blind. But the method of his cure they will not state. Maybe they had no first-hand evidence themselves, but in any event they were afraid of reprisals. For if they were led into a statement that Jesus was the Messiah they were in danger of excommunication. They therefore transfer the responsibility for that part of the answer to their son.

Notes: V. 14: the cripple was also healed on the Sabbath (**5.**9). The two stories have much in common, but at this more advanced stage of the ministry this man is much nearer to a full faith in Jesus, and gives a far more spirited defence of his own experience and of Jesus than does the healed cripple. V. 21: the age of legal responsibility was thirteen. The idea may, however, simply be that he is old enough to tell his own story without their intervention. V. 22: this would probably not be more than a temporary ban. What an eternal opportunity they may have lost because of it! Open confession of Christ is the essential accompaniment to faith in Him (cf. Rom. **10.**9 f.). Tragically, there have been many times, too, in the history of the Church when the issue has virtually been whether a man is cast out of the institutional Church or out of the Kingdom of God.

St. John 9.24-34

The religious leaders decide to examine the man a second time and on this occasion they are in a tougher mood. He must make a clean breast of what had actually happened. They clearly could not believe his story, for they knew that Jesus was a sinner. The man will not be browbeaten. He is not concerned with technicalities which are beyond his understanding. He knows one thing with full conviction—the reality of his change from a state of blindness to one of sight—'though I was blind, now I see' (25). They inquire again how it happened.

Now it is the turn of the man to be tough with them. He had already stated the facts quite clearly. They had taken no notice then. There was no point in repeating them unless they too wished to become disciples of Jesus. The crushing retort follows that they are disciples of Moses, a known recipient of God's word; he is a disciple of someone utterly unknown (cf. **7.**48 f.). Yet the man will not abandon his defence of his experience. His eyes have been opened, there is no doubt about that. And if they must force him into theology, into his own simple theology he will go. God does not answer the prayers of sinners. No one has ever heard of the healing of a man *born* blind. Such an extraordinary miracle therefore proves that He is not a sinner but is from God.

But as the man born blind moves steadily into clearer sight, the Pharisees plunge into deeper darkness. There is no attempt to answer the man. Assessing of evidence gives way to prejudice. Living experience is rejected by the dead hand of tradition. Those with a vested interest in the religious establishment put themselves beyond responding to the word of God proclaimed through a humble sinner. 'Would *you* teach *us*?'

Notes: V. 24: NEB: 'Speak the truth before God'. It probably suggests making a confession (cf. Josh. **7.**19). V. 28: 'We are disciples of Moses' (cf. **8.**33: 'We are descendants of Abraham'). But their discipleship of Moses was very blind (**5.**45–47). V. 29: ignorance of His origin is the ground for rejection of Christ just as supposed knowledge of it was before (**7.**27).

Meditation: 'Though I was blind, now I see' (25). This simple conviction has brought strength to many Christians, persecuted, reviled, laughed at or out-manoeuvred in argument. What does it mean to you?

St. John 9.35-41

Hitherto in this chapter the whole discussion has been concerned with the physical healing of a blind man and the identity of a person who was able to perform it. Now Jesus draws out the further lesson of His spiritual mission to the world and to individual people. Not even a miracle was sufficient, by itself, to create faith—a personal meeting with Christ was required.

Jesus had disappeared from the scene (**9.**12) but had kept an interest in the man, and on hearing that he had been thrown out by the Jews, He found him (cf. **5.**13 f.). He now asks him the direct question whether he believes in the Son of man. The man is baffled as to who such a person might be and Jesus has to explain that it is He Himself (cf. **4.**26). The man gives Him his trust and his reverence up to the limit of his understanding.

Jesus then utters one of His hard sayings. His purpose in coming

into the world was judgement. There has just been a perversion of
the judicial process. He will set things right by giving sight to the
blind and blindness to the seeing. Some of the Pharisees were
disturbed enough by the whole affair to ask whether they too were
in some measure blind. Jesus replies that the really incurable
blindness is that which has convinced its victims that it is in fact
sight.

   Notes: V. 35: some MSS read 'Son of God' but 'Son of man' is
more likely to be correct. Jesus is still revealing Himself cryptically.
V. 38: these words may not have their full Christian content yet,
for 'Lord' may be only 'Sir' and 'worshipped' need only mean
'bowed before' (NEB). To us, who know the risen Lord, they mean
so much more. V. 39: a hard saying, but all the Gospels allude to
the saying about blinding in Isa. **6.**9 f. Though salvation was the
primary purpose of His coming (**3.**17), judgement was its inevitable
consequence and so could be said in one sense to be its purpose.
'Those who see' are those who have some understanding of spiritual
truth which they regard as sufficient, and so they fail to see the true
message of the Gospel.

**Questions for further study and discussion on St. John chs. 8.12—
9.41**
1. How has Christ's claim to be the Light of the World been fulfilled in human history (**8.**12)?
2. How does the truth make us free (**8.**31 f.)? Is your life demonstrating freedom as one of its characteristics?
3. How much does Christ's claim to pre-existence affect our
   attitude towards Him (**8.**58)?
4. If men are spiritually 'born blind' (**9.**1) how do we try to deal with
   this fact in evangelism?
5. 'Would *you* teach *us*?' (**9.**34). What occasions arise when we, at
   least in heart, take this attitude?

St. John 10.1-10

Chapter divisions in the Bible can be misleading. While in a sense
the story of the man born blind is rounded off at the end of ch. **9,**
there is no evidence that the evangelist intended a break there. The
blind man and the Pharisees are mentioned again in ch. **10,** and,
while the main figure changes from light and darkness to the
shepherd and his sheep, the theme of judgement is still prominent.
   First, Jesus distinguishes between two kinds of people who go
into sheepfolds—there are those who use the door put there for the

purpose and those who choose some other way in. The shepherd is known to the gatekeeper and to the sheep. Because of the shepherd's personal knowledge of the sheep they are willing to follow him wherever he leads. They would do the opposite for strangers. This allegorical parable is lost upon the Pharisees. They are unable to apply the teaching of Ezek. **34** about the true and false shepherds of Israel to their own situation.

Jesus therefore has to be more explicit. He identifies Himself first of all with the door and then with the shepherd in two further 'I am' sayings. Other claimants to spiritual authority over the people of God had a destructive purpose in coming. The purpose of His coming was to bring life—life in far fuller measure than they had ever had it before.

For the people listening to Christ, the picture of a shepherd calling his sheep one by one, by name, was familiar (3,27). It is a vivid picture of the fact that God knows people as individuals. In 1929 Dr. L.P. Jacks wrote a prayer which ended 'Help us to regard each son of man not by his number but by his name'. Since then, vast increases in the population have made the impersonal numbering of people and the placing of them under tighter control, almost inevitable. But God has not changed, He still knows His people by name—an indication of His loving care for us as individuals.

Notes: V. 1: 'the sheepfold' was probably the enclosed courtyard of a house. Some have seen significance in the description of Judas as a 'thief' (**12.6**) and Barabbas as a 'robber' (**18.40**), but it is false spiritual claimants who are in view in the first instance. V. 4: 'brought out' comes from the same word as 'cast out' in **9.34**. It may suggest His bringing His flock out of the fold of Judaism. V. 6: 'figure'. This is not the same as the sort of parable usually found in the Synoptic Gospels. It means a symbolic utterance but not every detail is necessarily symbolic. V. 9: here as in v. 7 a second metaphor is introduced, comparing Jesus to the door as well as to the shepherd. This 'I am' saying is similar to that recorded in **14.6**. Access to God is through Christ alone.

St. John 10.11-21

Now we come to the specific identification of Jesus with the shepherd. The proof that He is the good Shepherd is shown not by any outward office or external display of strength but by the fact of His sacrificial love for the sheep. There is a clear contrast between Him and those whose supposed work of shepherding is done not for love but for financial or other reward. When it comes to the crunch, they do not really care about the sheep. Jesus, on the other hand, has such a knowledge of His sheep and such a love for them, that He is prepared to lay down His life for them. Not all His sheep are to be found within the fold of Palestinian Judaism. He will unite His flock which is at present scattered all over the world.

The secret of all this is not that Jesus will accept a martyr's death which He cannot avoid. It is rather that He lays His life down voluntarily and with a specific purpose. He lays it down in order to take it up again. This is a fulfilment of His Father's command and a reason for His Father's love. Once again His claims bring division and a charge of demon-possession and madness (cf. **7**.43; **9**.16). Once again a gap opens between those who have written Him off and those who will consider the evidence.

Notes: V. 11: 'good'—the particular word used here (*kalos*) suggests a moral beauty and attractiveness. This is shown to every generation in His love to the death for us. The figure of the shepherd was applied frequently to God in the O.T. and also to such leaders of Israel as Moses and David. It is not by itself necessarily a Messianic title. V. 12: 'wolf'—there is no need to try to identify this precisely. The point at issue is the different attitude of the true and false shepherds. The point, so far as Christian ministry is concerned, is well made in 1 Pet. **5**.2–4. Vs. 14 f.: the relationship between Christ and the believer is derived from the relationship between the Father and the Son (cf. **15**.9; **17**.21; **20**.21). V. 16: 'one flock'—the AV (KJV) translation 'one fold' could be seriously misleading. The people of God is one, even if denominational and other differences exist. The 'other sheep' may in the first instance be the Jews of the Dispersion but the thought of the Gentiles lies in the background.

St. John 10.22-30

The visit of Jesus to the Feast of Tabernacles, which has occupied a large section of the Book of Signs (**7**.10—**10**.21), has ended in division. This is the inevitable effect of light coming into the world (**3**.19–21). After a further two or three months, He comes back to Jerusalem to make His last challenge before the final crisis. The festival in question was the Feast of Dedication (or *Hanukkah*). The Temple, which had been desecrated by Antiochus Epiphanes in 168 B.C., was rededicated by Judas Maccabaeus three years later and this was commemorated annually in late December. (It is of course possible that the visit to the Feast of Tabernacles ended

309

earlier, and that to the Feast of Dedication began earlier, perhaps at the beginning of ch. **9**.)

It seems that Jesus did not take the initiative in pressing His claims but was available to be questioned further about them. The uncertainty and speculation had evidently not abated and He is now pressed to make an unequivocal statement as to whether or not He is the Christ. But an apparently straight answer would be misleading in view of the climate of belief and Jesus points them yet again to His deeds as the evidence (cf. **5**.36; **10**.37 f.; **14**.11).

What is wrong is not the evidence but the fact that they do not belong to Him. If they belonged to His sheep their obedience and discipleship would be evident and there would never be any doubt about their salvation. The unity of Father and Son meant that if they enjoyed the protection of the Son, they enjoyed the protection of the Father also.

Notes: V. 23: 'winter'—as this was always a winter festival perhaps this is an eyewitness touch which is meant to emphasize the particularly cold weather. The reference to the portico and to the Jews gathering round in a circle seem to be similar touches. Vs. 26–28: the fault of unbelief is in them and not in Him. There is in this passage as strong a strain of predestination as there is in the Pauline epistles. The positive side of it provides the only foundation for the Christian life. V. 30: the oneness is more than just of will. But the two Persons are still distinguished.

St. John 10.31-42

This last assertion of Jesus is such that for the second time the desire of the Jews to kill Him actually got as far as their picking up stones to throw at Him (cf. **8**.59; **11**.8). Jesus again reminds them of the evidence of His deeds. For which of them does He deserve to be stoned? For none of them, they tell Him, but for blasphemy. The charge of blasphemy is put in its most succinct form—'You, being a man, make Yourself God'. Here is one of the great ironies of the Gospel. The one who was 'God' (**1**.1) had become man (**1**.14) in an amazing act of loving condescension. Such is their failure in perspective through their moral blindness that they see everything the wrong way round.

Jesus answers their objections with a piece of rabbinic argument. If they look at the Scriptures they will see that the name 'gods' could be applied to the judges of Israel because they were exercising a divinely appointed function. They accept the authority of the

Scriptures which allow such a title. Why then object to the application of the title 'Son of God' to one sent by the Father? The proof
of it all is again His deeds. Their attitude to His words was of less
importance than what they made of the evidence before their eyes.
Again argument gives way to an abortive attempt at arrest (cf.
7.30,44; 8.20).

Jesus then retired briefly before the final conflict. Many people
came to see Him there and on meeting Him confirmed that John,
though no miracle-worker, had achieved his purpose in giving
faithful evidence about Jesus. So they believed in Him (cf. 1.6–8).
'Where the preaching of repentance has had success, there the
preaching of reconciliation and gospel grace is most likely to be
prosperous. Where John has been acceptable, Jesus will not be
unacceptable' (M. Henry).

Notes: V. 34: this would be a most unusual argument for any
Christian to invent, because it does not distinguish Christ from
other men clearly enough. He argues with them on their own terms.
V. 36: 'consecrated'. He in His own person fulfils the Feast of
Dedication. This consecration will reach its climax in His death
(17.19). V. 42: their faith must still be imperfect as He has not yet
fully revealed Himself through His death and resurrection.

*Meditation: 'John did no sign, but everything that John said about
this man was true' (41). The secret of spiritual success is not in the
spectacular but in a consistent witness to Jesus Christ. Have we the
humility to accept this role for ourselves?*

St. John 11.1-16

The stage is now set for the greatest of all Jesus' signs other than the
resurrection itself. He has shown mastery over the natural order and
over disease. If death had previously had a potential victim snatch-
ed from its jaws (4.46–54), now it must yield up a man who has been
in its domain for four days. Here is the Prince of life in action as He
goes to His death.

The last sign, like the first, takes place within a family circle and
is specifically said to show the glory of God and of Christ (2.11;
11.4,40). Despite the urgent call of Mary and Martha and His
special affection for the family, Jesus delayed visiting the sick
Lazarus, for He saw the divine purpose in the whole incident.
Eventually He told His disciples that He was going to Judea again.
Despite the protests of the disciples about the dangers facing them
in Judea, He insists that His work must be done at the right time.

311

As they misunderstand His allusions He has to tell them outright that Lazarus has died and that the purpose of their visit was to raise him. Thomas sees only death ahead and urges his fellow-disciples to come and face it with Jesus.

Notes: The historical character of this story has been more questioned than that of any other in the Gospel. The real problem is not whether Jesus could raise the dead (that was part of the Messianic claim—Luke 7.11–17,22) but why such a vivid demonstration of this power, which had such important consequences, was not recorded in the other Gospels. It must be said that the vivid detail speaks strongly for the story's being factual. The simplest possible reason for its not being mentioned in *Mark* is that Peter was not present, but that is merely speculation. V. 1: Lazarus and his sisters are the only persons named in a miracle story in the Gospel apart from members of the Twelve. Lazarus means 'God helps'. Mary and Martha are mentioned in Luke 10.38–42, and the name Lazarus is used in a parable in Luke 16.19–31. V. 4: 'not unto death'—death would not be the end of it. As an opportunity of glorifying God, cf. 9.3. Every affliction is an opportunity. Vs. 5 f.: the reason for His delay is surprisingly His love for the family. His absence will be the means of their faith (15). V. 16: Thomas is quite prominent in the latter chapters of the Gospel as a man of action slightly bewildered by the events around him (14.5; 20.24,26,29; 21.2).

St. John 11.17-27

Jesus arrives on the scene, not only too late to save Lazarus from dying, but also to find him already buried for four days. Many people from Jerusalem have come to console the sisters. The news then comes that Jesus is on the way. It is Martha, the active and aggressive sister, who goes out to meet Him and apparently rebukes Him for His slowness in coming. She and her sister do not have faith like that of the centurion, that a word spoken from a distance would suffice. They expected Jesus to come back with their messenger, and the fact that He did not do so must have seemed to them hard and inexplicable. Even so Martha's faith in Him remains and she knows that He will be able to do something to help.

Jesus tells Martha that her brother will rise again. This is taken by her as merely an orthodox statement of belief. She knows that he will in the end. Jesus then speaks to her the fifth of the 'I am' sayings. He is the resurrection and the life—faith in Him means in one way the overcoming of death and in another the avoiding of it.

When He asks whether she believes this, her reply is a confession of faith in Him as Christ and Son of God without any reference to His claim to raise the dead.

Martha and Mary both say the same—'if you had been here . . .' But if He had, their faith would not have been tested, and neither they nor the other people with them would have seen the great sign of eternal life. God delays for a purpose, and this is surely an encouragement to us in those trying times when His failure to intervene seems to us both endless and purposeless.

Notes: V. 17: he would have been buried on the day he died. V. 18: this fact may be recorded in order to show that He was not far away from a still greater raising of the dead from which alone all other signs drew their significance. V. 19: there would be seven days of solemn mourning. 'The Jews' are representative of the Judeans who are about to be given their last chance to believe. V. 21: even if there may be a note of reproach, it is more in sorrow than in anger, and her faith in Him remains. Vs. 25 f.: the relationship of physical and spiritual life and death has already been foreshadowed in 5.25–29. Here was the proof that the hour was not only coming but had actually arrived. Martha's orthodox faith had to be turned into a living experience through seeing Christ in action. So has ours today.

St. John 11.28-37

Martha may at times have been a difficult person to live with (Luke 10.40), but she had a sense of responsibility. She went to Mary, and aware of her sensitive nature she called her quietly, saying that Jesus had specifically asked for her. She too had to be involved in the amazing event that was to happen. Mary went off, not, as the Jews supposed, to weep hopelessly for her dead brother, but to meet the Lord of life. Her words to Jesus are the same as Martha's. They both believed that He could have prevented the tragedy, and fail to understand why it was that He had not come when they had called for Him.

Jesus is deeply affected by the sight of mourning which confronts Him. When they take Him to the tomb, He too weeps. To the Jews this is evidence of His love for Lazarus and some of them too wonder why He did not intervene sooner. But it seems that Jesus' weeping goes a good deal deeper than sympathy. There is an anger about it. This is probably, at the deepest level, anger against sin and death and the terrible hold which they have on the human race. Perhaps there was also anger at the unbelief or half-belief of those who could not see that He was able to fulfil His claims to raise the dead. His weeping, in any event, is not on the same level as theirs. It is His preparation for grappling with the power of death here and on the cross (Heb. **2**.14 f.; cf. Heb. **5**.7–9).

Notes: V. 28: 'The Teacher' may have been the name by which He was known to the family. It is an inadequate description of Him at this crisis. V. 32: Mary's action is more impetuous than Martha's. Jesus does not try to explain things to her but goes straight into action. V. 33: for His being troubled as He faced His passion, cf. **12**.27; **13**.21. Our redemption was achieved at tremendous cost to Him. V. 34: the only occasion in the Gospel on which He asks for information. V. 36: it was not His weeping but His death which was to show His love, not only for Lazarus, but for the whole world.

St. John 11.38-44

Jesus is inwardly stirred again as He prepares to wrestle with sin and death. He gives the simple order that the stone should be removed: Martha keeps her feet firmly on the ground. This is an impossible command. A putrefying body will give off an appalling stench after four days in a warm climate. Only the firm assurance of Jesus that faith is necessary and the glory of God is the object, causes them to obey.

Jesus then addresses a prayer to His Father, acknowledging His dependence in this particular action and thanking Him that He has already heard. He adds words which emphasize His confidence that His Father always hears His prayers. He has said what He has in order that the crowd should see this, not as a display of wonder-working, but as the most impressive of His signs to show that He was sent by God to do God's work.

Action has been taken, prayer has been offered, now comes the word of life. There is no mystical formula but a straightforward command (cf. **5**.8; Mark **5**.41). So the dead hears the voice of the Son of God and hearing lives and comes forth from his tomb (**5**.25–29). The trappings of death are still all over him. Jesus tells them to untie them and release him. The liberation He brings is meant to be complete. ·

Notes: V. 39: 'Take away the stone'—this and the unwinding of the graveclothes needed human co-operation. In His own resurrection no human agency was involved (**20**.1–10). Further than that, of course, Lazarus had his natural body restored to him and, though we hear no more of him, after **12**.10, in due course died again, Jesus was raised in His spiritual body, the mortal put on immortality (1 Cor. **15**.54). Vs. 41 f.: apart from the long prayer of ch. **17,** there is only one other occasion in the Gospel when Jesus is clearly recorded as addressing His Father (**12**.27 f.). However, it is quite probable that His words from the cross (**19**.28–30) were spoken primarily to His Father and not to men.

St. John 11.45-57

Surely this supreme and incontrovertible demonstration of Jesus' power will lead to His acceptance by those who have seen it and those who hear their evidence! Many who had come with Mary believed. But others, no doubt still bewildered, went to tell the Pharisees. They joined together with the chief priests to call a council. They do not now deny that Jesus is doing signs. The evidence is too strong for that. Nor, however, will they accept what the facts are shrieking at them, that this man is acting with the power of God, for He has been sent by God (cf. Mark **3**.22).

There is no attempt now at theological assessment. They have already made up their minds and they are confirmed in their resolution now that such an obvious threat to their position is developing. There is such a danger of a popular uprising that it will lead to counter-action by the Romans and that will be the end of both Temple and nation. It is the high priest, of all people, who with cynical expediency chooses the victim for sacrifice. In this master-piece of dramatic irony he decides that one man should die that the people should live. He spoke far more than he could ever know, for that was the purpose of Jesus' mission, which stretched far beyond the confines of Palestine to all God's scattered children (**3**.16). Now the issue is settled and they will pursue Him relentlessly to death.

The statement of Caiaphas, and the decision and subsequent action of the Council, illustrate what is frequently stated in Scripture—that God can take the evil that men do and weave it into a larger pattern which is for His glory and the good of other people. Caiaphas acted as a free agent, personally responsible for what he did. God, however, used his action without destroying his freedom, and turned evil into glory.

Jesus knew the situation clearly enough and withdrew to Ephraim. When the Passover came there was widespread specula-tion as to whether He would come to Jerusalem or not.

Notes: V. 47: the chief priests, who were Sadducees, were thrown into alliance with their rivals the Pharisees through common opposition to Jesus. The priests now take the leading role and the

Pharisees are only mentioned in **12**.19,42. V. 48: ironically this is just what the Romans did do in A.D. 70. They thought of *'our* holy place' as if it belonged to them, not God (cf. Matt. **23**.38). But Jesus made a new temple (**2**.19–22) and gathers the people of God on a new basis (**3**.16; **10**.16). V. 49: the high priest was unwittingly exercising his power of prophecy, despite his arrogant claim to knowledge (cf. **7**.47–49; 1 Cor. **2**.8). The office did not change annually—he was high priest that memorable year.

To think over: '**You** *meant evil . . . but God meant . . . good' (Gen.* **50**.*20).*

Questions for further study and discussion on St. John chs. 10 and 11
1. What principles of pastoral care may be found in **10**.1–18?
2. What effect should the knowledge of belonging to Christ's sheep have on us (**10**.25–30)?
3. Can illness and a delay in answer to prayer still be to God's glory (**11**.1–6)?
4. How far has the living experience of Christ, the resurrection and the life (**11**.25 f.), transformed our attitude to life and to death?
5. When did we last let our vested interest in the religious *status quo* dull our response to new truth (**11**.45–53)?

St. John 12.1-11

Now there begin the momentous events of the last week of the ministry of Jesus. While the ordinary people are divided and the Roman authorities have not yet been asked to show their hand, the Jewish leaders are inexorably committed to getting rid of Him and well aware that they must take action at the time of the Passover festival.

Jesus still goes calmly on His way and enjoys a meal with Lazarus and his sisters. The domesticated Martha sees to the arrangements while Mary, in an act of extravagant devotion, anoints His feet with expensive ointment and wipes them with her hair. Sensitive people, whose capacity for grief and sorrow is great, have the compensation that they can also rise to great heights of love and devotion. Judas fails to see the point of such seeming waste. Far better use the money for charity, though his idea of charity seemed to be concerned more with himself than with the poor. But Mary had kept the ointment for this significant and unrepeatable moment, in preparation for the burial of Jesus. There would be many further opportunities of helping the poor, many of them inspired in fact by His death for mankind.

316

News soon got round that Jesus was after all in the vicinity, so the crowds turned out to see Him. They were also interested in seeing the unusual phenomenon of a dead man who had come to life again. This living evidence of the truth of His claims was winning supporters for Jesus, so the chief priests decided that he too must be got rid of.

Notes: V. 1: the raising of Lazarus is emphasized again, as being a major cause of the crucifixion. V. 3: the story relates the same event as that recorded in Mark **14**.3–9, but a different one from that in Luke **7**.36–38. V. 6: it looks as if Judas had been made treasurer of the band because of financial ability, but his strength was also his weakness. V. 7: a very difficult construction. Most probably it means: 'Let her alone (she has not sold it for the poor) that she may keep it for the day of My burial' (which she was here anticipating). V. 10: a natural reaction from Sadducees to remove a man whose very presence refuted their disbelief in resurrection (Mark **12**.18).

A point to ponder: If, as we have suggested, temptation frequently comes to us along the lines of our greatest gifts and sin is often the perversion of our ability, how can we ensure that God is in complete control of all our abilities?

St. John 12.12-19

A great crowd of the Jews had come out to Bethany to see Jesus and Lazarus. Now a great crowd of those who had come as pilgrims to the festival hear that Jesus is coming to Jerusalem and set out to meet Him. They took with them branches of palm trees such as had been used to hail Simon Maccabaeus after his victory (1 Macc. **13**.51). They greeted Him with words from Psa. **118,** which was in use at the Passover, applying the words to Him as the King of Israel. There is no doubt that they were giving Him a Messianic welcome into the city. He could not now avoid being King as He had done before in Galilee (**6**.15).

But Jesus will not have Messiahship of the sort that they are looking for. He must come into Jerusalem but He does so, not on a regal charger, but on an ass, the beast of burden symbolizing peace. His interpretation of the incident was based on Zech. **9**.9 and was more far-reaching than theirs. For the passage was in a context of the Messiah's universal reign of peace and His liberating mission through the blood of the covenant. No wonder the disciples did not understand this until after the resurrection (cf. **2**.22; **14**.26). The excitement of Messianic expectation had spread from crowd to crowd until it seemed to the despairing Pharisees that the whole

317

world had gone after Him. They, like the high priest, were prophesying unwittingly.

Notes: The story occurs in all four Gospels. There are some minor differences between the account in John and the others. V. 13: 'Hosanna'—a Hebrew word meaning 'save now'. It had the general force of 'Hail!' V. 15: this is a free rendering of Zech. **9.9**. 'Fear not' could be an echo of Isa. **40.9**.

St. John 12.20-26

The world seems to have gone after Him in the Pharisees' eyes. And so it is because some of the pilgrims at the festival were Greeks. Whether these were Gentile proselytes or Greek-speaking Jews is not certain. What is important is that the mission of Jesus is shown to extend beyond the confines of Palestinian Judaism. And it is a Galilean with a Greek name—Philip—whom they approach with their request to see Jesus. The Judeans had had their chance to see Him during His ministry, and these pilgrims seem to want the same privilege. He is soon to hide Himself finally (36).

We are not told whether their request was granted. But Jesus sees it as an extremely significant occasion. Now was the hour of glorification. And glory was to come to the Son of man through death. It was only in death that there lay the possibility of growth. It was only in the death of one Man for the people that there lay the hope of the salvation of the whole world. What applies to the mission of Jesus applies also to the mission of His disciples. The willingness to lose our lives in the cause of Christ is the only true way of serving Him. Nevertheless, we still find His teaching hard to understand and harder still to follow. Almost everything in 'this world' conditions us to think that the man who 'loses his life in this world' has lost it. We need to remind ourselves of the grain of wheat—the simple, true fact of everyday life, which is also a most profound truth of spiritual life.

Notes: V. 20: it is unlikely that these were Gentile 'Godfearers' as they would probably not come up to Jerusalem for the festivals. The principles of the Gentile mission are firmly laid in the Gospel even if the Romans may be the only Gentiles with whom Jesus comes in contact. V. 23: 'the Greeks' may be included in this as well as Philip and Andrew. 'Glorified': this term covered the whole redemptive action which Jesus was about to perform. In the divine paradox the cross was no less glorious than any other part of His work. V. 25: the paradox of redemption applies also to discipleship. Only in its death does the self discover what it is meant to be.

For meditation: 'To serve Jesus is to follow Him, and He is going to death' (26, Barrett).

St. John 12.27-36

As Jesus enters into the supreme crisis, not only in His own ministry but in the history of the world, He cries out to His Father for strength and guidance. However tempting it might be to try to avoid the horrors that lay ahead of Him, He will not do it. He knows it is His hour at last. He knows that the purpose of it all is to glorify His Father's name. It is for that that He asks, and a heavenly voice assures Him that His prayer has been and will be answered. As usual the bystanders misunderstand. They no more grasp the meaning of the heavenly voice than they have done the meaning of the words of Jesus.

If this had seemed a strange time to be speaking of glory, it is an equally unusual one to refer to judgement when it is not judgement of Jesus but judgement of the world and the devil which is meant. But paradox cannot be avoided and it is His exaltation in death that will be the means of life for all.

Still people do not understand. Still they do not know who this mysterious Son of man is. So Jesus can only give them an urgent exhortation concerning the need to act while the light is there with them in His person. Faith in Him will change their whole being. And with that final challenge He goes, hidden from them until He appears as a prisoner about to be put to death.

Notes: V. 27: John does not describe the agony in the Garden of Gethsemane. This passage shows that he is aware of the real moral struggle which Jesus had to undergo as He faced death for the sins of the world. V. 28: the nature of the heavenly voice is not clear. The crowd heard the sound without distinguishing the words (cf. Acts **9**.7; **22**.9). V. 31: for the cross as a victory over the devil, cf. Col. **2**.15. V. 32: the idea of being 'lifted up' was important because of its double meaning (cf. **8**.28; Gen. **40**.20) and also because it specified death by crucifixion rather than by stoning or in any other way. V. 34: the passages in the Law referred to possibly include Psa. **89**.4,29,36; Isa. **9**.7; Ezek. **37**.25.

St. John 12.37-43

We are now coming to the end of the 'Book of Signs' and the evangelist gives us a brief summary of the lack of success of Jesus' mission and the reasons for that. Signs were meant to be an aid to faith so that men should have life. That is why the evangelist himself took the trouble to write them down (**20**.31). But for the majority of the people the signs did not have this effect. All sorts of excuses were made at various stages of the Gospel why men should not believe in Jesus. It was possible to question the evidence in one way or another, or to form *a priori* theological opinions that Jesus could not be a man of God, or simply to crush the suggestion from a position of ecclesiastical privilege.

But it would be wrong to look for the whole cause merely at the human level. The trouble went deeper than that. For this was a fulfilment of prophecy. In Isa. **53**.1 the fact of unbelief had been stated, and when the suffering servant of the Lord came, that had to be fulfilled. In Isa. **6**.10 the prophet went further and attributed unbelief to the action of God who blinded them.

Despite all this, there was not a clear-cut rejection of Jesus' claims. There were many secret believers who were anxious not to lose their position in Judaism, especially those of them who were among the authorities. They come under the devastating condemnation that they preferred to be praised by men than by God.

Notes: This brief review of the ministry by the evangelist is similar to the writer's assessment of the history of the northern kingdom of Israel in 2 Kings **17**. V. 40: the apparent failure of the mission of Jesus was accounted for in the Synoptic Gospels also by the quotation from Isa. **6**.10 (cf. Mark **4**.11 f.; **8**.17 f.; also Acts **28**.26 f.). The sense of the fulfilment of the divine purpose is supposed to complement rather than override human moral responsibility (cf. Acts **2**.23). V. 43: Nicodemus and Joseph became bolder later (**19**.38–42). Perhaps someone like Gamaliel was also a secret believer (Acts **5**.34–39).

St. John 12.44-50

'The Book of Signs' finally closes with a summary of Jesus' message, as if in a final presentation of it to an unbelieving or half-believing Judaism. Here we have, in concentrated form, themes which have been dealt with at greater length previously. Here there is faith and sight, the Son as the representative of the Father, light, judgement, authority and life.

For this reading it would be well to 're-cap' over 'The Book of Signs' and see the way in which these themes have been developed previously.

Vs.44f. Believing in and seeing Jesus is the equivalent of believing in and seeing God: cf. **1**.14–18; **6**.27–29,35–40,44–47. (Look forward also to **14.**1–11.) It is not necessary to establish the fact of God's existence before beginning to talk about Christ. We can begin the other way round—with the Man, Jesus, with His life, His words and His actions. 'God is Christlike and in Him is no unChristlikeness at all' (Ramsey). This is why history is of such importance and Christian truth is unique. It is the truth that in the man Jesus, God Himself was known, seen and heard.

V.46. Jesus is the light of the world, and those who believe in Him are delivered from darkness: cf. **1.**4–9; **3.**21; **8.**12; **9.**4 f.; **11.**9; **12.**35 f.

Vs. 47 f. Jesus did not come to judge the world but to save the world: cf. **3.**14–18; **8.**15; **10.**9 f. Nevertheless His word will judge those who reject Him and do not keep His sayings: cf. **3.**19 f., 34–36; **5.**19–30,45–47; **8.**26,31–51; **9.**39–41. (Look forward also to **14.**23 f.)

Vs. 49 f. Jesus' words have been spoken not on His own authority but according to His Father's command: cf. **3.**31–35; **5.**19 f., 30–37; **7.**16–18; **8.**26–29,39–47. (Look forward also to **14.**10.) The Son's word, spoken according to the Father's command, gives life: cf. **1.**4; **3.**16 f., 36; **4.**46–54; **5.**24–29; **6.**35–40,47–58,63,68 f.; **10.**10,27 f.; **11.**25 f., 43 f.; **12.**25. (Look forward also to **14.**6,19; **17.**2 f.; **20.**31.)

In view of the reference to Jesus' hiding Himself in **12.**36, there seems little doubt that this section was not supposed to have been spoken by Jesus at this time, but that it is a summary of His words by the evangelist in the way that vs. 37–43 are a summary of the response to His works.

Questions for further study and discussion on St. John ch. 12

1. How should we aim to achieve a balance between time and money spent on worship and on charity (**12.**1–8)?
2. Do people ask us to help them to see Jesus (**12.**21)? If not, why not? If so, can we help them effectively?
3. How has Jesus' statement in **12.**31 f. been fulfilled in the history of the Church?
4. What do the principles of life through death (**12.**24–26) mean in practice in your life?
5. What is our attitude to the light (**12.**35 f.)?

St. John 13.1-11

So far Jesus has been putting His claims, by deed and word, before the people of God, whose response has been largely negative. Now the last appeal has been made to the Jews. The rest of the Gospel

has been called 'The Book of the Passion'. The great sign is that o
His death and resurrection. This is preceded by the discourses which
explain it and its consequences. The teaching is now no longer
given openly to the world but privately to His disciples.

The Feast of the Passover gives us the theological setting for what
follows. The festival which commemorated the great act of redemption of the Old Covenant was to be the setting of the great act of
redemption of the New. The hour, which Jesus or the evangelist
had referred to earlier as not yet having arrived (2.4; 7.30; 8.20), has
now come (12.23). Jesus must return via death to the Father. His
mind was fully assured of His divine origin and destination. The
necessary work of the traitor, inspired by the devil, was already in
hand. In this context, where so many other emotions may have
been present, His dominant characteristic is love. This is shown in a
demonstration of humble service towards His disciples.

The foot-washing also had a symbolic meaning. Peter at first
impetuously refuses to be washed and then asks to be washed all
over! But Jesus explains that when a man has once been made clean
all over, then this is all that is necessary afterwards. All His disciples
apart from Judas had been made clean.

Notes: V. 1: NEB: 'now He was to show the full extent of His
love'—not only in the foot-washing, but in the cross. V. 2: for the
devil and Judas, see 6.70 f.; 13.27. 'His own' are now the disciples
rather than the Jews (1.11), but it is the member of the Twelve, who
was probably the only Judean and who bore the very name of
Judah, who was to betray Him. V. 4: 'laid aside'—the same word as
is used for laying down His life (10.11,15,17 f.). V. 7: the Spirit
would enlighten them and show them that they needed to accept
service from Christ before they could serve. V. 10: there is a once-
for-all cleansing, symbolized by baptism and dependent upon the
'baptism' of Christ in His death (Mark 10.38; Luke 12.50). There is
also the need for daily cleansing and forgiveness. Some MSS,
however, omit 'except for his feet'.

St. John 13.12-20

Jesus now takes His clothes again and resumes His place. The whole
action suggests that it is, amongst other things, a vivid demonstration of His death, resurrection and exaltation. He laid aside His
clothes as He lays down His life (10.11,15,17 f.), He takes His
clothes as He takes His life again (10.17 f.), and He resumes His
place as He returns to His Father (6.62; 13.1). The pattern is such as
is described in Paul's great 'Christological hymn' (Phil. 2.5–11).

322

It is not, however, the theological movement which He wishes to make explicit at this juncture. It is rather the moral and social consequences. They rightly put Him in a place of authority and yet He had done a menial service for them. How much more then should they be willing to serve one another! There is not much in any of the Gospels which is specifically referred to as 'an example', therefore all the more importance must be attached to this. Blessedness was promised to those who knew this—but on one important condition—that they did it. Jesus reaffirms that He knows that not everyone even of the Twelve will do this. The Scripture had to be fulfilled concerning the traitor, and His foreknowledge of this fact should help them to understand that He was the Messiah. Receiving them was receiving Him, and was also receiving the Father.

Notes: V. 13: Jesus is elsewhere called 'Teacher' in **11**.28 and 'Rabbi' in **1**.38,49; **3**.2; **20**.16. The idea of Him as 'Lord' is a prominent one in the Gospel and comes especially frequently in chs. **13** and **14**. Rabbis could expect some acts of menial service from their disciples, and masters could demand them from their slaves. Here the roles are strikingly reversed. V. 16: 'he who is sent' —the Greek word *apostolos* (apostle) is used here only in the Gospel and in a non-technical sense. V. 18: 'lifted his heel'—this either pictures a horse kicking back at a man or someone shaking the dust off his feet. V. 19: 'I am He'—cf. **8**.24. V. 20: this is what gives the work of the disciples such significance (cf. Matt. **10**.40). Their mission from Him is similar to His from the Father (**20**.21). For reaction to the Son being reaction to the Father, see **5**.23; **8**.19; **12**.44 f.; **14**.7,9; **15**.23.

For meditation: The call to service (14 ff.) is based on the fact that Christ first serves us, even to the point of dying for us. 'Every disciple and every company of disciples need to learn that their first duty is to let Christ serve them' (Temple).

St. John 13.21-30

There have been a number of allusions in this chapter to the traitor. Now Jesus, in distress of spirit, confronts the disciples openly with this fact. He solemnly asserts that one of them would betray Him. 'One of us? Surely not! Who on earth could it be?' Peter is determined to find out, so he asks the beloved disciple to ask Jesus. Because of his position of closeness to the Lord (literally 'in His bosom'—cf. **1**.18) he is able to ask Him. Jesus tells him that it is the person to whom He will give a morsel of bread. So Jesus hands it to Judas. As such an action showed that the recipient was an honoured

323

guest, this was in effect a last appeal to Judas as well as an indication to John of the identity of the traitor.

If there had been any chance of a change of heart from Judas, it now disappears. Satan takes possession of him. So Jesus bids him do his deed quickly, as the agony of the last struggle comes increasingly upon Him. Apparently Judas was not suspected by the others, who simply thought Jesus was sending him on an errand. In an action full of tragic symbolism Judas went out from the room, from the circle of the disciples, from the presence of the Saviour of the world (cf. 1 John 2.18 f.). No wonder, as he turned his back on the Light of the world, it was night! (cf. 3.19). Divine love could go no further. Pursued to the very end by the love of Christ and yet still free to choose, Judas is typical of every man.

Notes: V. 21: while John does not record the agony in the Garden of Gethsemane, he emphasizes as much as the other evangelists the tremendous pressure there was upon Jesus as He prepared Himself to bear the sin of the world. V. 23: we assume that 'the beloved disciple', named here for the first time, is John. (See Introduction.) V. 26: it seems likely that Judas occupied the place of honour on the left of Jesus and that is why He was able to give him the morsel. This is, however, by no means sure. V. 29: this does not necessarily mean that the Passover had not begun, for the feast lasted for seven days.

St. John 13.31-38

When the Greeks had asked to see Him, Jesus had said, 'The hour has come for the Son of man to be glorified' (**12.**23), and His soul had been troubled as He considered what the 'hour' would mean (**12.**27). At the supper He is troubled again (21) as He contemplates the betrayal, and when the traitor has gone out into the night He repeats in similar terms, 'Now is the Son of man glorified' (31). Each step that brings death nearer brings glory nearer also, for there is glory even in His death. What is glory for the Son of man is glory also for God, for it is the final result of perfect obedience to His will.

Jesus now speaks, as He will do frequently in this discourse, of the fact that He must leave the disciples very soon and go to a sphere of existence which they will not be able to penetrate. If He is to be absent in body His presence may still be known in their midst. It will be demonstrated clearly to all men by the new Christian virtue of love. This was a love that was to spring out of His love for them (**13.**1,15,35).

Peter inevitably wishes to know where Jesus is going and to follow Him even if it means laying down his life. Fine words and sincerely meant. But he does not know what lies ahead and, Jesus, with sounder knowledge of coming events and of human nature, has to tell him sadly that he will deny Him three times before morning.

Notes: V. 33: 'little children'—this is the only time this word is used in the Gospel, though it is used seven times in *1 John*. A similar word is found in **21.5**. 'A little while'—cf. **14.**19; **16.**16–19. 'As I said to the Jews'—see **7.**33 f.; **8.**21. V. 34: 'a new commandment'. This was not new in the sense that it had never been commanded previously, for the Law had told them to love their neighbours as themselves (Lev. **19.**18). It was new in the sense that the love of God had been demonstrated by the sending of His Son (**3.**16) who had Himself loved them right to the end (**13.**1). Their mutual love was to be a reflection of that, which gave it a new dynamic. V. 38: Peter's failure to submit patiently to Christ and obey Him, shown already in his attitude to the foot-washing, will have shameful consequences. So does ours!

St. John 14.1-7

In the face of the disturbed atmosphere among the disciples—His saying that He will leave them and His prediction of Peter's denial—Jesus tells them not to be troubled. Such a situation was an occasion for faith in the Father and the Son. There were many places in heaven. His departure was in order to make them ready for His disciples. Nor did He intend to leave them for ever, for He would return and take them to Himself so that their fellowship might be restored and continue.

When Jesus asserts that they know the way where He is going, Thomas protests that as they do not know the destination they cannot possibly know the route. This gives Jesus the chance to deliver another of the 'I am' sayings. He Himself is the way, the truth and the life. Because He is the truth and the life, He is the exclusive way to the Father. No one can reach the Father except through Him. The bewilderment about the Father was due to their state of muddle about who Jesus was. To know Him as what He really was would be to know the Father too (**8.**19).

Notes: V. 2: 'rooms'—the word means places to stop and remain in rather than progressive halts on a journey (cf. v. 23). The NEB renders as the AV (KJV): 'if it were not so I should have told you.' The difficulty with the RSV translation is that Jesus has not specifically been recorded as having told them that He was going to

325

prepare a place for them. V. 3: 'I will come again'—the primary reference seems to be to the second coming or to His receiving each disciple at death. But the succeeding passages show a great emphasis on His coming through the resurrection and the Holy Spirit (**14.**18,28; **16.**16,22). V. 6: 'the way, the truth and the life'—in the context it is clear that the second and third words explain further what Jesus means by the first. He is the true way and the living way. 'Life' is a word which occurs with particular frequency in the first twelve chapters, 'truth' an almost equal number of times in chs. **1–12** and **13–21**.

St. John 14.8-14

Even at this stage of the ministry the disciples are still baffled about many of the leading themes of Jesus' teaching and they still fail to understand the nature of His relationship to the Father. If Jesus talks darkly about knowing and seeing the Father, Philip is not satisfied. Let us have a proper revelation of God (a 'theophany' such as Moses had had—Exod. **24.**10). We shall see Him with our own eyes. There will no longer be any doubt. We shall really be satisfied then.

Jesus sadly has to point out to Philip his failure to grasp who He is. The mutual indwelling of Father and Son was a basic thing which the disciples ought to have grasped. This was shown by His teaching which was not given simply on His own authority. It was also demonstrated by His miracles which were not the deeds of a mere man.

Having used His doing the works of God as evidence of His relationship to the Father, Jesus, no doubt to their great surprise, goes on to say that the disciples will do even greater deeds because of His return to the Father. The glorification of the Father in the Son was not to end with the earthly life of the Son. Through prayer it would be continued, and the scope of prayer is vast, limited only by the important condition that it should be in His name.

Notes: V: 8: Philip is mentioned on four occasions in the Gospel (**1.**43–48; **6.**5–7; **12.**20–22). He seems to have been enthusiastic but uncomprehending. V. 9: to see Jesus is to see the Father (cf. **12.**45). The same applies to honouring Him (**5.**23), knowing Him (**8.**19; **14.**7), believing in Him (**12.**44), receiving Him (**13.**20) and hating Him (**15.**23). This was due to their mutual indwelling. V. 12: 'greater works' because more far-reaching in their scope throughout the world and to all men. V. 13: 'in My name'—on My authority. It assumes obedience to His will, as He was obedient to the Father's

326

will, and a true desire for the glorification of Father and Son. The promise has never been withdrawn and if it were taken seriously the effects would be incalculable.

Listening point: 'I cannot think what we shall find to do in heaven,' *mused Luther. 'No work, no eating, no drinking, nothing to do. But* *I suppose there will be plenty to see.' 'Yes,' said Melancthon. '"Lord,* *show us the Father, and we shall be satisfied" (8).' 'Why, of course,'* *responded Luther, 'that sight will give us quite enough to do.'*

St. John 14.15-24

Much of what Jesus says in the final discourse can only be understood in the light of the coming of the Holy Spirit. A new coming of the Spirit had been referred to by the evangelist in 7.39. Now Jesus devotes some time to explaining the personality of the Spirit, the nature of His coming and the work which He would do in the world.

The promise of the Spirit's coming is made in the context of the disciples' loving, and therefore obeying, their Master. The coming was to be in answer to the Son's prayer to the Father. The Spirit was described as the 'Counsellor'. He was to be there to stand by them and to help them. Despite the reality of the coming and the presence of the Spirit, the world at large would not recognize His presence or His existence. But the disciples would know from their experience.

Jesus now goes on to say that the Spirit's coming will be His own coming. As the days of His flesh come to an end the world will not be able to see Him any longer. His disciples, however, will go on seeing Him because His life will be in them through the Spirit. Only in the Spirit will they learn the mutual indwelling of Father and Son, and of themselves with Him. But this is not religious experience without moral consequences. Love and obedience are necessary for the continued enjoyment of the love of Father and Son, and for the reception of His revelation. There will be no fleeting visit. The man who loves and obeys will have the tremendous privilege of having Father and Son coming to make their home with Him through the Spirit.

Notes: V. 16: 'Counsellor'—the Greek word is *paraklētos*. It sometimes has the meaning of 'advocate' (so NEB). Christ is described as the believer's Paraclete or Advocate in 1 John 2.1. The Spirit is 'another' because He continues what Christ has done. There may be some connection also with the idea of Christian *paraklēsis* ('prophetic exhortation' to accept the Messianic sal-

327

vation; see Barrett's commentary ad loc.). V. 18: 'desolate'—literally 'orphans'. The word was used of disciples who had lost a teacher as well as of children who had lost a father.

St. John 14.25-31

Not only was the presence and power of Jesus limited in the incarnation, His teaching also had to be restricted. There were such obvious limitations in the capacity of the disciples to understand. One of the functions of the Holy Spirit was therefore to be that of teaching them further and also reminding them of what Jesus had said. In the new situation after the resurrection, with the new aid of the Holy Spirit, they would be able to grasp His message and the meaning of His own person and mission in a new way. We too live in this privileged position.

In the midst of so much that was disturbing, He promised them peace. Not the superficial co-existence which the world allows at times. This peace would reach through to the troubled heart. There should be joy also from contemplation of the fact that He was returning to the Father. The greatness of the Father meant the exaltation of Christ and the fulfilment of the blessings which He had promised would come to them through the Holy Spirit.

It was necessary for Jesus to let them know where He was going, because they could easily have been confused (as in fact they were) by the impending crisis. Satan was about to have his hour. He had no power over Jesus. What was going to happen was done in obedience to the Father's command and was a demonstration to the world that He loved the Father.

Notes: V. 26: for the teaching function of the Spirit see also **15.26**; **16.**13 f. For the disciples' understanding later what they could not understand during the ministry see **2.22**; **12.16**; **13.7**. V. 28: this does not imply any inferiority (see **10.30**). The Father is the source and origin of everything and He is greater than the Son in the sense that Jesus' mission was one of obedience to His Father's will. It is a reference to the incarnate Jesus. V. 30: 'ruler of this world', cf. **12.31**. Whatever the role of Satan, the fact remains that in one sense Jesus' death was voluntary (**10.18**). V. 31: 'Rise, let us go hence.' The presence of these words at this stage has caused a number of scholars to suggest that chs. **15** and **16** should come before this point. It may be, however, that the words should be taken closely with the rest of the verse and are a moral exhortation to go and meet the advancing enemy.

328

Questions for further study and discussion on St. John chs. 13 and 14

1. How far are we prepared to submit to Christ even when we do not understand (**13.6–10**)?
2. In what way can you follow the example which Christ gave in the foot-washing (**13.14 f.**)?
3. Why are the claims of Christ exclusive (**14.6**)?
4. Have we, in answer to prayer, experienced the power to do greater works than Jesus did (**14.12 f.**)? If not, why not?
5. Why is there such a close connection between love, obedience, and the presence of the Father and the Son (**14.21–23**)?

St. John 15.1-11

Mutual indwelling and mutual love have been the keynotes of ch. **14.** They are now strikingly illustrated by the figure of the vine and the branches, which provides the last of the 'I am' sayings and is further expounded in this chapter. Israel was frequently described in the O.T. as a vine (Psa. **80.**8; Jer. **2.**21; Hos. **10.**1) or as a vineyard (Isa. **5.**1–7). The metaphor suggests something belonging to God and tended by Him and expected in due course to yield fruit. This expectation was not fulfilled (Mark **12.**1–9). Israel, however, had only been a prefiguration of the Messiah, who was the true, genuine, real vine. Christ must not be thought of here simply as an individual, for by faith His people belong to Him and are united with Him. Consequently, He is the vine and they are the branches (5).

The main thrust of the figure now ceases to be the relationship of the vine to the vinedresser and becomes the relationship of the vine to the branches. The branches must be fruitful and become increasingly so. Fruit-bearing is only possible through the close union of vine and branches. When that occurs things will happen. The close union depends upon love and obedience. Fruitfulness brings glory to the Father and joy to the disciples, as we should discover for ourselves.

Notes: V. 1: the figure of the vine may have been suggested by the 'fruit of the vine' at the Last Supper (Mark **14.**25). V. 2: perhaps Judas and Peter are respectively in mind. V. 3: the disciples are in the position of having been pruned by the word of Jesus. V. 5: the metaphor is similar to the Pauline idea of 'in Christ' and his metaphor of 'the body of Christ' with its members. The fruit which is borne is first and foremost the fruit of Christian character (cf. Gal. **5.**22–24). V. 7: another striking promise about the efficacy of prayer but the basic conditions must not be forgotten (cf. **14.**13 f.). V. 8: it is important that there should be concrete evidence of their

329

discipleship of Him (cf. **13.**35). V. 9: the relationship of Father to Son is repeated in the relationship of Christ to the disciples also in the sphere of mission (**20.**21). V. 11: 'My joy', cf. 'My peace' (**14.**27). For the fullness of joy, cf. **3.**29; **16.**24; **17.**13—see also Psa. **16.**11.

St. John 15.12-19

Once again we return to the all-important theme of love. The link between love for God and love for one's neighbour is so strong in John's Gospel that Kittel's 'Theological Word Book of the Bible' states: 'Love to God and Christ takes second place after love to the brethren.' There is some strong evidence for that rather surprising statement. But this love is no mere sentiment which can be worked up by a man at will or which comes irrationally upon him. Its source is the love of God shown in Christ and only those who have first meditated on, and responded to, that love are able to reflect it in their attitude to others. Jesus' love was proved by laying down His life. It was also proved by the way in which He treated His disciples as His friends, keeping them informed about what He was doing. His friendship to them was also shown by the fact that it was He who had chosen them, rather than the reverse.

If it was previously impossible to speak of light without mentioning darkness (**1.**4 f., etc.), now it is impossible to mention love without in the end coming on to hatred. Men hated the light (**3.**20) and the 'Book of Signs' showed how many of them came consequently to hate the One who was the light of the world. Jesus acknowledged that the world hated Him, though it could not hate His unbelieving brothers (**7.**7). But where His disciples are faithful, the hatred will spread to them (cf. **17.**14). The reason for the hatred was that He had picked them out from the world, and nobody likes a convert taken away from his own side.

Notes: V. 12: 'My commandment' is singular, perhaps summarizing all commandments (10). V. 13: there is no reason to suppose here that Jesus did not die for the whole world. It is His friends who specifically benefit from it and appreciate it. And it is by receiving His sacrifice for themselves that they become in a real sense His friends. V. 15: the contrast between servants and sons had been made in **8.**35. Here it is servants and friends. The friends need to do His will just as much as servants, but because they have a different relationship and a fuller knowledge, it is done on a different footing. V. 16: the friends of Jesus are not marked off by natural attractiveness nor even by their own moral choice. His sovereign will initiates and maintains the relationship.

St. John 15.20-27

The new relationship which Christ offers to His disciples is such that it makes all the more inevitable that they will stand alongside Him and share the world's reaction to Him. They have been called friends, but there is still a proverb about servants which fits their case. 'A servant is not greater than his master'. There will be identification, at least to some extent, with His fate. While the note of warning predominates—that there will be persecution—there is also a note of encouragement—that some, at least, will keep their words. Yet the emphasis seems to be on the adverse reaction, which happens for His sake, through people's failure to know God (**8.**19,55; **16.**3).

What is the root cause of sin? The Jews might have been able to make excuses for their sin had not the light come and shone in their midst, and had not the words and deeds of Jesus been witnessed by them. Their hatred of the light, their hatred of Jesus, was hatred of the Father. This is a hatred which fulfilled Scripture, being without any valid cause.

All this must be seen and understood in the light of the great new fact—the personal coming of the Holy Spirit. The Paraclete was to be sent by the Son from the Father. He was the Spirit of truth sent to combat the falsehood and unbelief in the world. It was one of the functions of the Holy Spirit to bear witness to Jesus. It was also the task of an apostle to bear witness to Jesus. They were qualified to do this because they had been with Him from the beginning of the ministry (cf. Acts **1.**21 f.) and were consequently able to testify to the truth of the apostolic preaching (*kerygma*) about Him. So we in our generation rely on this twofold witness— the historical witness of the apostles to the facts and their meaning, which by the inspiration of the Holy Spirit is recorded in the N.T., and the 'existential' witness of the Holy Spirit at work in the world today.

Notes: V. 20: see **13.**16. V. 21: 'on My account'—cf. Matt. **5.**11; **10.**22; Mark **13.**13. V. 22: for the Law also as a revealer of sin, see Rom. **7.**7 For the guilt of unbelief, cf. **9.**41. V. 25: '*their* law'— which they profess to belive in (cf. **5.**45–47). V. 26: there is no reason to suppose from this verse that the Spirit does not come from the glorified Son as well as from the Father (cf. **16.**7).

*For prayer: See Phil. **1.**12 ff. as an example of vs. 26 f., and pray for Christians who are being persecuted today.*

St. John 16.1-7

Jesus had been aware all along, not only of the presence of a traitor in the apostolic band, but also of the great weakness both in understanding and in character of those who sought to be loyal to Him. This teaching, He tells them, was to keep them from falling away. There were going to be many temptations for them to do that. Excommunication from the synagogue could be a powerful pressure on them. But things would go much beyond that. The time was coming when religious bigots, no doubt convinced in themselves of the rightness of their attitude, would do their best to kill them and really believe that this was something which was for the service of God. This was an attitude well illustrated by Saul of Tarsus who was convinced that he ought to act in the way that he did (Acts **26**.9–11). Jesus Himself was threatened with death on grounds of God's honour (**10**.31–33) as well as of the welfare of God's people (**11**.50). The reason for persecution of the Christians will be theological—lack of knowledge of Father or Son.

Jesus emphasizes that He is telling them things now which they did not need to know before when He was with them. These things must be said because of His imminent departure. They had not asked where He was departing to, but the fact that He was going had become a source of sorrow for them instead of one of joy (**14**.28). Paradoxical as it may have seemed to them it was for their benefit that He went. Without His departure the arrival of the Paraclete would be impossible. In view of what had already been said about the Holy Spirit, they should have realized how they (with all Christians who followed them) would be better off. So long as their love for Christ, their knowledge of Him and their joy in Him, were links to His physical life, they were vulnerable. Separation or death could destroy everything at a stroke. Now, 'nothing can separate us from the love of God in Christ Jesus' (Rom. **8**.39, cf. John **16**.22).

Notes: V. 2: cf. the threat of expulsion in **9**.22. There was a Jewish saying that 'everyone who sheds the blood of the godless is like one who brings an offering'. V. 4: cf. **13**.19, where such information would help them to believe in Him. V. 5: they had of course asked in **13**.36 and **14**.5 but they had become so involved in their own sorrow that they had not pursued the question further on this occasion. V. 7: ironically enough Caiaphas had seen the advantage of Jesus' going away (it is the same Greek word in **11**.50; **18**.14).

St. John 16.8-15

Jesus now expands upon the reasons why it will be advantageous to have the Holy Spirit. There is a great deal of concentrated teaching on the person and the work of the Spirit in these few verses. The first task of the Spirit is the threefold conviction of the world on the counts of sin, righteousness and judgement. This will be an exposure of the attitudes of the world in such a way as to touch the conscience of men. As the world cannot receive the Paraclete (**14.**17), it will, presumably, normally be effected through the witness of the apostles (**15.**26 f.). Counsel for their defence becomes through them counsel for the prosecution of the world.

It is interesting to note the substance of these charges. The charge of sin was connected not with wrong actions but with unbelief. The people of Israel had long ago been condemned for stifling the national conscience. God had given them prophets and Nazirites to remind them of His truth by their words and by their deeds, but they made the Nazirites drink wine and told the prophets not to prophesy (Amos **2.**11 f.). God's people had done the same again in refusing to accept the words and deeds of Jesus (**15.**22–24). The Spirit would show them also that they had the wrong idea of righteousness. True righteousness was the divine vindication of the righteous life of Jesus through the resurrection and ascension. Likewise with judgement. Despite all that was to follow, they could not judge Jesus. It was the devil and those who followed him who were judging and condemning themselves in the death of Christ.

In addition there was the teaching function of the Spirit. He would guide them into all the truth about Jesus. It would be His function to pass on to them all that Jesus wished to reveal, and so to bring glory to Him.

Notes: V. 13: this does not mean that the Holy Spirit guided the apostles or the Church into the fullness of truth about everything. It was a specific promise to those whose business it was to record, interpret and pass on the once-for-all events connected with Christ's ministry, death and resurrection. 'The things that are to come' may be specifically the cross and resurrection, rather than a general power of prediction.

St. John 16.16-24

Jesus now tells His disciples about their not seeing Him and then their seeing Him again. This will be in a little while. The disciples are puzzled and do not know what He means by the expression. Interpreters of the Gospel since have not been in much better case! The question is whether the two references to 'a little while' denote different periods of time. Some have suggested that within a few hours they would not see Him because of His death. Then a few hours later they would see Him again because of His resurrection.

More probably, both instances of the phrase refer to the brief period between cross and resurrection which was a time of not seeing but of being about to see Jesus again.

Because of their difficulty in understanding, Jesus gives them a short parable. The time will be one of sorrow for them and of joy for the world, but their sorrow will be turned into joy. For it is like the anguish of childbirth. This time of crisis is sorrowful but soon turns into joy with the advent of new life. So their brief, temporary sorrow would turn into deep and permanent joy. Then they would start to ask the Father things in His name. If they asked they would receive and their joy would be full.

Notes: V. 16: the seeing may not be altogether unconnected with the seeing of Christ in the end (1 John 3.2). Seeing Him after the resurrection gives us a foretaste of the final vision. V. 17: the expression and reiteration of the doubt in this and in the next two verses suggest that some ambiguity may. have been intended. V. 21: this is not merely an illustration of any sorrow giving way to joy. In the O.T. the Messianic age was expected to be like childbirth, delivering God's people from their afflictions (Isa. **26**.16–20; **66**.7–14). Vs. 23 f.: there would be direct access to the Father, though prayer would be made in the name of Christ and on His authority, because of His effective work of reconciliation.

St. John 16.25-33

The circumstances of the ministry and the degree of understanding which the disciples have had have been such that Jesus has had to use a great deal of figurative language. The time would soon come when He would speak plainly of the Father. Not, of course, that it is possible to speak of divine truth without some use of human metaphor. But the possession of the Holy Spirit and the new degree of understanding which would come to the disciples would make much more direct teaching possible.

Jesus returns to the subject of prayer. After His exaltation, prayer would be made in His name. It would depend on His opening up of the way to the Father, but there would be no idea of the Son having to plead with an unwilling Father for the needs of His disciples. This would be unnecessary because of the Father's love for them. Their own love for and faith in Jesus were tokens that they were recipients of the Father's love. There was this close connection between attitudes to the Father and the Son because He Himself had His origin and destination with the Father, only being in the world for a time.

The disciples profess now to see the plain truth. They say that they understand His supernatural knowledge and therefore His divine origin. But Jesus warns them that such belief will be tested soon. For they were about to be scattered and to desert Him. In the face of the assault of the world He offered them peace and the confidence that He had already won the victory. This would be, and still is, a proof of His claims.

Notes: V. 28: this may be, in very summary form, the plain truth which Jesus tells them. The reply of the disciples seems to suggest it. V. 31: the implication is of a completely inadequate faith. V. 33: for the cross and resurrection as victory over the powers of the world, cf. 1 Cor. **15.**57; Col. **2.**15.

Questions for further study and discussion on St. John chs. 15 and 16
1. 'Apart from Me you can do nothing' (**15.**5). What in fact do we do in Christian or other activity apart from Christ? What difference would there be if Christ were really called upon to direct and help us in it?
2. Ought we still to expect hatred from the world (**15.**18–20)? If it does come, what form is it likely to take?
3. What are the advantages which we have in our day as opposed to those who lived before the Holy Spirit was given (**16.**7)?
4. Is our joy full and can no one take it from us (**15.**11; **16.**22)?
5. How has Christ overcome the world and what difference does this make to our lives (**16.**33)?

St. John 17.1-8

After the final discourse with the disciples, Jesus now turns to speak to His Father. This is often called the 'High-Priestly Prayer', as Jesus, the great High Priest, consecrates Himself to His coming death through which He will make atonement for the sin of the world (cf. **1.**29). Yet there is a good deal more to the prayer than just this theme, for it deals with some of the great doctrines of the Gospel—the relationship of Father and Son (1–5), the relationship of the Son to the disciples and of the disciples to the world (6–19), and the relationship of the Son to later generations of believers and their relationship to the world (20–26).

The hour towards which the clock of destiny has been ticking throughout the ministry has now come. In the mind and will of Jesus His work is already finished (4). He has accepted the Cross and taken it upon Himself as the full and perfect expression of love. So now He asks His Father that it may be an occasion for the glory of both Father and Son (**13.**31 f.). The object of the Son's mission

335

was to give eternal life in the knowledge of the Father and the Son. That mission had been accomplished and so had given glory to the Father. As it has been accomplished Jesus asks that He may now return to His Father and the glory which He had before the incarnation, and which had been His from the beginning before the creation of the world.

The mission of Christ was partly to make the name or character of the Father known to His disciples. They belonged to the Father and were given to the Son and they had been faithful. Now they also had knowledge of the divine origin and authority of Jesus.

Notes: V. 2: this is a strong reminder of the divine sovereignty. For the giving by the Father to the Son, cf. **3**.35; **6**.37–39; **10**.27–29. The last passage also speaks of giving eternal life to the disciples. V. 3: this is the only attempt in the Gospel at a definition of one of its leading concepts—eternal life. It is shown to be a personal relationship with God based on the historical mission of the Son, to know whom is to know God (**14**.7). V. 4: complete obedience to the Father's will was a characteristic of the ministry (**4**.34) and was sealed in His death (**19**.30). V. 6: the manifestation of the name or character of God was necessary for a true knowledge of Him which was not mere religious emotion.

St. John 17.9-19

Having described something of what He has done for the disciples, Jesus now turns to praying for them. He clearly distinguishes them from the world, for they belong in a special way to the Father and the Son. Because Jesus is leaving the world, their position as His representatives is of special importance. So He prays that His Father will keep them united and faithful. The unity of the disciples should be such as the unity of the Father and the Son. He also prays that they may have joy such as He had and would have in His return to the Father.

The passing on to them of the Word of God meant a calling of them out of the world. Their true allegiance was now elsewhere and they would therefore incur the hatred of the world. But He does not pray for their withdrawal from a hostile world but rather for them to be kept safe in the world from the attacks of the evil one. Just as Jesus Himself had a heavenly origin and destination, so in a sense the disciples have too. But just as He had a mission to the world, so have they. And His consecration of Himself was also a consecration of them for service.

Notes: V. 9: this does not mean that 'the world' is not still the

336

object of God's love for whose sake the Son came (**3**.16). In the writings of John 'the world' means, not the created order as such, nor the gifts of God in nature and human life, but human life and society lived in disregard of God and under the power of evil. In the divine strategy the outreach to the world is always through the disciples (20 f.). Almost all prayer in the N.T. is prayer for Christians, but it includes the request that they should be ready to take evangelistic opportunities (cf. Acts **4**.29 f.). V. 10: cf. the dependence of the love of Christians (**15**.9) and their mission (**20**.21) on the relationship of the Father and the Son. V. 12: 'the son of perdition'—NEB, 'the man who must be lost' (cf. 2 Thess. **2**.3; 1 John **2**.18,22; **4**.3). In some sense he is almost an incarnation of Satan. Vs. 17,19: the consecration of the disciples for the service of God depends both on the truth of God's word (maybe a reference to Jesus Himself **1**.1; **14**.6) and on His consecration of Himself. It is not a mere human effort at self-improvement.

St. John 17.20-26

If the prayer had earlier been confined to the disciples as against the world (9), now it is extended to future generations of believers. The faith which they will have is expected to come through the word of the apostles. The prayer, for what will in due course become a very diverse company, is for their unity. It was to be a unity with its origin in the unity of Father and Son. It would be sustained by a continuing relationship to Father and Son and its object would be that the world should believe in the mission of the Son from the Father.

Even the glory which belonged to God is in some way passed on to the disciples to assist the perfection of unity and the demonstration to the world that they are recipients of God's love. So He prays that they may see His true glory. Because He has known the Father and they have known the mission of the Son, He has made the Father's name known to them and will continue to make it known. This revelation of the Father's character was to further their experience of the Father's love of the Son and deepen the Son's unity with them.

Notes: V. 20: His own mission to the world was to evoke faith in response to His word (**12**.47 f.). The apostles were to bring men to faith through the apostolic preaching (*kerygma*). V. 21: the reference is to a unity of will and purpose rather than one of organization. The dynamic relationship of Father and Son is the pattern. Mutual love and joint action are the best answer to this prayer, and

337

when those are showing themselves, separate organizations will become irrelevant. It must never be forgotten that the object of Church unity is the glory of God and the evangelization of the world rather than administrative tidiness or comfort for Christians. V. 24: the disciples cannot fully follow yet (**13**.33,36) but there would be a foretaste of His glory before the full enjoyment of it (cf. Eph. **2**.6). V. 26: 'in them'—not only as individuals but in their midst also.

St. John 18.1-11

After three chapters of discourse and one of prayer, we come back now to action. But the Passion narrative in John, which we now begin to read, is different in emphasis from those of the other Gospels. Glory dominates. Even in the darkest moments there is triumph and victory. Jesus had warned His disciples about what was to happen, so that they would believe in Him (**13**.19). He had summoned them to rise and go out to the conflict (**14**.31). Now, after setting the coming affliction in the context of the whole plan of God and consecrating Himself and His disciples for this affliction and its consequences, He goes forth across the Kidron valley to a garden. Judas, having been identified and sent off to do his deed quickly, had gone out into the night (**13**.21–30). With the inner knowledge that he had from having belonged to the Twelve, Judas takes a band of Roman troops and Jewish temple police, and goes there to find Jesus.

Because of His foreknowledge of what was to happen, Jesus takes the initiative by coming forward and asking them whom they are seeking. To the reply 'Jesus of Nazareth' (His human designation) He replies, identifying Himself, but in terms which probably carried overtones of His deity, 'I am He' (cf. **6**.20; **8**.24,58)—a deduction supported by their immediate response in withdrawing and falling to the ground. When the question and answer are repeated, Jesus tells them to let the disciples go. The impetuous Peter draws his sword and cuts off the right ear of the high priest's slave. But Jesus rebukes this worldly attempt to frustrate His drinking the cup of suffering given to Him by His Father.

Notes: V. 1: 'a garden'. John alone describes it as such and does not name it as Gethsemane. Perhaps we are meant to see a conflict between Satan (**13**.27) and the Son of man, the second Adam. V. 3: religious and secular authorities combine against Him. 'A band' normally means a cohort of some six hundred soldiers. However, it is not necessary to presume that a force of this size

338

was used. Lanterns and torches were unnecessary to find the Light of the World (**8**.12) who was no longer hiding Himself (**12**.36; **18**.4). Weapons were unnecessary against One whose kingship was not of this world (**18**.36). V. 4: 'seek' may mean seek to kill (**5**.18; **7**.1, etc.). V. 5: Jesus is named as a Galilean (cf. **7**.52). Judas represents His own people—Judah (**1**.11; **4**.44). V. 6: this shows Jesus in command, willingly laying down His life (**10**.18). V. 8: He performs the part of the Good Shepherd and gives His life for the sheep (**10**.10–15).

St. John 18.12-18

Despite the willingness which Jesus has shown to be arrested, civil and religious authorities combine to seize Him and bind Him. They take Him first to Annas, father-in-law of Caiaphas the high priest. The evangelist reminds his readers of Caiaphas' attitude of cynical expediency to the execution of Jesus (**11**.49–52).

While Jesus goes alone as the prisoner, Simon Peter and another disciple follow. This disciple is known to the high priest so he manages to get into the court. Peter had stopped outside and has to be brought in by him. To a question from a maid whether he is one of Jesus' disciples the man of rock denies it. He then stands with the servants and officers trying to keep warm round a fire. He has denied the true light and stands with the enemies of his Master in the dark and in the cold.

Notes: V. 13: Annas was high priest from A.D. 6 to 15. Other references to him in the N.T. are in *Luke* and *Acts,* and both in conjunction with Caiaphas (Luke **3**.2; Acts **4**.6). He may have been the power behind the throne. Caiaphas (mentioned also in Matt. **26**.3,57) succeeded him after his deposition by the Romans and held the office until A.D. 36. There is some difficulty about this passage on the ground that there is no mention of a trial before Caiaphas (24,28) and Peter's denial comes into the examination before Annas. There is some very slight manuscript evidence for including v. 24 after 'Annas' in v. 13, but it is not strong enough to accept. Others have suggested that v. 24 has something of a pluperfect sense (as in AV [KJV]), stating that Annas *had* sent Him to Caiaphas. If we take the text as it stands it may be that there is no mention of a trial before Caiaphas because, in one sense, Jesus has nothing to say to such cynicism as Caiaphas had expressed (cf. Herod in Luke **23**.9). V. 15: it is natural to assume that this was the 'beloved disciple', but it is not certain. V. 17: 'I am not'—contrast the dignified reply of Jesus in v. 5. V. 18: standing with them, as

Judas had (5). How easily in our weakness we take the traitor's place!

St. John 18.19-27

The high priest begins his examination of Jesus, not by asking Him the basic questions about His origin and authority, but the more peripheral ones about His disciples and His teaching. Jesus has nothing to add to what He has already said in His public ministry. While He gave special teaching to His disciples at the Last Supper, His ministry was an open one. His message has been proclaimed in synagogue and Temple, places of public gathering. There is no point in His repeating it—His audience could tell them perfectly well.

Where argument fails, violence often takes over. An officer strikes Him but Jesus reminds them that the point at issue is the truth of His teaching and such a point is not solved in this way. Annas then sends Him bound to Caiaphas.

The scene switches back to Peter. Those with whom he has identified himself ask him if he does not in fact belong with the prisoner. For the second time he denies that he is a disciple. One of Malchus' relations then asks suspiciously whether he did not see Peter in the garden with Jesus. There is no glory here, only shame. For the third time Peter denies, and as Jesus predicted, the cock crows.

Notes: V. 19: certain questions are put to Jesus but hardly pursued. The decisions have been made secretly (not openly) without giving Him a fair trial (7.45–52). V. 20: Jesus' teaching has been done openly and to the world, though not in the way which His brothers had expected (7.3 f.). The word 'openly' could also mean plainly (16.29). But what was plain to His disciples would be hidden in meaning to the Jews, and even at this stage seems to have been lost on Peter. There is only one reference in the Gospel to His teaching in the synagogue (6.59). The main challenge to the Jews in their religious setting is made in the Temple. V. 21: the blind man had questioned the need to repeat his evidence. There was no possibility here of their wishing to become His disciples (9.27).

St. John 18.28-40

Jesus is sent from the religious leaders to the Roman governor; from the prejudiced judgement of His own people to the bewildered judgement of the world. With a supreme example of hypocrisy they refuse to run the risk of ritual defilement by entering Pilate's headquarters, though they are in the midst of defiling themselves morally (Isa. **59.**3). And in an amazing situation of irony they are preparing to eat the Passover without realizing that they are taking part in the putting to death of the true Passover Lamb in whose redemptive death the real significance of the festival is found.

To Pilate's tactful visit to them outside the praetorium and to his question about the charge which they brought, there is no reasoned answer. If He were not a criminal they would not have brought Him. Pilate wishes them to judge Him by their own law. But they say it is not lawful for them to put any man to death. They have determined that Jesus must die and die on a cross.

There is an inner stage as well as an outer. Inside the praetorium Pilate confronts Jesus and asks Him the question that matters as far as the Roman authorities are concerned. Are you the King of the Jews, a revolutionary leader? When Jesus tries to find out whether this is a conclusion Pilate has reached for himself, Pilate asks in desperation what on earth he could know about it all. What is this all about? Jesus puts the whole idea of kingship on to a different footing. Kingship, as Pilate knows it, is not the point at issue, it is truth. Outside Pilate has to face the demands of the Jews, inside he must face the claims of truth.

So Pilate with a despairing rhetorical question about truth, goes out in the cause of truth to tell the Jews that Jesus is innocent. But he wants to find a way around the problem and so makes use of the Passover amnesty. He has misjudged public opinion. They call out, not for Jesus their 'King' who was no threat to the Roman rule, but for a terrorist called Barabbas.

The way in which Jesus answered Pilate, and the things He did, are an example to all of us, and especially to Christians who are persecuted. Jesus renounced violent retaliation and even violent self-defence (36). His only weapons were supernatural and spiritual; so are ours (2 Cor. **10.**4).

Notes: V. 28: defilement would come by going into the house of a Gentile from which the leavened bread had not been removed. V. 31: their own law was in fact against them in their opposition to Jesus (**5.**45–47, cf. **7.**51). V. 31: it is uncertain whether the Jews had power to stone people at this time. V. 33: are *you* in all your weakness King of the Jews? V. 35: he feels quite out of it. The Gospel shows again and again that it is 'the Jews', 'His own people' (**1.**11) who are against Jesus. V. 37: 'Everyone who is of the truth'— cf. **3.**21.

To think over: 'Weakness is the only strength we have in presenting

341

the gospel. And if you rob us of that we are going to get in real trouble' (D. T. Niles).

Questions for further study and discussion on St. John chs. 17 and 18
1. The word 'give' appears sixteen times in ch. **17**. What encouragement can we derive from the various ways in which it is used?
2. Mission, unity and truth are three major themes of ch. **17**. What is the right order of priority for them?
3. 'Put your sword into its sheath' (**18**.11). How far is this a command to be obeyed on other occasions?
4. Do we ever deny our Christian discipleship by our words or by the company we keep (**18**.17)? How can this be remedied?
5. What religious scruples do we fuss over while permitting harm to others (**18**.28)?
6. 'What is truth?' (**18**.38). Are we prepared to face up to truth as it challenges us at a personal level?

St. John 19.1-7

Having failed to get rid of the responsibility for dealing with Jesus by means of an amnesty, Pilate now has Him flogged. This may be an attempt to get Jesus to give evidence (cf. Acts **22**.24), or an attempt to placate the Jews so that they would not go on asking for the death penalty (Luke **23**.16,22). The soldiers then do their utmost to humiliate this so-called king by mockery. They dress Him up in royal robes and proceed to call Him 'King of the Jews' and to strike Him.

Pilate goes out again in the name of truth on the level at which he understands it, and tells the Jews that he finds no case against Jesus (cf. **18**.38). Jesus then follows, a pitiful sight in His mock array, and Pilate offers Him to their view telling them to look at the man. Here is this poor fellow, your deluded and rejected Messianic claimant, is what he means. But here is 'the Man', the Son of man, the Second Adam, offering His perfect obedience for the life of the world (Rom. **5**.15, 19; Phil. **2**.6–8).

The religious leaders see Him and howl for His crucifixion. Pilate is still concerned enough for the truth not to be willing to order the crucifixion. He has, however, given in sufficiently to the pressure of the Jews to offer them the opportunity of performing it. But they continue to call out for Pilate to act. The true charge now comes out. It is a charge of blasphemy, which under Jewish law carried the death penalty (Lev. **24**.16). The 'man' has made Himself Son of God (cf. **10**.33).

342

Notes: V. 2: the crown was probably not so much an instrument of torture as a symbol of mockery. It was probably a 'radiate crown' which was sometimes used as a sign of divinity. V. 3: see NEB—'Then time after time they came up to Him'. V. 4: the Jews themselves had been unable to prove any moral charges against Him (**8.**46). V. 6: the Jews could not crucify Him, so this may have been a taunt by Pilate. He is anxious to make them responsible for the execution. But this is a 'buck' which no man can pass.

St. John 19.8-16

Against the apparent hardness and moral unconcern of 'the Jews', Pilate is clearly set as a man who is trying to make up his mind, trying on the level at which he understands them to come to terms with the claims of the truth. So he is afraid. Partly afraid because the title 'Son of God' was one that the Roman emperors claimed and this, therefore, had a smell of treason about it. Partly afraid no doubt because the 'man' (5) showed so many signs of being more than an ordinary man.

Pilate therefore asks Jesus where He came from. This may be simply a matter concerned with jurisdiction (cf. Luke **23.**5 f.). But it is the all-important theological question (cf. **3.**31; **8.**23). Jesus does not reply to this direct question (cf. **8.**25). Pilate then reminds the prisoner of his authority—power to release and power to crucify. But this is no absolute power. It comes delegated from above, not so much from Rome as from God (Rom. **13.**1–7) and Pilate has not realized that Jesus has power to lay down and take up His life (**10.**18). Pilate is in a way only doing his job, the real sinner is the one who handed Jesus over.

Pilate, endeavouring again to release Jesus, makes another attempt to follow the claims of the truth. But the Jews have another weapon—insecurity. They have acted to preserve their interests against the temporal power (**11.**48–50). Now Pilate is reminded of his interests with the one who had on the earthly level given him power. This is sufficient to sway Pilate finally, for like most men he has his price. He brings Jesus out and sits down on the judgement seat. He then offers Him to them again, this time as their king. When they call for His crucifixion, Pilate asks incredulously, 'Shall I crucify your King?', and receives the terrible reply, 'We have no king but Caesar'. So do the people of God abandon their heritage. Nothing remains but to hand Him over to them for crucifixion.

The decisive shout of the priests (15) marks the end of the continual conflict in John's Gospel between light and darkness—the

343

light and truth of Christ, and the darkness of the Jews. It is an
ironic end. The Jews reject their King-Messiah, whom they cannot
and will not recognize, by declaring their allegiance to an Emperor
and an army of occupation which they hate. It is always the same.
To reject Christ as King involves accepting or declaring allegiance
to some other master, who will turn out to be empty and unsatisfying at best, and a tyrant at worst.

Notes: V. 11: the last phrase could refer either to Judas or to
Caiaphas. Each represents Judaism as a whole with its claim to
sight (**9.41**). V. 12: ironically, in the end Pilate was removed by
Caesar. Just as ironically, the Romans ultimately came and
destroyed the Temple (**11.48**). V. 13: Gabbatha has recently been
discovered. V. 14: the day of Preparation might be the day before
the Passover or the day before the Sabbath of Passover week.
'The sixth hour'—John probably used the Roman (and modern)
time system.

St. John 19.17-22

The struggle between the two ideas of kingship is ended with
apparent victory for the rulers of this world. The argument concerning the truth is over, with the One who is true falsely charged
and sentenced, and the truth only shining out of the narrative
unintentionally or ironically. The decision has been made on the
human level and now comes the action.

Jesus went out carrying His own cross to Golgotha. There He
was crucified with two others, who were possibly associates of
Barabbas in his terrorist activity. So radically was Jesus misunderstood that they numbered the sinless One among the transgressors
(Isa. **53**.12), they crucified One whose kingship was not of this
world, and who abhorred the use of violence, between two violent
criminals.

There must be a reason why a man should receive the sentence
of crucifixion. Pilate, therefore, will have the last grim laugh. This is
'The King of the Jews'. So the title goes up in the three important
languages of the day. Aramaic (rather than Hebrew) was the
language of the Jews, Greek and Latin the official languages of the
Empire. The message of the cross is proclaimed to His own people
and to the world, of which He is the Saviour (**4.42**). So far as Pilate
is concerned He is Jesus of Nazareth, a description such as any of
his subjects might have. To that is added, in scorn of the whole
business, the title of king. The Jews, who have just declared that
they have no king but Caesar (15), naturally object. To show that

He was a false Messianic pretender would hurt no one, as this did. But Pilate stands firm and the title, unwittingly given remains. So in the end did they take Him by force to make Him King (**6**.15).

Notes: V. 17: 'bearing His own cross'. It is possible to harmonize this with Mark **15**.21. John is emphasizing that Jesus goes alone to accomplish the world's salvation. (Cf. also Isaac carrying the wood for his own sacrifice—Gen. **22**.6.) 'Golgotha'—the derivation of the name is uncertain and its location is not sure. V. 19: Pilate had already used this title five times. The Jews refuse to use it (cf. v. 12, 'a king'). In a sense it is a more limited title than 'the King of Israel' (**1**.49; **12**.13); and all the more ironic for the way in which 'the Jews' have been so opposed to Him in the Gospel. He is still King whatever men's response. V. 21: Jesus had, in fact, never said this.

St. John 19.23-30

To the soldiers Jesus is just another criminal to be dealt with, a political one with no very noticeable difference at the moment. So they carry on and collect the 'benefits' of the job—the prisoner's clothing. His tunic, the undergarment worn next to the body, was seamless and indivisible like that of the high priest (Exod. **28**.31 f.; Lev. **21**.10): there is no point then in trying to tear that. 'Let's toss for it,' they say. And so the soldiers, no doubt thinking of their good or bad luck in being on this 'job', commit themselves further to chance by gambling for the tunic. But there is no chance in the ways of God. This was to fulfil the Scripture, and in what a remarkable way, through the operation of those who did not know what they were doing, was Psa. **22** fulfilled in the Passion!

If the cross creates a false fellowship of gamblers trying to gain from the victim and from each other, it creates also a true fellowship of believers. Not only is there a group representative of the Church gathered around, but from the cross the word is spoken which puts Jesus' mother and the 'beloved disciple' into a new relationship with each other.

The mission of Jesus had been concerned with accomplishing the work which the Father had given Him to do (**4**.34). Here He knows that it has been accomplished, fantastic as this must have seemed to those who stood by. So He cries out, 'I thirst.' They come to meet His thirst on the physical level, so fulfilling the Scripture (Psa. **69**. 21). But His real thirst may be a spiritual one, for His Father (Psa. **42**.2). He who offers the living water, so that men need never thirst again (**4**.13 f.; **6**.35), Himself endures the agonies of thirst.

He who offers the Spirit and life (7.39) gives up His own spirit in death. Salvation does come to us freely, but not cheaply. The last cry from the cross (30) was one of triumph not of despair. He could die in peace. No one took His life. He gave it up freely, completing and perfecting His God-given mission.

Notes: V. 24: some have contrasted the divisions (literally 'tearings') of the Jews (7.43; 9.16; 10.19) with the untorn tunic and have seen it to be symbolic of the unity of the Church, but this seems rather remote. V. 25: the mother of Jesus had been dissociated from Him in 2.4 because His hour had not yet come. Now it has come and she is associated with Him. Our Christian witness is transformed when we can discern His time. V. 29: 'hyssop' would not be a very suitable plant to hold up a wet sponge. A similar word means 'javelin': so NEB renders.

For meditation: 'The Cross is the blazing fire at which the flame of our love is kindled, but we have to get near enough to it for some of its sparks to fall on us' (Stott).

St. John 19.31-37

So the hour has come, the work has been completed and Jesus has died. But that is not after all the end of the matter. For there are religious consequences for the Jews and for the disciples. The Jews have been busy with their Passover observances and while they go through with the removal of a Messianic pretender they do not intend to slip up in their religious observance (cf. 18.28). The Law had said that a hanged man's body should not remain all night upon the tree as that would defile the land (Deut. 21.22 f.). The Romans liked to leave the bodies on the crosses as a grim warning to potential troublemakers. Because the next day was the Sabbath of the Passover the Jews asked for the bodies to be taken away before nightfall.

The Romans could not, of course, remove the bodies until the victims were dead. In such cases, as an act of mercy, their legs were broken to hasten their death. This was done in the case of the two terrorists. When they came to Jesus they saw that He was dead already. So there was no need to break His legs, and one of the soldiers, probably just to check that He really was dead, thrust a lance into His side and there came out a flow of blood and water.

There was a witness of this and he gives true evidence for the faith of the readers. It was clearly something of importance. On the one hand, it was firm evidence of His death, particularly important as there were heretics who denied that Jesus had ever died. On the

346

other hand, water and blood are symbols in the Gospel. Water is applied for cleansing and new birth (**3.**5) and drunk for satisfaction (**4.**13 f.). The blood of the Son of Man must be drunk so that men may live (**6.**53–56). By what the soldiers did not do and by what they did they fulfilled Scripture.

Notes: V. 31: there is some doubt as to whether this means the day of preparation for the Passover or for the Sabbath. V. 34: Tasker, ad loc., quotes the medical evidence for what happened. Probably the two sacraments are in mind (cf. 1 John **5.**6,8). But the point is, as Barrett puts it, ad loc., that 'the real death of Jesus was the real life of men'. V. 35: this does not seem to be the 'beloved disciple'. V. 36: so revealing Jesus as the true Passover Lamb (**1.**29; cf. Exod. **12.**46; Psa. **34.**20). V. 37: quoting Zech. **12.**10, the whole context of which has bearing on the Passion.

St. John 19.38-42

While the fact of the burial of Jesus is mentioned as part of the apostolic preaching by Paul (1 Cor. **15.**3 f.), it is referred to very little in the N.T. As far as Paul is concerned it is probably only the link between death and resurrection which shows that both were real objective happenings. But John records a number of details about the burial which seem to have significance.

Joseph of Arimathea, a wealthy man and a member of the Sanhedrin, comes and asks Pilate to be allowed to take away the body of Jesus. No doubt due to his influential position he obtains permission. So he does what the Jews want, and avoids the defilement of the land. But he is also a secret disciple of Jesus, so that, despite his fear of the Jews, this is an act of courage and is done in order to honour Jesus. Nicodemus, who has not yet been described as a believer but who was at least an open-minded sympathizer (**3.**1; **7.**50–52), joins with him. They take a huge quantity of spices and treat His body according to Jewish burial custom.

It is to a garden that they go with Him, for it is here that the Second Adam must bring life where the first Adam has brought sin and death (1 Cor. **15.**21 f.). It is a new tomb, perhaps prepared for the use of Joseph's family and now given to Jesus as no other can be prepared in time. Here, free from corrupting influences, He is laid—the first to lie in the tomb and soon to be the first to rise from the dead to a new sphere of life (1 Cor **15.**20). Despite the honour paid to Jesus by these two men, outwardly the victory belongs entirely to the Jews and to the forces of darkness. A dangerous pretender has been disposed of by the Romans, Barabbas has been freed and no one has even broken the Law!

Notes: V. 39: the immense weight of spices seems to echo Psa. **45**.8. V. 42: the NEB follows the Greek in making 'Jesus' the last word of the chapter. 'The future lies with Him, and with the Father' (Fenton, ad loc.).

Questions for further study and discussion on St. John ch. 19
1. What pressures are there which come upon us today which might make us sin against the truth?
2. What does this chapter tell us of the claims of Christ in the spiritual and the temporal spheres?
3. How is it that the true kingship of Jesus is revealed in this chapter?
4. What effect does the cross have on our relationships with others (25–27)?
5. Does contemplation of 'Him whom they have pierced' (37) give us courage to act (38–42)?

St. John 20.1-10

The hand of legalism may seem to have triumphed as the drama must wait for a day while the Sabbath is observed. But after the Sabbath rest comes a new week and with it a new era in the history of mankind. Mary Magdalene comes to the tomb early, while it was still in every sense dark (cf. **13**.30; Luke **22**.53), but while dawn was imminent. She sees that the stone, such as would normally be placed across the entrance of a tomb to keep it safe, has been taken away. She naturally assumes that someone or other has violated the tomb and taken away the body of Jesus.

With this news she runs off to Peter and the 'beloved disciple'. The two of them then run as fast as they can to the tomb, and the 'beloved disciple', presumably the younger man, gets there first. He stoops to look into the tomb from the outside and sees the strange phenomenon of the graveclothes lying there. When Peter arrives he, as usual, is more impetuous and goes into the tomb. He sees the extra details—the different wrappings all lying in place. The boldness of Peter emboldens the 'beloved disciple' also, so he goes in and sees the evidence more closely and believes what has happened. This has come as a surprise because of their failure to know the Scriptural prediction that He should rise from the dead. So they go back home, thrilled no doubt but still mystified.

348

Notes: V. 1: Mary Magdalene was presumably not alone ('*we* do not know', 2), but is probably mentioned as the leader of the group of women and the one to whom the Lord appears personally (11–18). It is a forgiven sinner who makes the first discovery of the empty tomb and sees the first appearance of the risen Lord. V. 2: she probably thought of the enemies of Jesus, but the rifling of tombs was a fairly common crime. V. 7: Lazarus came out of the tomb with the wrappings still on him (**11.44.**) This was resurrection of a different kind, in which the form of the body seems to have been changed, so that it could slip out of the graveclothes without disturbing them. No one removing the body would have left the wrappings. V. 8: this is the first true Christian faith in the Gospel, because it is faith in the risen Lord. For an adequate confession we have to wait until v. 28.

St. John 20.11-18

If in a sense the 'beloved disciple' has come to Christian faith because he believes in the resurrection, it is Mary who comes to the first full Christian experience because she meets the risen Lord. For the fact of the empty tomb and the encounter with the risen Christ are the twin bases of the Easter faith.

As the Lord had gone, there was no point in staying at the tomb as far as the men were concerned. But somehow they had not communicated this to Mary. She remains weeping at the tomb as it was the place with which her Lord had last been associated, and she did not now know where to look for Him. Eventually she looks into the tomb and sees two angels. When they ask her why she is weeping she answers purely on the human plane. He has been moved from there and she does not know where they have put Him.

Turning round she sees the risen Jesus but does not recognize Him. To His question about the reason for her tears, she continues in the same vein of trying to discover where the dead Jesus is. Only the use of her name, no doubt in a familiar intonation, makes her realize that it is Jesus. Her apparent desire to cling to Him is forbidden. He must ascend to His Father. She must go and tell His brothers about this. So she goes off to the disciples, His newly-made brothers in the Christian family, and tells them that she has seen the Lord.

Notes: V. 12: it may be that she needed the evidence of the angels which was not needed by Peter and the other disciple. V. 15: a very different kind of seeking from **18.4,7.** V. 16: the Good Shepherd calls His own sheep by name (**10.3**). It helps us to think of Him

Photos: Church of the Holy Sepulchre and Gordon's Calvary

using our names. 'Rabboni' is an inadequate confession of faith
(cf. 28). V. 17: she may have touched Him (cf. 27). She was not to
cling to His body in this state because His abiding presence after
the ascension would be a spiritual one (14.18). 'My Father and your
Father'—they are brothers (cf.1.11) but His relationship to the
Father is still unique(1.14).

St. John 20.19-23

The disciples have now heard of the empty tomb, which some of
them at least have seen for themselves. They have also heard of the
appearance of Christ to Mary Magdalene. But they have not yet
met the risen Lord for themselves. To them the experience of the
Easter faith comes not at the tomb nor in the garden but in a room
where doors are shut through fear of the Jews.

Jesus passes through closed doors and greets them with a message of peace, now filled with new and wonderful meaning for them
(cf. 14.27). The evidence that He really is Jesus has to come not only
from His words but also from His body. The marks of crucifixion
are displayed to them. No wonder the disciples were filled with joy
(16.20–22). Jesus then repeats His word of peace and commissions
them for mission in His name. He breathes on them and imparts the
Holy Spirit to them. Their mission and the gift of the Holy Spirit
through which alone they could accomplish it (cf. Acts 1.8) are
connected with the forgiveness and the retention of sins.

Notes: V. 19: it is important to emphasize that this appearance to
the representative body of the disciples was on the first day of the
week, the first day of the new era. For fear of the Jews, cf. 7.13;
19.38. The emphasis here seems to be more on the power of Jesus
in His 'spiritual body' to pass through closed doors and yet be
recognized, than on the disciples' fear. But we can see how frigh-
tened men were transformed in preparation for their fearless mission to the world. It is not certain whether only the Twelve (minus
Thomas and Judas) were in the room. If this is so, then they are
there as representatives of the Church as a whole. V. 21: the mission
of the disciples from the Son is derived from and parallel to the
mission of the Son from the Father (cf. 17.18). V. 22: this is sometimes referred to as the 'Johannine Pentecost'. Jesus can impart the
indwelling Holy Spirit as soon as He has risen, though the full outward manifestation of the gift of the Spirit to the Church must wait
until the appearances are over. There is here a new creation (cf.
Gen. 2.7). The Second Adam is a lifegiving Spirit (1 Cor. 15.45).
V. 23: the forgiveness or retention of sins is the inevitable result

of men's reaction to the Gospel. What happened in His ministry (9.39–41) will happen in them through the Holy Spirit (cf. 16.8–11).

St. John 20.24-31

For some reason Thomas had not been present when Jesus appeared to the disciples on the evening of Easter Day. When the disciples tell him of the resurrection experience in the simplest terms—'We have seen the Lord' (cf. 18)—Thomas asks for more detailed evidence by sight and by touch before he will be convinced.

A week later comes the answer for Thomas. Again Jesus passes through closed doors and again He gives them His greeting of peace. Then He invites Thomas to put the evidence for the resurrection to the test which he had wished to make for it. It seems that touch was not necessary, the evidence of sight was sufficient. Thomas cries out in adoring wonder, 'My Lord and my God!'

The Gospel has reached its climax. An adequate confession of faith has at last been made, Jesus is confessed not only as Lord (cf. Rom 10.9; 1 Cor. 12.13), but also as God (cf. 1.1). Thomas' faith has been based on sight. But Jesus is concerned about those who will believe in later generations and in different places (17.20). So He pronounces His last beatitude upon those who will not have the privilege of sight but who will exercise the gift of faith.

As the climax has been reached the evangelist rounds off his work. He reminds his readers that the signs recorded are only a selection of all that Jesus did, and that they are selected for a purpose—to induce a faith in Jesus as Christ and Son of God which will bring life.

Notes: V. 24: Thomas, as shown earlier (11.16; 14.5), seems to have been loyal but to have lacked the perception of faith. V. 28: 'My Lord' contains much fuller meaning than Mary's expression of the same words in v. 13. Paradoxically, it is the doubter who in the end expresses his faith most completely. May our honest doubts find a similarly complete answer! V. 31: it is probably a present rather than an aorist. This would mean 'hold the faith' (NEB) rather than 'come to believe' (NEB margin). The Gospel would therefore be intended for Christians as well as non-Christians.

St. John 21.1-8

The Gospel proper ends with ch. 20. This chapter is a sort of appendix, the particular purpose of which is apparently to explain what Jesus had said about the destiny of the 'beloved disciple' (23).

It also has importance in showing the manner of Peter's restoration to the service of Christ, and the future which awaited him. So the relationship between Peter and the 'beloved disciple' is made clear. Both are represented as equal partners with complementary roles—Peter as pastor and evangelist, and the beloved disciple as guarantor of the truth concerning Jesus (25). These two leaders were obviously the subject of widespread rumours (23).

There were a number of different appearances to the disciples by the risen Lord (see 1 Cor. **15**.3–8) not all of which are recorded in the Gospels. As always, John has selected one which gets across an important point (**20**.30 f.; **21**.25). The disciples had apparently gone back to Galilee, uncertain of the way in which they were to carry out the apostolic commission (**20**.21). Seven of them are mentioned. Simon Peter decides to go fishing and the rest follow his lead.

Night was the best time for fishing, but a hard night's toil yielded nothing. At daybreak Jesus, unrecognized, asked them from the shore whether they had any fish. When they said they had not He told them to cast their nets to starboard. They made such a catch that they could not haul it in. The 'beloved disciple' is the very first to discern who the stranger is. But it is Peter who acts first, putting on his clothes and plunging into the lake while the others struggled in with the boat and the catch. Both types of people are found in the Church today. When they work together the cause of Christ prospers.

Notes: V. 1: the Sea of Tiberias was the same as the Sea of Galilee. V. 2: Thomas is prominent in *John*, Nathanael is mentioned only by him. This is the only reference to the sons of Zebedee in the Gospel and it helps us to assume that John was the 'beloved disciple'. But this is not certain, for it could possibly have been one of the two unnamed disciples. V. 6: Jesus probably saw a shoal of fish from the shore. It is not at all certain how far this story is meant to have symbolic significance with 'fishing for men' being illustrated (cf. Luke **5**.10 f.). V. 7: 'the Lord'—it is only after the resurrection that the disciples are recorded as referring to Jesus by this title in the third person.

St. John 21.9-14

Eventually all the disciples arrive, following Peter. They find that Jesus has already been at work. He has made a fire upon the shore and has cooked some fish and provided some bread. Jesus asks them to bring some of the fish which they themselves have caught and Peter goes back to the boat and hauls the net ashore. In it there were one hundred and fifty-three fish but the net was not torn.

Jesus then asks them to have breakfast with Him. There is about Him a numinous quality which stops them from asking who He is, but, in fact, they knew without having to ask that it was the Lord. In any event He can cope with shyness. He came and took and distributed both bread and fish as He had done to them and the five thousand beside the same lake before (**6.**11). It was in a meal, which must have reminded them of meals which they had shared with Him, as well as of the feeding miracle, that He revealed Himself. Luke too shows that 'He was known to them in the breaking of the bread' (Luke **24.**28–35). So in this informal fashion was Jesus revealed to them for the third time after He was raised from the dead.

Notes: V. 10: it is not clear why Jesus asked them to bring their fish when He had already prepared some for them to eat. It appears that their fish was not used on this occasion. V. 11: this number has long exercised the ingenuity of commentators. It may simply be that they counted up and this happened to be the total. But many have seen it to be symbolic. Some suggest that it represents the one hundred and fifty-three different species of fish known to ancient naturalists, or that, as factorial seventeen, it symbolizes perfection (as ten and seven were numbers indicating completeness). In either case this would be taken as referring to the complete apostolic mission to all men which would be carried out by the Church without the nets breaking. However, the primary meaning of the whole chapter must undoubtedly be sought on the plain literal level. V. 12: 'Who are You?'—this was the question the Jews had put to Him in unbelief (**8.**25). V. 13: while it would be wrong to see this as a celebration of the Holy Communion, our doctrine of the Lord's Supper should include the idea of eating together with the risen Jesus in our midst.

St. John 21.15-19

Simon Peter has been the leader of the band of the disciples. He has not always believed first (**20.**8) nor perceived first (7), but he has usually acted first. And through being in a prominent position it is he who has denied his Master three times. He has already hastened ashore to meet Jesus and it is clear that he wishes to put right his denial. First they eat the meal of fellowship and then Jesus takes the initiative in restoring Peter.

Three times Peter had denied that he knew Jesus (**18.**15–27), and

now three times Jesus asks him if he loves Him. It was only in reply
to Peter's threefold assurance that he did love Him that Jesus gave
him the threefold commission to feed His lambs and His sheep. At
the third question Peter is upset, but Jesus reminds him as He had
done before (**13.**6–10) of his need for submission. When he was
young he had the independence and opportunities of youth. When
he was old things would happen to him against his will. This was a
prediction of a martyr's death, in which he would glorify God as
his Master had done before him (**12.**23–26). This was to be his
destiny; it was for God's glory, it was the way Jesus had gone. So
the command comes, and echoes down the centuries, 'Follow Me'.

Notes: Vs. 15–17: despite NEB margin, most scholars do not
now try to distinguish between the two words used for 'love' in
these verses. John often uses synonyms and there is no reason to
suppose that he is recording reference to love at two levels—the
word used by Jesus in vs. 15 f. referring to Christian love, and the
word used by Peter in vs. 15 f. and by both of them in v. 17 to human
affection. Likewise there seems to be no real distinction between
'feed' (15, 17) and 'tend' (16), nor between 'lambs' (15) and 'sheep'
(16 f.). It was to this pastoral ministry that Peter, in fact, devoted
himself (1 Pet. **5.**1–5). 'More than these' refers to the other disciples
(cf. Mark **14.**29), rather than to his love of the trappings of the
fisherman's life. Peter has learnt enough humility not to make the
comparison in reply. V. 18: this is important early evidence for the
crucifixion of Peter.

St. John 21.20-25

It is always interesting to know what is going to happen to other
people too. Human nature being what it is, we enjoy comparisons
with others so that we can exult in our own virtue or grumble about
our own misfortunes. Sometimes we wish to find out about others
from sheer curiosity. Whatever the motive, Peter wants to know
what is to happen to the 'beloved disciple'. Jesus answered that
that is none of Peter's business, but puts it in such a way that He
seems to predict that that disciple would not die before the second
coming of Christ. The writer wishes to make it quite plain that Jesus
did not say that but only 'If it is My will that he remain until I come,
what is that to you?'

The book ends with the assertion that it is this disciple who is
bearing witness to all this and has written this, and that it is known
that his evidence is true. And in a charming concluding sentence the
writer adds that if all the deeds of Jesus were recorded the world

would not be large enough to hold all the books which should be written.

Notes: V. 20: it is not clear why such a long description is given of the 'beloved disciple'. It may be to contrast this incident with the other (13.21–30), when it seemed of considerable importance to both Peter and the 'beloved disciple' to know who was going to be the traitor. V. 22: perhaps this was deliberately expressed as the most different thing that could possibly happen to him, without any necessary implication that it would. V. 23: it is possibly necessary to state this because the 'beloved disciple' has recently died. If this is so, he is the witness behind the Gospel and the one responsible for its writing. Ch. **21** (or at least the last two verses) would then be edited by the disciples of the 'beloved disciple' ('we' in 24).

A final thought: While ch. **21** *may be something of a postscript to the Gospel, it is a most appropriate one. The transformation of an individual by Christ, through a personal encounter involving faith in Him, is what the whole Gospel is about.*

Questions for further study and discussion on St. John chs. 20 and 21

1. Compare the resurrection narrative in *John* with that in the other Gospels. Do the differences make the event seem more or less true?
2. Is belief in the empty tomb necessary for Christian faith?
3. In what way can we today meet the risen Lord personally?
4. 'Do you love Me?' Do we let Jesus ask us this question before we seek to do things in His service (**21**.15–17)?
5. Do we face the temptation of being more concerned with other people's progress than with following Christ ourselves (**21.** 21 f.)?

Acts

Name. Early Christian writers speak of the books of the New Testament as the "Gospel and Apostle". By this description they mean our gospels and the epistles which form the bulk of the New Testament literature. These are understandable groupings, but one further term is needed to explain how the Church came into being, and how the facts of the Gospel history are to be connected to their inspired interpretation in the apostolic letters. This "bridge" book which links the two chief parts together is the Acts of the Apostles.

Purpose. The main purposes of the book of Acts, apart from the obvious provision of a history of the Christian Church in its formative years of growth and development, are as follows:

(*a*) The first aim of the book is to provide a chronicle of the mighty and triumphant progress of the Gospel through the then-known world. This theme is clearly spelled out in Acts **1**.8, and pursued in each chapter of the book. It does not pretend to be a history of all the apostles, nor of the early church in all its parts up to the author's time, nor is it a series of biographical sketches. History and biography are included to serve a larger purpose—namely, to show the universal spread of the Christian faith which was begun and maintained by the Holy Spirit.

Certain emphases are given to spotlight the chief features of the Gospel's advance: the work of Stephen, who first made articulate (in his speech, ch.**7**) the worldwide scope of the message; the actual Gentile message (in ch.**13**), with its antecedents in the conversion of the Ethiopian (ch.**8**); the conversion of Saul (ch.**9**), and the conversion of Cornelius (ch.**10**); and the work of Paul, whose missionary task is implicit in his conversion-call (**9**.15).

(*b*) Another purpose is that which is stated by the author at the frontispiece of his book (**1**.1-4). In both his gospel and the Acts, Luke proposed to supply for Theophilus an accurate and progressive summary of the origins of the Church and its faith, about which he had already received as an interested enquirer some information. Theophilus is evidently neither a proper name nor a fictitious title (meaning "a man dear to God"), but a roundabout way of addressing a representative member of the intelligent middle-class public at

357

Rome whom Luke wished to win over to a less prejudiced and more favourable opinion of Christianity (so F. F. Bruce).

(c) There is an apologetic intention in this writing which aimed at defending the Christian cause against charges which were popularly brought against it in the latter half of the first century. Luke wants, in this historical narration, to demonstrate that a variety of officials, mainly Roman, bore goodwill to Paul and his friends, and that where they were appealed to and had to settle a dispute between Christians and Jews, there was no substance in the charges levelled at the followers of Jesus. Moreover, Roman military officials show a consistent attitude of interest and sympathy to the Christian message whenever it is presented to them. These factors prove—so Acts demonstrates—that Christianity is politically free from suspicion by the Roman authorities, and this political "innocence" would mean much to a man such as "Theophilus".

Dating. No certainty is possible in arriving at a precise date for the book of Acts, but certain historical factors make it likely that it was first published in the middle of the '60s of the first century. Two events of history in that period are decisively important for the understanding of the Church's life in the world: the persecution of Christians at Rome by Nero (A.D.64), and the outbreak of the Jewish war in A.D.66, which led to the Fall of Jerusalem in A.D.70. The first fact shows that Rome was beginning to be fearful of the Church's influence—a fear enhanced by the overt rebellion of the Jews in Palestine. This would be the opportune time for some statement from a Christian writer that showed that believers in Jesus, unlike the Jews, were not disloyal to the empire. The Acts provides just such a clear statement.

The omission of Paul's martyrdom in A.D.66-68 may be taken to indicate that Luke did not know of it when he wrote; and this may fix the date of the book as *after* A.D.64 and *before* A.D.66-68.

Writer. Early Church tradition associates the author of both gospel and Acts with Luke, the doctor of Colossians 4.14, and the "companion of Paul" (Irenaeus). The attestation which couples Luke's name with the book of Acts is both early (the first mention is given in the anti-Marcionite prologue to the third gospel, c.A.D.160-180) and widespread (including the Church Fathers from Irenaeus to Jerome).

The evidence from the book of Acts itself amply endorses this tradition, and there are clear indications that the author was the same as the man who composed the third gospel and was an associate of Paul.

Historical accuracy. Provided we do not ask from the book what it was never intended to give—*viz.*, a comprehensive and detailed account of the social origins of Christianity, we may have every confidence in the author's painstaking interest in securing a reliable record. Indeed, this is exactly the claim he makes for himself (Lk.**1.**3, R.S.V. marg.); and scholars like E. Meyer, Sir William Ramsay, F. F. Bruce, and E. M. Blaiklock have pointed to Luke's competence and accuracy in correctly reporting the proper official terms by which Roman governmental personnel were known in the first-century world. Thus *proconsul* and *procurator* are carefully distinguished, and this accurate usage suggests that Luke had first-hand knowledge and was concerned to make a careful investigation of his facts.

Helps. There are books on Acts to suit every need and taste. Historical allusions and much background material are given in E. M. Blaiklock's Tyndale Commentary (I.V.F./Eerdmans) and (with more devotional emphasis) William Barclay's *Daily Study Bible.* Larger works are those by F. F. Bruce (New London/International Commentary), and C. S. C. Williams (Black's N. T. Commentaries). An older commentary by J. A. Findlay has been used in our notes, to much profit.

Note. An occasional reference to the "Western text" of Acts in the pages which follow draws attention to this interesting fifth-century Greek manuscript (*Codex Bezae*) which represents the Western tradition. It has a number of unusual additions, some of them highly imaginative and colourful and possibly authentic.

Acts 1. 1—14

Vs. 1–5 connect Luke's account of how the Good News was brought from Jerusalem to Rome with his earlier record of how the Good News began, set out in his Gospel. The climax of that record was Jesus' resurrection and appearance to His apostles (3), followed by a warning and a promise (4, 5). Is this "baptism with the Holy Spirit" the same as that referred to in 1 Cor. **12.** 13—*i.e.*, marking our entry into the fellowship of the Church?

Vs. 6–11: The apostles are still bemuddled over the meaning of the kingdom (3) and the nature of their task (6, 7); and thoughts of an earthly reign fill their minds (see Mark **10.** 35—45). Jesus directs them to their immediate responsibility (8; what is it? Does it fulfil Isa. **43.** 10?). They must leave the future in God's hands, and attend to what He commissions them to be and do. This missionary task depends upon (*i*) the Lord's ascension (John **16.**5—11; Eph. **4.**8—13); (*ii*) the consequent gift and empowering of the Spirit (Acts **2.** 33 makes this clear, doesn't it?); and (*iii*) the sovereign purpose of God for His

Son in His world (Psa. **2**. 6—8)—a purpose to be completed at His return (11).

Vs. 12–14 show how the apostles interpreted the command to wait (4). What was their chief occupation? The upper room, often identified with the scene of the Last Supper, was to be a hallowed spot, and not least because Jesus had bound these men and women together in love and deep friendship. Even a former tax collector and a nationalist Zealot lost their traditional hatred for each other (13, who are they?) *Notes:* V. 4: "while staying with them" is literally "sharing a meal with them"; *cf.* Luke **24**. 41—43; John **21**. 12—14; Acts **10**. 41, one of the many proofs of His true resurrection. V. 8: the ground plan of the entire book. V. 9: the cloud is an O.T. sign of God's presence. He is received into His immediate presence (John **17**. 11, 24). Questions of how far is "up" are beside the point if God is omnipresent. The Ascension is the withdrawal of Jesus from our earth-bound vision, but not from our world (Matt. **28**.20). V. 12: 1000 yards is the extent of such a journey. V. 14: the women are those who were last at the cross (Mark **15**. 40, 47) and first at the tomb (Mark **16**. 1, 2).

Acts 1.15-26

Vs. 15–22 give the substance of Peter's statement, addressed to the first problem which faced the infant community. What anticipations can you find of Peter's leadership, in the Gospels? See Matt. **16**.17-19; Mk. **16**.7. The defection of Judas is described in Matt. **27**. 3-10 and should be read in the light of (*i*) his privileged position (17); (*ii*) the fulfilment of Scripture (16,20, quoting Psa. **69**.25; **109**.8); (*iii*) his infamous (16), yet self-willed treachery (25); (*iv*) the problem of a successor, created by his death (20b). This much is clear, but the character of Judas remains an enigma and a warning to us; and Scripture refuses to satisfy our curiosity as to his motivation, or to resolve the tension between Divine foreknowledge (John **6**.70,71; **13**.18; **17**.12) and human responsibility (Mk. **14**.10; John **13**.27; **19**. 11). See I.V.F. *New Bible Dictionary*, "Judas".

Vs. 23–26. Before the matter of a twelfth apostle is settled, some qualifications of the candidates are mentioned (21, 22). What are they? Two are important: (*i*) they must be well-known members of the apostolic band, associated with them during the ministry of Jesus; (*ii*) they must be witnesses *to* (R.S.V.) His resurrection. Why are these features necessary? *Cf.* Luke **1**.2; 1 Cor. **9**.1. Barsabbas and Matthias are nominated; and after prayer for God's guidance, the latter is chosen by the ancient practice of lot-casting (26). Was this the right method of making a selection? What is the significance of the fact that the use of the lot is never repeated after Pentecost, and that Matthias is never heard of again in Acts?

Notes: V. 17: the terms which Peter uses are intended to show a parallel with the election of Matthias. "Judas was numbered with us": God later added to the eleven (making again twelve of them). Judas was allotted a share in the apostles' ministry: his successor was chosen by lot. V. 25: perhaps the saddest and most revealing verdict on Judas. He "turned aside, to go to his own place"—*i.e.*, the place he had chosen for himself. And God confirmed him in that dreadful choice. "Then I saw that there was a way to Hell even from the gates of Heaven, as well as from the City of Destruction" (Bunyan's *Pilgrim's Progress*).

Acts 2.1-13

Vs. 1–4. Originally a festival marking the beginning of the wheat harvest in ancient Israel (Ex. **34.**22), the feast of Weeks was so called because it fell on the fiftieth day after Passover (see Lev. **23.**15*ff.* for the calculation). Hence the term "Pentecost", which means 'fiftieth' in Greek. It is interesting that the later Jews celebrated the giving of the Law at Sinai at this festival, and thought of the voice of God sounding in every nation under heaven. Is this in the background of vs. 6–8?

The disciples were gathered possibly in the Temple precincts or in the upper room when the promise of **1.**4, 8 was made good. There were two outward manifestations of the Spirit's presence and power (2, 3) —notice the guarded language, half concealing exactly what occurred. But the consequentials were unmistakable in Spirit-inspired utterances (4). Christianity lives by the communication of the truth of God to men by men.

Vs. 5-11. What was it that arrested attention among the motley crowd assembled in Jerusalem for the feast? Was it the universality of the Christians' message, each man hearing a language he could understand, although the hearers came from many parts of the ancient world of the Jewish dispersion and the speakers were Galileans who were noted for their guttural accent (Mark **14.**70)? If so, Pentecost witnesses the reversal of Babel (Gen. **11.**1-9). Otherwise, was it the remarkable speech of the disciples which expressed with rapture "the mighty works of God" (11)? This Pentecostal *glossolalia* is apparently different from the spiritual gift in 1 Corinthians **14** (which is to be used in private and public worship, and with caution and restraint).

361

Acts 2.14-28

Vs. 14-21. The secret of early Christian testimony to "the mighty works of God" (11) is the Spirit, giving them an exuberance and confidence which was mistaken for drunkenness (13; *cf.* Eph. **5**.18). And the Holy Spirit's presence and power are traced to the fulfilment of O.T. prophecy (16): "This is that which was spoken by the prophet Joel". This citation from the O.T. underlines a number of basic apostolic convictions:

(*i*) the Church is living in a new era of God's dealings with men, following directly upon the Cross and triumph of Jesus. These are "the last days" (17: Heb. **1**.1-2 is the best commentary on this phrase); (*ii*) the work of the Holy Spirit, restricted in the O.T. to special persons, is now enlarged to include *all* believers in Jesus as the Messiah (17,18); (*iii*) the Messianic age is often referred to in Jewish literature as the time of God's "salvation" (21). Peter goes on to declare that that promised time has arrived. The age-to-come has come! See 1 Cor. **10**.11.

Vs. 22-28. Peter goes to the heart of the matter by showing how the life, death, and resurrection of Jesus of Nazareth have inaugurated this new chapter in God's relations with the world. We must mark again some vital emphases of Christian conviction: (*i*) Jesus' ministry was that of 'a Man appointed by God'—*i.e.*, Messianic (22); (*ii*) His death at the hands of the Romans was no accident, but part of God's age-old plan (23); (*iii*) Peter's reference to Psalm **16** (25-28) illustrates again the use of O.T. "testimonies"—*i.e.*, Scripture passages which point to the Age of the Messiah, now begun. Paul will use the same thought in a later sermon (**13**.33*ff.*)

Notes: V. 15: "third hour" = 9 a.m.; and on that day a fast was observed until mid-morning. V. 17: the promised Spirit comes on all, irrespective of class and sex (Gal. **3**.14,28; 1 Cor. **12**.12,13). V. 21: the key word is "saved", but given here a richer meaning than in Joel **2**.28*ff.* V. 22: a reference to Jesus' Galilean ministry, evidently known in Jerusalem. V. 24: read "snares set by death".

To think over: What criterion decides the literal (27) and non-literal (19,20) fulfilment of prophecy?

Acts 2.29-36

We may take these verses as a single unit. They form the third and concluding part of Peter's Pentecostal address, and follow the earlier pattern—namely, a personal address (14,22) to his hearers (29:

362

"Brethren"); a statement of Christian conviction (29-33); and an
O.T. quotation which buttresses that affirmation (34,35). Note the
extra feature in this final section (36).

The allusion to Psalm 16 is now explained. Though written by
David, it cannot refer only to him because he died (29: note the
sombre finality of "and was buried"—a phrase which belongs also to
the earliest Christian creed of 1 Cor. **15.**3*ff.*). His psalm, however,
expresses the confidence that this will not happen to God's anointed
King, whom David typified. The only possible conclusion, then, is
that David was speaking prophetically of the Messiah (30,31). He
died—but, when men had done their worst, was vindicated by God
in the resurrection.

Three proofs are supplied of the reality of His resurrection here:
(*i*) only a bodily resurrection of Messiah can make sense of prophetic
Scripture: (*ii*) the apostles themselves are living witnesses to His
personal victory over death (see especially the strong statement of
Acts **10.**41 in the light of v.32): and (*iii*) only the exaltation of the
living Christ can satisfactorily explain the phenomena which his
hearers have seen and heard (33). John **14.**16; **16.**7 should now be
read.

The mention of the Lord's exaltation requires justification; and
Peter finds this in Psalm **110.**1. The dialogue is between God (in His
O.T. name, the Lord=Yahweh) and His anointed. David prefigured
the Messiah (so all Jews and Christians believe; 2 Sam. **7.**12-14), but
David never ascended to heaven. He must, therefore, again have
been speaking of the Messiah, "great David's greater Son" (34,35).

The conclusion is irresistible (36). As Jesus of Nazareth alone fulfils
both Psalms, He is the true Messiah Who is now installed in the place
of honour. His Messiahship, once concealed, is now displayed; and
His title to worship, as Lord, is proved (Rom. **1.**3, 4; Phil. **2.**9-11).

Meditation: The head that once was crowned with thorns
Is crowned with glory now.

Acts 2.37-47

Vs. 37-42. On that day about three thousand persons entered the
fellowship of the Church through the gateway of repentance, forgiveness, and faith, expressed outwardly by baptism and inwardly by
the gift of the Holy Spirit (Rom. **8.**16; 1 Cor. **12.**3). St. Augustine, in a
memorable phrase, described this day as the Church's *dies natalis*, or
birthday. Those who were thus introduced to the saving benefits of the
Gospel remained in close association (42). Conversion was for them

no flash in the pan, or ephemeral, emotional upsurge of religious excitement. Having begun the Christian life, they continued—and doubtless made good progress. Which of the Pauline churches does this remind you of? So unlike the Galatian Christians (Gal. **1.6**; **3.**3,4; **5.**7).

Vs. 43-47 are verses which paint a cameo picture of the first Christian fellowship. Note who the leaders were (43). And how the "common life in the body of Christ" was expressed, both in social responsibility (44,45) and spiritual exercises (46). It is a travesty to set these against each other as mutually exclusive. Right at the beginning of the Gospel age, in a Church fellowship which had come straight from the Lord's hands, there was a "holy worldliness" *and* a "sacred worship" in the Temple. Both were important—and still are today! Let us notice too the spirit which prevailed (47a) and the popularity of the young movement (47b), with "a conquering new-born joy" suffusing it all.

Notes: V. 38: baptism "in the Name of Jesus Christ" means a calling on His Name (Acts **22.**16) or, possibly, a claiming of the new believers for Him Who henceforth "possessed" them as their Lord (Acts **10.**48). Faith in Christ is implicit in both meanings, leading to forgiveness and incorporation into the Holy Spirit (1 Cor. **12.**13). V. 39: allusions are made to Isa. **57.**19 and Joel **2.**32 to stress the inclusiveness of the appeal. The Gentiles will eventually be evangelized. V. 42: four aspects of church life are mentioned: "teaching"—a ministry of instruction; "fellowship"—like our church or parochial meeting; "breaking of bread"—a common meal, called later the *agape* (1 Cor. **11.**20,21,33, 34; Jude 12), with which was joined a remembrance of the Lord in His death; "the prayers"—the definite article shows that believers observed the Temple worship. V. 46: the common meal again, practised in the people's homes.

Acts 3.1-10

Acts **2.**43 speaks of the apostles' "wonders and signs", wrought in proof of the divine reality of the Christians' claim to be the people of God. This section gives one illustration of what is meant; and contains a directory of evangelistic "method" which all Christians may profitably study. Luke's purpose, however, in recording the incident, is to indicate the important consequences which followed, leading to a rupture of the Church with Judaism, as Jesus had foreseen (Mark **2.** 21,22).

The scene is laid at the Nicanor gate of the Jerusalem Temple, specially noted for its magnificence. Hence the title, Beautiful Gate. The impotent beggar is a picture of dire need, whose only virtue is an awareness of his sad condition. Peter's response is twofold, in what he said (4,6) and no less important, in what he did (7). The action of the Gospel matches the word of the Gospel; and this is ever the pattern of meaningful evangelism.

The need is met (7) as the Name of Jesus Christ is invoked to release the power which attended His healing ministry in Galilee. So it is seen that the once crucified Jesus is alive, not only as an affirmation of faith or a statement of personal testimony (given in 2.32), but as a dynamic force at work in this world and effective in transforming the lives of those who call upon Him. Similarly, the apostolic message which may have seemed to be so much talk is invested with a new significance. Peter speaks "in the name of Jesus Christ"—and miracles happen. *Cf.* 1 Thess. **1.**5, where the miracle-working accompaniment of Paul's preaching was more in terms of a dedicated group of men than spectacular happenings as in this story. But is the "age of miracles" past?

Notes: V. 1: the Jews observed two hours of daily prayer. The "evening" one was at 3 p.m. V. 2: the Jewish historian Josephus describes this Temple gate as one that "far exceeded in value those gates that were plated with silver and set in gold." V. 6: what could not be bought with money is freely offered. The same phrase in 1 Pet. **1.**18, however, may point to a deeper meaning. Judaism was powerless to meet the beggar's case; the Gospel is able. V. 8: a fulfilment of Isa. **35.**6 and a sign that the Messianic age has arrived, according to Matt. **11.** 4-6. V. 10: there was no mistaking the identity, and so no possibility of explaining away the miracle.

Acts 3.11-16

The sequel to "a notable sign" (4.16) gives Peter a chance to improve the occasion with a speech which, in this passage, explains the reason for this event. Disclaiming all personal kudos (12), he attributes all the glory to God. More specifically, the grounds of the miracle are (*i*) God's purpose in glorifying His servant Jesus (13); (*ii*) the efficacy of Jesus' Name, when invoked by His people and trusted by those in need; and (*iii*) the presence of human faith (16, R.S.V. is certainly helpful here, in what is at best a difficult verse).

This short section is rich in its teaching on God and His purposes in Christ. There is no disparity between God's revelation in both O.T. and N.T. He is still "the God of Abraham, and of Isaac, and of Jacob" to the N.T. writers as to our Lord (Mark 12. 26). The person of Jesus is described in terms of Isaiah's picture of the suffering servant (52.13—53.12), once humiliated but now exalted (Isa. 52.13 in the Greek O.T. uses the same word as v.13). His other titles bear witness to His blameless character, and have parallels in O.T. and in the Inter-Testamental literature which expected a Deliverer for Israel. A more obscure title is "the Author of life" (15) which is found again in Heb. 2.10, which may suggest His eternal existence (as in John 5.26) or His ability to grant eternal life to His people (as in 1 John 5.11,12). Either way it is an expressive term, betraying a high estimate of His person; and in a paradox shows the wonder of His resurrection victory. "You killed Him"—although He was the pioneer of life: "but God brought Him back from death" (15). And He is still at work in healing the lame man.

Notes: V. 11: Solomon's colonnade lay to the east of the outer court, or court of the Gentiles, of the Temple. V. 12: "stare", a different word from that in v.4. V. 13: a liturgical description of God, current in Temple and synagogue worship. Possibly Peter had been reminded of it during the service. V. 13: "Servant", admittedly the Greek word could mean "child" (as R.S.V. marg.), but the reference to Isa. 52—53 seems clear. V. 16: a verse which in its obscurity shows that it is a translation from Peter's original Aramaic language. "Prince of life" in v.15 can equally mean in Aramaic "Prince of salvation", which includes both bodily health and spiritual renewal.

Acts 3.17-26

Peter addresses his Jewish hearers as (*i*) those responsible, through their human leaders, for the Messiah's death (17); and (*ii*) men who could be forgiven, because they acted in ignorance, if they reversed their attitude to Jesus (19), and could be included in the scope of God's saving purpose for Israel (20), declared first to their forefather Abraham (25,26).

Old Testament prophecy is again appealed to in order to show that the Cross was part of a divine plan (18), and also that God's offer in sending Israel's Messiah, likened in v.22 to a second Moses, is not to be trifled with (23). Indeed it is not simply that there are individual prophecies of His coming: the entire fabric of O.T. Scripture is a preparation for the events which have recently taken place, Peter declares (24).

God's redeeming purpose began with Abraham whose family is blessed in succeeding generations (25). Ultimately, as Paul shows in Galatians, this promise will embrace the Gentiles (Gal. 3.6-9,29). But both apostles agree that the offer of Messianic salvation is sent "to the Jew first" (Rom. 1.16: v. 26). This fact stamps all missionary work among the Jewish people with an importance which is unique.

Notes: V. 17: a reference to Luke 23.34 seems intended. Who else "acted ignorantly in unbelief" (1 Tim. 1.13)? Vs. 19,20: "times of refreshing" and the "establishing (of) all that God spoke by the mouth of His holy prophets" go together, and relate to the full joys of the Messianic era, to be consummated at the return of Christ (20). V. 22: John's Gospel enshrines references to this aspect of the Messianic hope, current among the Samaritans who awaited a "restorer" (John 4.19,25,29). V. 26: The verb speaks of Jesus' mission, not His resurrection. He is God's Servant as in Isaiah's prophecy. Just possibly He may be likened to Isaac (25) whose "binding" (Gen. 22) was understood by the Rabbis as atoning for sin.

Questions: In relation to vs. 19,20: (i) Does this section belong particularly to Israel in the future, as in Rom. 11.26-28? (ii) Did Peter expect that His return would occur in the near future, as v. 20 seems to mean? (iii) If "establishing" is translated "restoration" of all things (so R.V.), the thought of cosmic renewal and the renovation of Nature (Rom. 8.18-23; 2 Pet. 3.8-13) may be in mind. Is this the same as Matt. 19.28?

Acts 4.1-12

Such an offer as 3.26 contains seemed too good to be true. It gave the Jews a "second chance" and opened the door to God's Messianic salvation. Many entered in (4). But the Jewish leaders were disturbed (2). Note what it was in the apostles' preaching which upset them most (2). The Athenians found this also hard to accept (17.32); and it is still a rock of offence to modern minds.

The description, "a good deed", is not boastfully made, for Peter's explanation makes it clear that the risen Jesus is the Agent of healing (clearly in v.10). Peter has thrown down the challenge to the Jewish religious leaders in an unmistakable way: Jesus is the Christ, and the Author of Messianic blessedness. The "good time coming", yearned for by prophets and seers, has come in Him. By His death and resurrection God has visited His people with His grace; and has reversed the verdict of those who cried, "Away with Him" (Luke **23**.18), prompted by the evil designs and accusations of their leaders (Mark **15**.11). Peter's vivid illustration of this reversal (11) would not be lost on those who remembered Jesus' own teaching (Mark **12**.10*f.*)

Notes: V. 1: "captain of the temple" means probably a police official in charge of the soldiers who guarded the outer court and prevented Gentiles from crossing into the sacred (inner) enclosure. The Sadducees formed a Jewish party of aristocratic priestly leaders. They held a commanding place in the Temple's hierarchy and also in the governing body of legislature, the Sanhedrin. Conservative in belief, they objected to the doctrine of the resurrection (see Mark **12**.18). Hence their twofold opposition to the apostolic ministry in the Temple courts. V. 6: Annas was in fact the ex-high priest, but he continued to exert a considerable influence through his son-in-law Caiaphas (Luke **3**.2). An important manuscript tradition (the Western text) gives Jonathan for John here. If this is correct, it refers to Jonathan, Annas' son, who succeeded Caiaphas as high priest in A.D.36. Alexander is otherwise unknown to us. V. 7: the two terms "power" (Gk. *dynamis*) and "name" characterize the Church's early days. The apostles were powerful in word and work because they invoked a mighty Name (12: "name" carries its Biblical sense of "revealed character", the person known to others. *Cf.* Ex. **34**.5*ff.*). V. 11: the "stoneship" of Christ derives from Ps. **118**.22 and is found in Rom. **9**.33; Eph. **2**.20; 1 Pet. 2.6,7.

Acts 4.13-22

"Enchanted but not changed" is a title of one of Oswald Chambers' studies, and the same description applies here. The leaders were impressed by the apostles' (*i*) boldness of speech, which they could not explain in view of their lack of Rabbinical training; and (*ii*) likeness to Jesus Himself Who was for them no figure of the past but a personal presence Whose spirit they had caught. He also had no formal Rabbinical education (John **7**.15).

But that was as far as it went. Reduced to silence by the incontrovertible evidence standing by (Luke's gentle irony), yet unwilling to accept the logical consequence of the miracle and its significance (16) they rather tamely tried to quash the whole matter by muzzling the apostles (18). Men with a crusading and missionary zeal like Peter's and John's will never go meekly home and forget all about it! So they press home the unwelcome logic of vs. 19,20. And further threats do not move them, either (21).

Notes: V. 13: the Greek word means "forthright public speech"; for such a gift Paul prayed in Col. **4.**3,4 and Eph. **6.**19,20. Many a Christian preacher may very well emulate this, especially when the temptation to compromise or water-down the truth of God is strong. Commentators draw the parallel with Mark **14.**67. "A servant-maid of Caiaphas recognizes Peter has been with Jesus because of his over-wrought condition; her master comes to the same conclusion for a precisely opposite reason" (Findlay). V. 16: the miracle was common knowledge in the city and no-one could deny it. At a deeper level, the failure of the authorities to challenge the apostles' preaching of Jesus' bodily resurrection is of tremendous interest. "The silence of the Jews is as significant as the speech of the Christians." Why did they not produce the remains of His buried corpse, and silence the apostles for ever? The alleged mythical origins of Christianity as a slowly growing legend, wrapt in obscurity, and a hole-in-the-corner affair are frankly incredible. See Acts **26.**26; 2 Peter **1.**16. V. 17: how did Luke know what the Council said? The answer may lie in Acts **6.**7; or **26.**10; or through Gamaliel to Saul of Tarsus, **22.**3. V. 19: "listen to" has the common O.T. meaning of "obey" (see Deut. **6.**4). Socrates gave an almost identical reply to his accusers. The freedom of the conscience is a foundation-stone of all morality. The tragedy is that over-zealous religious folk often deny it to those from whom they differ. V. 22: his age shows that he was a responsible witness (*cf.* John 9.21).

Acts 4.23-31

The Church which meets us in the pages of the N.T. is a worshipping and witnessing community of believing men and women. The passage in these verses gives a notable example of corporate prayer, offered by the church as it welcomed back the apostles from their interrogation by the Jewish Council (23). The same verb, translated "reported", is found at **14.**27 at the close of the first missionary journey. What was the church's reaction then?

Three thoughts are suggested by the record of this earnest petition: (*i*) its Scriptural language (24-26) both in the invocation of God as Creator of the world and (therefore) in control of human destiny, and in the citation of Psalm **2**. The fulfilment of this ancient text is seen in the recent events which had brought Jesus to His cross (27), and incidentally stirred up the hostility of the authorities to the first preaching of the message. Yet Christians took comfort from the fact that all these events were under Divine control (28). There may be incidents in the Church's struggle and hardships; but there are no accidents. Rom. **8.**28 is still the great sheet-anchor of faith.

(*ii*) The specific request which the Church voiced (29,30) is related to the need of the hour. Some people find difficulty in justifying this type of prayer by suggesting that God is not interested in our trivial needs. Paul, however, found no such objection: see Phil. **4.**6.

(*iii*) A spectacular consequence followed (31) as the Hearer of prayer answered the need with the Holy Spirit's presence and strengthening power. The very thing they asked for (29) God gave— as Jesus had promised (John **14.**13,14).

Notes: V. 23: Christian footsteps knew the way back to their friends. V. 24: to the R.S.V. refs. add Neh. **9.**6; Isa. **42.**5; Jer. **32.**17 (especially). V. 25: Psalm **2** was one of the Messianic passages in current use (especially Ps. **2.**7). It is quoted again at the Lord's baptism (Mark **1.**11) in conjunction with Isa. **42.**1—a "servant" passage. Vs. 27,30 also connect Jesus with the Servant of God. His "Christhood" (27: "thou didst anoint") is that of God's obedient Servant and royal Son, destined to have universal dominion.

Acts 4.32-37

This is another summary of what life was like for the earliest Christian company. Body, mind, and spirit were involved. For the first, there was a pooling of material resources. Was this a good thing, do you suppose, involving as it did the liquidation of capital assets (34,37)? And was it the cause of the poverty of the Jerusalem church in later years (Acts **11.**29: 2 Cor. **8.**9)? Luke is content simply to report the facts as a proof of Christian concern for the well-being of all, at least for the immediate future, and as a lesson in generosity.

The unanimity of the church is marvellously portrayed in the words "of one heart and soul" (32), fulfilling Jer. **32.**39. And this oneness of mind is the more striking in view of the growth of the church. The term "company" is literally "the multitude" (R.V.), an evidence of the rapid expansion of the Gospel's influence.

On a spiritual level, v. 33 testifies to the effectiveness of their ministry. Note again the central doctrine in the preaching and witnessing. Is it prominent in the Church's proclamation today?

Joseph or Barnabas, a Levite from Cyprus is picked out for special mention. He is related to John Mark (Col. **4**.10); and Acts **12**.12 may indicate the family connection in Jerusalem where he owned some land. He sold this estate, and turning the asset into money, brought the purchase-price as a gift to the common fund. By this introduction the way is prepared for the later part which he will play in the missionary outreach of the Church (Acts **9**.27; **13**.2).

Looking back over this section, we may ask one or two questions, to which no settled answer is possible, but which provoke our thinking. Was it an expectation of the Lord's near return which motivated the selling of land and houses—and perhaps therefore the teaching to the Thessalonians (2 Thess. **2**.2; **3**.6-13; 1 Thess. **5**.1*ff*.) was a needed corrective? What were the specific aids to Christian unity which these believers used? Fellowship in prayer and service; an agreed gospel message and apostolic teaching; a common meal, at which their unity was symbolically expressed (1 Cor. **10**.17)? *How* did the apostles give their testimony (33)?

Notes: V. 36: Barnabas' name means strictly speaking "son of Nebo" = son of the prophet. The Greek term for "prophecy", however, includes encouragement (1 Cor. **14**.3).

Acts 5.1-11

Just as the idyllic setting of the first man was destroyed by sin's presence, and its effect in Cain's crime, so the fair beauty of the church's life was spoiled by unworthy members. Their sin lay not in keeping back part of their proceeds (as v.4 makes clear), but in trying to deceive others (and God!) that they were in fact more generous than they were. They pretended to give all—the full price of their property—but they had kept back a portion for their own use (2, 8). Their sin was one of vain pretension and hypocrisy; their unholy motive was discerned by Peter (4) whose stern verdict (4b) had a startling effect (5). Peter is no less severe with Sapphira, although he does give her a chance to confess and put things right (8).

"To our minds the whole tone of the story seems un-Christian." So one commentator passes his judgment of this passage, while others find it "frankly repulsive". How would you justify Peter's severe actions? Indeed, how would any of us escape, if our hidden motives and secret sins were laid bare and openly punished (Psalm **130**.3)?

Certain features should be kept in mind in interpreting this passage: (*i*) peculiar significance attaches to this sin because it is the *first* recorded offence in the "new creation"; (*ii*) these early days of Church history were charged with a vivid awareness of God's presence.

Ananias and Sapphira really *believed* what Peter said; and reaped an immediate harvest of their deed (Gal. **6.**7); (*iii*) Paul's teaching is that there is something worse than physical death which may be a chastening experience to bring the soul to its true repentance (1 Cor. **5.**5; **11.** 30-32; 1 Tim. **1.**20); (*iv*) Church discipline meant far more in the early Church than it does to us today. It may be significant that the word "church" occurs for the first time in Acts at verse 11.

Notes: V. 3: this explains the gravity of Ananias' act (*cf.* 4, 9). V. 6: these young men may have been public buriers (like undertakers' assistants today). *Cf.* Ezek. **39.** 12-16.

Acts 5.12-21a

Vs. 12-16. God accredited the apostles as His true servants by accompanying gifts of power and healing miracles. Paul later claimed the same credentials (Rom. **15.**19; 2 Cor. **12.**12). Some suggest that these miraculous powers served a limited function (*i.e.*, to accredit the apostolic Gospel) and were then withdrawn, as B. B. Warfield taught. For others, they are an available accompaniment of the Gospel preaching in every age.

V. 13 is a puzzle, as it stands; and it is not easy to connect the popularity of the young movement with the statement that "none of the rest dared join them." The last verb may carry the sense, "meddle, interfere"; and some scholars wish, with a slight alteration, to read "Levites" for "the rest": "but no one of the Levites dared to interfere with them" by preventing them from holding their meetings in the Temple courts. But the text may mean simply that, in spite of the believers' popularity with the people, those who were attracted to them hesitated to join them because of the judgment-power on insincere motives and hidden sins (exemplified in the case of Ananias and Sapphira). But it must be conceded that verse 14 hardly reads as a natural sequel to this thought.

Vs. 17-21 report another outburst of opposition from official Jewry. The Sadducees (as at **4.**1,2) are again the active fomenters of trouble. Why was it that this Jewish party was stirred to hostility?

Notes: V. 12: see **3.**11 for this part of the Temple: a spot hallowed by Jesus' earlier ministry (John **10.**23). V. 14: *cf.* **2.**47. V. 15: "pallets", like the one used in the story of Mark **2.**4*ff.* V. 15: Peter's healing shadow is not a piece of superstition or magic. Luke doesn't actually say that the apostle's shadow healed, but that the people associated with it the presence of a man of God and, therefore, God's presence.

Cf. **19**.12. V. 17: the phrase sums up the composition (along with the Pharisees, in verse 34) of the Sanhedrin, the Jewish legislature. V. 19: angelic deliverance of this sort will be more fully described in **12**.7*ff.* Paul, too, was released from prison in remarkable circumstances (**16**.25*ff.*). V. 20: "life" and "salvation" both translate the same Aramaic word.

To think over: Do we remember in prayer enough those imprisoned contemporary Christian leaders for whom there is no supernatural release?

Acts 5.21b-32

Vs. 21b-26. The Sanhedrin had evidently expected a full arraignment of the apostles, and a summons to bring them out for trial was issued (21). To the dismay of their foes and captors, the apostles had disappeared and could not be traced anywhere—until it became all too apparent that they had not fled into safe hiding, nor slunk away in abject fear, but were to be found and heard in a public place (25). There is gentle irony here, as Luke records the reactions of those concerned.

Vs. 27-32 give both the command to desist from preaching and the reply that Peter's conscience found this injunction intolerable. The accusation which the high priest makes reminds us of what the Jews said in Matt. **27**.25, and shows how widespread the Gospel's influence was spreading, much to the consternation of the Jewish leaders who saw their own place being undermined. We may recall a similar fear about the effect of Jesus' ministry (John **11**.48).

The brave response of Peter, again spokesman for the rest, in the face of such a threat, is quite in character—that is, in line with the new Peter, who has shed his pre-Easter cowardice and has received a baptism of the Spirit's courage and strength. He repeats his earlier affirmation of loyalty to God (**4**.19); and proceeds to give the urgent reason why his voice cannot be silenced.

The story of Jesus is told again in its impressive simplicity: "God sent Him to Israel as their Messiah; the Jewish leaders rejected Him and engineered His crucifixion; God stepped in, and reversed this judgment of condemnation by raising Him from the dead and installing Him as a life-giving Saviour; we are the eyewitnesses of these facts under the guidance and empowering of the Holy Spirit." How succinct and compelling is this statement! Note the effect it had.

Notes: V. 21b: the "and" explains what follows. Translate "the Council, that is, all the senate." V. 28: the high priest refrains from

373

saying Whose name it is. V. 30: "raised" refers to the sending of Jesus to Israel (as in 3.26); the resurrection is mentioned in the next verse. "A tree"=the cross of Calvary is meant, but the implication is clear. Jesus died under a curse (Deut. 21.22,23; Gal. 3.13) voluntarily assumed for the sake of sinners, as Peter was later to teach (1 Pet. 2.24). V. 31: see on 3.15. *Cf.* Luke 24.47*f.* which includes the note of witness (in 32). The apostles were fulfilling their commission to the letter.

Acts 5.33-42

At Pentecost the reaction to Peter's Gospel call was penitent acceptance; here it is enraged hatred and refusal. The Gospel is ever a divider of men (see 2 Cor. 2.14-16).

The intervention and speech of Gamaliel offers an interesting sidelight. Its first effect was to save the apostles from their fate (33). Gamaliel was a Pharisaic member of the Council, and greatly esteemed. He belonged to the liberal wing of his party, as a disciple of Rabbi Hillel; and was the teacher of Saul of Tarsus (22.3), who quite probably supplied Luke with the information here recorded.

His policy speech is typically Pharisaic in temper and content. It picks up the leading point in their theology—that God rules the world by a wise providence which is over all. "Everything is in the hand of heaven, except the fear of heaven," the Rabbis taught. That is, all is under divine control, but man is required to obey God and leave the issues with Him.

Two notable uprisings had already proved abortive, Gamaliel reminded them. Let the new movement work itself out; if it is not of God, it is bound to fail, as did the Messianic rebellions of Theudas and Judas the Galilean. If God is really in it, no human opposition can break it. Is this really a valid argument (*i*) to test early Christianity; (*ii*) to test later movements in the history of the Church?

Notes: V. 36: there was a rebel named Theudas whose disaffection against Rome was crushed in A.D. 44-46, according to Josephus. But this is an impossible identification, for at the time of Gamaliel's speech it had not happened. The name Theudas was common, and it is likely that an earlier (pre-A.D. 6, when Judas of Galilee was defeated, v. 37) uprising is referred to. V. 37: the census in this verse occurred in A.D.6-7, but is not the one mentioned in Luke 2.2, which was before 4 B.C. V. 38: the counsel is "wait and see", but at least one of Gamaliel's students was not willing to accept this restraint. See 8.3.

V. 41: "the name", almost a substitute word for their Christian principles and faith, as in 3 John 7.

To think over: (*i*) *"The same sun which softens wax hardens clay"—is this an adequate explanation of the difference referred to in the first paragraph of this comment?* (*ii*) *How may we know where loyalty to civil and religious authority ceases in obedience to a higher allegiance? See Rom.* **13.***1f.; 1 Pet.* **2.***12-17.*

Acts 6.1-7

Today's verses sketch the background to an important innovation in the early Church. Within the Jerusalem community where (*i*) a pooling of material resources was practised (**2.**44*f.*; **4.**34*f.*) and (*ii*) the influx of new converts was a notable feature (**5.**14; **6.**7), dissension arose over precisely these two developments, as v. 1 makes plain. The church, moreover, was divided on a cultural and linguistic basis, one side holding fast to its Palestinian tradition and speaking Aramaic, the other side being more open to the influences of Greek culture and using that language. Hence the two terms, "Hebrews" and "Hellenists". In later years this difference of emphasis hardened into clear opposition. The Hebrew Christians were fearful that a denial of the Law would lead to a relaxed morality; the more liberal Hellenistic Jewish believers saw the opportunities for missionary expansion, and under Stephen and Paul caught the vision of a worldwide Christian Church, reaching out to all nations.

The matter of the allotment of funds to necessitous widows was immediately attended to by the apostles. They gave the Hellenists a share in the administration, for, to judge from their names (5), all seven men belonged to that wing of the fellowship. They were commissioned with the full blessing of the Twelve (6).

A further note is added to call attention to the ongoing life of the Church, and its influence among even the priestly families in Jerusalem. There have been recent attempts to define more closely the identity of these priests (in the light of the Dead Sea scrolls and the Epistle to the Hebrews), but they are all speculative.

Notes: V. 2: the duties of the seven men are given as "serving tables". This is usually taken to mean some financial work in connection with the common fund. But it may be that they were to have responsibility for the *agape*-meal (see note on **2.**46) or love-feast, which also meant the task of sharing out the food to the poor (1). Of the seven in verse 5, two are more renowned for their preaching ministry. Which two? Notice the exemplary spiritual qualification needed. V. 5: all have

Greek-sounding names; one of them was not a born Jew, namely Nicolaus, a proselyte=a convert to Judaism. V. 6: the people chose and appointed the men, often called "deacons" (in view of the description in 1 Tim. 3.8-13); the apostles confirmed the choice by a solemn rite of ordination, after the Jewish pattern of "setting apart".

Acts 6.8—7.1

The most prominent member of the "seven" who were appointed to represent the Hellenists was Stephen. He is a key-figure in early Christian history, chiefly because of the powerful grasp that he had of the universal character of the Gospel which went beyond all national and racial boundaries. For that reason, his speech is reported in detail.

In these verses Stephen is introduced. His personal "charm" (8) and effective ministry (8) are mentioned. He stood in a true apostolic succession (*cf.* the wording here with **5.12**). His opponents, drawn from a synagogue which called itself "a meeting-place for Freedmen" and who represented Hellenistic Jews from the world of the Dispersion, challenged him to debate. When they failed to answer him by fair means, they resorted to foul (11,12). The indictment was the same as that which was brought against Jesus: a remarkable fact, and one further proof of the continuity of the witness against Judaism, begun by the Lord and maintained by His servants who had grasped the inner meaning of His mission (Mark **2.21,22**).

But false witnesses sometimes correctly hint at the truth. It is quite likely that he had spoken out against the sacrificial system, the venerable place of the Temple and the final authority of the Law—to judge from his later speech in chapter **7**. He certainly made it clear that God's ultimate word was to be found in Jesus, not Moses (14). And that was a blasphemous remark in any Jew's ears (11).

Notes: V. 8: "grace" in Luke can often mean "graciousness" (Luke **4.**22). V. 9: the place names indicate the original homes of men who had either received their civil freedom and citizenship or inherited it from their fathers. Saul of Tarsus is a notable instance of such a case (**22.**28), and it is tempting to find his presence in this dispute in view of the reference to Cilicia (see **21.**39) and his later appearance at Stephen's martyrdom (**7.**58; **8.**1). V. 10: *cf.* Luke **21.**15. V. 11: Moses came to stand for all that was holiest and most valued in Rabbinic religion. Hence to deny him was to strike at the divine authority and validity of the entire Jewish system. This was a radical attack on

Judaism, which the earlier apostles had not made (*cf.* Peter's observance of the Temple worship). V. 14: Stephen had evidently perceived the inner significance of the Lord's promise (in John **2.**19-21), and the thought of a new temple (Eph. **2.**20*f.*; 1 Pet. **2.**5). V. 15: his face, no less than Moses' (Ex. **34.**29*f.*), shone with a heavenly glow.

Acts 7.2-29

What Stephen said to the Jewish council is sometimes called his defence (*i.e.*, an answer to the legal charges brought against him); but it is clearly more of an *apology*—that is, a statement of the teaching which had led to his arrest and prosecution. And as his doctrine touched the vital questions of Judaism's validity and his own "blasphemy" against God, his address turns out to be an *apologia* for his own life.

There are three chief ideas which his lengthy re-telling of the Old Testament story is designed to emphasize: (*i*) the Jewish people, throughout their long history, have been inveterately rebellious against God and His accredited messengers; (*ii*) God does not live in, nor does He desire, a material and fixed shrine. His presence is not confined to sacred sites, but accompanies His people, who are to be always a "pilgrim Church" on earth; and (*iii*) as a subsidiary theme, the Jewish people have not only rebelled against God and their leaders, they have consistently rejected the saviours whom God sent to them—the outstanding proof of this trait is to be seen in their recent rejection of their Messiah.

In Egypt Joseph was God's answer to the threat of patriarchal extinction; but he suffered much indignity at the hands of his brothers (9). Moses, too, in a later period appeared as a heaven-sent deliverer, but he met opposition and misunderstanding (23*ff.*).

So far Stephen has been patiently laying the foundations of his argument. Later, he will draw some unwelcome conclusions, as far as his hearers are involved.

Notes: V. 2: the call to Abraham, given in verse 3, is placed *before* his removal to Haran. Gen. **11.**31*ff.* give it *after* his arrival there; but Gen. **15.**7 shows that God was responsible for his leaving Ur, and this implies some communication with the patriarch. V. 4: see note in the I.V.F. *New Bible Commentary* on Gen. **11.**26—**12.**5. V. 6: "aliens"— "a theme throughout the speech" (F. F. Bruce). *Cf.* Heb. **11.**8-16. V. 14: the Hebrew text of Gen. **46.**27; Ex. **1.**5; Deut. **10.**22 gives the number as seventy; but the Septuagint reads seventy-five. V. 20: an addition to the Old Testament account found in Philo. V. 22: again, extra-biblical sources (Josephus, Philo) comment on the wisdom and accomplishments of Moses in Egypt. Stephen shows acquaintance with these traditions.

Acts 7.30-53

Stephen's recital of Israel's history continues. The purpose of the long paragraph on Moses' call by God and his unique place as both deliverer (30-36) and lawgiver (37,38) is simply to show that Moses, of all Israel's national figures, enjoyed divine appointment and authority. But, in spite of these clear signs of attestation from God, he met with opposition and disbelief. Notice the asides which Stephen cleverly inserts: (25,35,39).

As a further indication of the failure of the Jewish nation, even when blessed with such an outstanding man of God as Moses, is given in the positive act of idolatry and apostasy which they committed (40,41,53). It was bad enough that they rebelled against Moses; it was far worse that they lapsed into flagrant idol worship and astrology (42).

At the same time as they practised a heathen worship, they imagined that God could be localized in a man-made shrine (built by Solomon, 47), and, further, they contrived to placate God by a multitude of sacrifices. Both these errors indicate bad religion, as the eighth-century prophets in Israel were quick to expose. But this prophetic protest went unheeded.

Stephen found the same hard core of resistance in his hearers; and his impassioned peroration (51-53) drove home the personal application in the light of the ample evidence. What precise points in his speech made them so angry (54)?

Notes: V. 34: with God's summons to send him to Pharaoh, Moses is thus uniquely qualified (35); and his later exploits demonstrated his authority from God (36). V. 37: see **3.22**. V. 39: Stephen indicts the *motive* which inspired the worship of the golden calf. V. 42: *cf.* Rom. **1.24,26,28** for this fearful sentence. Vs. 42 and 43 are quoted from a Greek translation, of Amos **5.25***ff.* This explains the difference in wording from our English version. V. 44: God's intention is expressed in the making of a mobile tent (suitable for a pilgrim people); the permanent structure of Solomon's temple was a second-best, for reasons given in Isa. **66.1***f.* V. 51: as the unfaithful Jews did, according to Isa. **63.10**. V. 52: *cf.* Matt. **23. 29-37**. "The Righteous One" is a name for the Messiah (**3.14**).

Acts 7.54—8.1a

A colourless neutrality was impossible in view of the forthright declarations in Stephen's speech. The violent language of verse 54 makes it clear that he had touched his hearers on a tender spot; and they reacted by cutting short his sermon in an outburst of rage.

Note the one final "blasphemy"—from their point of view—which called forth the murderous spite of verses 57 and 58.

Stephen died, like his Master, with a prayer of committal and forgiveness on his lips (Luke 23.34,46). His death was probably more a lynching than a judicial execution for blasphemy; there was no trial, and Jewish law had an elaborate arrangement to safeguard the guilty person, accused of blasphemy and therefore condemned to death by stoning, if he should recant or if a witness for the defence should suddenly appear on the scene. Then the stoning must be stopped. It seems clear that no such precautions were made for Stephen's benefit; and he fell victim to the mob violence of an uncontrolled crowd. The most impressionable person in this sordid scene seems to have been Saul, who both looked after the witnesses' clothes—these witnesses for the prosecution were to carry out the sentence, according to Lev. 24.14; Deut. 17.7 (*cf.* John 8.7)—and, by his complicity, agreed with the rough "justice" meted out. He never forgot this awful sight (Acts 22.20), and his personal involvement in such violence (1 Tim. 1.13). Yet this martyrdom may have been the turning-point in his life, as Augustine believed: "If Stephen had not prayed, the Church would not have had Saul".

Notes: V. 55: Stephen's vision is full of meaning, and gives the key to his whole thought. He sees the exalted Jesus as victorious Son of Man, destined like the celestial Figure of Daniel 7.13*ff.* to possess world-dominion, and worthy of worship. Here is the clear statement of Stephen's Christology: he "saw that the Messiah was on the throne of the Universe" (W. Manson), and so by implication the Head of a worldwide Church. His characteristic name for Jesus is "Lord", which has the same implication, and he calls upon Him in prayer (so confessing His place within the God-head). Vs. 59, 60: the links with Luke's Passion story are important. He has captured the spirit of the dying Jesus, Who rises to greet the first Christian martyr. Contrast 2 Chron. 24.22.

Acts 8.1b-8

As a direct consequence of Stephen's speech and its sequel, an anti-

Christian outbreak scattered the Jerusalem Church. Why were the aposiles exempt from this (1c)?

Some slight relief comes in the record of the kindly action of some Jews (or Jewish-Christians, 2) who buried Stephen, thus showing their abhorrence of this deed. By stark contrast, Saul felt no such regret—or, if he did, he silenced the voice of conscience by redoubling his efforts against the Church (3).

Vs. 4-8 take the reader into Samaria, the scene of Christian activity under the ministry of Philip, one of the "seven" (6.5). Again it is the Hellenistic-Christian representative who blazes a trail of evangelism outside Judea, and it is a further step in the onward and outward march of Christ's kingdom, according to the programme of 1.8.

"A city of Samaria" was probably Gitta, where, according to an early Christian (Justin Martyr, who was a native of Samaria), Simon Magus (9) was born. Some features of evangelism in such a situation are recorded: the proclamation of the message which centred in the Messiah (5); the evidential accompaniment of signs (6,7) both in exorcism of foul spirits and in bodily healings—note that these two aspects seem to be distinguished; and an upsurge of spiritual "joy", as a direct gift of the Holy Spirit according to Rom. 14.17; 15.13; Gal. 5.22. *Consider how far these features are to be expected today in the Church's evangelistic work? Are they in fact found in your church?*

Notes: V. 1: persecution leads to further expansion on the principle that (*i*) "the blood of the martyrs is seed" (Tertullian); and (*ii*) dispersed Christians share their faith over a wider area. The Greek verb in v. 4 is the farmer's word for sowing seed across a field. Collect some of the N.T. passages on the theme of sowing and reaping, like Mark 4; 2 Cor. 9.6-15; Gal. 6.7-10; 2 Tim. 2.6. V. 2: "devout men" is a term usually associated with Jews (as 2.5; Luke 2.25), but occasionally it is used of Jewish-Christians (22.12). V. 3: "laid waste", lit. "ravage"—or even "savage"—the lexicon gives it in regard to a wild beast's tearing at a carcase. There are four references in the epistles to Saul's persecuting zeal. Can you discover them? One is given in yesterday's portion.

Acts 8.9-24

Vs. 9-13 concentrate on one special case among the multitudes (6) who showed interest in Philip's preaching and healing. Simon had already acquired a reputation before Philip appeared (10,11), and quite likely saw his popularity about to wane and his livelihood to be in danger by his competitor's success. He therefore suggested an alliance, and feigned belief (12,13; but v. 21 is clear on his motive) even to the extent of openly identifying himself with the Christian cause.

Vs. 14-24 show how Simon fared when the apostles came to visit Samaria. Note the purpose of their coming. And what followed in regard to those Samaritans who had professed faith in Christ. Were they believers *before* Peter and John laid hands on them?

The clash between Peter and Simon well illustrates the spiritual gift of percipience which the apostle had (see 5.3,4). Simon betrays his secret motive in a request for the Holy Spirit's power as though it were like a piece of magic (19). He wanted the power to enhance his own reputation as a wonder-worker. Peter tartly refuses, and speaks right to the point (20-23). Verse 23 means in modern language: "I see you are still an unconverted reprobate" (J. A. Findlay)—so much for his earlier profession of belief and his acceptance of baptism! Simon's reaction is vague (24), but probably it means a weak plea to escape punishment, like King Saul's (1 Sam. 24.16; 26.21).

Notes: V. 9: Simon the magician plays an important role in early Christian literature as the father of heresy. V. 10: means that he regarded himself as the unique agent of "the supreme God" (probably a syncretistic name for God in some Oriental-Greek religions). V. 13: was he sincere, or (as suggested above) a charlatan? Lucian was later to write about such bogus "believers" who traded upon simple Christians and made an easy living that way. V. 14: John had been to Samaria before (*cf.* Luke 9.54). V. 15: for other sequences of believing, baptizing and receiving the Spirit, see Acts 10.44*ff.*; 19.5*f.*; Eph. 1.13. V.16: "it"—R.S.V. needs correction here. The Holy Spirit is a Person. V. 17: this has been called a Samaritan "Pentecost" (by G. W. H. Lampe), and apostolic authorization is thus given to a new phase of the Church's outreach as "a new nucleus of the missionary Church has been established" (Lampe).

Questions: Did Simon receive the laying on of hands (17, 18)—or was his "wickedness" (22) detected before that? What is today's counterpart to Peter's gift of discernment (1 John 4.1-6)?

Acts 8.25-40

The Church's leaders leave Samaria (25) once their mission is achieved. Philip, however, received a direct summons to keep a lonely rendezvous on the Gaza road (26). The other party in the interview was a well-connected courtier, an official in the service of the Candace (a hereditary title borne by Ethiopean queens; "Ethiopia" = Nubia). At Jerusalem where, probably as a "God-fearer" (see comment on 10.2f.), he had worshipped Israel's God, he had also acquired a scroll of the book of Isaiah in Greek. The ensuing conversation proceeds by the method of question and answer. Note the three queries which the Ethiopian expresses (31,34,36). The evangelist's answers are straightforward and of immediate help (a lesson here for all Christian counsellors today). Philip becomes the interpreter of Scripture, the evangelist with a single text (35), and the baptizer of a new convert (38).

The Spirit of God Who first directed Philip's footsteps (26: here called "an angel of the Lord") and gave him accurate guidance to the place of human need (29) now separates the two men (39). Why?

Notes: V. 26: "desert" may refer to Gaza, in which case the road ran from Jerusalem to Old Gaza, destroyed by Alexander the Great in 332 B.C. and in ruins at that time. V. 27: Ethiopia is not the modern Abyssinia, but North Sudan. Vs. 32, 33: a citation from the Suffering Servant poems in Isaiah, interpreted by Philip as fulfilled in Jesus' life and death, following the example of Jesus' own application of these passages to His ministry (*e.g.*, Mark 10.45). V.35: "opened his mouth" —rabbinical idiom for a lecture on Scripture. V. 36: some instruction on faith and baptism is clearly implied, leading to the eunuch's request. V. 37 is relegated to the R.S.V. margin as an addition of the Western text. It represents, however, an early baptismal procedure of interrogation and response of faith. Notice the "creed" which the eunuch confessed. V. 39: the same Western text adds a reference to the Holy Spirit's coming on the new believer. V. 40: in a walking trance, Philip came to himself at Azotus—was it a spiritual elation which upheld him?

Meditation: Consider Philip as "the evangelist" (21.8).

Acts 9.1-9

Saul of Tarsus,. briefly introduced at 7.58, now re-appears in what is a turning-point in the narrative of Acts. Indeed, what this section describes is the turning-point in the life of this man, destined to become the dominant character in the remainder of Luke's history as the divinely-chosen apostle to the Gentiles (Gal. 1.16). The Lord's intention in 9.15 is the key to what is written in today's portion. And it is indisputable that "What happened on the Damascus road is the most important event in the history of Christianity from Pentecost to our own day" (F. F. Bruce).

The right of extradition was given to the high priest by the Roman authorities; and Saul had already shown promise as an able persecutor of the Christians (8.3).

The encounter with the living Christ is told with a simplicity and naturalness of any reported conversation (4-6); but the circumstances of both the vision and the voice are altogether remarkable. Which Old Testament prophet(s) received a heavenly summons by what they saw of God's glory and what they heard from the heavenly throne?

The "light from heaven" (3) outshone the noon sun (22.6; 26.13) and is a frequent Old Testament symbol of the divine presence. The voice (4) has a counterpart in the Rabbinic *bath qol* (lit., the daughter of a voice) by which when God speaks in heaven an echo of His voice is heard on earth. The supernaturalness of what Saul saw and heard is clear. His companions were arrested (7), but only Saul was able to understand the *meaning* of what the voice said (v. 7 is expanded in 22.9) and Whom the vision represented. Moreover, only he was affected by the excess of light (22.11).

Not much was revealed at that time to the future apostle (6); but he was "a new man in Christ" (2 Cor. 5.17) from that moment. In that brief encounter his past life flashed before him—a thought he could never efface (1 Tim. 1.12-14); and his terrible crime of wounding the Christ in His people appeared in a heinous light—which again he always remembered (1 Cor. 8.12). Above all, this was his moment with the living Lord who called him by name (John 10.3,14) and was answered "Lord, what wilt Thou have me to do?" (Verse 6 in A.V. which translates an inferior text, but the thought is found in 22.10).

Acts 9.10-19

Everything we learn about Ananias, the Jewish-Christian disciple (22.12), is commendable and edifying. He is human enough to express incredulity that such a notorious arch-enemy as Saul should have been converted (13,14), but believing enough to go without hesitation and fear (17) upon the Lord's errand, and charitable enough to greet his former persecutor as "Brother Saul", a word which would have stuck in the throat of any lesser man than Ananias. Ananias goes down in history as the first Christian influence on a newly-awakened Saul, by what he said (17) and what he did (12,18; 22.14-16)—the first in a

383

line of men and women to whom Paul later paid tribute as his predecessors in the faith (Rom. **16.**7). The formative influences we receive in the first days of our Christian life greatly influence our subsequent future. Hence the exacting role of Ananias which he performed admirably. Two visions, one conveying instructions to Ananias of what he was to do, and the other making known to the blinded Saul the person he was to expect, brought the two men together. Moreover, Saul would be recognized by what he was doing in Judas' house. Note what it was (11).

Saul's future destiny is carefully described in v. 15, which strikes the notes which the later record will amplify: he will fulfil a ministry, like that of Isaiah's elect Servant, and bring the news of salvation to the Gentiles (**13.**47, quoting Isa. **49.**6), but the price to be paid will be costly (16). Col. **1.**24 and his ultimate martyrdom (2 Tim. **4.**6 looks forward to this) tell us something of that cost.

Notes: V. 12: the "laying on of hands" was a Jewish rite with many meanings. Here the sense is one of solemn ordination or setting apart for God's service (as Jewish rabbis were ordained). The gift of the Holy Spirit (17) is associated with this commissioning, but the Head of the Church alone can impart this, as **26.**16 and Eph. **4.**7 make clear. In any case Ananias was no priest! He seems to have administered the baptism (**22.**16).

Acts 9.19-25

Vs. 19b-25 show how seriously Paul took his new vocation as a man "saved to serve". Mark the word "immediately" (20). Where does the record of Gal. **1.**15*ff.* fit in to this period? The answer is supplied in 2 Cor. **11.**32. See below.

The preaching of the Christian apostle is set in the synagogue, which may be a little surprising. Yet Saul was a Jewish rabbi, albeit now converted to the Messiah, and entitled to address the assembled congregation at their worship. Saul's first opportunities came in this way, during his first missionary tour (**13.**14*ff.*). The rift came at **18.**4-7. Some idea of what Saul said in these messages is given in verses 20, 22: Jesus as Son of God (in the sense of Psalm **2.**7; the enthroned Messianic King, and Rom. **1.**3,4: a pre-Pauline confessional formula) and the true Messiah of Israel Who fulfilled the prophecies.

Vs. 23-25 describe the first of the many hazards to which his life was exposed. Perhaps we should insert before these verses a departure for "Arabia", inhabited by the Nabatean Arabs. Their leader was Aretas, who heard something of his ministry in his kingdom as Saul preached to the Nabateans (Gal. **1**.17). When he returned to Damascus, Aretas' ethnarch was instructed to seize him with the help of evilly-disposed Jews in the city (23). But Saul too had his helpers, called "his disciples", since his powers of leadership were already being felt, who assisted his escape through a hole in the city wall (2 Cor. **11**.33).

Notes: V. 21: titles for early Christian believers are interesting. Those "who called on this Name" (*cf.* 14) means men and women devoted to the worship and service of Jesus as their God. The exact expression comes from the Old Testament—*e.g.*, Genesis **21**.33—and lasted on into the Pauline church vocabulary (1 Cor. **1**.2). The title "saints" (**9**.13), meaning "dedicated to God's service", is mainly employed in describing the Jerusalem community (Rom. **15**.26).
To ponder: "Are you a converted Jew?" a Hebrew-Christian was once asked. "No," he replied, "I am a completed Jew." So Saul preached.

Acts 9.26-31

Vs. 26-30. This short paragraph is full of men and movement. Saul, the Jerusalem disciples and their leaders, the apostles, Barnabas and Hellenistic Jews are mentioned; and from the parallel account in Galatians **1**.18-24 we can identify the apostles as Peter, and James the Lord's brother.

Saul removes from Damascus to Jerusalem (26) where he meets a natural suspicion on the part of those who only recently had cause to fear his bitter persecution (**8**.3; **9**.21). How could they trust his motives? He finds an advocate in Barnabas (27), who disarms all criticism on the score that (*i*) Saul had met the risen Lord Who spoke to him—observe the naturalness of this conversion-description; and (*ii*) he had "won his spurs" in his bold witnessing for Christ at Damascus. Saul could never turn back now.

His further movements at Jerusalem are recorded. "The words 'coming in and going out' at Jerusalem do not mean that he visited places outside the city, but that he moved about freely and fearlessly in and out of houses in the city" (McNeile-Williams); and continued an intrepid ministry of forthright proclamation. His approach to the Greek-speaking Jews, however, met with some opposition. Like Stephen before him, he found himself embroiled in religious contro-versy (the bitterest sort of controversy!) (V. 29: "disputed" is the same verb as in **6**.9). Not for the first time (**9**.23), his life was threatened. Again, Christian friends came to his aid, and conducted him to

Caesarea, the Mediterranean sea-town. Thence he sailed to his home city of Tarsus in Cilicia (Gal. 1.21). I wonder what his family and their friends would have made of him at this time, as he did according to Mark 5.19.

V. 31. Paul leaves the stage at this point, later to re-enter at **11.25.** Peter comes back into the chief role; and the transition is marked by this summary of the (Palestinian) Church's progress and expanding influence.

Notes: V. 27: the plural "apostles" is not in conflict with the two names of Galatians 1.18*f.*; and "the churches of Judaea which were in Christ" describe (as in 1 Thess. 2.14) Jewish-Christians *outside* the holy city to which at that time Saul was personally unknown. V. 29: Hellenists are Jews of the Greek-speaking world (R.V., Grecian Jews), like Saul himself. (See Acts 6.1 and comment.)

Acts 9.32-43

Saul's conversion and its aftermath has been a significant interlude to Luke's history. Now the historian returns to one of his central themes, namely, to chronicle the progress of the Gospel as it embraced the non-Jewish world. Peter's adventures, continued in chapters **10, 11** and **12,** point forward to the subsequent Gentile mission. Indeed, the rather vague phrase "Peter went here and there among them all" (32) may look back to 8.25, where Peter and his companions are last mentioned.

Bedridden Aeneas may have belonged to the Christian group at Lydda, perhaps formed following the evangelistic work of Philip in **8.40** in those parts. In words which are reminiscent of the healing stories in the gospels (*e.g.,* Mark 2.11) Peter bids the paralyzed man get up and "get yourself something to eat" (34; this translation, preferred by some translators, then re-echoes Mark 5.43). Can we see here an attention to a patient's needs agreeable to the professional interest of Luke "the dear doctor" (Col. 4.14)?

Vs. 36-43. Joppa was originally a Philistine city, and populated in New Testament times by Greeks. Peter's message and ministry are reaching out with a remarkable breadth of sympathy and concern; and we may ponder the fact that he is willing to lodge with Simon, a tanner—*i.e.,* one engaged in a ceremonially unclean and defiling occupation from the Jewish point of view.

Tabitha's name is similar to the call "talitha" (in Mark 5.41) as two forms of the same name, meaning "my gazelle"; but this coincidence is not significant, even though the Lord's raising of Jairus' daughter and Peter's ministrations follow a similar pattern. What points of correspondence can you spot? The disciple has caught his Master's spirit.

Notes: V. 37: washing was a Jewish practice as a rite of purification. V. 39: a touching scene, especially if we give full value to the verb's true meaning: they showed *on themselves* the coats and garments which Dorcas had made—a Petrine memory, passed on to Luke. V. 41: Peter's helping hand is again outstretched (3.7).

Acts 10.1-8

Cornelius's status is referred to in a few verses in this chapter— verses 2,4,22 and 35. What sort of picture can you build up of this man's character from these descriptions?

From a professional standpoint he was a Roman centurion and a Gentile (1), but a Gentile who was attracted to the Jewish faith and way of life, although not a fully committed proselyte. Persuaded by Jewish monotheism (belief in one, righteous God) and morality, he is known by the technical term of "God-fearer" (2), and this for him was no empty profession, as an angel, and his servants, and Peter, all confirm. What an excellent set of character references he had!

Cornelius is chosen for the signal honour of receiving the Gospel and its benefits at the hands of Peter as the latter exercises the "power of the keys". See Matthew **16.**19. He is the first-fruits of the great Roman world to be led to faith in Christ under the apostolic ministry; and his conversion is a notable watershed in the book of Acts, as **11.** 17,18 recognize.

Notes: V. 1: "Italian Cohort"—a company of six hundred men. There is evidence that *Cohors II Italica* was stationed in Syria in A.D. 60-70, and Caesarea was the military headquarters of Roman government in Palestine. V. 2: these are the marks of Jewish piety, characteristic of a "God-fearer" (see too in **13.**16,26; **16.**14; **18.**7). V. 3: at 3 p.m. the vision came, but probably it was too late for the men to set off for Joppa, some thirty miles away, that day. So they left on the next day (9) and arrived at noon. V. 4: almsgiving is likened to a Levitical sacrifice (Lev. **2.**2,9,16; *cf.* Psa. **141.**2: Heb. **13.** 15*f.*; Phil. **4.**18). V. 6: Simon lived by the seaside where (*i*) he used sea-water for his trade, and (*ii*) caused no ceremonial (nor social!) offence to the Jews who abhorred that odorous trade.

387

Question: But His angels here are human,
(*Not*) the shining hosts above.

Which line fits the visitor of verse 3? Verse 20 suggests the second, but verse 30 could be taken in the sense of "angel" = messenger = human agent, sent by God.

Acts 10.9-16

Cornelius' vision at Caesarea has its counterpart in Peter's vision at Joppa to which the messengers have been sent. While they are making the thirty-mile journey Peter is made ready to receive the request they bring by a special revelation in the form of a symbolic vision.

The noon hour (9) probably indicates the second period of prayer in the Jewish habit of prayer three times daily (see Psa. 55.17; Dan. 6.10). The heavenly vision consisted of a large object resembling a sheet (a ship's sail?) let down from above and holding a menagerie of the animal kingdom. The point to notice is that clean and unclean animals, according to the levitical rule (Lev. 11), jostled together indiscriminately; and the divine command of verse 13 makes no discrimination. This accounts for Peter's horrified disavowal (14) and the answer to his objection (15: which verse in the Gospel of Mark does this call to mind? Perhaps Peter is responsible for the editorial note which is what Mark 7.19b really is, as R.S.V. makes clear). Lest he should mistake the meaning or imagine that he was dreaming, the vision is renewed three times (16).

But what is the meaning? Clearly it has to do with the cancellation of the Jewish food-laws which allow some diets and forbid certain others. That in itself was revolutionary enough, as the debate between the Lord and the Pharisees (in Mark 7.1-23) illustrates. But there is a deeper sense which Peter was later to grasp more fully. As a Jew he would at the time of the vision regard the Gentile people as religiously "defiled" (the description in Galatians 2.15 is an apt summary of Jewish mentality and exclusiveness) and so beyond the reach of friendship. And to have a meal with a Gentile would be unthinkable, for meal-time was a solemn and sacred occasion, begun in a prayer of blessing over food and continued by religious conversation. The abolishing of the ancient dietary laws is a token from God that there is no barrier to keep the Jews and Gentiles apart any longer. As Paul put it, the middle wall of partition has been broken down in Christ (Eph. 2.11-18).

Notes: V. 10: literally, "he experienced an ecstasy". V. 11: "four

Photo: Caesarea

Photo: Roman Aqueduct at Caesarea

corners", obviously metaphorical. V. 12: see Gen. **6.20**. V. 14: it is a
foolhardy man who contradicts the Lord. *Do we ever try?*

Acts 10.17-33

Notice that the angelic visitor's message is attributed to the Holy
Spirit (19-20) Who spoke to His servant both in the trance-vision
(10*ff.*) and through the inward monition of his own reflection (17,
"inward perplexity" required Peter to "ponder the vision", 19).

Peter's hospitality—an important virtue in early Christianity—
delayed the departure until the following day (23a).

Vs. 23b-29. The time-notices are not easy to follow; and it is
possible that "the next day" of verse 23 is the same as "the following
day" of verse 24, if the journey of thirty miles took the same time as
that of the early messengers. The Western text in verse 30 reads, "It
is *three* days ago". Otherwise, if we read "four days ago", the reckoning
is inclusive or the return trip for the messengers took longer.

In this way Peter the Christian apostle and Cornelius the Gentile
enquirer were brought together. Why did the latter prostrate himself
and do homage (25)? What steps had he taken to ensure a good
reception of the message from God which Peter was to bring (24,27,
33)? The courtesy and modesty of verse 33 should be particularly
noted. (Are these excellent qualities found in us in our correspondence
and conversation with other believers?) "Did ever a preacher of the
Gospel have a more promising audience than this?" (F. F. Bruce).

Notes: V. 20: the key phrase is "without hesitation" (*cf.* similar
words in v. 29). This is explained by v. 28. Peter as a Jew might well
hesitate before accepting the invitation to visit a Gentile, and object
to eating under his roof. Such an act would lead to a ceremonial
defilement. But the vision of verses 9-16 had changed all this. V. 25:
cf. Rev. **19**.10; **22**.8,9. V. 28: Jewish rules virtually forbade loyal
Jews from accepting Gentile hospitality, chiefly because of the fear that
the food provided might not be *kosher* (*i.e.*, ritually slaughtered,
with the blood drained away) and perhaps harmful, if it had previously been used in idol-worship. 1 Cor. **8** may be compared.

*Question: The whole question of God's revelation to man is involved
here. How does God speak to us today?*

Acts 10.34-48

This memorable sermon is important for a variety of good reasons:
(*i*) it represents the *first* offer of the Gospel to the Gentile world, and

so paves the way for a full-scale Gentile mission; (*ii*) it gives an outline of what the early Christians believed about the significance of Jesus' ministry, death, and triumph. Not by accident, therefore, it contains a ground-plan (in 37-40) of the later Gospel of St. Mark, which Christian tradition has associated with Peter's preaching. "Peter related, Mark wrote" (Jerome); (*iii*) addressed to a Gentile congregation (35), it received the approbation of God in a way which few sermons do. The preacher's voice was silenced by a gracious interposition (44) and a remarkable outpouring of the Holy Spirit (45). The main point to grasp lies in the phrase "even on the Gentiles". In an apt phrase, this has been called the Gentile Pentecost, and shows the fulfilment of what Peter had hinted at in 2.39. Work out the steps by which God prepared the Church for this decisive turning-point.

The structure of the sermon is worthy of close study. Peter begins by declaring that recent events have shown that there is no "most favoured nation" clause in God's covenant with His people. The Old Testament prophets had taught the same, with a doctrine of the remnant (the faithful Israelites within the larger group of the nation) and a universalistic outlook which comprehended the Gentiles within the scope of God's mercy and care. (There is no conflict between Israel's election and God's mercy to the nations; precisely *through* His elect people His love was intended to reach out to the Gentiles. Israel was elect for the sake of mankind.)

The terminal points of Jesus' ministry are John's baptism (37) and the witnesses to the empty tomb (41). He was the Messiah (38), marked out as God's saving Agent in His life, death, and vindication by God. The apostles are the accredited witnesses to all this (39,41), and the commissioned representatives of the Gospel message (42) whose offer fulfils the promise of the Old Testament (43). Turn up *one* Old Testament promise of forgiveness, now made good in the Gospel.

The effect of the preacher's words is notable. Peter compares it to his own experience on the day of Pentecost (47; *cf.* **11.15-17**). These Gentiles gave evidence by the use of "tongues" (46), and received Christian baptism (not administered by Peter, however, 48) as initiation into the visible fellowship of the Church. No mention of circumcision is made.

To think over: Go through Peter's sermon again and compare it with what the Apostles' Creed says of our Lord Jesus Christ.

Acts 11.1-18

The good work of Peter's ministry now comes under fire! Note who its critics are (2). And what charge they bring against him (3).

The apostle's defence occupies the next section, and goes over the same ground as in ch. **10**. Why has Luke taken obvious pains to repeat the details of this incident? Certainly this account, in Peter's own words, has a vividness and colour all its own. Pick out some of the interesting additions and personal turns of phrase which Peter's own account gives: for example, "it came down to me" (5); "looking at it closely" (6); and verse 14. From verse 15a it seems that Peter was only getting started with his sermon when God's intervention took him and his congregation by surprise! Verse 17 implies that the Twelve became full believers and Christians only at Pentecost—*i.e.*, when they grasped the saving significance of the Cross and the risen Lord. The defence concludes on a note which could hardly be controverted. God Himself had borne witness to the rightness of His servant's action (17), and any refusal to accept the response as genuine and in line with His will would be tantamount to opposing Him.

In the face of such irrefutable logic, the Jewish-Christians accepted the conclusion of verse 18. Probably they did this with sincerity, but a more serious and sustained criticism was bound to arise once the evangelization of the Gentiles and their acceptance as church members without circumcision was made the rule rather than the exception. The Judaizers here were prepared to receive Cornelius and his group as an exceptional and isolated case; they were utterly opposed—as later history records—to the Pauline principle of a Church in which *all* distinctions of race were abolished (Gal. **3.27-29**). What is the bearing of all this on the civil rights/colour question in the modern world?

Notes: V. 2: the tenets of this party are given in **15.1**. Hence their name. But at this stage their accusation is that Peter broke the ritual rules and ate with Gentiles. The issue over circumcision came later, and was raised as a bulwark against the prospect of a predominantly Gentile Church once the mission to the Gentiles got under way (**11. 20,21**) so auspiciously. V. 6: adds a fourth group to the list of **10.12**. V. 18: an admission that Peter was right--for the moment.

Acts 11.19-30

This is a short section, but packed with dynamite. It carries forward to the next crucial stage the widening expansion of the Church's out-reach. At Antioch an unprecedented step was taken (20). Members of Stephen's school, who had caught and preserved his spirit and who represented the wide sympathies of Hellenistic Judaism, began an evangelistic approach to rank outsiders. Cornelius had been a God-fearer (*i.e.*, interested in the Jewish faith) before his conversion; the Greeks whom these men appealed to were completely untouched by Jewish influences. Yet they made a dramatic response to the proc-lamation of Jesus as Lord (21). Consider the significance of this title at this juncture (*cf.* 1 Cor. **12.**2,3).

The Jerusalem headquarters wanted to keep this movement under surveillance; and Barnabas was sent to Antioch, a city destined to become the springboard for the full-dress mission to the Gentile world (**13.**1).

It is not surprising that this city played such an important role in early Christianity. Situated near the coast of Syria, it was the capital of the Roman province. Its earlier history was shaped by Greek influences, yet it had received a great influx of Jewish popula-tion during the centuries of its life. It was thus the cosmopolitan centre of the Syrian world, a meeting-place of east and west. Greek culture and Jewish faith met and intermingled in a busy commercial emporium, and provided just the right conditions for the rise and growth of a Hellenistic Christian Church (24b).

Vs. 27-30 provide an interlude, chiefly to explain how it was that the churches came to contribute to the relief of the poverty-afflicted mother church in Jerusalem. The famine in Judea is dated by Josephus between A.D.44-48. The missionary apostles of Antioch are dele-gated to bring the gift to Jerusalem (30)—a visit probably to be equated with that of Galatians **2.**1*ff.* if the letter to the Galatians is the first of the Pauline letters to be written.

Notes: V. 19 picks up the reference in **8.**4. The mention of Stephen's name is important in showing a continuance of his posthumous influence. V. 20: "preaching Jesus as Lord" (so Rom. **10.**9). V. 21: "turned to the Lord"—a characteristic description of Gentile conversions (**15.**19; Gal. **4.**9; 1 Thess. **1.**9). V. 23: the Gospel's effect upon human lives was *visible*! V. 26: first mention of "Chris-tians"="partisans of Christ", as pagans viewed them (**26.**28; 1 Pet. **4.**16).

Acts 12.1-11

The next incident of the onward sweep of the Gospel which the

reader expects is the kind of episode which chapter **13** narrates—
namely, the first missionary journey of St. Paul. But one indication
that the events of **11.**22-30 occupied a longer time than the text at
first suggests may be that Luke places next a full account of Peter's
adventures. At all events, our attention is switched from Paul to
Peter.

"Herod the king" (1) is Herod Agrippa I, who found a friend in the
Roman emperor Caligula who gave him the control of territory
which belonged to the former's uncle Philip (Luke **3.**1), adding to it
the district of Abilene governed by Lysanias. In A.D.37 Herod received
the kingdom, and thereafter acquired the domain of Herod Antipas,
the territories of Galilee and Perea. In A.D.41 he received the control
of Judea; and this is the period indicated by the chronological note of
verse 1: "about that time".

Two Christian leaders fell foul of Herod's violent pogrom. James
was killed (fulfilling Mark **10.**39), Peter was arrested with a view to a
later execution after the seven-day period of the Passover festival (3).
Herod's malevolent design is darkly hinted in verses 4 and 6, where
"to bring him out" implies an intended execution.

Peter's case seemed to be hopeless (notice the emphasis on "prison",
"soldiers", "chains", "sentries" guarding the door in verses 4-6). But
the Christians' secret weapon was being silently and secretly forged.
What was it (5)?

Deliverance came in the form of a supernaturally-timed visitor's
arrival (7). No barred doors prevented his entry; no guard impeded
him and the bewildered Peter as they threaded their way through the
gaol (10); no key was needed to open the last gate to freedom (10b).

Notes: V. 3: Passover lasted from Nisan 14 to Nisan 21 (Ex. **12.**18).
Luke uses the term Passover (4) for the entire festival season, as in his
gospel (**22.**1,7). V. 5: "earnest prayer"—this description is found
in Luke **22.**44, *lit.*, "in a stretched-out manner". Prayer meant hard
work for these devoted believers (Col. **4.**12). V. 7: "angel" and "messenger" are the same Greek term. Whichever translation is preferred,
the deliverance was miraculous at every point.

Acts 12.12-17

The bewilderment of Peter was quickly dispelled as he came to himself (11) and took stock of his position (12: the same verb for his
awareness is used again at **14.**6). The address he sought out is evidently
(as a fourth-century tradition confirms) the place where the Last

Supper was held and the gift of the Spirit was awaited (1.13,14); and this was the scene of the church at prayer (5).

Some life-like touches make this one of the most gripping narratives in the New Testament. Each subsequent action is true to experience; the recognition of his Galilean accent; the disbelief with which her announcement was greeted; the attempt at rationalization ("it can't be Peter himself; it must be his guardian angel, impersonating his voice", 15); and at length, as he kept on knocking, the decision to find out who it was by the simplest method—to open the gate! Then Peter came in, and with a characteristic gesture of the hand damped down the hubbub of excitement. ("If only you'll be quiet, I'll explain and tell you all about it".) What followed was a thrilling testimony to the Lord's grace and power—and an indirect rebuke to those who had met for specific prayer (5) and who wouldn't believe that the answer they sought was to be found outside the door, waiting to come in. The epistle of James has something to say on this topic (1.6-8).

Peter then departed for "another place", but no one knows exactly where. He is back in Jerusalem at chapter 15, but at that time James, the Lord's brother, holds a commanding position in the church there. Perhaps he had filled the gap of leadership when Peter was in prison. Hence verse 17b.

Notes: V. 12: John Mark is the author of the gospel which bears his name and is the man of Col. 4.10; Philem. 24; 2 Tim. 4.11; 1 Pet. 5.13 as well as Acts 13.5. V. 15: the idea of a guardian angel is found in Matt. 18.10; Heb. 1.14, and goes back to Gen. 48.16. V. 17: no mention of the other apostles. They had left Jerusalem, as is possibly implied in 11.30.
Questions: (i) What problems of providence does this chapter raise? James is killed, but Peter survives by a miracle. Can we say why? Should we try? (ii) What lessons in prayer may we learn from this story?

Acts 12.18-25

Not unnaturally there was an immediate sequel to the news of Peter's escape from prison. His guards suffered as a result of Herod's displeasure (19). But Herod himself was soon to meet a fateful end; verses 20-23 are a piece of secular history which is also recorded by Josephus in *Antiquities*, Book 19. Both accounts agree that he suffered a divine sentence of judgment on the score of his pride. In fact, both records are complementary, and throw light on each other.

It appears that the "appointed day" in Caesarea on which the people of Tyre and Sidon were to make a representation to the king

(20,21) was a festival in honour of the emperor, possibly the emperor's birthday (August 1). Both historians describe how Herod was greeted as a god (22), and Josephus adds: "He did not rebuke them, nor did he repudiate their impious flattery". His story goes on: he saw an owl, which he recognized as a messenger of evil tidings, and a pang of grief pierced his heart. Luke attributes this to a divine action (23), and his terrifying phrase, "he was eaten by worms and died", corresponds to the description which Josephus gives of violent abdominal pains which led to his eventual death five days later. The date is about A.D.44.

By vivid contrast "the word of God grew and multiplied" (24)—a reminder that earthly tyrants come and go, but even their cruel animosity is powerless to arrest the onward progress of the cause of God and His Church. In the bitter days of Julian the apostate, a scoffer asked a Christian, "What is your Carpenter doing now?" His quiet reply was: "Making a coffin for your emperor".

V. 25 poses a difficulty; the R.S.V. and R.S.V. margin giving two different versions of the direction in which Barnabas and Saul moved. As the story left them last at Jerusalem (11.30), the R.S.V. reads more naturally, but it translates a corrected text. As a third possibility the phrase "at Jerusalem" might be taken with what follows rather than with what precedes. Translate, then: "Barnabas and Saul returned (to Antioch), having completed their task in Jerusalem".
Meditation: Philippians 1.28,29.

Acts 13.1-12

The N.E.B. heads this chapter and new section: *The Church Breaks Barriers*. This is an accurate summary of the new phase of missionary activity begun by the Church at Antioch.

Vs. 1-3 describe how the new impetus was given. Note what the Church's preoccupation was when the Spirit's summons came (2) and why these two men were chosen. How were they commissioned (3)?

The first missionary tour is then detailed. From Seleucia, the port of Antioch, they came to Salamis, the chief town of Cyprus. Christian witness was made in the Jewish synagogues, mainly (so we may judge from verse 15) by seizing the opportunity which came to give a sermon to the assembled congregation in each place. *Cf.* Luke 4.15-30. John (Mark's) assistance suggests that he was a catechetical teacher, engaged in follow-up work (5).

Paul's First Missionary Journey

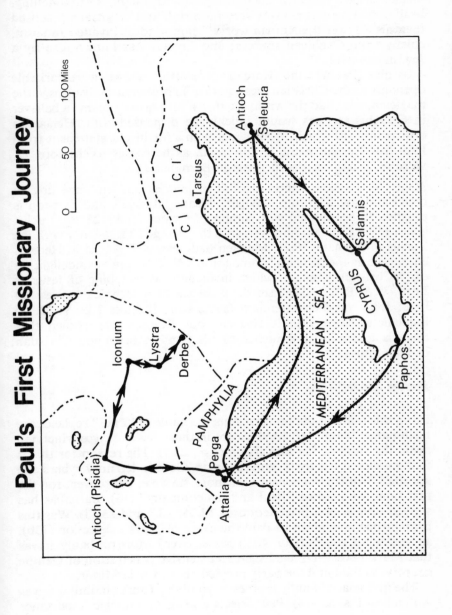

The encounter with Elymas at Paphos is a reminder that the Gospel of Christ had many rivals in the ancient religious world. The lure of magic—which included such things as astrology, fortune-telling, healing and exorcism—was very powerful, and magicians practised their art all over the Roman world. Magical ideas invaded Judaism, chiefly from Chaldean sources; and Elymas was known also by a Jewish name (6).

Sergius Paulus, the Roman proconsul, shows a remarkable openness to the Christian message (7). This obviously displeased the magician, who had the wit to see that if his master became a believer in God his services would quickly be dispensed with. Hence his obstruction (8) which, in turn, met with a forthright statement from Paul (his Roman name is now used, as he comes to the fore, *cf.* verse 13, and takes precedence over Barnabas).

Notes: V. 1: these names are full of interest and embrace diverse racial and social groups. "Niger" means "darkie", and Symeon is possibly to be equated with Simon of Cyrene (Luke 23.26). Lucius is not to be equated, however, with the evangelist Luke, nor with the Lucius of Romans 16.21. Manaen had been well placed in Herod's entourage as the prince's "companion". V. 2: a precious sidelight on early Christian worship, which included a worshipping of Jesus as Lord. V. 5: R.S.V. disguises the presence of a technical expression here: John was their attendant (same word in Luke 1.2). V. 12: no immediate conversion is explicit, but Ramsay has shown that there is inscriptional evidence of his family's becoming Christian in later times.

Acts 13.13-41

From this point in the book of Acts the name of "Paul" replaces the birth name "Saul" (*cf.* 13.9) except in those few passages which tell again the story of his conversion (*e.g.*, 22.7). The reason for this is that missionary activity moved on to Gentile territory where the apostle's Roman *cognomen* was more suitable. Moreover, for the first time, we read of "Paul and his company" (13). Barnabas has slipped into second place (contrast 12.25; 13.2 and 13.43). Was this prominence now given to Paul the cause of Mark's defection (13b), as he saw his cousin (Col. 4.10) passed over? More probably, it was that Mark never envisaged such an extensive penetration of Gentile country, as Paul and the party pressed on into Asia Minor.

The first goal of Paul's journey beyond the Taurus mountains was Antioch in Pisidia (14). Paul selects a place of strategic importance as a centre and base of apostolic ministry—Pisidian Antioch was a Roman colony. He makes full use of the synagogue as a sounding-board from which his message may go out.

Jewish worship gave opportunity for any qualified visitor to expound the Scriptures in the form of a "homily". Hence the invitation of verse 15. The apostle's sermon is an appeal to God's revelation under the old covenant. "The law and the prophets" (15; Rom. 3.21) were his source of authority—at least as a preparation for, and witness to, the coming Christ of God. In this sermon his chief point rests with David (22), who prefigures his greater Son, Israel's Messiah (23).

The Gospel facts (27-32) cover the same details which are given in Peter's earlier addresses (2.22ff.; 3.13.f; 10.37-41), and the prophecies of Psalms 2 and 16 are again laid under tribute (33,35). Two prophecies are new. Which?

At the heart of his message lies the characteristic Pauline emphasis on (i) the resurrection of Jesus as God's vindication of Him, and (ii) the provision of righteousness by faith, which meets the demands of the Law. Verses 30 and 39 are pivotal; and *Romans* is the later elaboration of these vital themes.

Notes: V. 21: King Saul doesn't often figure in O.T. testimonies to Jesus. Did the speaker have a personal interest, coming from the same tribe (Phil. 3.5)? V. 26: an appeal to born Jews and "God-fearers". V. 32: a favourite Pauline expression (Rom. 1.16; 1 Cor. 9.16).
To ponder: Neglect of spiritual truth is not always due to ignorance. Sometimes we can know it too well (27).

Acts 13.42-52

"Good news" (32) is meant to be shared. Many Jews and proselytes were won over and were encouraged to persevere (43). To judge from the next paragraph, they came back the next week with a great crowd of interested Gentiles (44,45). Did Paul see in this sequence a divine confirmation that this was Israel's destiny and mission—to be a light for the Gentiles (47)? National Israel—the Jewish people of old, represented in their synagogue officers of verse 45—had failed to seize this opportunity; the task therefore fell to the Christian apostles to accept the vocation of the servant and as "elect for the sake of mankind" to reach out to the distant peoples. So "we turn to the Gentiles" (46). This solemn announcement sounded the death-knell of Jewish exclusiveness and selfish particularism which said,

"What we have as a special privilege we want to keep to ourselves". It equally proved to be a manifesto and charter of Christian liberty and a promise of a worldwide Church. No longer could the Christian movement be thought of as a sect within Judaism—whatever misunderstanding their enemies might have; Acts 24.5 shows that this is what the Jews would like to have believed about the Church—but, having burst the cocoon, the missionary Church showed itself to be no inert chrysalis, but a living creature, ready to fly to earth's extremities with a message and a ministry to all (47). Small wonder that the Gentiles, regarded by official Judaism as beyond the pale and hopeless (Eph. 2.1-3 picks up this sorry plight, but doesn't stop there), were overjoyed to receive the news of their salvation through Israel's Saviour.

Notes: V. 43: these converts are the God-fearers of v. 26 (see comment on 10.2). V. 43: a follow-up ministry is intended, as at 11.23. V. 46: "necessary" because of a priority stated in 3.26; Rom. 1.16; 11.11*ff.*, which Paul adhered to. But he refused to stay with obdurate Israel; he moved on to attend, in his own apostolic labours, to Israel's mission to the nations in the light of (*i*) his own call as apostle to the Gentiles (22.21), and (*ii*) the Servant prophecy of Isaiah 49.6, with its primary application to Jesus but carried on by His people. V. 51: a symbolic action for a decisive break with human indifference (Mark 6.11).

Acts 14.1-7

From Antioch the apostles moved on to Iconium, now called Konia, and a junction of several routes. Commentators draw attention to the Greek phrase (in v. 1) rendered "together". This should be translated "in the same way" with a backward glance at the apostolic procedure at Antioch. There the two apostles used the Jewish synagogue as a springboard for their evangelism; so too, in like manner, in spite of the declaration of 13.46, they began their work at Iconium by visiting the Jewish assembly. A tiny word in verse 1, translated "so", speaks volumes of the way they conducted themselves. Their manner of life had a powerful effect in conjunction with the truth of their words.

Opposition also was encountered (2). Who were the "devil's advocates"? Which church in Asia Minor at a later time met this animosity from the Jews? (See Rev. 2.8-11; and note the martyrdom of Polycarp which tells of Jewish opposition and evil designs in fomenting trouble for the Christians in the same place.) And in which other city did Paul feel encouraged to stay on because there was opposition to the work of the Gospel (as vs. 3, 4 imply)? (See **18.**6-11; 1 Cor. **16.**8).

A critical point was evidently reached when Paul learned of a concerted effort put in hand to attack him and his company (5,6). Then the principle of Matthew **10.**23 was invoked; and they took refuge in Lystra and Derbe, where fresh scope for evangelization was given (7).

Notes: V. 2: this disaffection was possibly caused by Jews who came on to Iconium from Antioch. Paul ignored their hostility (3), but felt it wise to move on when the local Gentile inhabitants seemed adamant in their resistance, even to the point of mob-violence (as verse 5 implies). V. 6: Lystra and Derbe, with the Phrygian city of Iconium, most probably (on Sir William Ramsay's view) represent the churches of Galatia to which the epistle of that name was written.
Study: Pick out some verses from Galatians which speak of the founding of the church in the teeth of hardship and opposition (e.g., Gal. 3.4) and with accompanying "signs and wonders" (e.g., Gal. 3.5).

Acts 14.8-18

Both parts of Paul's ministry at Lystra are full of interest. His action in healing the crippled man recalls Peter's work at the Temple gate (3.1—10). Both apostles evidently had a presence which commanded attention and drew out the earnest hopes of the needy invalids they encountered (note the double reference to intense longing—3.5 and **14.**9–which was matched by a direct look from the apostles).

The behaviour of the crowd (11-13) was typical of the people of Lycaonia whose district, so tradition reported, had once upon a time been favoured by a visit from Zeus (the king of the Greek gods) and Hermes (his messenger). Recent archaeological finds in that area of Asia Minor have shown that the cults of Zeus and Hermes flourished in the third century A.D. and go back earlier. In fact, the priests of Zeus (*cf.* v. 13) are referred to in the inscription unearthed by W. M. Calder of Manchester in 1922.

The second point of interest in Paul's speech (15-18). This brief and impromptu statement is the first opportunity Paul had to address a Gentile audience; and it is important to observe the features of the Christian message which it highlights. It cannot be complete in itself and was probably never finished, for Paul had still to mention the distinctive elements, such as the Cross and resurrection of Jesus, when he was stopped (18). The verses, therefore, contain a preamble to the Gospel, and lay the foundation for it in a concise summary of "natural theology". What are the chief points which he makes (15-17)?

Notes: V. 9: how could this man's "faith to be made well" be evident to Paul? Was it a look in his eyes or any expression on his face? V. 11: the statement is at first not understood by Paul and Barnabas because of its strange language which they did not know; only when the Lystrans began to give them divine honours (13) did they realize the purport of it all. Hence their horrified rejection of what the people intended to do (14). V. 14: a sign of mourning: here it is expressive of disgust that the Lystrans should have regarded them as gods come to earth. Such actions were idolatry (15; 1 Thess. 1.9), which is inexcusable in view of God's creatorship (15), past forbearance (16), and general revelation in Nature (Rom. 1.19-23).

Further Study: Continue a comparison between Paul's experience with these people in Galatia and the letter he later wrote to them. For instance, see Galatians 4.14 (in the light of the name of Hermes given to him); 1.6; 3.1 (the Galatians' fickleness); 6.17 (cf. verse 19).

Acts 14.19-28

Experiences at Lystra left a permanent mark on Paul's mind (2 Tim. 3.11)—and his body, if Galatians 6.17 is interpreted as the scars of his suffering in missionary service. Not for the last time did he face imminent death (19,20); and this successful attempt at rescue, as the disciples formed a ring around him, permitted him to escape, and, undeterred, to press on to the next town, Derbe.

Preaching and making disciples go hand in hand, according to the missionary manifesto of Matt. 28.19, Mark 16.15 (A.V.). The divine order and intention is that converts should become disciples. So it happened at Derbe (21).

"Tribulations" sounds an ominous note for the Church in every age and place; and there is no legitimate short-cut to avoid such a

Notes: V. 19: Paul's stoning is part of his apostolic hardships recorded in 2 Corinthians 11.25. Note the sudden change in the Galatians—from enthusiastic hero-worship to a bitter attack on Paul's person. V. 22: a pastoral follow-up is indicated in the verbs (cf. 18.23 and 11.23; destiny. "Suffering, then, is the badge of the true Christian . . . Luther reckoned suffering among the marks of the true Church, and one of the memoranda drawn up in preparation for the Augsburg Confession similarly defines the Church as the community of those "who are persecuted and martyred for the Gospel's sake" ... "Discipleship means allegiance to the suffering Christ (Bonhoeffer).

Further pastoral provision was made in the appointment of a simple church leadership (23). What was the prime responsibility of these "elders" (see 20.28; Titus 1.5-9; 1 Tim. 3.1-7)?

Vs. 24-28 complete the story of the missionary circuit. Paul and his party return to the place from which they were valedicted (26). 13.43). The key-verb is "must"—not an optional vocation which may be bypassed. Similarly, 2 Tim. 2.3; 3.12; Rev. 7.14. V. 23: "elders" represent an oversight of the local congregation, as at Ephesus (Acts 20.17) and Philippi (Phil. 1.1). Other functions are given in Romans 12.8; 1 Thessalonians 5.12; Hebrews 13.17. V. 27: indeed an "open door" (Rev. 3.8). Where else did Paul use this metaphor for a ready scope for the Gospel? *To think over: Look back over Paul's provision for the new converts—in verses 22 and 23. Are we sufficiently attentive to such needs?*

Acts 15.1-5

The immediate occasion of the Council was the success which attended Paul's missionary journey. Jews and Jewish proselytes had been won, but, more significantly, the Gospel had made a noticeable inroad into pagan territory and (chiefly in Galatia) a ready welcome to the message had been received. So much so that Paul had introduced a rudimentary church organization for the maintaining of congregational life and growth (14.22,23). News of this had reached the Jerusalem church, where alarm was felt. Why?

The "dissension and debate" centred on the admissibility of Gentile believers to the Church. Cornelius was clearly a special case, and at all events, he was half-way to becoming a Jew before his conversion to Christ. The issue was whether Gentile converts were to be welcomed *en masse* the moment they were converted—or to be gradually introduced to full Christian standing by receiving the imposition of certain Jewish rites and rituals. Note the chief qualification which the strict Jewish Christians were insisting upon (1).

The danger of a divided Church, split into two factions and with two headquarters, at Jerusalem and at Antioch, was present. So to settle the question (2) a consultation was arranged. Clearly Paul and Barnabas stood for a liberal attitude, which Paul strenuously argues for in his Galatian epistle; while at the opposite end of the scale, a rigid policy of turning Gentile converts into good Jews before according them a full Christian status was adopted. *Who were the spokesmen for this line* (5)?

Notes: V. 2: the precise relation between this visit and an earlier one (11.30) in the light of Galatians 2.1-10 is much canvassed. The simplest solution is that the Galatians 2 visit is the same as that of 11.30, and that the letter to the Galatians was written *before* this council in A.D. 49. This explains why there is no reference to the decree in Galatians. It is less easy to account for its omission from 1 Corinthians. Probably Paul accepted it in principle, but based his appeal to the Corinthians on other grounds (1 Cor. **8**; *cf.* Rom. **14.1—15.6**). V. 3: Paul evidently enlisted much sympathy, including Luke's. V. 5: this restriction was intolerable, and a betrayal of the Gospel of God's free grace, according to Paul's (earlier) letter to Galatia. Why?

Acts 15.6-12

Much debate evidently led nowhere (7); and Peter's statement was intended to cut through the knot by an assertion that the grace of the Lord Jesus was the sole requirement for salvation (11).

His rehearsal of God's dealings with him served to underscore the important points of conviction: (*i*) God Himself had taken the initiative in the choosing and calling of Cornelius (7); (*ii*) the proof of His pleasure was the giving of the Holy Spirit in the same way and on the same basis as the blessing of Pentecost which inaugurated the Christian era (8, 9); (*iii*) as there was no distinction in the gift of Messianic grace, there must be no "extra" necessity which would obscure the gracious way in which God chooses to act (9, 11); and (*iv*) in any case, to insist on a Jewish prescription is an invitation to bondage from which Christ has set us free (10). Which verse in *Galatians*, with its ringing tones of freedom in Christ, does this echo?

Peter had profited from the rebuke administered by Paul at Antioch (Gal. 2.11-21). At that earlier time he had vacillated by, at first, welcoming the Gentiles as brothers and sharers in a common table; but later, when put under pressure, he had "played the Pharisee" (Gal. **2.12a**) by a deliberate withdrawal and refusal to share fellowship. Note his motivation then (Gal. **2.12b**). And its effect on others. What exactly was at stake in Antioch?

Notes: V. 7: "early days"—the Cornelius episode happened some ten years before. The divine "choice" recalls the election of Abraham

(Neh. **9**.7); Cornelius is the firstfruits of a new people of God. V. 9: "cleansed", as in **10**.15; **11**.9. V. 10: "a yoke upon the neck" re-echoes a familiar Jewish phrase ("to take up the yoke of the kingdom of heaven") for accepting the Jewish religion. Peter here reflects the attitude of Galilean Jews to the burdensome regulations of Phari-saism. Jesus too offered release from this heavy "yoke" (Matt. **11**.29, 30; *cf.* Matt. **23**.4; Luke **11**.46). V. 11: a clear statement of free grace, unencumbered by any "works", of which Paul would not have been ashamed.

Meditation: In a day when theological discussion and debate get more and more complicated, let us ponder the apostolic declaration (11) with its note of (i) impressive simplicity—"the grace of the Lord Jesus"; (ii) triumphant certainty—"we believe . . . that we shall be saved"; and (iii) unconfined universality—"we . . . as . . . they".

Acts 15.13-21

It is James'·turn to contribute to the discussion. He expresses cordial acceptance of Peter's statement (14: Symeon is Peter's first name, John **1**.40-42) by discovering a Scriptural precedent for the thought that God intended to include the Gentiles in the assembling of His people. This is part of the missionary message of the Old Testament.

The quotation from Amos **9**.11*f.* is taken from the Greek Old Testament and makes two points: (*i*) the rebuilding of David's dwelling (16 in James's speech) speaks of God's covenant of restora-tion with Israel after the exile. This is now fulfilled in Messiah's coming to His people; (*ii*) verse 17 relates to "the rest of men"—*i.e.*, the Gentiles who are called by God's Name—and the promise is that they too find a place within the fold of God's people. The upshot is the statement of verse 19, which is a clear counter-statement of the Judaizing proposals of verses 1 and 5.

One consideration of a practical nature required some attention, however. Exactly what this is depends upon how we construe verses 20 and 21—the text of the so-called "apostolic decree". In the R.S.V. there are four items of "prohibited practices", all of them having to do with practices which mean much to orthodox Jews—*viz.*, idolatry, immorality, eating meat from animals which had been improperly (by Rabbinic standards) slaughtered—*i.e.*, by being strangled, and from animals which still retained the blood. If these prohibitions were imposed on Gentile believers, the intention will have been to make possible table-fellowship between Jewish and Gentile Christians. If the latter would accept this code, the former would not be scandalized.

The difficulty with this reconstruction is that in Paul's dealings with Gentile churches (at Rome and Corinth) he refuses to legislate in this formal way and leaves the question of "unclean foods" to be settled by considerations of conscience (see I.V.F. *New Bible Dictionary*, "Idols, meat offered to"). The R.S.V. margin, which adopts the "Western text", may, therefore, be preferred. Then, with the omission of a reference to what is strangled, the remaining *three* items may be taken as parts of an ethical code, *viz.*, idolatry, adultery (probably by marriage within the prohibited degrees of Leviticus **18**), and bloodshed (=murder). Paul would have had no scruple about accepting such elementary moral regulations for Gentile believers, whereas his "fight for Galatia", already won, is not likely to have been thrown away by his tamely accepting some ceremonial rules (on the R.S.V. text reading). Therefore we may prefer the R.S.V. margin; and Church practice in the second century confirms this.

Acts 15.22-35

A delegation of four men is appointed to carry this letter containing the terms of the "apostolic decree" from Jerusalem to Antioch. It was at Antioch that Christian fellowship between the two branches of the Church had been disrupted by the arrival of certain Jerusalem teachers (called Judaizers) who, claiming to speak with James's authority, insisted on a separation of Jewish Christians from uncircumcized Gentile believers, and brought pressure to bear upon Peter (Gal. **2.**11*ff*.). It was therefore necessary that (*i*) these Judaizers should be checked (24); (*ii*) Paul and Barnabas who had put matters right at Antioch should be vindicated by the general assembly (25,26); (*iii*) some independent evidence of the assembly's decision should be provided, lest the Antiochians should imagine that Paul was inventing all this. Two impartial witnesses are commended (27); and it was further required that (*iv*) the terms of Christian moral practices should be spelled out clearly, so that the high moral tone of the Church which was quickly becoming the spiritual home of Gentiles who were converted to Christ from a world of licence, immorality, and self-indulgence should be preserved (28,29). The guidance of the Holy Spirit is acknowledged in this epoch-making decision (28).

How was the decree received (31)? Further explanations were given by the two accredited delegates, who had a spiritual gift of prophecy (*cf.* 1 Cor. **14.**3).

Notes: V. 22: Judas Barsabbas—was he brother to Joseph Barsabbas (**1.23**)? Silas (or Silvanus) is first introduced. He played an important part in the Pauline and Petrine correspondence (1 Thess. **1.1**; 2 Thess. **1.1**; 2 Cor. **1.19**; 1 Pet. **5.12**). V. 24: "unsettling your minds"—a military term for plundering a town. V. 26: "risked"—the Greek verb is the same as in Galatians **2.20**; Romans **4.25**; **8.32**. Perhaps we should translate: "men who have dedicated their lives". But the R.S.V. thought recurs in Philippians **2.30**. V. 33: "in peace"=with the good wishes of the congregation, and in prospect of Silas' return to Antioch (40; v. 34 in the margin simply confuses).

Question: "The Acts of the Holy Spirit" is one apt description of this book. Here we see His guidance in the business and decisions of a church assembly (25, 28). How shall we make provision for Him to lead our denominational and united Church conferences today?

Acts 15.36-41

Six verses which offer a fascinating study in early Church personalities!

Paul and Barnabas both agreed that it was opportune to re-visit the churches of Galatia (36); but that was as far as the *entente* went. Both men had different opinions of John Mark, who had accompanied them on the earlier journey, but had retired somewhat unceremoniously (**13.13**) at what proved to be only the outset of the tour. The result was a distressing situation—Luke calls it by a strong name, an altercation (Greek, *paroxysmos*, 39) which could only be settled by the two men going their several ways.

Who was right? Probably both men were right—up to a point. Paul, no mean judge of men, saw that Mark's character at that time was not suited to the strains and stresses of another missionary journey (considering the importance of this venture in the light of the council's ruling and the need to press onwards resolutely into the heart of the Greco-Roman world with the Gospel). Barnabas, on the other hand, was prepared to overlook one lapse in the hope of a stronger character yet to emerge, and perhaps the axiom "blood's thicker than water" controlled his decision to give his relative a second chance.

At all events, two happier notes are struck in the later story. First, by a division of labour, *two* missionary parties set out and so more territory was evangelized. Secondly, "all's well that ends well", and the final chapter in Mark's story is that of a recovery. "Failure is not final" (E. M. Blaiklock)—see 2 Tim. **4.11**, with its glowing tribute to Mark's usefulness at the last; 1 Pet. **5**.13 for Peter's special interest; and, of course, the Gospel of Mark—

> *The saint who first found grace to pen*
> *The Life which was the light of men.*

Notes: Vs. 37,38: the commentators draw attention to a subtle change in the tenses here. Barnabas wanted to decide *to take* (aorist, implying a single action), but Paul foresaw the risk of having *to take* Mark as a continual partner (present tense)— and liable at any moment to desert them. V. 40: Silas was admirably qualified as a Jerusalem Christian and a Roman citizen (**16**.7*ff.*).

To think over: "*An unedifying episode*". *Yes, but are there no redeeming features?*

Acts 16.1-5

Paul received some compensation for the indignity he suffered on his first visit to Lystra (**14**.19,20). At least one convert had gone on in the life of the Spirit—and so was ready for the touch of God upon him. He was Timothy. Notice some points of special commendation: (*i*) his progress since his conversion is perhaps indicated in the name "disciple" (1)—*i.e.*, learner and student in the school of Christ. He had matured to that extent. Who, elsewhere in the New Testament, had failed to grow in the Christian life (Heb. **5**.11-14)? (*ii*) Verse 2 is an important feature to be observed in any young person who feels the call of God to full-time service. Timothy had a good reputation, and was *persona grata* with the leaders of the neighbouring churches. The reason for this character reference is given in 1 Tim. **4**.12. (*iii*) The will of God was made known to Timothy by the agency of Paul, who addressed to him the summons to divine service (3a). The apostle must have been able to perceive in him the makings of a real man of God; and he was not disappointed.

Two subsequent developments confirmed the correctness and wisdom of Paul's choice. First, Paul was able to send Timothy more than once as his personal representative—and almost as an extension of his own personality—to the churches (1 Cor. **4**.17; Phil. **2**.19-24; 1 Thess. **3**.2). And, at the last hour of his life, Paul requested Timothy's presence (2 Tim. **4**.9,21).

The mention of Timothy's circumcision comes as a surprise in view of the apostolic decree (referred to again in verse 4). But there were evidently special circumstances to be respected—*viz.*, Timothy was a half-Jew already (1), and Paul simply "regularized his status"

(F. F. Bruce) in having him circumcized. Besides, the question of salvation was not in view here, as in the Galatian churches at the time of the (earlier) Judaizing controversy. Then, the avoidance of circumcision was a prime requirement (Gal. **5.**2,11). Does 1 Cor. **9.** 19-23 bear upon this distinction?

Notes: V. 1: mixed marriages, then as now, create a problem, and not least for the children. In Jewish eyes Timothy would be regarded as illegitimate—hence Paul's desire to remove the stigma by this minor surgical operation. And this would be important if Timothy's future ministry were to be acceptable to the Jews for whose salvation Paul still yearned (Rom. **9.**3; **10.**1). On Timothy's Jewish ancestry, see 2 Tim. **1.**5.

Questions: Are we (i) as ready as Paul was to encourage young people in the Lord's service? (ii) as alert as Timothy was to respond to His call through older Christians?

Acts 16.6-10

There are some points of particular interest in this passage: (*i*) The ministry of the Holy Spirit is seen here in both restraining (6,7) and constraining the Christian missionaries. The verbs used indicate clearly the Spirit's personality and His intimate association with the person of Jesus (especially verse 7: a unique description, but it is hinted at in John **14.**16). (*ii*) Guidance came in the form of a human voice, heard in Paul's night-time vision. The circumstances of this encounter with the Macedonian "man" whom Sir William Ramsay suggested was Luke himself, and the clear direction given in the call to cross over the Aegean sea, led Paul to the firm conviction that this was the guidance he sought. In fact, he needed such guidance, because the way ahead was blocked. Why? (*iii*) At this point in the narrative the literary form changes, and verse 10 introduces a new, unheard-of feature in Luke's history. Can you spot it?

Few sections of the Bible hold such useful teaching on the theme of guidance. Re-read the passage in the light of the following suggestions: (*i*) We may confidently expect a guided life as the children of God. He will direct us *away* from the second-best, if we are faced with a choice; (*ii*) He may lead us through some fellow-believer, some "man of Macedonia" whose word comes to our prepared and responsive minds; but we must cultivate a sensitivity to *hear*; (*iii*) when circumstances combine to indicate a course of action, we are expected to use a God-given faculty of common sense and perception (10).

Notes: V. 6: the "South Galatian" view interprets this phrase as meaning the region of *Phrygia Galatica,* evangelized by Paul on his earlier journey (**13.14***ff.*) and inhabited by the readers addressed in the epistle to the Galatians. Paul was checked from turning west towards Ephesus (6) and north-eastward into Bithynia (7). V. 9: the first extended "we" section, indicating the presence of Luke. V. 10: the verb normally means "to put together" (*cf.* our colloquial "putting two and two together"—*i.e.,* concluding.)

Acts 16.11-24

Philippi had two claims to fame (12). What were they? A more illustrious and enduring claim was begun on the day of Paul's arrival, for this city was honoured as the first "European" city to hear and to receive the good news of God. Perhaps this thought lies behind Philippians **1.5**; **4.15**. Two notable conversions are described:

(*i*) *Vs. 13-15.* Lydia hailed from Thyatira, a centre of the dyeing trade in Asia Minor. She was evidently on business in Philippi, and had some attachment to the Jewish faith as a God-fearer.

Her conviction illustrates what the theologians call "prevenient grace"—*i.e.,* that God took the initiative, "went before", in her readiness to hear the word by pre-disposing her to give a ready acceptance to the Saviour's call (14b). Notice her confession of faith in baptism and her gracious, if firm, offer of hospitality. Perhaps Paul was unwilling to accept the hospitality, but she had her way (15b) as the first convert in Europe. If Lydia is an example to follow, which other woman of Thyatira gives a warning to avoid (Rev. **2.** 18-20)?

(*ii*) *Vs. 16-24* remind us that the world of Paul's day was peopled by men and women who made a living out of religious humbug and chicanery. The girl fortune-teller found release from her spiritual bondage "in the Name of Jesus Christ" (18). On a quickly-invented charge Paul and Silas fell victim to her masters' annoyance at the loss of their profits, the crowd's venom, and the magistrates' indifference to elementary justice. Even the jailer seemed hostile, as he placed his prisoners' legs in the torturing stocks. But their deliverance—and his too—was shortly to appear!

Notes: V. 12: "a Roman colony"—see Phil. **1.27**; **3.20** for the use Paul makes of this fact. V. 13: a prayer-meeting in the open air. V. 17: the girl perceives that these are "holy men" offering a spiritual message. V. 20: Luke is accurate with his term for the magistrates, *praetores duoviri.*

Paul's Second Missionary Journey

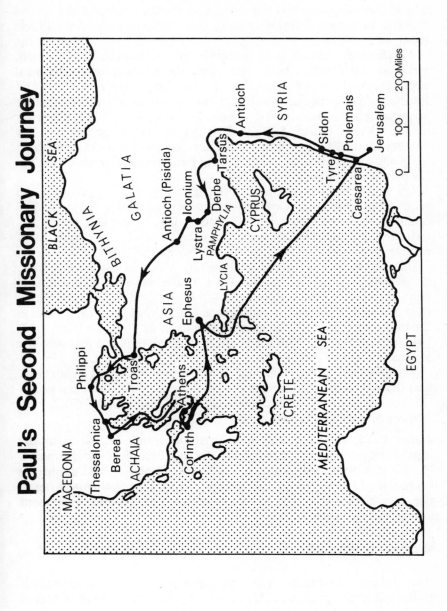

Acts 16.25-34

Three miracles disturbed the citizens of Philippi during the day and night when they presumed to place the Christian preachers in their local jail:

(*i*) The first miracle is in the realm of the human spirit, which, renewed and fortified by Christ, rises above the grim and painful experiences of the prisoners' cell and the instrument of torture, and finds a song of praise to God (25). Paul and his companion took their adverse circumstances as a challenge to faith (Rom. **8**.28); a clarion call to victory (Rom. **5**.17; 2 Cor. **2**.14); and a springboard for witness (25b). Many a man would have cursed his luck, renounced his gods, and tried to bribe the jailer; Paul found a better outlet for his pent-up feelings (Phil. **4**.6,7).

(*ii*) The earthquake came at the right time and for precisely the required purpose—to release the prisoners from their chains and to open the cell doors, but not to destroy life. Moreover, the supernatural disturbance struck terror into the jailer's heart, giving him a salutary fear and anxious concern for "salvation" (30).

(*iii*) Terror betrays a bad conscience, which in turn stems from disharmony with God because of sin. Therefore, all need is comprehended in man's first requirement—to know God as Saviour, which stamps Christ's Gospel as uniquely suited to that need (31). Here is the miracle of grace, as the jailer passes from death to life (Col. **1**.13, 14), with his family, from the solitude of alienation and fear into the joyous family of God (33,34).

The apostles' "joy in suffering", the phenomenon wholly from God, and the wonder of the simple Gospel—these marked out the establishment of the Philippian church as God's "good work" (Phil. **1**.6). Is there anywhere a nobler work?

Notes: V. 25: an O.T. psalm or a Christian canticle. V. 26: the moorings of the prisoners' fetters fixed to the wall became loose (Ramsay). V. 27: suicide would vindicate his military honour, and avoid the reproach of having failed in his duty. V. 30: perhaps he had heard the slave-girl's cry (17). V. 33: note the two uses of water. Sacrament and service go together.

Acts 16.35-40

Why did the magistrates change their minds and send the policeman to discharge the prisoners (35)? And why did Paul refuse to accept his freedom in this way (37)? Was it a fit of pique which made him disgruntled? Or a desire to see justice done by demanding a full apology? Or (more likely) an insistence on an official release and admission of error so that there would be no recurrence of this kind of hindrance to his missionary labours?

Anyhow, he acted clearly within his civil rights and got what he demanded even to the full apology and regret that they had blundered into beating and imprisoning Roman citizens whose case had not been investigated (37).

There are some pointers here to aid our thinking about the Christian's civil and social responsibility. Notice how Paul and Silas stand for their civic rights (Rom. **13.**1*ff.*), yet, once they have attained their aim, they comply with lawful authority and refuse to be an "odd ball" or social misfit (1 Pet. **2.**13-17).

Notes: V. 35: the accurate terminology is again to be seen. The "praetors" send their "lictors" (lit. rod-bearers) who carried as a badge of office bundles of rods bound together round an axe. V. 37: Paul uses the technical term "uncondemned" (*re incognita*, "without investigating the case")—a monstrous crime against Roman citizens, though not without precedent. Paul and Silas (37: "us") may have claimed their exemption from punishment on the previous day, but have been shouted down by the mob (22). V. 39: a noticeable change of face from v. 35. V. 40: Lydia's home was possibly the church's meeting-place, and housed a virile and affectionate company of believers to whom Paul became specially attached. Read his letter to the Philippians, detecting its warm, pastoral tones.

To think over: "One cannot help feeling that this is the best story Luke has given us so far" (Findlay). Do you agree?

Acts 17.1-9

The apostolic band (minus Luke, who evidently stayed on at Philippi to consolidate the work there; the "we-narrative" abruptly breaks off at **16.**17) moved southward, calling at Amphipolis (30 miles from Philippi) and Apollonia (27 miles further on) *en route* to Thessalonica (another 35 miles). The excellent Roman roads—this one was the useful *via Egnatia*—made travel both safe and speedy, and both factors were of incalculable importance for the spread of the Gospel message in the early days of the Church.

At Thessalonica a three weeks' ministry at the local Jewish meeting-place (2) gave Paul a chance to set out the Scriptural basis of his message. Note the three chief emphases he made (3). The reaction was true to previous experience. Some were convinced and won over to faith in Jesus as Messiah and Lord; this response angered the Jews, who raised the rabble against the visiting missionaries on the handy charge that they preached a subversive message which called for disloyalty to Rome (6,7). The evidence for this accusation was the proclamation of the Kingship of Jesus, which the Jews interpreted in a malicious way to mean that the Christian preachers were political agitators, offering a rival emperor to Caesar. The authorities, however, were not easily taken in by this specious allegation, but did investigate the claim. Jason, at whose house the apostles were lodging, was required to give an assurance that his guests were not seditiously-minded (9); and to make sure, Jason agreed that the apostles should be "bound over" and prevented from speaking in Thessalonica. This explains their immediate departure for Beroea (10).

Notes: V. 2: R.S.V. margin gives "sabbaths" as an alternative translation. On successive sabbath days Paul was the invited preacher. Perhaps the three themes (of v. 3) were handled on these consecutive sabbaths. V. 4: the adherence of some influential women reminds us that Christian ladies play a significant part in early Church life. Which names come to mind? Priscilla, Phoebe, Lydia . . . Turn up Romans 16 for many more. V. 5: the "loafers" (lit. those who hang about the market-place). V. 5: Paul was not there when Jason's house was attacked.
Meditation: "These men have turned the world upside down" (6).
Christian preaching is not a sedative, but social and spiritual dynamite.

Acts 17.10-15

We have Paul's later comment on the turn of events which made him rather suddenly have to quit Thessalonica (1 Thess. 2.18). Possibly he would not have accepted the dismissal so tamely, but Jason had given his word to the magistrates (9) and he would abide by that.

So he came to Beroea, 60 miles away. Here the previous pattern of his ministry was repeated. His preaching was evidently conducted in no "take-it-or-leave-it" manner, for it encouraged people to investigate the Scriptures for themselves. Not surprisingly, when this happens, "many of them . . . believed" (12). Truth, personally sought out and discovered by us, is always more vital and dear than thoughts which are handed to us "on a plate".

Meanwhile, the infant church at Thessalonica was facing much hardship (see 1 Thess. 1.6; 2.14; 3.3) and yet it did not cease its witness to the Gospel (1 Thess. **1.**8). A later reference in that letter implies that persecution had caused the premature death of some believers (1 Thess. **4.**13); and the Jewish leaders, determined to crush every outcropping of the Church, moved on to Beroea (13).

Paul had to face fresh opposition from the Thessalonian Jews, and felt it wise to travel on to Athens, using Silas and Timothy as his delegates to encourage the believers in the place he had been forced to flee (15). So much is clear; but it is very likely (from 1 Thess.) that Paul had to meet another kind of insinuation. Perhaps he had been accused of cowardice and running away from danger; or of double-dealing, by staying at Thessalonica only long enough to get a money-gift from Philippi, and then quickly moving on, hoping to collect more subscriptions from rich ladies *en route*. So he seeks to vindicate his character and to account for his actions in the Thessalonian letters. And, to make matters worse, he couldn't come in person to Thessalonica while the promise and pledge given by Jason was still in force. So he sent two men as his personal representatives.

Notes: V. 11: "noble"—in their attitude to the message? Yet Paul never hints at a defect in Thessalonica. The Greek can mean "more generous": can it refer to their support of the missionaries by gifts? Hence the defence (in 1 Thess. **2.**5,9,10) of being disinterested and above-board. V. 14: *cf.* 1 Thess. **3.**1*ff.*

Acts 17.16-21

The apostle's first reaction to what he saw at Athens led to a public ministry of disputation, both in the Jewish synagogue and in the market-place. No record is given of his appreciation of the city's objects of beauty; what fastened itself on his mind was its senseless idolatry (16)—a judgment called forth by the excessive religiosity of the Athenians (22) and their custom of dedicating shrines to a variety of deities (23).

There are two settings of his encounter with the philosophers who met him. In the market-place they overheard his preaching, which they couldn't understand. To their ears he kept on referring to "Jesus and the resurrection" (18), which they probably misconstrued as an allusion to two deities: Jesus and His consort *Anastasis* (the Greek word for resurrection). Others seemed to have dismissed him with the disdainful term "babbler" (lit. seed-picker, a slang expression for a worthless person who picked up scraps of food in the markets). But some wished to hear more.

Photo: Parthenon at the Acropolis, Athens

Photo: Erechtheion at the Acropolis, Athens

The second scene is the Areopagus (19), a venue for the Athenian court and a meeting-point for religious discussion and debate. Luke evidently had a pretty poor opinion of the value of what usually went on there (21); and his verdict was not unshared.

Notes: V. 16: Athens, the cultural centre of the Greco-Roman world, renowned for the sculpture of Pheidias. But Paul's spirit was provoked by its idols. The verb occurs in the Old Testament for God's anger at Israel's apostasy (Deut. **9.**18; Psa. **106.**29). V. 18: these two groups held beliefs which Paul touches upon in his sermon, *viz.*,—the Epicurean notion that God is all-sufficient in Himself; and the Stoic doctrine that He gives life to all (*cf.* v. 25). The word "preacher" means "herald" and was a technical expression in the Greek mystery religions. A different term is used at Romans **10.**14. Vs. 19,20: "new teaching", "strange things"; *cf.* the reaction to our Lord's ministry (Mark **1.**27; Luke **5.**26), but for different reasons. Why? V. 21: Demosthenes, the Greek orator, had accused his fellow-Athenians of "going round and asking, Is anything new being said?" This is a human trait in every age, based on the false assumption that the latest vogue is the best. Theologians are not exempt.

Acts 17.22-34

Paul's apologetic or defence of the faith before the Athenians is a classic statement of "natural theology". An earlier and shorter specimen was given at **14.**15-17. It aims at laying a foundation on which the special revelation of the Gospel may be built; but no foundation is ever complete in itself and requires a superstructure to explain it *raison d'étre*. Paul, taking his text from an altar reared to an "Unknown god" (23) proceeds to state the answer to the basic question of all theology, Who is God?

(*i*) He is Maker, Lord of heaven and earth (24); (*ii*) who is Spirit, unimprisoned in any earthly temple (25,29; John **4.**24); (*iii*) He is self-existent, in whom all creation lives (25). This answers the children's insistent question, "Who made God?" (*iv*) He is Creator of men, whose span of life and dwelling-place on earth are determined by Him (26). If the last phrase of verse 26 refers to territorial ambitions, then God is seen as Lord of history, concerned with the rise and fall of national powers; (*v*) moreover, He is the source and goal of man's spiritual life (27,28).

Two final attributes (30,31) are logically connected with this list. As God is One and almighty, with no visible image, all idolatry stands

417

under His judgment since He is a righteous Lord who summons men to repentance. As Lord of history and of the Universe, it is His design to bring the world to its consummation at the final day of reckoning. The proof of this final judgment has been given in Jesus' resurrection from the dead.

Paul's hearers would follow him in the preliminary stages of his case, but mention of repentance (which implies sin), judgment (which involves moral responsibility), and the resurrection and return of Jesus (which ran counter to all Greek ideas of immortality and union with God) was too much for most of them. Some derided (32); some deferred (32); only a few decided for the Pauline Gospel (34). Had Paul failed in this situation?

Notes: V. 23: there is independent evidence of altars at Athens "to unknown gods" set up in time of civic distress, and as a feature of man's incurable religiosity (22). Paul accepts this as a fact of experience (27), confirmed by man's being created by God in His image (28). V. 28: a quotation from Aratus, and an allusion to a line in Cleanthes—both Stoic poets. Aratus hailed from Paul's place of origin. V. 30: *cf.* Rom. **3.25f.**

Meditation: Universal kinship with Adam (26) and the world's future judgment by the last Adam (31)—these are the terminal points of the sermon, and of Christian doctrine today.

Acts 18.1-4

When he later reflected on his ministry in this part of southern Greece, Paul later wrote of "the household of Stephanas" as the first converts in Achaia (1 Cor. **16.**15)—and Stephanas was a Corinthian. This suggests that no church—certainly no thriving community—was left in Athens after his departure.

Some scholars infer that, on reflection, Paul regretted the philosophical and cultural approach which he made to the Athenians, and that 1 Corinthians **2.**1-5 was written out of a new resolve henceforth to focus his preaching on "Jesus Christ and Him crucified". We may doubt this inference, but it does seem clear that, in direct contrast to a somewhat barren ministry in Athens, the initial response at Corinth was a tremendous encouragement to him. In fact, from his letters, the evidence is that the church at Corinth turned out to be his main pastoral concern.

The exigencies of the situation at Corinth also may have contributed to his desire to proclaim the "simple Gospel" in full reliance on the Holy Spirit. For Corinth was a flourishing seaport, notorious for its moral laxity and crude ways, the "Vanity Fair" of the Roman Empire. The verb in Greek "to corinthianize" means "to go to the dogs"!

In such an unpromising setting Paul directed his ministry to both Jews and Greeks (4), and found support in two friends, husband and wife, who had been forced out of Italy by an imperial edict aimed at the Jews (c. A.D.49-50). Jewish rabbis were taught a trade, so it is not surprising to read this reference to Paul's craftsmanship (3).

Notes: V. 2: these two Christians play a significant, if secondary, role in the New Testament literature. Paul was later to owe much to them (Rom. **16**.3,4; *cf.* 1 Cor. **16**.19; 2 Tim. **4**.19). The decree of Claudius is that mentioned by the historian Suetonius. V. 3: the trade was that of leather-working. Paul's occupation to support his ministry is well attested (*cf.* **20**.34; 1 Cor. **9**.12,15; 2 Cor. **11**.7*ff.*; 1 Thess. **2**.9; 2 Thess. **3**.8).

Question: Consider the apostle's example at Corinth and its bearing on (i) lay ministry, and (ii) part-time pastoral ministry.

Acts 18.5-11

We may pick out a number of features of Paul's labours at Corinth:

(*i*) His evangelism. Verse 5 reads, "Paul was engrossed in this preaching of the word" (Moffatt) once Silas and Timothy arrived. Probably their coming and work freed him from the necessity of dividing his time between preaching and his craft, and made a full-time ministry possible.

(*ii*) His decision, following on the hardened attitude of the Jews (6,7), to divert his energies into the channel of a mission to the Gentiles (8) and to set up a rival meeting-place next door to the synagogue. Would this arrangement have been approved by modern missionary policy-makers? But Crispus' conversion seems to have been a direct fruit of this bold venture, to be followed by that of many Corinthians.

(*iii*) His encouragement (9,10). In spite of some success and the strength of Christian fellowship in the work, Paul grew depressed, and needed the enheartening reminder and caution of a night-time vision. The message is precisely suited to his immediate situation: "Stop being afraid, and go on speaking". A special promise of the Lord's protecting hand implies that his life was in some peril; and the assurance that his work was not to be in vain (1 Cor. **15**.58) must have breathed fresh courage into his jaded spirit. (Compare 1 Kings **19**.18.) The effect on Paul was notable (11).

Notes: V. 5: perhaps Silas and Timothy brought him gifts from the Macedonian churches (2 Cor. **11**.8; Phil. **4**.15) and this made possible a full-time ministry. V. 6: "he shook out his garments"—an act of protest (*cf.* Neh. **5**.13). For the following phrase, see Matt. **27**.25. V. 7: Ramsay identifies this man with Gaius (Rom. **16**.23). What we do know is that he was a Roman citizen and a God-fearer. V. 8: Paul refers to this conversion in 1 Corinthians **1**.14 (baptism following conversion) and Gaius (?Titius Justus) is mentioned there also. V. 9: notice the translation above, which brings out the Greek tenses. Something of Paul's fear is reflected in 1 Corinthians **2**.3. For the Church as God's people, see 1 Peter **2**.9,10.

Acts 18.12-23

Vs. 12-17 give details of the kind of opposition which Paul met at Corinth (10), and his policy of setting up a rival centre next door to the Jewish synagogue led, not unnaturally, to this "united attack" on him. He was haled before the tribunal of Gallio, who was proconsul of Achaia in A.D.51. In his capacity as local magistrate, Gallio heard the charge (13), but did not stay for the defendant's reply (14). He just couldn't be bothered, as verse 17 implies, even when a flagrant injustice was done before his eyes.

Vs. 18-23. Paul's itinerary took him from Corinth *via* Ephesus to Antioch, and then back to Galatia to re-visit the churches in that province. At Ephesus he parted company with Aquila and his wife (26; and in 1 Cor. **16**.19, written from Ephesus, he conveys a greeting from them to their friends at Corinth). The allusion to a vow (18) is interesting. Based on Num. **6**.1-21, the custom of taking a Nazirite vow was followed by a man before setting out on a dangerous journey. The traveller would vow not to cut his hair until the trip was completed; then he would shear his head at a ceremony of thanksgiving in the Jerusalem Temple (**21**.23,24). It was Paul's intention, once his hair was cut at Cenchreae, not to have it cut again until he reached Jerusalem in safety. Then the hair would be offered as a token of thankfulness for "journeying mercies". Probably we may understand a visit to Jerusalem in the phrase "went up" (22). This is Luke's ending of the second missionary tour, the final stage being told with breathless rapidity.

Notes: V. 12: Gallio was the brother of the famous philosopher Seneca, who in turn was a tutor of Nero. V. 13: it is not certain what this accusation means; whose law is Paul supposedly contravening, Jewish or Roman? Gallio replies that on both counts Paul is no criminal, as far as he can see. He clears Paul of breaking a Roman law, and professes no interest in the domestic issue of Jewish affairs. V. 17: Sosthenes may be the same as in 1 Corinthians 1.1. If so, he too (like Crispus, 8) may have then been converted, and the Jews show their anger at losing *two* leaders to the Christian cause. But it may have been *Greeks* who gave Sosthenes a beating, taking advantage of Gallio's unconcern (so the Western text). V. 22*f.*: "in these two verses and 19.1 is compressed a journey of 1,500 miles" (F. F. Bruce).

Acts 18.24-28

Apollos' gifts were considerable: (*i*) "learning", by which we are probably to understand a gift of public speaking—*i.e.*, eloquence (24); (*ii*) a close acquaintance with the Old Testament Scriptures, which he used in a ministry to the synagogues (26); and (*iii*) an ardour (25) which drove him to share with others the knowledge he had of Jesus. Something of the infectiousness of his zeal is hinted at in this memorable description: "fervent in spirit", or perhaps, "bubbling over with enthusiasm" (*cf.* Rom. 12.11 for the same phrase). Yet he possessed a commendable trait which must have endeared him to all; his humility and teachableness which did not refuse to accept fuller instruction of "the way of God" (26). The maxim of Prov. 9.9 sums it up.

Following this "course of instruction" which Priscilla and Aquila (note the order of names) gave him at Ephesus, there was an increase in Apollos's influence as he crossed over the Aegean sea to southern Greece. Here he was welcomed, and exercised a two-sided ministry. He stimulated and strengthened the believers (27), probably at Corinth (where unhappily his name became associated with a clique in the church, 1 Cor. 1.12; 3.4,22). Incidentally Paul pays a warm tribute to his work at Corinth (1 Cor. 3.6: "Apollos watered" the spiritual shoots and slips planted by the apostle). Then, he conducted a public campaign of "Christian evidences" against the denials and contradictions of the Jews (28).

Notes: V. 24: Apollos' culture derived from the advantage of living at Alexandria, the Sorbonne of the ancient world, famed for its library and letters. Apollos' knowledge of the O.T. would be that of the Septuagint version, and his religious experience seems to have been that of a pre-Pentecostal nature. Possibly he was a member of a group which venerated John the Baptist, although recognizing the existence of Jesus' Messiahship and an experimental knowledge of the Holy Spirit (see on ch. **19**). This explains the effectiveness of his later ministry, based on his ready aptitude to learn (28). V. 27: a "letter of commendation" is meant, like those referred to in 2 Corinthians 3.1.

*Question: To be a leader, without becoming a party-leader, is not easy. How does Paul deal with factions at Corinth (1 Cor. **1-4**)?*

Acts 19.1-7

The first verse takes up the story of Paul where **18.23** left off, and brings him to Ephesus. His work there falls into the following categories: (*i*) as apostle (1-7); (*ii*) as apologist (8-10); (*iii*) as miracle-worker (11-20).

The disciples who professed to be ignorant of the Holy Spirit (2) must have been Gentiles if we take their statement in a precisely literal way, for all Jews would recall the Old Testament teaching of Psalm **51**.11; Isa. **63**.10, *etc.* These men were believers (2) and had been baptized as disciples of John the Baptist (3). Possibly the description "disciples" (1) is meant to fit this case, as in Matt. **14**.12, though it is just conceivable that they were disciples of Apollos, whose earlier life as an incomplete believer seems to have matched theirs (**18.25**). At all events we are clearly meant to see here: (*i*) An exceptional circumstance of a small (hence the number is given, 7) group of men who had believed in Christ (as the coming One, heralded by John) and had received a pre-Pentecostal baptism in anticipation of Messiah's coming. Their Christian knowledge and experience therefore, while sincere and genuine, was defective. (*ii*) A transition from the anticipatory baptism of John (and Apollos?) to the fulfilment—baptism which is the norm in the Gospel age. In Eph. **1**.13 Paul states explicitly the accepted sequence, with the same aorist participle in the Greek ("having believed") to be construed as coincident in time with the action of the chief verb. So, "Did you receive the Holy Spirit at the time of your believing?" corresponds exactly to the Pauline teaching: "At the time of your believing you were sealed with the promised Holy Spirit". No interval is envisaged, and the possibility of believing without the sealing of the Spirit is not entertained. This is why the Ephesian disciples are an exceptional case. (*iii*) A

Paul's Third Missionary Journey

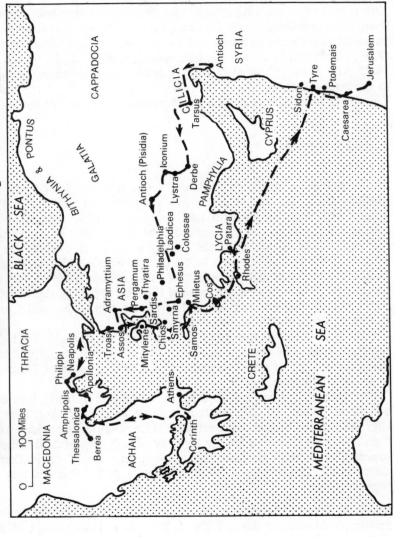

polemic against remaining content with John's baptism and a pre-Pentecostal faith and experience. The men were encouraged to submit to *Christian baptism*, which was followed by apostolic ordination and the gift of "tongues" (6).

Notes: V. 1: the wording implies that Paul's attention was drawn to these men and their needs. Hence his query (2). Vs. 2,3: the intimate connection between baptism and the gift of the Holy Spirit is plain (2.38; 1 Cor. 12.13). John's baptism is described in 1.5; 11.16; 13.24*f.*; 18.25, and John's Gospel, 3.23*ff.* A Johannine movement persisted in the later centuries.
Question: Is it possible to be a pre-Pentecostal believer today?

Acts 19.8-20

Paul's Ephesian ministry took on some features which are now familiar from our earlier readings. A ministry in the Jewish synagogue met with opposition and defamation (8,9), which obliged him to continue on neutral ground. The lecture-hall of Tyrannus is the new meeting-point, made available to Paul during the hot afternoon hours from 11 a.m. to 4 p.m. (a credible addition, supplied by the Western text, printed in R.S.V. margin) when the room would be unused. The townspeople would then be enjoying their midday siesta, while Paul and his devoted followers met to present Christ's claims to any who cared to come.

Paul gained some notoriety as a worker of miracles (11). This reputation induced some itinerant Jewish magicians to capitalize on his success, and to try their hand at using the name of Jesus as a formula of exorcism (13).

The spiritual power released by the apostolic ministry had other beneficial effects (18-20), with a notable display of the Gospel's effectiveness to counter and overcome false religion. No price was too high to obtain release from the tyranny of bad religion and crippling superstition which plagued the first-century world of Hellenistic man—and still grips modern man in spite of his technocracy and sophistication.

Notes: V. 8: "the kingdom of God": not a very common theme in the epistles, but we may refer to 1 Thess. 2.12; Rom. 14.17, and Col. 1.13. V. 9: "the Way", as at 9.2, a name for the early believers who were committed to the way of life ruled by Jesus Christ. Tyrannus was evidently a professional lecturer who hired out his room during its

424

unused hours. Vs. 9 and 11 tell us that he had a very full day! V. 12: these garments are described in trade terms and refer to items which Paul used in his manual work. V. 13: a surviving papyrus has a list of such exorcisms, including "I beseech you by Jesus the God of the Hebrews". V. 14: possibly "high priest" was a pretentious claim Sceva made for himself, not to be taken too seriously.

Questions: (i) How did Paul use his leisure hours (9)? How do we? (ii) "the folly of second-hand religion" (13,15). Are we ever guilty of this sort of borrowed vocabulary?

Acts 19.21-41

Vs. 21, 22 are an intimation of Paul's future plans, including the expression of his desire, which henceforward runs like a thread through the rest of the book of Acts, to visit the imperial city, Rome.

The evidence for opposition here is partly factual (like the story here of the riot in the amphitheatre), and partly inferential (*e.g.*, the hints of a terrible danger to his life in 1 Cor. **15.**32; 2 Cor. **1.**8-10 and, probably, Phil. **1.**30; **2.**17).

Paul's preaching (26), as in the report of his Athenian sermon (17.24,29), was seen as a danger to the silversmiths; and a second occasion of Demetrius' protest may very well have been a period of social anarchy and unrest, following the assassination of Junius Silanus in A.D.54. The murder of this proconsul of Asia at the instigation of Agrippina may possibly have been carried out by two men who afterwards stayed on in Asia to oversee the imperial business until a successor to Silanus was appointed. G. S. Duncan makes this interesting suggestion in his book on *St. Paul's Ephesian Ministry*, and so explains (*a*) the reference to proconsuls (plural) in verse 38; and (*b*) Paul's grave danger in which his Roman citizenship failed to protect him from the venom of the mob and the authorities.

In God's providence, however, the apostle was able to call upon local influential friends (31). A moderating voice was raised by the Ephesian "town-clerk" (35-40). Luke did not fail to note the irony of the situation (32), though it may have been an ugly scene for a time until reason prevailed (41).

Notes: Vs. 25,27: "business is business" was Demetrius' ruling motto. V. 29: the Ephesian theatre has been excavated; it seated 25,000 persons in its day. Gaius may not have been a Macedonian (so the textual authorities grant) in view of **20.**4, where he is called a man of Derbe. Possibly, however, there were two men of this common

425

name. See comment on the later verse. V. 32: the Greek word translated "assembly" is the regular word for "church" (so 41). V. 35: the image of Artemis was supposed to have fallen (like a meteorite?) from the sky.

Acts 20.1-6

From Ephesus Paul's journeys took him to Macedonia and then to southern Greece. Later as he faced opposition he decided to return northwards and to sail from Neapolis, the port of Philippi (6), across the Aegean to Troas on his long trip to Jerusalem (3: "set sail for Syria").

In a section which deals with Paul's uneventful travels we shall do well to dig a little below the surface, for this *was* an important period in his life. His visit to Macedonia (1) evidently was the same as that spoken of in 2 Cor. **2.**12 when he halted at Troas where he had arranged to meet Titus. This was a critical period in his apostolic service, for he had been insulted at Corinth (2 Cor. **2.**5) and had written a "severe letter" to rebuke a factious minority in the church which had opposed his authority. But this letter was not composed easily, as 2 Cor. **2.**4 makes clear. At Troas he was anxious to receive news of the letter's effect.

Indeed, so concerned was he and sorry that Titus had failed to rendezvous with him at Troas that he crossed over into Macedonia (2 Cor. **7.**5-13). There good news awaited him as Titus arrived with the report that the Corinthian disturbance was over and the church had voted confidence in him. From Macedonia, he wrote *2 Corinthians*, therefore; and followed it up with a visit (2), when he composed the *Epistle to the Romans*, which was sent out from Corinth.

The return trip, through Macedonia to Troas, brought him a further stage on his eastward journey. It was a slow journey (compare v. 6 with **16.**11, 12), and meant a hurried "stop-over" at Miletus instead of a diversionary visit to Ephesus (**20.**16). Why was he in a hurry (16)?

Notes: V. 4: the names of Paul's travel companions are interesting. Sopater may be the same as Sosipater of Romans **16.**21. Aristarchus was mentioned earlier at **19.**29, while Gaius may be the Macedonian of that verse if we accept (with N.E.B.) the variant reading "the Doberian" instead of "Derbaean" (N.E.B. marg.). Doberus was a Macedonian town, near Philippi. Tychicus is well known in the later imprisonment epistles as Paul's courier; and Trophimus recurs

426

as the sick man of 2 Tim. **4.20**. V. 6: Passover days numbered a week, and probably a date in April A.D.57 is intended.

Acts 20.7-16

Vs. 7-12 are a description of the New Testament church at worship, and help to fill a gap in our knowledge of what went on when the early believers met in congregational assembly. Significant aspects: (*i*) the day is "the first day of the week"—*i.e.*, our Sunday (if, as is likely, Luke is using the Roman, not Jewish, calculation of the days of the week; *cf.* N.E.B.). This day became known as the Lord's day (Rev. **1.**10) in commemoration of His resurrection (Luke **24.**1; John **20.**19,26) and in contrast to the Jewish sabbath. Another feature of the Christians' holy day is given in 1 Cor. **16.**2. (*ii*) The time of this gathering at Troas is evidently evening ("he prolonged his speech until midnight" (7). (*iii*) The purpose is set out in the technical expression "to break bread" (7)—*i.e.*, to share a common meal which was held in order to observe a solemn remembrance of the Lord's death. The sense of this expression is given clearly in v. 11 and 1 Cor. **10.**16; and at this early stage of development, Christians observed a common meal (the *agape* or love-feast) in the framework of which there was a communion service (the Eucharist). This pattern seems clear from 1 Cor. **11.**17-34, and other Christian writings. (*iv*) In the context of this assembly Paul gave a "sermon" which was interrupted by Eutychus's unfortunate accident. An inland trip to Ephesus was not made because Paul had his eye on the calendar (16).

Notes: V. 7: "the morrow" refers to a new day, begun at "day-break" (11). Luke is therefore using the Roman system of reckoning, whose day was from midnight to midnight; not the Jewish, from sunset to sunset. V. 8: "lights" were torches which gave off heavy fumes. It is not surprising then that one young man nodded off (9) and fell down. V. 10: Paul acts like Elijah (1 Kings **17.**17*ff.*) and Elisha (2 Kings **4.** 34*f.*). V. 10: his "soul" (in O.T. sense of life's vital principle, *nephesh*) was still alive, although he was unconscious and concussed.

Acts 20.17-27

Opportunity to make contact with the Ephesian churches was not altogether lost; and if Paul couldn't come to them, they—or their leaders—could travel to meet him at Miletus. Ministers and church leaders should find special relevance and challenge in these words. Today's reading covers the first half of Paul's address, the only example of its kind in Acts as a speech delivered by him to a Christian community. "Almost certainly Luke heard it himself, and may even have taken shorthand notes" (F. F. Bruce). Certainly it carries all the marks of a Pauline composition.

Vs. 18-21 are mainly in the past, and relate Paul's type of ministry in Asia. This would be well known to his hearers, who, as "elders" (17) or "overseers" (28) would have special reason to be grateful for his "all-round" (20,21), if personally costly (19), ministry. "The plots of the Jews" (19) remind us of some far more serious danger to his life than Luke has recorded, as we observed earlier.

Vs. 22-27 are in the form of an announcement of what the future holds. Paul is on his way to Jerusalem, fully alive to the perils which beset him (22,23). In fact, he does not anticipate a return to Ephesus (25). His life is forfeit, yet expendable if only the divine purpose for which he was called and chosen may be realized (24). What was that purpose (9.15; 26.16-18,22)? Was it achieved (2 Tim. 4.6-8)?

Notes: V. 17: the "elders" are apparently to be equated with "guardians" (Gk. *episkopoi*, A.V., "overseers", 28), although the former may be the name of an office, the latter a function. V.19: *cf.* 1 Cor. 15.32; 2 Cor. 1. 8-10; 11.23. V. 20: relevant to the pastoral office: "in public", and privately in the people's homes. Equally the two themes (21) still need strong emphasis. V. 22: "under the constraint of the (Holy) Spirit". V. 23: by inward monition or through the guidance of prophets like Agabus (21.11). Vs. 24,25: testifying to the Gospel and preaching the kingdom—are one and the same activity. V. 26: like Ezekiel's watchman (Ezek. 33.1-6).
Meditation: Consider Paul's fidelity to his ministerial tasks.

Acts 20.28-38

Vs. 28-35 are the concluding part of this pastoral charge, in which exhortation and example meet and mingle. Paul's encouragements are given in such verses as 28,31,35. He holds himself up as a model to emulate in verses like 31,33,34. The call to vigilance and faithfulness is made all the more insistent and urgent because of the attacks of heretical teachers (29, 30) whose influence in the later church became only too apparent (*cf.* 1 Tim. 4. 1-3; Jude; 2 Pet 2.1-22; 1 John 4. 1-6; Rev. 2.2 in particular). The saddest warning is given in the announcement that these men will arise "from among your own

428

selves"—*i.e.*, they will be apostate teachers who desert the Church's faith and introduce some distortion of Christian doctrine and ethics. Can you think of some modern counterpart to this "false teaching"?

Vs. 36-38. The elders escorted him to the quayside—the place of many tender farewells.

Notes: V. 28: the Church as a flock (John **10**) has a natural complement of its leaders as "overseers" (*episkopoi*) whose job it is to tend it and to protect it from marauding wolves (29). The Holy Spirit appoints such pastoral leaders over the Church, purchased (as Israel of old, Psa. **74**.2; Ex. **15**.16) by the blood of God's only Son (R.S.V. margin gives the best sense in the light of Jesus' relationship to God as His well-beloved, *cf.* Gen. **22**.2; Rom. **8**.32). V. 29: heretical leaders are often likened to wolves (Matt. **7**.15). V. 33: Samuel made a similar protest of disinterested concern (1 Sam. **12**.3). V. 34: "these hands"—one can almost *see* Paul point to his toil-worn hands as he spoke. The two words are in an emphatic place in the sentence. V. 35: a saying of Jesus not recorded in the Gospels, but evidently widely known. This suggests that a collection of His teaching was already in circulation among the churches.

Thought: The elders are to be built up (32) so that they may defend and tend the flock. The measure of one is the key to the other.

Acts 21.1-14

Vs. 1-6 narrate a further stage in the apostolic sea voyage from Miletus to Tyre. *En route* they called at various ports of call (1-3) until they reached Tyre on the Syrian coast. There a lengthy process of unloading the ship's cargo meant some delay (4), but Paul redeemed the time by making the acquaintance of Christian friends at Tyre. The church was formed there probably as a result of the missionary dispersal of **11**.19. A warning came to Paul, possibly by some inspired utterance in the church assembly, that he should not proceed to Jerusalem (4b); but he recognized some higher constraint (**20**.22) impelling him onwards. The cameo picture (5, 6) is a most touching scene, filled with tenderness and pathos. The final parting came as the two groups of Christians went their own ways: "*we* went on board the ship . . . *they* returned home". Many a missionary's valediction today is like this!

Vs. 7-14 take up again the theme of prophetic warnings given to Paul. This time it is Agabus—a noted prophet in the Judean churches

(11.27,28). Both Paul's companions and the Caesarean church sensed the imminent danger, and Paul's refusal to follow their advice was not made lightly or in a foolhardy manner (13). Like his Master, he was answerable to the divine will of which he had an assurance (Luke 13.31-33). The church eventually accepted his firm persuasion (14) of God's will with a note of concurrence.

Notes: V. 1: lit., "we tore ourselves away from them". V. 7: the sea voyage ended at Ptolemais, the Roman port of Palestine, and thence Paul proceeded to Caesarea by road. V. 8: Philip and his family had settled at Caesarea (8.40). His unmarried daughters had the spiritual gift of 1 Corinthians 11.5; 14.3. V. 10: if we translate the time-phrase literally, with J. A. Findlay, it will mean "we stayed there more days (than we intended)". Perhaps it was congenial company or profitable discussion which detained the Pauline party; certainly Luke would benefit from the extra 'stop-over' by assembling materials for his literary works. V. 11: Agabus performs a symbolic action, like that of O.T. prophets, to lend extra force to his spoken message. V. 13: lit. "bleaching my heart by pounding it like a washerwoman" (Findlay) —a vivid metaphor in Paul's verb.
Question : Both Paul and his Christian friends claimed the Spirit's guidance (20.22; 21.4,11), yet reached opposite conclusions. What do we learn from this?

Acts 21.15-26

James, the Lord's brother and leader of the Jerusalem church, gave the apostolic travellers a cautious welcome (18*ff.*). Their response to Paul's celebration of the Gospel and its success among the Gentile peoples (19) matched his enthusiasm with a sobering reflection that his ministry had been a source of embarrassment, partly based on a false report (21) and partly caused by the logical conclusion of Paul's doctrine of salvation by faith alone.

"What then is to be done?" was a natural question, demanding some action (22) to allay Jewish suspicions that Paul was advocating a wholesale rejection of the Jewish law and its relevance to Jews who became Christians. Underlying the fear of the Jewish party was undoubtedly a healthy regard for moral standards, and the insinuation that the Pauline message led inevitably to antinomianism— *i.e.*, a casting-off of all moral restraints in the interests of a supposed freedom and championing of divine grace (as in Rom. 6.1*ff.*; Gal. 5.13)— which dogged Paul all his life.

430

In fact, Paul had never quarrelled with the use of the Law for Jewish believers (see Rom. **2.25**; **3.1ff.**, **31**; **7.12**) and had never renounced his Jewish heritage (1 Cor. **7.18**, **9.20**; 2 Cor. **11.21ff.**). It was an attempt to shackle *Gentile* converts with the Law which called forth his loudest protest, as in *Galatians*, which was written directly to a Gentile-Christian church in a controversial situation.

The evidence for his deep loyalty to his ancestry was provided by his acceptance of a Nazirite vow, both for himself and four men whose expenses—eight pigeons and two lambs in all (referred to in v. 24)—he paid. He is reminded of the earlier apostolic decree, made binding on the Gentile churches; and since this code (see on Acts **15**) did not infringe Gentile liberty in Christ, he was willing to comply (26).

Notes: V. 16: Mnason is called "an early disciple"—*i.e.*, a foundation-member of the church since its beginnings. V. 19: "he related . . . the things God had done among the Gentiles"—as on a previous occasion (**15.3f.**, 12). V. 20: a true report of what was said, but was the statement exaggerated? V. 21: "the customs" are ethical standards. Hence the suggestion that Paul was leading people astray. V. 23: Paul had taken such a vow earlier (**18.18**). He had no need to purify himself from defilement (24), but conceded the point (26) out of deference to the elders. 1 Corinthians **9.19-23** is well illustrated.

Thought: Two powerful ideas dominate Paul's thinking and action: the freedom of the Gospel, and the unity of the Church. Consider these in the light of today.

Acts 21.27-39

There is an indirect element of pathos in today's passage. Paul was arrested (33), and as far as the story in Acts goes, he was never again a free man! Verses 27-32 therefore tell of the apostle's last days of freedom.

Vs. 27-32. Paul's fulfilment of the vow in company with four Jewish Christians (23,24) was done openly—to serve as a notification of his ancestral loyalty. But he paid a heavy price for such notoriety. Certain Asian Jews spotted Trophimus, a Gentile from Ephesus, in his company, and drew the conclusion that Paul had taken him into the most sacred and restricted part of the Temple. This was a serious breach; hence the outcry (28). The gates were shut (by the Temple police chief presumably, 30c: he is referred to at **4.1**) to prevent further trouble; and the Roman tribune took Paul into protective custody (32,33).

Vs. 33-39. The fury of the crowd is seen both in their uncontrolled demonstration (34) and their determination to get at Paul, who was carried into the safety of the barracks on the backs of Roman soldiers (35).

Claudius Lysias (23.26) was the tribune's name. He thought that he had carried off a notable prisoner (38); and before the incident closed, Paul was given a chance to speak to the angry mob. But to no avail (22.22, 23).

Notes: V. 27: the seven days of the Nazirite vow (Num. 6.9*f.*) are meant. V. 28: the Romans honoured Jewish scruples about the sanctity of the Temple; a "middle wall of partition" (Eph. 2.14) separated the Court of the Gentiles from the Court of Women and the Inner Court to which no Gentile could come. The penalty was death. Asian Jews had already proved (20.19) that they meant business in their enmity to the apostle of the Gentiles. V. 38: "the Egyptian" was evidently a man with a police record and wanted for his part in a Jerusalem uprising, quelled by Roman soldiers in A.D.54 (Josephus tells us the story, and Klausner identified him with a false prophet named Ben Stada). He led the "Assassins" (lit. dagger-men). V. 39: Paul speaks up, giving his identity.

Acts 21.40—22.21

Paul's speech from the steps (40) was given to a quietened audience. The reason for this dramatic change which turned a restless, turbulent mob into a subdued body of listeners is found at 21.40 and 22.2. Speaking in Aramaic, Paul, with great tact, gained his audience's attention while he presented his "apology" (1) for his faith in Christ Jesus.

It falls into three parts: (*i*) his conduct before conversion (3-5); (*ii*) the circumstances of his conversion (6-14); (*iii*) his commission at conversion (15-21).

Paul adopts a frankly autobiographical pose, recalling his past life in the same way as in Gal. 1.13-17; Phil. 3.4-11, and 1 Tim. 1.12-16. Confining our attention to the record in Acts, we note how Paul's pre-Christian life was seen from different points of view. The revered Jewish teacher Gamaliel (*cf.* 5.34) no doubt saw in Saul of Tarsus an apt pupil, known for his zeal (3; Rom. 10.2 puts this ardour in its true light). The early Christians saw in him a notorious enemy and persecutor, greatly to be feared, and the embodiment of undying hatred (4,5). Paul's own estimate of his former way of life is contained in the hints of (*a*) his diligence as Gamaliel's pupil, and (*b*) his all-consuming zeal for what he then believed to be God's honour.

Vs. 6-21. The circumstances of Paul's conversion are set in three different scenes: (*a*) on the road (6-11), where the living Jesus met him, captured his will, and claimed him as His servant. Note the new features recorded here, supplementary to the account in 9.3-9. (*b*) In the house (12-16), identified earlier as Judas' home in Straight Street (**9.**11). (*c*) In the Temple (17-21). From this revealing piece of autobiography we can see the tremendous impression Stephen's martyrdom made on him (20), and Paul's appointment as apostle to the Gentile world was confirmed (21; Gal. **2.**7-9).

Notes: V. 14: "the Just One" = the Messiah (**3.**14). V. 15: his witness was grounded in personal experience, which no one could deny to him (*cf.* **26.**16). V. 16: Paul's baptism followed his conversion, imparting an assurance of forgiveness as he called on His name (**2.**21,38).
Meditation on Paul's conversion:
> *Nay, but I yield, I yield,*
> *I can hold out no more;*
> *I sink by dying love compelled,*
> *And own Thee Conqueror.*

Acts 22.22-29

The trance-vision in the Temple is of some importance both in its immediate impact on Paul (perhaps 2 Cor. **12.**2-4 refers to the experience; more likely 1 Cor. **9.**1 seems to indicate this occasion, when he *saw* the Lord) and its bearing on his future service. The commissioning word was "I will send you far away to the *Gentiles*" (21). The Roman tribune, evidently mystified over a speech (in a language foreign to him) which produced such a violent result (23), determined to get at the root of the matter, even if it meant torture (24,25). Paul appealed to his civil rights, and used his Roman citizenship to extricate himself from further indignity and suffering. He had no love of pain for its own sake – contrast with some of the later martyrs (*e.g.*, Ignatius) who took positive delight in their prospective sufferings.

The issue of verses 26-29 turns on Paul's possession of Roman citizenship, gained by inheritance from his parents (28). This automatically exempted him from such torture as the tribune intended to apply—a cruel method of "third degree" to extract a confession of guilt (24). The Roman soldier was amazed that a man like Paul could have afforded to buy his citizenship (27,28); but accepted the explanation that he gave.

Notes: V. 23: the offending thought was that Paul was claiming a divine commission to offer God's salvation *directly* to the Gentiles—*i.e.,* without requiring them to become Jews first or to become subservient to Jews (as in Isa. **61**.5). Throwing dust into the air, along with tearing clothes, is a sign of horror at blasphemy (Job **2**.12). V. 25: as at **16**.38, Paul reminds the Romans of his right to a fair trial. The flagrant mistake was that they had dared to bind him "uncondemned"—*re incognita:* without investigating his case—and were ready to flog him (from which he was, even if guilty, exempt). V. 28: the venerable Bede preserves an interesting reading: "It is easy to *say* you are a Roman citizen: I know how much it cost me!" In other words, the tribune speaks ironically, and marvels that such an undistinguished fellow as Paul could be a Roman. But appearances are often deceptive.

Acts 22.30—23.10

The Roman tribune's curiosity was further stimulated by the remarkable prisoner he had taken into custody. He was a man who knew his privilege as a Roman citizen to a trial (25,29), and at the same time had acquired a reputation as a trouble-maker among his own people (30). The simplest procedure, Claudius Lysias thought, was to bring accusers and accused together. So Paul was placed before the Jewish Sanhedrin (1).

Evidently Paul's protest divided the council, and Sir William Ramsay even suggests that, at verse 6, the Pharisees in the Sanhedrin walked across to take their place by the prisoner's side, as if to associate themselves with him. At all events two things stand out in the sequel: (*i*) Paul henceforth addresses the Pharisees by appealing to a doctrine which they and he as a Christian shared—the resurrection of the dead (denied by Sadducees, the high-priestly party, **4**.1,2; Mark **12**.18, *etc.*), and in response he gains the approval of this part of the Jewish legislature (9). (*ii*) In the subsequent outworking of his relations with the Jewish leaders, his main enemies are the Sadducees (**23**.14).

Notes: V. 1: see **26**.9; Phil. **3**.6. V. 2: Ananias is known to history as an unscrupulous ecclesiastical politician who held office and wielded influence for a long time. He was finally assassinated in A.D.66. by the nationalist terrorists referred to in **21.38** Vs. **3, 5**: Paul's retort seems to mean, "I couldn't recognize the high priest in the outrageous behaviour and speech of such a man as that!" The quotation from Exod. **22.28**, however, is half-apologetic. V. **3** reflects Matt. **23.27**, which confirms the view given above. The high priest may have worn the clothes of his office, but his spirit was *not* that of God's servant and leader of the people. V. **9**: the Pharisees show, as at earlier times, a readiness to accept the message (**5.34-40, 15.5, 21.20**). The Sadducees, as at the trial and condemnation of Jesus, are the inveterate enemies.

Questions: Is the test of verse 9 valid today? How may a claim to fresh revelation and new truth be judged?

Acts 23.11-22

V. 11. Paul must have wondered what the issue would be. His life seemed to hang on a fragile thread, with three serious attempts made upon it in two days (**21.31, 22.22, 23.10**). "often near death" (2 Cor. **11.23**) was no poetic expression! The Lord's encouragement was, therefore, timely and to the point.

Vs. 12-15 give the "inside" story of a plot to put Paul out of the way once and for good. Fanatical Jews had made this compact to kill him. They had taken an oath on the matter (**14**), and sought the ready co-operation of the religious authority (**15**).

Vs. 16-22. The conspiracy was discovered by Paul's nephew— one of the rare sidelights on his family connections. The following scene, set in the Roman garrison-house, is a drama of suspense and mystery, with hurried exchanges of information, quick decisions, and sworn secrecy (**22**). The name of God doesn't appear in the swift-flowing narrative; no moral is drawn from the drama, and the characters act and speak like "men of the world" who might be found in any modern spy tale. The Bible doesn't moralize unnecessarily, nor is it tediously "pious" (as though as every character in its story is constantly talking about religion). Yet the undertone of divine providence runs throughout; and God is *there*, if unseen and unrecognised, in the plans and counter-plans of enemies and friends. Of which Old Testament book does all this remind you?

Notes: V. **11**: "take courage"—the Greek word is that used of Jesus' concern for His disciples' needs, in the Gospels (*e.g.,* Mark **6.50**). Paul's own desire to visit Rome (**19.21**; Rom. **1.10,11**) blends with the Lord's will for His servant. Such a combination has irresistible force (Psa. **37.4, 5**). V. 12: abstinence from food and drink was a mark of earnestness in carrying out a purpose. Evil men can be thorough-going in their designs and often display a zeal which shames the Christian's half-heartedness (see, for illustration, Luke **16.**1-9). V. 18: "Paul the prisoner"—a state in which he later rejoiced to be (Eph. **3.**1; **4.**1; Col. **1.**24).

Thought: "All who take the sword will perish by the sword" (Matt. **26.**52). The irony is that the assassins whom Ananias abetted (14-16) ten years later claimed him as a victim.

Acts 23.23-35

The counter-plan, devised to foil the conspiracy of murder, was to abduct Paul by night from Jerusalem to Caesarea (23,24). A formidable bodyguard of foot soldiers, cavalry, and light-armed troops was detailed to escort the prisoner on the way to Felix, the Roman procurator at Caesarea, the headquarters of Roman authority in Palestine.

Lysias wrote a covering letter (26-30). The commentators, impressed by the realistic style of writing, wonder if Luke had actually seen a copy of this letter. Certainly it bears the imprint of what a Roman official may well say in such circumstances, including a touch of embellishment (27) designed to enhance *his* own reputation for prompt and decisive action. Strictly, Lysias did not learn of Paul's Roman status until later than the time of the arrest, and his motive in rescuing Paul was hardly that of verse 27! He tactfully omits an incident which had clearly embarrassed him (22.24-26)!

The apostle was ushered into the presence of Felix, whose predecessor in the governor's office—Pilate—is well known. Felix's term began in A.D.52, and was marked with uprisings and fierce counter-measures. As a result of one such commotion and its harsh treatment by Felix (24.27), he was recalled. A contemporary historian sums up his character: "He exercised the power of a king with the mind of a slave". Luke is more kindly in his record (especially 24.22,23), but picks out some basic flaws in his character (24.26,27).

Notes: V. 23: about 9.30 p.m. From the size of the escort, it is clear that Lysias was taking no more chances. Contrast Ezra 8.22. V. 24: the plural "mounts" (horses or mules) implies that Paul had his friends, including Luke, with him—*cf.* 24.23. V. 26: a title of respect, also given to Luke's first reader (Luke **1.**3;) V. 34: a similar question, put for purposes of identification, was asked concerning the Lord at His trial (Luke 23.6, 7). V. 35: Paul spent two years at the official residence of the governor, built by Herod the Great; hence the name.

To think over: Our letter-writing is a revelation of character. How does Lysias' character shine through his letter to Felix?

Acts 24.1-9

In today's reading we see Paul through the eyes of his enemies (particularly 5), and learn something of how the earliest Christians had to contend with misrepresentation and implacable hate.

"The speech of Tertullus is a delightful parody of the oratory of the second-rate Greek hired pleader; Luke must have enjoyed writing it. It begins with a high-flown compliment, and then quite suddenly subsides into the baldest colloquialism, as if the poor creature could not keep it up" (Findlay).

Tertullus's rhetoric leads him into (*i*) culpable exaggeration (2, "much peace" is sharply contradicted by the series of uprisings and punitive retaliations which had disgraced Felix's tenure of office); (*ii*) a distortion of the facts (5, which tried to denigrate Paul by making him no better than a Messianic revolutionary, like the man of 21.38, whom Felix, aided by Jews, had put down); and (*iii*) a perverted sense of justice (7, which is relegated to the R.S.V. margin, but many editors believe it to be authentic). Clearly something more needs to be added to explain the reason for Paul's "arrest" by the Jews. Notice the slant which Tertullus gives to the recent events, silently glossing over any thought that the Jews were ready to lynch their enemy, and putting the blame for "violence" on Lysias' head (7). His hint ("we would have judged him according to our law", 6) may suggest that there was no need for Felix to bother himself overmuch with this case —let him just release Paul, for them to deal with!

Notes: V. 4: "briefly"—at least one redeeming feature of the speech, and he kept to his promise. V. 5: a threefold charge is brought against Paul. He is accused of being (*i*) a troublesome pest—*i.e.*, a seditious agitator against the Roman authority; this was designed to get Felix's interest: (*ii*) a ringleader of Nazarenes—*i.e.*, a heretical Jewish sect, based on the teaching of an executed false prophet: (*iii*) an attempted violator of the Temple, whose claim to sanctity the Romans respected. How much was (*i*) true? (*ii*) false? (*iii*) distorted? V. 7: *cf.* John 18.31. *Thought:* Read again the account of Paul's encounter with the Jews (**21.27***ff.*). Both Claudius Lysias (**23.26***ff.*) and Tertullus (**24.2***ff.*) have given their own—different—versions of it. Shall we turn this thought into prayer for all who influence public opinion in our newspapers, radio, and TV, that *facts* may be clearly distinguished from *comment*.

Acts 24.10-21

The defence which Paul makes before the governor's tribunal deals point by point with the accusations levelled against him. The main intention, however, is to show that he is innocent of all *political* charges, and that the real issue between him and the Jews is a *theological* one (20,21). We may take up the individual rebuttals he makes to the list of accusations which faced him: (*i*) Paul's visit to Jerusalem was a recent happening and the facts of the case should be known to all (11); (*ii*) he denied all responsibility as a trouble-maker at that time. He was going about his lawful occasions (12,18); (*iii*) in any case, the men who confronted him at Felix's palace were not the same as the real assailants (13,18b,19: "Jews from Asia" were the disturbers of the peace); (*iv*) The nub of the dispute between Paul and the Jews who supported Tertullus' castigation (5,9) was found in a conflicting interpretation of Scripture (14,15) and a debate over theology (21). The implication which Paul intended is clear: he himself had a clear conscience over the charges of supposed agitation (16) and the matter before the governor had no political significance. The "one thing" was a domestic affair which ought to be settled peacefully.

In the course of this brief statement Paul has indirectly made his position clear. He was and always had been—a loyal Israelite (14) with a faith built on the Old Testament revelation which, as prophetic Scripture, looks beyond itself to the fulfilment of divine promises. Part of that faith is an expectation of resurrection (15,21)—a Pharisaic tenet also. From this belief it is an easy step to the central *Christian* article of faith: the resurrection of Jesus, which validated His Messiahship as Israel's King and Saviour. Paul is no iconoclast, with a relish for acting irresponsibly and upturning his ancestral beliefs (16). In fact, the opposite is true. He had come to Jerusalem with money for *Jewish*-Christians, as a token of charitable concern and a proof of unity among the one people of God (17).

Notes: V. 14: non-Christians may call them a "sect" (*i.e.*, heterodox party within the Jewish fold), but the correct title was "the Way",

438

9.2; 19.9,23; 22.4; 24.22). The qualification "God *of our fathers*" is important. Like Moses (Ex. **3.**13) and the prophets of Israel (Hos. **12.**9,13; **13.**4,5; Amos **2.**10, *etc.*) Paul harks back to God's earlier revelation, at the same time pointing forward to its future consummation. V. 17: the collection for the saints occupied much of his time and attention (2 Cor. **8–9**; Rom. **15.**25*ff.*).

Acts 24.22-27

Felix was in no mind to settle the dispute there and then, and deferred the case (22,23). One notable interview which brought the two men together is described (24,25). Felix's intention was clear; he wanted to hear the Christian missionary speak on a vital theme. (What could have been more congenial to Paul than to expound "faith in Christ Jesus"?) Paul, however, refused to fawn on his distinguished audience and to ingratiate himself with those who had the power to set him free. The trio of "justice" (better "righteousness", in the sense of Romans 1—4, as a divine standard by which human life is tested and condemned and a divine offer in the Gospel), "self-control" and "future judgment" was hardly calculated to make the preacher popular. It formed "the very subjects that Felix and Drusilla most needed to hear about" (F. F. Bruce), but not what they *wanted* to be reminded of, as is apparent from their known characters at that time. Small wonder, then, that Felix was terrified, and cut short the interview on that occasion. Paul, however, was given further opportunities (26b), but evidently without making much of a deep impression upon this interested dilettante. At least, he saw no injustice in holding in detention a blameless man (27). So much for his religious interest!

Notes: V. 22: apparently Lysias never came, or else this was Felix's way of postponing proceedings and the verdict *sine die*. Paul had no redress and no choice but to hope for a discharge. When this became unlikely, he played a trump card (**25.**11). V. 23: the Roman term for this detention *libera custodia* ("free custody") shows that it was not irksome, but Paul must have wondered why, in God's providence, his active ministry was curtailed. V. 24: Drusilla had been enticed away from her husband, Aziz, by Felix and persuaded to join his *harem* as his third, polygamous wife. V. 26: Paul's financial state gives the mark of some affluence at this time of his life (implied in **21.**24 and **28.**30).

Meditations: (i) Two men's consciences are dramatically sounded: Paul's (16) and Felix's (25). (ii) "When I have some spare time I'll send for you" (25). Does "spare-time religion" ever satisfy?

Acts 25.1-12

Festus succeeded to the office of procurator at Caesarea in A.D.58. Little is known of him—in fact, virtually nothing apart from what Luke and the Jewish historian Josephus tell us.

Paul's fortunes seem to be unchanged. The Roman authorities were unwilling to decide his case; one motive for such tardiness is given in **24.27**. The next scene is fraught with momentous consequences. A second deputation of Jews, sent from Jerusalem, had nothing new to say and repeated the unfounded charges as on the former occasion (7). Paul simply denied any complicity (8). Then came the decision-laden question. "Do you wish to go up to Jerusalem?" (9). The prisoner was clearly at the crossroads. If he said yes, he would play himself nicely into the hands of his accusers, perhaps admitting that there was a case to answer and that they were competent to act in this matter. Besides, his safety was involved, and he must have known something of the attempt which was planned on his life (3). On the other side, to refuse now might alienate Festus and lose the protection of Roman custody.

Paul gave a deliberate reply, probably using the technical phrase to which he was entitled as a citizen of the empire: *Caesarem appello*— "I appeal to Caesar" (11). This exercise of his privilege at once quashed all local proceedings, and transferred his case to the imperial court of Nero in Rome, as Festus perceived (12). So, in a roundabout way, the divine purpose was strangely carried forward (**23.11**).

Notes: Vs. 3,9: Festus, having been asked this favour, grants it. His motto seems to have been "Anything for a quiet life". Considerations of justice and fair play don't seem to have weighed much. Herod Agrippa is more forthright (**26.31**). V. 8: "against Caesar"; this shows that the Jews were accusing him of a political offence. V. 11: a final plea of innocence, implying that there were no charges to answer. The appeal to Caesar indicates that Paul had despaired of any justice at such a crooked court where a plaintiff's "favour" influences the presiding judge on the tribunal seat (3,9).
Today's prayer: For all who make and administer our laws.

Acts 25.13-27

Vs. 13-22: Agrippa visits Festus. Herod Agrippa II was a political figure, important as a tetrarch of some districts in north Palestine, and also as the secular head of the Jewish church who appointed the high priesthood. He was a character of some influence, therefore.

A state visit of Herod, along with his sister Bernice, gave Festus a chance to mention Paul's case (13,14). This was not to re-try him (which was now beyond his power, since Paul had appealed directly to the emperor), but simply to get Herod's views and thereby to have information for the dossier to be sent to the imperial court. One cardinal Christian truth had penetrated into his mind (19), which proves that the general debate over the resurrection of the dead (**24**.15,21) turned upon the case of *one* particular resurrection— *viz.,* that of the Messiah. This special application of a principle was more than the Pharisees could allow or believe; but at least the pagan Roman had the wit to see what Paul was continually talking about.

Vs. 23-27. Luke was evidently in close touch with these proceedings, as his detailed descriptions show (23).

Notes: V. 13: Herod Agrippa and Bernice were related, but rumour darkly hinted at their immoral ways. V. 19: "superstition"; the Greek word may carry a neutral sense, "religion", as well as a derogatory one, as R.S.V. gives. Festus, perhaps unwittingly, goes to the heart of the matter. The tenses of the verbs he uses are interesting: one Jesus Who *has been dead* (for some time), Whom Paul *was repeatedly saying* to be alive. V. 26: "examined"—*i.e.*, by this enquiry. This would provide information to send off to "my Lord" = the emperor, concerning the prisoner.

Exercise: Look back over the previous chapters, and notice the fundamental importance of the resurrection of Jesus both as a central affirmation of faith and a living experience in the early Christians' fellowship and service.

Question: Do I know a living Christ today?

Acts 26.1-18

After a brief introduction (2,3), designed to pay deference to "King Agrippa", whose Jewish ancestry would give him a special sympathy with Paul's case, the apostle opens up his "defence" in the three main sections of our portion.

(*i*) The story of his past life (4-11). This may be summed up as "sincere, but wrong", with verse 9 as its epitome. Yet, in a strange way, the Christians were simply announcing in Messiah's resurrection (8) a special application of a tenet cherished by all good Pharisees (6,7).

(*ii*) The crisis of his conversion (12-15). His encounter with the living Lord was indeed a crisis—*i.e.*, a judgment upon his past life and a new beginning, memorably stated in 2 Cor. **4.**6; **5.**17 as a new creation. In the darkness of his ignorance and folly, the light of God had shone (13); and the real meaning of his persecuting zeal was made known (14,15), for in attacking His people, Saul was wounding Christ Himself—a fearful possibility which he never forgot (1 Cor. **8.**11-13) and which very probably became the basis of his teaching on the Church as Christ's body (see 1 Cor. **12.**12; Eph. **5.**23,29,30).

(*iii*) The terms of his commission (16-18). The account of what was said to him is here given in its fullest detail, and repays close study. The life-work of the future apostle to the Gentiles is admirably sketched, from the initial experience of personal knowledge of Christ (16, "in which you have seen me") to the establishing of Pauline churches (18: "those who are sanctified", 1 Cor. **1.**2, *etc.*). Notice the effect of Gospel ministry, which includes conversion, deliverance, forgiveness, and a place in the new society of Christ's people (18). All these benefits recur in Paul's writings.

Notes: Vs. 2,3: intended to put the speaker *en rapport* with his hearer, but not the flattery of **24.**2*ff.* V. 4: Paul's essentially Jewish upbringing and training in Jerusalem is important, as W. C. van Unnik has shown, to dispel the notion that Paul took over a Greek mystery religion and turned it into his version of Christianity! V. 7: "observe that Paul knew nothing of the fiction of the 'lost' tribes" (Bruce). V. 10: does this mean that Paul had been a member of the Sanhedrin—and therefore at one time a married man? V. 14: note the addition to **9.**4 of a proverbial line, reminding us that his zeal masked a disquieted conscience.
*Meditation: Try to match the parts of verse 18 with the teaching of the epistles (e.g., Col. **1.**12-14).*

Acts 26.19-32

When the facts are examined—Paul concluded—there is nothing anti-Jewish in the message he brought; rather, it complements and brings to fulfilment the Old Testament hope of a Messiah, humiliated yet vindicated and the author of God's blessings to all men, both the Jewish people and the Gentile races (22,23).

Festus was plainly out of his depth. Much study, the Preacher remarked, is a weariness of the flesh (Ecc. **12.**12); the Roman governor pronounced it a danger to sanity (24). Paul repelled that charge, insisting that his Christian knowledge and experience were based on the opposite of "madness"—*viz.*, soberness, the possession of a right mind (see 2 Cor. **5.**13 for the contrast). There is nothing irrational in Christianity in the sense of claims which are contrary to reason (*cf.* 8), although there is much that is *above* human reason, and may be known only by faith.

The interchange of conversation between Paul and Agrippa (26-29) is full of interest. The Christian preacher confidently appeals to what is public knowledge—thereby incidentally dispelling the latter-day idea that Christianity is wrapt in the mists of obscurity and legend; and presses home the appeal (27). Agrippa eases himself off the horns of such a dilemma with a facetious retort: "In short, you are trying to persuade me to play the Christian". Paul picks up the king's words: "The short and the long of it is—I wish that you and all who hear me today could *become* (as opposed to "play a part") as I am—but not as a prisoner!"

Notes: V. 19: the vision is that mentioned in **22.**17*f.* which (as implied in 16-18) assured him of his call to be a missionary to the *Gentiles.* V. 22: Paul appeals, as elsewhere (Rom. **3.**21), to the united witness of the two major sections of the Jewish scriptures. V. 23: *cf.* Luke **24.**25*ff.*, 44. His resurrection is spoken of as a "first instalment" (1 Cor. **15.**20), guaranteeing that of all His people (2 Tim. **1.**10). V. 24: Festus speaks angrily with a loud voice; Paul's reply is restrained. V. 28: the best parallel is 1 Kings **21.**7: "Is it like this that you play a king's part in Israel?"

To ponder: Four characters are here: Bernice, Herod Agrippa, Festus, and Paul. How do they come out of this exchange of views and convictions?

Acts 27.1-12

Commentators praise the vividness and accuracy of this narrative which describes Paul's sea voyage from Palestine to Italy; it is "one of the most instructive documents for the knowledge of ancient seamanship". In this way Paul's long-cherished ambition to get to Rome

Paul's Journey from Caesarea to Rome

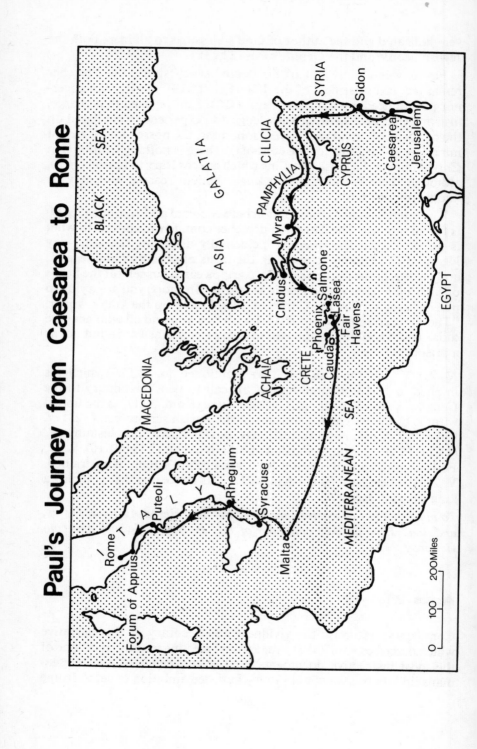

is made good, though in circumstances (1) which he did not relish. And by this long journey the divine promise was realized (23.11).

Paul had travelling companions all the way; one of them is named (2) and at least one other was in the party—Luke the narrator (2; "*we* put to sea").

The Roman centurion Julius showed consideration to the Christian prisoner he had in custody, even to the extent of permitting him to make contact with his fellow-believers at Sidon. We should probably, however, understand verse 3 to mean: "allowed his friends to visit him" on board before they disembarked.

Having trans-shipped at Myra, the party sailed on a corn-ship bound for Italy. The next stage of the voyage was slow and difficult, owing to unfavourable winds and the need to negotiate dangerous coastal rocks.

At Fair Havens (8) Paul came forward with a suggestion. The inference is that the ship's captain should have anchored in the security of Fair Havens bay during the stormy season. Instead, with Paul's advice ignored (11), the decision of the ship's personnel was to sail on, hoping at all events to get to Phoenice (or Phoenix) and to winter there (12).

Notes: V. 1: there is evidence of the presence of this cohort in Syria in first-century A.D. V. 2: Aristarchus is found later as a companion of Paul's at Rome (Col.4.10; Philem. 24), and we may suppose that he travelled with him all the way. V. 9: "the fast" is the Day of Atonement, to be dated about the 5th October in that year. Ancient sailors regarded the 14th September as the beginning of a two-month period when all navigation was hazardous, so it was particularly risky to venture out of harbour in mid-October. Paul was overruled by the various officials—the helmsman and owner (11)—whose decision influenced the centurion.

Acts 27.13-32

Vs. 13-20. The sailors were deceived into thinking that a gentle southerly wind was a good augury (13). The ship put out from Fair Havens and coasted along the shore of Crete, only suddenly to be struck by the fearsome Euraquilo—a fierce north-easterly gale which, sweeping down from Mount Ida in Crete, quickly had the vessel out of control (15). The danger was that the strong waves would overwhelm the ship or smash her structure (hence the measure which was taken of undergirding the ship, 17); or else she would be driven helplessly on to the Syrtis, a dreadful whirlpool and quicksands off the North African coast.

Vs. 21-26. Paul's commanding position is evident. Not for the first time he had faced the perils of the storm (2 Cor. **11.**26); and out of his past experience and present faith he speaks words of (*i*) cheer (22); (*ii*) explanation, giving grounds for his confidence and courage (23); and (*iii*) testimony (25). One man's presence and faith made all the difference.

Vs. 27-32. After two weeks of drifting at the mercy of the elements, the first signs were recognized that Paul's promise (26) was true. The sailors sensed that they were nearing shore as they took soundings (28) and possibly heard the sound of breakers on the shore. Anchors were dropped to brake the vessel (29); and Paul again showed his leadership in preventing a party of sailors from saving their own skins at the expense of the rest (30-32).

Notes: V. 17: the measures included passing a cable round the ship several times, pulling it taut, to ease the strain and prevent the timbers working loose and the seams opening (Findlay). V. 18: as in the scene of Jonah **1.**5. V. 21: perhaps the food was sodden—or the mariners were seasick! Paul's remarks are a mild "I told you so". V. 24: *cf.* Gen. **18.**26 for the principle that good men protect the community (Gen. **19.**22).

Question: "I have faith in God" (25). How did Paul's faith show itself in this critical situation?

Acts 27.33-44

The apostle's leadership is again seen, and among a crew and passenger list of 276 men he stands out as a man of practical faith and sturdy common-sense (34). The angelic vision (23) and the divine promise of safety (24) were food enough for him, and he was prepared·to act upon the assurance which had come to him (34b). With his splendid example to encourage them (35), the rest of the ship's complement took fresh heart (36).

The shipwreck scene is dramatically painted in the remaining verses of the chapter (39-44). The sailors severed the cables and left the anchors in the sea; at the same time unleashing the steering-paddles, and hoisting the foresail to catch a wind, they drove the ship on to the shore (40).

The beaching operation worked. The ship struck a spit of land which jutted out where the two seas met (41, R.S.V. marg.), and the

446

prow became embedded in the sandbank of the promontory, while the stern was broken up by the force of the sea (41).

The soldiers' plan to kill off the prisoners lest they should escape in the confusion of the shipwreck was thwarted—for Paul's sake, to whom everyone owed a great deal. We can only guess by what method—swimming, clutching a plank, or holding part of the ship's spar—Paul and Luke reached land.

Notes: V. 34: the Greek term, elsewhere rendered "salvation", here means physical well-being (as in Phil. **1.**19). The next sentence is an O.T. proverb (1 Sam. **14.**45; 2 Sam. **14.**11; 1 Kings **1.**52; *cf.* Luke **21.** 18). V. 35: an acknowledgment of God's goodness in providing food, though the Western text adds that Paul shared this meal with "us" (presumably Luke and Aristarchus) and understands it as a sacramental meal (so Ramsay). V. 37: R.S.V. margin gives smaller numbers, but the figure of 276 is only half the complement of a ship on which Josephus travelled to Rome, so there is no inherent difficulty in the larger figure. V. 44: the Greek *may* mean :"some on the backs of members of the crew"—a vivid touch!

Acts 28.1-6

The island on which the storm-tossed sailors found refuge was Malta —a Phoenician word which, by a strange coincidence, means "escape". It has been suggested that Luke was aware of this correspondence when he wrote verse 1: "We recognized that the island deserved its name". Rain and cold added to the miseries of their experiences on board ship and then in the water; so the warmth of a fire (2) was especially appreciated, as the historian records.

The incident of the viper's sudden appearance from among the brushwood which Paul was helping to gather for the fire well illustrates popular opinion on the island. The first reaction was to see in the event a judgment on Paul the prisoner, recognized as such possibly by his dress, or perhaps by the chain he was still wearing. The viper, however, was shaken off his hand and as no ill-effect followed, the Maltese changed their tune, and hailed him as a divinity, like the people of Lystra (**14.**11, 12). Such is the fickleness of human opinion, which oscillates with great ease between the two extremes of branding Paul a murderer and then of greeting him as a god come to earth. "The sudden reversal of opinion about Paul may be compared and contrasted with the attitude of the Lycaonians in **14.**11*ff.*, who first acclaimed him as a god, and later nearly stoned him to death" (Bruce).

Notes: V. 2: "natives": lit. barbarians, but not in the sense of un-civilized (which Maltese were not), but meaning "not speaking Greek". Their dialect was Phoenician, which sounded to Greek ears as *bar-bar*, a cacophony of strange words! None the less, Luke pays tribute to their hospitable welcome. V. 4: there is an ancient tale of a murderer who escaped from a storm at sea and was shipwrecked on the North African coast, where he died from a viper's sting. *Cf.* Amos 5.19. "Justice"—the Maltese natives associated Paul's pre-dicament, with a snake hanging on to his hand, as a piece of Nemesis which had at length caught up with him. The narrative does not specifically state that Paul was bitten, but their reaction certainly suggests this.

Thought: "*Hospitality is variously regarded as a 'fine art', a joyous privilege, an unwelcome necessity, or an opportunity for display. The New Testament writers emphasize its importance as a Christian grace and as a species of evangelistic service*" (C. R. Erdman). *Consider Rom.* 12.13; *1 Tim.* 3.2; *Tit.* 1.8; *Heb.* 13.2; *and 1 Pet.* 4.9.

Acts 28.7-16

Vs. 7-10. "One good turn deserves another". On the one side, Publius extended to the apostle some friendly hospitality which lasted three days (7), and, on the other hand, he received the added happiness of seeing his father cured of gastric fever and dysentery, following the visit and prayer of Paul (8).

Paul's healing ministry became widely known, and sick folk throughout the island saw a chance to be healed by this Christian leader whom the ocean had washed up on to their beach. They showed their gratitude by the offer of gifts and ship's stores (10).

Luke doesn't comment on any deeper spiritual significance of these incidents: did Paul preach the Gospel as he exercised a ministry of prayer and healing? Were any Maltese won for Christ? Did the apostolic party leave behind a Christian community? The record is silent; but we may surely believe that here was an evangelistic opportunity too good to be missed.

Vs. 11-16. The Roman writer Pliny informs us that the winter season when the seas were closed for navigable traffic ended on February 7th; and we may infer that the three months' stay on the island ended about that time of the year (11). The ship in which they resumed their journey was another Alexandrian grain-ship which bore as a figure-head the "Heavenly Twins" (Castor and Pollux, the patron saints of navigators in the ancient world).

The course led them at last to Puteoli in the Bay of Naples. In this flourishing seaport a Christian fellowship was contacted, and Paul and his company had a week with them. The last "leg" of the long journey brought them *via* the Appian Way to within sight of the Imperial City.

Notes: V. 7: "chief man of the island"—Luke's accuracy is confirmed by inscriptions which show that this was the title of the Roman governor. Paul's citizenship would be his passport to the governor's residence. V. 10: it could mean "paid us handsome fees" for the medical treatment received, as Luke the "dear doctor" (Col. 4.14) may have observed. V. 15: Christian fellowship meant much to Paul, and he was obviously touched by this "welcome party" which came forty-three miles to greet him.
Question: God used Paul's ministrations to heal (8,9); but he worked no magical cure and was not always successful (2 Tim. 4.20). Why?

Acts 28.17-30

Rome at last! The narrative moves to its zenith, as Bengel observed in his commentary written in the mid-eighteenth century: "The victory of the Word of God: Paul at Rome, the climax of the Gospel, the conclusion of Acts". Paul's attempt to put himself in the clear with Jewish leaders at Rome failed, although he was able to (*i*) make plain the reason for his being in Rome as a prisoner (17-20) and (*ii*) testify, at a conference called for the purpose, concerning "the hope of Israel" (20) and the central theme of the Gospel message (23).

As on so many previous occasions, his preaching divided men into two camps (24; *cf*. 1 Cor. 1.18; 2 Cor. 2.15,16). As the unconvinced Jews left in total disarray (25,29, R.S.V. marg.), Paul clinched his point with a quotation from the Old Testament and with a hint of his teaching, amplified and worked out in Romans 9—11, that the Gentiles have received mercy because of the disobedience of Israel (Rom. 11.30)—another leading *motif* in the preceding record of how the Gospel was brought from Jerusalem to Rome.

"They will listen" (28): this is the final thrust of the Pauline testimony. Israel's salvation, rejected by her national representatives and leaders, is now offered to the Gentiles, and nothing can stop the onward march of God's truth to the "uttermost part of the earth" (1.8, A. V., K.J.V.). Paul's "free custody" (as the Romans called it, 30,31) gave him opportunity to do the work of an evangelist among an audience which had free access to his hired room, which was his prison-cell; and the closing words "quite openly and unhindered" stress both his personal confidence (*cf.* Phil. 1.20 for the same expression, "with full courage") and the unrestricted scope he enjoyed to proclaim the message of Christ.

These two elements—the preacher's boldness and an all-embracing proclamation—are interwoven in the fabric of the history of Acts as it speaks of the good news: "it began at Jerusalem; it finishes at Rome. Here, O Church, is your model. It is your duty to keep it and to guard your deposit" (Bengel).

Questions: (*i*) What do you understand by Paul's preaching of the kingdom of God (23,31) to his hearers? (*ii*) Trace the way (*a*) Israel refused the Gospel offer in Luke's story; and (*b*) the Gentiles received it.